STUDIES IN THE MEANING OF JUDAISM

Eugene B. Borowitz

JPS דורדור
SCHOLAR ודורשיו
OF DISTINCTION
SERIES

EUGENE B. BOROWITZ

STUDIES IN THE MEANING OF JUDAISM

THE JEWISH PUBLICATION SOCIETY

Philadelphia *2002 • 5763*

The Jewish Publication Society
2100 Arch Street, 2nd floor
Philadelphia, PA 19103

Composition by Book Design Studio
Design by Adrianne Onderdunk Dudden

Manufactured in the United States of America

02 03 04 05 06 07 08 09 10   10 9 8 7 6 5 4 3 2 1

Library of Congress Cataloging-in-Publication Data

Borowitz, Eugene B.
Studies in the meaning of Judaism / Eugene B. Borowitz.
p. cm.
Includes bibliographical references and index.
ISBN 0-8276-0721-0
1. Judaism—Doctrines. 2. Reform Judaism—United States. I. Title.
BM602 .B67 2002
296.3—dc21
2002009464

The publication of this book
was made possible by a gift from

Betty Golomb

in memory of her husband

Dan Golomb

This book is dedicated to

The New York School
of the Hebrew Union College
Jewish Institute of Religion

for the pleasures of forty years of teaching full-time,
in appreciation of its
helpful administrations and staff,
and in joyous celebration of its admirable faculty
who have transcended individual striving and diversity of opinion
to create a community of mutual concern and affectionate regard.

Contents

Acknowledgments

Every book comes to its public because many unheralded hands abetted the author's intentions, and this work, gathered from many places, certainly demonstrates that. In the half-century span of these papers, the names of many who were instrumental in their publication have now slipped from active memory. I can only thank them now by this blanket statement of appreciation for their help to me and my writing. Fortunately, a number of others can be directly addressed.

I gladly acknowledge the cooperation of the copyright holders of my older articles for granting permission to reprint the following works:

"Creating Commitment in our Religious Schools." Reprinted with the permission of the Union of American Hebrew Congregations. Copyright © UAHC all rights reserved.

"Faith and Method in Modern Jewish Theology." Reprinted with the permission of the Central Conference of American Rabbis.

"Creative Worship in the Computer Age." Reprinted with the permission of the Union of American Hebrew Congregations. Copyright © UAHC all rights reserved.

"Why We Went" by Sixteen Rabbis and One Layman. Copyright © 1964 Christian Century Foundation. Reprinted by permission from the Aug. 26, 1964, issue of the *Christian Century*.

"On Celebrating Sinai." Reprinted with the permission of the Central Conference of American Rabbis.

"The Problem of the Form of a Jewish Theology." Hebrew Union College Annual 40–41 (1969–70).

"The Postsecular Situation of Jewish Theology." First published in *Theological Studies* 31(1970) 460–475.

"Education Is Not I-Thou" and "*Tzimtzum*: A Mystic Model for Contemporary Leadership." Reprinted with the permission of The Religious Education Association.

"A Jewish Response: The Lure and Limits of Universalizing Our Faith." Originally published in *Christian Faith in a Religiously Plural World,* edited by Donal G. Dawe and John B. Carman. Copyright © 1978 by Orbis Books, Maryknoll, NY 10545.

With few exceptions, the papers and the glossary are as they appeared in their original. As a result, there are variations in spelling and language style from piece to piece. In some papers, text originally in Hebrew has been transliterated in this printing, always utilizing the contemporary Sephardic pronunciation. Special apologies for the sexist writing in the earliest articles and later in translations in historical fidelity to classic Jewish texts. The term *op. cit.* in the notes indicates that I have previously identified the publication of the thinker cited there.

The library of the New York School of HUC-JIR has always been most supportive of my work. Its librarian, Dr. Philip Miller, has often taken personal charge of my frequent demands for uncommon materials, responding to them with unflagging good will, great bibliographic skill, and a remarkable ratio of success. For all this and the friendship that accompanies it, many thanks.

Special thanks as well to Amy Helfman, who, while serving as Associate Librarian of the Klau Library at HUC-JIR, New York, kindly agreed to do the bibliography of my writings, which was my seventy-fifth birthday gift to myself. Amy is now a librarian at the Jewish Theological Seminary, and her list of my writings 1944–1999, now added to by me, is a welcome supplement to this book.

In these scholarly endeavors over the decades, I have regularly had the support of the Hebrew Union College Faculty Research Fund and remain grateful to its donors and administrators for the aid. My old friend and one-time congregant, George Lotker, amplified the resources available to me by making possible the establishment of the Ilona B. Samek Institute for Theology and Liturgy at the Hebrew Union College and, through its various publications has, I hope, vicariously achieved his dream of becoming a philosopher. Another friend from our youthful days together in the Port Washington Community Synagogue, Betty Golomb, who has long given leadership and support to various activities in Reform Judaism, has now with her customary graciousness and generosity made possible the publication of this book; may many blessings continue to enrich her years.

Elsewhere in this volume I have expressed my thanks to The Jewish Publication Society and to Dr. Ellen Frankel, its editor and CEO, for the invitation to participate in this exclusive series. Here I wish to record my appreciation of the mix of generosity, tough love, and genial efficiency with which she and Carol Hupping, publishing director of the Society, managed the details of bringing this book into reality. Thanks also for the attention to detail shown by Sarah Dunn, copyeditor, and proofreader Marsha Kunin of this volume.

My academic intern for 2001–2002, Shoshana Nyer (to be ordained a rabbi in 2003), really deserves the title of managing editor of this project. No request that I have thrown her way, arcane or complicated as it might have been, has given her pause. Rather, with intelligence, good humor, hard work, and unfailing grace, she has transformed what easily could have been drudgery for both of us into something of a fun exercise—at least for me. I have been lucky to have had her help. I am also grateful to Eric Eisenkamer for his perceptive help in reading the page proofs.

Over the decades, the Jewish mindfulness I have sought to cultivate has been, in large part, an effort to remain conscious of God, the enabler of my existence and continuing activity. Perhaps at age seventy-eight, the piety that I intermittently manifest is somewhat more poignant than when I was younger, but clearly it is its ongoing extension. So I continue in the custom I long ago learned from medieval Jewish authors: of not publishing a book without some words of deep gratitude.

People may order their thoughts,
But Adonai's is the answering speech.
All their ways seem right to people,
But Adonai probes the intentions.
Entrust your projects to Adonai,
And Adonai will establish your thoughts.

לְאָדָם מַעַרְכֵי־לֵב
וּמֵיְהוָה מַעֲנֵה לָשׁוֹן׃
כָּל־דַּרְכֵי־אִישׁ זַךְ בְּעֵינָיו
וְתֹכֵן רוּחוֹת יְהוָה׃
גֹּל אֶל־יְהוָה מַעֲשֶׂיךָ
וְיִכֹּנוּ מַחְשְׁבֹתֶיךָ׃

(Prov. 16.1–3; my rendering)

Eugene B. Borowitz

Preface

In most academic disciplines, the balance between accepted method and individual creativity is weighted heavily toward the accepted ways of doing things. The researcher's special insight expresses itself largely in finding new modes of applying the established methodology, or finding new materials that merit consideration, or some other productive new take on carrying on this work. Only rarely does an academic in such a field hope to create a significantly new manner of thinking about and studying the old discipline. This pre-understanding led to my first intellectual shock when I came to rabbinical school in 1942.

What interested me was something that I naively, and for want of a better term, called "Jewish theology." The Hebrew Union College (HUC) was unique in those days because it had a Professor of Jewish Theology, one professor who did not limit himself to investigating the history of Jewish ideas. But his unique title meant that there were no colleagues whose cognate work could set the standards for estimable ways of "doing" Jewish theology and whose evaluation of each other's thinking could create a field of discussion. Worse, most of my fellow students derided the area as Jewishly inauthentic, its very name testifying that this activity was but another fawning effort to gain favor with the gentiles.

I felt differently. Even as a youngster I exasperated my synagogue schoolteachers and my rabbi with my questions about the general nature and content of contemporary Jewish belief and its validation. Something, too, helped me reject the inflated self-confidence that led my university teachers of philosophy and the social sciences to scorn religious belief while confidently preaching that reason was the real messiah. Instead of becoming another confirmed mid-century agnostic, I became convinced that only belief could now found, even mandate, our strong sense of personal and human values. So I wanted to know what a thoughtful, informed Jew was expected to believe and how that truth could be cogently explicated today. Fortunately, my soon-to-be HUC roommate, Arnold Jacob Wolf, shared that passion, as did our friend Steven S. Schwarzschild, *z"l*, and, as we gradually discovered, so did a handful of other young rabbis.

That situation lies behind the uncommon chronological, rather than thematic, ordering of the papers selected for inclusion in this book. The steady movement of their publication during half a century seeks to highlight the fact that my work as a thinker has proceeded on two interconnected levels. I have worked at creating an academically credible field called Jewish theology (or, as some prefer to term it, Jewish religious thought) and, simultaneously, sought to inaugurate a new and less inadequate manner of understanding and validating the truth of contemporary Jewish belief. The discipline-determining effort dominated my work for nearly thirty years, though only late in that period did it dawn on me that I had long been seeking a systematic overview of the field and that I could now finally provide one. (For Lawrence Hoffman's generous estimate of my work in this regard, see *Jewish Spiritual Journeys*, edited by him and Arnold Jacob Wolf, Behrman House, 1997, p. ix.) After some years of refining this insight by letting it structure my work in one of my courses, I finally was able to set down a major statement of my view, *Choices in Modern Jewish Thought: A Partisan Guide* (Behrman House, 1983). Since, happily for me, others gradually began devoting themselves to this area, their cogent work has occasionally stimulated me to further structural writing and to a second edition of my descriptive book, one that, just as I finished it, I realized was already in need of further updating.

All during this time, I had also been devoting considerable effort to clarifying my sense of my Jewish faith and the intellectual manner in which it might best be communicated. At first, what I came to call religious existentialism seemed adequate for that role because its embrace of the whole person and not merely of mind made it possible to talk about God in relationship with persons and not as an abstract idea or concept. Yet it was of little help in speaking of the truth of being not a person-in-general but a Jew-person/a person-Jew, in short, a Jew. Realizing that the radical intellectual individualism of most Western thought in our time was the impediment to a fuller statement of my Jewish theology did not come easily. Somehow, about the time that I published my description of the field of Jewish theology, I came to realize that I needed to speak in terms of the (religious) sociality of the self and then, in turn, to discover that the language of the emerging world of postmodernism made it possible to do so cogently. A decade's deliberation then brought me to a major statement of a new Jewish theology for our time, *Renewing the Covenant, a Theology for the Postmodern Jew* (Jewish Publication Society, 1991). In the decade plus since, this relational vision of Jewish faith has proved most stimulating, giving me greater insight into Jewish belief and practice both as expressed in our traditional literature and in our own lives. The final paper in this collection, one conceived and carried through while this volume was being brought together, confirms again for me the intellectual and religious fruitfulness of this point of view.

The present volume, for which I am heartwarmingly grateful to The Jewish Publication Society, its editor-in-chief, and its editorial committee, has no excerpts from any of my books, though some of the papers selected for inclusion in this volume have appeared in my previous books. The chronological arrangement of the articles mixes the more descriptive with the more substantive articles—as do many of the papers themselves. Nonetheless, it has the special virtue of allowing a patient reader to see how, in this discipline, a scholar struggled to overcome incomprehension and inched ahead as the accretion of insight only slowly appeared. (The reader who prefers to follow the steps to the goal in terms of a more global sense of the journey will find it useful to begin by first reading paper 26 of this volume, "A Life of Jewish Learning: In Search of a Theology of Judaism.")

The intellectual process, much like life, does not proceed with linear efficiency. Rather, thinkers lurch forward, they hope, prompted as much by external circumstance—an invitation to speak here or write something there—as by internal purpose; even orderly thinkers entertains a jumble of impulses. These papers therefore often deal as much with issues of Jewish doing (*halakhah, musar, minhag*—education, ethics, interfaith dialogue) as they do with abstract, philosophic themes; the fuller evidence of these various doings-thinkings is in the bibliography.

To emphasize the dynamic, developmental nature of the ideas presented here, I have metaphorically divided the papers into four stages of a journey. I briefly introduce each of these stages and hope that my comments as your tour guide will make the intellectual trip more pleasurable.

A GLIMPSE: WHEN AGNOSTICISM AND RATIONALISM COULD NO LONGER GROUND OUR VALUES

Perhaps the most direct impetus to thinking is dissatisfaction with someone else's statement of the way things are or ought to be. Young writers generally claim a place in intellectual discussion by their critiques of certain established figures in their field. What passed for Jewish theological thinking at mid-century was generally a watered-down version of Hermann Cohen's conception of Judaism as religion of reason par excellence. A minority preferred Mordecai Kaplan's more-science-than-philosophy-based sociological understanding of Judaism, particularly because it, unlike Cohen's view, had a strong ethnic component. Most Americanized Jews had never heard of either Cohen or Kaplan but they shared the rationalistic, optimistic ethos of those post-Depression days and believed that people, at their best, were rational beings and hence had a strong ethical impulse in their lives.

Two difficulties with the dominant rationalisms caused me and some other young thinkers to seek a radically different mode of conceptualizing Judaism. First, with human reason primary, God and the Jewish tradition—the truths on which we based our lives—were superfluous to being simply a worthwhile person, a goal more directly attained via rationality and ethics. Agnosticism, therefore, became the standard if covert belief of those who, for whatever reason, stayed Jewish; the commandments that now spoke to many others in our community mandated politics and social betterment causes, not Jewish piety. Second, the link between thinking logically and a demanding ethic (of some recognizable Judeo-Christian substance) was broken by two concurrent challenges. Practically, how people actually behaved in the first half of the twentieth century belied the essentially rational-ethical nature of human beings. Theoretically as well, Marx, Freud, anthropology, and the advocates of scientific-mathematical philosophy denied the Kantian insistence upon the imperative ethical quality of pure reason. These were not purely abstract issues for me and my friends; Judaism was surely more interested in how one lived than how exactly one thought about it. So, as God became a living reality for us, prayer and classic Jewish texts became critical to our lived Judaism, a direction that only toward the end of the century became more common among modernized American Jews.

The intellectual issues underlying Jewish life must have been troubling other rabbis because in 1950 the Reform rabbis' group, for the only time in its history, invited its members to a special conference on "theology." There was no significant suggestion—in either the call for that meeting or in its major addresses—that the founding of the State of Israel or the post-war definitive evidence about what later came to be called the Holocaust demanded this rethinking of belief. What brought people to the meeting was a vague sense that the older philosophic ways of talking about God and relating to the Jewish tradition were no longer adequate. No new understandings of Judaism emerged in that conference—theology rarely if ever can be done by committee or by plenum votes—but I was encouraged to discover in the Reform rabbis' group rabbis who shared my sense of unhappiness with the established ways of understanding Judaism and who were seeking something substantially different. My first major article (paper 1 in this volume) described that meeting and, by being published in the leading Jewish intellectual journal of the time, encouraged me to try to write more.

A sense of the truer, richer Judaism that animated me began to surface in the following years, though I had little awareness of it at the time. Nonetheless, the focus of two of my papers in the following years reflects it. My 1956 address to the assembly of educators, a group that went on to found the National Association of Temple Educators, was directed to "Creating Commitment [*sic*] in Our Religious Schools" (paper 2), a concern utterly foreign to the rational-ethical or ethnic interpreters of Judaism. In 1957 I was invited to give a paper to the Central Conference of American (i.e., Reform) Rabbis CCAR, on the classic topic, "The Idea [*sic*] of God" (paper 3). Rather than provide what the rationalists anticipated of such a presentation—namely, a new philosophically validated conception of God—I sought to radically change our theological frame of reference. I asked, instead, how we would recognize a Jewishly authentic notion of God, and—my systematic sense of theologizing here manifesting itself—I proceeded to analyze the clashing theologies of Kaplan and Buber in terms of their Jewish religious yield. Unbeknownst to me, I was insisting that particularity, Jewishness, was as central to modern Judaism as was universality. By 1963 I could talk directly about "Faith [*sic*] and Method in Modern Jewish Theology;" paper 6. (This essay was presented as part of a series of presentations to the CCAR conference that year on the newly emerging existentialist approach to Judaism.)

During these years, this intensifying glimmer of the root nature of Jewish truth had been leading me to what was then the most responsible, non-rationalistic way of thinking about life and reality, existentialism. I embraced it in a religious form unacceptable to its Parisian star, Jean Paul Sartre, but vaguely traceable to the Danish Christian thinker Sören Kierkegaard. Existentialism provided me and my theological companions with a non-rationalistic way of understanding Judaism that allowed us to speak of God in terms of a living relationship and not merely as a grounding cognitive premise. An early statement of this emerging Jewish theological language is seen in my 1959 essay, "Existentialism's Meaning for Judaism" (paper 4). Later in the decade it would make possible the publication of my first four books.

A further word needs to be said about the articles gathered here and in later sections of this book that seem to stray from my central intellectual pursuits by their concern with practical issues. As indicated above, a Jewish intellectuality radically detached from Jewish duty and observance belies the classic Jewish fixation on lived spirituality. For that reason I have long consciously sought to check the adequacy of my understanding of Jewish belief by seeing how it played out in Jewish living, not only in my private and familial life but also in my varied Jewish and American communal activities. My chief concerns have been ethical duty and educational practice. Two further clarifications must also be made. First, I was only the principal drafter, not the author, of paper 8, "Why We Went," the 1964 statement issued by those of us in the CCAR who were jailed overnight for our participation in Martin Luther King's St. Augustine, Florida, campaign. The group emended but largely retained the draft I did that night at their request in our joint cell. Second, so much of this book being serious to the point of near-grimness, I think it fair to note my proclivity to use humor in order to humanize and deepen oral theological instruction. On occasion, however, as in "Creative Worship in the Computer Age," paper 7, I have sought in print to summon laughter to touch the Jewish soul in ways that reasoning hardly ever can.

1 / Theological Conference Cincinnati, 1950: Reform Judaism's Fresh Awareness of Religious Problems

1950

If the purpose of the Institute on Reform Jewish Theology, held at the Hebrew Union College on March 20–22, was to formulate a declaration of belief, then it was a failure. The general as well as the Jewish press had carried stories declaring this to be its aim, and the American Jewish community is accustomed to seeing all assemblies of more than two persons bring forth some such statement, tailored to the moment and complete. Yet it can be fairly said this Institute was a success—perhaps just because it did not proclaim a credo.

Had there been no serious problems unsolved by the theology that has been current for the past fifty years or so, there would have been no need to convoke this Institute. Had the rabbinate or Reform Judaism as a whole had the answers to the questions perplexing us, had the Institute not recognized the profound seriousness of modern man's situation, then a platform could easily have been prepared to order and canned for quick mass consumption. Happily, the Institute was neither so shortsighted, smug, nor "practical."

The "religious crisis of our time" is no stock phrase restricted to the theological journals—that it is a sharp day-to-day reality any man knows who ministers to individuals in their hours of need. The unexpectedly large attendance of rabbis at this mid-season conference can be directly traced to congregants—not a few, but very many—who confess they are unable to accept the old replies, who cannot cease questioning, who have no secure goals but a persistent anxiety and a deep, if hidden, fear of the future. Rabbi Levi Olan of Dallas, Texas, in his paper on "Theology Today," described the situation accurately: "Modern man is in search of a faith that is resourceful enough to give meaning to chaos, and reliable enough to encourage hope for the future. . . . The world seems to have lost its direction. . . . Though we cannot comprehend with precise clarity the nature and extent of the upheaval in Western culture, we are faced with fundamentally radical changes."

As the institute split into its constituent round tables, it became evident that liberal Judaism today is confronted by four basic religious questions.

First, is the belief in God as an objective, divine reality indispensable to modern Judaism, or must it be replaced by something more agreeable to the modern temper?

The traditionalists insisted that God is either unique, eternal, and absolute, or He is nothing. Faith need not have rigorous proof. Only a God who is Lord of this world can give it universal standards and a universal meaning. Judaism without personal piety, meaningful prayer, and divine sanction, without an immanent and transcendent God, is no Judaism.

But some felt that the traditional Jewish belief in a God who exists in His own right, who is independent of man, is too much at variance with modern knowledge to be acceptable. His existence cannot be proved. It must be of an order which is completely foreign to our experience. Moreover the recent tragic course of Jewish history makes it difficult to believe in a God of justice who rules history.

Clearly, without a convincing answer to this question, no Jewish theology is possible.

Second, is it possible for man to believe that an existing God is active in our world? As modern men we cannot deny the rational structure of our universe. Any incursion of God into the normal operations of the universe is then a miracle—if not of the natural kind, as the dividing of the Red Sea in the Bible, then of the theological kind, as providence, election, and revelation. Everyone conceded the emotional efficacy of prayer, but whether it actually "worked" was a matter for great doubt. While all affirmed that the people of Israel had a moral and spiritual mission, Israel's choice by God in any active sense was questioned by some. It was generally agreed that revelation was central to Judaism and that revelation involved man's ability to perceive the ultimate principles governing his existence, but whether such a perception involved the idea of God was debated.

Third, to what extent is there authority within Reform Judaism? From its earliest days Reform had introduced into Judaism the idea that modern man had the right to select from tradition whatever elements remained meaningful in his belief and practice. Though Reform insisted upon the authority of Judaism's moral teachings, it seemed to sanction anarchy in regard to everything else in Judaism. Indeed, recent Reform rabbinical deliberations have been one long continuing effort to bring order into this chaos.

Yet if part of our tradition is still binding, what are the criteria by which it is to be recognized? Who are the true and who are the false preachers? Furthermore, is there any divine authority in the sphere of custom and ritual? Do we believe "who has sanctified us by His commandments and commanded us"? Certainly no guide to Reform Jewish practice will pretend to have ecclesiastical authority. But what, then, will be the source of its authority?

Fourth, can we still believe in progress as "salvation"? The awesome tragedy of the first half of this century seems to stand as a refutation of the halcyon hopes of the late nineteenth-century thinkers. If we believe man is able to perfect himself without God's intervention, then Reform teaches that history is a march, now slower, now faster, toward the Messianic era. If we believe man can never reach ultimate goodness, then Reform must hold that it is God who will bring about salvation in the "end of days" or else that history is simply endless movement toward an unattainable goal. Ten or fifteen years ago there was no doubt about the Reform belief in man's march toward the Messianic age. Today some rabbis are wavering in this faith.

Originally, too, Reform was convinced that revelation was universal in time. God spoke to us today even as he spoke in Biblical days, and we had to be as obedient as our forefathers. Moreover, man's knowledge progressed qualitatively, and the reform of Judaism was no mere convenience but a demand born of intellectual honesty. Because we are better informed today than in the past, the sacred literature of tradition could occupy only a subsidiary place in the determination of modern Judaism.

Today, this outlook has become problematic. This is not to say that there has been any hint of a compromise with the fundamentally liberal attitude toward tradition. Yet some rabbis at the Institute felt that the Bible, for example, contains a revelation of truth which has not changed and will not change. They concede that the historical context in which that truth was expressed has changed, and their attitude toward the Bible as a text is still critical. But they insist that there is A Truth in the Bible, and that this truth is as important to us as our knowledge of God. The latter expresses the same truth in the concrete terms of our own time and specific conditions. The former serves as a guide and check. There must be a tension between the two. This attitude denies essential progress but not change and reform.

A special word is necessary on the impact of the Existentialist interpretation of Judaism offered by Rabbi Emil L. Fackenheim, both in the round tables and by his formal paper. He held that the brutal facts of the past fifty years had demonstrated conclusively man's inability to "save" himself. To those who believe that the universe is without plan or purpose, existence is a tragedy without relief which one should meet with as much courage as one can muster. The religious man, convinced that life has a meaning, believes in a real, transcendent God who will eventually "save" man. Salvation by progress is an error of nineteenth-century idealism which was grafted onto Judaism by the theological speculation of the last century. To the question of authority, Rabbi Fackenheim felt that only a tentative answer could be given at the moment. While the religious man's relation to God was something certain and necessary, rising above the flow of time, the ceremonial and ritual practices and institutions of Israel could only be defended as a means of accepting one's particular position in the contingencies of history and fulfilling it.

Existentialism came as a profound philosophical shock to the assembled rabbis. But the immediate reaction of annoyance at a new terminology and a new way of thinking soon changed to appreciation of the direct response this point of view has to offer to modern man's perplexity. Religious Existentialism considers man's innate inadequacy and anxiety as the norm of human existence. This view makes our modern bewilderment seem less the result of a catastrophic regression than the natural return from an unwarranted optimism. While there was no mass conversion to Existentialism, most of the rabbis agreed with Rabbi Fackenheim that it would be useful to Reform even if only as an antidote to the nineteenth-century idealist interpretation of Judaism.

It is not surprising that the forty-eight hours allotted for discussion were insufficient for more than a tentative exploration of the various problems. Though it was decided not to issue any comprehensive statement, the

Institute as a whole, in plenary session, gave unanimous approval to the acceptance and publication in its name of the following paragraphs on the mission of Israel:

> As touching the life of the Jew, our mission challenges us to win back to positive participation in Jewish religious life (1) those Jews who are unsynagogued; (2) those who have roamed away from traditional Judaism and who are groping for an expression of religion more congenial to their modern outlook; (3) to bring our own concept of Judaism to those Jews who live in non-progressive, religiously static areas of the world; (4) to assist Reform, or Progressive, congregations that are struggling to achieve self-sufficiency, wherever they may be; (5) and to assist in the creation of such congregations wherever the need for them may be expressed. The resuscitated State of Israel, whose spiritual potentialities seem unlimited, presents an important challenge and unique opportunity to Reform Judaism.
>
> As touching the world in general, our mission has been to some extent fulfilled in the acceptance by Christianity and Mohammedanism of our Bible. However, the practical fulfillment of our mission requires firstly, a recognition that we have been derelict in our devotion to our mission; and secondly, a resolve that we implement the ideals of our faith by supporting every positive and progressive endeavor seeking to establish social justice, in cooperation with all men of good will; and thirdly, to promote within the congregations of Israel projects of social justice and social service among the despised and rejected, regardless of race or creed.

This definition of the practical tasks of Israel was given point by the personal presence and powerful preachment of Rabbi Moses Weiler of Johannesburg, South Africa, who was in the United States for his first visit in the seventeen years since he was graduated from the Hebrew Union College. He spoke to the rabbis of his struggles in establishing Reform synagogues, first in Johannesburg and later in other communities, and of his continuing fight to win a place for them in the South African Jewish community. He emphasized with great force on several occasions during the Institute that it was a real belief in Israel's mission, and the practical activity which the liberal congregations had undertaken because of it, which had vitalized the movement in South Africa. They had tried to win the unaffiliated back to Judaism. They had undertaken projects for their white Christian neighbors and had even made the unprecedented step of opening a non-missionary, self-run school for Negroes. If the American congregations were not alive, he insisted, it was largely because they had lost the sense of mission.

It was not only Rabbi Weiler's vigor which influenced the rabbis to give their unanimous assent to the statement on the mission of Israel, but the corroboration offered by their common experience and thought in the past decade or more. What is perhaps more significant is that, while there was no agreement as to the theological basis of Israel's mission, there was complete unanimity as to its pragmatic meaning.

The same disparity between the theological and the pragmatic was found in the treatment of the question of a guide for Reform practice. Since the late thirties there has been an increasing clamor for such a guide. At the moment it is the most hotly debated issue in Reform Judaism, both in the rabbinate and among the laity.

As soon as the first registration cards were mailed to the chairman, Rabbi Ferdinand Isserman of St. Louis, Missouri, it was clear that the round table on Reform Jewish practice was to be the best attended of all the round tables scheduled to meet. The chairman had also solicited statements of theological belief from a number of rabbis on the subjects to be discussed at the Institute. Almost unanimously the statements he received on "Reform Jewish Practice" avoided theology and dealt instead with the practicality of a "Guide," or the merits or evils of its adoption. The discussions of the round table at the Institute continued this pattern.

Not only was this non-theological round table one of the best attended at the Institute on Theology; it was also, to speak strictly, a non-theological paper which was best received. Rabbi Lou H. Silberman of Omaha, Nebraska, delivered a lecture on "A *Shulchan Aruch* for Reform Judaism" (a title not of his own choosing). It was a most eloquent *kaddish* to the memory of his beloved teacher, Dr. Jacob Z. Lauterbach, whose eighth *yahrzeit* occurred that day. After a brilliant if brief introductory analysis of the criteria which should be employed, he discussed the significance of the form in which such a guide should be presented. He also decisively demonstrated by examples taken from the history of Reform in America—from its experience with the Union Prayer Book and the Columbus platform, both of which had been the occasion for (unwarranted) fear and trembling—that such a work would not congeal the freedom of the movement or render it a new orthodoxy. It was a mature paper, deserving the warm reception it received.

Shortly thereafter the Institute voted, with but two negative ballots, to accept a resolution of the round table on "Reform Jewish Practice." In effect this statement declared that there was a need for a "Guide to Reform Jewish Practice" and formally asked the Central Conference to take steps to create one. Again it should be noted that while there was no agreement as to the meaning of revelation in modern Judaism, its practical consequences—ritual, ceremonial, law—were almost unanimously desired.

Because psychiatry has only recently become a matter of great interest to the rabbinate, the discussion on "Judaism and Psychiatry" indicated even more clearly the distance between rabbinical experience with practical matters, and systematic theological thinking.

While no round table discussed this subject, part of an evening was devoted to it by means of a paper by Rabbi Julius Gordon of St. Louis, Missouri. Unfortunately the lecture was an informal one and hence did not pretend to comprehensiveness. It dealt almost entirely with the apparent similarities between the teachings of Judaism and psychiatric dicta, and only partially with the question of the compatibility of the two. On the basis of Freud's *The Future of an Illusion,* Rabbi Gordon felt that while Freud did not accept religion, he did not reject it either, and that harmony was possible.

After the lecture a number of rabbis stated the problems they have had in relation to psychiatry, ranging from lack of cooperation by psychiatrists in practical matters to conflicts with psychiatric theory and therapy on the basis of Jewish belief. The standard reply to these questions by Rabbi Gordon and others who spoke was that psychiatry is necessary if we wish to cure the ill and the maladjusted. Its therapy has marvelous accomplishments to show, and the rabbinate in its traditional Jewish appreciation of *r'fuo* (healing) cannot but accept it. Moreover, it was asserted, every rabbi who deals daily with congregants in the moments of their greatest emotional crises values the insights that psychiatry has given him and which make it possible for him to accomplish his spiritual tasks more successfully. Psychiatry was regarded as a "creative ally," but there was no attempt to make sharp and explicit the terms of the alliance.

It became obvious to the rabbis themselves, as the Institute progressed, that while their practical maturity had grown in their years of experience, they had neglected to maintain a corresponding theological growth.

This observation will come as a shock to those who have assumed that Reform Judaism is a theological movement. Was not "Jewish theology" a product of Reform, which sought to establish its validity by theological research and formulation? It was Kaufman Kohler, a president of the Hebrew Union College, writing for the cause of Reform Judaism, who produced *Jewish Theology*, the first systematic work on the subject. Even today the works of Baeck, Montefiore, Cohon, and Buber (who must certainly be classed with the liberals) make up nearly all the advanced works in the Jewish field.

Yet even a cursory examination of the history of the movement shows that Reform, like traditional Judaism, has been occupied mainly with the practical problems "of living a Jewish life." Dr. Joseph Silverman, president of the Conference, at the Bar Mitzvah meeting of the Central Conference of American Rabbis in 1903, was proud to say that it had devoted itself to the questions of: "Public Worship, Marriage and Divorce, Confirmation, Proselytism, Cremation, Zionism, Interpretation of Bible and Talmud, Funeral Reforms, Rabbinical Ethics, Religious Instruction, Circuit Preaching, Religious Propaganda, the Unaffiliated, etc." The index of the Conference Yearbooks has few references to theology, almost all of them in connection with the early (1903-1908) discussions on a synod. As Rabbi Hyman G. Enelow so pithily put it in 1904: "The Conference is not a summer school of theology. Its purpose is practical."

The Reform movement today, then, is just emerging from a period in which the rabbis rejected theology almost completely. A Hebrew Union College graduate of the twenties remarked at the Institute that in his day almost everyone was "for religion and against theology." They had a real faith in God as the guarantor of human dignity, but beyond that they had little interest. Their concern with Jewish existence was directed at halting assimilation, fighting anti-Semitism, or enlisting in the ranks of the Zionists or anti-Zionists. Social justice and the prophetic role were the rabbinic order of the day, and the rabbis dedicated themselves to the fight for civil rights and social reform. Theology smacked of "pie in the sky" and was viewed with the traditional Jewish skepticism towards preoccupation with hidden things when there was so much to be done with what had already been revealed. That skepticism still persists.

The Hebrew Union College itself was unable to bring to its students a realization of theology's function and significance. Not in any one department of the college alone, but in every area where the ideas of Judaism were taught, there was detailed scientific investigation and thorough historical training, but no inspiring theological creativity. The imagination neither of the rabbinate nor of the laity was captured for liberal Jewish theology. But to be sure, it is asking a good deal of any group of men that they reverse completely the social currents of their hour.

In the very opening hour of the Institute, the venerable Rabbi Leo Baeck gave an inspiring and authoritative analysis of "Jewish Theology Today."

Jewish theology, he said, is always, at the hour of its creation, Jewish theology for today. When the time is explosive, when frightening events belie the old questions and the old answers, then a new theology is needed.

The questions which are asked in these times of stress, Rabbi Baeck continued, are not really new ones, for only four or five basic questions have troubled man since the beginning of time. One of these questions may, in a sense, be called the "Jewish question": "It is the problem of the transcendent becoming immanent, of the being entering into the passing, the eternal into the transient, the infinite into the finite, the creator into the creature, of the rational growing up out of the non-rational, the fathomable out of the unfathomable, the distinct out of the secret, the commandment out of the mystery. However we call it: creation, revelation, prophecy, law, hope, messianism, it is always the same problem, the problem manifested by Judaism."

This question, or one of the others, will on occasion take hold of a man, and he will be compelled to struggle with it, to make it his own, to join it to his individual way of thinking and speaking. Through this grappling, his thought and language are re-created and the question itself assumes a new form. He is then finally able to give it new expression. These three factors, the problem, the personality, and the resolve of the personality to struggle with the problem are all necessary to bring about a new expression of the problem, a new theology.

But the problem itself is neither new nor without historical experience. To be Jewish theology, the new thinking must be an expression of Jewish tradition. This includes not only the Halacha ("the sphere of law") but also the Aggada ("the sphere of the idea"), the poetry, the philosophy, the customs, and all the rest of our religious treasure. In the sphere of the idea there must be constant change, for its very production is for and through the individual. In keeping with this, the tradition of Judaism has been handed down not from one exclusive authority to any single authoritative body, but to the many congregations. Hence no *Schulchan Aruch* is possible in Judaism in the realm of the idea as there is in the realm of law.

The old liberal theology based on nineteenth century idealism might have weathered the tumultuous thirties, but it could not survive the bestial forties. We are concerned because we are in crisis. And what we require is not a single, fabricated statement of belief but bold theological thinking to make clear the relevance of Judaism today.

If this be the way that Jewish theology must take, then the Institute can be said to have made a significant contribution. The rabbis who attended the round table on "Revelation" were well enough satisfied to report to the Institute that they had found their discussions "fruitful and stimulating," even though they were able to arrive at no more than a delineation of the eight major problems they felt existed in that area. What is more, the confrontation with the problems had had a profound personal effect upon the rabbis present. An older member of the rabbinate was able to say with sincerity that it was "one of the most moving spiritual experiences I have had since I was ordained." Equally impressive was the insistence of the rabbis that the Institute's work had been too important to be ended in one three-day meeting. They voted unanimously to formally recommend to the Conference the establishment of a permanent Institute on Theology to meet annually. The problems had captured the men.

2 / Creating Commitment in Our Religious Schools

1956

It is a sign both of some modest success in Jewish education and of some emerging maturity in the ranks of Reform Jewry that we can devote ourselves to this particular problem: the creation of commitment in our religious schools.

It is not so long ago that we Jewish educators would have felt happy if we were transmitting to each child the facts of Judaism. Let the child know the Ten Commandments and memorize some of the more beautiful passages from the Bible. Let him be familiar with the prayer book and be able to read at least its more important prayers in Hebrew. Let him be acquainted with the history of our people, the cycle of its religious year and the important events in each man's life. Indeed, this list of information is impressive and there are many who would still consider this their sole goal.

But a little reflection reminds us that there is a considerable gap between the mind and the soul. It is one thing to know the facts of history, the terms for our ceremonies and the words of our prayers, and quite another to want to live by them. It did not take long for Jewish educators to recognize that more important than information was attitude—and the attitude of most Jews to Judaism in our society was decidedly negative. If the Jew was unhappy in his Jewishness he could scarcely be receptive or retentive, nor would he allow what Jewish information he absorbed to enter into his life. More important, the addition of knowledge would not of itself change the attitude, and unless a change was made, the system was self-destructive.

POSITIVE JEWISH CONDITIONING

So Jewish educators and Jewish parents (the true Jewish educators) set to work to condition a generation of Jews positively to Judaism. The Jewish holidays became the focus of this effort. Chanuko became a major Jewish festival as did Purim, and every Jewish pleasure from *hakofos* (synagogue Torah scroll circuits) to *homontaschen* (Purim pastries) was brought to bear upon our impressionable charges with wonderful results. By and large our children today have a sense of security in their Jewishness and, more than that, a positive attitude toward things Jewish. This success, let me add, stems not so much from the ingenuity and talent of Jewish educators as it does from two other essential factors. First, the very decision of our parents to relate their children affirmatively to their Jewishness and hence to take a stand themselves; and second, the innate value and worth of the Jewish heritage itself which, given a chance to be heard, has again asserted its ability to speak with meaning to us as it did in the past.

But this in turn has brought us to our present embarrassment. Is Judaism a psychological gimmick we use to counterbalance our sociological maladjustment, an emotional sinking fund we lay up to offset the deficits we incur by being different—a means to self-delusion by which we hope to achieve some peace of mind? Or is Judaism today what it was in the past, a faith to live by, a set of values to judge by, and our primary source of truth about God, man, and the universe?

If Judaism is more than a means toward adjustment, if it is more than an analgesic for our minority status, if it is an end in itself, if it is still meaningful, if it is still *true,* then we cannot settle for conditioning. Instead we require commitment.

WHAT IS MEANT BY RELIGIOUS COMMITMENT?

We require a Jew whose Judaism is a part of his very self, his identity, his life—one whose Judaism is no separate bundle of feelings or emotions which stands apart from what he is. We require a Jew whose Judaism is not something special or additional in him, but an essential part of him, as inseparable from him as his sense of duty, his reaction to beauty and his attitude toward right and wrong. His Judaism is what he is, because he has committed himself, his life, his talent, his knowledge, his hopes, his fears to Judaism, and, through it, he will live his days.

Jewish educators who believe in Judaism are dedicated to making every child in their schools become this kind of devoted Jew.

The goal of commitment is not a substitute for conditioning. We still require it. Surely we cannot expect a normal person to unite his life with a faith he despises. But commitment goes at least two steps beyond conditioning. When we achieve commitment, we strive to live by Jewish standards, for these are now our standards, inseparable from our own goals. But conditioning can only predispose one to accept them. It creates the favorable attitude—but one does not condition another into making a decision. The gap between disposition and decision remains wide and unbridged.

Moreover, the conditioning we practice is based on the pleasantness of Jewishness. But being a Jew is often not pleasant. To be a Jew in our society takes a special effort, an effort not required of others. For many in our own day, the pleasures of Judaism are not worth the effort being Jewish requires—and this in a pleasant, prosperous decade. In another decade filled with the turbulence say of the thirties, how many buyers would Judaism find in a market where prices were high and dividends small?

In a larger sense, what would have been the outcome of Jewish history with its record of suffering and martyrdom if our generations had been trained to live by the credo: I'm glad I'm a Jew, for Judaism is enjoyable. No one wants the dark ages to return, nor should we set our goals as if we had to live in them. Nonetheless, it is remarkable how easy it is in this fluorescent twentieth century of ours for the darkness to reappear.

If it is true that Jews have suffered for their Judaism and may have yet to suffer in the future, is positive conditioning an honest preparation for Jewish life? Is it even an honest approach to everyone's life as we know it? Are not disappointment, frustration, pain, even tragedy, a real part of every man's life? And if my life and my Judaism are to be one, then my attitude toward Judaism, my relationship to it must be shaped in such a way as to include this harsh truth and prepare me to face it in my own life.

WHAT DOES GOD REQUIRE?

In the last analysis, we stand before the simple question which faces the Jewish educator in everything he does: Can God be satisfied with this? Can God require less than commitment? Can He be satisfied with positive conditioning or does He require the soul of man, the whole of the man devoted to Him—as the prayer which follows our declaration of faith says, "Thou shalt love the Lord, thy God, with all thy heart, with all thy soul and with all thy might. . . ."

When I am committed to Judaism, I am not committed to its pleasures or its delights but to it, itself. I know of no finer example of Jewish commitment, particularly as distinguished from positive conditioning, than that quoted in the wonderful little anthology edited by Nathan Glatzer for the Schocken Press, *In Time and Eternity,* taken from Solomon Ibn Verga's *Shevet Yehudah:*

> I heard from some of the elders who came out of Spain that one of the boats was infested with the plague, and the captain of the boat put the passengers ashore at some uninhabited place. And there most of them died of starvation, while some of them gathered up all their strength to set out on foot in search of some settlement.
>
> There was one Jew among them who struggled on afoot together with his wife and two children. The wife grew faint and died, because she was not accustomed to so much difficult walking. The husband carried his children along until both he and they fainted from hunger. When he regained consciousness, he found that his two children had died.
>
> In great grief he rose to his feet and said: "O Lord of all the universe, you are doing a great deal that I might even desert my faith. But know you of a certainty that—even against the will of heaven—a Jew I am and a Jew I shall remain. And neither that which you have brought upon me nor that which you will yet bring upon me will be of any avail."
>
> Thereupon he gathered some earth and some grass, and covered the boys, and went forth in search of a settlement.

Some I imagine will be puzzled at this goal I am trying to describe. It sounds rather fanatic, narrow-minded, irrational. And this reaction only goes to show what a sorry state religion is in in our day. Can a truly religious man be any less than this? Can he be truly religious for part of the time or with part of himself? We are a little afraid of such commitment because for most of us the picture of the religious man often connotes harshness, unreason, bigotry and atavism. Unfortunately, there do not spring to mind readily a hundred memories of the modern religious men we desire, dedicated to their own faith yet not intolerant of that of others, devoted to their own religious system yet not parochial in their interests, devout yet not medieval. Such a man does not require explanation but exemplars.

This is what Judaism wants of the Jew. Indeed this is what every religion wants of its adherents for this is what God truly requires of us.

Then how shall we try to reach this goal?

RELIGIOUS COMMITMENT CANNOT BE TAUGHT

Let me first give the negative prescriptions. No principal, no teacher, no human being can "commit" another to a religion, a faith, a way of life. Commitment comes from within. It is something you will, consciously or unconsciously—and as the will is finally free, so genuine commitment must be freely arrived at. It cannot come from without at the insistence or persuasion of another. It is for yourself that you are being asked, and only you can give it.

Hence we cannot "teach" commitment or "transmit" it in our religious schools. We can only hope to create a situation in which commitment is possible, or better still, likely. The inner act itself remains beyond us.

There is, in fact, no direct way of creating commitment. You cannot make it a subject, or set definite times when you can ask each child whether he really wants to live as a Jew. People seem to take such frontal attacks on their intimacy rather hard, and instead of helping create commitment, such indelicacy on the part of the one who presents such questions often tends to postpone or prevent decision. As in all such deeply personal questions, the only pathway is indirect and tangential, except in the most exceptional and personal situations. Since we generally cannot be direct, we cannot be sure of being the effective influence we would like to be. This is the risk that honesty dictates we undertake in religious education.

If this is not difficult enough, let it be noted that since the very nature of what we desire is personal and subjective, what will be helpful or decisive for one person may be meaningless for another. Foxholes made as many atheists as believers, though I think it made momentary thinkers of all. Some come to decision in a moment of drama and crisis; others are never involved in doubt or ambiguity; while most must move along adding impressions here and reactions there until eventually a patchwork tower of Jewish faith is created. We require the *individual*, and because we do, we cannot make rules that will pave the way to universal success.

Jewish education is really so improbable a task even before we begin it, it is not strange that so many fall so easily into the traps of verbalization or emotional manipulation.

COMMITMENT IS NOT A CATECHISM

Let us say without qualification that we are not talking about intellectual indoctrination. A child can memorize many a fine phrase about what he believes, Confirmation classes can stand before the open ark and speak beautiful vows of faith, Bar Mitzvah boys with their hands on the Torah will pledge to continue their study in sincere voices that turn grandparents into sentimental slush, but this is a far cry from genuine commitment as their lives and subsequent actions show. Words are not decisions, nor does committing phrases to memory commit the self to God through Judaism. Verbalization remains our best rationalization for not bringing our children to true commitment.

By the same token it is not hard to manipulate the emotions of children so as to win psychological victories for ourselves. They can be made to cry, to laugh, to thrill, to exult by any reasonably effective group technician and it takes an antiseptically honest leader to place the needs of the group before his own. The effects of group manipulation are transitory in nature, but commitment does not so easily disappear. And while commitment is of necessity linked to the truth, such manipulation of group emotions is linked only to the false goals and standards of a selfish leader. The knowledge of his dishonesty and betrayal, unconscious though it be, makes difficult identification with his cause. There is a real need for honest emotional experiences in Jewish education, but we must not substitute small experiments in group hysteria for authentic emotional participation, simply because the former is easier to achieve.

If it seems that the goal of Jewish education is impossible of achievement, then it should be said in all honesty, it is indeed a most difficult thing to accomplish, perhaps the most difficult in all the world, and yet at the same time the most precious. The religious man, the creature who is able to come to know God and to link his personal destiny with the purposes he sees operating about him, this animal is the climax of creation, the purpose for which the world was called into being. It is no easy thing to achieve this goal, to help complete creation, but there is none more worth striving for—and there are some definite directions we can take toward it.

INFLUENCING BY PERSONAL EXAMPLE

First, and most important, commitment can be caught from one who already has it. The sense of his dedication seems to project beyond the religious man, and those around him are strongly influenced by it. Thus it is a universal religious phenomenon, unrestricted to one religion or another, that the great religious men have attracted circles of disciples.

Often what these common people were unable to accomplish on their own, they could do in the presence of the man who truly believed.

Among the many examples of this in Judaism, the outstanding one is the Chasidic movement which made this principle the basis of its institutional organization. The Chasidim grouped themselves around the various Tzaddikim, and if one could not live near one's rebbe, so as to be in his presence often, one at least made pilgrimages to his home to renew the contact. While the Chasidim considered the preachments of their rebbe important, more important was being with him. It was not so much what he said but what he was; not so much his teaching, but his being, that had its effect. As Rabbi Leib the son of Sara said: "I did not go to Rabbi Dov Ber of Mezritch to hear Torah from him but to watch him tie his shoe-lace." It is not as important to teach Torah as to be Torah. The truly religious man is religious in all he does, because he is religious in all he is, and sometimes the spark jumps the gap from him to me.

THE TEACHER'S ROLE IS CRUCIAL

This means then that the most important method or technique of religious education is the being, the person, the soul of those who represent it to the child. The indispensable ingredient of our schools is the genuine and thoroughgoing commitment of our rabbis, our supervisors and our teachers to Judaism. When they are Jews in this full sense of the term, there is some hope that our children, too, may make Judaism a real part of their selves. Without our religious school leaders feeling this way, how can our children be expected to find their way?

So professional competence is no substitute for personal commitment. We do not have such things as lesson plans to bring about ultimate decisions. We cannot have them, and, even if we could, the most competent direction by a non-participating teacher would doom them from the start.

But the rabbi, the principal, the teacher who is a committed Jew will make his commitment felt in whatever he does—whether it be in his relations with other teachers, while talking casually before or after class, while dealing with the material of the lesson or by participating with a full and believing heart in the activities of the school and of the synagogue.

Such persons are truly rare in our day and there can be no doubt that on the practical level we must often accept far less. But this should not obscure either the truth or the goal. The most important means of religious education is the being of those who conduct it. Hence our first and most important task as Jewish educators is to search deep within ourselves and be certain of our own commitment to Judaism. Only then can we hope to play our proper role with faculty and students alike.

In another age one might hope that the student could pick this up at home and thus relieve the school of this tremendous challenge. The facts of our day place this burden, as well as many other equally improbable ones, upon the school. But if the desired rabbis, principals and teachers are rare, if we do not have many such living persons around us, at least the school possesses stories of such persons.

What makes a great Jew great is his Jewish living. When we tell stories of Moses and Jeremiah, of the real man struggling to do what the real God wants of him; when even for an instant we catch a glimpse of the soul of Ben Zakkai, Akiba or Maimonides, living Judaism in their day in their own way, our own lives are influenced.

The trouble is, of course, that the man is dead, not alive; gone, not present; not having the effect his person would if he were right before you. And the teacher who does not feel the same reality in his soul that our great Jewish heroes did will have a difficult time making this clear or convincing, and probably even of identifying this as the point of the story, the goal of what he is trying to do in class.

REMOVING INTELLECTUAL BLOCKS

Which brings us to the second positive approach, the intellectual side of achieving commitment, for it should be obvious that to try to commit one's self but to withhold one's mind makes no sense. Here the first and most important thing that we must do is to make commitment possible by clearing the way to it of untruth and hypocrisy. One cannot ask a man to dedicate himself to a cause his reason tells him is not true and to a lesser degree to express it in forms that his aesthetic sense tells him are objectionable and tasteless. Hence we cannot teach that the miracles of the Bible happened just as the Bible describes them. Hence we must teach the story of Creation and affirm all its religious truth while still making possible the truths of evolution and paleontology. Hence we must dispense in our society with such practices as requiring the mourners or worshippers on some occasions to go about in their stocking feet.

When we do what we can to keep the road toward Judaism free of blocks and detours, we can hope the individual will then find his way.

But we can do more than this. Through our teaching we can help him feel again and again the truth, the worth, the appeal of the Jewish religious experience and insight. That is to say, the Jewish tradition has reacted to the universe and its meaning in a certain way. It has formulated certain ideas and patterns of action. Whenever a child hears of these and they strike a chord within him so that he responds almost instinctively, almost intuitively, from his depths, "This is true, I believe this," he has, for a moment, identified Judaism with himself and hence been brought closer to our goal.

Some of our favorite lessons operate on this level. The primary child really understands and believes with Abraham that the idols are not God but only statues. The idea of one God for all the world is true for them in the same way that tolerance, love of neighbor and peace are accepted with a whole heart by an older child. But while these are the common merchandise of our schools, they do not by any means deplete Judaism's spiritual inventory. Judaism's attitude toward man, his nature, his responsibility, his goals, his sins, his repentance, his hope—its attitude toward history, toward law and discipline in religion, toward a hundred other things could also well be taught. These, too, would raise the sense of truth within the child and help him see that Judaism and his deepest sense of truth and right are one. But to effect this, our theologians must make these and our other concepts available in readily understandable forms, so that our teachers can then find those of relevance to the child and devise techniques for making them clear.

USING THE BIBLE AND OTHER TEXTS

And lastly, in this series, it may be of some help, though this is clearly the least promising suggestion of the lot, to make available to the child some of those materials which have had a direct influence on other religious persons in the past. Here one says simply, this seems to have worked before, and as long as we do not transgress our other rules, let us try this, too. The Bible was once a great influence in Jewish piety but today it is probably our most difficult subject to teach. Yet people are still affected by the Bible—not just its heroes, but by its other stories, its poetry, its prophecy, and its laws as well. To many people the Bible still speaks, and we should try as best we can to find a way of acquainting our children with it.

Yet we need not limit ourselves to the Bible alone. One of the most effective pieces of Jewish religious writing with children is almost contemporary, not more than sixty years old, the prayer for peace in the *Union Prayerbook.* Despite the almost utter failure in the classroom of every anthology of Jewish literature, there is a place for contact with the writings that have helped other Jews become and remain religious—though exactly what that place should be or which writings we should choose remains to be carefully worked out within the context of all that we have said.

All of which should make it abundantly clear that the great game of curriculum tinkering does not have very much really to do with bringing us to the goal of Jewish religious education. As long as the curriculum offers a reasonably well-rounded introduction to Judaism of the past and the present and is reasonably well geared to the interests and abilities of children on a given age level, one curriculum will be as satisfactory as the next. To announce the salvation of Jewish education simply by shifting the same old courses around from grade to grade and calling them by different names is to avoid the true goal which is the achievement of the personal, intimate and free commitment of the individual Jew. It is not so much the pattern of the courses that counts, as who teaches them, and it is not so much the sequence of the courses, as the ability of the teacher to evoke affirmation through them that is crucial. We have enough curricula now that satisfy these minimal requirements to keep us busy for a long time to come. What we do not have is the proper people to exemplify and teach them, or a very good knowledge of how to bring such people into being.

If there is anything that should be said regarding curriculum, it is, and this is the third positive suggestion, that we should emphasize those activities which involve the whole person. If we can bring our children even for a little while, to live as Jews, to "be" Jews in the full sense that our education is reaching toward, then we have given them an insight, a personal experience of what we are driving at, which will serve them both as a motive and a goal.

SUCCESSFUL EXPERIMENTS AT SUMMER CAMPS

So far this has been accomplished best in camp situations. The success of the National Federation of Temple Youth in its specifically Jewish objectives, has been due largely to its camp program. It has done this by going to camps, where, cut off from normal society, it could create a modern, yet Jewish community, in which one lives as a modern Jew for a number of days. In such an environment one need not preach much about being a modern Jew—one simply is, or soon becomes one for the duration of the camp. The experience of such days, the meaning they give to personal existence as man and Jew, reaches down to the realities of existence and remains to stimulate and uplift for long afterward.

This kind of program has been tried with younger children to a limited degree at camps associated with the Wilshire Boulevard Temple of Los Angeles and Temple Emanu-El of Denver. We also have the experience of a camping program for religious school children at the Camp for Living Judaism in Saratoga, sponsored by the West Coast Region of the Union of American Hebrew Congregations and at Oconomowoc, conducted by the Union's Chicago Federation of Reform Synagogues. There is still much room for trial and experiment in this area and every forward-looking synagogue should consider what it can do in its own locale to make possible such total experiences by groups of its children for even short periods of time.

Of course the two- or three-hour religious school session cannot hope to accomplish anything like the total life experience of the camp, but it can involve the whole child in many activities. Normally we would think of such things as pageants, plays or dances as involving the total personality. But insofar as these are labeled, categorized, cut off from the other things the child does in the school, they, too, are but partial experiences. However, the teacher who can move out of the intellectual and social activity of learning to create something which involves the child in thinking, planning, executing and evaluating, particularly when in the course of these activities all the student's talents are required, that teacher has brought the child closer to our goal.

THE PLACE OF PRAYER

It may seem strange to say so, but the one activity in which the whole person is truly involved is prayer. If you can get a child really to pray, then you are bringing him all in all to face whatever there is to be found in the world. For one cannot speak honestly with half a heart or with mental reservations—to speak truly with another is to speak with all one's self. But how does one get a child truly to pray? How strange that after all these years of religious education, we do not know how to answer that question!

Yet, two things can be said: First, pray with your children when and how you yourself can truly pray—and more difficult, encourage them to help you know when they want to pray. Second, there is in preparation now a book of children's services sponsored by the Central Conference of American Rabbis which strives honestly to provide prayer services which can be of meaning and inspiration to different ages of children each on their own level. This, most regretfully, is all that can be said on so important a subject.

Yet one thing more remains to be said about what can be done, and that is to remind us to be ever mindful of and watchful for the sensitive moment. There are such moments, times when suddenly a sense of wonder comes to the fore, when a desire to know causes one to ask the full-hearted question, when, for a change, you really care and really want to know. The right word or phrase at such a time, the answer which comprehends the question and the questioner, which speaks a truth known and lived, will reach a depth normally inaccessible with a directness otherwise impossible.

One never knows when such moments will come for the smart boy with the broken home, the cute red-headed girl with every luxury, the listless, barely average kid whose home is as dull and colorless as he is. Sometimes it happens after class when someone stays to ask something that he could not say before the class and which he wants to talk of now, when the teacher is in a hurry to get home and started on the outing he has been promising his family for weeks. Sometimes it comes with unexpected suddenness in class when you strike, for no good reason you can see, a chord in the heart of this or that child. Sometimes you see there is something troubling a child or making him quite happy and a remark will start a chain that leads to a moment of inquiry and receptivity. Sometimes (how rarely) a lesson will catch fire and involve you and almost every person in the room in an experience of sympathy and understanding which none of you could have predicted, or can now explain.

RARE MOMENTS IN THE RELIGIOUS SCHOOL

They come, such moments. The great teacher is one who, from time to time, creates such moments though he does not himself know how or why. The good teacher, even if he cannot produce them often, will at least wait for them to appear, recognize them when they do, follow them wherever they may lead and, if possible, let them result in a form of expression which will involve his students, heart and soul.

Is this not the true purpose of pedagogy—to bring the student to the point where he wants to know, when he calls from his depths for information to take into his soul? If he asks such a question, and if you have arrived at such a mood, then the lesson plan is unimportant and the subject matter, having served its purpose, may be forgotten.

The principal who is too rigid and inflexible for such deviations from the curriculum does not belong in a religious school but in a factory—and in one where automation has replaced human beings. Anyone who insists on rules and regulations by which to regiment and determine all, or even most of the factors of religious education, is doomed even before he begins, for what we seek is an individual, personal, private decision. No matter how necessary the rules, or how helpful the administrative procedures, it is the individual whom we require—every precious individuality of the masses of dull and bright, disinterested and interested, maladjusted and happy children we see. Nothing less can satisfy God, and hence satisfy us.

Does Jewish religious education now seem impossible, its approach so tenuous, its attainment so unlikely? Then recognize, too, that anyone who has had the experience of the sensitive moment in the classroom, who has helped children come close to the truth and relevance of Judaism, has in the moment of their affirmation been renewed himself. Such single moments of contact and reality make up for the many days when only information or some slight emotional charge passes between you and your students, and you wonder if the process is worth the pains of its seeming failure. But let such a moment come, and the doubt is quenched in the immediate sense of certainty of the value of the process.

THE TEACHER'S REWARD

And even when it does not come as quickly as one desires it, there is consolation in the experience of most older teachers. How many times in later years will a student return to tell you of things you did which you can no longer recall, or of casual incidents or comments you cannot remember which meant a lot to him and have been a source of strength or inspiration in his life. The truth of teaching in so personal a field is that we and our students alike cannot tell whether we have succeeded or failed, for what the individual in the depth of his being selects and saves from all that we offer him is mostly hidden from us and often from him as well.

And if this be but small consolation and seems but an attempt to save our defeat from being complete, then we must reply that Jewish religious education cannot fail despite us, though it can hardly succeed without us, for God requires Israel. It is He who says that Israel shall exist and serve Him. Indeed He is the true religious educator of us all, for history is no more than His classroom and we, all of us, His recalcitrant students.

If we are devoted to Jewish religious education, it is because we have faith in Him and His purposes, because we know we want to help Him—as difficult and unlikely as that seems—because working with Him, we cannot fail.

From the calculating, the hardheaded, the realistic point of view, Jewish religious education cannot succeed. From the standpoint of faith it cannot fail. Commitment, then, is not only the goal, it is the means, the motive and the source of hope as well.

3 / The Idea of God

1957

Ledor vador nagid godlecha
Ulenetzach netzachim kedushatcha nakdish
Veshivchacha Eloheinu mipinu lo yamush leolam vaed

Our genial chairman has with most uncharacteristic severity insisted that this paper must not extend *ledor vador*, from generation to generation, nor to *netzach netzachim*, from eternity to eternity, nor even *leolam vaed,* forever and ever, but must end in forty-five minutes. Under the circumstances, then, I am grateful that his kind invitation was not to speak to you about God, His greatness, His Holiness and His praise, but only, *nebbach,* about the idea of God.

Now it is clear that Judaism requires a belief in God, but what kind of idea of God, what sort of mental construct or intellectual picture of Him does it deem necessary? What is the Jewish idea of God?

The answer to that question would seem, at first, to be the purpose of this paper. But I am troubled by a question which logically demands prior consideration. How will we recognize the Jewish idea of God when we find it? Among the concepts proposed by Mordecai Kaplan, Martin Buber, Hermann Cohen, Eric Fromm and others, how shall we judge which may properly be called Jewish? What are the criteria by which we may determine whether this formulation rather than that is truly the Jewish idea of God?

This crucial question, as far as I have been able to ascertain, has rarely been dealt with in our day. Yet unless our standard of judgment about the idea of God is first made clear, unless we can establish with reasonable certainty what Judaism requires of an idea of God, our partisanship of this or that concept is equally meaningless. Hence I must request that it is to the question of the proper form of the idea of God in Judaism, not to the delineation of its correct content, that I may devote what I hope will seem to you the less-than-eternity that I have been given.

Where shall we begin this investigation of ideational form? We must, I think, first find the place of the idea of God within the structure of Jewish religion as a whole, remembering that it is not belief in God, or the reality of God, or the existence of God with which we are concerned, but only the idea of Him which we create. Once we have found the relationship of this idea to the other elements of Judaism, we will then be able to establish the criteria which we seek.

We turn, first, to the place of the idea of God in Judaism.

It will, I think, help us clarify our perspective to begin with a brief look at how some other religions have dealt with this matter.

In Christianity, it seems clear, not just belief in God, but one's idea of God is crucial. This is not due simply to Christianity's early conquest and absorption of Greek philosophy. The idea of God has been of vital significance to more than Christian theologians alone. Paul made faith in the crucified and risen Christ central to Christianity. It is through his faith in the Christ that a man becomes a Christian, that he lives as a Christian and that he achieves salvation. But the Christ is God, God become man, God who suffered and died, God who saves us from our sins. Not every faith will save a man. It is the specific content of his faith which determines his Christianity and his salvation for all eternity.

It is no wonder then that for its first five hundred years Christianity devoted a major part of its intellectual energies to defining its idea of God. The great controversies and heresies of those years all center about the precise meaning of God in Christianity. With but a small stretch of the imagination one might view all the intellectual history of Christianity as one continuing effort to define its idea of God. The Protestant rebellion, for example, is, intellectually, basically a dispute as to where the body of Christ, the indwelling presence of God in our world, is to be found: in the Roman church, the gathered church, the church spiritual, the Spirit acting in the church, the heart of the believer, or the like.

The very term Christianity uses for an exposition of its faith, "theology," literally "the science of God," shows that for it there can be nothing of greater importance.

But because this is so emphatically true of Christianity, we should not be misled into thinking it must be true of all religions. To Theravadin Buddhism, the school of the older, more authentic Buddhist tradition, the idea of God is totally irrelevant. Its concern is the universal suffering of mankind; its goal, to overcome that suffering. The means of doing this the Buddha discovered and proclaimed. He taught four noble truths: that all is suffering; that suffering comes from desire; that when desire is ended, suffering is ended; that desire can be ended by following the eight-fold path. But as to God, he maintained what the Buddhist sages have called a "noble silence." On this subject he did not speak, for as he is reported saying about such matters, "Because this profits not, nor has to do with the fundamentals of religion, therefore I have not elucidated this."

Theravadin Buddhism has no place for the idea of God because it has no place for God Himself. The four noble truths were not revealed by any God. They were the product of the Buddha's own mental achievement, his inner enlightenment as he sat under the famous Bo tree at Budhgaya. The eight-fold path does not at any step depend upon the grace, the mercy, or any other help from God. They are all acts which man by his own effort can do, if he will. No wonder, then, the Buddha could maintain a noble silence about God. Let Him be there or not—it makes no difference to your escape from suffering. Let Him be this or that—it does not matter in your search to find release.

And what of Judaism? What is the place of the idea of God within our religious faith? Clearly we are not religiously agnostic as are the Theravadin Buddhists. We are more like their brothers of the other Buddhist school and would insist that God is indispensable to our religion. But what place do our ideas of Him have within the structure of our Jewish belief? Shall we say it is the same one Christianity has assigned to the idea of God?

To answer this we must ask ourselves a most difficult question. Christianity is focused upon redemption from sin as Buddhism in both branches is devoted to release from suffering. What is it that Judaism is centered upon? What is the axis, the pivot, of the Jewish religion? I think we must respond, not an idea of God, but the life of Torah. The root religious experience of Judaism, it seems to me, is not the negative one of escape from sin or suffering. It is the positive one of hearing God's commandment that we serve Him, as a people and as single selves. It is the sense that God wants us to act in Godlike ways. It is the feeling of mitzvo. It is Torah.

Torah in its widest sense is the substance of that continuing Jewish religious experience, elaborated on many different levels. Here I use it in the narrower sense of the content of the commandment and its explicit application to all of life.

Is it not Torah in this sense that almost all the great Jewish controversies have centered about? Not concepts of God, but the implications of Torah separated the ethically sensitive prophet from the ritually centered priest; the pioneering Pharisee from the reactionary Sadducee; the law-loving Gamaliel from the antinomian Paul; the evolutionary rabbanite from the reductionist Karaite; and in our own day, it is their concepts of Torah, not their ideas of God, that separate Reform, Orthodox and Conservative Jews.

It is to Torah in this sense, to the never ending effort to make more precise the definition of how God would have us live, that the Jewish intelligence has dedicated itself. Until modern times it is almost impossible to find a Jewish book whose major purpose it is to expound the idea of God. Even the works of medieval Jewish philosophy seem to deal with the idea of God rather as a prelude to their discussion of Torah, as a requirement for establishing the origin and authority of Torah, and in this way the truth of Judaism.

Nor should we be surprised to note, therefore, that it was in the area of Torah, and here alone, that Judaism chose to make exact decisions and to exercise religious discipline. The official definition of Torah was binding upon the Jew and carried behind it all the power the Jewish community could muster, from fines to whipping, from excommunication to death. The closest thing Judaism had to the authority of Christian dogma was the rigor of the halacha. The nearest thing Judaism had to the Christian creed was the accepted code of law.

But the halacha is clearly limited to questions of action, which Judaism considers primary. It does not embrace the field of thought, which in Judaism therefore is secondary. Ideas of God as such do not come within the domain of the halacha. Their place is in another realm of discourse, the realm of the aggada.

The halacha strives for completeness and precision. The aggada gives these up in advance for illumination of the partial and brief insight into the whole. The halacha insists on resolving opposing views. The aggada is quite tolerant of apparent contradictions and will not coerce the assent of either "a" or "non-a." The halacha labors to fix the authoritative path for all to follow. In the aggada the Jew is always free to seek an ever more adequate expression of the meaning of his faith. He may spend all of his life in this quest confident that, except for certain minimal conditions, Judaism will not demand of him ideas he has not reached on his own, nor legislate him out of Israel by the adoption of an authoritative code of beliefs. Judaism has given the aggada, its world of ideas, an extraordinary freedom. Though the aggada abounds with ideas about God, we may not expect to find in Judaism one systematically integrated idea of God.

This placement of the idea of God in Judaism within the realm of the aggada is not a historical accident. It is rather a basic decision with regard to that kind of theological structure which would alone be true to the Jewish religious experience.

To have placed the idea of God in the realm of the halacha would have meant that Judaism believed the human mind as capable of reaching authoritative decisions about God as about Torah. The Torah does say of the commandment that it is neither too hard for us, nor too far for us. It is not in the heaven nor over the sea, but very nigh unto us that we may do it. The halacha, Judaism feels, is clearly within man's power to understand and extend. Yet the Torah does not speak this way of God. Indeed it emphasizes rather the opposite, that though we may know the will of God, we may not see His face and live.

Judaism purposely confines the idea of God to the realm of the aggada because it knows the limits of human reason in this regard. The aggada should not then be thought of in a negative way, as only that which is not halacha. In the aggada, Judaism created a unique structure of thought, a special realm of discourse, complete with its own distinct standards and style, its own proper logic and language. By this ingenious mental architecture Judaism allows reason to extend itself continually, without the danger that it might overextend itself and its authority. Or to put it more positively, Judaism invented the aggada as the proper vehicle for Jewish religious ideas because its respect for reason did not transcend its awe of God.

Even medieval Jewish philosophy, whose language sought for something like the precision of the halacha, must be considered a branch of the aggada, specialized and sophisticated though it be. We see this clearly, for each philosopher felt he had complete freedom to reject and reformulate what his predecessor had thought were the required beliefs of Judaism. And despite Maimonides' immense authority, his creed down to our day is but a voluntary addition to the service, except as it occurs in the more overtly aggadic form of song.

Thus in Judaism, we must conclude, all efforts to speak of God must be understood as aggadic speaking, and all Jewish theology must be conducted in this domain. The freedom of the aggada, then, makes it a contradiction in terms to speak of "the" Jewish idea of God. Judaism has but one God; but not one idea of Him.

Hence our original decision not to speak of the content but of the form of an idea of God in Judaism has by this very investigation been justified. To have spoken here of what seems to me or to someone else the essential ingredients of an idea of God with contemporary relevance would have been to substitute a Jew's view for a Jewish view of God and to strive for the authority of the halacha in an area which requires the humility of the aggada. How much so-called Jewish theology has been of little lasting worth because its author's thought was structured in alien categories!

In the aggada Judaism created a form of thought which anticipates in essence what modern philosophy of religion has now come to. Through the positive emphasis of Kant and Cassirer on the way in which reason necessarily shapes knowledge, and through the negative criticism of the logical positivists that propositions are meaningful only insofar as they are verifiable, a revolution has taken place in our understanding of philosophic language and meaning. Gone are the days when philosophic propositions, particularly in reference to ethical or religious issues, could be taken at face value as accurate statements of fact. Today it is generally conceded that such language is a symbolic form of speech. The significant phrases, ideas or events around which religion centers carry their meaning in a way which cannot be taken literally or understood denotatively, but must be recognized as reaching a level of reality otherwise closed to us by pointing to something beyond themselves, in which they at the same time participate.

The most philosophic of contemporary Christian theologians, Paul Tillich, has been able to rear so lofty an intellectual structure only because he has been one of the foremost investigators of the meaning of symbolism for philosophical theology. From my outsider's point of view, it is this philosophic insistence that the word of God when spoken by man must be understood symbolically that will increasingly split contemporary Christian theology into two wings. Many now speak frankly in the realm of philosophic myth as Tillich does, treating the Christ as the ultimate symbol. Others, following Karl Barth, reject philosophy entirely and speak only of the Kerygma, the message of the New Testament, whose burden is the real, if rationally inexplicable event of the God who truly became a man in history and died that those who would believe in him might be saved. This "scandal" needs preaching, not philosophic exposition, for it seeks faith, not understanding. These differences are deeply troublesome to Christian thinkers because they tend to result in two views of the Christ. This is a matter of the highest intellectual importance to us since one of these views may be surprisingly liberal. It therefore seems to me no less than an intellectual felony to hear Jews indict these Christian thinkers indiscriminately (sometimes with Jewish thinkers thrown in among them). And why is this done? So that we may pronounce them guilty by their association with ideas we will not take the time to understand, because we are so eager to hang the witches of Existentialism.

Protestant theology may indeed be in great turmoil because of symbolic philosophy. Jewish theology, when it is true to its historic roots, when it remembers that it is part of the aggada, need not tremble. It has already known this wisdom.

Yet, though Jewish theology is relatively free, it is not formless. Despite the many contradictory statements of the aggada, what Solomon Schechter so perceptively called "a complicated arrangement of theological checks and balances," it has a kind of cohesive inner structure. The masters of this form of expression, Kohler, Cohon, Moore, Schechter, and the others, have by their researches elucidated the great central tendencies, the basic drift inherent in the prodigious number of ideas in the aggada. But as to what is crucial to our quest, these core ideas themselves cannot constitute the criterion of acceptability for a Jewish idea of God.

The criterion which we seek cannot be intellectual, for in Judaism, thought, as aggada, is essentially free. Our criterion must come rather from the primary realm, that of action or life. It must, because of the centrality of Torah, be a functional criterion, not an intellectual one. In Judaism an idea of God is judged by the way it operates in the life of the individual Jew, and, by appropriate additional standards, in the life of the Jewish religious community. Let us then look at this criterion in some detail.

For the individual Jew, first, his idea of God must be such as to make possible for him the life of Torah. It is not enough to think about Torah. The Torah must be done, continually. A fully adequate Jewish idea of God would move the Jew to fulfill the Torah by showing him the cosmic authority from which it stems and the deep significance of the acts it requires. The more completely an idea of God motivates the performance of Torah, the more acceptable to Judaism it may be said to be. The limits are reached in the opposite direction. When a Jew begins to think of God in such a way that it keeps him from fulfilling the commandments, then he may be said to have an idea which is not a permissible Jewish conception of God. That is to say, an idea of God which keeps a

Jew from observing Rosh Hashono or from giving to charity or the like is not a Jewish idea of God.

We Reform Jews, out of courage born of conscience, have reformulated the traditional conception of Torah, but we have not dispensed with it. Because we believe Torah is dynamic, not static, is not to say that there is no Torah here and now. We still believe that "our lives should prove the strength of our own belief in the truths we proclaim." We would agree, I think, that an idea of God which kept us from social action, prayer, study and the rest of what we know Torah is for us, had moved to the border of Judaism or beyond.

If this first part of our criterion seems vague, it is because we have kept our definition of Torah vague. We do not hesitate to chide our Conservative colleagues over their failure to show that Jewish law can do justice to the *aguno,* but having declared that there is continual revelation, what have we done to guide our people to what we believe has been and is being revealed to us here and now? Just what is it that Reform Judaism feels the Lord doth require of us specifically and concretely? When we have fulfilled our age-old rabbinic responsibility to make the Torah clear and understandable in our day, then, and only then, will we have more certain standards by which to judge our God ideas.

Yet the Torah is not meant to be carried out in isolation. It is given to a community, to a people, to Israel. A Jewish idea of God must also then imbue the Jewish mind with an assurance of the value of the continuing existence of Israel, the Jewish people.

The secularists will deny that the existence of Israel has anything to do with God. It is a people like all other peoples, they will assert, and has the same biological right to life and self-expression. The logic of these theoreticians would speedily doom all Jews outside the State of Israel to sterility and decay, while it would seek to make the Jewry of the state itself just like the non-Jew. But this was not the inner logic of our people from its birth in the Exodus, through the trials of the Diaspora, down to the continuing birth-pangs of our own emancipation era. It was Torah, not genetics, that transformed the Hebrews into Israel. It was Torah, not politics, which kept Israel alive and unified, which fashioned its distinctive character.

But why should Israel have the Torah and be a people of Torah? Because Israel felt that between it and God there was a mutual pledge, a bond, a Covenant, by virtue of which Israel became somehow His people, and He became their God. Israel exists as Israel because of its relationship with God. Whatever the Jew understands by God, it must make some kind of Covenant between that God and Israel possible; it must make Israel's continuing dedication to Him reasonably significant; it must explain Israel's suffering and make it possible for the individual Jew to intertwine his destiny with that of his people. To the extent it inspires him to be faithful to the Covenant among the Congregation of Israel it is an acceptable Jewish idea of God—but let his idea of God be such that it negates the value or significance of Israel as a continuing religious community, and it moves outside the sphere of Jewish belief.

Yet one thing more his idea of God must do for the individual Jew—it must make life with God possible for him, not just as a member of Israel, but as an individual as well. Life with God—the life of piety, when we see all our experiences in the perspective of their Divine dimension; the life of faith, when despite what happens to our plans and hopes, we know His rule has not been broken and we are not deprived of His presence; the life of prayer, when we turn and speak to Him out of the fullness of what we are and long for, knowing we shall always find His strength and inspiration. An idea of God which will not let us speak to Him, nor let Him be of help to us in meeting the varied experiences of life is not an idea for Jews. But insofar as it makes possible for us a rich and intimate relationship with God, the idea is welcome within Judaism.

The life of Torah within the congregation of Israel in the presence of the Lord, this is what a Jewish idea of God must make possible. This is the standard by which an individual Jew's idea of God is judged.

It is not hard to see that the God implied in this standard would have the characteristics the scholars have found generally attributed to God in the aggada. A God whose relationship with man could be by way of Torah must be a God who cares for man, whose standards are ethical and whose nature is holiness. A God who could call a people to His service must be a God who trusts in man's powers, who is the master of history because He is its author. A God in whom man may confidently trust must be as present as He is distant, as forgiving as He is just, as revealed to the eye of faith as He is hidden to the eye of reason. Yet though our criterion implies a content for the Jewish idea of God, we must always remember it does not legislate one. The content itself is at issue only as it affects the way the Jew lives Torah. As long as it makes this possible, its elaboration may be naive or philosophic, simple or extensive. This is his private privilege.

Yet while one does not need to be a theologian to be a believing, practicing Jew, there are many persons for whom ideas form an important part of their lives. For them systematic thought is basic to motivation, and they feel obliged to think out their faith clearly and logically or else abandon it. It is with them that Jewish theology is born. They send their ideas from the private into the public domain, and in the process must meet new criteria. These cannot any longer be naive and unreflective concepts and hope to endure the scrutiny of the community. They must now come forth with a maturity equal not just to the best that Israel still contains, but to that which it still remembers.

Israel, on its part, needs such persons and their theological activity for it is only through their ideas that its faith is made clear and manifest, subject to analysis and criticism, open to creativity and intellectual progress.

It is here that Judaism gives reason its full due. Judaism exalts reason as the corrective of unreflective faith, questioning its consistency and coherence. In the rabbinic period when the direct intervention of God through miracles to decide issues of halacha was sought, the rabbis insisted that miracles could not replace logic. In the same way, Maimonides used every philosophic means to expose the superstition of those Jews who insisted on the corporeality of God. We Reform Jews have gloried in the important role assigned to reason in our faith. Unfortunately we have often tried to make it the whole of Judaism. Reason is significant in Judaism as the corrective of faith, but Judaism makes history the arbiter of both.

Any public idea of God in Judaism must stand not only before the test of intellectual coherence, but before the test of Jewish history as well.

No basic idea comes to Israel now as a complete surprise. We have a long history of theological thinking behind us in which no significant aspect of life has been omitted. Israel will always want to know how this modern concept relates to what has been thought before. As aggada it need not be a duplicate or exact derivative of what has gone before, but it must somehow appear to be a meaningful continuation of the Jewish past, or Israel will deny its Jewish relevance. This is particularly true of areas in which Judaism, challenged by rival systems of thought, filled the aggada with its vigorous affirmation of its own belief, as in the struggles against dualism and gnosticism.

But here a bridge is set up between the aggada and the halacha. Not infrequently this reaction was sufficiently strong to pass over from the aggada into the halacha and from a matter of thought, become a matter of law. Thus the aggada is more than a domain of formulation and criticism. It is in due course the intellectual breeding ground of the halacha. It is because aggada can on occasion be transmuted into halacha that even the individual Jew is limited in part in the freedom of his God idea, by the experience of the Jewish past built into his practice of Torah.

Yet the final arbiter is not past history with its literature and its law, but history yet to come. The generations yet to be, they will finally decide the adequacy of this idea for Israel. They will decide it by testing it in their lives. They will live it for a century or more wherever life may take them, no matter what it may bring. Then perhaps they will reject it as they did the idea of original sin, or accept it as they did that of life after death, or continue to struggle with it if they find it meaningful though incapable of resolution, as with the problem of human suffering and the justice of God.

History is the laboratory of Jewish theology.

This is why reason has never triumphed over life in our religion. This is why Judaism at its best has not been afraid of the freedom of the aggada or the discipline of the halacha. It has them yoked in a dynamic tension which keeps them both alive, and it relies on the experiences of history to lead them both closer to the truth.

An idea of God set before Israel must then meet the criterion of history past, present and future. It must demonstrate it is an authentic development of the Jewish past. It must be logical enough in contemporary terms and standards to make the present generation want to live by it, and its content must be such that this life is recognizably Israel's life of Torah before God. And it must be willing to stand before the judgment of the lives of the generations yet to be. Past, present and future; the aggadic freedom is given—but the responsibility is great.

Such, it seems to me, are the standards Judaism sets before an idea of God. To make certain that we understand them and their implications, let us briefly apply them to some of the great public formulations of our day. There are not many.

Despite the Pittsburgh Platform's emphasis that "Judaism presents the highest conception of the God-idea," none of the great early leaders of our movement ever expounded it with the systematic philosophic attention we would require. They devoted their research to the history of the God-idea in Israel, assuming that by showing this, they were clarifying its present difficulties and establishing its meaning to our generation as well. While their research is still of enormous value to us, to know the history of an idea is one thing, and to be convinced of its validity for our time is another. The contemporary theological task was but peripheral to their interests, hence we must turn elsewhere for our examples.

Mordecai Kaplan has devoted himself to the exposition of his idea of God with a thoroughness unique in Jewish history—and with similar individuality he has not hesitated to define God. God is the power that makes for salvation. By power is meant those real processes of nature which operate so as to produce salvation. By salvation is meant the maximum fulfillment of man's capacities and abilities both in an individual and social sense.

Kaplan derives this idea from the life experience of most men as well as from the motifs he finds implicit in the Torah. The origin and need of Torah itself he derives not from God, but from Israel. Our people as a historic entity can fulfill themselves only through living out the values they have created in the past, as these continue to have meaning. But the group also requires the belief that carrying out its Torah has real value in our universe, and so an idea of God is created to supply this.

In defining Israel's traditional concepts in this way their inner relationship to one another has changed, and Kaplan, for the sake of relevance, does not lack the intellectual courage to invert the traditional structure—where God once chose Israel by giving it the Torah, here Israel creates the Torah and chooses for it a suitable idea of God. This is aggada of unusual creativity and ingenuity.

In the generation since its enunciation this idea has drawn many fine and sensitive individuals to Torah, both in study and practice, made them loyal to Israel and eager to take leadership in its affairs, and helped them live in piety with their God.

As a public idea it has been charged with being too great a departure from the Jewish past. It is true that Kaplan uses familiar words in a new and highly individual way, but the desperate need to translate Jewish theology into modern idiom inevitably requires the development of a new or renovated Jewish religious vocabulary. To attempt this is precisely the poetic freedom characteristic of aggadic discourse. While he may have stretched aggadic freedom to its limits, there can be little question that our generation must say *Eilu divrei Elohim chayim:* These are words of the living God.

What the future generations of Israel will have to say of his loyalty to the past, or, which is more important, his meaning to them, we cannot now know. Let me only indicate why this one Jew finds this idea of God intellectually confusing and functionally obstructive.

While Kaplan refers to God in the singular, "The Power" as such, as a single entity, has no individual existence. It is merely a singular usage. The unity of God means only the oneness my mind imposes on the diverse natural forces which make for salvation. But if God, insofar as He is objectively real, refers to what are but fragmentary forces of the universe, whence did these come, and what is their relation to those other forces which exist about us and which do not make for salvation?

If God as a unity is the creation of my needs and my imagination, how can I know that He is as real in the world as He is to my mind? Where will I find the certainty, which alone will make me act, that He is indeed dominant in the universe? Why should I do His bidding against much of my will when I know that His will is but another part of mine?

To me, too, it is a contradiction in terms, or at least an enormous paradox, that a "power" or a "process" should make for moral ends. The terms "power" and "process" are useful precisely because they are natural, that is, objective, impersonal, mechanical. But moral ends are inevitably tied up with personality, with freedom, will and choice. If God, insofar as He is an objective reality, is somehow personal, we can understand how He can make for a salvation which is intimately personal. But what is real in the universe in this idea of God are natural forces or processes which are by definition impersonal. How then can we understand them as making for moral ends and stake our whole existence on the outcome?

I find I cannot pray to this God, particularly in the language of the tradition. Shall I address forces that cannot hear? Shall I speak to myself and my ideas about the universe and call this prayer? I cannot even say a simple blessing like the one for the Chanuko candles when my mind, without which I cannot pray, understands by the Hebrew words: *Baruch ata, Adonai Eloheinu, melech haolam, asher kidshanu bemitzvotav, vetzivanu lehadlik neir shel chanukah*, "I acknowledge those processes in the universe which make for my highest fulfillment, which predominate in it, and to which our people has been devoted, thereby creating activities which help the individual and group achieve self-fullfillment, one of which ennobling activities is to kindle these Chanuko candles." To this I cannot say "Amen."

Martin Buber, on the other hand, has said far less about God, though far more about how God may be known.

Most of our knowing is of things. We inspect them, peruse them, gather our sense impressions and unify them into concepts about things.

Most of the time we know persons in this way—their hair, their height, the birthmark on the cheek. But not always. On occasions we cannot predict or produce at will, we meet them not as objects, but as selves. At such times all that I am and all that you are, Buber says, stand over against one another in complete mutuality. No words need pass between us and yet there is real understanding. No data or concepts are communicated for what I now know is you, as you now know me. It is a separate kind of knowing characterized by its immediacy, intimacy and privacy. It is the kind of knowing in which I participate as a whole or not at all. Hence it cannot be observed or accurately recorded, but only experienced.

We know God in this way, meeting Him even as we meet other persons, encountering Him in the midst of life. Though we may not often find Him, each time we stand in relation to a "Thou" we meet something of Him. Though they must speedily become an "It" for us, He never can. He is the Eternal Thou. I know Him as a person, or what I know is not God.

To know God in this way is not to indulge in mental delusion. This is the same means which tells me you, not just your body, is real.

Nor is this some kind of mystic union or absorption into the great ineffable One, Buber would insist. I do not disappear as a self when I truly know you—indeed it is just this experience of being addressed as a person by you which brings me to know that I am a self, that I as "I" really am.

Nor is the fact that one cannot put what he has experienced into literal terms or exact ideas to be taken as sign that this knowing was simply irrational. Persons cannot be reduced to strictly rational terms. We cannot define our mothers, or give the concept of our wives. More than reason is involved here, for reason is but part of a person—but reason is involved as well. To leave my reason behind would keep me from being my self in any relation. Hence reason participates in the meeting, though not autonomously. And after the event, it is indispensable in helping me understand clearly what it was that happened and what I now must do.

Thus Buber rejects all definitions of God, even refusing to say that God is a person. We know only that we meet Him as we meet persons; that, *kivyachol,* so to speak, He lets Himself be a person for the sake of the encounter.

As the knowing of other persons makes us wish to do things for them, so the encounter with God leaves us with a sense of commandment and commitment. This is a particularly liberal understanding of Torah, for God is the Eternal Thou, who may be met in every age.

Israel's covenant with God was the result of such meeting. In the history of man, only Israel had such an encounter with God as a people and not merely as a collection of individuals. Israel pledged itself as a people to proclaim in history the Sovereignty of God by serving Him alone. From generation to generation Israel renews its continuing commitment to God and their covenant.

Yet though this makes the role of Israel in history unique, Buber's primary religious emphasis is on the individual's personal relationship with God. To pray to this God is to reach out for the dialogue, or at least to speak to One we know is real and near. To have faith in Him is to know between the moments of encounter that He is not lost, that in another moment we may meet Him again as the Source of all that is.

Though spoken of in modern terms, this God Buber points to is not so different from the God pictured in our tradition. Future generations may well reject this formulation, but never on the grounds that it created a barrier between them and their God. Its greatest virtue is its self-transcendence. It does not show us God, but only where He may be found. It is aggadic, not only in form and language, but in its very content as well. Then surely we must say to him, *Eilu divrei Elohim chayim*, these are the words of the living God.

Time will not permit us to apply our criterion to the rationalist God-idea propounded by Hermann Cohen, the enlightened humanist strivings of Eric Fromm, or the ideas of others. Our purpose, however, was only to make the standards of judgment clear. Now let each one refine the instrument that he may use it in his own search for the most adequate Jewish idea of God. To test further will lead us only to more or less acceptable Jewish ideas of God, not to "the" Jewish idea of God.

Can we be content with the emphasis upon form rather than content? Can we be satisfied religiously with only the search and not the solution? We can, if we will remember that the search cannot be ended now, for history is not yet ended. Jewish theology will have the solution to all of its problems one day, the day Elijah comes preceding the Messiah, and answering all our questions. On that day Israel's great aggadic search will cease, for on that day, and on that day alone, the Lord shall be One and His name shall be One.

And until then?

Until then, as best we can.

Ledor vador nagid godlecha
Ulenetzach netzachim kedushatcha nakdish
Veshivchacha Elocheinu mipinu lo yamush leolam vaed
Baruch ata Adonai hael hakadosh,
We bless you Adonai, the holy God.

4 / Existentialism's Meaning for Judaism: A Contemporary Midrash

1959

Why has existentialism had so little impact upon the leaders of American Jewry? The educators and social workers move in another philosophic universe entirely. The laity is barely conscious of its existence—as it is barely conscious of philosophy in general—though it occasionally manages to recognize some such name as Franz Rosenzweig. The rabbinate has heard this or read that about the Jewish existentialists, but tends to see them as a menace deserving only of excoriation and denunciation. What has happened to that immutable principle of modern Jewish life that the Christian fashion after a little while becomes the Jewish ideal? Surely nothing has excited and invigorated contemporary Christian thought, Catholic as well as Protestant, as much as existentialism. It has been the major excitement in academic and religious circles for over a decade, and even before World War II its influence had been felt in a number of intellectual-religious circles in America.

Perhaps stating the problem that baldly is already to give the most obvious answer. Existentialism, as no other philosophic movement since the emancipation of European Jewry, is of Christian religious origin. It was born out of Sören Kierkegaard's violent protest against the Christianity of his day, and against what he saw as its intellectual foundation, Hegel's all-encompassing rationalism. If Kierkegaard attacked Hegel—"attack" is perhaps a mild word to describe the venom, satire, invective, and irony of his philosophic enterprise—it was to make possible a renewed Christian life. Existentialism was born to renew the Protestant affirmation. No wonder it has had such influence on contemporary Protestantism, and on some leading Roman and Eastern Catholics.

But how could Jews be expected to respond sympathetically to a philosophic tendency of Christian religious origin? It is indeed a sign of the increasing self-respect which has characterized American Jewry since World War II that it has resisted existentialism on Jewish grounds and for apparently Jewish reasons.

Yet the grounds for the Jewish rejection of existentialism involves much more than a simple judgment of guilt by association. Most of the polemics against existentialism have held that its very content is un-Jewish. All existentialism is characterized by a critique of human reason, climaxed not, as in Kant, with a reaffirmation of its areas of power and certainty, but with a thoroughgoing delineation of its limitations. It is the humility of human reason before the realities of human existence which is the major theme of existentialism. Man's mind is incapable of solving all his truly significant problems. Indeed, it cannot even explain the most fundamental datum of his life—that he exists.

It is this anti-rational strain in existentialism which alarms the few who take Jewish thought seriously; they see in it an insidious threat to all the progress of the past century in making Judaism rational. In their eyes, the existential delineation of reason's limits quickly leads to "irrationalism," "mysticism," "a first step toward superstition and every danger of medievalism." The fury of the attack indicates that more than just an idea is at stake.

The two principal strains of liberal Judaism have each been associated with philosophies that strongly emphasize mind as the measure. One strain, Reform Judaism, has been dominated from its beginnings by the tradition of German rational philosophy. It leaned heavily on Kant in justifying its emphasis on ethics over ritual and on universal preachments over particular practices. With Hegel it saw in the forward movement of history the progressive self-revelation of the absolute, and looked forward to the triumph of spirit, as enlightenment and education inexorably brought brotherhood and peace. Reform prided itself on logic and scientific investigation, the elimination of superstition and atavism, and the possession of a faith as reasonable as it was intelligible. Though their views varied in emphasis or detail, the early intellectual leaders, Abraham Geiger, David Einhorn, Kaufmann Kohler, and the later teachers of today's Reform rabbinate—David Neumark, Samuel Cohon, Henry Slonimsky, Samuel Atlas—all spoke out of German rational idealism. It was rationalism that validated liberal Judaism. Without it, there could be no right to reform. Without it what would deter the resurgence of magic and superstition?

Conservative Judaism, the other liberal Jewish tendency, has been notorious for its studied refusal to clarify its ideological position. It would be most unfair to associate all of Conservative Judaism with Mordecai Kaplan's rationalist religious philosophy. For one thing, there is a significant minority of Reform rabbis who espouse his Reconstructional theology with enthusiasm, at the same time as the preponderant majority of Conservative rabbis look askance at it. Nevertheless, the rationalist emphasis of Kaplan's forthright reinterpretation of Jewish belief and practice typically distinguishes the thinking of his former students at the Jewish Theological Seminary, who now make up the body of the Conservative rabbinate—this rationalism is the result of his influence on them as a teacher, and, of their years of exposure to nearby Columbia University, the shrine of American naturalism.

Kaplan is as emphatic in insisting on the role of mind in shaping contemporary Judaism as any of the Reform thinkers. But he borrows from the American intellectual idiom where they borrowed from the German. Where the Germans sought for the elaboration of the "spirit," with its strong intellectual connotations, the Americans sought rather to introduce the scientific method into the realm of philosophy. Naturalism implied an intellectual questioning of everything which could not be understood as part of the natural order as conceived by science, using that word in its broadest sense. The supernatural God of the religious tradition was by this mental effort transformed into a process in the universe; God's choice of Israel became but a typical folk-conceit, acceptable only in the sense that it encouraged the Jewish people to choose God.

Here, far more than in the austere formulations of early Reform, room was made for the emotions. The Jewish people—an obvious datum of the natural order—invests its rationally validated beliefs with its particular folk feelings and associations, thus giving full scope to man's emotive as well as his rational capacity. Thus Kaplan has emphasized the broadest cultural expression of Jewish religious belief, and is clearly an inspirer of the revived interest in Jewish art and music. Yet despite the acceptance of Jewish folkways and appreciation of the depth of Jewish traditional feeling, it is reason alone that is the arbiter of belief and that establishes the criteria for religious practice. Impressed by the success of science, and by the scientific direction of American philosophic thought in the thirties, Reconstructionism established itself on a rationalistic foundation which it has never felt required to re-examine seriously.

Thus the left wing of Conservative Judaism consciously, and much of its thinking center often unconsciously, have associated American rationalism with their contemporary Judaism. For Conservative Judaism as for Reform, to challenge the adequacy of reason in the religious sphere looks like an effort to turn back the clock, a failure of nerve that imperils the continuing development of Judaism.

It is something of a corroboration to find that a reverse process has occurred among the Orthodox. To be sure, Orthodoxy has been more concerned with defending traditional Jewish practice against the enticements of the contemporary American milieu than with dwelling on the mystery of the unique revelation at Sinai. There is also the notable history of rationalism in traditional Judaism. Nevertheless, the events at Sinai, which are basic to Orthodoxy, are not now and never have been rationally explicable. Their authority and uniqueness are inseparable. One can accept or reject the miraculous event. To explain it is to rob it of precisely that which makes it precious. The Torah and the Halachah, with or without rationalistic apologies, are the basis of the Orthodox faith. While it can accept such corroboration as reason might offer, as in Maimonides' day, it does not see its life as being dependent upon philosophic explanations, but rather on acceptance of the yoke of the kingdom.

Thus it is in the Orthodox movement alone that we find a leading figure who is apparently a committed existentialist. Rabbi Joseph Soloveitchik serves as chairman of the Rabbinical Council of America's Committee on Law, is professor of Talmud at Yeshiva University's seminary, and is widely hailed as the spiritual leader of the American-trained Orthodox rabbinate. Unfortunately, he has published very little, and the few articles that have appeared about him have only hinted at his philosophic views. For the past few years he has been lecturing weekly on the Jewish view of man at a seminar of rabbis investigating the relations between Judaism and psychiatry. Neither Rabbi Soloveitchik's written lecture notes nor the tape recordings of each session are available to the public. Yet if the reports of those in attendance may be relied on, and they seem consistent with the little else that we know, Soloveitchik's position lies clearly within the existential camp, representing a view of man and revelation that seems analogous *(l'havdil)* with that of Karl Barth.

Like Barth he begins with a refusal to reduce religion to philosophy, psychology, ethics, or anything else. For Barth the crucifixion and resurrection of the Christ are unique acts in history through which God has let Himself be known. They are the measure for the rest of history, rather than measurable themselves according to the value placed on their antecedents and effects. Soloveitchik takes a similar position toward the Halachah. The justification of *kashrut* is not the danger of trichinosis, the "point" of religious ceremony is not the subjective one that it is a means for arousing emotion. The Halachah, like the Christ, must be taken in all its objectivity, in all its legal specificity; it must be seen as God's instrument and the means of His service. Seen in this way, the Halachah implies a whole body of meaning and teaching which becomes the basis for encountering and grasping reality. Here too the criteria and standards derive from the unique historical event, the giving of the Law at Sinai, which makes the rest of history intelligible but must itself be accepted on faith.

Both thinkers see man desperately in need of faith, to save him from himself and the self-destruction inherent in his natural existence. Barth is the more radical here: every human effort to cope rationally with the problems of existence is for him a de facto rebellion against the sovereignty of God. Human reason is not only inadequate to the task of resolving man's profound anxieties, it in fact strengthens them by holding out the delusive hope that it can somehow overcome finite existence. That way lies only sin and further estrangement from God, the fullest spiritual as well as natural death. But the man of Christian faith may hope through God's promise to find true life. His acceptance of God's condemnation of his sinfulness, and his hope in the promise God has made available through Jesus, have freed him from delusion and given him the one firm ground for a man in a shifting universe.

Soloveitchik would not denigrate human reason to this extent, yet he too insists upon its limitations and fundamental inadequacy. There is nothing inherently evil in the growth of human knowledge so long as man is willing to recognize the mystery which he thus continually uncovers. Science need not be considered a source of sin if it is accompanied by a growing sense of astonishment at the extent of order in the universe. When we confront human reason honestly, our humility increases with our self-esteem. It is the effort to rely on ourselves alone, to hide from the mystery and the wonder, that produces the alternate idolatry and dejection of our inner life. He makes a devastating analysis of modern man's situation, using every sociological and psychological technique to expose the falseness, the hypocrisy, and, ultimately, the intense anxiety which fill our lives. The alternative to such a life is that of the man of the Halachah; Soloveitchik moves through the entire range of the tradition to show how Judaism tames its faithful adherents beyond anxiety to the only kind of security of which man is capable. It is the act of faith, the personal appropriation of Sinai and the life built upon it, which makes the difference. It is the revelation and the revelation alone which can transform man's life. Such, as best it can be made out from a distance, is Soloveitchik's argument. It is not just Orthodox Judaism. It is orthodox existentialism as well.

One cannot help speculating why Soloveitchik refrains from publishing or publicly discussing his ideas. The astonished reception they would in all likelihood receive doubtless plays a part in his reticence. It is true that Orthodoxy could easily benefit from existentialism, but most of its leaders are unprepared for so radical a readjustment of their conscious or unconscious intellectual commitments. In general, they tend to follow the Reform and Conservative pack in noisily hunting out exponents of this view.

It is Will Herberg who has borne the brunt of the attack. The public Jewish reactions to his theological writings have been almost invariably negative, the private ones even worse. Again it is the Christian origins of Herberg's thought that arouse the opposition. Were Herberg himself not so honest as to acknowledge the debt he owes to Reinhold Niebuhr, who showed him this pathway back to Jewish belief, the informed reader of *Judaism and Modern Man* would discover as much soon enough. Yet it is what Herberg says, not where he got it, that arouses the real resistance. Perhaps the best part of Herberg's argument is his exposure of the pseudo-faiths, the substitute religions, of our time. He examines politics, science, and psychiatry to show how each in turn has served as a religion for many modern Jews. Each has seemed to offer salvation. And each has thereby been a means for modern man to evade the real religious problems, the ultimate issues which every man discovers in the depths of his existence.

Herberg is at pains to show that politics, science, and psychiatry each have their truth and value, but his main point is that they can never be legitimate substitutes for the act of faith. By destroying contemporary intellectual idols he in fact destroys the hope that anything man's mind alone might ever create could be considered adequate as religion. The reliance on rationality obstructs the way to God.

What remains is the "leap of faith." With his old false faiths gone, the individual now stands naked before the universe. The one positive step left him is the personal acceptance of God and Judaism. But it is just here that Herberg deserts us. What the "leap of faith" means, how it is to be accomplished, what keeps it from ending in Zen Buddhism, Christianity, or ghetto Judaism, is not made clear. As one might expect, this is precisely where all the liberal critics of Herberg have taken him to task. Indeed, the rejection has been so complete that while non-Jews and especially non-Jewish seminaries and colleges regard Herberg as an authoritative spokesman for Judaism, it is difficult to find any Jewish leaders who might think of themselves as being his intellectual disciples.

However, the criticism of Herberg is more than a rationalization of the various Jewish ideological positions. It is also a valid argument. Most existential analyses of man's condition, after eliminating every seeming absolute, arrive like Herberg's at a point where they must decide what to commit themselves to. But not all of them then make the religious commitment. Some of them insist, in face of the absurdity of existence, that no mysterious plan beyond man's reason finally gives it meaning. They prefer rather to accept this existence with all its unreasonableness than to anesthetize themselves with comforting illusions about God or the good. Atheistic existentialism is as legitimate an existentialist response to the unmasking of man's pseudo-religions as is the leap of religious commitment. Herberg conveniently ignores this.

It is surprising that no major statement of a Jewish atheist existentialism has been forthcoming so far. With many old-line Zionists and other secular Jews anxious to escape from the increasing identification of Jewishness with religion in America, a Jewish atheist existentialism might well provide a personally meaningful, culturally exciting, non-religious Jewish point of view. Its outlines do not seem difficult to discern.

A logical beginning would be to view the Bible as a classic, but misunderstood, existentialist analysis. It would see its centuries of religious striving as a people's effort to abolish anxiety by projecting an image of God into the world. Yet as the generations passed, the impossibility of maintaining this belief against the realities of existence becomes clearer. The outcry of the righteous in the Psalms, Jeremiah's troubled confessions, Ecclesiastes' assertion of the futility of history, and finally Job's struggle for meaning in the face of suffering indicate there cannot be a God. There is no meaning to existence in this world and, as the Bible preponderantly knows, no after-life.

Yet man finds himself confronted by the continual need to make decisions. Every law of the Torah is a recognition of this fact. And every action, as the prophets show, stands under the judgment of "might have been" or "why not the other way?" Nonetheless, the Jewish affirmation of life, simply because it is given, as the schools of Shammai and Hillel agreed, remains basic. The Jew then seeks to redeem the unreasonableness of existence by sharing in the existence of family, folk, and mankind.

Here we have the outlines of a position that, all in all, might compete favorably with many a secular existentialism and yet consider itself fully Jewish at the same time. The fact that such a philosophy has not yet made an appearance speaks eloquently to those who are religious about what it means to be a Jew. The Jewish people and its destiny can be separated from God only by prodigious and unnatural effort.

The rejection of Herberg because of his failure to show why the religious commitment is necessary has convinced the defenders of rationalism that it is philosophic, not ideological, considerations which underlie their opposition to existentialism. As a result they have proceeded with double incentive to decry all those who might seem to share the existentialist view. Here they err in failing to appreciate the scope and variety of views which pass under that label.

Paul Tillich has made a distinction which can serve us well at this point. Commonly, when we think of existentialism, we think of it in terms of the typical existentialist content, the conclusion that human reason is finally inadequate to grasp the problems of existence. But, Tillich reminds us, existentialism is also a philosophic method whose results may vary quite considerably from the customary ones. Thus, as a matter of fact, much of Kierkegaard's most searching criticism of Hegel and the German idealists was directed at their method. It was in subjectivity, he argued, in a truth that involved the individual, that truth was to be found, not in an objectivity that produced a so-called truth to which one might well remain indifferent. It was in the concrete, specific, and therefore personal realm that truth was to be discovered, not in some splendid universal abstraction that encompassed the entire universe but left out the individual doing the thinking. Philosophy therefore should proceed from, build on, the individual, on the realities of his existence. It was the application of this method which has led to results as different as Kierkegaard's passionate Protestantism and Jean-Paul Sartre's atheism.

It is clear that those Jewish thinkers who accept the existentialist conclusion about the inadequacy of human reason cannot be expected to influence the liberal wing of Judaism. But other than Herberg there are few who hold this position. The other representative Jewish existentialists, Martin Buber and Franz Rosenzweig, employ its method but are far from embracing its usual content. This has not, however, saved them from the calumny visited on Herberg. If they are not members of his party they are at least his fellow travelers and deserve to be exposed. This explains the peculiar circumstance that while Buber is known, studied, and respected by Protestant and some Catholic thinkers, he has still to find recognition in most Jewish circles.

Buber himself seems to share something of the liberal's suspicion of the anti-rationalism of existentialism. Two years ago, in a colloquium he conducted at Columbia University, he was asked if he considered himself an existentialist. His immediate reaction was not only negative, it indicated a certain amount of surprise that he should be so identified. The questioner, however, was more shaken by the answer than Buber by the question. After a moment's embarrassed stuttering he rephrased the question in terms of philosophic procedures, emphasizing the immediate, concrete, and personal. This quickly relieved the situation. "Oh," said Dr. Buber, "if that is what you mean, then of course I am an existentialist. I thought you meant whether I agreed with certain thinkers associated with that term."

Buber's thought leads him far from the usual existentialist content, though by a method clearly to be classified as existential. His well-known analysis of knowing as carried on in terms of either an I-It or an I-Thou relation bears all its hallmarks. An "I" is always involved, and this subjective content is matched with an emphasis on the individual's immediate experience in knowing. In all things Buber will sacrifice the big abstraction to the concrete experience.

Yet Buber is not thereby a foe or denigrator of reason. In the realm of I-It, reason is of course the indispensable master, but even in the realm of I-Thou, it is not denied or despised. In a truly personal relationship, the participants must be wholly involved. My mind or my social facade is not me, any more than my wanting to know you is a desire to become acquainted with your conversational talent or your artfully attired body rather than with you yourself. If I am to be involved in an I-Thou relation, I cannot leave my mind out of it and still be me. Yet I cannot simply think my way into it for I am more than a mind; I am a person.

Love, as always, supplies the best analogy to religion. To love only with my mind, or only my beloved's mind, would not be the love of heart and soul and might that most men seek. On the other hand, to love without one's mind is to commit the follies of which love has often been accused. It is a dangerous and difficult matter, to be sure. This is what is meant by existential risk. But every truly important human choice faces the same danger. So religious faith is not simply a matter of reason, nor can it yet proceed without it. God requires the whole man.

Thus the existentialist Buber, against the dire predictions of his critics, has not rejected man's efforts to improve society. On the contrary, it is just his philosophic understanding of what the relations between men should be that has made him a religious socialist. One of his major works, *Paths in Utopia,* is an analysis of various social philosophies; and his Zionism, particularly his complete dissociation from the formal Zionist organizations, is founded upon his convictions about what men can and what Jews particularly ought to do to create a worthy community. It was not just Israeli politics that led him to be appointed professor of Social Philosophy at the Hebrew University.

Buber's attitude to change and development in Judaism is like his attitude to social change. He is no bringer of a new orthodoxy. If anything, his insistence on personal experience as the criterion for Jewish observance is too free for most Jewish leaders. Here Rosenzweig's emphasis upon the discipline of the Law, understood in a developmental sense, can serve as guidance for the more traditionally inclined. In either case it is clear that existentialism can, like rationalism, provide a firm basis for the liberal traditions in Judaism.

What seems to disturb Jewish religious liberals most about Buber, though, is not his theory of Jewish practice, but his return to the older Jewish theological terms. To speak of God as a Thou is to return to a personal God, to a concept of prayer as a dialogue between persons, to revelation as communication between God and man. To require the involvement of the total individual in his religion, to emphasize the importance of personal faith and devotion, is to reach for the intimate in a way to which modern men are unaccustomed and which makes them feel uneasy. This is not the cool rationalist tone that seemed the essence of liberal Judaism and the hallmark of the sophisticated American.

But rather than being a fault, this may be just the contribution existential interpretations of Judaism can give us now. It is just such questions of personal faith, of the meaning of prayer, of the authority of revelation which are making their way to the fore of the lay consciousness. The warmth and feeling which American Jews have found missing in the older expressions of their liberalism cannot be supplied for long simply by renewing ceremonials or *kashrut,* and certainly not by a host of congregational gimmicks. What is needed is a statement of Jewish meaning that involves the emotions as well as the mind, that helps us understand how we may give ourselves entire without losing the gains rationalism has brought us. The existentialist method, if not the existentialist content, seems to offer the best prospect of meeting this need.

Since existentialism insists upon exposing illusions, and by doing so forces us to make genuine decisions, it perhaps helps us see most clearly how far the American Jewish community must go to become a community of the Jewishly religious. And it must go very far indeed. The decision to create a meaningful American Judaism, rather than just to go on building buildings, enrolling members, and making a great communal stir, is beset by all sorts of risks. But the existentialist realizes that there are no decisions without risks. He realizes too that truth is known only in the wholehearted acceptance which for a Jew must mean its living out in deeds. As Rosenzweig insisted, it is life that validates truth, and it takes the lives of generations to validate the greatest of them.

Here then is a call to American Jews which says nothing about defense activities and social acceptance, which does not use the carrot of mental health or the stick of intermarriage. It faces the realities of our possible failure, but knows that the promise of our own existence is bound up with our accepting the risk in a commitment to live by God's law as Israel has come to know it.

To be sure, existentialism has its internal difficulties. It has not yet successfully grappled with the problem of communication—how the realities of one man's existence may be harmonized with those another finds. In this respect Protestant thinkers, notably Paul Tillich, have already tried to go beyond existentialism. And there is of course a danger in too closely identifying Judaism with any philosophy, as Rudolph Bultmann seems to have identified Christianity too closely with existentialism. Judaism is not existentialism and it has much to say in the way of correcting and supplementing existentialism. Yet Judaism has always found value in midrash; it has considered philosophy not the equivalent of revelation, but a key to its meaning. Existentialism should yet prove to be the most meaningful midrash of our day.

5 / Crisis Theology and the Jewish Community

1961

A dozen years have passed since Irving Kristol, in a savage critique of Milton Steinberg's *Basic Judaism,*[1] sought to demonstrate that Jewish thought in America was powerless to answer the great questions—questions about man and his condition, about destiny and the meaning of history—that the war had raised in the troubled minds of so many intellectuals in the West. Kristol's article challenged Jewish thinkers to face these questions instead of taking refuge in the kind of calm, confident faith that he accused Milton Steinberg, and most American rabbis, of preaching. To this challenge a group of younger theologians—among them Emil Fackenheim and Will Herberg—soon responded, and for a time it seemed that a new Jewish theology, a theology concerned with the crisis of the age, was in process of being born. But the effort miscarried. Aside from a few articles and one book, perhaps two, the promise of these first few exciting efforts remained unfulfilled.

Now that over a decade has passed, it may be useful to ask why this new Jewish theology failed to develop. To do so we must return to Kristol's argument and set forth its basic thesis. What disturbed him was the relative indifference of American Judaism to the extent and complexity of the problem of sin. He wrote that "the spiritual distress of the modern world does not arise merely because man perversely chooses to do evil rather than good. If it were as uncomplicated as all that, present-day Judaism—even Rabbi Steinberg's Judaism—would have the answer right at hand. The horror that breathes into our faces is the realization that evil may come by doing good—not merely *intending* to do good, but *doing* it."

Jewish theology to be meaningful in the postwar world would have to speak to this problem—to man's talent for creating evil, to his capacity for deluding himself about the strength and subtlety of his evil inclination. Contemporary Jewish thinkers, of whom Steinberg was the most articulate, lacked the courage or the vision to see the problem, much less to provide the answers. Books, journals, and sermons seemed quite satisfied with the liberal formulas and melioristic illusions of the thirties. To read or hear them was to experience the eerie feeling that their authors had been suspended in time or that in their limited vision they had remained oblivious to what meanwhile had happened to mankind. Thus for men like Irving Kristol who were preoccupied with the ordeal of Western culture, a Judaism without an emphasis on the problem of sin was "still catastrophically narrow," and was characterized by "intellectual timidity, cultural immaturity." So went the appraisal and the challenge.

It is not difficult to recall the circumstances which engendered this troubled concern with religion and with its failure to take sufficient account of the realities of human evil. By 1948, the mood of which Kristol's article was only one of many expressions was already prominent in American Protestant circles which were experiencing the same disillusionment that their European colleagues had learned a war earlier. A few years before, everything had seemed so clear. The professors had swept out the dead dogmas of tradition and had confidently pointed the way to a better world. The politicians, particularly the radicals, had been even more convinced that their revelation was truth. Political action, scientific investigation, man-for-himself—such notions became the Messianic hopes, the pseudo-religions, which were shattered by the realities of World War II and the cold war that succeeded it. Once these new idols had been discredited by the tragic complexities of what was now seen to be "the human condition," religion itself began to appear in a new role and to take on new meaning. If man could not play God successfully, then perhaps God was not dead. If man could not finally stand in effective judgment over his own pride and sinfulness, then God could and would—perhaps, indeed, had. To rebuild his life, to be true to his new view of history, postwar man needed to understand not only his limitations but also his profound capacity for evil even in the guise of doing good. And, with their continuing revelations of both democratic and Communist deceit and treachery, the years since World War II have but made the problem more pressingly relevant. As a result, the theology of sin—and related to it, the theology of the state and its functions, the theology of culture and of history—has continued to be a central concern of Western thought.

The impact of this vast change was felt with special power in the Jewish world, for the thirties had had a special significance for American Jews. They were the first years of rapid integration into American culture. Out of the ghetto neighborhoods had come great numbers of young adults intent on becoming true Americans and on making use of a freedom that had been won after long centuries of persecution. Their Jewish heritage, with its emphasis on intellect and self-assertion, also made the American opportunities for education and advancement particularly attractive. No liberal, scientific, or cultural movement was without its youthful Jewish zealots. No group should therefore have been more disillusioned by the experiences of the forties or have been more attuned to the appeal made by Kristol's article.

Yet the record of the fifties is clear. The prevalent mood of the Jewish community since World War II has not been one of concern with human sinfulness or with man's inability to transcend evil. It has not been characterized by resignation or despair. On the contrary, though the American Jew may be politically less naive, even to the point of near apathy, and though he may not be as trusting as he once was of those who have simple solutions for our society's ills—the dominant accent of his life is still his faith in the Good Deed.

Indeed, what stands out in a review of the life of American Jews during the fifties is not a mood of indecision or even hesitation, but a clear and simple knowledge of what they needed to do—and then did. Marriage, children, decent jobs, and homes—these often led them to new neighborhoods, or to communities which had not existed a few years before. There were no established institutions, no patterns of community life, waiting to receive them. Still, even in the presence of communal nothingness they knew what needed to be done. There must be Jewish schools for Jewish children, Jewish centers for Jewish youth, synagogues and temples for—of all people—them! There must be organized Jewish communities, if for no other reason than that they might work together to rescue brother Jews from refugee camps, from lands of oppression, or wherever they were in distress. And American Jews did what they could, from sending telegrams to running rummage sales, from attending mass meetings to offering quiet prayers to create, build, and maintain the State of Israel. It was not the Jewish professionals or the great national organizations which developed this attitude—though they often take credit for it. Their role, however significant, was shaped in response to a process that was already under way in the Jewish community. In short, without ever having to think about it, the masses of American Jewry emerged from World War II not with a sense of man's helplessness before the evil consequences of his well-intentioned behavior or of the powerlessness of his will before his own evil inclinations, but rather with what can legitimately be called an unshaken faith in man's capacity to know the righteous act and accomplish it successfully.

To be sure, one may condemn much of what American Jews have done in the past decade as merely the exuberant response of those newly admitted into the suburban middle class. Yet it seems to me that it is not middle-class morality so much as a history of commitment to the concept of *mitzvah* which has asserted itself in contemporary American Jewish life. *Chupah v'kiddushin,* marriage, *pru ur'vu,* progeny, *talmud torah,* study, *tz'dakah*, charity—these and a hundred other commandments may be unacknowledged as such by the American Jew, but they still guide his life. He does not, of course, study the codes of Jewish law as his great-grandfather did, and he may even believe that they no longer have relevance. Nevertheless, it seems clear that centuries of Jewish devotion and observance have conditioned his psyche so thoroughly that virtually no amount of rebellion, flight, and camouflage has been able to purge him of the conviction that a man is capable both of knowing and doing the good. This conviction—which forms the very basis of Judaism and which is one of the main points on which Christianity split from its mother-religion—has continued to dominate the life of American Jewry in our day, despite wars, crises, and intellectual disillusion.

Starting with that faith—obscure though it may be—the "ordinary" American Jew has raised his own theological questions. Though he may not practice the *mitzvot* which one observes him practicing out of any conscious religious commitment, still the acts themselves lead him to inquiries about their origin, purpose, and authority. From within the Jewish community, from Jewish living and devotion, there has thus arisen a distinct and indigenous desire for theology—only this is for a theology of *mitzvah,* a rationale of the Jewish way of life and belief. Thus, first by the witness of its life and then by the questions which that life poses, American Jewry has in effect rejected the kind of question raised in Irving Kristol's article.

This is not to say that the problem of sin has disappeared from Jewish *intellectual* life. Along with the related questions of culture, the state, and history, it still comes before the handful of thinkers who take the discipline of theology seriously. Yet to expound a Jewish theology relevant to our day, one must decide whether to begin with the problem of sin or the value of *mitzvah.* In the one case, man's continued failure is taken as the basis of religious experience. In the other case, the need and the ability to do the righteous act become the concern in thought that they have previously been in life.

Contemporary Jewish thought in America, confronted by these two paths of theology, has chosen the latter, the one which has always been characteristic of Judaism. Traditionally it is Christianity which has been most preoccupied with the problem of sin, for to Christianity the most basic and overwhelming fact of human existence is man's sinfulness before God's law. Man, said St. Paul, cannot perform the Commandments though he exert himself to the fullest. Because man's will is corrupt, the Torah is inherently self-defeating: if anything, God's purpose in giving it was to prove that it was impossible to reach Him through merit. Salvation can only come to the unworthy sinner through God's grace, and even after the sinner has been redeemed, he continues to be dependent on divine grace for living the good life. In Christianity, then, first comes the theology of sin, then the theology of redemption, and finally the theology of justification and sanctification (the theology of righteous living).

Judaism has traditionally faced life from a different point of view. What has amazed the Jew, leaving him in awe and trembling, is his declared ability to know and to do a righteous act. That he, an ant, a grasshopper, is privileged to know God's will and to perform it; that he, a mote in the vastness of creation, is still by reason of this knowledge and this capacity "but little lower than God" (the Hebrew says *elohim)*—this has been the primary source of his religious inspiration. His Bible is filled not with philosophic disquisitions, with metaphysical analyses, but with laws and commandments, histories of how he lived under this regimen, and prophetic harangues that criticize his performance and refine his responsibilities. The vast libraries of rabbinic literature are not filled with guides to religious introspection, but rather seek to make ever clearer the details of the religiously responsible act. Even the medieval philosophers discuss the existence and attributes of God primarily as a basis for validating and authorizing the life of Torah.

Judaism knows sin and sinfulness, but understands them within the context of *mitzvah,* not vice versa. When the Jew sins, he is not overwhelmed by the event, nor does he anticipate that God will be. The Jew knows that he is but an animal. Surely this cannot come as a surprise to God, his creator, who fashioned him of dust. Hence He will understand the lapse; and because what He wants, more than punishment, is the righteous act, He will allow man to turn from his evil and pursue righteousness again. Even in his sinfulness, the Jew does not simply wait for God to act. Even then, there is a *mitzvah* to perform. The Jew acts. He does *t'shuvah,* he turns his life to righteous living with an immediate act of repentance. And he knows his heartfelt turning to his maker will be accepted.

Thus it is not especially difficult to understand why the demand for a new Jewish theology, the Jewish theology of man's sinfulness, has had little effect. Instead there has been another concern, a concern which arose from within the Jewish community, based upon its commitments, and one which Judaism has always considered more elementary. To this theology of *mitzvah,* Jewish thinkers, particularly the younger ones, have increasingly given their attention. It is symptomatic that the articles by Emil Fackenheim which have appeared in *Commentary* during the past twelve years have moved from the consideration of human limitations to the possibility in liberal Judaism for authoritative guidance of Jewish living. Fackenheim's intellectual odyssey is similar to that of most postwar Jewish theologians.

It would be premature to call this effort to articulate a theology of *mitzvah* a distinct school of thought. At the moment there is no book, personality, nor institution around which it might be organized (though it owes much to the writings of Franz Rosenszweig and Martin Buber). However, it has enlisted the interest of such diverse Jewish thinkers as Lou Silberman, Steven Schwarzschild, Jacob J. Petuchowski, W. Gunther Plaut, Herschel Matt, Monford Harris, and Samuel Dresner; and the broad outlines of one emerging system can be sketched. This system might be called "Covenant Theology," for it rests upon a reaffirmation, in contemporary terms, of the Covenant of Sinai and its renewal during the centuries of prophetic leadership. It seeks to explore and understand the implications of defining religion as a covenant relation, and specifically to make manifest the nature and meaning of the Jewish Covenant with God.

Covenant Theology, then, understands Judaism in frankly existential terms. Judaism does not involve only a set of ideas, a concept of God, or even a set of practices. It is also a way of living one's life based on a relationship with God, a relationship in which the whole self is involved. But it is not simply the private faith of an individual. The Jew is the man who shares the common faith in the mutual promise existing between God and Israel—that is, the Jewish people as a whole. The Covenant was not made between one Jew and God, but between God and the entire House of Israel. The individual Jew shares in his people's relationship with God as a matter of birth. He may also share in it as a matter of will when he makes this historic Covenant the chief article of his faith.

The Covenant, begun with Abraham, sealed at Sinai, renewed a dozen times over through the prophets, and reaffirmed by succeeding generations of Jews, thus provides the base for the new theology. Under that Covenant the Jews have acknowledged *Adonai* alone as God and have pledged themselves to live by His law. Here the new theologians emphasize the *mitzvah,* for it is through this service, individually and communally, that Israel testifies to God's reality, nature, and existence through all of history. Israel will remain faithful to God and His service until all men come to know Him; that is, to live by His law. Israel does not believe that any other religion has been or would be able to carry out that function. And it believes that God will preserve and protect the Jewish people through all of history—though that care is not extended from the people as a whole to each Jewish family or individual, as we have so bitterly learned. And Israel knows that God will vindicate its striving on His behalf on the day when all men indeed do come to know Him.

The central task of modern Judaism, according to this theology, is to win the conscious, willed loyalty of the modern Jew to the Covenant. Other generations could take the Jew's acceptance of the Covenant for granted. Yesterday's Jew grew up in a community which lived by it, and it so informed his personal and group life that he did not even have to articulate it. If he had begun to question it, the whole force of his intellectual orientation would have led him to a resolution. Today's Jew does not have the benefit of living and thinking within this pattern. If the Covenant is to bind his children and his children's children, he must come to accept it as his personal Covenant as well. By making it inform his life and the life of his family along with seeing that his children receive a proper Jewish education and encouraging them to marry within the religion—by living a life of Torah—he must work to ensure that the Covenant will be transmitted to future generations.

In the eyes of the new theology, then, the modern Jew must be not only an ethical man, not only a religious man, but the man of the Covenant as well. He is a Jew because he affirms that Covenant and has made it the basis of his existence. Once he does so, his life becomes an effort to sanctify time, to redeem history through following the Commandments, by performing other righteous deeds. Each Commandment becomes a way not only to personal improvement and fulfillment, but also helps to satisfy his responsibility to God and to mankind. Similarly, in performing the *mitzvot* he makes his own life more holy and brings the world that much closer to the Kingdom of God. And as he becomes more observant, ethically as well as ritually, in his practical life as well as in study and prayer, he not only comes to know his God more intimately but speaks of Him to all mankind.

Moreover, the Covenant explains to him that great mystery of which he personally has been a witness and participant—Israel's continuing survival. Only twenty-five years ago, some Jews were calculating how soon American Jewry would disappear. Today they complain because education and observance do not go far enough, and their concern is that Judaism must become more profound. Having suffered the worst calamity the Covenant people has ever known, the House of Israel has responded with new will and determination. No answer is given by the "Covenant Theology" to why God demands such suffering from us under the Covenant, and it neither condones nor minimizes Jewish persecution. The new thinkers do, however, point to the fact that the ties which bind us one to another have not been broken by persecution and suffering, but continue to be strengthened in the course of meeting common Jewish problems. The creation of the State of Israel and its continuing survival, they affirm, is also moving evidence that the Covenant continues.

The specific details of what is meant by "God's law" will vary among Jewish groups. They do not differ over the abiding relation between God and Israel, but—as is traditional in Judaism—about Torah: that is, the specific ways through which the Covenant shall be made manifest in life. The Orthodox will insist that traditional Jewish law, subject to change only within carefully circumscribed limits, is the only authentic expression of the relationship. The Conservative will agree that the institution of law must continue but will insist that Jewish law has historically adapted itself to new circumstances, and that it contains within it all the necessary means for defining how one should live under the Covenant and still be part of American society. The Reformers will insist on the freedom of the individual to decide questions of ritual observance in terms of his conscience or his personal encounter with the divine. But just as the other groups will benefit by the emphasis in the new theology on God's role, so the Reform Jew will find that the role of Israel asserts itself more deeply in his consciousness. By seeing Judaism as the Covenant faith, he will regard it not as a private religion, but as one he shares with his people. Hence his right to decide what is Torah-for-him, which might lead to anarchy, will be expanded to what is Torah-for-him-as-a-member-of-the-Covenant-folk. From the point of view of Covenant Theology, then, what binds Jews together is far more important than what separates them. Their differences, particularly as modified by the role of the *mitzvah* in the lives of families and communities, become far more a matter of degree than of kind.

Understanding Judaism as a Covenant can also explain why modern Jews believe in the continuing worth of righteousness despite the ubiquity of sin. They know that religion always involves two partners, God and man. Jewish history has seen the doleful results of overemphasizing the role of either. The reliance upon God alone in times of oppression and persecution has often acted to reduce the role of *mitzvah,* to relieve the people of its responsibility to use its own powers for justice and peace. And the insistence upon man as the master of history explains the continuing stream of false Messiahs and of the spiritual ordeal which inevitably follows their exposure—for example, the prophets of social change and scientism of the thirties, followed by the despair of the forties. It is true that despite our best efforts the Messianic era does not arrive. But we do not then conclude that it can never come. God, too, has a share in its coming, and in His own good time, if not our own, that great Messianic day will dawn. This sure faith that God stands with him in history can give the individual Jew the patience, the holy obstinacy, to endure and to act. God moves through history, working out His will for the creation, and man has the privilege of serving as His partner, though not as His surrogate.

Sin might destroy the Jewish will to act if the Jew believed that sin might destroy the Covenant, that it might nullify the relationship between God and man. But Judaism long ago affirmed that its Covenant was eternal—that is, unconditional. God may punish, exile, decimate Israel. Still the Covenant remains. The prophets may denounce Israel in His name, they may insist that He will render judgment upon it as upon any other sinful nation, and perhaps even more severely—still they do not say He will revoke His Covenant. Israel's obligations under that continuing Covenant are precisely what call forth the prophetic denunciation and the punishment of God.

The Jews, then, have traditionally rejected Paul's thesis that the Covenant is obsolete and that a new Covenant is required. The living reality of their relation with their God despite their failures, their experience of the response of their God to them in their sin, their trust that He has taken upon Himself part of the responsibility of history, all combine to bring them to assert faith in the Covenant despite their inability to fulfill it on their own.

There is much more to be said both about *mitzvah* and sin. Still in true Jewish fashion it is life which must strengthen and intensify theology, so that theology may in turn direct and order life. Only as American Jewry comes to live by the Covenant in a rapidly shifting culture can Jews determine its lasting significance for Judaism. But should that life of the Covenant become real and pervasive—whether in its rationalistic, humanistic, or existentialistic form—the foundation will have been laid for Jewish theology to reach out to the broader questions of culture, of the state, of the history of non-Jewish peoples. Until then the primary task of the Jewish thinker remains within the community of Israel. Some will still find this devotion to be as "catastrophically narrow" as Kristol did twelve years ago. But the Jew, the man who through the Covenant has survived the Hellenistic, Persian, Moorish cultures, and a dozen more—the man who, as it were, has survived the forces of history itself—will but marvel at such myopia. For in reaffirming the Covenant, in making it his own, in reestablishing his people's loyalty to it, the Jew enables himself and his people to transcend geography and politics, civilization and time.

And perhaps the greatest contribution Jews can make to Western culture is simply in living by the Covenant of their fathers, in patiently pursuing righteousness until God's kingdom comes. Western man reels between the poles of "forcing the end" and despairing of man's power. The people of Israel has in great part learned to avoid both evils. It knows its role in history as it knows God's. That it can affirm such faith in man and God, that it can continue to live by that faith, should be a source of continuing wonder for all mankind, and, hopefully, a spur to similar faith and action.

NOTES

1. "How Basic Is Basic Judaism?" *Commentary* (January 1948).

6 / Faith and Method in Modern Jewish Theology

1963

I

My assignment this morning is to discuss the role of faith in modern Jewish theology. In this context, faith may have three separate though related meanings: faith as commitment to action, faith as commitment to content, and mostly, faith as commitment to a beginning. Each level of definition has its particular implications for theological method and must therefore be treated on its own.

On the first level, to say that Jewish theology involves faith means, at least, that we expect the Jewish theologian to live what he teaches. Of the philosopher of religion we can demand only that he understand the reasoning of religious thinkers, not that he believe and live by all the diverse systems he expounds. A theologian should be no less academically competent and proficient, but in his case one critical requirement is added which radically changes the context of his scholarship. He shares the faith he expounds, and we expect his life to show his strength of belief in the truths he proclaims.

If faith for us must include both acts and thoughts, it is because of our frequent experience with those whose concepts are persuasive but whose behavior is repulsive. Not all men who think bright thoughts, not even those who are persuaded of their truth, actually live by them, even most of the time. This gap between cognition and decision, between idea and resolve, cannot be ignored. We may not ourselves believe much, but we will judge the man who says he believes, more by his performance than by his preaching.

In Judaism, in which action has traditionally been valued above thought, the theologian's life must be the first evidence of his teaching. And for a Jew that must inevitably mean not just his private and familial existence, but his participation in the ongoing activity of the synagogue and the Jewish people as a whole. Those of us who attended school in Cincinnati in the forties saw Samuel Cohon's vast Jewish learning in the classroom—but when we spent a Shabbos evening in his home, then we had a touch of Samuel Cohon the Jew, and in his living saw his theology fulfilled. No wonder, despite the Pauline associations he vigorously opposed, he suggested as a verse for one of the then new stained glass windows in the College chapel Habbakuk's proclamation: "the righteous shall live by his faith."

At this level there is virtual unanimity among us. The Jewish theologian should live his understanding of Judaism, and through his Jewish living he should test and refine his Judaism. But Jewish action stems from an understanding of the content of Judaism, and that content is itself established through faith. Surprising as it may seem, that is the almost unanimous conclusion of contemporary Jewish thinkers. Let us take, for example, the absolutely central question: "How do we know there is a God?" Even those Jewish theologians who are committed to the utmost use of reason acknowledge that at a given point reason will carry us no further. It may prepare the way. It may be necessary for clarification afterward, but reason itself does not lead us to the conclusion that there really is a God. The only way to get to Judaism's position is by faith.

Mordecai Kaplan has said: Belief in God "is an assumption that is not susceptible of proof"[1] and "Whence do we derive this faith in a Power that endorses what ought to be? Not from that aspect of the mind which has to do only with mathematically and logically demonstrated knowledge. Such faith stems from that aspect of the mind which finds expression in the enthusiasm for living, in the passion to surmount limitations."[2] Elsewhere he speaks of it as an intuition or an affirmation of one's whole being.[3]

Levi Olan similarly acknowledges that "The God faith is not subject to proof in the rational or scientific sense. . . . Ultimately, as Judaism learned at the beginning, God is an affirmation and a postulate."[4] What affirmations and postulates involve is made clear by him in another connection: "Faith by its very nature involves affirmations *beyond the rational* [italics mine, E. B. B.] and the Hebraic spirit is not characterized by a rigid syllogistic encasement."[5] Similarly, Roland Gittelsohn, in the course of his argument for the existence of God, says: "The mind . . . by itself, unaided by the heart, . . . can never provide total answers. . . . We need faith. Man cannot live by reason alone. . . . Of course we need faith to carry us beyond the bounds of reason."[6]

We are so accustomed to hearing these men called "rationalists" that we tend to accept that appellation naively. We begin to believe that they are true philosophic rationalists, that if we follow their views we may hope to dispense with the kind of faith which they themselves categorize as "beyond the rational" or "beyond the bounds of reason." But we have only ourselves to blame for this illusion. The thinkers themselves have been far more rigorous and honest. They say plainly: "We need faith." Their claim to the title "rationalist" does not derive from their elimination of faith but from their effort to control faith by reason, as we shall see.

There have been Jewish thinkers in ages past, not only in medieval times, but as recently as Hermann Cohen, who were thoroughgoing philosophic rationalists. These men sought to demonstrate the truth about the existence of God out of a rigorously intellectual argument. In this, the simple philosophic meaning of the term, it would be true to say, there are no rationalists among liberal Jewish theologians today.

This description is not limited to naturalists. Leo Baeck, often considered a "rationalist" by the uncritical, is rather to be found with those who clearly confess reason's inadequacy to establish a Jewish view of God. One might have expected Baeck, as a faithful if independent follower of Hermann Cohen, to restate Cohen's philosophical demonstration of the necessity of the idea of God. Baeck completely avoids this and instead, following Schleiermacher, bases his discussion on inner experience, grounds which would have been repugnant to the Marburg neo-Kantian. Thus it is not God as idea, but God as Exalted One, as Mystery, as Secret, that Baeck often speaks of Him. Moreover, Baeck does not wait for the end of a long rationally ordered argument to introduce faith as the means of reaching a triumphant conclusion. God in all His shroudedness as well as His righteousness is present from the very beginning of Baeck's discussion. When in his chapter on "Faith in God" he discusses faith directly, he says:

> In Judaism faith is nothing but the living consciousness of the Omnipresent. . . . This conviction is not sustained by speculation and gnosis, or by facts and proofs. Hence there is in it nothing subtly reasoned out, nothing demonstrated or expounded. On the contrary, it is the opposite of the faith which has to be set forth by arguments or established by victories.[7]

Only Martin Buber, among contemporary thinkers, finds God by knowledge, so to speak, rather than by faith. Buber manages this by an epistemology which has two categories of knowing, object-knowing and subject-knowing. The latter is as natural and everyday as the former. It involves no special state of consciousness and is clearly not to be compared with the mystic's special experience. Buber says we know God as we know other subjects, save that He is non-corporeal. Thus faith for Buber is not a way of reaching convictions about God, but the life which comes from knowing Him.

Philosophically, we cannot insist *a priori* that it is impossible that knowledge is available in two modes each with its appropriate structure and value. If Buber's categories are right, it would seem just as rational to know subjects by subject-knowing as it is to know objects "objectively." In those terms one might facetiously suggest that Buber is the only "rationalist" among Jewish philosophers today. But the title has now lost all meaning. Though faith has become knowing for Buber, what he has really shown us is that all subjects are known by faith, and that faith is more common to life than most modern men had thought.

Thus, there is almost universal agreement among contemporary writers that faith is basic to Jewish theology, not only on the level of action, but on the more fundamental level of content as well.[8]

Once faith has been admitted to Jewish theology, we are led to a third and deeper plane of discussion. Faith brings us to such fundamental Jewish affirmations as the existence of God, His goodness and its eventual triumph. But what else will it bring us of Judaism? As modern Jews, are we prepared to accept everything that has been characteristic of believing Jews over the centuries? Admitting faith to our religiosity raises the danger of Orthodoxy and sets the liberal Jew in search of a principle by which to regulate the content faith may contribute to his liberal Judaism.

The need of a regulative principle is prompted too by our knowledge of human history. Summoning the deepest of men's passions, faith may lead to superstition, fanaticism and oppression, and it has done so among Jews as among other peoples. Perhaps a liberal Jew could somehow reconcile Orthodox Jewish observance with his liberalism, if his personal decision so demanded. But that his faith might bring him into conflict with his sense of morality is as intolerable as it is a realistic possibility. For this reason, even more than because of Orthodoxy, a means of controlling faith must be found.

In traditional Judaism the search would quickly be over. The halachic tradition of authentic interpretation would do this in theory, even as the sanctions of the observant, organized Jewish community would do so in practice. But for us liberal Jews, who have neither a unifying law nor an observant community to channel our faith, but who rather require a firm faith so that we may rally our community and re-establish standards of Jewish living, the regulating principle must be found on the personal, not the communal level.

How has this need been met over the past one hundred or so years of liberal Jewish theology? For Geiger, the progress which history displayed in its systematic evolution was the criterion of his Jewish faith. In its name he could abandon the personal Messiah. For Leo Baeck, God's will is always understood as an ethical demand, and ethical monotheism is the test of Judaism. For this reason he makes the Jewish people a means to preserve and foster ethical monotheism, and Jewish observance a secondary means to preserve that primary means. With Buber, though faith is a kind of knowing, one is commanded only as one encounters or is personally encountered. Thus Buber is halachically more radical than the most radical Reform Jew and rejects any practice which stems from community tradition rather than personal experience.

For Mordecai Kaplan, the modern, naturalistic, particularly social scientific understanding of man and society are indispensable. This, he believes, requires him to posit an impersonal God. Roland Gittelsohn's argument carries this view of reason as the arbiter of faith to its fullest and clearest exposition. Now, let us read the sentences which follow our previous citation and thus give his thought his own completion:

> Of course we need faith to carry us beyond the bounds of reason. But that faith must be built on a foundation of reason, must be consistent with the reasonable and the known, not contradictory to them. If the direction of the knowledge yielded by experience and reason be represented by a solid line, faith must be a dotted line which continues in the same general direction, not one which goes off at a capricious and contradictory angle.[9]

Here faith is strictly bound by reason and Gittelsohn's reason can permit him to have faith in only a limited God.

We may, with some hesitation, summarize this cursory survey. Liberal Jewish thinkers have generally sought to regulate their faith by finding a universal standard of truth and reinterpreting Judaism in its terms. This standard has usually been borrowed from the philosophy current in the theologian's time and place, though Cohen and Buber created their own. If liberal Jewish thinkers, excepting Cohen, deserve to be called rationalists, though they rely on faith and cannot dispense with it, it is because they have regularly sought to control their faith by some rational principle.

II

But now let us turn to our own case. What principle is most appropriate to our day?

Before responding to this question, the responsibility involved in making our decision should be made abundantly clear. The choice of a principle to guide the operation of faith is not a modest technical matter. It involves the very heart of our Judaism. As we select one concept pattern over another we are already committing ourselves to a certain character in our Judaism, not just its beliefs, but the balance and weight of its observances as well. This principle changes the nature of God, alters Israel's character, and reforms the hierarchy of Jewish values, as we have seen above. This is the most fundamental decision we can make with regard to our religion.

For some men the response is relatively easy. They recognize in one or another contemporary philosophic system man's best guide to truth, and they interpret Judaism through it. But for most of us the choice is not that simple, particularly when we look at the views which previous thinkers have espoused.

If we turn to the vaguely Hegelian trust in historic progress of either a Geiger or a Kohler, we find ourselves in most uncongenial territory. History is not always progressive and we find it difficult to say with conviction that we know the truth of man and God better and more clearly than did a previous age. We do know, however, that we cannot, as they did, unselfconsciously choose what we wish in history and, by calling it "the highest," "the noblest" or "the best," consider it validated by the historical march of truth.

The rational idealism of a Cohen, even as modified by Baeck, is similarly problematic. In the former case, we are troubled by its relation to the real world. How shall we make the transfer from the philosophically necessary idea to the concretely existing reality? And in both cases, how can we today re-establish a philosophic certainty which derives from the clarity and independence of the ethical demand? We obviously do not wish to compromise the significance or the authority of the ethical. But it is another thing to make ethics the one sure and self-substantiating foundation of all our other affirmations of value. The varying apprehensions of ethical responsibility among different peoples, and even in different social classes within Western society itself, as well as the role education and personal exposure play in determining conscience, all make of the ethical a problem to be dealt with, rather than an unshakable base on which to build.

Nor is the scientific naturalism of Kaplan, Olan and Gittelsohn any less troublesome. Perhaps in the thirties it was possible to hold simply and self-evidently, as Kaplan did, that to be modern necessarily meant to think in terms of naturalism.[10] Today there are clearly other ways of being sophisticatedly modern, particularly since naturalism has floundered in dealing with the key philosophic problem of our time, the identification and authorization of values. One can take a thoroughgoing scientific view of reality and come up a moral neutral, as the atomic bomb so dramatically illustrated. Such an uncommitted naturalism is far more "rationalistic," that is, internally consistent, than is Kaplan's theism. His response to this charge is that such a naturalism cannot motivate morality, and therefore must be rejected.[11] Philosophically, if the morality is prior, Kaplan should, like the neo-Kantians, first rationally establish the realm of the ethical, which he never does. Practically it is simply not true that naturalists, agnostic philosophically of God or ethics, cannot be morally active, as the case of Bertrand Russell and others makes clear.

Gittelsohn's more tightly drawn argument from science suffers from a similar difficulty. If scientific reason knows anything, it is that superfluous hypotheses are rigorously to be excluded. To add God to a strictly scientific view of the universe is therefore not to continue in a direction previously established but to add a new and rationally unnecessary direction. It is not just adding a bit of spice to the food stuff, but radically changing the menu.

Of course, if what Gittelsohn means is that God seems a "reasonable" addition to the scientific view of the universe, that is another matter. It is a far cry from the philosophically ordered "rational" to what I personally can believe, the "reasonable." What makes the addition of God so "reasonable" to Gittelsohn is that he already believed in Him before the argument began. Indeed, it would be difficult to explain why Gittelsohn prefers the scientific data and opinions which will make the addition of God reasonable to all that which would not, if it were not that he begins with faith in God. Thus while Gittelsohn claims faith only completes a line which rationality itself drew, it seems clear to me that faith here preceded reason and guided it.

Levi Olan, who has given a similar argument about man's place in the universe, has been far more precise on the matter of presuppositions. While insisting that reason is a fundamental ingredient of truth, in his discussion of faith and reason he has frankly noted: "Reason, of itself, is never the source of truth."[12] Thus he correctly calls his evidence from modern science neither proofs nor even indications but resources. In other words, having established by faith that he believes in man, he can then find much substantiation in modern science for such a view.

These previous choices—historic progress, idealism, naturalism—do not easily commend themselves today as a means of guiding our faith. Perhaps then we should turn to the current fashions in philosophy: linguistic analysis, Tillichian ontology, or one of the varieties of religious (not atheistic!) existentialism? Perhaps, dissatisfied with all the alternatives, we ought instead to begin by creating our own system of universal truth.

Which of these living if troublesome options shall we choose?

But considering what is at stake, should we not first ask: "*How* shall we choose?" On what basis shall we decide whether to adopt one principle or another to regulate our faith? This question may with equal significance be asked of the man who is not troubled by our uncertainty but knows which philosophy he must follow. How does he know it? How did he determine it?

Three possibilities suggest themselves. At one time it might have been possible to suggest that certain truths were self-evident, or so clear and distinct that one could not doubt them. Obviously a philosophy which based itself on them was sound. Such a view could be accepted by only a few in our day. We have learned to doubt everything, not the least ourselves, our certainty and our intuition. To be modern is, to begin with, to be critical.

Perhaps then we should prefer to see our choice more as a hypothesis, an educated guess, a temporary venture whose validity we will determine as we experience the results of its use and its application to life.

In many ways that is an attractive suggestion. Surely we do not consider ourselves in possession of absolute truth here and now. We, as liberals, do not want to take up a dogmatic stand, one which is not open to change and the possibility of whose further refinement is rejected in advance.

But while we are determined to remain open to new and keener truth, it is difficult indeed to call the principle we seek but a tentative surmise. Let us remember what is involved in this decision. On this "hypothesis" our whole religion hangs. What is at stake is simply—*everything*. A commitment of such intense involvement and immense consequence is not merely an enlightened hunch about what might possibly turn out to be right. In all its momentariness, in all its openness to readjustment, I do not see how we can call our choice less than an act of faith.

Indeed the very structure of the decision itself makes that clear. When we are judging among alternate possibilities of reason (in fact when we stand before any single system of reason asking ourselves whether we shall use it), we cannot use reason itself as the basis of decision. The criterion of the adequacy of reason cannot be reason itself, for it is precisely reason which is being judged. Or, to put the matter more directly, every philosophy begins with an act of faith. That is what we mean when we say that each one inevitably has its own assumptions. Assumptions are not validated by reason. They are an expression of faith.

On this point, too, Olan has been far more clear and consistent than other naturalists. Beginning in 1947 (as far back as I have been able to trace the matter), he has openly referred to liberalism as a "faith." His essay in the collection by the alumni of our school called "Reform Judaism" is appropriately entitled: "Rethinking the Liberal Faith."[13] And his address to our Conference last year was on the theme: "New Resources for a Liberal Faith."[14] Olan does not seek to prove the rational necessity of liberalism. He rather admits that liberalism is a faith, one which is consistent with reason but clearly not established by it. Faith first establishes a matrix, and then, within its frame, reason is free fully to operate.

In short, in choosing a regulative principle we confront a paradox. We know we do not arrive at the content of Judaism without faith. But we also believe that we cannot affirm everything to which believing Jews in the past few centuries have been committed. Hence we seek to limit our faith in Judaism by some sort of regulating principle. Only now it is clear that no self-justifying, autonomous principle exists, but all the possibilities before us themselves involve a prior act of faith. Thus, we can delimit our Jewish faith only by acknowledging that we have a *prior* faith, in whose name we are willing to alter and revise traditional Judaism. This is the third and deepest level of faith on which the Jewish theologian must take a stand, commitment not only to action or to content, but to one particular beginning. Thus the structure of Jewish theology is tripartite or even reduplicated. It begins in faith, and this makes possible the work of reason which, in turn, ends with faith—from this point on it is always faith followed by reason followed by faith in infinite—better, messianic—progression.

So, to return to our theme, I ask again in which approach shall we today put our faith?

III

From this point on I should not speak of what "we" should choose. Rather, in accord with what I said on the first level about the theologian's thought and life, I should rather speak of what I must choose and of the method which derives from it. If I say "we," it is in the hope that there are others who share my commitment and that, hopefully, I am articulating their views, consciously held or not, as well as my own.

My position is simple. I believe the general method of Jewish theology over these past hundred years no longer makes sense. It reflects a point of view that may once have been necessary or even desirable, but is so no longer. And it is time we consciously confronted this issue and radically altered our course.

Perhaps I can clarify my position by a question, hypothetical, to be sure, but not unrealistic. Suppose we follow the traditional method of liberal Jewish theology and choose an intellectual medium for our faith, say neo-Kantianism or existentialism. We carefully work out the meaning of our Judaism in its terms, adding some insights on the one hand, but also refusing to believe this or observe that, on the other. Whereupon, over the years, we discover that the philosophy in which we had placed such faith is not nearly as adequate to life as we thought. Indeed, we now wish to replace it with a better one. But wait. We had based our Judaism on that philosophy. In its name we had both justified and revised our Judaism. Once we have lost faith in our philosophy, do we lose our faith in Judaism as well? Would we, in the face of this intellectual setback, conclude that Judaism itself no longer had meaning for us?

Some men have indeed given up their Judaism under such circumstance, but I would like to believe that I would not, and the majority of Jews would not either. Despite such an intellectual catastrophe we would insist that we know Judaism is still true. And we would do so despite the crash of reason and the tragedy of this experience, because our belief in Judaism was deeper than our trust in any philosophy.

Let me be blunt. Our theologians in the past century have acted as if they knew a truth superior to Judaism. But I do not know a body of knowledge or a system of understanding God and man and history superior to Judaism. I do not have a faith more basic to my existence than my

Judaism. I believe in Judaism not because there are such good expositions of its content and its meaning, but despite all the inadequate and clumsy statements of its substance, including my own. I should be delighted one day to have a philosophically tenable exposition of the truth of Judaism, but I shall not wait for one to believe in it. I want faith in Judaism to come before any other faith, and I want to make this priority of faith in Judaism my methodological starting point.

Perhaps in these remarks you find me insensitive to the nature of the group I am with. After all, we are rabbis, students, teachers and servants of Judaism. Surely we do not have to be reminded of our commitment to Judaism. But what is of critical concern to me is the level on which we make that commitment. This question of primacy is not only crucial to our theological method, but explains our great difficulty in dealing with our congregants. Let me take two examples.

All of us have had to deal with intellectuals whose approach to life was genuinely framed in terms of a given mental pattern. When such a man inquires seriously about Judaism, we are eager to tell him of its truth but usually have great difficulty in doing so. The reason is clear. This man has a prior faith. The only way we can make ourselves understood and, hopefully, convincing to him, is to translate Judaism into the terms of his prior faith. And that is just the trouble. Often his private faith is so constructed that it does not make possible a belief in God or, to him worse, an institutionalized religion. But whether he already has a hospitable or inhospitable point of view, we must recognize its priority in his life. We must talk to him in his terms and that is why we have such difficulty doing so to our own satisfaction.

This task of explaining one's faith to a man with another faith has an old and honorable theological history. Its name is unfortunate. It is called apologetics. Much of our work not only with intellectuals but with our members as well is apologetic theology. And, in general, liberal Jewish theology this past century has been apologetic theology. Perhaps unconsciously it seems to have assumed that it was addressing non-believers. It then took up its argument in terms the non-believer could hopefully accept and sought to explain Judaism convincingly in them.

Apologetics is an important practical task, not only for the Jew who does not believe but also for all those men of good will who seek its truth. We have a responsibility to share such truth as we have found. But apologetics cannot be our primary intellectual task today. Before we devise a theology for the outsider, we must clarify what those inside the circle of faith share.

If our faith in Judaism is prior to any other body of truth, then it is entitled to receive our attention in its own right, not just as explanation in terms of another point of view.

More critical to this issue of priority is the case of our more loyal members, those who have some faith in Judaism. Why does their Judaism generally have so little impact on their lives? Why do we so often find it difficult to communicate to them the overwhelming importance of Jewish belief and observance? Here too the answer may be found in analyzing the level of their Jewish faith. They do believe in Judaism but they have other faiths of greater importance. As long as Judaism can be explained in terms of their private world of belief, they will accept it. We win their willingness to Jewish action when we explain it in their terms, say mental health or the image of themselves as good parents, dutiful children or loyal Americans. But let the demands transgress their private norms, say we suggest mid-week Hebrew, daily prayer or public agreement to racially integrated housing, and Judaism has become a bore, a chore, a nag.

That is the danger of marketing Judaism in the consumer's terms, of our informal apologetics. We are covertly endorsing the private faith by which our member lives. We never shake him loose from his more basic faith. We never make Judaism the foundation of his faith, and he lives out his days, using Judaism when it suits his purposes, rejecting it when it does not.

Many people are attracted to Reform Judaism for just this reason, not because it is "convenient," but because they know we stand committed to freedom of individual conscience. We will not deny each man's right to spiritual self-determination. The result in many cases has been that our members believe first in themselves, their needs, their goals, their image, and only on a secondary level in Judaism, its God, its commandments, its aspirations. And that is why every sensitive servant of the God of Israel suffers so as he works with his people. A religion that takes second place is no religion. Unless we make Judaism primary in our lives and in the lives of our people, we shall not have accomplished that first step on which all the rest of the journey depends.

Liberal Judaism is committed both to the self and to the tradition. Previous generations sought regularly to put the self first, to work from the self back to the tradition. In part they were right. The individual must always be the foundation of belief and thus retain the right to disbelieve. Our full respect for his freedom makes the right of dissent inalienable.

But many of our people have gone one step further. We taught them that Jewish tradition was not absolute, but that they had the duty to reach their own religious conclusions. They have transformed this, mostly unconsciously, into a whole view of life. They have made their selfhood the ultimate source of their religiosity, and their individuality the determinative principle of their faith. They confidently judge such truth as comes to them from without in terms of their goals and their predilections. They may occasionally find themselves confused and troubled, and this may turn them to Judaism for help. But mostly they seek a new fad, a new recreation, for they cannot abandon their operative faith that they personally know more about man and his destiny than does Judaism. "The anxious shall live by his faith in himself." This position is a logical outgrowth of liberalism, but it is at the same time the source of a superior, sometimes patronizing attitude to Jewish belief and Jewish action. As long as Judaism is not primary to the existence of our people we cannot hope to see their inertia and apathy disappear.

But can we give primary allegiance to a tradition we cannot accept as absolute? Can we retain the self's right to judge and to dissent, without turning it into a rival principle of faith? That is indeed what I am suggesting. By faith in Judaism I mean the conscious, personal assent to the unique meaningfulness and significance of the Jewish religious tradition for our lives. Such faith affirms a qualitative distinction between the body of truth given us about God, man, and history in Judaism and in any other system or structure, without thereby insisting that Judaism is always right or cannot learn on this or that issue. Being founded on individual assent, it likewise guarantees the right to dissent without thereby raising the self to the status of a prior principle.

IV

The faith by which I seek to live as a liberal Jew is therefore a vigorous affirmation of the primacy of Judaism for my life if not of its absolute character. If I am consistently and rigorously to carry on the work of theology in its terms, a fourfold process suggests itself.

First, it should be obvious that such Jewish theology begins not with an idealist, naturalist, ontological or linguistic philosophy, or an existential diagnosis of the self, but with the tradition and its affirmations. Nor will the disciplined detachment of a Buchler or a Marmorstein, or the quiet appreciation of a Schechter or a Moore, suffice us. They saw the Jewish past as an object of investigation. I see it rather as having a claim upon me and my life reasonably similar to that which it had upon other generations of Jews. Their careful objectivity can only be a beginning for a search which now must also ask: What did it mean once to believe such a faith? What did it mean to try to live such a faith? And, most important, what does it mean for me to join my forefathers in this belief? We begin with the tradition not as an interesting curio from the past or a source of quotations to illustrate some modern view, but as a living content of belief which confronts us in authority and challenge.

Nor can we, in the second place, say in advance that we should limit our attention and concern to just those aspects which are relevant to us. Because we assert no principle prior to Judaism we cannot know beforehand what no longer has the power to speak to us and to guide our lives. We must pay attention to the priesthood as to the prophets, to the rabbinic apocalypses and mysticism as to their ethics. And we must, if we would be true to our faith, remain as open as possible to what Jewish tradition can teach us, even if that means we might end up believing it all. The methodological principle here is that we seek to make our faith in Judaism self-regulating. Once prophecy was that judgment-from-within that helped the tradition transcend itself. Our hope is that a living Jewish faith can show the way to an ever truer Judaism.

Third, our openhearted search of the tradition may from time to time lead us to dissent. Because we do not wish to make a faith of dissent, we should not search to disagree or study to disavow. In our affirmation of the primary value of Judaism we would not easily or peacefully dissociate ourselves from its teachings. When we are in all seriousness moved to disagree, the responsibility now rests upon us to justify that disagreement. Previous generations of liberal Jews often acted as if Judaism had to justify itself to the Jew. I am arguing that making Jewish faith primary calls on us to justify ourselves when we dissent from it.

Nor do I worry that this shift of responsibility will make it difficult for the liberal to remain free and selective. We can rely not only on his decades of autonomy and the influence of the American environment to strengthen his will to think for himself, but on the instinctive human disinclination to accept duty and responsibility freely.

This affirmation of the right to dissent is the reason we cannot follow the theological methodology of Abraham Heschel. Omitting now all questions of the literary form in which he puts his arguments, the content does seek to be true to the Jewish tradition in its own terms. Heschel's favorite response to the questions of modern thought is to point out how the reverse may be asked if we only begin from within the circle of Jewish faith. But while he is no fundamentalist and makes allowances for the humanity of the channels of revelation, he does not understand genuine dissent. Again and again he asks whether it is believable that a Biblical author should lie or misrepresent. Again and again he characterizes possible alternative thoughts as unthinkable, unbelievable, irrational, even insane.[15] We can recognize the consistency of his theology with one variety of Jewish believing, but it is one whose certainty liberals do not share. Perhaps this contrast with Heschel's full-fledged neo-Orthodoxy will make clear why I believe the position enunciated here, with all its emphasis on the priority of faith in Judaism, is yet fully a liberal one.

Fourth, from this dynamic process of confronting the claims of the tradition in its fullness, and working out concurrence and dissent, the individual will come to know himself fully. It is not just that Judaism will teach him what a man is and ought to be. In thinking through his disagreements with the tradition, in seeking to justify and explain his necessary difference of opinion, he will find himself revealed. Both Judaism as accepted guide and as rejected standard will call forth the mixture of person and tradition that should mark the modern Jew.

This living interchange between the self and the tradition can thus provide the base from which the individual can reach out to all that diversity of modern life and culture which the tradition could not know. Again the order is reversed. We do not here begin with psychiatry or democracy and come to find what in Judaism agrees with them. Rather, in confrontation with the tradition we create a matrix of value with which to reach out to modern culture, willing to learn from it where we can, but sufficiently secure that we shall not also hesitate to criticize it. The firmer our roots are in our Judaism, the freer we will feel to participate in modern society in its most varied activities. Knowing with reasonable clarity who we are and for what we stand, we can go our way as critics or enthusiasts with quiet confidence.

This approach seems to me to be theoretically sound, if by that we mean consistent with the faith from which it sprang. It is far more difficult to say whether it can work practically. I believe it can, but my assignment this morning does not permit me to proceed further. Were I leading the session on sources, I would discuss with you how it is possible to assert, despite the obvious difficulty, that there is such a thing as an integrated tradition of Jewish belief. True to my faith, I mean that in a Jewish, not a philosophic way, and I associate myself with Lou Silberman's remarks on this topic last evening. And were I leading the session on reason, I would discuss the problems raised by the impossibility of coming to the tradition without preconceptions or in explaining it without a frame of meaning. In both cases our aim is not to avoid the use of reason, but to keep the rational patterns subject to the prior authority of our faith in Judaism. The discussion could then take up the important role of contemporary philosophy in the work of theology and the way in which various systems might be usefully employed.

But this is a session on faith. What I have tried to do is to make clear the way in which method necessarily depends upon faith, for all of us. The critical question then becomes: "What is your primary faith?" For some of us that faith is Judaism, and, as a result, we feel that a new methodology is needed in liberal Jewish theology. Men of other basic commitments will take other directions. That is their privilege and their right. If anything can characterize the proposal given here, it is this: for me and for many of us the crucial question of our existence has shifted from "How can a Jew truly be a modern man?" to "How can a modern man be truly a Jew?"

NOTES

1. *The Meaning of God in Modern Jewish Religion,* the Jewish Reconstructionist Foundation, New York, 1947, p. 28.
2. *The Jewish Reconstructionist Papers,* Behrman's Jewish Book House, New York, 1936, p. 98.
3. *The Meaning of God in Modern Jewish Religion,* p. 84.
4. *Yearbook* of the Central Conference of American Rabbis for 1962, New York, 1963, p. 238.
5. *Judaism,* 5.2, Spring 1956, p. 114.
6. *Man's Best Hope,* Random House, New York, 1961, pp. 61–62.
7. *The Essence of Judaism,* Macmillan, New York, 1936, pp. 118–119.
8. Obviously this does not mean that all the content of Judaism is derived from or reached by faith but that its major premises, such as the existence of God, His goodness, the ultimate triumph of righteousness, revelation, and election, all involve faith.
9. *Op. cit.,* p. 62.
10. *Judaism As a Civilization,* Reconstructionist Press, New York, 1957, pp. 36–45.
11. *Ibid.,* pp. 309–310.
12. *Op. cit.,* p. 114.
13. *Reform Judaism,* Essays by Alumni of the Hebrew Union College, HUC Press, Cincinnati, 1949, pp. 28ff.
14. *Op. cit.,* pp. 226ff.
15. Although I cannot associate myself with Ben-Horin's own exaggeration and the dogmatism which he brings to his pragmatic criteria, the reader will find a useful collection of some of Heschel's most disturbing habits in Meir Ben-Horin's "The Ultimate and the Mystery" in the *Jewish Quarterly Review,* vol. LI, no. 1, July 1960.

7 / Creative Worship in the Computer Age

1964

Fifteen years have passed since creative worship was introduced to Reform Jewish Youth at the first NFTY National Leadership Institutes. Much good has come from the notion that services should be designed by the worshippers themselves, based on their present needs and utilizing all relevant materials, not just the prayerbook. By this direct appeal to their concerns, stated in their language, appealing to their taste, our young people have learned to feel at home in prayer, to articulate their deepest longings and their highest hopes to God. And they have experienced the broad variety of forms: music and dance, choral speech and pantomime, in which worship may find adequate expression.

Yet with the passage of the years some problems have arisen. As the Methodists, Baptists, and even the Quakers have discovered in their practice of free and unregimented liturgy, spontaneity is difficult to combine with regularity. The persons charged with creating the service find they are using the same themes over and over again. Their knowledge of the resources of prayers and music is finite and they soon run out of fresh material. Even their sensitivity to the needs of their fellows begins to dull and they cannot meet their congregants' desire to pray on any but the most obvious level. Often then, the efforts at creative worship end up a tasteless mixture of the customary and the new, with neither the lovers of the tradition nor those who want a more personally oriented service happy with the result.

The problem is largely one of human limits in time, energy, knowledge and inspiration. Why not, however, utilize modern technology to expand the range of creative capacity to the fullest and thus make this modern style of worship more fully effective? No committee, regardless of its scholarly or artistic membership, could be as effective in identifying the inner needs of worshippers and creating a service responsive to them as a properly programmed computer.

The inability of most leadership to diagnose the congregations' living needs week after week has obviously been a limiting factor in previous creative services. The computer can render great aid here. On the simplest level, congregants could be given a check list of varied moods and emotions, which, according to a specific code, could be phoned in to the computer before each service. Less superficial would be a series of Rorschach-like designs which would allow the worshipper to project his depth desires. The extraordinary speed of the computer would make it possible to keep this information quite current and prevent the creation of services expressive of needs which might have already passed. Brief experimentation could easily indicate how close to the beginning of services the worshipper could still make his concerns manifest. This process has the advantage that, having personally participated in creating the service, the congregant is more likely to attend. For its part, the computer would do what no rabbi ever could—accept every suggestion, whenever it might come, regardless of its content, gratefully and patiently, even several simultaneously.

At the last moment possible the computer would, by mathematical computation, determine the exact proportion of needs to be manifest at that service. This would be analyzed in terms of all the possible patterns of worship which have previously been programmed for the computer by a panel of experts in Judaism, other religions and the arts. These various structures are now quickly considered to see which would be most appropriate to the mood of the congregation. The possibility of too much repetition can easily be guarded against through the machine's memory device which will retain a record of the previous weeks' patterns.

A fitting form for the service having been determined, the computer would draw forth appropriate materials with which to give it substance. Again, a vast range of religious literature and music has been stored in its circuits. In a liberal movement this would obviously include suitable selections from the greatest of mankind's writing, regardless of their author's own race or creed. Here too, the proper proportion of Jewish to non-Jewish materials could easily be fixed or even varied from week to week within a given mathematical range.

One other factor might also be taken into account: the congregation's response to the previous services. A truly sophisticated installation would include provision for feedback after each service, indicating to what extent the service designed had actually met the needs of the congregation. These responses could be included as part of the computer's guidance in creating future services. Over a period of time the computer would not be working out of the expert's theory alone but out of its own real experience with this congregation.

Some practical problems are worthy of consideration. The computer should be attached to a high-speed printing device which would make it possible for each congregant to have a nice-looking copy of the service on his arrival. By determining mathematically how many people actually come in ratio to the number of calls received, at a given time of the year, in relation to the weather, the machine could produce an efficient number of copies.

Since the cost of computers is beyond the reach of most congregations, they might well be located on a regional basis, serving the various communities via the telephone installations so common to big businesses today. Perhaps the Union might undertake this valuable service. However, some provision should be made for an occasional hook-up between the computers to exchange information, lest regional differences eventually come to disrupt the unity of Reform Judaism.

Preaching too, might benefit from the use of the computer. Surely the sermon should speak to the living needs of congregants. The computer might well guide the preacher in his choice of text or approach. Since time is a critical factor in meeting needs, it would be better if the energetic preacher could stock the computer with a variety of sermons. (He too could benefit from the computer's memory and analysis of previous congregational reactions in preparing these more effectively.) In this case, the computer, while selecting materials for this service, could also choose the sermon most appropriate to it. And the electronic brain could be relied upon to keep the manuscript, if not the delivery, down to a length adjusted to the congregation's attention span.

Many exciting possibilities, open up once the computer is brought into the planning process. More will undoubtedly be revealed once it is actually in use. Serendipity has proved to be one of the major factors in the attractiveness and utility of these electronic brains. Of course the costs involved in even a pilot project are very substantial. But surely in a dynamic and progressive movement such as ours there must be some individuals or foundations who would underwrite what may well prove to be a decisive breakthrough in twentieth century religious practice. The electronic age is here. Will not someone step forward to enable us to meet it with courage?

8 / Why We Went: A Joint Letter from the Rabbis Arrested in St. Augustine

1964

St. Augustine, Florida
June 19, 1964

Dear Friend:

St. Augustine is the oldest city in the United States. It was here on St. Augustine's Day, August 28, 1565, that Pedro Menendez de Aviles first sighted land. In 1965 it will celebrate its 400th anniversary—indeed it has requested federal funds to enhance this historic observance. St. Augustine has other distinguishing characteristics. In American history books yet to be written, this small, neatly kept Florida community will long be remembered as a symbol of a harsh, rigidly segregated, Klan-dominated, backward-looking city which mocked the spirit of the doughty African-born, dark-pigmented priest for whom it was named.

St. Augustine is a tourist town. By far the highest percentage of its income comes from the visitors who walk through its quaint streets staring at "excavations" from the eighteenth century only now being restored. Most visitors stop at the Slave Market, supposedly only a relic of bygone days. True, they no longer sell slaves in that market, but let no one be deceived into thinking that there no longer exists among this town's white residents the mental attitude and the psychology which first put slaves on those trading blocks. The spirit of racial arrogance persists and is reinforced by the sway of terror long exerted by hooded and unhooded mobsters.

We went to St. Augustine in response to the appeal of Martin Luther King addressed to the CCAR Conference, in which he asked us to join with him in a creative witness to our joint convictions of equality and racial justice.

We came because we realized that injustice in St. Augustine, as anywhere else, diminishes the humanity of each of us. If St. Augustine is to be not only an ancient city but also a great-hearted city, it will not happen until the raw hate, the ignorant prejudices, the unrecognized fears which now grip so many of its citizens are exorcised from its soul. We came then, not as tourists, but as ones who, perhaps quixotically, thought we could add a bit to the healing process of America.

We were arrested on Thursday, June 18, 1964. Fifteen of us were arrested while praying in an integrated group in front of Monson's Restaurant. Two of us were arrested for sitting down at a table with three Negro youngsters in the Chimes Restaurant. We pleaded not guilty to the charges against us.

Shortly after our confinement in the St. John's County Jail, we shared with one another our real, inner motives. They are, as might be expected, mixed. We have tried to be honest with one another about the wrong, as well as the right, motives which have prompted us. These hours have been filled with a sense of surprise and discovery, of fear and affirmation, of self-doubt and belief in God.

We came to St. Augustine mainly because we could not stay away. We could not say no to Martin Luther King, whom we always respected and admired and whose loyal friends we hope we shall be in the days to come. We could not pass by the opportunity to achieve a moral goal by moral means—a rare modern privilege—which has been the glory of the non-violent struggle for civil rights.

We came because we could not stand silently by our brother's blood. We had done that too many times before. We have been vocal in our exhortation of others but the idleness of our hands too often revealed an inner silence, silence at a time when silence has become the unpardonable sin of our time. We came in the hope that the God of us all would accept our small involvement as partial atonement for the many things we wish we had done before and often.

We came as Jews who remember the millions of faceless people who stood quietly, watching the smoke rise from Hitler's crematoria. We came because we know that, second only to silence, the greatest danger to man is loss of faith in man's capacity to act.

Here in St. Augustine we have seen the depths of anger, resentment and fury; we have seen faces that expressed a deep implacable hatred. What disturbs us more deeply is the large number of decent citizens who have stood aside, unable to bring themselves to act, yet knowing in their hearts that this cause is right and that it must inevitably triumph.

We believe, though we could not count on it in advance, that our presence and actions here have been of practical effect. They have reminded the embattled Negroes here that they are not isolated and alone. The conscience of the wicked has been troubled, while that of the righteous has gained new strength. We are more certain than before that this cause is invincible, but we also have a sharpened awareness of the great effort and sacrifice which will be required. We pray that what we have done may lead us on to further actions and persuade others who still stand hesitantly to take the stand they know is just.

We came from different backgrounds and with different degrees of involvement. Some of us have had intimate experience with the struggle of minority groups to achieve full and equal rights in our widely scattered home communities. Others of us have had less direct contact with the underprivileged and the socially oppressed. And yet for all of us these brief, tension-packed hours of openness and communication turned an abstract social issue into something personal and immediate. We shall not forget the people with whom we drove, prayed, marched, slept, ate, demonstrated and were arrested. How little we know of these people and their struggle. What we have learned has changed us and our attitudes. We are grateful for the rare experience of sharing with this courageous community in their life, their suffering, their effort. We pray that we may remain more sensitive and more alive as a result.

We shall not soon forget the stirring and heartfelt excitement with which the Negro community greeted us with full-throated hymns and hallelujahs, which pulsated and resounded through the church; nor the bond of affectionate solidarity which joined us hand in hand during our marches through town; nor the exaltation which lifted our voices and hearts in unison; nor the common purpose which transcended our fears as well as all the boundaries of race, geography and circumstance. We hope we have strengthened the morale of St. Augustine Negroes as they strive to claim their dignity and humanity; we know they have strengthened ours.

Each of us has in this experience become a little more the person, a bit more the rabbi he always hoped to be (but has not yet been able to become).

We believe in man's ability to fulfill God's commands with God's help. We make no messianic estimate of man's power and certainly not of what we did here. But it has reaffirmed our faith in the significance of the deed. So we must confess in all humility that we did this as much in fulfillment of our faith and in response to inner need as in service to our Negro brothers. We came to stand with our brothers and in the process have learned more about ourselves and our God. In obeying Him, we become ourselves; in following His will we fulfill ourselves. He has guided, sustained and strengthened us in a way we could not manage on our own.

We are deeply grateful to the good influences which have sustained us in our moments of trial and friendship. Often we thought of parents, wives, children, congregants, particularly our teen-age youth, and of our teachers and our students. How many a Torah reading, Passover celebration, prayer book text and sermonic effort has come to mind in these hours. And how meaningful has been our worship, morning and evening, as we recited the ancient texts in this new, yet Jewishly familiar, setting. We are particularly grateful for what we have received from our comrades in this visit. We have been sustained by the understanding, thoughtfulness, consideration and good humor we have received from each other. Never have the bonds of Judaism and the fellowship of the rabbinate been more clearly expressed to us all or more deeply felt by each of us.

These words were first written at 3:00 A.M. in the sweltering heat of a sleepless night, by the light of the one naked bulb hanging in the corridor outside our small cell. They were, ironically, scratched on the back of the pages of a mimeographed report of the bloody assaults of the Ku Klux Klan in St. Augustine. At daybreak we revised the contents of the letter and prayed together for a new dawn of justice and mercy for all the children of God.

We do not underestimate what yet remains to be done, in the north as well as the south. In the battle against racism, we have participated here in only a skirmish. But the total effect of all such demonstrations has created a Revolution, and the conscience of the nation has been aroused as never before. The Civil Rights Bill will become law and much more progress will be attained because this national conscience has been touched in this and other places in the struggle.

We praise and bless God for His mighty acts on our behalf.

Baruch ata adonai matir asurim. Blessed art Thou, O Lord, who freest the captives.

Rabbi Eugene Borowitz
Rabbi Balfour Brickner
Rabbi Israel Dresner
Rabbi Daniel Fogel
Rabbi Jerrold Goldstein
Rabbi Joel Goor
Rabbi Joseph Herzog
Rabbi Norman Hirsh
Rabbi Leon Jick
Rabbi Richard Levy
Rabbi Eugene Lipman
Rabbi Michael Robinson
Rabbi B. T. Rubenstein
Rabbi Murray Saltzman
Rabbi Allen Secher
Rabbi Clyde T. Sills
Mr. Albert Vorspan

A TRACK: LEADING ON FROM GOD, THE GROUND OF OUR VALUES

In the near twenty years spanned in this section, the fruit and ultimate inadequacy of my early existentialist approach to Jewish theology manifested themselves. Having a fresh standpoint and becoming a full-time professor empowered me to publish four books in the late 1960s. The first, *A Layman's Introduction to Religious Existentialism* (number 71 in the bibliography) set Jewish existentialism alongside its more plentiful Christian exponents, made a case for Yehuda Halevi as its Jewish progenitor, and identified Franz Rosenzweig and Martin Buber as its modern representatives. Hindsight suggests that, despite the ripe sense of relationship with God that this stance made possible, I was already struggling with existentialism's inability to validate the truth of Jewish particularity. That discontent emerges in the constructive statements in my second book, *A New Jewish Theology in the Making* (number 101 in the bibliography). There I call for an effort to do Jewish theology as much or more from the standpoint of Jewish faith as from one of modern culture's preferred ways of structuring a vision of truth—or as theological jargon epitomizes it: as much from the inside out as from the outside in. Paper 15 in this collection, "The Authority of the Ethical Impulse in *Halakhah*," exemplifies the limits non-Orthodox believers run into when they try to theologize from the inside out. Studies like this clarify the mixed commitments that must shape a statement of Jewish faith hoping to be persuasive to Jewishly rooted but significantly self-determining members of our community.

Ironically enough, it was the general existentialist emphasis on authenticity that spurred my intellectual allies and me on to this newly assertive Jewish self-regard. That second book, which contained some chapters previously published, also evidences my growing concern to give structure to the entire Jewish theological enterprise in our time, a classification that would help me find my place within this communal cognitive endeavor. The most notable exemplar here of this continuing interest in theological systemics is found in "The Problem of the Form of a Jewish Theology" (paper 10). That investigation not only classifies the major Jewish thinkers by the different hierarchical orders they assign to the major beliefs of Judaism but then also identifies the religious problems created by each kind of systematization. It concludes by suggesting another, more satisfactory structure, Jewish theological holism (but not by that terminology). In the physical sciences, that sort of study is an experiment that helps clarify the larger problem the investigator is working on but is itself not appropriate for inclusion in the final, encompassing statement. This collection of papers consists largely of such scouting exercises, important for what they clarified as I moved beyond them, yet significant enough today to be of more than historical interest (according to the judgment of the generous but demanding JPS editor). My third book, *How Can a Jew Speak of Faith Today?* (number 110 in the bibliography), was a collection of diverse articles that were originally intended to exemplify the foundations laid in *A New Jewish Theology in the Making* and were a part of that manuscript. They became a volume on their own at the publisher's suggestion. Two further collections of my papers were published in later years: one thematic, *Exploring Jewish Ethics* (number 264 in the bibliography), and one extending the insights of my postmodern theological statement, *Judaism after Modernity* (number 322 in the bibliography).

My fourth book of that early period, *Choosing a Sex Ethic: A Jewish Inquiry* (number 109 in the bibliography), forced me to confront the problem of how to communicate and, therefore, how to lay out and validate religious teaching in a largely secular society. I wanted to explain to college students and those who guided them what Judaism had to say about sexual freedom. They, of course, were non-believers or semi-believers, heady with skepticism. Meeting them "where they were" would require me to speak a language largely inhospitable to Jewish truth as I understood it; speaking in my terms—Judaism from the inside—would make me an intellectual alien. I met them halfway, addressing myself to their staunch desire to think for themselves—hence "choosing"—and introducing my Jewish message along the way as relevant. But I could not settle for that alone, so I ultimately ventured a statement from the inside out. Reflecting on that exercise now, I would guess that the discovery of the critical importance of clashing "universes of discourse" for the nature of theological truth (today we would easily say "language") subsequently affected my thinking more than did the exact pattern I followed in that pioneering positive effort.

My growing Jewish intellectual self-understanding in this period made possible my active involvement in interfaith theological discussions. Two examples occur in this collection: "A Jewish Response: The Lure and Limits of Universalizing Our Faith," and "Recent Historic Events: Jewish and Christian Interpretations" (papers 14 and 16 here). In both, an emphasis on the particularity of all religions is strongly projected; in the former case against what I saw as David Dawe's excessive universalizing of Christianity, and in the latter (my Presidential Address to the American Theological Society) as to the different approaches that Christian and Jewish theologians have taken to such events as the Holocaust and the founding of the State of Israel. The most unusual manifestation of this interest was in my 1980 book, *Contemporary Christologies, a Jewish Response* (number 192 in the bibliography). That unique foray into the heart of Christian faith (as contemporary Christian theologians explicate that doctrine) resulted from an invitation of the American Theological Society to present a paper during a meeting devoted to Christology. I agreed to do so if the Society's program committee would indicate who were then the leading interpreters of this teaching and if they would make sure their list spanned the contemporary theological spectrum. Preparing this paper for and presenting it to an extraordinarily prestigious group of Christian scholars made plain to me that while there are difficulties in discussing the trans-rational elements of our faith with those who do not share it, much can be accomplished by informed people of good will without dumbing down the specifics of our belief to the platitudes of a tepid tolerance.

The climax of these years of intellectual maturation came in two diverse publications. The first was my 1983 book, *Choices in Modern Jewish Thought: A Partisan Guide* (number 213 in the bibliography). In it I was finally able to give voice to my conception of the field of modern Jewish thought and the alternative systems in which our thinkers had tried to present the lasting truth of our ancient faith. Perhaps seeing the alternatives so clearly enabled me to produce my 1984 breakthrough paper, "The Autonomous Jewish Self" (number 17 here). It had finally become clear to me that as long as one maintained that, in some Descartesean fashion, the individual was the ultimate judge of truth and the source of all legitimate authority, the Jewish group (or any other, for that matter) could not be given its proper due. A strong individualism regularly created a weak sense of communal responsibility. Besides, the social sciences had made it increasingly difficult to deny the corporate role in creating our vaunted selfhood, and feminism had already begun to unmask the sexism driving the male insistence on each individual's universal rational capacity. But the modern emphasis on self-determination had led to much good, as functioning democracy made clear; selfhood needed to be modified and socially recontextualized, thus my initial effort to speak of what I could now visualize as the "Jewish self." It would then take until 1991 before I could give that insight a reasonably full, book-length exposition, as I did in *Reviewing the Covenant: A Theology for the Postmodern Jew* (number 273 in the bibliography). My existentialism had taken me beyond rationalism, but now, to remain true to my belief, I had been forced to grow beyond its individualism.

9 / On Celebrating Sinai

1966

The past century and a half of Reform Jewish thought should have taught us, it seems to me, that observances remain more meaningful than our analyses of them can disclose. Liturgy and ritual are a significant language of their own and not merely a primitive substitute for the philosopher or social scientist or theologian's self-consciousness.

We ought not try, therefore, to limit our religious practices only to those whose message can be framed in verifiable propositions. The validation of the observance must come in the practice itself, not in its abstract discussion. Yet the elucidation of the meanings implicit in our religious activity has an important place in our lives: we are morally obligated to increase the responsibility of our decisions by knowing what we can know, for our knowledge may shape, even if it does not determine, our decisions as we seek to live our faith. This discussion, then, does not seek to exhaust or to delimit the meaning of Shavuot but, in accordance with this heuristic understanding of the theology of ritual, to expose and elucidate it.

Our starting point is phenomenological, the reality of the given situation. It has the advantage of preventing that continuing regress to basic assumptions which soon undercuts every attempt to analyze a complex, synthesizing theological symbol, such as Sinai. To be sure, the phenomenological basis chosen will necessarily seem arbitrary to some and may therefore appear to provide a skewed or perverted sample of experience to be analyzed. Such subjectivity is not to be avoided, and with apologies to those included or excluded against their will, the following is the foundation for this discussion. (1) We celebrate the Festival of Shavuot essentially in a communal, liturgical manner, and though its observance does not resolve all our questions concerning it, we know it expresses the truth of our relation to our God. (2) We observe Shavuot in our way as a continuation of a traditional observance of the Jewish people. Our Reform movement did not originate this day, neither did it reject it as it did certain other Jewish practices. Such institutional guidance as exists commends the celebration of this traditional festival on its traditional date.[1] (3) At the same time, it is precisely the Reform innovation in the commemoration, the Confirmation ceremony, which gives the day it greatest meaning. We seek to clarify, insofar as we can, the meanings we find as we solemnize this traditional festival, particularly in this new way.

It may help if we clarify what we are not celebrating on Shavuot day. We do not celebrate the legendary associations of the revelation at Sinai. Here already the tradition was quite clear. The halachic regimen for the observance of Shavuot does not obligate the Jew to affirm the historicity of every aggadic hyperbole on *matan Torah,* i.e., that the world was silent or that the Decalogue was heard in seventy different languages around the world when God spoke.[2] The authority of the halachah does not extend to such details despite the occasional efforts of zealots to turn aggadah into dogma. Such midrashic allusions occur only in the *piyyutim* and not even in all of them, for these hymns are far more concerned to stress the greatness of the Ten Commandments and the Torah than the legends which surround the day.[3] Since the legendary is limited to this poetic context it should be clear that they need not be taken literally. Reform Jews, whose passion for the chronological is well developed, should have little difficulty distinguishing rabbinic elaboration from Biblical account.

The problem of Shavuot for Reform Jews is both the biblical story itself and the halachic discipline which claims to derive from it. The question is hardly whether the mountain was on fire, a horn sounded or the people "saw" thunder.[4] The Bible reports and the holiday service celebrates God's giving words of instruction to His people. Some He himself said for all the people to hear; the rest He spoke to Moses to say to them. The rabbinic tradition authorized itself by saying that He also gave Moses either in principle or detail, the teaching which was to be handed down orally but authoritatively from generation to generation by the teachers of the law. Shavuot celebrates God's giving of the words of the Torah, both Written and Oral, and I cannot celebrate that. With all the love and respect I have for the Jewish tradition and its wisdom, which regularly far surpasses my own, I cannot believe that God reveals Himself in words. My reasons, once again, cannot fully explain the reality of my faith as I try to live it, but two considerations may be mentioned which affect me. Even in the moments of which I can say I have been closest and most intimate with my God, I have not found Him to speak words—though that may only prove what I well know, that I am no prophet. And when I consider the words which others have heard which they said were God's own (though of course put in human terms), it seems far more consistent with everything else I at this point know of man's history and God's nature, that these are men's own words in response to God, not His dictation.

In my opinion, the most characteristic theological assertion of liberal Judaism is that such knowledge as we have of God is subjective, a human response to Him, rather than objective, a human reception of His formulations.[5] It is this personal grounding of revelation which makes for the fundamental liberalism of Reform Judaism, that is, its effort to maximize religious freedom of choice and its trust in the responsible individual. Theoreticians may disagree to what extent God is actively involved in the process of man's coming to know Him, arguing in humanistic versions that religious knowledge is really self-knowledge for which "revelation" is hardly an appropriate term. Because I believe God still has an active role in such human experience, I still want to speak of "revelation," though I do not believe in verbal revelation. Regardless of the term used and its special nuances, the liberal Jewish thinkers, almost without exception, are united in their insistence on the subjectivity of man's knowledge of God.

If Shavuot is traditionally the great Jewish commemoration of God's objective revelation, how can those who affirm its subjectivity celebrate Shavuot? I must preface my answer with a brief digression on the theology of Jewish "law" (in some liberal Jewish sense of that term).

One advantage of the many varieties of liberal Jewish thought that we have had over the past century and a half is that they have explored a number of alternatives available to us. By exposing the consequences implicit in various theological perspectives, they have made it easier for succeeding thinkers to know which ones reject or require the sort of Jewish religious existence which they somehow know to be true for them (though often in need of further clarification and greater integrity). That is particularly true in that most perplexing of all liberal Jewish theological problems: what does God still require us to do? A typology of the answers given thus far would find them clustering around two poles. The one set seeks to derive practice largely from a conception of God. The other speaks more of the peculiar practice of the people of Israel.

The earlier Reform Jewish view sees religious practice as a celebration and rehearsal of the unity of God—as eternal ethical principles derived from the acknowledgment of His overarching oneness. Shavuot thus celebrates the supreme ethical discovery and commitment of the Jewish people. True monotheism (the first three commandments) is the necessary foundation for all true morality (the last six commandments). The difficulty with all such theories is the logical inconsistency of seeking to justify particular actions by universal values. They can never satisfactorily explain why, now that the universal values are known in a truly universal way, anyone need bother to practice them in a highly particular fashion, e.g., on the 6th of Sivan, which falls on a Wednesday (as in 5726). The answers attempted have never been convincing. Some have argued that the Jewish idea of God was unique, or that Jewish ethics were unique, or that Jewish ethical monotheism was unique and required the Jewish people to make it manifest in history.[6] Yet if God and ethics are truly universal, they cannot be especially Jewish, except by accident of discovery. Hegel, the unwitting source of the concept which most connects universal ideas with a particular people (and its celebrations) already provides its refutation. Now that the ideas have risen to the state of full, self-conscious, philosophic reflection, their religious elaboration, less pure and less universal, effectively is superseded. Since one knows, one need not celebrate. Pragmatic arguments (the help religious observances give in opening man to ethical monotheism or keeping him faithful to it) will not help much. Try justifying the fourth commandment this way! The Sabbath is not directly an ethical activity and surely one could get more direct aid for one's ethical aspirations in contemporary society by Sunday rather than Saturday observance, and by recreation and education rather than liturgy and sanctification, though the Reform movement has steadfastly called for the primacy to the latter. The argument is even weaker with a Shavuot which falls on a Wednesday. The theological reasoning the average Jew derives from this universalist, God-centered view is impeccable: if he believes in the one God and does the right thing, isn't he really a good Jew though he doesn't come to temple or observe Shavuot? We taught him well, unfortunately, and we must bear intellectual responsibility for his minimal observance.

The counter-argument seeks to emphasize the ethnic element in Jewish existence and, by authorizing the particular group, to motivate the Jewish form of observing. This position is even less satisfactory to the American Jew whose sociological strivings to be an equal reinforce his intellectual insistence on validation in terms of universals. The ethnicists are led either into chauvinism, social determinism, or social utilitarianism. So we hear that Jews have a racial talent for religion; or that one is required by the laws of sociology to express one's religion through one's people; or it is best for one's mental health not to reject one's group; or it will be a way to enrich one's cultural existence by amplifying it with these old folk functions.[7] An individual might well derive some personal satisfactions from joining his people's folk festivals, though I doubt that one would get very far with a Wednesday Shavuot by such reasoning. Moreover, why, unless God is somehow real and present to this people, should they make His formal worship the focus of their late-spring festivities? After all, the holiday traditionally celebrates His doing, more than the Jewish people's being, and it gives them little positive to do other than to pray to Him and rehearse His goodness toward them.

Contrasting these ideas vis-à-vis our Jewish practice (a good Jewish way of pursuing this unaccustomed intellectual enterprise), we may learn that any theology of Jewish observance which does not include both a real and present God and some sort of special relationship between Him and the people of Israel will not result in any meaningful continuation of traditional practices. If there is no God, we can at best celebrate ourselves or be that antiquarian-minded remnant of humanity which still takes time out (on a Wednesday?) to remember one interesting day in an Arabian peninsula (though rationally we should free ourselves of this cultural laggardness and give over our limited celebration time to more directly significant events in man's self-understanding, i.e., Freud's discovery of the unconscious). At the same time, if Israel does not have some special link with God, then we might just as well celebrate our private belief all by ourselves. Private celebration will not only be more convenient for us but less fraught with the risks of boredom and personal irritation which are the steady threat of public worship. Because many of us are not willing to face up to what we believe about God, many a Shavuot celebration quietly substitutes the aesthetic experience for the liturgical, the impressive dramatic reading for the communal reliving of what God did with us at Sinai. And because others—though far fewer, I think, than once was true—are not clear about the corporate nature of the Jew's relation to God, such liturgies as we do create for our children sound, but for a few Hebrew sentences and modes, more like public high school baccalaureate exercises than the people of Israel renewing its Covenant and its task. Thus a Jewish theology which will be adequate to my continuing observance of Shavuot must somehow know a real God and a significantly unique bond between Him and the Congregation of Israel. And that experience/knowledge is the framework within which I seek to clarify what I solemnize at Shavuot.

Though I cannot commemorate the giving of the Torah in the objective sense that traditional Judaism understood it, I celebrate the establishment and the continual re-establishment of the relationship between God and Israel. I rejoice in *kiyum berit* rather than *matan Torah* but as one who affirms that Covenant as the foundation of his existence, I acknowledge that I therefore stand under the Law. Only for me the Law is not simply the Written or the Oral Law of tradition, but that living discipline which flows from the consciousness of standing in direct personal relationship with God, not merely as a private self, but as one of the community with whom He has covenanted. While I cannot agree that the pact between God and Israel established at Sinai was fixed then in immutable, contractual terms (together with the principles of their extension and elaboration over the generations), I know that a relationship is meaningful only insofar as it results in action, that Covenant without responsibility, faith without deed, is meaningless. In that sense, *keyom berit* is my equivalent to *matan Torah*.

This understanding clarifies, it seems to me, the nature of my observance.

I celebrate the traditional holiday, on the traditional date, with liturgical forms that are substantially traditional. The Covenant did not begin with me. I came into it when I was born; it was, so to speak, there waiting for me. It belongs to history. If it depended on me and my abilities to initiate such a Covenant from the human side, I do not think there would be a Covenant. I know I am not what Father Abraham was; but because he was, I can try to emulate him.

The Covenant is not carried through history or renewed by me alone. It did not remain the possession of one family for long. Indeed, the first man of the Covenant was promised that he would become a father of nations, a mighty people. He had to be in order to enter and survive and transform human history. Sinai is the culmination of the Covenant with Abraham, the inception of its full form, not a Covenant with Moses, but one with all the Household of Israel. So I, who affirm that relationship, am not free to choose a private date or time to celebrate the establishment of my people's relationship with God. I celebrate it on our day, in their midst, and, essentially, by liturgy, for our relationship is with Him, the real and present God, the living God. We rejoice not simply with one another, but with Him, for what we celebrate is that we know Him and continue to serve Him, that of all human communities ours has been permitted to have had this intimate and continuing experience of Him.

The traditional Jew, looking at my observance, will find many of its features strange. He will be particularly perplexed that I interpret *brit* in personal rather than in legal terms.[8] But he should be able to recognize (and that is increasingly my experience) that what unites him and me is greater than what separates us. We stand as part of the same Jewish people united in the same basic relationship with the same God. (Because one does not need to define someone to have an authentic relationship with him, the issue of the identity of our concepts of God is as irrelevant to this dimension of the discussion as to the traditional aggadah.) We both believe that this Covenant relationship authorizes and requires communal and individual action. We differ only—though it is a great Jewish "only"—on what constitutes that required action, its substance, hierarchy and religious weight.

Because the partners of the relationship remain substantially the same over the centuries, though the terms used to describe them will differ, the sort of action which derives from the relationship will remain recognizably continuous with what went before. But new social circumstances and intellectual insights may make it possible to enrich and enhance, as they may require us to modify or to reject, the old patterns of living the Covenant. The Confirmation ceremony is an excellent example because its proper practice is already its justification.

The tradition knows no such group rite:[9] for girls as well as boys; at the conclusion of a prescribed course of study; at an age well past 13; as part of the Shavuot liturgy; climaxed by an act of dedication on the children's part. Reform Jews may have dropped the celebration of the second day, the *musaf*, the additional holiday prayers, and the customary *piyyutim*. We may have modified the *birchat hashachar*, the daily blessing on arising, and condensed the *shacharit*, morning service. None of these, we feel, touches the heart of our relationship to God or deprives us of the central remaining means of sanctifying the day. To the contrary, the reality of that Covenant relationship comes alive for us precisely because its ancient feel is conveyed in the modern mode by an air of serious attention, harmonic music, understandable prayers, family seating—and, most of all, by the Confirmation ceremony itself.

What are we doing with these young people? We cannot now induct them into the Congregation of Israel and its millennial responsibilities, since they have been part of it from birth. That was imposed upon them, a necessity, so to speak, of being born to just this family. Now, however, they may turn destiny into personal choice. At Confirmation we welcome them to conscious, individual affirmation of God's Covenant with Israel. That is why we wanted them to study before they ascended this pulpit; they must know what history bequeathed them so that they can know what burdens they must carry. That is why we wanted them to be of a more mature age than thirteen, so that their understanding could be fuller and their affirmation more responsible. (Why not the end of high school, an even more mature and critical time?) That is why we have girls as well as boys. The Covenant relationship is as real with women as it is with men. That is why we do it by the group, in the presence of a great and numerous congregation, for the Covenant is no private matter, but one which binds private souls to Israel's pact. And that is why it takes place on Shavuot day, for that is the day when the Israelite folk itself had to decide whether to accept God's Covenant relationship. Now each year the Sinai-day rolls round and the faithfulness of Israel to that ancient pledge is once more tested (as in so many other ways) and—how surprisingly for this stiff-necked folk—once again renewed. These children join all the Children of Israel in this rededication, only they do so publicly, formally, in a way which therefore marks a turning point in their Jewish development. They may soon not care, or rebel, or quietly turn to things that are more fun. It is their privilege, to use their freedom for good or ill. Yet the people of Israel did its duty by them and by their God helping them to know that precious, sacred history and inviting them to personal appropriation of that untiring messianic task.

And that is why we, the congregation, are so moved. Of course it is sentiment mixed with guilt, the consciousness of our aging fused with the illusions we associate with our children. Yet these are not base emotions, unworthy of bearing God's truth or sensitizing us to His presence. We may not have been the Jews we ought to have been, the Jews our parents or grandparents or rabbis wished us to be. We may have failed our children often as we sought to guide them; and we cannot bear to acknowledge what we have repaid God for all His benefits. But on this Shavuot day, in the sanctuary, seeing our children on His altar, this Sinai, hearing them affirm and avow and depose and declare, we know we have not been altogether faithless. By bringing them to Confirmation, we have confirmed our loyalty, and confirming them, we are confirmed as well. And that is true not only for the parents of the confirmands but for every Jew who identifies himself with the Jewish community and shares in its mutual responsibility for the education of all Jewish children. These confirmands are all our children, the next necessary step in our people's purposeful history, the hope that our Covenant-effort will continue yet further into history, working and waiting for the Kingdom of God.

Traditional Judaism knew no such ceremony as Confirmation, but if Shavuot day celebrates the establishment of God's Covenant with Israel, what act could be more relevant? Indeed it illuminates and upholds the rest, for we still love our children, though we find it difficult to understand, much less practice, the love of God. (And that is why some Shavuot services are exercises in the manipulation of congregational emotions rather than an openness to confrontation with the covenanting God.)

There remains one last question, the most crucial of all. Its several forms are one: Did God really make a Covenant with Israel? Is it true God has a special relationship with Israel? How do you know? How can you believe this? "Really . . . true . . . know . . . believe . . . how," these are the words which chart the regress of every theological assertion back to ontology, epistemology and beyond, to those fundamental assertions which turn the chaos of the fully open mind into the creation we call premises or assumptions. To answer requires a radical return to the first questions of theological methodology and thence a gradual working out of these initial principles until they bring us to Sinai and thus Shavuot. That is, no less, the demand for a systematic Jewish theology. Yet the question cannot altogether be set aside here for if nothing really happened at Sinai, if nothing could have happened at Sinai, then for all its intellectual utility, the Covenant theory is meaningless.

Without seeking to duplicate in Jewish circles the debate that Rudolf Bultmann's radical rejection of historicity continues to evoke among Protestants, this much may be said: what "really" happened at Sinai lies outside the sphere of the modern academic discipline known as history.[10] The historian, as historian, can tell us something about the records and traditions of the Sinaitic Covenant. He will want to have his say in the continuing argument over the likely date of the Exodus and how many of the Hebrew tribes were involved in the Egyptian experience. He may even be able to tell us something about how the events described as taking place at Sinai compare with similar events in the history of other peoples. What he cannot tell us, as long as he sticks strictly to historic evidence, is whether God and Israel did in fact make such a Covenant. This question involves fundamental metaphysical questions to which historical evidence is irrelevant: Is there a God? Does He act? Does He make covenants? Normally, historians are reticent about their implicit metaphysics, admitting that what they offer is an imaginative reconstruction of the past which is as valid as their premises about what "really" powers and shapes history. The latter, being a metaphysical matter, they generally do not argue but accept as a matter of modern methodology or good academic discipline. What is vital to this discussion is that good modern methodology involves leaving God out as an active factor in history. It is one thing to state this as a methodological procedure. It is quite another to claim it as a statement of reality. A "modern" historian cannot tell us about what happened at Sinai because his very methodology prevents him from knowing a God who acts in history. But because he cannot detect this reality with his specialized instruments does not yet mean that what the texts say took place did not take place.[11]

The same is true of the contributions of the psychologist, the anthropologist and other social scientists. They may tell us much about religious behavior; what they cannot assess is whether religion is true. Their very methodology (since it is empirical) prevents them from seeking to know God and hence they are incompetent to deal with the most vital of all religious questions. They do not know what is "real" because they cannot know it until they forsake scientific method for metaphysics.

Philosophy then stands between me and Shavuot services. In recent Jewish history, philosophy was less a menace than a friend.[12] Neo-Kantian ethicism and post-Hegelian historicism seemed ideal means of expressing ancient Jewish themes in modern tones. They could do this because each in its own way could show what then seemed rational access to metaphysical reality. Kant knew no metaphysics of the natural order but he clearly asserted the validity of the noumenal order reached via ethics. Hegel saw the one absolute spirit making itself manifest in the zig-zag of historic development. Religion therefore could be substantiated by philosophy and yet remain reasonably true to its own personal and historic genius.

Contemporary philosophy is nowhere near as hospitable to religion. If anything, its anti-metaphysical compulsion makes it downright hostile. Linguistic analysis is generally as atheistic as its parent, logical positivism. Phenomenology and existentialism are resolute in their rejection of the claims that there is a God. Such occasional metaphysical assertion as is still heard labors mightily to bring forth some sense of ultimate reality, but does so under the handicap that most modern philosophers consider that task, much less their results, well outside the limits of the acceptable use of the term "rational."

These metaphysical issues are not to be dismissed. They are not trivial. If what religion is speaking about is to be made meaningful it must somehow come to terms with modern philosophic idiom, even if that means to fight, refine or even break modern philosophy's constricted sense of what can be "real." And while the average man or the educated man to whom we speak is unaware of this technical philosophical discussion, he nonetheless reflects it in the covert metaphysics upon which, quite unwittingly, he builds his life. Religion cannot altogether ignore the issues posed by contemporary philosophy even though these seem in our day, as against what they were in another generation of liberal Judaism, to reject the possibility of meaningful religion.

But now, as I begin to ponder these questions for the hundredth time, I realize that the 5th of Sivan is drawing to a close. Shavuot is upon me with its claim for observance. I will not have time to resolve these metaphysical problems before the holiday is here. If I insist on doing so I shall almost certainly never observe the festival this year. My insistence on clarifying all the premises of religion before I move on to religious practice will, in effect, be the equivalent of denying belief in God and the Covenant He entered into with Israel at Sinai.

Yet to affirm the Covenant need not mean one has resolved all the metaphysical issues inherent in that belief. I have not. The question of my response to the coming of the 6th of Sivan hinges rather on whether, despite all my doubts and difficulties, I still manage to believe enough that I can accept the advent of the festival; whether my sense of what is finally real in the universe is such that I can still go to meet my God as one of His Covenanted people.

I do not go to Shavuot services out of dogmatic security, but despite my unanswered questions and unresolved conflicts, out of a knowledge of what has happened to me there before, and not just on this festival but day by day as I have tried to live under the Covenant. And I am grateful to have discovered that, though some of my problems with Judaism deepen as the years go by, the question of whether I possess sufficient affirmation to attend to this observance, as to many others, has grown less difficult to answer positively.

If I am to lead the service, this knowledge that the service justifies itself imposes special responsibilities upon me. It cannot today be only a fulfillment of the previously existing Jewish piety; it must be an experience in Jewish rediscovery and reaffirmation. It cannot simply count on what the modern, secularized congregation brings with it; it must reach out to them so that they know as they can in so few other ways truly know, that God and Israel still stand bound in Covenant.

The reader must manage the service. But if his mind is on the organist's cues, the undependable PA, the inattentive ushers or the nervous class, he will never bring to bear the personal *kavannah,* mindfulness, which will mold sound and music, silence and movement, reading and response, into living liturgy. No wonder the Roman Catholic mass prescribes a "master of the ceremonies" to stand beside the officiant and guide him through the intricate order of the special mass so that he may concentrate on the meaning of what he is doing rather than on keeping order. The *sh'liach tzibbur,* service leader, cannot shirk his leadership in transforming an audience into a congregation, but only as he transcends techniques and leads the praying will the congregation come jointly to face its God.

That too is why the service itself is no time for reflection. Precise meanings and integrated intellectual structures will have to wait for later. Now is the time to say what can be said and see what happens. Of course one phrase or another may stick in the throat or be rejected by the mind as an honest expression of the whole self. Sometimes a whole paragraph may seem unsayable—though I am inclined to believe that many of us so enjoy the posture of complaining about the *Union Prayer Book* that we cannot pray what, if we left off nagging, we could pray. Even to interrupt the service with many comments about the prayers, their meaning or origin, is to objectify the mood and shatter the developmental integrity of the service, thereby defeating the hope of making the festival worship a personal experience of Israel's communal Covenant reality. Thinking is no less present to the person for being subordinated now to what the whole man finds himself in this congregation, at this moment, able to say.

Yet any possibility of accomplishing this small liturgical miracle depends on what happens in the prayer leader himself. Jewish worshippers may once have been far more self-sufficient. Today they are, and we have made them, highly dependent on the man who stands before them. Most of the time his person will establish the context of what may happen at the service. He cannot not know this. In part that is what attracted him to the rabbinate or cantorate, that he might be the focus of this community. Now he will read or sing or bless or speak and they will attend to him—and there will be many, many, watching, listening, in a special mood of attention. If he does not gratify himself on this occasion he will surely not be able to give to it the fullness of self on which all else hinges. But if he does so only to gratify himself, he has required his people to covenant with him rather than with God. True, he cannot deny his ego and its needs. Yet he can and must find a way in this vortex of institutional, intellectual and emotional demands to be a transparent witness to the reality of the Covenant which binds this people to its God. Standing beyond drive and mind and ego, he must serve God with a whole heart.

Such accomplishment is not credible. The Household of Israel is too impious, the synagogue too bourgeois, the rabbi too human, God too distant. That is all true—and yet it happens. It has happened in the past—were the vessels of God's Covenanting inhumanly saintly in biblical times? And it has happened to us as we, on and off, found ourselves one Shabbat, one holy day, one weekday, entering the service just people and becoming in it once again the people of His Covenant.

We cannot know whether it will happen once again this 6th of Sivan. We cannot even tell what difference it will make if nothing special happens. For we know that if without tears or tongues or thrills or sparks something does happen, we shall probably recognize it as something old and familiar to us. It will not be altogether new and strange to us. We shall not be converted but only returned, restored, renewed. We shall discover what was ever ours. We will find what we brought with us. We shall gain what we always had.

NOTES

1. *C.C.A.R. Yearbook* for 1927, vol. 37, resolution VII and subsequently reaffirmed.

2. For a typical collection see, Louis Ginzberg, *The Legends of the Jews,* vol. 3, p. 90ff. and vol. 6, note 198, p. 35.

3. A complete list with brief description is given by Abraham Idelsohn, *Jewish Liturgy* in Appendix C. See especially pp. 336–37. It is noteworthy that the Hertz and Birnbaum prayerbooks for the entire year and the Rabbinical Council of America prayerbook for Sabbath and Festivals consider only the *Akdamut* of sufficient importance to warrant inclusion in their volumes. It contains no legendary material.

4. Exodus 20.18 and note the characteristic difference of interpretation between Ishmael and Akiba in *Mechilta Bachodesh,* ch. 9, lines 1–5 in the Lauterbach edition.

5. Gunther Plaut's insistence on the reality of revelation to the early Reformers is not in any way a contradiction of what is being asserted here as the excerpts he gives demonstrate. *The Rise of Reform Judaism,* p. 125.

6. The Pittsburgh Platform in its very first article asserts the superiority of Israel's God-idea and then goes on in articles 3 and 4 to set up universal ethics as the criterion of religious practice. David Philipson, *The Reform Movement in Judaism,* p. 491. Despite Ahad Ha'am's championing of the idea of a unique Jewish ethical understanding and the many Reform Jewish neo-Kantians who have placed great stress on Jewish ethics, no work since Moritz Lazarus has appeared which would seek to define those ethics or to indicate their unique approach. For the last view, see Leo Baeck, *The Essence of Judaism,* pp. 281ff. (in the first English translation) and the entire first book of *This People Israel.*

7. So Geiger (see note 5) and Kohler are racialists, though they used the term far more loosely than we do. *Jewish Theology,* pp. 325ff. See the justified attacks by Kaplan in *Judaism As a Civilization,* p. 119, and the return to the attack over two decades later, as if the idea were still

wide-spread, in *The Greater Judaism in the Making,* pp. 291ff. Kaplan's own position is a mixture of the last two views, that one cannot fight social necessity and can benefit by accepting it. See *Judaism As a Civilization,* pp. 48, 184, 261.

8. In biblical usage it often carries the connotation of specified law rather than relationship, e.g. Ps. 25.10 as contrasted with 44.18.

9. Though already in 1831 a prominent Orthodox rabbi began conducting regular confirmation ceremonies for classes of boys and girls. Article "Confirmation," *The Jewish Encyclopedia,* vol. IV, pp. 219ff.

10. For a survey of the question, with excellent bibliography, see James M. Robinson, *A New Quest for the Historical Jesus,* particularly pages 1–25. For a Jewish reaction, see Lou Silberman, "The New Quest for the Historical Jesus," *Judaism,* vol. 11, no. 3, Summer 1962.

11. The many problems relative to the creation of a philosophy of history can only be noted here. For a good, brief summary of the range of issues from the standpoint of philosophy of religion, see John Hutchison, *Faith, Reason and Existence,* pp. 167ff. A review of the problem, which sketches the history of philosophy and theology of history from the earliest time to the present, is Alan Richardson, *History, Sacred and Profane.*

12. This theme is discussed in greater detail in my *Layman's Introduction to Religious Existentialism,* pp. 69ff.

10 / The Problem of the Form of a Jewish Theology

1970

Methodological problems have been the concern of Jewish theologians only in recent years. Other than holding sporadic discussions of the place of dogma in Judaism, thinkers of previous generations seemed to take the initial steps and dominating principles of their work for granted. In contemporary Jewish thought as in almost all other humanistic fields there is, by contrast, an intense self-consciousness about every move, particularly the first one. The difficulty of finding or creating a generally acceptable framework for Jewish theological discussion has been a major factor inhibiting such work. For that reason largely, though others might well be adduced, it has been suggested that this generation may not be the time to do systematic Jewish theology. Rather the most useful task for the theologian would be to concentrate on significant aspects of Jewish belief and elucidate them. Such atomistic work could well serve as a corrective to and as progress from the time of the theological system builders: Tillich, Barth and Bultmann among the Protestants; Baeck, Kaplan, Buber and Heschel among the Jews. Hopefully it would prepare the way for a new time of synthesis which lies in the future.

Prudence alone would seem to make such a procedure desirable. Yet on reflection it is difficult to see how one can escape the holistic question altogether. While much can be learned by concentrating on a single religious motif and studying it in depth, its proper function and general significance emerge only when it is seen in the total context of the thought of which it is a part. Rabbinic literature is notorious in this regard. It contains such a dialectic of opinions, not excluding flat contradiction, that it is difficult to believe that there is any overall form to rabbinic thought at all. Without some such sense of the general balance of rabbinic sensibilities, however, one hardly knows what to make of an isolated rabbinic statement, or teacher, or study of a single idea.[1] Novices in the literature have often failed to notice that hyperbole is almost the customary tone of aggadic rabbinic utterances and hence have been led to claim as central to rabbinic Judaism something which a more experienced scholar, out of his comprehensive sense of rabbinic thought, would consider only representing what the rabbi happened to be emphasizing at that moment. A collection of all the many things which some sage at some time said was equivalent "to the entire Torah" would bring in many odd items, particularly when compared to what the same rabbi said were the halachic requirements that each Jew should minimally fulfill, much less the whole Torah. That is why we are grateful when theoreticians like Kadushin and Heschel help us to acquire a sense of the general form of rabbinic thinking, though the former's system is quite cumbersome to work with while the latter's, though charting two significant modes of thinking, does not yet help us to see what is the greater framework which keeps this dialectic, like all the rest of the rabbinic aggadic dialectic, within its bounds.[2]

It may help to give a more modern example. Each of the modern Jewish thinkers referred to above has an understanding of God as mystery that is highly significant for his view of Jewish faith and life. A comparative study of this concept in their thought will show that much of what they have to say about it is quite similar. Yet when this motif is seen in the context of the thinker's overall view of Judaism, specifically of revelation, of man, of the nature of the Covenant between God and Israel, it turns out to mean something quite different to each of them.[3] Thus it is common practice in the study of individual ideas to show their scope by indicating how they function in relation to other important religious ideas. Since most writers are unconscious of such definition by contextual delimitation, the holistic aspect of their work tends to remain implicit. They believe they have merely adumbrated one idea, whereas, in fact, they have understood it in terms of a more inclusive view of Judaism which they do not realize they have or are not able to bring to expression. One cannot for long escape the question of the whole of a Jewish theology.

Once that question is raised, the related one of the form of the thought pattern suggests itself. Now one wonders not merely where one will begin one's conceptual structuring of Jewish faith, but how the various commitments will be fitted together and with what rank or weight. The question of form is essentially one of the relationship of one area of belief to another: which beliefs stand in dialectical tension with one another, which are subordinate or superordinate to others, which are determinative and which derivative. Out of these judgments of value location, a specific shape is created for the intellectual structure as a whole. Because then the topographic characteristics of a theology are critical even to working with individual ideas much less to undertaking the holistic task, it should be useful to do a morphology of contemporary Jewish theologies. To that end a typology of four structures will be utilized. These have been derived from the major thinkers of the current scene but the types go far beyond them. Nonetheless this entails no presumption that this is the only possible typology or that it is as comprehensive as it might be.

The premise for this study will be the not uncommon one that the three major factors in Jewish faith have to do with God, the people of Israel and the Torah, the latter understood more as a teaching about living than as a historical record or literature. Heschel, Baeck, Kaplan and Buber will each be used to illustrate a different way of imposing form on a Jewish theology. Respectively, beginning with the one closest to the structure of Tannaitic Judaism, they are: (1) a theology in which Israel is subordinated to the reality of God and Torah, i.e., revelation; (2) a theology in which Torah as more-than-ethics is subordinated to Israel which in turn is subordinated to universal ethics which are derived from God; (3) a theology in which God, understood primarily as a functional concept, stands in dialectical tension with Torah but both are subordinated to the people of Israel; (4) a theology in which God and Israel stand in dialectical tension with one another with the Torah derivative to them. Let us examine each of these designs with a view to seeing what some of its virtues might be and what problems it suggests.

The theology of Abraham Heschel centers around the concept of revelation.[4] Because his writing about God's immediacy is so impressive in an age when men have been carefully conditioned to rule Him out of nature, one is often tempted to connect Heschel's thought with some form of natural revelation. That is true only on the first level of his thought about the knowledge of God. He is quite explicit about its ultimate inadequacy, however, and specifically wishes to control what is given on the natural level by what was given at Sinai and through the prophets derivative from it.[5] That in turn is understood as the revelation of the oral law as well as the written in the full traditional sense.[6] That is what enables him to look at all the questions modern thought asks from a human point of view and reverse them so that they may be seen as they should be, the questions God puts to man. So the content of his "Philosophy of Judaism," *God in Search of Man,* is divided into a third devoted to "God" and two-thirds devoted to "Revelation" and "Response," what we have roughly called Torah. So, too, his study *The Prophets* is essentially concerned to explicate his theory of revelation as pathos and thereby justify the biblical view of God as feeling and reactive, rather than impassable.

Because of its reverent attitude toward the Bible and the oral law, this would appear to be a fully traditional form for a Jewish theology. That judgment becomes questionable when one asks what has happened in this system to the people of Israel and, particularly, to its land. The people, as such, is barely discussed in Heschel's various books. What is said reduces its full-bodied ethnicity to what may be predicated of it as the recipient of the revelation. It is "a spiritual order," "living in a holy dimension," at most "the existence of the community of Israel."[7] There is no discussion of the nature of that community or of what it might imply even today that an *am,* people, or *goy,* nation, was summoned into covenant by the Sinaitic revelation.

Before the furor raised in the Christian-Jewish dialogue over the Six-Day War, the discussion of the Land of Israel was similarly limited, though it occupies an even more explicit place in the Torah.[8] Now with the publication of *Israel: An Echo of Eternity,* one can see quite clearly the implications of subordinating the people to the relationship of God and Torah.[9] Heschel takes great care to elucidate the historic attachment of the Jews to the Land of Israel and the variety and seriousness of the religious observances in which it was kept alive. He makes a moving case for what it meant to the Jewish people as a whole after the Holocaust to found and build the State of Israel and he communicates brilliantly the alternate despair and elation of world Jewry during the Six-Day War. To the meaning of being in Jerusalem and before the Wall, he brings his unique inner ear and gifted tongue. I do not see how one can fail to be persuaded by the book of the intimate relationship between Jewish faith and the Land of Israel. But what Heschel does not do, what the form of his theology prevents him from doing, is showing what is the theological place, the reason or necessity for the Land of Israel in the faith of Israel as he has described it. His difficulty is that, basing everything on revelation, he has previously made Judaism a religion of time rather than space.[10] Now this specific locale, just this land and just this city, must be explained and he cannot find a simple way to bring them into his system as they are in his heart. So he must rely on the significance of paradox, that the people of universal history should need one particular land as its own, or on a statement of the validity and nonallegorizable quality of biblical revelation.[11] Both square somewhat oddly in their flimsiness as argument with the extraordinarily effective case he makes for the emotional place of the land and Jerusalem in a living Judaism. That is why, apparently, he does his best to make the city of Jerusalem and the Wall, even the Land of Israel itself, active factors in the religious life, as it were, channels for the continuation of revelation. Here he is again imaginative and evocative, but he does not indicate how one can justify geographic particularity for such efficacy in producing religious experience.[12]

The form of Heschel's theology would seem then to conform more to the medieval structuring of Jewish belief than either to the biblical-rabbinic or the contemporary. None of the medieval Jewish creeds makes the people of Israel a significant factor as such in their précis of Judaism.[13] In their day, before modern nationalism, the major dividing lines among men were on the basis of revelation. In medieval Jewish literature the word *dat* often has the connotation of "people" as well as of religion or revealed faith. Such subordination of people to revelation was entirely responsive to the needs of a Jewry which had long been and seemed long destined to be in the Diaspora. They did not lose their attachment to a land and city they had little practical hope of reaching, for it was included in their revealed literature and way of life. What was necessarily the heart of their Judaism was Torah and the God who gave it. These could function for them anywhere, and because they were in reality a people with no present geographic roots, their religion was necessarily one which emphasized time at the expense of space.

It is difficult to find that form to a Jewish theology adequate in a time when a State of Israel is not only a fact but a deeply moving reality to almost everyone who bears the name Jew. That conflict of reality with thought is exactly the basis for Jakob Petuchowski's recent shift of theological position.[14] Having previously been working with a form of theology in which revelation was central, albeit a non-orthodox variety of revelation, he now has come to the conclusion that the people of Israel must receive, as a people, a far more adequate place in his thinking.[15] In this he has gone a step beyond Rosenzweig, the creator of the liberal model of Jewish theology centered on a theory of revelation.[16]

There is a sense in which the classics of liberal Jewish theology are related to the preceding pattern. In Hermann Cohen and, with important differences, Leo Baeck, the idea of God is central but it is intimately related to a conception of human ethics.[17] The God-Torah focus of the more traditional form of Jewish theology here becomes universalized to God as a unifying concept and ground of universal ethics. Revelation no longer is largely a movement from God to man as it is from man to God by what may, though with exaggeration and some distortion, be called conscience.

A theology cast in such a form has great appeal because of its emphasis on what is common to all true religion yet is abundantly to be found in Jewish literature and practice. Since ethics is necessarily universal, God, its ground, must be resolutely undivided and thus the oneness of God is emphasized in such a theology. Because ethics has been separated from all the rest of Torah and raised to a superior level, concern for one's fellow man now becomes the chief of all religious duties, and what lies at the heart of Judaism unites it with all men in the world who have risen to the level of enlightened reason. The social function of such a theology in a time when Jews were striving to legitimate their presence in general society is obvious.

The very strength of this patterning of Jewish thoughts, as usual, is the source of its problems. With universality the dominating motif, the problem of justifying any particularity becomes almost insuperable. As the people and the Land of Israel were problems in the preceding form, so they are here. Only now the difficulty is much more severe because there is no divine sanction for anything other than the strictly ethical materials of Torah. Heschel can, at the least, argue that God gives the land as is revealed in the Torah, hence it has a significant, albeit marginal role in his Judaism. The God who only, so to speak, gives the ethical has no special involvement with a particular land. If anything, Zionism is an embarrassment to proponents of this view. It not only seems to limit the horizons of social concern, but it raises the old doubts about the universality of Jewish faith.[18] (Cohen's own attachment to Germany was a notorious inconsistency to this position.[19])

Baeck's more positive attitude toward the Land of Israel, which made him only a non-Zionist, is derivative of his assigning an important if secondary role to the Jewish people in his theology.[20] Indeed Baeck's deviations from Cohen seem most easily explained in terms of his concern to validate Jewish piety and observance in a way that did not seem possible in a more strictly neo-Kantian interpretation of religion in general and Judaism in particular. Baeck could not give up the universalism which was the validating basis of the Cohenian approach to Judaism but he made an effort to link Jewish particularity to it. He argued that the idea of ethical monotheism is brought into history fully by the Jews and that it has since become fully identified with them to the point that if they do not survive it will not survive in purity. Hence the Jews are justified in terms of their universal idea which they represent in history, and their particularity as a people can consequently be justified as necessary to keep them and their idea alive through history.[21] Jewish law can now also be validated not only because so much of it is ethical at heart and thus directly mandated but because even where it is not directly ethical it serves to shield and protect the people of Israel.[22] That pattern of subordinating the people to its idea and in turn then the law (in its trans-ethical dimension) to the people did not change in Baeck's thought even after the Holocaust. Though he is now concerned to write about people and existence rather than idea and ethics, the formal design of his theology remains unchanged.[23]

Despite Baeck's heroic effort to validate such particular aspects of Judaism as people and practice the very form of his theology inevitably brings his secondary argument into question. Justifying particularity as instrumental to the belief in, and continuity of, ethical monotheism makes a good deal of contemporary Jewish practice seem inefficacious. One could easily argue that there are groups and activities which better accomplish this because they more directly work toward the universal goal. The only answer to such a charge from this point of view would be some sort of argument making the people of Israel a necessity. Baeck sometimes sounds as if he is a Hegelian, arguing, as did Krochmal, that the great ideas must have peoples to carry them and every great people is the bearer of such an idea, that of the Jews being infinite or absolute, and hence the people of Israel is eternal.[24] Yet Baeck does not produce an argument from the workings of Absolute Spirit in history. His whole approach to God through mystery and religious consciousness rather than cognition would militate against his being able to predicate such inner workings in the divine. Without an argument for particularity on a metaphysical level it is difficult to believe that it can ever find an effective motivation in a system dominated by universalist conceptions. Alvin Reines, utilizing a similar form for his philosophical theology, seems consistent with this judgment. In his work thus far he empties Jewish symbols, not excluding the word "Jew," of any particularistic significance and validates theologically only universal questions and concerns.[25]

In determined rejection of the loss of particularity generated by the previous model of Jewish theology, Mordecai Kaplan radically reversed the order of the major beliefs. Kaplan was fully self-conscious of the need for a new form to Jewish theology if particularity were somehow to be kept central to Judaism. He explicitly describes his new step in topographic terms, calling it his "Copernican revolution."[26] It consists in subordinating everything to the people of Israel, with Torah and God held in tension on a derivative level. (Kaplan's self-image and the form he envisages for his theology will not, in my opinion, stand up to close scrutiny, but the previous description seems accurate to his ideas.) Kaplan realizes that this is a radical revision of previous efforts to think through a Jewish theology but he justifies it on the grounds of the radically new social situation in which the Jews find themselves and in terms of modernity's reliance on science to explain things. Sociology explains the new conditions of Jewish life and suggests how one should now think about the Jews and Judaism, that is from the point of view of the group as the creator of human values and the forms of their expression.

With the people of Israel dominating his understanding of Judaism, all the previous problems of particularity are solved at one stroke. The people is the creator of its idea of God, the shaper of its religious institutions, the deviser of the forms in which its human values are given expression and effectively transmitted from generation to generation. This is but one part of a total culture or civilization which it brings into being, yet this religious aspect of the civilization is the most important part, giving authority to all other assertions of value and bringing to a high self-consciousness the society's image of its aspirations. By making the idea of God and the religious forms subject to the people, Kaplan provides for growth and development in religious thought and form. By requiring them to be expressed in particular, that is socially conditioned form, he keeps them Jewish.[27]

Many problems have been raised with this construction; the two treated here are related to the form of the theology rather than to Kaplan's special way of filling it out. The first question one may raise is that of making the group a primary source of authority, to say that one should do something because that is the way one's group does it. The two previous models have made the source of authority God as He makes Himself known to man, in the varying ways they understand this.

Accepting the guidance of the Master of the Universe or following one's own truest sense of right and wrong seems reasonable. However, why should one do something simply because one was born into a given group? Kaplan has given a variety of answers to this question: that man is by some sort of necessity of nature, social or human, a member of a group and bound to express himself through it; that it is unhealthy not to utilize one's group forms for expressing one's religiosity; that his theory is only for people who are ready to accept Jewish group identity and are looking for a believable philosophy to show how this best can be done.[28] In a day of increasing concern for autonomy none of these will serve to transfer the sense of ought from the self to the community. Thus the most important accomplishment of this position is upset by what is revealed to be its fundamental sociological dogmatism.

That crisis of value theory is only extended when one asks, if the group is supreme, what is to prevent it from making Satan its God and turning its biblically oriented ethics into what previously would have been called demonic values. That is not a hypothetical matter in a century of totalitarianisms of every sort. If the people is the basis of all else in the theology, then what limits are there to its willfulness? It is here that Kaplan's hidden agenda emerges. He will not allow the group to do away with the one, universal God or with similarly universal ethics.[29] Apparently he takes them for granted, as if in the modern age one could hardly doubt either. Yet it has been precisely the burden of death-of-God theology that the former can no longer be taken for granted, and there is substantial philosophic doubt that anything like the older sense of ethics can be rationally established these days. What is critical however is the recognition that if the model is followed strictly and the people is superior without any superordinate entity, one cannot set ethical limits to its acceptable creativity. Anyone devoted to the moralizing of society and social relationships to the point of making this the burden of Israel's vocation, as Kaplan does, should, if he is logically rigorous, give up this "Copernican revolution" and subordinate the people of Israel to God and the ethics derived from Him. That will bring us back to the problems of the previous model for which the notion of a necessity of human or social nature was introduced to solve this problem. It is difficult to see how any theology which continues the Hebraic concern for righteousness can ever adopt a model in which the people is in fact the foundation of all else. That is the basis for the continuing objection in the Jewish community to all extreme forms of Zionist nationalism.

Kaplan's positive sense of what the Jewish people as an ethnic entity contributes to Judaism is already present in Martin Buber's liberal religious Zionism of the World War I period.[30] In the subsequent development of his thought, particularly through his understanding of the I-thou relationship and its meaning as revelation, Buber created a fourth form for a Jewish theology. In it the concept of relationship is critical. Neither God alone nor Israel alone is the determinating entity of Judaism but rather God-and-Israel in covenant. What Israel knows about God it knows only out of its quite human and natural, albeit directly person-to-person experience of God. That is why this is not an orthodoxy. Yet since the experience is of God Himself, the relationship must be taken with full personal ultimacy. What Israel knows about itself it knows in terms of its unique and transforming relationship with God. So while Israel is as fully ethnic as any of the seven nations it dispossesses from the land, its ethnicity, as for example its right to occupy its land, is fully qualified by its faithfulness to its relationship to God. Religion and ethnicity, universalism and particularism are here kept together in a harmony which does justice to each of the themes but makes something new of them both as they are placed in counterpoint to each other.[31]

Torah is subordinated to the Israel-God relationship in a way that has a strong initial appeal to many liberals. All the texts—narrative, legal, prophetic, or wisdom—are men's record and response to the encounter. Hence when they are only human it is no embarrassment, and when changing sensibilities or situations call for a change in Jewish practice, that is not only permissible but mandatory.[32] The law is always subject to the present command of God to the people. But now it is difficult to see how, particularly in a time of continuing rapid social change such as ours, there can be any valid law at all, or even general patterns of practice or continuity of traditions. Buber's own interpretation of the distance between God-and-Israel and Torah as practice almost dissolves the latter conception altogether. Fearing corporate domination of the individual as one of the abiding sins of the century, he insisted that what he meant by God addressing nations, which he fully believed in as he moved to the end of his life, was to be understood in an atomistic way.[33] God, in fact, only speaks to individuals, and it is only when these individuals, hearing God call them, know themselves to be called to act together, that their simple ethnic identity becomes a meaningful national identity.[34] The commandments at Sinai are addressed to single selves but the individuals who heard it knew themselves to be one in hearing and accepting.[35] So it was at all the great covenant renewals in Israel's history, down to this day. But he who does not hear God commanding today cannot be expected to do something merely because other Jews once heard and did. For Buber attention to the old ways today generally creates barriers between the individual and God.[36] Buber's own consequent lack of traditional Jewish observance has always seemed to many believing Jews strangely at odds with his lively sense of God's living relationship with the people of Israel.

For the diaspora Jew, who cannot count on land, language, the Bible and a Jewish environment somehow to channel this inwardness, the absence of a doctrine of general practice is quite critical. Without some structure of activity linking such a Jew with other members of the Jewish people covenanted to God, it is difficult to believe that they can long survive. Radical individualism over against the demands of the Jewish tradition is hardly the problem of contemporary diaspora Jews. Taking Buber at his most reductive level they would willingly substitute the I-thou relationship for that of God and Israel. Then not only has Torah been dissolved but the people of Israel as well. That, however, is not so much a requirement of this form of a Jewish theology as of Buber's radical fragmentation of the people of Israel into a collection of individuals as far as law is concerned.

This investigation has tried to show that as difficult as the holistic question is one cannot leave it aside. The overall form of a Jewish theology inevitably affects the meaning of the component parts. A shift in subordination or superordination changes the impact of the teaching and the sort of Jewish life it will produce. Contrariwise, if one has some sense of what Judaism must come to mean in our time, that will be critical in determining the form his theology ought to take.

For me, as for many others, today's Judaism cannot be an orthodoxy even in the rather open and theoretically flexible form in which the new Orthodox Left is speaking.[37] For all its promise, such an interpretation of Judaism still gives the halachah and, more significantly, the interpreters of the law, priority over the individual so that his autonomy becomes a heteronomy. Because I cannot see that heteronomy as the equivalent of a theonomy and thus the fulfillment of my autonomy, I cannot be orthodox. Nonetheless, as I have argued elsewhere,[38] I do not see autonomy as a self-substantiating value, to be accepted as a self-evident, unquestioned basis for philosophizing, as did Kant. In an intellectually oppressive atmosphere, where reliable reason seems in shackles, freedom might quickly qualify as an end in itself. In a permissive age, where almost everything is tolerated or considered worthy of some serious attention, autonomy can as well become a means to self-destruction and the debasement of everything philosophy until recent years seemed to prize. And if everything is permitted, why not the negation of autonomy itself? So for me autonomy is inevitably linked to a relationship with God. That cannot simply be a personal matter, for not every relationship with God would be such as to ground personal autonomy and yet give it proper scope for fulfillment. That sense of the individual in relation to God I find implicit in the traditional Jewish understanding of the covenant Israel has with Him. In typical modern reinterpretation, I understand the God-Israel covenant more as a personal relationship than as a legal contract.[39] What passes between God and Israel determines what is Torah, and where what another generation called Torah does not reflect the reality of this relationship, it needs to be changed to do so or dropped in practice if it cannot so be changed. To that extent I follow the Buberian reformulation of the nonorthodox position so as to rescue it from ethicism or ethnicism.

Yet I wish to go beyond Buber by refusing to reshape Jewish theology as he does when he reduces the concept of Israel to that of man. Subordinating the people of Israel in that way makes sense if one is doing theology for universal men who are interested in seeing how Jewishness might fit into their world view. There is still a useful place for such theologizing when it is recognized for what it is, apologetics, and particularly when it is directed toward Jews speaking from the stance of universalism. However, as a simple matter of self-respect, there ought to be Jewish theology for Jews whose Jewishness is neither incidental nor accidental but a very part of their existence. The incredible drama of recent decades, both its tragedies and its accomplishments, has made many a Jew recognize that universalism was true as an ideal but not as a state, and that considering what Western civilization was making of man in general he was proud to see himself primarily as a Jew. I am concerned to do Jewish theology for such people, for I am one of them.

Such a Jew is a quite particularistic sort of man. So are all men, none of whom can live outside the finitudes of history. Yet as one of the covenant people his style of existence aims at universalism, messianically achieved, and is founded on autonomy called into being by a God Who commands him to live out their relationship but does not deprive him of his freedom in responding.[40] He knows autonomy is basic to living, for his people teaches him its significance through an embracing community style of individualistic existence and strengthens him in its pursuit by its concern for his proper response to his freedom in covenant. So even as he comes to a life of autonomy via God and the people of Israel, so he fulfills it not merely in terms of what is law for his private good alone but what is an appropriate act for a member of the covenant people serving its God.[41] Torah is still subordinated here to the God-Israel relationship as in all nonorthodoxies. It is not thereby reduced to ethics, folkways or a response to the purely personal situation. In this formulation, Israel is not merely a historical or social category but an existential one. So Torah is kept from becoming an individualistic matter, tending to communal anarchy. Rather by linking the individual situation indissolubly with that of the people of Israel as God's covenant folk, a new foundation for corporate, yet individualistically centered patterns of behavior becomes possible.

From the modern point of view that is an exceedingly difficult position to take. Descartes' myth of the mind which can free itself from all particularity and thus think its way through to what alone one really must believe is so widespread as to have become itself, ironically, not subject to systematic doubting. Rosenzweig's genius was that he made his way from Hegel's grand universalism to the particularity not of Jewish ideas or of folk but of Jewish existence.[42] Then, having become the first existentialist Jew, he could illuminate every aspect of Jewish life, even as he fulfilled his primary Jewish responsibility to live it. Rosenzweig made that move without any mystical experience or leap of faith. (One does not need such radical transformation to become what one has always been though not attended to.) Even as he learned idealism was untenable and Christianity unnecessary, he found himself, existentially, a Jew. Our frustration with him today is that we, living in another cultural situation, cannot follow his way back. Speaking to the problems and in the style of a culture relatively alien to us, he does not help us find our way from the periphery of fragmented, pseudo-universal existence to the center of that real world where the people of Israel lives in the authenticity of its unending relationship with God.

The apologetic task of contemporary Jewish theology is to show the reasonableness of that movement from the margin to the middle. That can hardly be done, however, without some knowledge of the God-Israel-Torah relationship which characterizes authentic Jewish existence. Describing that relationship in a rather internal way would then seem to be the primary task of Jewish theology today.

NOTES

1. Solomon Schechter was fully aware of the complexity of rabbinic thought as the double modesty of the title of his book on rabbinic thought indicates. Yet having excused himself from being complete, chronological or systematic, he then proposes to give the enduring beliefs which form the general opinion of "the Synagogue." So it is no surprise that the table of contents compares well with the sort of topics normally treated by avowedly systematic Jewish theologians. *Some Aspects of Rabbinic Theology,* New York, 1923, Preface, particularly pp. xif., and chapter 1, particularly p. 17. Cf. Herbert Loewe's Foreword to Roy A. Stewart, *Rabbinic Theology,* Edinburgh and London, 1961, especially p. vi, and the author's own comments on selectivity, climaxed on 10. The historical versus theological questions involved in trying to give a comprehensive view of Judaism are most cogently raised by Jacob Neusner, "What Is Normative in Jewish Ethics," *Judaism,* vol. 16, no. 1, Winter 1967, pp. 3–20.

2. Max Kadushin, *The Rabbinic Mind,* New York, 1952, chapter 11. Abraham Heschel, *Theology of Ancient Judaism* (Hebrew), London and New York, vol. 1, 1962, summarizes his position in the Introduction pp. 37ff., and first chapter.

3. For Mordecai M. Kaplan, God's mysteriousness means that one should not indulge in metaphysical speculation but should confine oneself to speaking functionally and only of the idea of God. Though it remains necessary to intuit His reality, Kaplan does not make such sensitivity a central concern of his Jewish religious living. *The Meaning of God in Modern Jewish Religion,* New York, 1937, p. 29. *Jewish Reconstructionist Papers,* New York, 1936, p. 98. *The Future of the American Jew,* New York, 1948, p. 182. For Leo Baeck the mystery, once sensed, is not subordinated to the demands of living, but because it is understood as significant consciousness it becomes fully equivalent to ethics in Jewish living. *The Essence of Judaism,* New York, 1936, beginning on p. 5, then *passim.* He develops the idea more explicitly in "Mystery and Commandment," *Judaism and Christianity,* Philadelphia, 1958, pp. 171ff. Albert H. Friedlander relates this to his scholarly interest in Jewish mysticism; *Leo Baeck, Teacher of Theresienstadt,* New York, 1968, pp. 154ff. For Abraham Heschel the mystery by which man can be radically amazed is too great to be controlled by ethics and finds its fulfillment and transformation in biblical revelation. *God in Search of Man,* Philadelphia, 1955, p. 57, and the entire context. For the relation of wonder to the Bible, see p. 31 there. Martin Buber also has a sense of mystery because he knows the I-thou relationship cannot be forced but has a spontaneity of its own. Since, however, the sense of mystery preceding its coming is dispelled by the encounter itself, any concentration on the mysterious rather than the meeting itself becomes pseudoreligion. *I and Thou,* Edinburgh, 1937, pp. 11 and 81.

4. What Fritz Rothschild calls a polarity in Heschel is more precisely called by Edmond Cherbonnier an effort to explicate a coherent philosophical outlook contained in the Bible. The revelation, in other words, sets the content and frame of the philosophy. See the respective articles "The Religious Thought of Abraham Heschel" and "Heschel As a Religious Thinker" in *Conservative Judaism,* vol. XXIII, no. 1, Fall 1968, pp. 12ff. and 25ff., and the former's introduction to *Between God and Man,* New York, 1959, pp. 7ff.

5. *God in Search of Man,* pp. 90ff., and then the progress of the argument to revelation, chapter 17, and Sinai, chapter 20.

6. Ibid., p. 274.

7. Ibid., p. 423.

8. Ibid., p. 425.

9. New York, 1969.

10. This appears at the very beginning of the section on revelation in *God in Search of Man.* Judaism is defined "as a relation between man with Torah and God," p. 167. Judaism as, consequently, a religion of time rather than place is picked up on p. 200 and cf. pp. 312 and 417f. The latter restates briefly the eloquent statement of *The Sabbath,* Cleveland, 1962, where the Epilogue and Appendix should also be consulted.

11. Israel: *An Echo of Eternity,* pp. 127ff.

12. Ibid., pp. 5ff.

13. For a concise statement, see Solomon Schechter, "The Dogmas of Judaism," *Studies in Judaism,* First Series, Philadelphia, 1920, pp. 147ff. For a more modern treatment, with highly useful bibliography, see Louis Jacobs, *Principles of the Jewish Faith,* New York, 1964, pp. 1ff.

14. "More Than a Plank," *CCAR Journal,* October, 1968, pp. 76ff. The whole burden of this article is that the shift of emphasis on one idea was not merely significant for that idea alone but

for all of the theology of Reform Judaism. I will await the judgment of historians of the period as to whether the attitude toward Zion was as causative in relation to the totality of Reform Jewish thinking in the formative period as Petuchowski seems to believe. I only call attention here to the significance of this form of a theology which I see so dominated by an attitude toward revelation that it has little room, without significant alteration, for the people and Land of Israel. Though Heschel is as good as orthodox in his theory of revelation, and Rosenzweig and Petuchowski are nonorthodox, all utilize the same design in their thinking.

15. The fullest statement of position was given in *Ever Since Sinai,* New York, 1961, which must be read, particularly in view of subsequent publications, as a statement of personal commitment and not only scholarly description.

16. Revelation "became the central idea of his theological system." Nahum N. Glatzer, *Franz Rosenzweig: His Life and Thought, second edition,* New York, 1961, p. 63. Glatzer is referring to his theory of religion in general, here used to distinguish Judaism and Christianity from all other religions. For the way in which this emerges from the trinity of creation-revelation-redemption to become dominant, see my *A Layman's Introduction to Religious Existentialism,* Philadelphia, 1965, pp. 80ff. The historically significant Rosenzweig essay on theology without revelation, "Atheistic Theology," (see the comment by Glatzer, p. 31) has recently been translated by Goldy and Holch, *Canadian Journal of Theology,* vol. 14, no. 2, April, 1968, pp. 79ff. Revelation, however, is central also to Rosenzweig's Judaism and the basis for his transhistorical sense of the Jewish people and his objection to Zionism. Steven Schwarzschild has best brought out the attraction-repulsion struggle in Rosenzweig toward Zionism. *Franz Rosenzweig,* London, Education Committee of the Hillel Foundation, n.d., pp. 29–31. See, too, the significant letter to Hans Ehrenberg in Glatzer, pp. 157f., the attack on modern Hebrew, pp. 263ff., but the corrective later letter p. 358. J. Guttmann makes the movement from revelation to religious people to problems with ethnicity and land quite clear. *Philosophies of Judaism,* New York, 1964, pp. 390ff.

17. Guttmann (*supra,* n. 16), pp. 354ff., gives an architectonic view of the place of God in the Cohenian philosophic system. Friedlander connects Baeck and Cohen in this regard (*supra,* n. 3), p. 79, though he is careful to note the differences between the two, pp. 148–54.

18. Guttmann is too faithful a disciple to raise the embarrassing issue of Cohen's relationship to Zionism and Germany, though he does not hesitate to show how Rosenzweig's existentialism led him astray with regard to peoplehood. If one reads Guttmann's warm discussion of the Cohenian ethics and its emphasis on universality recognizing that the people of Israel is subordinated to these concepts, he will get the constructive reason for Cohen's opposition to Zionist ethnicity and nationalism (*supra,* n. 16), pp. 360–64. A similar effort to protect Cohen against himself is made by Samuel H. Bergman, *Faith and Reason,* Washington, D.C., 1961, pp. 52–54. For a more balanced view see Ephraim Fischoff, "Hermann Cohen," *Great Jewish Thinkers,* Washington, D.C., 1963, pp. 126–29.

19. Emil Fackenheim has sought to find the philosophic basis for this in his Leo Baeck Memorial Lecture *Hermann Cohen—After Fifty Years,* Leo Baeck Institute, New York, 1969.

20. Friedlander seems to understand that God's relation is primarily with man in general and with Israel only in a derivative way, but in his desire to stick close to Baeck's own wording he gives an emphasis to the people of Israel in the primary relationship which may be misleading. Because Baeck identified Israel with humanity and himself with Israel, he could speak this way without realizing the problems this might cause in obscuring his intellectual design. Friedlander (*supra,* n. 3), pp. 64ff. My own interpretation is given in *A New Jewish Theology in the Making,* Philadelphia, 1968, pp. 89ff. On the other hand, Arthur Cohen has almost no appreciation whatsoever for the systematic integrity and intellectual thoroughness of Baeck's theology. He never manages to overcome the distaste which comes through in the opening pages of his chapter on Baeck. *The Natural and the Supernatural Jew,* New York, 1962, pp. 102ff.

21. *The Essence of Judaism,* pp. 255, 263, 266.

22. Ibid., pp. 268ff.

23. The opening pages of *This People Israel* immediately link the Jewish people to the one, universal God as a matter of their inner experience, consciousness and intuition. Only the emphasis, not the ranking of beliefs, has changed since the earlier great book. The formal relationship of the doctrines remains the same, New York, 1964, pp. 5–16, in particular. Cf. Friedlander (*supra,* n. 3), pp. 220ff.

24. "If it (Israel) had no future, humanity had none" (p. 11). So too the last pages of the book. *This People Israel,* pp. 401-403.

25. To understand the word "Jew" as "an ontal symbol" means that it is a term for having being, in this connection, human being. Jew, then, equals man. So what was understood generally as a particular form of being (i.e., one of the folk covenanted to God) has now been universalized and emptied of specific reference. This would seem to be the only consistent attitude toward particularistic forms of being for one who follows the philosophic existentialist emphasis on human freedom, and one finds the idea well developed in Sartre. "God and Jewish Theology," *Contemporary Reform Jewish Thought,* Chicago, 1968, p. 73. The same is done with the Sabbath in "The Sabbath As a State of Being," *CCAR Journal,* January, 1967, pp. 29ff., where the very title indicates the departicularization which the article then carries through. A more recent example is the question of Jewish survival which is treated as only another instance of survival in history in general and without any particular reference to the nature of Israel or its special place in history. "A Theology of Jewish Survival," *CCAR Journal,* October, 1968, pp. 45ff.

26. *Judaism As a Civilization,* New York, 1957, p. xii, and the comparison of himself with Pasteur in the new Foreword, p. x.

27. Ibid., pp. 385ff. and 431ff. Despite an intensive study of Kaplan's writing in succeeding years (from the first edition, 1934), I have not seen any substantial change in his attitude to the ordering of these ideas.

28. Some typical expressions will be found ibid., pp. 83, 184, 327, 335; *Judaism in Transition,* New York, 1941, p. 298; *The Future of the American Jew,* pp. 95–96, 108; *Questions Jews Ask,* New York, 1956, p. 434.

29. Beginning already in *Judaism as a Civilization,* pp, 109ff., where he generously accepts the Reform Jewish teaching about universalism, particularly in ethics, as basic to a modern Judaism, and pp. 305ff., where the necessity of religion and belief in one God as a matter of universal human nature is insisted upon. These always form the context of his discussion of Israel as the chosen people and are the intellectual reasons for his inevitably polemical attitude toward it; pp. 42ff. Again, the early statement of order remains stable over the years.

30. See "The Early Addresses (1909–1981)," *On Judaism,* New York, 1967, for an idea of what this meant to Buber in a relatively racialistic stage of his thinking. His nationalism continued to be important to him even after the shift of his general position produced by his understanding of the I-thou relationship. This is evidenced by the many later addresses to Zionist groups, as a perusal of the sources of the several collections of his papers will show. (See *infra,* n. 31.) One of the problems with the treatment Buber has received at the hands of his popularizers has been their failure to give his Zionism an adequate place in their thought.

31. Most simply accessible in the collection of papers, called *Israel and the World,* New York, 1948; particularly parts IV and V. The list of sources of the various papers is itself of great interest.

32. Ibid., part II, "Biblical Life," gives the general positive attitude. For Buber against the Bible, see *Eclipse of God,* New York, 1952, pp. 149–56, and *The Philosophy of Martin Buber,* eds. Schlipp and Friedman, La Salle, Illinois, 1967, pp. 31–33. On law, see the following note.

33. The basis here is the theory of revelation clearly stated in the Buberian understanding in *I and Thou,* pp. 109ff. The classic explication of its problems as too radically individualistic is given in the exchange between Buber and Rosenzweig, beginning with the latter's essay "The Builders" and the ensuing correspondence. *On Jewish Learning,* New York, 1955. Yet Buber believed God spoke to nations. He not only said this in his Zionist-racialist period, *On Judaism,* p. 155, but continually to the end of his life, pp. 216ff.

34. On the individual and his community, the central discussions, which are quite abstract, are in *Between Man and Man,* New York, 1948, especially pp. 30ff. and 58ff. The same theme repeats itself, only from a positive point of view, in *Moses,* Oxford, 1947.

35. Ibid., pp. 130ff.

36. For Buber's most positive statement on law, one must turn to his defense of Moses against Korah. Yet even in accepting law he states the situation in which revolution is justified. Ibid., p. 188. The results and his present judgment emerge in the debate with Rosenzweig, referred to in note 33.

37. In this connection see Charles Liebman, "Left and Right in American Orthodoxy," *Judaism,* 15, 1966, pp. 102ff., and Emanuel Rackman, "A Challenge to Orthodoxy," *Judaism,* 18, 1969, pp. 143ff.

38. *A New Jewish Theology in the Making,* pp. 197ff.

39. *How Can a Jew Speak of Faith Today?* Philadelphia, 1969, pp. 143ff.

40. This matter is given thoroughgoing and convincing treatment by Emil Fackenheim, *Quest for Past and Future,* Bloomington, Ind., 1968, pp. 204ff. The background for that discussion will be

found in Fackenheim's direct confrontation with Buber on the nature of revelation as dialogue in *The Philosophy of Martin Buber.* Fackenheim's essay begins on p. 273 and Buber's responses to him are on pp. 691f., 707ff., and 716.

41. I tried to give this matter systematic expression in an article, "Toward a Theology of Reform Jewish Practice," *CCAR Journal,* April 1960, pp. 27ff., but I now find that statement premature, in large part because it denied the holistic question and dealt only with the issue of criteria for Torah-as-practice.

42. *A Layman's Introduction to Religious Existentialism,* pp. 86–87, but see the entire context to understand the nature of the struggle against idealism and then against Christianity. The difficulties in following Rosenzweig's path as contrasted to appreciating his point of arrival are nowhere made more clear than in his famous correspondence over Christianity with his would-be converter, Eugen Rosenstock-Huessy. The letters, despite interpretive essays by Harold Stahmer, Alexander Altmann, and Dorothy Emmet, and an epilogue to the correspondence recently penned by Rosenstock-Huessy himself, are essentially impenetrable. Very little substantive exchange, only an increasing over-againstness of the letter writers, both using a highly idiosyncratic style, comes through to me. The issue is finally joined in letter 11 on p. 109 of Eugen Rosenstock-Huessy ed., *Judaism despite Christianity,* University, Alabama, 1969. I was also unable to comprehend Rosenstock-Huessy's purposes in including a 1945 article on "Hitler and Israel, or, On Prayer" as the closing and apparently climactic word of the book.

11 / The Postsecular Situation of Jewish Theology

Simply to report the situation I discern in contemporary Jewish theology often leads to grave problems in communication; for in considerable measure it is taking a direction substantially opposed to that of contemporary temporary Protestant thought and at even further variance from most Roman Catholic thought. Hence I believe it to be almost as important to set the context within which Jewish theology is operating today as to depict its major concerns. I hope that will account for what I feel as a grievous omission from this article,[1] namely, a consideration of what Jewish thinkers are learning from their Christian colleagues. I think there is still a good deal of which we are the beneficiaries, but I cannot say that the dialogue with Christian theology is, at the moment, either central to, or deeply influential in, Jewish thinking. Within the limits of this article, then, I must confine myself to what is transpiring within our community. Yet I do so with the clear hope that our apparently insular experience will be of direct relevance to the current revolution in Roman Catholicism. Indeed, I have permitted myself this restricted focus because it is my conviction that the experience of Judaism in the modern world has much to teach Roman Catholics in their present state of change and anxiety.

Jewish theology does not begin with a consideration of dogma, for Judaism has none—not even that one. Every time a scholar has taken the field to claim that Judaism has or does not have dogmas, he has drawn the heavy fire of equally learned and admired teachers. It is, then, quite difficult to know where Jewish theology does start, and, in our present age of methodological skepticism, taking the first step has become the most difficult of all our acts of faith. Yet I venture to suggest, with all the ages of Jewish history stretched out before us by several generations of modern historians, that Jewish theology can most easily be understood when approached through its social context. That is, from biblical times on, Jewish faith and reflection upon Jewish faith are intimately connected with the Jewish people. And because they are a people like all other peoples, though covenanted to God, it is in their social and historic experiences primarily that they have come to know who they are and whither they are destined. Thus the Bible is not so much a book of theology or spiritual exercises as it is an account of the history of the world, of the Hebrew people, of the prophets who arose to criticize their behavior in history, and of various other books reflective of man's place in that process. Moreover, it is quite clear that the sort of abstract, rigorous thinking about the content of faith which we normally call theology is neither native nor central to the Jewish religious experience. Aside from Philo, who was unknown to traditional Judaism, theology—or philosophy, as we often prefer to call the medieval writings—comes into Judaism only in the last thousand years. With the passing of the great Moslem Jewish centers it fades out of Jewish intellectual life for several centuries, only to re-emerge in the modern world. Apparently, then, it is less an inner need of Judaism than a Jewish response to a given social situation, namely, being immersed in a culture in which Greek-style rationality is highly esteemed. Thus Philo is a reaction to the Alexandrian Hellenistic culture, just as Maimonides and his medieval colleagues are a result of the hybridization with Islamic society in the period of its philosophical creativity. And Jewish theology today is awakened and shaped by the emergence of the Jew into the modern Western world.

One can hardly overestimate the importance of understanding the process we call the emancipation, if one is to understand modern Judaism or the modern Jew. The Jew was emancipated from a situation of physical, social, and economic segregation. From roughly 315 until the time of the first Crusade, the Jews were degraded but lived in relative personal safety. With the Crusades, riot, forced conversions, expulsions, and other forms of terror were added to Jewish existence. About 1500, what had for long been Jewish sections in a town were often walled in and provided with a gate behind which the Jews were locked each sundown—the infamous ghetto. That originally Italian invention became the symbol for the whole pattern of living imposed on the Jews until the time of the French Revolution. With the proponents of liberty, equality, and fraternity in power, freedom was extended even to the Jews—though it took a debate of nearly three years to agree to it. Then slowly, and by fits and starts, with much variation in given areas, the Jew began to come into Western society as an equal.

As the transition took place, the cultural shock was enormous. The Jew was now to wear the society's clothes, speak its language, follow its manners, accept its sense of good taste, read its literature, hear its music, go to its universities, participate in its economic endeavors, and be a citizen in its social undertakings. A tradition of fifteen centuries of segregation, reinforced by a virulent, irrational, and often deeply unconscious hatred, was now, in theory, radically altered. And the Jew, having been given these rights, was expected to take full advantage of them, adapt himself to his new social context, and be a credit to those liberals who had fought so hard for him and his rights.

Wherever the emancipation was at all honest, the Jews responded with eagerness and will. They rushed from the ghetto into the modern world. But the authoritative leaders of the Jewish religion were not equipped personally or institutionally for such radical change. The heartland of Jewish existence was, in the nineteenth century, Eastern and Central Europe, and there simply was no emancipation there. The rabbis in an unaltered social situation could not see any need for great change or even flexibility. Worse, the last few ghetto centuries had been so oppressive that the Jews had been robbed of their energy and sapped of their spirit. It had taken about all they had to survive with dignity. Even in the West they could not cope with the rapidity of the change and the newness of the arrangements. Of course, one should also keep in mind that we are not speaking of a hierarchical, structured, institutionalized pattern of authority but an essentially atomized, localized, and informal one. Almost everyone was afraid or unwilling to institute change. The authorities stood pat in what they said Judaism demanded of Jews even in the new social situation. As a result, the Jewish community overwhelmingly, as it moved into the modern world, deserted traditional Jewish law and its authoritative interpreters.

Hindsight, focused through the lenses of the sociology of change, does not see the many Jewish conversions to Christianity or the wholesale assimilation of Jews to the Western cultural style as surprising. Considering what the majority was now offering this tiny group, what strikes me as remarkable is that so many of them insisted on remaining Jews. They somehow wanted the best of both worlds, the modern and the Jewish, and that is the continuing problem of all Jewish thought. How is it possible to reconcile the freedom which is so central to the contemporaneous ethos with a religious tradition that one does not create but inherits? How is it possible to view religion as a matter of the most inner personal commitment and determination, and yet have it come to one heavy with historical freight and institutional rigidity? For the Jew those questions were doubly poignant, for without the modern commitment to freedom, he would still be in the ghetto. And if he elected to continue in his Judaism, he had identified himself with a religion that might be tolerated in the modern world but that was, at the same time, a peculiar and alienating religion to hold.

The result of this position, more intuited than thought through for some decades, was the birth of nontraditional forms of Judaism. First Reform Judaism, and then Conservative Judaism, came into being with varying mixes of freedom and tradition. In reaction to them, a self-conscious Orthodoxy emerged and the basic institutional manifestations of present-day Judaism were established. That is to describe the situation in its religious aspects only. What is equally important for our twentieth century and, particularly, our American situation is the concomitant secularization which Jewry underwent.

THE PROCESS OF SECULARIZATION

Harvey Cox has identified the two major spurs to secularity as the city and the university. The process of emancipation is intimately involved with both of these. For the Jew, prohibited from farming in the Middle Ages, the town and then later the city became his normal habitat in Western Europe. And it was the towns, growing in size and in commerce in the seventeenth and eighteenth centuries, that made it possible for the Jews of Eastern Europe slowly to make their way back into the Western countries from which they had been expelled. So as the towns grew to cities, their Jewish population grew too. And as the cities became increasingly the place where pluralism developed into the modern secular style, the Jews, as they were freed, were immediately involved in it.

To the emancipated Jew the university quickly became the surrogate for the yeshivah, the advanced academy of Jewish study. All the old Jewish drive and passion for learning was now channeled into modern disciplines, and the result was a burst of productive scholars and professional men that was as remarkable then as it is taken for granted now. But being largely urban dwellers, this increasing proportion of Jewish university graduates led to the thoroughgoing secularization of the modern Jewish community.

One special Jewish motivation needs to be taken into account. Secularity has been particularly congenial to the modern Jewish spirit because it is directly associated with Jews having rights. When states are Christian, as they were in the Middle Ages, the non-Christian has no legitimate place in them. The Jews had to be outsiders in the feudal ages because they could not swear the feudal oaths, based as they were on Christian beliefs. Only as states became secular, only as society made religion a private matter and opened up large nonreligious, that is, secular areas of existence, could the Jew have a fully authorized place in things. For the Jew secularity has meant belonging, equality, opportunity. No wonder he has embraced it wholeheartedly.

Of course, it needs to be added at once that the secular style is not nearly so strange to the Jewish tradition as it seems to be to some kinds of Christianity. Since the Jews are a people and not a church, their sort of religiosity has always included elements that from a Christian perspective might appear to be secular rather than religious. But since the full dimensions of Jewish folk existence were not finally separable from the covenant with God, then the rather sharp distinction which Christians tend to draw between the religious and the secular are simply not applicable within the Jewish frame of reference. And that is still true today.

It may be of some help to show, first, how that affected the style of modern Jewish religiosity. In two separate but not unrelated areas, it is continually involved with what seem like worldly things. The first of these has to do with the status of Jews. Unless the Jews have rights and are allowed to exercise them fully, the entire enterprise of modern Judaism is a fraud. Hence, in its most central religious manifestations, modern Judaism necessarily is involved in fighting anti-Semitism and working to secure the rights of Jews and thus by extension of all other minority groups, in the United States. Those are social and political matters, it would seem, but for a Jew they are obviously matters of the most primary religious concern. By the same token, the threat to Jews in other parts of the world is equally a danger to Jews here, so the protection of world Jewry, with all the political implications involved, is a major religious obligation. Thus the Jews of the United States, as Jews elsewhere in the world, become deeply involved in what was Zionism and today are deeply tied to the State of Israel. This strange sort of spiritual-social mixture, what Martin Buber so perceptively called the theopolitical thrust of biblical religion, may seem odd to Christians who think of religion in rather strictly churchy forms. It is, for Jews, the most authentic way of expressing their peculiar sort of faith.

The other area in which modern Judaism is shaped by the secular style is in its role as mediator of the surrounding culture. It is not just that Judaism takes on some of the forms of the surrounding society, but rather that in the creation of a new, hybrid style of Jewishness the Jew is brought into close contact and personal familiarity with it. Consider the most immediate changes in the synagogue. The liturgy is translated into the vernacular. The organ and the mixed choir are introduced. The rabbi is not only expected to lecture in the vernacular and cite copiously from modern literature, his training soon requires that he be a university graduate, preferably with Phi Beta Kappa key and ultimately a doctorate. That makes the religion seem modern and supposedly more acceptable. It is equally to be seen as a means of taking a community from its ghetto and getting it to accept the standards of the general culture.

What is less easy to appreciate for those who have not grown up in the Jewish community is the effect of secularization in creating that perplexing yet widely observable creature, the irreligious Jew. Indeed, so many Jews so regularly and so emphatically tell you how little they believe that one sometimes wonders if there are any believing Jews left! Part of that strange phenomenon comes from the fact that Jews, thinking of their pious grandfathers and conscious of their own radically different practice, cannot see themselves as "religious." But a greater part of it derives, I have become convinced, because they do not recognize how large a measure of belief remains in what was, long before Rudolf Bultmann ever coined the term, an emerging demythologization of Judaism.

The urban-dwelling, university-trained, secular-minded Jew can easily think of a dozen good reasons why traditional Jewish belief is no longer tenable in the modern world. He reduces God to nature, law to ethics, sin to error, repentance to psychotherapy or education, Torah to culture, and salvation through commandments to a new society through good politics. He does not give up Judaism for hedonism, self-seeking, or the pursuit of power. In distinctive statistical disproportion, he devotes himself to what, in effect, he considers the best of Judaism, the myths having been cast aside. He is now concerned with high intellectuality, liberal politics, and the pursuit of culture. So many Jews would not be so frequently involved in such activities in all the decades since the emancipation began to take effect, were it not for the fact that in this pattern they see the modernized continuation of traditional Jewish faith. If one wants to see what a thoroughgoing demythologization and politicization of Christianity would lead to, if one would like to weigh all its ultimate virtues and failings, I suggest one take a look at the contemporary American Jewish intellectual. He is, in the flesh, everything Harvey Cox was looking for in the last chapters of *The Secular City*. I shall have more to say about him below.

The most important form this demythologized, secularized Jewishness has taken is Zionism. Here the thrust toward modernity utilized the nineteenth-century form of nationalism and projected it through the twentieth-century historical situation to establish the State of Israel. That state is surely not what traditional Judaism had in mind when it set prayers for the return to Zion, yet in all its modernity it cannot be understood, nor can the concern for it of Jews around the world be understood, unless one can see it as a continuation, in modern transformation, of the Jewish religion. The Zionism that brought the State of Israel into being is largely the creation of Eastern European Jews. If they were to opt for modernity in their special social and political situation, it could not be via the liberalization of the Jewish religion. There was no Reform or Conservatism available to them; for as the Christianity around them was essentially monolithic, so the government and the cultural mood would not tolerate religious innovation. Their only hope to carry through emancipation was to think of themselves in ethnic terms. Like the Ukrainians, the Georgians, the Finns, they wanted the right to develop their language, their culture, and their customs. If some of their number wanted to be religious—and that meant to continue the segregated, inner-directed style of existence—then that was their privilege as part of the folk. But the group itself was now entitled to exercise cultural self-determination, free of clerical control and open to any truth that the modern world was ready to teach it. It was only one step to full-scale political claims, that the people should go back to its ancient homeland and there re-establish itself as a sovereign nation. And with the destruction of European Jewry by Hitler, the desperation of the Jewish survivors and the guilt of the European nations somehow made that possible.

The State of Israel claims to be thoroughly secular, and the overwhelming majority of its inhabitants are nonbelievers by traditional standards. Yet the ethos of the State is a far cry from simple nationalism. The Israelis expect of themselves and their government a high standard of ethics and a thoroughgoing commitment to enhancing their social welfare. And I would judge that world Jewry takes the greatest pride, not in any material Israeli accomplishment, certainly not in any military victory, but in the high humaneness the Israelis have exhibited in the midst of the most excruciating power realities. As the Bible again and again makes perfectly clear, it is one thing to write or preach about ethics and another thing to have to confront the terrifying pressures of history, knowing one stands under the judgment of the Almighty.

Again, if one wishes to see what might happen to Christianity were it radically demythologized and radically committed to social and political existence, then one might well turn to the State of Israel. And seeing it now as a special case of emancipation and transformation of Judaism, I think one will be able to appreciate why what appears to be so secular by Christian standards, is, by Jewish standards, still firmly part of the Jewish religious tradition.

THE INFLUENCE OF MODERN THOUGHT

In all this process of modernization, philosophy has played a role quite different from what it has in traditional Roman Catholic thought. There, philosophy has been (at least till the recent past) the handmaid of theology. It has been studied and cultivated as a means of establishing the heritage of the Church. The magisterium has gone so far as to commend the philosophy of Thomas Aquinas, dynamically viewed, as being of perennial significance. Thus philosophy, so to speak, has been a major instrument of maintaining the establishment. A major problem in contemporary Catholic thought, as I read it, is how to find a philosophy which will allow for movement away from the established positions of the Church and open up the rich areas of personal freedom and existential depth which are so important to modern religiosity.

In modern Judaism, philosophy has been the means of directing change and validating flexibility. It could serve that role because, as we have noted, it was not part of the core of Jewish religiosity, nor did the tradition rely on it to any great extent. Hence, when the Jews came into the modern world and discovered philosophies which they felt were reasonably congenial to Judaism while being acceptably modern, they utilized such thought systems to explain why an old tradition could now take a new form without contradicting itself. The earliest major accomplishment of this sort was the German idealist interpretation of Judaism created by Hermann Cohen before World War I. Here the neo-Kantian emphasis on ethics, and the need for an idea of God in the system to connect ethics to nature, became the essence of Judaism. According to Cohen, what is permanent in Judaism, then, is ethical monotheism. What changes are the customs and practices in which this fundamental truth is expressed, taught, and transmitted from generation to generation. In

Hermann Cohen, and in his more religiously oriented disciple Leo Baeck, modern Judaism was given a firmly universal ethical cast which distinguishes it to this day.

In the United States, idealistic philosophy was uprooted by various forms of pragmatism and naturalism in the twenties and thirties. These found their Jewish exponent in the person of Mordecai Kaplan. Using the newly emerging science of sociology as his foundation, Kaplan created a philosophy of Judaism which based everything on the Jewish people. This allowed him to remedy a serious defect in the theories of the idealistic interpreters, who could never quite explain why, when all truth was universal, one needed to be particularly Jewish, with all its minority handicaps. For Kaplan there now seemed a simple scientific answer to this question. Sociology showed how the group into which one was born shaped one and gave one values by which to live. A Jew, being born into the Jewish people, should normally utilize its modes of expression. Not to do so was already to be sick. Yet, at the same time, the Jews had been guilty of not recognizing that they were a people in the full sense of the word. They had been talking as if they were a church. What they needed to do was to rebuild a full-scale culture, or civilization, as Kaplan preferred to call it. This would include all the elements that a folk normally had in its way of life, the most significant of which would be its religion. Hence one could well find one's place in this sort of Judaism without making religious belief vital, though if it were completely left out, something would be lacking. This sort of ethnic humanism has great appeal to those Jews who still think that Judaism's major problem is adjusting to the truths revealed by science.

At the present moment, however, it would seem that science has become more of a problem than religion. That has led to the current popularity of various forms of Jewish existentialism which derive from Martin Buber and Franz Rosenzweig. The former, particularly, has become something of a cliché among Jewish college youth as among students generally, and it is difficult in conversations with them to long avoid such terms as "I-Thou," "relationship," or "real person." As contrasted with the American shift from German idealism to science-modeled philosophies, the existentialists in Germany came into being through their insistence on replacing mind as the medium and measure of all things, with the whole self, including rationality, but integrating it in the person entire. That brought about a substantial transformation of religious talk. Now ideas, and most specifically ideas of God, could no longer be the major concern of theologians. The problem was not conceiving

Him, an obviously impossible task, but learning to relate to Him and only then reflecting on what such relationship meant. That sounds more traditionally religious, even pious, than what previous modern philosophies of religion had made possible. The same sort of revivification was practiced with regard to most other religious terms, and that led on to seeing new virtue in older forms of practice. The continuing appeal of Jewish existentialism is its central emphasis on the person in a time of social depersonalization and its mode of clarifying how belief is primarily a noncerebral matter without at the same time being superstition. In a situation newly awakened to the possibilities of faith, such teaching will continue to have much to say.

In a very real way, all that is history. To be sure, it is still the content of what most thinking Jews talk about and it would surely account for the overwhelming bulk of most courses on Jewish thought being given in congregations or universities. But if we are concerned to know something of what is going on at the moment and what then is likely to be emerging in the coming decade, then we must move on beyond these great, accomplished systems to the area of experiment and creativity. There is great difficulty in doing so. I do not know how one could claim to give a reasonably objective account of what is going on. The judgment as to which efforts are significant and which are not is highly subjective. The paucity of the people involved makes such judgment more, not less, difficult, for it is difficult to know who, not now in the public eye, might soon emerge as a major figure. And being myself one of the dozen or so professionally concerned theologians and partisan to a position I am seeking to create, my judgment may be skewed. Nonetheless, while I may be wrong in what I am about to say, I think it fair to add that I am reasonably well informed about what is going on and do not refuse to listen to what may be happening that goes in directions uncongenial to me.

What seems to be central to the serious Jewishness of an increasing minority in our community is their recognition that they cannot remain as dependent upon the surrounding culture as they once were. The point is not that the culture has nothing to offer them or that they do not want to be acquainted with it. Remember, we are speaking precisely about Jews who emerged from the ghetto, who were delirious about the new autonomy, and who secularized themselves thoroughly. This is no obscurantist insistence on remaining in the past as society moves ahead. Rather, having been through all that the society has to offer, having sampled all its goods, indeed having contributed in overwhelming measure to the creation of a better civilization, has now brought some Jews to believe that traditional Judaism may have something to teach in its own right, that rather than always genuflecting to what modern man and modern science and modern culture say, one of the most useful things Judaism could do would be to stand up to them, correct their excesses, and shape their values.

The Jews of the United States, about whom we are speaking, have special historic reason for that. One must always remember, in speaking about this community, that it has undergone the emancipation process quite recently. The vast bulk of American Jews derive from Eastern and Central European immigrants who came to this country from 1880 to 1925. In their countries there had been no meaningful emancipation. Some of them had known the modernity of the large cities and some (fewer) had been to the gymnasium or university. Mostly, however, their style was that of a long segregated Jewry, the shtetl style, that of the small Jewish village. It was very often only their children who, having arrived in the United States, truly made their way toward a free form of living. Thus the twenties and the thirties may well be characterized as the decades in which Jewish acculturation substantially took place. The forties brought war, heightened social dislocation, and a subsequent upward movement of a great deal of the American population. In the fifties and sixties the emancipation of the Jews in the United States was pretty well realized and the results were felt in every branch of American culture.

THE POSTSECULAR STANCE

The major hopes of the past twenty-five years are now being brought into question. For the overwhelming segment of American Jewry, it was hope in secularity. They were willing to give up much of their Jewishness to benefit from the many good things that the American style had to offer. Now they have come to realize that, for all its benefits, there are many things wrong with the American society. What is so painful is the consciousness that we are not dealing with a specific problem or group of them. There have always been problems and it was not blindness to them that made the secular way of life so attractive. Rather it is obvious that many of the problems are inherent in the system itself, that the structure of our society, for all its greatness, is also productive of evil. And the root difficulty is that there is little or nothing in the secular approach to things today which is productive and empowering of human value. The civilization is in crisis because all its major instrumentalities are value-free or even antihuman. No amount of going to college or reading books or attending the theater or buying paintings will give us the kind of human beings we need. The dream that the cultured man would automatically be an ethical man, in some biblical sense of that term, has collapsed.

What is slowly giving way with it is the old religious accommodation to the culture. We really believed that we could win autonomous, modern man to religious faith and practice by changing the old, imposed forms of our faith and making them essentially voluntary and self-commending. There was a period of time when the innovations were met with great enthusiasm and it seemed as if a new mood had been created in the ancient faith. But our experience in the long run has been deadly. Orthodoxy, Conservatism, and Reform alike show pervasive apathy as the standard tone. Nonobservance of whatever standards are set is common, and an air of irrelevance is generally felt. But now it is difficult to believe that further modernization will solve anything. Having gone from monophonic to polyphonic music, from the cantor unaccompanied to adding mixed choirs and organs, from Slavic modes in minor keys to Western ones in major keys and thence on to atonal compositions, how can we now hope that we will solve something by introducing guitars, classical or electric? They obviously have their place in youth or experimental liturgies, but as solutions to the problem of a general lack of religiosity, we cannot remain so hopeful. Our experience is that, although liturgical and hierarchical and clerical tinkering may be useful, indeed necessary, to make it possible for modern men to take their religion seriously, they themselves do not resolve our problems. Having tried them all, the time comes when one must turn back to the questions of faith and belief. And when the culture can no longer be the surrogate for the old tradition, the time has come to bring all one's tattered social attainments with one and take another look at the commitments of one's fathers. That is the postsecular situation of what I see as the most significant minority working at Jewish theology today.

One of the things that gained Abraham Heschel justified renown was his being among the first to recognize this problem. Having made his way from the highly traditional, Hasidic milieu in which he was brought up, through the German intellectual world in which he gained his Ph.D. without losing his deep faith, Heschel made the further transition from Europe to the United States in the late thirties and not long thereafter emerged as a major interpreter of Judaism to a postwar America. His medium has attracted as much attention as his message. He writes with extraordinary grace, a gift most admirable in a man who wants to open us up to the inner reality of faith. Heschel is willing to reason with us modern men and it is remarkable how well and how deeply he knows our problems with belief. But he does not share them. Rather his own faith, for all his modern understanding and his vast modern learning, remains substantially that of traditional Judaism. So though he can illumine the assumptions of our skepticism and bring to the surface the unconscious presuppositions of our doubt, he never really responds to them. He can show us how for a believer these are not the real questions, and with his magic style he can momentarily open up to us his realm of certitude. Yet though he has touched many in the American Jewish community, he has persuaded very few. But if he cannot make a sophisticated traditionalism acceptable to American Jewry, it is difficult to believe that anyone else can.

That sets the dilemma for the contemporary Jewish theologian of this postsecular stripe. Cohen, Baeck, Kaplan, Buber, and Rozenzweig, all in their various ways allow the culture surrounding Judaism, mostly in the form of a general philosophy they accept or devise, to determine the content of Judaism in at least some critical areas. Entering the seventies, one must look back at them and say that they trusted modern education and modern intellect too much. Heschel, on the other hand, has accommodated it so little that, though we yearn for greater Jewish authenticity, we do not hear him speaking to us. We carry our secularization with us as we turn back to the tradition, but we know that without being firmly rooted in something like traditional Jewish faith our secularity will lead us and our society to human bankruptcy.

Since that is the core problem, as I see it, of contemporary Jewish thought, I am unable to dictate its solution. I can, however, point out three areas in which some directions begin to take shape.

The first of these has to do with belief in God, and it centers about the utter collapse of the death-of-God movement in the Jewish community. That was not primarily a philosophic question among us. There are occasional complaints against the philosophic adequacy of Jewish language about God, but nothing comparable to the sort of furor created among Protestants by van Buren or among Catholics by Dewart. Not having taken philosophy that seriously even in modern times, Jews were, on the whole, not terribly shocked that empiricist-oriented philosophers found it difficult to speak meaningfully about a nonempirical God. What did arouse the Jewish community, quite characteristically, was the question of God in history. The Holocaust under Hitler could somehow be ignored by Christian scholars talking about the reality of God, but for Jews it was the central question. Auschwitz and all the other death camps became an unanswerable protest against God's goodness or His very existence.

Those scars still remain. No amount of subsequent Jewish accomplishment can assuage them. But to say that God was dead, or neutral, or nothing, in a somewhat devouring sense, may have explained the matter cognitively, but it also destroyed the possibility of meaningful human existence. If there is no standard of value at the very heart of the universe, then Auschwitz is permitted. If anything, it is a reasonable indication of the reality in which man finds himself. By the same token, our utter revulsion at what took place is utterly unreasonable if the world is neutral or devouring and each man has as much right to do what he wants as any other. If it is our sense of protest which brings us to pronounce God dead, then we have contradicted ourselves. For having said the obsequies over Him, we have similarly deprived ourselves of any fundamental ground on which to oppose Him. That may be a paradox, but it will not be the first one in Jewish faith. We need God in order to be able to stand up against Him; without God, there is no reason to be righteously indignant about anything men do.

More, we know that if we now deserted God and the Jewish tradition He so centrally formed, we would be giving the worst possible reaction to the Hitler barbarity. Though Hitler could not succeed in putting an end to Jewry, we would now be doing that for him. The absurdity of that response seems reasonably clear to most Jews, though they rarely articulate it. They know they must go on being Jews and carry forward the Jewish tradition. Again paradoxically, that which should have been the most cogent reason for giving up Judaism now becomes a powerful commandment to continue it.

That tells us something about such commitment as remains among us Jews. The death-of-God movement and Hitler have, in effect, radicalized some Jews. They can no longer feel at ease in the old agnosticisms. Believing in human value as they do, concerned with Jewish continuity as they are, they must now ask, what is the ground for such tenacity? That is, it seems to me, the way that contemporary Jews are reaching for a God whom they may not understand but whom they find, partially to their own surprise, they still believe in.

The second focus of present theological concern is the people of Israel and, more specifically, the State of Israel. Modern religious thought has been quite personally centered and quite universally directed. At the moment, those traits have brought about a crisis in the validity of any religious institutions. Persons can be religious without them, and service ought to reach out to all mankind. Hence particular institutions seem anachronistic. In the same way, though for a much longer period, the peculiar social form of Judaism has been under modern attack. The problem is that the Jews are not a church but a folk, a people, an ethnic group. That may seem strange to Christian eyes, but it is clearly and quite unambiguously what our Bible proclaims the Jews to be. The defense of Jewish particularity, of the reasons for maintaining and continuing the Jewish group, especially when it is so tiny and disliked a minority, has been difficult in the face of modern individualism and universalism. But the Holocaust and the State of Israel have made clear that a good deal of the objection to Jewish particularity was quite spurious, often downright anti-Semitic, even when it emanated from those born Jewish.

One cannot understand the mood of the contemporary Jewish community if one does not realize how deeply it is committed to the fact that there will be no more Holocausts. The Jews under Hitler so trusted Western governments that they cooperated in what turned out to be their own destruction. And the Jews of the United States have now discovered that their government knew about the death camps but was not willing to do anything about them. Facing a hostile world, martyrdom has now been removed as a Jewish religious option. The fundamental Jewish duty is rather to survive. In the face of what the world has done to the Jews, in the face of what the world continues to be today, that needs no further justification. Just by being in history, the Jews are already carrying out a high mission. By refusing to disappear, they are already a unique testimony among the nations.

But all that holds doubly true of the Jews of the State of Israel. It is hard to think of religious imperatives more central to the contemporary religious consciousness than that the Jews of the State of Israel, the survivors of Hitler, the refugees whom no nation would admit, the refuse of a dozen backward and inhumane states, now brought to full humanity by their own efforts and against tremendous odds, have a right to live. And other Jews have a duty to see to it that they do. That seems like politics, and it is. Only, in the Jewish covenant with God, because the Jews are called to be a people and participate in the real history of the peoples of the earth, we are simultaneously dealing with a religious question. The two cannot be separated, the one from the other. So threats to exterminate the State of Israel and all its inhabitants are a major threat to adherents of the Jewish religion everywhere, and the refusal of the Israelis to become brutalized or militarized in the face of the stark power realities confronting them is one of the major glories of contemporary Jewry.

Third, the collapse of confidence in the culture has opened up the possibility that the old Jewish way of life may have more to commend it than the generations panting for Americanism ever realized. It is difficult to see in the culture surrounding us any institution which will produce the masses of consistently humane people that the Judaism which passed through the modern experience did and does produce, at least for some little time yet. But if those values are to be transmitted with sufficient power to resist the pernicious effects of the American culture, then perhaps they need not only the grounding of Jewish belief but the warmth and habituation of a rather traditional Jewish practice.

One sees this possibility most dramatically in the number of young Jews who consciously choose to be Orthodox. This is not something simply inherited or carried out because they do not know any other possibilities, but rather because, having seen whither the civilization is tending, they want to assert a full-scale Jewish authenticity. They voluntarily take upon themselves the full yoke of the commandments and carry them out with a will reinforced by knowledge concerning them. They are a small number as the millions of American Jews go. But they are such a repudiation of the vulgar antitraditionalism of much of American Jewry some years back that they are highly significant. One sees the same phenomenon among individuals and small handfuls of Jews in the Conservative and Reform movements as well. One is no longer surprised in community after community to run into the family or the few couples who want to know what it might mean to commit themselves to Jewish existence and how they might best express it. They are nothing like a decisive number or even recognizable enough to become a nucleus for change in the Jewish community. But they exist. They seem serious about their Jewish intentions. And their number seems to be increasing.

They are the social reality to which postsecular Jewish theology is addressing itself. With all the noise being made by liturgical swingers and institutional revolutionaries, by theological anarchists and professional mourners at the death of religion, it is good to know such people can arise. And for such as me, it is God's grace to be permitted to work at a theology adequate to their modern but authentic Jewishness.

NOTES

1. Originally presented as a paper in the Jewish-Christian lecture series cosponsored by the Pope Pius XII Religious Education Center, Detroit, Mich., and the Interreligous Affairs Department of the American Jewish Committee.

12 / Education Is Not I-Thou

1971

I

Five years ago, perhaps four, our problem was whether we could still be religious. William Hamilton assured us that the only religious experience moderns could have was of the absence of God, and Harvey Cox defined secular man as one utterly shut off from the sense of the numinous. Religious educators somehow managed to survive, in part because the enthusiasm of ecumenism gave us new life, in part because the death of God agitation died in the passage from theological fad to social reality.

But that was one sensation back. Today it is obvious one can be religious. The only problem is how. The utter accessibility of God's Spirit—at least to the young—makes institutions dispensable and education for religiosity a contradiction in terms.

(I do not think that is the whole truth of this moment. Those who have fled Western religion for Hinduism or Buddhism have often discovered there that discipline is a primary means to insight, a long and arduous training the normal way to enlightenment. Not every religious seeker today demands instant ecstasy. It will be interesting one day to see whether this encounter with Eastern forms of strict religious training has its effect on our relatively lax Western ways of instruction. But right now, I am convinced, the primary challenge to religious education is the demand for immediate rewards.)

The justifications for this mood are another inflated currency of our current intellectual recession: a pseudo-Freudian hope that less repression means more health; a Spockian commitment to demand-feeding and natural development; a Dewey-derived emphasis on child-centered curricula; a Summerhillian faith that out of the greatest freedom comes the greatest good nature; a Sartrean certainty that the self is its freedom and the one thing we must never surrender; all nourished by a society affluent enough to free education from its traditional role as the necessary instrument for making a living. Yet with all these reinforcements of contemporary infantilism, none is called upon more frequently or sanctimoniously than Martin Buber's teaching of the holiness of the I-Thou encounter. That most people who cite Buber have not read him, and even more misunderstand him, has little to do with his social effect. That Buber is "in" makes it all the more important to review his ideas. If there is any question of his continuing relevance, it will help to keep in mind that the essays I shall cite were written in 1926 and 1939 (as translated in *Between Man and Man*, Macmillan, New York, 1948).

Because Buber clarified the difference between being treated as a person and as an object—or, at the least, supplied us with the language by which we could now bring to self-consciousness what we had previously but dimly sensed—it is obvious that for him all "education worthy of the name is essentially education of character." However, our technologically oriented and exploitatively structured society makes the I-it relationship dominant, so it is critical that the educator exert a countervailing influence. He must not forget to teach the most important thing, that people are persons. Society generally wants the educator only to provide appropriately trained manpower. Particularly in economies of scarcity, education was content to be an exercise in compulsion. As long as men desperately needed what school or master offered, that was bearable. We honor today as the great revolutionaries of education men like Rousseau, Froebel and Pestalozzi who insisted that was not yet the education of men. So too, Buber says, "Compulsion in education means disunion, it means humiliation and rebelliousness" (p. 91). It can go further. "The situation of the old type of education is, however, easily misused by the individual's will to power, for this will is inflated by the authority of history. . . . The will to power becomes compulsive and passes into fury, when the authority [of the tradition or culture—EBB] begins to decay" (p. 93).

Thus, nearly fifty years ago, Buber saw the necessity of gaining freedom for the student. "Freedom—I love its flashing face: it flashes forth from the darkness and dies away, but it has made the heart invulnerable. I am devoted to it, I am always ready to join in the fight for it . . . I give my left hand to the rebel and my right to the heretic: forward!" But for Buber, contrary to Sartre, freedom is not an end in itself. He continues, "But I do not trust them. They know how to die, but that is not enough.

I love freedom, but I do not believe in it. . . . It is easy to understand that in a time when the deterioration of all traditional bonds has made their legitimacy questionable, the tendency to freedom is exalted, the springboard is treated as the goal and a function of the good as a substantial goal" (p. 91f.).

Freedom is the means to interpersonal relationship. That is its validation and significance. "At the opposite pole of compulsion there stands not freedom but communion" (p. 91).

The most important thing the educator can do is create genuine human encounter. In an anti-human time, he is a healer. "Trust, trust in the world, because this human being exists—that is the most inward achievement of relation in education. Because this human being exists, meaninglessness, however hard pressed you are by it, cannot be the real truth. Because this human being exists, in the darkness the light lies hidden, in fear salvation, and in the callousness of one's fellow-men the great Love" (p. 98).

To create such an experience under a system emphasizing compulsion is impossible. Rather, in proper education "there is only *one* access to the pupil: his *confidence.* For the adolescent who is frightened and disappointed by an unreliable world, confidence means the liberating insight that there is human truth, the truth of the human existence. When the pupil's confidence has been won, his resistance against being educated gives way to a singular happening: he accepts the educator as a person. He feels that he may trust this man, that this man is not making a business out of him, but is taking part in his life, accepting him before desiring to influence him. And so he learns to ask" (p. 106).

Therefore, "A conflict with a pupil is the supreme test for the educator. He must use his own insight wholeheartedly; he must not blunt the piercing impact of his knowledge, but he must at the same time have in readiness the healing ointment for the heart pierced by it. Not for a moment may he conduct a dialectical maneuver instead of the real battle for the truth. But if he is the victor he has to help the vanquished to endure defeat; and if he cannot conquer the self-willed soul that faces him (for victories over souls are not so easily won), then he has to find the word of love which alone can help to overcome so difficult a situation" (pp. 107–108).

Thus far, Buber would accompany most of the educational radicals. It is not a modest distance. Since most of our education today still damages persons where it does not outright ignore their existence, it needs to be radically revised. In that respect, Buber remains a revolutionary.

II

But for many people dialogue has become the content of education. Relationship takes the place of learning. Rapping is better than study. One even gets the impression that for some people, ignorance is to be cultivated to keep creativity uninhibited. They think Buber taught that the I-Thou relationship was all one ever needs. It somehow does not occur to them that a mindless thou is as little a person as someone who is all mind and method. Martin Buber, however, was not an orthodox Buberian. With regard to education, he made a major break with his own "system." Education, Buber taught, for all that it must center about the person, education is not I-Thou.

What concerned Buber here was the role of the world in the development of a person. "Self education . . . cannot take place through one's being concerned with oneself but only through one's being concerned, knowing what it means, with the world" (p. 101). Further, "The world engenders the person in the individual. The world . . . 'educ-cates' the human being: it draws out his powers and makes him grasp and penetrate its objections . . . [education is] *a selection by man of the effective world* . . . The relation to the world is lifted out of the purposelessly streaming education by all things, and is marked off as purpose. In this way, through the educator, the world for the first time becomes the subject of its effort" (p. 89).

The work of the educator is therefore directed to the world, to himself as its bearer and thence to the child whom he is addressing.

Education as a real person, then, begins not merely with a congenial other, but with the world, "that is, the whole environment, nature and society." So "the education of men means the selection of the effective world by a person and in him" (p. 101). Buber takes quite seriously that oft-repeated term "effective." It will not do simply to let things happen, to trust that in due course we will learn what we need to learn, or even that it makes no difference what we learn. On the matter of intellectual discipline, Buber is quite firm. "Every form of relation in which the spirit's service of life is realized has its special objectivity, its structure of proportions and limits which in no way resists the fervor of personal comprehension and penetration, though it does resist any confusion with the person's own spheres. If this structure and its resistance are not respected then a dilettantism will prevail which claims to be aristocratic, though in reality it is unsteady and feverish: to provide it with the most sacred names and attitudes will not help it past its inevitable consequence of disintegration" (p. 95).

The educator's first task, then, is curricular, to select that in the world which will bring his students forth. One of his major criteria in this and certainly his major means of influencing his students, is what this material does to him as a person. "The forces of the world which the child needs for the building up of his substance must be chosen by the educator from the world and drawn into himself . . . The educator gathers in the constructive forces of the world. He distinguishes, rejects, and confirms himself, in his self which is filled with the world. The constructive forces are eternally the same: they are the world bound up in community, turned to God. The educator educates himself to be their vehicle" (p. 101).

This, truly, is what has scandalized and radicalized modern students—they have seen the un-persons we have become by virtue of our learning. How stunted and misshapen as human beings appear those who have restricted themselves rigidly to being master technicians of an intellectual discipline. Worse, how many a man who teaches about society, politics, human behavior or personal values has ruled out of bounds the questions that a troubled world surrounds us with. By contrast, whenever we encounter a man whose discipline, no matter how technical, has somehow become the medium of his self-expression, we are deeply moved. Many a man has been led into zoology or statistics or some other apparently impersonal area by virtue of some such contact and the hope that the same would happen to him.

Buber can even go so far as speaking of the need for discipline in the classroom. He wants a discipline that is consistent with his major goal and thus is far ahead of what most practitioners today can envision much less achieve. The teacher "has to introduce discipline and order, he has to establish a law, and he can only strive and hope for the result that discipline and order will become more and more inward and autonomous, and that at last the law will be written on the heart of his pupils. But his real goal which, once he has well recognized it and well remembers it, will influence all his work, is the great character" (p. 113). In this connection too he makes one of his strongest statements on the importance of the "objective" study of ethics. "All this does not mean that the great character is beyond the acceptance of norms. No responsible person remains a stranger to norms. But the command inherent in a genuine norm never becomes a maxim and the fulfillment of it never a habit. Any command that a great character takes to himself in the course of his development does not act in him as part of his consciousness or as material for building up his exercises, but remains latent in a basic layer of his substance until it reveals itself to him in a concrete way. What it has to tell him is revealed whenever a situation arises which demands of him a solution of which till then he had perhaps no idea" (p. 114).

III

That would be enough, I submit, to disturb the average naive campaigner for the I-Thou in education. But Buber goes one extraordinary step further. He insists that in the educator's movement toward the student, he may not try to set up a fully reciprocal relationship with him. The moment the educator is as much thou to his charges as they are to him, education is over and friendship begins. There is obviously an important place in our lives for friendships but they are not the same as the education we should get from a teacher. Buber insists on a radically un-Buberian understanding of this peculiar situation called education. Though its goal is communion, it is not the usual I-Thou relationship.

At its inception, the teacher reaches out to the student to address him as a proper "thou." "In order to be and to remain truly present to the child he must have gathered the child's presence into his own store as one of the bearers of his communion with the world, one of the focuses of his responsibilities for the world" (p. 98). But the teacher goes no further. He does not present himself as a thou. The relationship remains a-symmetrical. That contradicts everything Buber ever said about the possibility of drawing forth the "thou." He taught that unless the encounter was fully matural and bilateral, it could not genuinely occur. The educational radicals are therefore more rigidly Buberian than was the master himself. It is possible, of course, that Buber could not bear the consequences of his teaching in this regard and that this lapse in his thinking is a failure of nerve on his part. Yet there is little in these essays or the subsequent four-plus decades of Buber's work to make one think he had reserved one reactionary enclave in his thinking. To the contrary, he had extensive experience in the classroom, was a teacher of teachers and an educational administrator. I suggest rather that Buber did indeed follow his methodological bent here. He did not argue from theory to life. Rather he tried to derive plausible intellectual structures for what life revealed when approached in openness. Self-contradiction was less important to him than trying to be honest to reality as he experienced it. That he was consciously willing to face the risk of being called incoherent in his teaching about dialogue only serves to emphasize how seriously he must have taken discipline and structure in education. He may have been wrong, but his opinion should be carefully considered by all those who think they are revising educational processes in his name.

IV

In all of this, you will have noted, I have not spoken specifically of religious education, but of education as a whole. Perhaps there might have been some shift in mood nuance in this discussion had Buber been asked specifically about religious education. I doubt it. He did not believe in religion as a special dimension of life. He believed God was present in all genuine encounters and thus, I would imagine, that all genuine education is, subliminally, religious education. Moreover, he did not limit his own religious development to the practice of the I-thou with persons or nature or forms. He was from his earliest years an intense student of world religious literature and the detailed nature of his studies of the Old and New Testaments in his later years sets a high standard for the contemporary personalist to attain.

This material in Buber is also useful, I believe, to help us with two difficult allied questions. If personal authenticity is everything, what shall we do about assuming a social role, and why should we have specific and particular religions?

For some reason, Buber never felt the need to examine or try to fit into his way of looking at things the concept of role. Perhaps that is because authenticity and role seem so contradictory. Indeed, the problems of being a genuine person when certain social expectations are forced upon one, has become a commonplace of existentialist cultural criticism. A role undoubtedly causes some constriction of self, for it requires, as with the teacher, sacrificing certain possible ways of acting to concentrate on some other ones deemed especially significant. Yet many good men, not at all wooden or unfeeling, have voluntarily sought to take on specific roles and have found themselves fulfilled in them as in nothing else. That is the phenomenon I believe Buber was forced to recognize with the teacher. The concentration provided by limiting the relationship makes possible a certain service to the other, education, and, at its best, a unique way of expressing the self that holding oneself open to all possibilities, as a normal person would, could not do. Some men are most themselves when they teach or sell or heal or play tennis. If that is all they are, they are nothing. To be the creature of one's role or discipline is not to be human. But Buber called on the teacher to transcend simple competence in his subject matter. He asked him to make his teaching an education of his self, to make his primary method the presentation of self-as-teacher and to make his goal a continual reaching out to the student as person. I think he was saying that role can be a means to humanhood, though that is not easy. But all of us have seen enough examples of its being true that we can hope to yet find a theory worthy of our experience here.

That in turn leads on to the question of particular religions and their specific disciplines. Those who have only read *I and Thou* are often surprised to discover how passionate a Jew, how fervent a Zionist, how utterly rooted in the Jewish people and its traditions Buber was. They assume that if I-Thou is the source of meaning there is no meaning elsewhere. And I do not see how anyone could meaningfully deny that if we all learned to treat one another as persons, if our society was organized to enable people to be human, if our world was not torn by senseless rivalries and prejudices, we would all be far more human. Buber's universalism remains of major importance for our time. Learning to live it is no less than a foremost duty.

But the concept of the person in role opens up the possibility that particularity too may have certain virtues. Of course man may stand before God as simple thou, as man-in-general, as one of the sons of Noah. How wonderful that would be! But men are wicked and history is the arena of their willfulness. What the simple I-Thou reveals must be carried through history, converting man's urge to evil, transforming the civilizations of men into the Kingdom of God. To stand before God as a Jew, to ground one's existence in his Covenant with his people, is to take on a particular and unique role in history. It is to give up the generality of being for what may be specifically accomplished for the self and for mankind through the limiting but liberating discipline called Torah. I do not see that the same could not be said of Christianity or Islam. For God's sake and our own, we are not content to be part of undifferentiated humanity. Through our particularity we will teach and realize the coming of universality. Through this specific role, we become whole.

If Buber is our teacher, then the tasks of religious education have just begun. And if he is our guide, it remains important that we work at them together.

13 / *Tzimtzum:* A Mystic Model for Contemporary Leadership

1974

If sex was another generation's "dirty little secret," as D. H. Lawrence termed it, surely ours is power. Now that we can admit we bear this primal lust, we see it operating everywhere, often more decisively than money, class, conditioning, genetics or the other usual determinants of behavior. The "purest" relationships reveal a political structure. In sex—and not only the rearing of children; in education—and not only in political dealing; in religion, art, literature and culture—and not only in business; most decisions are made on the basis of power. So our hope of accomplishment in most fields rests largely on how power is organized there or what can be done to change that arrangement.

Perhaps we should not have been shocked to discover the extent to which power determines most human affairs. It is more than a century now since Nietzsche proclaimed man's will to power as his dominant characteristic. Yet what has moved many in our generation to despair is neither the ubiquity nor the decisiveness of power but rather the recognition that almost everywhere we see power in action, we see it abused. Ethically we may be far more relativistic and contextual than our fathers were. But even if we have given up ethical absolutes and moral rules, many of us still cling to the notion that each of us is a person, not merely an animal, and that, à la Buber, we ought to be treated by others as persons and not as things. Hence we retain a strong ethical sense, though it often pits us against the forms which once claimed to make the dignity of persons explicit but today only operate to demean it, e.g., children should be seen and not heard. In an imperfect world, we could probably tolerate the fact that most relationships are inevitably hierarchical, particularly when more than a few people are involved for more than a few months. So we would not mind some people having power if they used it much of the time to enable us and others to be persons, that is, to be true to the self we know we ought to be. But they don't. Again and again, people—parents, lovers, teachers, politicians, chairmen, bosses, nurses, bureaucrats, scoutmasters, friends, therapists, children, hosts—force us to be something other than what we know we are. We despair because the abuse of power seems endemic.

Our constant experience is that we have not been consulted, or have not been listened to, or have not really had a voice in matters which deeply affect our lives. In short, we exist in the continuing consciousness of being the object of someone else's power rather than being a person in our own right though we are involved with people of greater status than ours.

Modern times brought democracy into human relationships. This change may properly be called a revolution, for, despite the varying forms in which it was effectuated, it gave those of little power some significant power. By contrast, the best previous generations had been able to do to humanize man's will to power was to appeal to his better nature, to beg the mighty to act with mercy. Thus, in the Bible's classic formulation, the test of the Covenant community's faithfulness to its gracious Partner-God is its treatment of the widow, the orphan and the stranger, the figures who epitomize social powerlessness. Much remains to be said for inculcating compassion in the possessors of power, that is, all of us. Yet the sad truth is that despite their occasional acts of charity, truly benevolent tyrants are rare. Rather than rely on a sovereign's good will we prefer to share his power. So today almost every social arrangement we know is under pressure to transform itself in the direction of more effective democracy.

I

The problems involved in moralizing the use of power are so great that any contribution to their mitigation should be welcome. While I believe that our best hope in this direction lies in giving ever greater power to the people, it also seems clear to me that we are nowhere near the stage where we can have leaderless associations. I therefore want to make a suggestion which might help ethicize the leader's role and which does so by going a step further on the road which turned the benevolent tyrant into the responsive chairman-executive. I believe we can find a fresh model for contemporary leadership in the mystic speculations about God of Isaac Luria (1534–1572) of Safed in the Holy Land. The reasons for utilizing Luria's extraordinary teaching will, I trust, become clear below. Here a word is needed about the methodological validity of transposing images of transcendent being into a purely human dimension. I hereby follow Ludwig Feuerbach's insight that statements about God are, in fact, projections of our sense of what it is to be a person. Hence to Feuerbach, concepts of God are essentially concepts of man, and theses about the way God relates to his creatures are implicitly theses about the way people ought to relate to each other. Feuerbach, of course, thought that theological assertions were assertions only about humankind. I think that aspect of Feuerbach's thinking is wrong, but surely it is not the only case in intellectual history of a useful idea being turned into an all-embracing absolute by its enraptured creator. Hence I propose to bracket the question of what God-talk says about God while still utilizing a Feuerbachian analysis to determine what Luria's visions of God say about us.

Luria's doctrine centers about two themes rarely treated so directly in traditional Jewish literature yet of intense concern to us today: God as creator and man as co-creator. Though creation grandly opens the book of Genesis, it and all the later texts are extraordinarily reticent, for ancient documents, of what was involved in God's creating. This anti-mythological bent became law, for the Mishnah (compiled about 200 of the common era) decrees that one may not publicly teach *Maaseh Bereshit,* the Work of Creation. So we can find only hints of this esoteric doctrine until, centuries later, mystic writings begin to record some of the possibilities, reaching a spectacular climax in Luria's rather detailed description of the process.

What appeals to our generation in the focus on God as creator is that his power is used to bring others into being. By contrast, the normal biblical/liturgical terms for him, Lord and King, speak of his status and power. This sense of God's power is modified by images which envision him as using it lovingly, e.g., God as Father, Husband or Lover. Yet remembering the realities of Near Eastern life and the continuing tradition of male dominance in Jewish life, even these symbols speak strongly of sovereignty and obedience.

Luria's teaching about God is appealing because it makes man, quite literally, his co-creator. His teaching involves so complete a shift to human activism that scholars can even speak of God becoming passive in the process.

The Lurianic doctrine is most conveniently discussed around three major terms: *tzimtzum, shevirah, tikkun.* Since these are three stages in the Work of Creation it will be best to explain the theory as a whole first and then draw its implications for leadership. (In the description which follows I work largely from the analyses of Gershom Scholem, the pioneering master of the modern study of Jewish mysticism.)

Creation is commonly thought of in spatial terms and is envisioned as a movement of externalization: what was God's will now is turned, by an application of his power, into a reality "outside" him. Think for a moment of Michelangelo's Sistine Chapel depiction of the creation of man. The mighty God stretches forth the full length of his arm to one fingertip and thus brings man into being. For us humans, creation is normally an act in extension of ourselves, of producing something "there" that was previously only within us.

Something of this picture is to be seen in the Biblical texts despite their apparent efforts to avoid the gross anthropomorphism of Near Eastern creation stories. Thus, in the first version, Genesis 1, God utters words in order to let the light be, and, if some modern translators are correct ("When God began to create the heaven and the earth—the earth being unformed and void . . ."), there already was material external to him to shape. The story in Genesis 2 simply begins with the dry ground and then, with explicit externality, has God mold man out of the dust of the earth before putting the breath of life into him. Creation as externalization is fully explicit in the neo-Platonic teaching (from the first century of the common era on) and thus in the Jewish mystic tradition which often borrowed from it (from the early Middle Ages on). Here creation is generally spoken of as emanation, the gentle but efficacious spilling over of the plenteous being of God. The usual image is of a fountain which, out of its fullness, pours water over its basin, thus creating new pools. God has such plenitude of reality that some of it emerges in a lesser form, which, in turn, makes possible an emergence in even lesser form, and so on, down a series of variously interpreted gradations, until our world exists. The neo-Platonists and mystics thought in this way to ease the problem of the infinite God creating finite beings. To us it seems reasonably clear that the very first movement from infinity to finitude—no matter how extensive the finite is thought to be—is as difficult to understand as the Universal God creating ants or pebbles. In any case, the doctrine of emanation, though it links all creatures to God by an unbroken progression of being, is a clear expression of our usual sense that creation is a species of externalization.

II

Luria felt otherwise. I cannot say to what extent his radical shift of creation images was due to the memories and continuing effects of the mass expulsion of the Jewish community of Spain in 1492. The fact is, Isaac Luria alone created a radically new mystic theory of creation. It will be simplest then to limit ourselves to his intellectual trail, and we may best prepare ourselves for his ideas by confronting a logical issue with regard to creation. If God is everywhere, how can there be any place outside him for him to create in? Michelangelo, for example, had to limit God to one majestic-sized human figure if he was to leave room to paint an Adam. But God is not a man and we are taught that he fills all space. If that way of speaking about God is unsatisfactory because spatiality is a poor metaphor for God, consider the question in ontological form; if God is fundamental being, fully realized, how can there be secondary being, that is, being only partly realized? Or, if God is all-in-all, how can the partial or the transitory, which must depend upon him for their being, ever come to exist?

One response might be to deny the reality of creation as much Hindu thought has done (and as, from the Divine perspective, the later Jewish mystic, Shneour Zalman of Lyady, 1747–1813, would do). Luria is too much under the influence of classic Jewish creation theory for that. Instead he boldly suggests that creation begins with an act of contraction, *tzimtzum.* God does not initiate the existence of other things by extending himself. There would be no place for them then to be, no area of non-being or partial being in which they might exist. Hence to create, he must first withdraw into himself. God must, so to speak, make himself less than he is so that other things could come into being. So great, says Luria, is God's will to create; so great is his love for creation.

It is not without interest that Luria has utterly reversed the older meaning of the term *tzimtzum.* In the rabbinic usage from which he almost certainly took the term, the verb form means "to concentrate" but in an externalizing way. The reference there is to God being especially present between the cherubim atop the Ark of the Covenant in the Holy of Holies. And the comment is made that the God of all universes "concentrates" himself particularly at that point in space. For Luria, *tzimtzum* is the exact opposite. God concentrates himself not out there, at a point in the world, but within himself. By this act he leaves a void in which his creatures can come into being.

Tzimtzum, then, is not itself creation but the necessary prelude to it. Now the externalizing act can occur, but with certain ultimately troublesome consequences derived from its taking place in a realm from which God has withdrawn. Of course, he could not have removed himself completely, for without something of his being present nothing at all could exist. Luria says he leaves behind, in the creation-space, a residue of his reality, something like the oil or wine, he nicely notes, that is always still there after we think we have emptied the jug.

The positive externalizing movement of creation begins with God sending forth a beam of light into the void he has left. From this light, in various extraordinary stages, the creation we know eventually took form. For Luria, then, creating is a two-fold process, a contraction which leads to an expansion. More, it is a continuing double movement, for God continues the work of Creation each day, continuously, and hence all existence as we know it pulsates to the divine regression and egression. Here Luria's sense of time and the opportune moves in a mystic realm no fine-tuned atomic instrument can ever hope to clock.

Perhaps we should already be prepared by the doctrine of *tzimtzum* for the next major stage in creation but most people find it not only dramatic but somewhat disturbing. Luria teaches that the creative act speedily results in a cosmic catastrophe, that creation begins with a calamity. Luria describes it in metaphors which today could easily be taken from our experiments to harness thermonuclear energy, specifically to find "containers" for the enormous heat of the plasma gases involved in the fusion process. As the divine beam of created light comes into the void, it goes through various transformations. Ultimately it produces certain "vessels" which are to come to full existence when they are filled with the creating light. But now, as God's great power fills some of the lesser vessels, it proves too mighty for them and they are shattered, the *shevirah* mentioned above. The result is an imperfect creation, one in which things are not as they ought to be or were intended by God to be, a cosmos which from almost its very beginning is alienated from itself, a created order where evil abounds instead of good.

Luria, however, is not a pessimist. Once again his sense of the dialectic implicit in all things reasserts itself and he turns the doctrine of a flawed creation into the basis of man's having cosmic significance. To begin with, the *shevirah* does not mean that the creation collapses into nothingness. It cannot, for God's energy was poured into it. True, what we see around us today is largely the "shells" or "husks" of what should have been, without their proper kernels of God's energizing light. But by their very existence we know that something of God's power is in them. Thus Luria speaks of the divine sparks which are to be found everywhere in creation. If all these sparks were lifted up from the husks and restored to their proper place in God's spiritual order for creation, then all things would become what they were intended to be. Creation can be restored and *tikkun* means restoration, the reintegration of the organic wholeness of creation, the reestablishment of the world in the full graciousness of God's primal intent.

What astonishes us here is Luria's bold insistence that *tikkun* is primarily humanity's work, not God's. In everything one faces, in every situation one finds oneself in, one should realize that there is a fallen spark of God's light waiting to be returned to its designated spiritual place. Hence, as people do the good moment by moment and give their acts of goodness a proper, inner, mystic intention—more specifically, as the Jew practices Jewish law and manifests Jewish virtues with full concentration of the soul on the task of uplifting the Divine sparks—the shattered creation is brought into repair. The ailing cosmos is healed. The Messiah is brought near. People do that, each person by each act. And if enough people did that enough of the time, Luria teaches, God would send the Messiah. Or, to put it with more appropriate divine passivity, if people, by their acts, restored the creation to what God had hoped it would be, then all the benefits of his gracious goodness would be available to them. Such a messianic estimate of human initiative is unique—so much so that some scholars have argued that Luria's ideas, transmitted by Christian Cabbalists and transformed by late Renaissance and early rationalist humanism, were influential in producing the heady confidence in humankind of the eighteenth-century enlightenment. But I do not think we need carry Luria's ideas any further.

III

The excitement of the Lurianic teaching arises from its radical shift in the application and hence the structure of cosmic power. Traditional creation theories focus on God and the effectuation of his will. God is understood in a transitive mode. In such an approach, the creatures are, so to speak, only the objects of God's activity. So, by Feuerbachian inversion, leadership comes to mean using power to achieve one's ends. The greatest leaders, then, are the people who mobilized massive energies to accomplish vast projects. And since, until recently, social power has been political-military, most of the great figures of world history were warriors or warrior-kings. Though today we might add executives or administrators to the list of those eligible for adulation, our ideal leader remains the achiever, the person who imposes designs upon reality.

The Lurianic God moves in radically other ways. He is understood in a reflexive mode. From the very beginning, thinking of him involves consideration of his creatures; how can their independent existence be assured? Where will they find sufficient emptiness of being to make their limited reality significant? With this in mind, the exercise of God's power is drastically redirected. It must first be applied to itself, to the extent of constricting its all-encompassing quality. Only when God withdraws can he create—if his creatures are to have full dignity.

This readily translates into contemporary human terms. We seek a leadership construed not primarily in terms of the accomplishment of plans but equally in terms of its humanizing effect on the people being led. Our ethics demand a leader who uses power to enable people to be persons while they work together. Such a leader, as against the stereotype of the cruel general or ruthless executive is not essentially goal oriented, but recognizes that people are always as important if not more important than the current undertaking.

The extension and the withdrawal visions of creation retain something in common. Even tyrants know that people can be pushed only so far, and the biblical God, who by his unlimited power could have been the greatest of tyrants, nonetheless creates a man independent enough to resist him. On the other hand, in the Lurianic theory, though the creatures are given initial consideration, the creation is not oriented to their satisfaction but by the divine will. Yet though these creation visions overlap, they assign quite different status to those of lesser power and so must be considered alternative models for exercising leadership. Think of the sort of leadership we all have known in groups of small to moderate size, the family, the classroom, the church or synagogue. (One could easily expand the list.) These institutions have goals to accomplish. Yet in being part of them, it has made all the difference in the world to us whether we felt our parents or teachers or clergy were using us to accomplish their purposes or helping us grow as we labored for our common ends. I suggest that the ability to practice *tzimtzum* can sharply distinguish accomplishment-directed from person-fostering leadership.

Leaders, by their power, have a greater field of presence than most people do. When they move into a room they seem to fill the space around them. We say they radiate power. Hence the greater the people we meet the more reduced we feel—though as in fascist or fantasy adulation we may hope that by utterly identifying ourselves with our hero, we can gain the fullest sort of existence. So in the presence of the mighty we are silent and respectful, we await their directions and are fearful of their judgments. Who we are is defined by what they think of us. Like God the preeminent have true existence and we, their creatures, exist only in part. In such a system the activists strive for the day when they will be god and others will have to serve them. Professors, who suffered through the indignities of the old Ph.D. apprenticeship system and have finally made it to full rank and tenure, today face students who increasingly demand to be treated as persons, that is, as partners whose independent reality is respected in the relationship. But the professors, having finally become Number One in the academic hierarchy, want to realize the benefits of that status, not the least as a compensation for the pain of achieving it. They want to rule as they were ruled—and that is only one of the many varieties of refusing to make room for others so neatly summarized in the term "ego-trip."

The Lurianic model of leadership has, as its first step, contraction. The leader withholds presence and power so that the followers may have some place in which to be. Take the case of a parent who has the power to insist upon a given decision and a good deal of experience upon which to base his judgment. In such an instance, the urge to compel is almost irresistible. Yet if it is a matter the parent feels the child can handle—better, if making this decision and taking responsibility for it will help the child grow as a person—then the mature parent withdraws and makes it possible for the child to choose and thus come more fully into his own. *Tzimtzum* here means not only not telling the child what to do but not manipulating the decision by hinting or "sharing" experience or "only" giving some advice. Leaving room for the other means just that, including allowing the child sometimes to make a foolish choice. Not ever to be permitted to choose the wrong thing means not truly to be free. Parents, like all other leaders, should seek to emulate God's maturity. He gives his children their freedom even though they may use it against him because he knows his dignity cannot be satisfied in the long run with anything less than a relationship in which we come to him freely rather than in servility.

Tzimtzum operates in a similar way in the leadership of teachers and clergy. Normally both are so busy doing things for us that they leave us little opportunity to do things on our own and thus find some personal independence. Both talk too much—so much so, that when they stop talking for a moment and ask for questions or honest comments, we don't believe them. We know if we stay quiet for a moment they will start talking again. We realize that their professional roles have been built around creation by extension of the self, so they will have to prove to us by a rigorous practice of *tzimtzum* that they really want us to be persons in our own right.

One common misinterpretation of this approach is to think it calls for a swing from dominance to abandonment, a sort of petulant declaration that if one's lessers do not want one's guidance then they should get no help at all and suffer the consequences of being on their own. There are many parents who vacillate between enforcing a harsh law and granting complete license. In school or church situations, withdrawal to give others freedom easily becomes a rationalization for indolence, the refusal to plan, or provide resources, or make proper demands upon the community. Luria's God does not indulge in *tzimtzum* to sulk or feel sorry for himself. He bears no resemblance to Aristotle's self-centered god who was not only pure thought, thinking, but did his thinking about the purest of things, himself. *Tzimtzum* is rather the first of a two-part rhythm, for it is always followed by sending the creative beam of light into the just-vacated void. The withdrawal is for the sake of later using one's power properly. Contraction without a following expansion, regression without subsequent egression does not produce creation. But once room has been made for an other, even simple applications of power can prove effective. How often it has been the seemingly casual word, the side comment, the quizzical look we got which, coming from someone we knew respected us, powerfully affected us. So in the classroom, though the teacher's summary of the data or interpretation of the material is regularly needed, it is also the good question, the challenge of stimulating options, the pause which is receptive that is the most effective means of educating. Indeed, perhaps the greatest effect one can have on someone seeking to become a person is to provide him with a model. Here the exercise of power is, directly speaking, all on oneself and only indirectly on the other. Yet in creating persons, the effectiveness of a good example, particularly as contrasted to laying down rules or verbalizing ideals, is immeasurable.

Leadership in the Lurianic style is particularly difficult, then, because it requires a continuing alternation of the application of our power. Now we hold back; now we act. To do either in the right way is difficult enough. To develop a sense when to stop one and do the other, and then reverse that in due turn, is to involve one in endless inner conflict. An example will make this clearer. In a seminar, though the teacher may have spent a lifetime on a topic, the teacher elects to sit silently so as to give the student an opportunity to speak. If the teacher does not keep still, allowing, say, slight errors of fact or misinterpretations to pass by uncontested, but regularly interrupts, the student's presentation, and his self, are as good as destroyed. At the same time, incompetence can be tolerated only so far. If the student is well on the way to ruining an important topic for the class or making such major misstatements that all which follows will be false, the teacher must interrupt. Danger lurks equally in action and inaction. Premature or too frequent intervention is as fateful as missing danger signs or giving insufficient aid. And with all this, we cannot help but realize that our judgment to intervene may only be a power-grab while our decision to stay silent may really mean we are unwilling to take the responsibility for interrupting.

The seminar situation illustrates well the complexities of functioning as a Lurianic leader. No wonder then that the call for a modern style of leadership throws many people into great anxiety. Their masters did not use their power this way and no one now can give them a rule as to when and how they ought to step back or step in. So failures in trying to exert the new leadership abound, and examples of successful leadership are rare even in face-to-face associations, much less in the giant organizations of which our society is so largely composed.

IV

Some implications for leadership of the ideas of *shevirah* and *tikkun* also deserve mention, though they are perhaps at greater distance from Luria's teaching than the ones mentioned above. Those who lead by *tzimtzum* must quickly reconcile themselves to the fact that leaving room for others to act is likely to mean their own purposes will be accomplished only in blemished form. The student will, in terms of the content presented or material covered, not lead the seminar as well as the teacher could. The children who write their own college application biographies or seek out summer jobs themselves are not likely to do as expert a job as the parent. The congregants who read or create a service will probably not reach the level of expression or educe the religious traditions in a way the clergy might have. *Shevirah,* imperfect creation, is the logical consequence of leadership by *tzimtzum.* Hence, if our eyes are only on what has been accomplished in our plans and we cannot see what has happened in the creation of persons, we are likely to be deeply disturbed. The next step is to take over ourselves. It is, indeed, often easier to get things done by doing them oneself rather than allowing others to do so, particularly in their way. But to seize power from others is to deprive them of the possibility of significant action and thus of dignity. We must learn to trust them if they are to be given a chance to be persons, and that means learning to "put up" with their bumbling ways. Of God we say that he "bears" with us. Without his forgiveness for our sins, we would not be able to continue as real shapers of history. The graciousness implicit in *tzimtzum* is not only the grant of space in which we might have being but the will to forgive the faults we may commit once we have that independent being. Anyone who would lead by *tzimtzum,* then, must know that *shevirah* is likely if not inevitable. Thus Lurianic leadership depends not only on an exquisite sense of interpersonal rhythm but a capacity to forgive and go on working with those whose need for independence is a major cause of the frustration of our plans.

The strength to persist in so frustrating a role can come from recognizing that the leader's *tzimtzum* and the resulting *shevirah* are the occasion for the followers' work of *tikkun,* restoration and completion. The group's objectives may not have been accomplished now but the leader may be confident that the effort will go on. Its continuation no longer depends upon the presence of the present leader. By the act of *tzimtzum,* confirmed in bearing with the *shevirah,* the leader has taught the disciples to work out of their own initiative and not by coercion from above. The painful process has created a new generation to carry on the work. And it, in turn, following the leader's model, will create another generation of workers, *ad infinitum,* until the goal has been accomplished. This is as much messianism as we are entitled to in human endeavors. So the parents who see their children able to make their own decisions maturely, though they choose a peculiar lifestyle; so the teachers who see their students become competent scholars, though they reach conclusions at variance from what they were taught; so the clergy who develop laymen committed to living religiously, come what may, though they transform the traditions they received; such leaders by *tzimtzum* know they have done as much as men can do to save a troublesome and treacherous world. Their hope, then, arises from seeing the present and the future as two parts of a whole. They are patient during the *shevirah* and endure the self-denial of their *tzimtzum* to create an indomitable commitment to *tikkun.* Leadership with so long a view is not muscular enough for

Michelangelo's God, or his heroes Moses and David. The great Florentine was a Renaissance man and believed power meant lordship, not person-making. We can still learn much from Michelangelo's sense of grandeur but we must move beyond it to implement our new sense of humanity.

Did Isaac Luria himself see, far before Feuerbach, that his vision of a withdrawing creator could be a model for personal leadership? We cannot quite tell. In some respects he seems to have been unassertive beyond the customary humility of the pious. Thus, we are told that he usually allowed one of his disciples to walk ahead of him—an act firmly prohibited in the etiquette of respect for a master—because the student considered it a special honor. He is also reported never to have bargained over the price asked for any object he needed for religious purposes or questioned his wife's requests with regard to household or personal expenses. So too, he emphasized to his followers that they were all parts of one organism and therefore needed to care and pray for each other. And he was quite uncommunicative about his deepest mystical doctrines, not only refusing to write anything down but apparently instructing his most trusted adepts only by hints and allusions.

But we dare not press this interpretation further. In most respects Luria seems to have exercised authority in the typical kingly fashion of one who is recognized as wearing the crown of the Torah. He organized his disciples into a group called The Lion's Whelps (a pun made on the initials of his title, Rabbi Isaac, gave him the title The Lion) and he set high admission standards which were stringently enforced. He then divided them into two categories, apparently according to how much mystic knowledge he felt he could share with them. The extent of his dominance of the group may perhaps be gauged from the fact that he refused Joseph Karo, the greatest authority on Jewish law of that time, permission to be part of the inner circle. Another intriguing fact gives us some indication that Luria's leadership had limited effectiveness. He arranged to have all his followers live together in a sort of commune, but within a few months, there was considerable difficulty among them. The texts say, typically enough, that the wives began to quarrel among themselves and this caused the disturbances among the adepts. Yet, if this seems to compromise Luria's stature somewhat, we should also keep in mind that his career as a mystic teacher in Safed comprised just three years, after which he died. In that short time he changed the course of Jewish mysticism and did so, apparently, by imbuing his disciples with so deep a commitment to his doctrine that they, and their followers in turn, spread it throughout the Jewish world. More, they brought it into the thought and lifestyle of much of Jewry, the first time that mysticism, which had always been an elitist interest, became part of mass Jewish living. So if we cannot know whether Luria led by *tzimtzum* we can nonetheless say that his leadership had an extraordinary effect in his day and his teaching retains a powerful message for our time.

14 / A Jewish Response: The Lure and Limits of Universalizing Our Faith

1978

Traditional Judaism has a reasonably well-defined attitude to non-Jewish religions. The Torah describes God as making a covenant with Noah and thus, through Noah and his children, with all of humanity. The rabbis made this covenant the basis of their authoritative rulings about the religious status of non-Jews. They and all the Judaism that flowed from them considered the covenant with Noah to be real and continuing. Rabbinic Judaism thus believes all people know what God wants of them and can achieve their salvation. But as the Torah story of Noah immediately makes clear, humankind regularly violates its covenant responsibilities to God. The rabbis generally believed that the children of Noah were obligated to carry out seven root commandments: not to blaspheme God, or worship idols, or murder, or steal, or be sexually degenerate, or cut limbs from living animals, and, positively, to set up courts of justice. Even as the descendents of Noah built a tower to enter heaven and gain a name, so the rabbis saw most of humanity behaving sinfully and thus deserving of God's judgment.

The Torah understands the covenant with Abraham as a compensation for the sinfulness of humanity. The covenant with Noah is not abrogated by God. Rather God establishes a special covenant so that the divine rule may be properly established among people. Covenant being essentially a relationship of obligation, the Jews fulfill God's special purpose by living in special intensity under God's law. They proclaim the reality of God's rule by doing the commandments, personally and communally; by example, they set a standard for humanity.

Proselytizing has little role in Judaism. People do not need to be Jews; they need only be pious Noachides. So the Jews have no command to convert anyone. They do accept converts and, in love of their faith, occasionally seek to have others adopt it. The rabbis acknowledged that unconverted individuals among "the nations" could be fully righteous and thus "saved." The comment, "The pious among the gentiles have a share in the life of the world to come," may be taken as the standard Jewish attitude. The rabbis, like the Bible, were, however, spiritually pessimistic about human collectives and freely speculated that they would not survive the post-messianic judgment day. In our own time, the experience of the Holocaust, perpetrated by a nation steeped in Christianity and a leader of modern culture, has reinforced those traditional attitudes. While still hopeful about individuals, we are skeptical if not cynical about claims for the goodness of human nature, the progress of civilization, or the way institutions will transform humanity. If I forbear from discussing the Holocaust further it is because I take it for granted that its horrifying reality is a motive for and an assumption of our discussion of world interreligious relationships.

Yet for all this doctrine, the only gentile religion the rabbis directly dealt with was idolatry. Succeeding generations have had to fill in Judaism's judgment of other religions. With regard to Christianity this involved a consideration of whether it was not another form of idol worship. Its use of icons, its veneration of saints, and particularly its doctrine of the Christ as a person of the triune God, seemed the equivalent of idolatry. The slow development of a relatively positive assessment of Christianity has been beautifully traced by Jacob Katz in his *Exclusiveness and Tolerance* and needs no further statement here.[1] Islam being radically monotheistic caused many fewer problems. Most Jewish thinkers today see pious Christians and Muslims as fulfilling the Noachian covenant, and thus as "saved." A minority opinion remains that their worship is the equivalent of idolatry; also some modern Jews have tried to give these religions a more than Noachian status, in line with their own claims, but no such view has gained even substantial minority support. This is as far as the Jewish theory of other religions has gone. In sum, humanity does not need to be Jewish but God needs Jews and Judaism to achieve the divine purposes with humanity. This sense of the Jews as chosen and special but only instrumental to the establishment of God's kingdom is so great that some rabbis can see the ultimate disappearance of Jewish distinctiveness at the conclusion of the eschatological drama, though most love the Jewish people too much to believe that God would do without them, even in the life of the world to come.

All this is, essentially, early rabbinic teaching. I find it remarkable how much of its nontriumphal universality Professor Dawe accepts and I cannot repress a Jewish sigh that it has taken so many painful centuries for Christian thinkers to do so.

I also think most believing Jews would find quite congenial, as I do, Professor Dawe's method for potentially accepting the religious legitimacy of many faiths. He does this as a matter of Christian faith and not as a matter of enlightenment universalism or secularist pragmatism. He does consider it critical to recognize that the world is incurably pluralistic religiously, but he does not argue as some have done that the multiplicity of religions itself demonstrates that none of them is true and that truth is more likely to be found in what they share. The logic of such quick derivations from comparative data escapes me. That there are many religions is, in itself, no basis for denying the truth claim of any one of them. Moreover, to argue that multiplicity demonstrates commonality is a simple contradiction in terms. Rather, to see unity when there is diversity before one requires a transempirical standard. The nature of that standard and its source are critical to our discussion. If the standard is open enough to reach out to most of humankind, one might end up with a fairly unrestricted relativism: "All religions or almost all religions are equally worthwhile." If, however, while recognizing that many religions might be true, one's standard of judgment discriminates between religions as being more true and less true, then one may find oneself denying the adequacy of certain peoples' faiths.

The origin of one's basis for asserting universality may have a great effect on its nature. Dawe is quite precise in this regard. He is a universalist, he contends, because he is a Christian. So I am a universalist because I am a Jew. Our specific, historic faiths teach the possibility that all people can know God. I do not know that all other faiths teach such a doctrine. Indeed, for many centuries it seems fair to say that Christianity itself did not. One of my concerns in the study of comparative religion is to know which particular faiths assert similar doctrines and what sort of standard of judgment they apply to other faiths.

In any case, without a particularistic grounding for universalism I do not see how it can arise. Since the history of religion is descriptive, it cannot move on to statements of what is real in all religions, or what is their essence, without becoming philosophy of religion. Since religious universality is not self-evident it would need some rational argument, most likely a compelling metaphysics or ontology, to establish it. I see nothing like that in the competitive pluralism of theories we call philosophy of religion today, though I remain open to the possibility that reason here comes to coincide with what I have been taught by revelation. My point is that if universality is grounded in particular faith it would seem odd that universality could ever fundamentally negate the truth of particularity, for in so doing it would destroy its own legitimation.

This concern for particularism leads me to raise some Jewish problems with Dawe's discussion of Christian universalism. I do so conscious of the fact that his paper is an exercise in outreach and inclusiveness, not a full statement of his Christianity. I concede that the timeliness and morality of his effort are not unimportant considerations. Nonetheless as all faiths move in a similar direction it is important to raise certain questions, essentially methodological ones. Coming to his universalism via Christianity, Professor Dawe has a standard by which to judge other faiths and says we cannot be undiscriminating. But being concerned to be inclusive he brings universalism to the brink of relativism. He gives us criteria for judging other faiths that are so broad—new being, human renewal, and fulfillment—that it is not clear what, if any, religious way of life might give him Christian pause. I suggest we shall not know whether Professor Dawe is not effectively a relativist until he tells us who he might conceivably exclude from his company of equivalent faiths.

The Jewish standard for such judgment is the Noachian covenant, and one asks whether a given religion, in fact, reflects it. Thus one of the major problems that would arise in Jewish discussions with other faiths, Islam most notably excluded, is idol worship. This being the root sin to Judaism, strict authorities would allow for no efforts to explain away the facts of the practice. Lenient authorities might conceivably seek some mitigation on this point, even as in the case of Christianity, the identification of God with a human being, once considered the equivalent of idolatry, was no longer so understood. Another matter of major Jewish concern would be the attitude toward and the practice of the rules of conduct taken to be part of the Noachian covenant. A religion that did not make them central would not, from the Jewish view, be a proper way for humanity to serve God.

Dawe's elaboration of his criterion raises major problems for me with regard to theological method. His argument rests on an interpretation of Christianity as proclaiming the name of God as the name of Jesus. His own universalizing translation of that name is justified by the flat assertion: "This is true because the 'name of Jesus' is the disclosure of the structure of new being." How does he know that this is what the Christ really means and apparently has always meant? I do not recall such language in the New Testament or in medieval statements about the nature and work of the Christ. Rather it seems reasonably clear to me that Dawe is presenting us with one of the most appealing modern interpretations of the Christ, a personalist or existentialist one of a decided Tillichian flavor. He equates all of Christian tradition with this modern interpretation of it. I wonder. We know a good deal about the rise and fall of theological systems, of the ephemeral character of modern hermeneutics of the old great symbols, and, equally, of the present pluralism among Christian interpreters of the Christ. Why Dawe wants such a view of the Christ I find commendable, but it is not clear to me how, from within the circle of Christian faith, he arrives at his equation of Christianity and humanization. Despite his summoning of key symbols I cannot tell to what extent this is a reasonable reinterpretation of Christianity. This issue is common to many faiths today: How much modernization can an old tradition admit and still be true to itself. In contemporary Judaism, for example, many of our most significant arguments rage over how much one may change the concept or practice of Torah, or the extent to which Zionism is a full translation of classic Jewish identity.

What is more troubling to me, however, is Dawe's full-scale universalization of the truth of symbols that traditionally were as true in their particularity as in their universality. Let me give two examples. Dawe turns the Bible's God into a radically monotheistic Lord. If radical meant that there was only one God and that God was *Adonai,* we would have no argument. But for Dawe radical monotheism means more than absolute sovereignty. It means that God is so universally Lord that God cannot really be connected intimately with particulars. Radical monotheism is thus a "Protestant principle" that denies particular divine covenants. But the Bible knows no universal God who does not at the same time radically participate in the election and chosenness of particular covenant partners.

With regard to the Christ, Professor Dawe is more circumspect. He does not deny that Jesus of Nazareth was a particular man of a given historical locus, and he does not denigrate the fact that a particular group of people, Christians, see in this individual, "the fullest disclosure of the relationship of God to the fulfillment of human existence." But when done translating Christhood into humanization, no particular truth, no special claim attaches to Jesus, the Christ, or to Christians. Instead, again and again we hear that wherever new being generates human fulfillment, wherever life is renewed and virtue expressed, one has the equivalent of the Christian's Christ. Thus, such truth as Christianity has is universal. What is particular about Christianity has been relegated to a second, perhaps valuable, but certainly not essential, level of truth and value.

On what basis is this done? Professor Dawe said he would speak from a Christian base. But Christianity itself has not previously authorized this emptying out of its particularity. Perhaps the issue is better put in logical terms: How does he know that particularist symbols can be fully translated into universalistic terms? In the face of previous failures to departicularize Christianity and show it as essentially universal truth, how does Dawe now validate this method and these results?

Perhaps it will be helpful to set these questions in a sociological framework, though I know I now border on the impolite. For which Christians does this sort of universalism speak? And what does Dawe think of the Christian legitimacy of those who will differ with him? Answering the same about myself, I am a Reform Jew whose liberalism is uncommonly traditional. Many Reform and some Conservative Jews would be far less particularistic than I am. At the other extreme few if any Orthodox Jewish thinkers would find congenial the sort of discussion of faith being engaged in here. The Jewish community as a whole, I suggest, is increasingly committed to the proposition that Judaism's symbols, while bearing high universalistic import, cannot fully be rendered in universal terms. From late in the nineteenth century to our own time, Jews have lived with the effort to translate Torah into simple human ethics. This produced some strikingly positive results in terms of Jewish contributions to the welfare of humankind. It also laid the intellectual foundations for generations of unconcern with Jewish identity and belief. Now we are beginning to see the cumulative effect of this denial of our roots: With the erosion of our particularism, our ethical commitments have now also begun to slip. Our non-believing Jews—a high proportion of our community—do not seem to care much about this. I obviously do not speak for them. For most of the rest of us, seeing what has happened to our people's conduct has ended the quest for articulating Judaism as universalism in these pre-messianic times.

I suppose my ultimate objection to Dawe's method is its apparent consequences. To humanize Christianity he has made it dispensable. Jews, not acknowledging the occurrence of a messianic resurrection in history, take the potential death of a covenant partner more seriously. I wonder if Professor Dawe would object if his children adopted humanizing, non-Christian faiths, married their adherents, and raised his grandchildren in them? To his mind, would there be any *theological* loss if Christianity should disappear as an identifiable religion? Or would it mean the loss of merely another socio-cultural humanizing faith? We Jews are much more particularistic than that. We want our children to be Jews and marry Jews so there can be Jewish homes so that Jewish people and its faith can survive, set an example of covenant faithfulness, and ultimately give birth to the Messiah. Paradoxically enough, even those rabbis who justify performing intermarriages generally do so as helping to keep the family and its children within the Jewish community! Our concern for particularity goes that far.

This leaves Jews, and I think all major religious traditions, with a perplexing methodological problem. Contemporary Western intellectuality has no good contexts for validating particularity. A proper explanation or proof always involves relation to a universal rule or truth. Individuality is significant only as an instance of a class or category. It has the worth of a necessary accident, finitude being our lot, though it may also have instrumental value. As soon as one seeks to raise particularity above this level one must have recourse to generally denigrated patterns of legitimation. One can utilize terms like "revelation," "tradition," "dogma," "authority," or, more philosophically, "fideism." These have almost no persuasive power among sophisticated Western university academicians. Becoming a professor apparently commits one to universalize truth. Take the case of existentialism. Kierkegaard thought that he was validating truth as a particular, individual matter. Today we turn that into a general theory of what it is to be a person, and existentialism is used, as in Dawe's case, to departicularize.

My Jewish faith leads me to assert that there is no inherent need to departicularize one's faith because one is drawn to its universal vision of humanity. I suggest that we may find it far more valuable and authentic to acknowledge our simultaneous assertion of particular and universal truths and see how we can envision our particularity so as not to violate our universality. This is not easy. The tension between the particular and the universal will always plague such a paradoxical faith as it does Judaism. And the human will to sinfulness and self-service being so great, chauvinism and fanaticism can easily blind us to our intimate involvement with all human beings.

Our particularism may then need some special limits and I can suggest four that faiths might insist upon. First, we can limit the role of our particularity, applying it only to ourselves, as in the Jewish assertion that only Jews, not all people, need to serve God in the specifically Jewish way. Second, one may adopt the liberal religious stance and acknowledge that one's sense of religious truth, while great enough to stake one's life on, is not absolute. One must then allow room for others with a different sense of truth. Third, whether one can accept the liberal stance or not, one may recognize that religion today stands under the moral judgment of its secular critics. For pragmatic reasons, then, we must not act so as to discredit our claims to serve a universal God. Such a concern for what others think would undoubtedly change as we found ourselves in a position of power, precisely when we need the greatest restraint. Perhaps then, fourth, we can admit that the fullness of the truth we affirm can come into being only in God's eschatological redemption of all human history. Until then we must do our share while recognizing that we ourselves stand under God's present judgment and must leave to God what God alone can do. In fact, as a liberal Jew, I believe all four of these theses. This does not resolve the paradox of my simultaneous Jewish particularism and universalism or relieve me of the need in each decision not to transgress against either of my commitments. But paradox is the sign of expulsion from Eden and only in the new Eden will it finally be taken from us.

NOTES

1. Jacob Katz, *Exclusiveness and Intolerance: Studies in Medieval and Modern Times* (London: Oxford University Press, 1961).

15 / The Authority of the Ethical Impulse in *Halakhah*

1982

A good deal of attention has been given to the turn to Jewish tradition among those who at one time identified the essence of Judaism with universal human ethics. With the loss of confidence in the authority of Western civilization, the possibility arose that classic Jewish teaching might be the best guide to the good life.[1] The question is then often asked, in the all-or-nothing terms beloved by those who like to use intellect coercively, "Why do you not then fully embrace rabbinic teaching as developed over millennia and as amplified in unbroken tradition today?" Much of the response to that query hinges on the place of ethics within Jewish teaching or, to be more precise, on the authority given to the ethical imperative within classic Rabbinic Judaism. (On this term, a euphemism for the unbroken tradition of interpreting the Torah in inherited fashion, see below.)

This issue has been treated most intensively from within traditionalist circles by Aharon Lichtenstein in his widely read paper, "Does Jewish Tradition Recognize an Ethic Independent of Halakha?"[2] Lichtenstein has surely clarified the issue before the community, but in my opinion, has not satisfactorily faced up to the issue troubling many Jews about their heritage.

Lichtenstein focuses on an internal problem of Rabbinic Judaism. It recognizes that its legal procedures occasionally do not directly produce ethical results. It thus includes various measures for overcoming such impasses. He takes particular pains to point out that some of these special processes were actionable, that they could be enforced by a Jewish court. He can then conclude that though Jewish tradition does not recognize an ethic independent of Halakhah, it contains within itself all the ethical resources its notion of God and humankind would expect us to find in it.

The issue of the internal ethical adequacy of Jewish tradition is not a minor one, both for theological and practical reasons. Ethical demands come with an imperative quality. They lay an authoritative claim upon us. If Rabbinic Judaism were to recognize an ethics independent of it, that would be to recognize a second source of authority to the Torah. Or, to say the same thing differently, Jews would have to admit that God had given them only a partial, not a complete, revelation. The former notion conflicts with the common identification of the one God with the one Torah, the latter with the Jewish understanding of the completeness of the Torah revelation.

Practically, too, the notion of an external ethics would raise methodological problems for a contemporary *posek*, legal authority. His expertise is in Torah. He will certainly recognize the internal ethical impulses and goals in Torah and respond to them as he deems appropriate. Should external ethical considerations be included in determining authoritative Jewish duty, he would have to transcend his received methodology and learning and become expert in general ethics and its relation to rabbinic tradition. No established institution would easily accept such a radical challenge to its accustomed ways of proceeding.

David Weiss Halivni's statement on the halakhic status of a universal ethics seems more motivated by pragmatic than theological reasons in rejecting the concept of an external morality with authority within Halakhah.[3] Maimonides' famous insistence that Noachides must accept their commandments as revealed by the Torah and not as given by their own reason, while a somewhat different case, is relevant here. Why he should rule this way despite his practical identification of revelation with reason has not yet been made compellingly clear.[4] The pragmatic explanation, in his case securing the ultimate foundation of the social order, is perhaps the easiest to accept, particularly if we are influenced by the "two doctrines" interpretation of his thought. Yet that would require us to accept that, in terms of the higher doctrine, such a sociological "external," if revealed, ethics exists and is authoritative. Our only other alternative would seem to be to take a radically fresh approach to the nonrational or transrational aspect of all of his philosophy, a reading often spoken of but not yet done.

Lichtenstein's treatment of the issue, however, proceeds beyond these issues to analyze the way in which an ethical impulse makes itself felt and operates within Rabbinic Judaism. For our purposes, it will help to grant immediately what appears to be one of Lichtenstein's main points: Rabbinic Judaism has a fundamental ethical thrust, not only manifested in the law itself, but most notably in the methods and motives it has for overcoming internal conflicts between its ethical values and its legal procedures. The vulgar contrast made in older Christian polemics between Jewish legalism and general ethics betrays ignorance of Judaism and insensitivity to its own prejudice (in the name of ethics!). Leaving that question, I wish to focus on the problem that I see arising when one speaks about the internal ethics of Judaism as Lichtenstein has done.

Critical to understanding Lichenstein's argument is his special use of the term "Halakhah" (note the capital "H"). He does so in a way different from that commonly found in North American English-language writing on such matters. Through most of his paper he means by Halakhah the totality of the rabbinic tradition. (To conform to his meaning but to avoid the linguistic confusion which can result from his usage, I shall use the term "Rabbinic Judaism" to refer to the same phenomenon.) Lichtenstein's choice of terms is certainly justifiable, but the question posed by many interlocutors asking about an ethics independent of Halakhah often has a somewhat different issue in mind. That is, one regularly sees the word "Halakhah" used as referring to only one part of Rabbinic Judaism, the legal part, as contrasted to *aggadah,* the non-legal part. The *aggadah* obviously contains much ethical material. To ask about an ethic independent of Halakhah means, then, to ask whether ethical impulses arising outside the law carry full imperative quality either in their own right or, more threateningly, against provisions of the law.

Lichtenstein knows that his usage is somewhat uncommon and on the last two pages of his article makes mention of the more common understanding of the term "halakhah" (note the lower-case "h").[5] He thinks we would be better off calling *din,* law, what people usually call halakhah. In sum, he argues that this is only a matter of semantics and that, while one may define as one thinks best, the outcome will be the same: Rabbinic Judaism has a vital, effective, internal ethics.[6]

What may go unnoticed as a result of Lichtenstein's unusual terminology is the problem of the several levels of authority within Rabbinic Judaism. Lichtenstein is too careful a scholar not to refer to this along the way, but it does not serve as one of his major foci. The best example of an accurate statement which may perhaps be misleading is found in one of his summary sentences. Referring to various ways of speaking of

Jewish tradition, he concludes that it makes little difference as long as we "issue with the thesis that traditional halakhic Judaism demands of the Jew both adherence to Halakha and commitment to an ethical moment that though different from Halakha is nevertheless of a piece with it and in its own way fully imperative."[7] The critical yet easily overlooked part of this statement is the qualifying clause, "in its own way." That is, Lichtenstein does not say: "and commitment to an ethical moment that though different from Halakha is nevertheless of a piece with it and fully imperative." No, the "ethical moment" that is "nevertheless of a piece with" Halakhah is "fully imperative" only "in its own way." Just what is that distinctive way? And what are its implications? These questions will be critical to a mind sensitized by general ethics, now seeking to understand how ethics functions within Rabbinic Judaism.

Let us now retrace Lichtenstein's argument insofar as this will help us see his answer to these questions. Much of his paper deals with the sort of imperative involved in acting *lifnim mishurat hadin.* Lichtenstein is at pains to point out that this "is no mere option." It has "obligatory character" as shown by the verses Nahmanides uses to ground his argument about it.[8] Obviously, were this matter merely optional, it would not have any serious ethical standing. That it is "obligatory" would seem as good as guaranteed by its being part of the Oral Torah, God's revelation not being a matter of mere play. Our question, however, is just what sort of obligation is involved.

The matter is not settled, as Steven S. Schwarzschild believes, by the term itself. He writes: "*lifnim mishurat hadin* is 'within,' not as the usual rendering has it, 'beyond,' the line of the law; i.e., the very term indicates that we are here dealing with a dynamic function that operates within the system."[9] As I see it, Schwarzschild confuses the meaning of the term *din* here. The reference is to the particular legal right which one could now exercise. One is rather directed to restrict one's right in this particular case and not do that which one might otherwise properly do under the law. He correctly reads *lifnim* as "within," that is, not at the limit of what one might do. But that differs from the issue here: the status of this precept as a whole. Does it itself come to us as part of the law, the *din,* or is it in another category (though admittedly part of Rabbinic Judaism and "in its own way fully imperative")? If the reference of the term *din* was the whole legal system and not the specific *din* at issue in this instance, the phrase and its effect would be contradictory. One would be enjoined to act legally—*lifnim mishurat hadin* read as "stay

[well] within legal limits"—and yet be told not to do what the law clearly entitles one to do. Lichtenstein apparently does not consider this the meaning of the phrase, and this explains why he struggles to show the imperative nature of the injunction.

To continue, Lichtenstein notes: "With respect to the *degree of obligation,* however, *rishonim* admittedly held different views" (emphasis added).[10] Apparently, only Rabbi Isaac of Corbeille considered it to have the full "degree of obligation." He alone lists the need to act *lifnim mishurat hadin* as one of the 613 commandments. We can understand the issue of degree better if we attend to Lichtenstein's succeeding sentences: "Nahmanides did not go quite this far, as he does not classify *lifnim mishurat hadin* as an independent *mitzvah,* as binding as *shofar* or *tefillin.* However, he does clearly posit it as a normative duty, incumbent upon—and expected of—every Jew as part of his basic obligation."[11]

The treatment of Maimonides' position which then follows is of interest to us, despite the difficulty in giving a consistent interpretation of his position, only because he posits a somewhat different degree of obligation. Depending upon one's interpretation, Maimonides proclaims either a higher or lower level of responsibility than does Nahmanides, but in either case not as strong as that of Rabbi Isaac.[12] Regardless of the interpretation, Lichtenstein is satisfied that a "supralegal ethic" exists within Rabbinic Judaism. What remains unclear is the precise status of the "supralegal," that is, the specific way in which it is "supra" or, alternatively, just how much authority it has and how it is brought to bear upon the full legal requirements of Judaism.

Lichtenstein approaches this issue by inquiring whether *lifnim mishurat hadin is* actionable.[13] He notes that while the Rosh, and therefore probably the whole Spanish school, did not consider it actionable, some Tosafists held such action "could indeed be compelled."[14] He then immediately sets the necessary limits to what might otherwise lead to a gross antinomianism: "Of course, such a position could not conceivably be held with reference to all supralegal behavior. *Din* has many ethical levels; and so, of necessity, must *lifnim mishurat hadin.* Surpassing laws grounded in, say, the concept that 'the Torah has but spoken vis-à-vis the evil inclination' is hardly comparable to transcending those with a powerful moral thrust." This retraction, however, does not lose his point, for he concludes: "Nevertheless, the fact that some *rishonim,* legal authorities before the *Shulchan Arukh,* held *lifnim mishurat hadin* to be, in principle, actionable, indicates the extent to which it is part of the fabric of Halakha."[15] For our purposes, the very division of opinion and the need to qualify such opinion as coercive indicates that there remains a considerable question about just where this "ethical moment" stands within the Halakhah. And we shall not know very much about its actual ethical status until we know a good deal more about the already qualified way in which it is "fully imperative."

Once again Lichtenstein enables us to clarify an interpretation of Steven S. Schwarzschild's. Citing Hermann Cohen to substantiate philosophically his interpretation of *lifnim mishurat hadin,* Schwarzschild writes, "Equity is not a factor additional to the *jus strictum,* but a judgment-procedure which makes sure that the application of the law in each individual case is proper (i.e., moral); thus all of the law, statutes as well as the procedures, operationalizes ethical values *(aggadah)*."[16] Schwarzschild wants us to consider *lifnim mishurat hadin* as part of *din* and, for Cohenian reasons, necessarily so.

The facts, as Lichtenstein makes plain, are otherwise. Most Jewish authorities do not consider the need to act in this ethical fashion a *din.* And Lichtenstein indicates why. A law, or *din,* which directs one to override the law (for significant ethical reasons) might soon destroy the fabric of the law as a whole and reduce it to morality. As commendable as that might be, Judaism has classically been a religion where morality takes the form of law, not one where moral law effectively dominates the Torah's precepts. Of course, in an ideal Kantian legal system, morality and law would be identical. Cohen has in mind just such a rational ideal. Perhaps Schwarzschild means to argue that in Jewish law an inner essence makes itself seen which corresponds to the ethical ideal and slowly works its way out into reality. In that case, in addition to validating philosophically the notion of essence or ideal, he will have to deal with all the contrary historical data, in this instance, as forthrightly detailed by Lichtenstein. Until then, the famous gap between "religion of reason" and "the sources of Judaism" will continue to loom before the eyes of many contemporary students of the Jewish tradition.

Lichtenstein extends his argument by associating *kofin al midat Sodom*, we punish for general immorality, with *lifnim mishurat hadin,* particularly by way of a striking excerpt from the Maharal. He then asks a double question which closely approximates the issue I have been calling attention to: "If *lifnim mishurat hadin* is indeed obligatory as an integral aspect of Halakha, in what sense is it supralegal? More specifically, on the Ravya's view, *what distinguishes its compulsory elements from* din *proper?*" (emphasis added).[17]

He eventually answers his questions, thus apparently telling us what he means later by the ethical moment being "in its own way fully imperative." "It is less rigorous not only in the sense of being less exacting with respect to the degree and force of obligation—and there are times, as has been noted, when it can be equally demanding—but in the sense of being more flexible, its duty more readily definable in light of the existence of particular circumstances." To the average reader, I should think, that provides so many loopholes that it seems to indicate a far less significant sort of imperative. For that reason, I take it, Lichtenstein immediately continues: "This has nothing to do with the force of obligation," though he said the opposite in the prior sentence. And: "Once it has been determined that, in a given case, realization of 'the right and the good' mandates a particular course, its pursuit may conceivably be as imperative as the performance of a *din*."[18] To me that seems to indicate that though the ethical impulse is there, it has much less imperative status than the *din*. It is explicitly termed "less rigorous." Moreover, it only gains "the full force of obligation . . . once it has been determined" that an ethical issue is involved. This determination is not a matter left to the general conscience, but is assigned to competent decisors and permitted to function by them in only a limited number of cases.

Because of this administrative structure, we note that Lichtenstein cannot say more than that, when operational, "its pursuit *may conceivably* be as imperative as the performance of a *din*" (emphasis added).[19]

In a later discussion he indicates that this is the case, for he can summarize the dialectic between formalist *din* and contextualist *lifnim mishurat hadin* as follows: "Quite apart from the severity of obligation, therefore, there is a fundamental difference between *din* and *lifnim mishurat hadin*. One, as a more minimal level, imposes fixed objective standards. The demands of the other evolve from a specific situation; and, depending on the circumstances, may vary with the agent."[20]

I do not think anything further in Lichtenstein's paper impinges upon the issue at hand.

Perhaps it will help us to expand a bit the way in which the "ethical moment" in Rabbinic Judaism makes itself felt. It surely is not confined to the notion of *lifnim mishurat hadin*, though this theme constitutes a particularly interesting and even dramatic instance of it. There are a number of other rubrics under which the rabbis act in order to extend or amplify what the *din* requires, so that one may more clearly do that which is "good and right." Isaac Herzog, in *The Main Institutions of Jewish Law*, lists a number of these.[21]

In a recent article, J. David Bleich gives a striking instance of the different levels of rabbinic injunction to action. The case will set into bolder relief the problem of the varying levels of authority within Rabbinic Judaism. Bleich notes that Rashi considers Num. 33:53 merely God's prudent advice to the Jewish people about how they should go about conquering the land.[22] Nahmanides, on the other hand, considers the verse a positive commandment. Maimonides, however, is understood by Bleich as essentially agreeing with Rashi.[23] I do not think that Bleich is suggesting that Maimonides considers the advice to Jews about settling on the land of Israel "merely optional," to return to Lichtenstein's formulation. Rather, Bleich here resolves the issue of the "degree of obligation" by invoking the notion of merit, *zekhut.* That is, he suggests that Maimonides believes that while there is no law requiring one to immigrate to the land of Israel, he follows abundant rabbinic teaching in holding that to do so brings one great reward.

The sages often sought to get people to behave ethically not as a matter of full legal prescription, but by suggesting that certain acts, while not required, were highly meritorious. These exhortations, too, are part of God's Oral Torah and, therefore, in some sense not "merely optional." But I do not know whether Lichtenstein would consider them within his category of being fully imperative though only in their own way. Bleich does not help us further with this issue, for he notes that "this issue of merit, as distinct from compensation of fulfillment of a Divine commandment, is difficult to elucidate."[24] Again, let me suggest that we shall not properly understand the place of the ethical within Rabbinic Judaism until we clarify the weight of ethical obligations encompassed by such nonlegal rabbinic injunctions to action as that of *zekhut,* particularly because they so often are used in relation to ethical concerns.

The introduction of the notion of merit, however, has taken us away from Lichtenstein's purpose. While he would not deprecate preaching, education, model-setting, and the like as rabbinically desirable, he recognized that the key issue in this discussion was showing that its proper form was *not* the relation between a required law and an optional ethics. That would not only fly in the face of the facts as he sees them, but could not suffice as an adequate defense of the ethical impulse in Rabbinic Judaism. With commandment the dominant Jewish religious sense, an ethics that was less than required would hardly have much Jewish status. Then, too, ever since the time of Kant, an ethics which does not take the form of law has hardly seemed to most Jewish thinkers an ethics at all.[25] (I would add that though ethics does not take the form of law in

Buber, by being God's own behest it is clearly "fully imperative.") Lichtenstein, therefore, took great pains to show that the ethical thrust in Rabbinic Judaism was a species of command.

The result of Lichtenstein's discussion, however, leaves me, and, I would judge, some considerable portion of the Jewish community, troubled by the balance between the law and its supralegal ethical imperative. The disparity between the different levels of authority restricts the operation of conscience in a way that seems to us unacceptable. No one questions the commanding quality of the law. The ethical normally operates on a different, secondary level, with its degree of obligation not clearly known. The law is authoritative unless occasionally supervened. The ethical must make a case for itself should there be a conflict between them. Even then its legitimacy and functioning will be defined by the legists. The law is clear, with much precedent and institutionalized patterns of procedure. The supralegal functions in a hazy area, with few guidelines as to its proper application and handicapped by needing to make its way against the well-entrenched patterns of community practice, the law.

All this is not astonishing for a legal system. Rather, an open-minded student would probably show great admiration for the Jewish community in creating a legal structure which is so highly ethical. But to one who takes seriously the obligatory character of ethics—whether understood in the Kantian sense of law or the Buberian-Rosenzweigian and perhaps Heschelian sense of personal response to God—a major problem arises. The ethical, which ought to come as a categorical or unmediated imperative, operates within Judaism in a quite qualified, mediated way. A substantial difference exists between a system of action in which ethics is commandingly primary and one in which, though it remains imperative, it can often be a subsidiary consideration. The matter is not merely one for academics to ponder as the continuing agitation over the classic issues of *agunah* and *mamzerut* makes clear.

With some hesitation, permit me to suggest that in claiming a pattern of subsidiary but still "fully imperative" ethics, we seem to contradict our polemical argument against Christianity. Jews have charged that by subordinating works to faith, Christianity seriously compromises the impulse to righteous action.[26] Does not, in the argument we have considered, Judaism do something similar, if not to works of law, then to its own ethical moment?

Let us take the issue presently disturbing a good portion of the Jewish community, the status of Jewish women. Two major lines of thought on this issue seem to emerge. The one finds ethical reason within Rabbinic Judaism for recognizing a problem with the present formulation of the *din* with regard to women, as well as the expectations contained in contemporary Jewish practice. Based on much internal conflict, various authorities seek remedies within the law. On the whole, the more traditionally inclined interpreters who see the problem, though recognizing the ethical need to seek solutions, find that little remedial action can be taken. That is, though the ethical moment has here made itself felt within the system, it is of such limited power in the face of law and precedent that it has no supralegal effectiveness. Such reasoning has brought some Conservative Jewish legists to challenge this classic balance between law and ethics in Judaism. In this instance, they wish to make the ethical thrust of women's equality in Judaism "fully imperative" and not allow it to function in so qualified a fashion as to rob it of any ability to shape community action. For them, the ethical issue is so categorically felt as to require the vaunted flexibility inherent in Halakhah to operate and accomplish an ethical revision of existing law and practice.[27] They believe, as do many in the Jewish community, that the gap between ethics and law must now be bridged so as to make our understanding of our obligations under the Torah worthy of being called the service of God.

The other line of thought illumines our difficulty even more clearly. Some authorities deny that there is a women's ethical problem at all. That God ordained a different scope of obligation for Jewish men and women is not at all contravened by notions such as God creating humankind equally as male and female, or bestowing these creatures with dignity. The diverse yet allegedly unequal categories of commandment are so well established in Torah teaching that these authorities do not even see an issue. No possibility of an "ethical moment" arises for them. They claim that the so-called ethical impulse behind the women's issue is a Gentile importation into Judaism. Had it not been for the influence of non-Jews, they charge, we would not be concerned about this question.

Historically, I think, this judgment is correct. I cannot in this paper seek to determine whether, though the issue was raised by non-Jews, the fresh reading of the rabbinic tradition prompted by them proves that women's equality was all along present in the Torah or whether substantial Jewish basis exists for moving toward it. What we can usefully do here is to inquire about our attitude toward ethics.

The broader theoretical issue concerns the status of non-Torah ethics. Is all that Jews can call ethical fundamentally given in the Torah, or may we ever gain significant ethical insight from Gentiles? Factually, we American Jews should acknowledge that the Gentile notion of universalism and common humanity has reminded us of the Torah's teaching that there is, in fact, but one human family—though some in the Jewish community would as good as say that, although Gentiles remain God's children, they are by God's will inferior to Jews. The issue of democracy takes us a step further. This extraordinary notion, with its corollaries of pluralism and tolerance, did not arise within Rabbinic Judaism. We have yet to hear a good theological argument, as against a pragmatic case, being made within the terms of Rabbinic Judaism to endorse, much less to mandate, the practice of democracy. And this matter would immediately leave the hypothetical realm should the Orthodox parties of the State of Israel come to power.

The more restricted, communal issue concerns the present balance between *din* and the ethical moment within Rabbinic Judaism. To many Jews today, the Torah's ethical behests come with such imperative quality that they can consider them properly heard only when they are accepted categorically. To qualify their functioning as substantially as do the spokesmen of contemporary Rabbinic Judaism cannot be seen by them as other than less than what God now demands of the people of Israel. They therefore cannot consider Rabbinic Judaism, as presently interpreted, God's will for the people of God's covenant.[28]

To be sure, on a vulgar level, almost all human beings prefer personal convenience to heavy responsibility. But not being tainted by original sin, they also have a strong sense of what is good and just. Though it has been difficult to call their attention to it and more difficult to get them to live up to it, many people have acknowledged that slavery is unethical and racial discrimination is immoral. In a similar ethical way they came to realize that keeping Jews from equal rights was unjust. And most Jews who have modernized agree that any proper contemporary sense of the good ought to emphasize the equality of all human beings and, in the present case, to give women the status and opportunities hitherto available only to men. The matter is so compellingly clear to these Jews today—as other matters were in recent generations—that if this impulse cannot function supralegally, that is, to change Jewish law, they will find it necessary, for all their Jewish devotion, to function extralegally.

One reason that they will do so is that they feel they have a more satisfactory understanding of Rabbinic Judaism than it offers of itself. Watching it struggle to confront ethical issues and not be able to move very quickly to resolve them, they do not see it as God's own institution, albeit a human one, for mediating the divine will. Rather, it discloses to them the same traits they find everywhere in thoroughly human institutions. It is regularly more concerned with form than with content, with precedent than present need, with regulations than with persons, with what authorities and peers will say than with what, as best we can tell directly, God wants of us now.

In a prior generation, some such belief caused many serious-minded Jews to make general ethics, rather than Torah, the law by which they lived. Even those of us who know that the universalistic path is unreliable without the corrective guidance of Torah are not willing to forsake the way of ethics entirely for a Rabbinic Judaism which, by construing its ethical concerns as it does, appears to us to vitiate them substantially.

NOTES

1. See my "Rethinking the Reform Jewish Theory of Social Action," *Journal of Reform Judaism,* Fall 1980.
2. Aharon Lichtenstein, "Does Jewish Tradition Recognize an Ethic Independent of Halakha?" in *Modern Jewish Ethics,* ed. Marvin Fox (Ohio State University Press, 1975).
3. "Can a Religious Law Be Immoral?" in *Perspectives on Jews and Judaism,* ed. Arthur A. Chiel (Rabbinical Assembly, New York, 1978).
4. For two recent discussions, see Isadore Twersky, *Introduction to the Code of Maimonides* (Princeton, N.J., 1980), pp. 454ff. and Lawrence V. Berman, "Maimonides on the Fall of Man," *AJS Review* V (1980), 3, note 6.
5. Lichtenstein, "Jewish Tradition," pp. 82–83.
6. In his remarks to the December 1980 meeting of the Association of Jewish Studies, J. David Bleich argued in a somewhat similar linguistic fashion. I am grateful to him for allowing my student, Mr. Marc Gruber, to tape his remarks.
7. Lichtenstein, "Jewish Tradition," p. 83.
8. Ibid., p. 71.
9. Steven S. Schwarzschild, "The Question of Jewish Ethics Today," *Sh'ma,* 7/124, p. 31.
10. Lichtenstein, "Jewish Tradition," p. 71.
11. Ibid.
12. Ibid., pp. 71–74.
13. Ibid., p. 74.
14. Ibid.
15. Ibid., p. 75.
16. Schwarzschild, "The Question of Jewish Ethics," p. 31.
17. Lichtenstein, "Jewish Tradition," p. 76.
18. Ibid., p. 77.
19. Ibid.
20. Ibid., p. 79.
21. Isaac Herzog, *The Main Institutions of Jewish Law* (Soncino Press, 1936), vol. I, pp. 379–86.
22. "Judea and Samaria: Settlement and Return," *Tradition* 18:1 (1979), 48.
23. Ibid., p. 50.
24. Ibid.
25. See, for example, the criticisms of Martin Buber by thinkers as diverse as Marvin Fox and Emil Fackenheim in *The Philosophy of Martin Buber,* ed. Schilpp and Friedman (Open Court, 1967).

26. For a recent discussion, see my *Contemporary Christologies, a Jewish response* (Paulist Press, 1980), pp. 127–29; 133–34.

27. See the bold, general statement by Seymour Siegel in "Theology for Today," *Conservative Judaism* XXVIII, no. 4 (1974), 47–48. He had previously asserted these views in "Ethics and the Halakhah," *Conservative Judaism* XXV, no. 3 (1971), and projects them as part of the ideology of Conservative Judaism in his anthology *Conservative Judaism and Jewish Law* (Rabbinical Assembly, New York, 1977), p. xxiiif. Since then this position has come under increasing attack from the Conservative rightwing as a result of which Siegel was ousted from his position as chairman of the prestigious Rabbinical Assembly Commission on Law and Standards.

28. I have dealt with the liberal Jewish affirmation of personal autonomy despite an increased regard for the guidance of Jewish tradition in chapter 11 of my *Modern Theories of Judaism* (Behrman House). A fuller statement of my views of the proper process of liberal Jewish decision-making will be found in my paper, "The Demands of the Autonomous Jewish Self," in a collection of conference papers sponsored by the National Jewish Resource Center and the Center for Judaic Studies of the University of Denver.

16 / Recent Historic Events: Jewish and Christian Interpretations

1983

Several discussions about my book on contemporary Christologies[1] suggested to me that I occupy an uncommon situation in the field of contemporary Jewish thought. Most of my professional colleagues are philosophers, specializing in the medieval Jewish or modern general areas. I am one of a tiny number identifying themselves as Jewish theologians and, rarer still, one with postrabbinic training in Christian theology. Standing between these two disciplines, then, I propose to undertake a comparative theological inquiry here, hoping thereby to gain insight into the distinctive faith of each tradition. Somewhat recklessly, I should like to work holistically and try to characterize the current situation in each faith by focusing on one broad theme. I can, perhaps, reduce the risk of so grandiose an enterprise by starting from a description of the Jewish situation, which I know better, and then moving on to what appears to me to be its closest Christian parallel. I hope the heuristic gains of this effort compensate for its substantive shortcoming.[2]

JEWISH INTERPRETATIONS

For about two decades now, Jewish religious thinkers have centered most of their attention on the theological[3] implications of recent historic events. Five distinct interests can be delineated. The first two, the "death of God" and the State of Israel, aroused far more participation than the three other topics I shall explicate.

The early novels of Elie Wiesel and the first group of Richard Rubenstein's theologically revisionist articles appeared in the late 1950s.

Yet it was not until the mid-1960s that large-scale Jewish discussion of the meaning of the Holocaust began.[4] I remain convinced[5] that an important factor in finally legitimating this topic was the emergence of the Christian death-of-God movement then. In any case, the debate continued vigorously for about ten years and still sporadically resumes, though in rather ritualized fashion.

What moved the Jewish theoreticians was less the classic issue of theodicy than responding to the actual, awesome events under Hitler. Rubenstein's argument and title made Auschwitz the symbol for the new form of an old problem.[6] He, Wiesel, and Emil Fackenheim asserted that the Holocaust was unique in the history of human evil. It therefore demanded totally new responses from Jews. It was, for all its negativity, our Mt. Sinai. Wiesel insisted that its singularity took it far beyond our ability even to frame proper questions about it, much less to provide answers. Rubenstein demanded a radical rejection of the received God of Judaism, in whose place he now saw the Holy Nothing. Fackenheim, after years insisting that God's revelation (understood in Buber's contentless I-thou terms) must be the basis of modern Judaism, could no longer speak of God's presence in history. Instead, he built his Jewish commitment on the unconditional command to nurture Jewish life which came to the Jewish people from Auschwitz though no commander was discernible.[7] The responses to these views were based on new ways of restating the old defenses: it is good that people are free and responsible, even to be Nazis; God is finite; having some reason to have faith, we can trust in God even though we do not fully understand God.

The second major discussion arose out of the Holocaust controversy as a result of the 1967 Israeli Six-Day War. In the weeks prior to and during the news blackout of its first two days, the possibility of another "holocaust" loomed before world Jewry. This mood was intensified by our first experience of war by television. Those experiences were sufficient to arouse Jewish ethnic concern to levels previously unprecedented. They were then heightened by the details of an incredible victory—deliverance—and, even more miraculously, by seeing Jews enter old Jerusalem and, for the first time since the State of Israel had been established, being permitted to pray before the Temple Mount Western Wall.

The effect of those weeks on American Jewry was profound, lasting, and utterly unanticipated. Our new affluence and success in an expanding American economy had made us lukewarm to our ethnic identity and rather indifferent to the State of Israel. The frightful threat and wondrous triumph of the Six Day War made us realize how deeply Jewish we were and wanted to be, and how organically we were bound to the State of Israel. Once again, we were not alone in changing our social self-perception. The growing urban strife in America and the consequent burgeoning of ethnic consciousness in all groups undoubtedly influenced us.[8] And the ensuing years of international isolation for the Israelis and the rise of a new international anti-Semitism strengthened a post-Holocaust community's determination to make Jewish survival primary.

Theologically, the issue became what spiritual weight one should attach to the State of Israel. To Irving Greenberg it was, with the Holocaust, the second irresistible imperative transforming Jewish modernity into a new pluralistic traditionalism.[9] Fackenheim went further. He proclaimed the State of Israel the contemporary absolute of Jewish life. This followed logically on his evaluation of the Holocaust. The Commanding Voice of Auschwitz had laid an unconditional obligation upon the Jewish people to deny Hitler a posthumous victory. The State of Israel was Jewry's collective, life-affirming fulfillment of that commandment. Hence keeping it alive and flourishing was the unimpeachable, overriding Jewish responsibility.[10]

Opposition to this Israelocentrism faced the difficulty of communicating the difference between the extraordinarily important and the essential or indispensable. Specifically, the protagonists of the opposing view sought to establish that, on the biblical model, Jewish statehood must be subordinate to other beliefs, certainly in God, but also in the Jewish people itself.[11] Two political tangents of this discussion deserve mention. The one had to do with the right and criterion of criticizing the Israeli government. The other considered the long-term viability of Diaspora Jewry should the State of Israel disappear.

A third recent theme, notable mainly because our Orthodox writers rarely debate theology, centered about the possible eschatological implications of Old Jerusalem coming under Jewish sovereignty for the first time in nearly two thousand years. Some thinkers, taking seriously their daily prayers for God's return to Jerusalem, saw the spectacular events of 1967 as possibly the first glimmers of the messianic redemption. Other thinkers, chastened by the long, bitter Jewish experience of premature messianism, cautioned against this view, despite its special appeal in explaining our recent experience of terrible travail as "the birth pangs of the Messiah.[12]

Fourth, a broader segment of our community has seen the Vietnam War, Watergate, and other socially disillusioning events, requiring them to rethink the old alliance between Judaism and modernity. This has a social as well as an intellectual aspect. American Jews have long considered themselves fully at home here. Some thinkers now suggest that we must revive the category of Exile. To a considerable extent, they argue, Jews are aliens in this society. They propose utilizing the term Exile not merely in its existentialist, universal connotation of alienation but in a particular Jewish fashion, in the Bible's nationalistic usage, without thereby yielding to the Zionist secular definition, which is purely political.[13]

A rather more compelling question addresses the balance between the authority of American culture and Jewish tradition. If, in our new realism, our culture is less worthy of religious devotion, then our tradition newly commends itself to us. Not only does it suggest itself as the antidote for our society's ills but as an independent source of human value we have long ignored. We therefore need to be "more Jewish" in belief and practice than we have been.[14] The two most exciting spiritual phenomena in our community during the past decade have been the new traditionalism of liberal Jews and the ground-swell founding of *havurot,* small communities for Jewish celebration and experience.[15] Unexpectedly, too, Orthodoxy has emerged as an option for modern Jews desirous of living an authentic Jewish existence. Both movements have parallels in the general American turn to the right. The specific Jewish contours of our developments arise from considering the failures of America and the re-emergence of anti-Semitism against our memories of the Holocaust.

Fifth, our most recent issue has come out of our everyday experience in these years. Not long ago many writers were saying that our entire Jewish way of life must now be rebuilt around the Holocaust. With most of us day by day finding normality the basic condition of our lives, that older view seems faulty. Frightful disasters occur and dreadful horrors are still regularly perpetrated. We must never be blind to the hells about us or to the potential of their occurrence. But our lives are very far from a recapitulation of Auschwitz or even greatly illuminated by its uniqueness. Even God, who in Rubenstein's formulation was absent to us—"we live in a time of the Death of God"—has reappeared in the living search of at least a minority of the Jewish community.[16]

This transition can most readily be seen in the thought of Irving Greenberg, who has devoted himself wholeheartedly to the intellectual and communal tasks imposed by the Holocaust. In his earliest writing it was not clear whether he seriously dissented from Wiesel, Rubenstein, and Fackenheim that Auschwitz had taken the place of Sinai for us. Before long he not only gave it equal rank but began speaking of moment-faiths and the continuing place of God in our lives.[17] Most recently he has given further prominence to Jewish continuity, though with the radical revisions required by living in a post-Holocaust age.[18]

It seems to me that abstract, academic themes dominate contemporary Christian theology, save for liberation theology (of which more later). By contrast, Jewish thinking overwhelmingly centers on living social questions prompted by recent historical events. In theological language, my Jewish colleagues are asking, "What is God saying in what has happened to us?" To be sure, we do not hear that question articulated in those words. Jews retain a certain traditional reticence about speaking directly of God. Surely, too, some of our thinkers remain so sensitive to the agnostic Jewish environment in which they grew up and continue to move that they habitually bracket out the God-question, preferring instead to speak about the Jewish people or Jewish duty. Nonetheless, our debates involve more than ethnic interests or social concerns. They inevitably reach down to our ultimate convictions about Jewish responsibility. In the typical selectivity of a secular generation, we tune out the most important frequencies of our "signals of transcendence."

Before asking how Christian theologians approach recent events, I think it important to test and thereby try to strengthen the comprehensive hypothesis I have sought to establish. Let us inquire to what extent historic events are a long-term or only a recent Jewish religious interest. The evidence from biblical-Talmudic Judaism is unambiguous. One might even argue that this religious concern with history is as unique to Hebrew tradition as is monotheism. The prophets and rabbis regularly sought God's hand in the major historic occurrences of their time. While the theophany at Mt. Sinai may ground and limit Jewish life, the Bible spends comparatively little time on what transpired there and devotes itself in great detail to what happened in later centuries when Jews sought to live by the Torah. Though the rabbis restrict where revelation may be found,[19] they quite organically react to the destruction of the Temple or to rulers such as Hadrian by indicating what God is teaching the Jewish people through these calamities.

This pattern of interpreting the triumphs and trials of Jewish history as the operation of God's justice continued until Jewish modernity. Characteristically, it now surfaces among us only in the speeches of one or another of our European-oriented *yeshivah* heads, that is, the leaders of that part of our community which has resolutely refused to modernize. For the rest of us, as early as the nineteenth century, modernization meant secularization, substituting a scientific worldview for a religious one. Those modernized Jews who maintained some effective belief in God quickly gave up the old mechanistic, Deuteronomic reading of history. The modern concepts of God made history almost entirely the domain of social forces and human moral decision, not God's direct action.[20]

This modern demythologization of history is of some importance for our theme. Consider, for example, the response of Jewry to the "Holocaust" of its time, the 1903 Kishinev massacre. Jews worldwide could not imagine such an act occurring among civilized people, and the conscience of much of Western civilization motivated almost universal protest. Despite the pain, the modernists did not try to explain this tragedy in terms of theological verities they had long given up. Rather, the outrage was blamed, variously, on a failure of conscience and reason, a cynical governmental diversion of the masses, a capitalist plot against the proletariat, or a result of the Jews not being expected to stand up in self-defense. Rubenstein's charge, half a century later, that the Holocaust made it impossible to believe in the old God of history may have applied to the Jewish traditionalists who still affirmed Deuteronomic justice in history. (Factually, some recent data dispute this charge.)[21] However, this interpretation of the death of God simply did not apply to the mass of modernized Jews. They had secularized long before the Holocaust and were largely atheistic or agnostic. Those who had liberal concepts of God knew nothing of a God who was "the ultimate omnipotent actor in history."[22]

If so, did secularization mean the end of the classic Jewish perception of history as a continuing scene of God's self-manifestation? A surface examination of liberal Jewish theologies in the early decades of this century bears out that surmise. Hermann Cohen, whose neo-Kantian, philosophic reinterpretation of Judaism set the standard and problematic of most of the succeeding thinkers, described Judaism in terms of its central, that is, its regulative "idea," ethical monotheism. His younger German compatriot Leo Baeck yoked religious consciousness to the master's rationalism and spoke of "the essence" of Judaism. Both notions derived from German idealism, in which the empirical is radically subordinated to the rational—as good as dissolving history into concept.

I wish to argue that, on a deeper level, this seeming ahistoricalism is itself their response to what God was doing in their history. Their idealistic Judaism arose, though they do not remind us of it, as a means of coping theologically with Jewish Emancipation. The political and social enfranchisement of the Jews in the general society was not one event but, by their time, a century-long process. While most Jews enthusiastically accepted their new human equality, many doubted they could adopt a way of life determined by their society and yet remain authentically Jewish. The decades of experiment in worship, observance, and rationalization finally reached maturity in the thought of Hermann Cohen. If the University of Marburg philosopher did not discuss his system as a response to Emancipation, it was only because he took that move for granted even as he exemplified its benefits. Note that his philosophy of Judaism elevates Judaism's eternal idea against the books tradition says were given at Sinai. He thus validates the authority of contemporary reason in Judaism, making rational relevance the criterion of Jewish authenticity. Baeck employed a similar strategy to reach similar goals. He only expanded the dimensions of the immediate experience which Jews would now make sovereign.[23]

As the twentieth century moved on, the succeeding philosophers became more historically self-conscious. Our other great rationalistic system-builder, Mordecai Kaplan, is a good case in point. Kaplan justifies his radicalism by pointing to the reinterpretations brought on by the prior major turning points in Jewish history, the Exile and the destruction of the Second Temple. He argues that the Emancipation is another of these, requiring us to rethink and reshape Judaism stringently to our democratic social situation. Since our cultural ethos is scientific, Kaplan reconstructs Jewish institutional life, practices, values, and ideas in naturalistic terms. In this system, American naturalism replaces German philosophic idealism but the function of reason remains the same: to establish the emancipated Jew as the master of the Jewish past, though also its beneficiary. This, once again, is a philosophy of the "revelation" given by historic events.[24]

A decade earlier in Germany, Martin Buber had reached his unique insight about the reality and authority of genuine interpersonal encounter. In this nonrationalist "system," history has renewed importance. The homogenized chronology of rationalism now is accompanied by the personalistic experience that some moments are far richer in meaning than others. By this theory Buber reached the same goal as the rationalists: he had acknowledged the revelatory authority of the Emancipation and met it by giving the present encounter hegemony over tradition.

At the same time, Buber had provided modernized Jews with a non-Orthodox understanding of how God might be speaking in contemporary events. Israel, the people, can today, as in the past, encounter God, this time in the wilderness of contemporary history. Buber responded to events in his lifetime from this perspective. Zionism was to be the modern counterpart of the ancient Hebrews' corporate relationship with God; the *kibbutz* was the noble Jewish effort to live community in full dimension; the Israeli need to reach out and make common cause with the Arabs was the test of Zionism's Jewishness; though Eichmann was guilty of the most heinous crimes against the Jewish people, Buber argued that it did not befit our character to take his life. The Holocaust so troubled him that he rethought his theory of evil, acknowledging now the terrifying biblical truth that, on occasion, God withdraws from us, "hiding His face."[25]

The other two distinctive system-makers of this century, Franz Rosenzweig and Abraham Heschel, would seem the exceptions to my hypothesis. Since I believe I can somewhat mitigate the refutation by way of Heschel, I shall speak first about him, though Rosenzweig wrote nearly half a century earlier.

Heschel interpreted Judaism as a religion centered on time rather than space.[26] But he did not initiate the contemporary Jewish theological interest in historic events. Before 1967, the opposite was actually the case. In his system, which was fully elaborated prior to that fateful year, contemporary history has no role, except perhaps as secularizing villain. I read Heschel's work as a religionist's protest against the desanctification of the world and, in particular, against the liberal secularization of Jewish faith. In quite classic fashion, therefore, Heschel made the recovery of revelation the goal of his apologetics. He thereby returned Sinai and the prophets to their authoritative place and made the rabbis their legitimate interpreters. In his Judaism contemporary history was only another arena for the application of these eternal truths. At that stage his attitude to recent history merely involved him in reversing the liberal Jewish manner of accommodating to modernity, though he retained its ethical thrust.

The return of Old Jerusalem to Jewish sovereignty changed that. Heschel's book *Israel: An Echo of Eternity* movingly describes what this place, Jerusalem, means to him as a Jew, and therefore what this event of return means to Judaism.[27] Intriguingly for so traditionalistic a thinker, he makes no messianic argument. Rather, he limits himself to the theological significance of geography. He provides a phenomenology of standing on the sites which constitute some of the people of Israel's most sacred symbols. Thus, though Heschel's thought was based on the classic tenet that ancient revelation determined contemporary Judaism, he too was religiously overcome by a modern event.

We cannot say the same for Rosenzweig, though it must quickly be noted that he died in 1929 after a meteoric intellectual career, in the last few years of which he was incapacitated by an almost total paralysis.[28] Like Heschel, he saw revelation as the heart of Judaism, though Rosenzweig posited a nonverbal, "contentless" (by classic Jewish standards) encounter with God.[29] As a result, Rosenzweig too had no significant doctrine of the Jewish people and, alone of all twentieth-century Jewish thinkers, turned his back on contemporary events (though accepting the Emancipation).[30] He made history a Christian domain, with authentic Jews already participating in eternity by living the Torah. They thus had no religious interest in what passes for history.

Rosenzweig's thought clearly counts against my argument concerning the centrality of history to modern as to ancient Jewish theology. If he is correct, the concerns of my generation are an accident of our situation but not Jewishly essential. I think it fair to rejoin that this aspect of Rosenzweig's thought has been an embarrassment to those who would follow him. On the issue of eternity, not the moment, he has been almost totally rejected by the Jewish community on the basis of its lived experience. Any theory that would render the Holocaust and the State of Israel peripheral to being a Jew cannot be right. I suggest that Rosenzweig came to his extreme stand because of his heavy polemic agenda against the opposing views of Judaism, the Orthodox, the liberal, and the Zionist. This caused him to emphasize God and contentless revelation to the detriment of the folk and human aspects of Judaism. Consequently, the philosophical idealism which Rosenzweig was seeking to escape managed to reassert itself and frustrate the protoexistentialism he had creatively initiated to take its place.

Let me sum up my Jewish case by adducing one further piece of evidence. With the exception of Buber, the great system-builders give almost no attention to the Mt. Sinai experience. The rationalists as good as dissolve it into mind and conscience. Heschel assimilates it to his general theory of revelation as sym-pathos, despite his commitment to Sinai's uniqueness. Rosenzweig, describing revelation as love, speaks of Sinai only symbolically. Buber, applying the I-thou relationship to the national level, searches the Exodus account with intriguing personalistic openness. [31] But having devoted one chapter of one work to the topic, he does not return to it. Thus the Jewish concern for history in these thinkers is not attention to a unique occurrence in the past but to the events of their time.

It may well be countered that this is so because the thinkers I have analyzed, except Heschel, are liberal Jews. If only Orthodoxy can be Judaism, my argument again fails. But I see no useful way of debating the issue of what constitutes authentic Judaism. I would only point out how Orthodoxy itself has changed as a result of events. Particularly notable is its about-face toward Zionism. What was almost a complete rejection of this irreligiosity when modern secular Zionism arose, has now become almost total support, mainly enthusiastic but partially grudging. This transformation was not the result of a changed philosophy of history but of a realistic response to what happened. Moreover, I cannot here treat any Orthodox Jewish philosopher because there are no twentieth-century systematic expositions of traditional Jewish faith comparable to those of the liberals. The least that can be said of my hypothesis, then, is that it characterizes such Jewish theology as we have. I gladly acknowledge that I am speaking about liberal Judaism. I must add that the systems I have described raise to the level of academic reflection the beliefs of the overwhelming majority of concerned American Jews.

CHRISTIAN INTERPRETATIONS

In turning now to contemporary Christian theology, let me identify a methodological problem. The differing Christian attitude toward recent events, I perceive, is not totally distinct from that of the Jewish theoreticians. Polemicists prefer to draw battlelines sharply. They force a decisive choice—and then the advocate is tempted to delineate the two stands so as to make the decision well-nigh irresistible. I think no false sense of ecumenism secretly makes me see only indistinct lines of dissimilarity between us. Even in disagreement the positions partially overlap. Living in the same culture, brought ever more closely into contact by democracy, media, and travel, utilizing the same repertoire of civilization symbol-structures, we are bound to be alike. That does not rule out genuine, fundamental opposition, but it explains why seeking to discern where our disagreements begin and leave off is a most subtle and often frustrating task.

To some extent, the greatest similarity in dealing with recent events may be seen in the attitudes of some evangelical Christians and

Orthodox Jewish thinkers. Both can discern in the happenings around them signs that the eschaton is breaking in. I do not know how much weight to attach to the different historical valences they consider meaningful. The Christian thinkers work with the negative aspects of events and resonate with vibrations of the power of the Antichrist. Because of Jerusalem, the Jews are overwhelmed by a positive indication the Messiah may be nigh.

Even in this convergence I detect somewhat contrary evaluations of the pre-Messianic history in which we stand. The evangelicals seem to me to esteem the Second Coming and its salvation so highly that present events are, by comparison, of small significance. Accepting the Christ and remaining steadfast in one's faith, while devotedly awaiting, even anticipating, his speedy return are the religiously desirable virtues. Obviously, these will affect one's everyday life. But the time frame radically distinguishes between the value of this era and that which was when Jesus walked this earth and that which will be when he returns.

Jews, for all their commitment to the coming of the Messiah, are less eschatologically oriented. God's Torah directs them to the here-and-now, not to the life of world-to-come, though it awaits them. Their sense of the Messiah remains so human that figures as ordinary as Bar Kochba and Sabbetai Zevi could be taken for the Shoot of Jesse. Though the great eschatological drama of resurrection, judgment, and eternal life ensues in due course, the advent of the Messiah will occur in profane, not transformed, history. I suggest, then, that even on the right we can distinguish between the faiths on this theme. With some hesitation, I find here what I see more clearly elsewhere: the Jewish thinkers can be deeply moved by *specific* happenings, while the Christian theologians seek to read the signs of the times *in general*.

The contours of difference emerge more readily when I read less orthodox thinkers. The most dramatic confrontation with contemporary history would seem to occur in the European praxis theologians like Moltmann and Metz, and the South American liberationists. In the late 1960s I would have described the European movement as a response to the student revolution and the prospect of great social change. But for more than a decade now, no particular occurrence—the Polish worker's revolt, for example—has had anywhere near similar impact. And Hispanic liberation theology likewise seems far more socially than historically oriented.

Something also must be said now about the power of events to reshape theology. For the Jews, the Emancipation, the Holocaust, the

State of Israel, the gaining of Old Jerusalem, and, potentially, other happenings can cause fundamental revisions in our thought. These events changed the thinkers' teaching concerning God and Torah and, most markedly, their doctrines of the people of Israel. I do not see historical incidents impinging as strongly on Christian thinkers. Recent experiences may transform Christian witness and the tone of Christian existence, as in recent years, but I do not see events causing so fundamental a rethinking of faith among Christians as among Jews. Somewhat less hesitantly now, I would identify the Christian concern as responding to the culture generally, while the Jews have reacted more directly to specific historic occurrences.

Perhaps I can go a step further. The socially oriented Christian theologians seem to me to be answering the Marxists' legitimate criticism of the society and the church. The leftists co-opted and perverted the church's social ethics. Now that the ethical duplicity of the secular critics is plain, the church can reclaim its social values, challenge the Marxists for their institutional failure, and, by co-opting the Marxist social analysis, renew its mandate of stewardship. My ethical admiration for that stance does not change my judgment about our diversity in theologically confronting our time.

Somewhat similar attitudes emerge in two lesser themes of Christian writing. One is the continuing effort to create a theology of culture. While this activity seems less lively to me in recent years than it did in the exciting days of H. Richard Niebuhr and Paul Tillich, little similar work surfaces among Jews. Far less predictable is the outcome of contemporary Christian thinkers' engagement with Asian religions, now freshly seen as dialogue partners rather than as objects of missionary zeal. I read this as a broadening of contemporary Christian theology's cultural horizon from barely beyond the West to include the whole globe. Accompanying it has been an enlarged sense of the equality of humankind and the universality of genuine spirituality. This poses a new challenge to Christianity as to other faiths' particularity. But these activities fit in well with my earlier speculations about the central orientation of Christian thought.

Even clearer insight is yielded by a retrospective look at the Protestant death-of-God agitation of the mid-1960s. The four theoreticians who formulated the issues under discussion then—Paul Van Buren, Thomas J. J. Altizer, Gabriel Vahanian, and William Hamilton—based their positions, different as they were, on cultural considerations. Altizer's cyclical view of opposing spiritual epochs, based vaguely on Mircea

Eliade's view of religion, yielded a negative judgment about Western civilization and contemporary religion. Van Buren called for demythologizing the Son to conform to the philosophic temper of the times. Vahanian and Hamilton examined immediate religious experience and found it empty. In our culture, they proclaimed, God was dead. Not until Richard Rubenstein's writing came to their attention did it occur to them to argue that an event in their lifetime, the Holocaust, was an immediate refutation of the existence of a good and omnipotent God. And the Nazi experience never did play much of a role in their subsequent discussion.

In the near twenty years since those days, some Christian thinkers have acknowledged that, at the least, this event requires some reconsideration of theologies formulated before evil like the Holocaust could be imagined. Roy Eckardt, Franklin Littell, John Pawlikowski, and others have tried to rethink their Christianity in terms of this human and Jewish horror. Paul Van Buren has gone even further and now has begun to study what it might mean to think rigorously of Christianity as an offshoot of Jewish religious experience. Such Christian theologians are doing very much what Jews have done, but I shall not further consider their work. I cannot tell to what extent they are responding to what happened or to the challenge of Jewish colleagues for whom attention to this matter is a condition of dialogue. How such an event might find a proper place in Christian thought remains unclear to me. My doubts arise from the fact that the overwhelming majority of Christian theologians do not yet consider the Holocaust a sufficiently significant event to merit much attention in their thinking.

I have come across only two Christian thinkers who have responded to historic events somewhat as Jews have. Karl Rahner has pondered the theological implications of the declining world influence of Christianity and its potential fall to a minority impulse in Western civilization. To Jews, long accustomed to Christian apologists arguing that the success of Christianity demonstrates its truth, the change in Christian power over the past two decades has been striking. Rahner resolutely rejects all such temporal criteria of worth as contrary to the kenotic traditions of the church. To the contrary, Christianity most authentically fulfils its mission as a servant church. It may now well be required by God to become a church in diaspora, serving in the humility befitting a relatively powerless, scattered institution. But that will only confirm, not contradict, its central truth.

Rahner's effort here is comparable to the reconsideration forced on Jewish thinkers by the Emancipation drastically changing their social status. But where their experience could compel them to rethink radically the nature of their Jewishness, Rahner's reaction to this apparently substantial historical shift barely impinges upon his central understanding of Christianity. The notion of a church in diaspora is only hinted at in his comprehensive volume *Foundations of Christian Faith.*[32]

A far more direct investigation of the meaning of historical events in Christianity may be found in Wolfhart Pannenberg's *Human Nature, Election and History.*[33] Pannenberg's interest in history is well known, since he contended in *Jesus—God and Man* that an academic historical approach to the evidence available validates the factual occurrence of Jesus' resurrection. In the last three of these lectures he probes the meaning of historic events since the Christ. He deplores those tendencies in Christianity, from Augustine through Luther and beyond, to separate the true domain of Christian existence from the commonplace realm of sociopolitical affairs. This led, after the collapse of the medieval effort to establish a proper Christendom, to the secular modern state, where religion is reduced to a private activity. Pannenberg calls for a proper recognition of the social dimension of Christianity. He emphasizes the importance of the "people of God" motif in the New Testament and Christian belief, holding it to be more important even than the notion of church, but, in any case, equally significant a doctrine as that of individual salvation.[34]

I was particularly curious to see what he made of this as he applied it to our time. Permit me to explain my special interest. In my paper on contemporary Christologies, I had excoriated Pannenberg for his religious anti-Semitism. He had continued the old Christian-Protestant-Lutheran charge that with the crucifixion the religion of the Jews died. I was outraged that he, a post-Holocaust theologian, in Germany of all countries, seemed to have no consciousness of the social consequences of centuries of such teaching. The anti-Semitism of Christian theology had made it possible for secularists to transform "Judaism is dead" into "Jews should be killed." While reworking this material into book form, I learned that in a work of the early 1970s Pannenberg had modified his earlier view. He then described his prior statement as "the resupposition of a view widespread in German Protestantism, that the religion of the Law and the Jewish religion are identical."[35] But when Richard John Neuhaus kindly brought us together to discuss this matter, Pannenberg could not understand why I should assess his thought in terms of the previous German generation's actions, which, plainly enough, he considered totally reprehensible. I therefore was particularly interested in what he might say about recent historic events.

In his final lecture Pannenberg devotes one long paragraph to the meaning of the two World Wars, which he discusses in terms of modern nationalism. Because it has been secularized, nationalism has been affected for evil as well as for good, as has the other chief organizing principle secularism utilized, liberalism. (Both nationalism and liberalism have Judeo-Christian origins, he argues.) The evil effects on nationalism have been most pronounced, leading to World War I's orgy of European self-destruction and an end to Europe's world domination. Worse, "It meant that the divine vocation that was perceived earlier in experiences of national chosenness, had been forfeited by nationalistic self-glorification." He then continues:

> That judgment became definitive with World War II. Among the hardest hit was the German nation. The single most serious reason for that in theological as well as in historical terms may have been the persecution and attempted annihilation of the Jewish people. This attempt disclosed to the world the radical nature of that nationalism. The German case demonstrated in a particularly decisive way the dangerous potential of nationalism, but it is uncertain whether the general significance of that experience has yet been properly understood in the contemporary world.[36]

The ethical import of this passage is admirable. But it leaves a Jewish reader troubled. Events can apparently teach a Christian theologian something about nationalism, in this case particularly about German nationalism, though here that instance is sublimated to the world's problem with it. Events do not, in this instance, cause the theologian to take a hard look at his own religious tradition. Surely, that such an evil made itself manifest in the birthplace of Protestant Christianity and still one of its most important intellectual centers, is not a trivial matter. How could a nation with such a vigorous church life, Catholic as well as Protestant, have become so demonic? Should there not be a thorough critique and rethinking of the intellectual factors in the church which made this possible?

If we follow the Talmudic dictum of judging others by looking only at the scale of merit,[37] we may say that Pannenberg's lectures, for all that they do not say so explicitly, are a judgment on and a reconstruction of Christian theology. While Pannenberg does not discuss Christian theological anti-Semitism here, he does isolate and correct the basic error he sees in prior interpretations of Christianity: it was too individualistically oriented and now needs to take more direct responsibility for the nation in which it functions. If that is the proper understanding, Pannenberg is one of the few Christian thinkers I have encountered who have allowed their basic faith to be modified by recent events.

Can we now provide some reasons for the dissimilar interests of contemporary Jewish and Christian theologians?

Let us say the simplest yet most important thing first: we do not know when or where or why God acts. All religions know moments highly charged with meaning and long stretches when memory must take the place of revelation. Who is to say that perhaps in recent years God chose to act toward the Jews with a directness and significance God did not in the same period manifest to Christians? In other centuries one might have made the same observation the other way around. Let us therefore proceed with great humility. We may be seeking to fathom matters which radically exceed our depth of penetration. But let that not keep us from seeking to explore that which mind and soul make available to us.

In this spirit of tentativeness, two sociological caveats ought to be introduced. To begin with, the distinctive Jewish theological concerns may reflect the situation of those who do it rather than Judaism's essential faith. Most Jews writing in this area are not professional theologians. Their agenda is not set by a well-established guild and they are not centrally concerned with the academic challenges one's seminary or university colleagues may raise. Even those of our writers who are academics work in disciplines other than Jewish theology. As a result, we are far more likely to attend to the realities faced by our community than to the abstract issues made significant by generations of learned, abstract, academic debate.

Second, our community is small, conscious of being a tiny minority everywhere but in the State of Israel and sensitive to the perils to its survival. We magnify every trauma, and having recently undergone previously unimaginable pain—even in terms of the long, anguished history of Jewish suffering—we have been humanly and spiritually changed. But we have also been overwhelmed by several unbelievable triumphs in our time. We can, therefore, often find ourselves quite confused as to how such extremes as we have known can testify to one ultimate reality.

By these familial Jewish standards we find it almost incomprehensible, for example, that when the Christian Lebanese were under severe assault by their Moslem Lebanese brothers and their Syrian allies, there was no Western Christian outcry. Perhaps the vastness of Christianity simply gives a different scale to any individual event. Thus, for all Rahner's genuine humility, he can know that even a diminished church will contain some hundreds of millions of remaining believers. That should surely keep it alive until the Spirit manifests itself again in the church's social status. We do not have this numeric assurance. Nonetheless, Jews may well ask what God is saying to them in keeping them so few and so imperiled. However, with this question about the theology of Jewish sociology, we have moved on to the more important level of our analysis.

I wish to suggest that the differing responses of Jewish and Christian theologians to recent historic events is largely due to their different paradigms of religious reality. For Jews, that is the Covenant with the people of Israel begun at Mt. Sinai; for Christians, it is the New Covenant made through the life and death of Jesus the Christ and carried on through the church. If we contrast these two religions to Asian faiths, the many similarities between Judaism and Christianity quickly stand out. The structure and content of the relationships with God clearly show a "family resemblance."

Yet there remain major differences between them. For our purposes, let me point to the rather diverse balance each faith gives to God's role and to that of God's human partner in the covenants. I believe we will find this theological divergence determinative of the phenomenon to which I have been calling attention.

In Judaism God initially fulfills the Covenant promises to the patriarchs by expanding Jacob's family to a populous nation, by taking them out of Egypt, giving them the Torah, and setting them as a people on their own Land. The act of receiving the Law-and-Teaching climaxes the early relationship and sets the conditions of all that is to follow. But it includes a commitment to the everyday history which will come after Sinai, in which God's care will regularly make itself felt. Then, too, the people of Israel, though utterly subordinate to their King/Lord/Creator/Only-God-of-the-universe, are active agents in the Covenant-making process. More, by assenting to being yoked to this God, they agree to bear the personal and corporate responsibility of living out God's Torah in history. By rabbinic times and the emergence of the doctrine of the Oral as well as the Written Law-and-Teaching, the rabbis become the effective shapers of the continuing meaning of Torah. They then richly endow the ordinary Jew with duties to sanctify life as perhaps only priests had thought of doing in prior times.

With secularization, modern Jewish thinkers transformed the ancient notion of the Covenant. Under the impact of science, God's providence was reinterpreted as less active, while the formerly limited role of human agency in the Covenant was extended almost to the point of dominance. As I analyze it, this transition did not negate the old covenantal faith that God was continually involved in the people of Israel's efforts to live by Torah. Thus, despite modernization, Jews could remain open to the possibility that contemporary history might be revelatory. To put this in the less tortured language of a simpler age, they could still ask what God was saying to them in their history.

It seems to me that Christianity's New Covenant does not as easily provide for such a modernized religious interest in recent events. What is involved, I am suggesting, is a sense of time which, for all its similarity to Judaism, here exposes its difference.

At the heart of the New Covenant lies God's utterly gracious and incomparable generosity in sending the Son and thereby assuming personal responsibility for atoning for human sinfulness. God's act-of-love in the Christ is so extraordinary that God's action cannot have the same sort of continuity in Christian lives that God's partnership has after God's gift of the Torah at Mt. Sinai. To be sure, when the Parousia comes, all that was promised and foreshadowed in the life of the Christ will be gloriously fulfilled in ways beyond our imagining. In the interim God does not, of course, forsake the newly called-forth people of God. The Holy Spirit is with them, acting in their lives, their institutions, and their history. But I am suggesting that the interim work of the Spirit, though real and powerful, is of a different order than that of the God who gives a Teaching rather than a person of the triune Godhead. For the God of the Sinaitic Covenant remains personally involved with those who, alone in all the world, seek to live by God's Torah.

To better understand the differentiating thrust which will influence contemporary Christian theologians who seek to modernize the classic doctrine of the Holy Spirit, we must first seek what the traditional notion of the New Covenant makes of the role of the human partner. To Jewish eyes, Christianity's overwhelming sense of God's graciousness renders human beings in the New Covenant more thoroughly subordinated and passive in relation to God than are the Hebrews of the Covenant of Sinai. To be sure, there are major differences here between Catholic and Protestant teaching. Yet, in terms of the Jewish religious self-perception, Christianity as a whole seems to create a rather different balance between God and humankind. Christianity does call on us to open our hearts to faith and be ready to receive God's truth. In various interpretations it stresses the importance of the church and the life of sacraments as crucial to salvation. Yet, as Jews view it, in classic Christianity the balance is radically weighted toward God's side by the utterly unparallelable act-of-love God once did. Moreover, it should be noted that Christian salvation is primarily directed to the individual by God, though in varying interpretations the group, that is, the church, plays a role in it. Hence what happens to individual Christians is likely to have more significance to them than what happens to their community. Thus, Rahner appears to be predominantly occupied with the individual human being and God, and only secondarily with the church. By contrast, when Pannenberg needs models for his newly socialized Christianity, he draws them almost entirely from Hebrew Scripture.

The modernization of the New Covenant pioneered the radical activation of the human role and the de-emphasis on God's providence which is typical of liberal religion. What happens to the Holy Spirit in this, and where it is now seen to operate, I am speculating, keeps contemporary theologians from envisioning recent events as "revelatory." This is not to argue that events can never play such a role in Christianity. In a previous time, when Providence was strongly activist, the Holy Spirit might be seen in happenings as varied as the Crusades or the Reformation. Today, with our scientific view of existence making the Holy Spirit less likely to be seen as objectively active, historic events retreat in importance for Christians. Rather, with salvation understood in primarily personal terms and religion now conceived of largely in experiential terms, the Holy Spirit is more likely to be seen acting in the inner life of individuals than in the occurrences which befall the church as a whole or some significant part of it. But I have now strained my thesis to its limit. In extenuation, I ask you to remember my intention: I have been trying to clarify why what seems so obviously critical to one faith, Judaism, has not been so to another faith, Christianity, though both lived through the same history.

At least we can say that this investigation illustrates again the notion that we are apt to perceive about us that which our perspective on reality permits us to see. Perhaps in the clash of all the other factors which affect our perception, understanding our theological lenses does not explain very much. But if it helps enable once contentious religions to understand and live better with one another despite their differences, that will be accomplishment enough.

NOTES

1. *Contemporary Christologies: A Jewish Response* (New York: Paulist, 1980).

2. In many ways I see this paper as an extension of the method utilized in *Christologies* (cf. #1–9).

3. When Jews can bring themselves to use this term, they do so in a sense far looser than that of Christians. Not having dogma or creed as Christians do, working instead out of the rabbinic openness to ideas and images which is structured by required action rather than by confessions of faith, Jews tend to be wary of theology lest it mean required statements or specifications of belief. Yet we have always had thinking people who, while living by this believing way, have tried to determine what it meant to them abstractly. In our time of high intellectual activity and social challenge, there has been a great deal of such thought. This matter recurs in this paper. Note, e.g., the discussion below of the people who work at what I would call Jewish theology.

4. The Eichmann trial and Hannah Arendt's provocative thesis on the effect of Jewish cooperation with the Nazis gave the discussion initial impetus. That was under way by 1963, but it was not until 1966 that the first major Jewish gathering dealt with the issue, the then annual symposium sponsored by *Judaism.* Fackenheim, Popkin, Steiner, and Wiesel participated, and their remarks were published in *Judaism* 16 (1967) 269–84, under the telling title "Jewish Values in the Post-Holocaust Future."

5. This theme has concerned me in a number of my articles and books where I have dealt with the change which has come over Jewish thought in the past two decades. With Jews anxious to protect the status they had gained as one of America's three major religions, they could never admit the widespread agnosticism of secularized Jews. Hence the Protestant death-of-God movement seemed for a time a positive liberation from the long-repressed hypocrisy of Jewish religiosity. And it is the collapse of that self-perception (of not needing religion) which has brought about the new Jewish interest in personal spirituality.

6. Note the title of his book, which became the focus of this discussion: *After Auschwitz* (Indianapolis: Bobbs-Merrill, 1966).

7. For a summary discussion of this material, see chapter 9, "Confronting the Holocaust," in my book *Choices in Modern Jewish Thought* (New York: Behrman House, 1983). Most of the distinctive positions in the debate are discussed there. Note particularly the contribution of Michael Wyschogrod, who has given the most careful analysis of Fackenheim's argument, originally in "Faith and the Holocaust," *Judaism* 20 (1971) 286–94. My own argument concerning the uniqueness of the Holocaust is given at the end of the chapter noted above.

8. My treatment of this material may be seen in *The Mask Jews Wear* (New York: Simon and Schuster, 1973) 58ff., and see the context.

9. The most easily available statement is in *Auschwitz: Beginning of a New Era?* ed. Eva Fleischner (New York: Ktav, 1974), in his statement "Cloud of Smoke, Pillar of Fire" (31ff.).

10. See, e.g., his paper "The Holocaust and the State of Israel: Their Relation," in Fleischner, *Auschwitz* 205ff., and passim in his papers collected under the title *The Jewish Return into History* (New York: Schocken, 1978).

11. My rejection of this position may be found in two articles, originally one long paper, published as "Liberal Judaism's Effort to Invalidate Relativism without Mandating Orthodoxy," *Go and Study,* ed. Samuel Fishman and Raphael Jospe (New York: Ktav, 1980), and "The Liberal Jews in Search of an Absolute," *Cross Currents* 29 (1979) 9–14.

12. See the symposium "The Religious Meaning of the Six Day War," *Tradition* 10, no. 2 (Summer 1968) 5–20. A further exchange between Shubert Spero and Norman Lamm in the wake of the Egyptian-Israeli Yom Kippur War of 1973 is instructive: *Sh'ma* 4/73 (May 3, 1974) 98ff. Also Shubert Spero, "The Religious Meaning of the State of Israel," *Forum,* 1976, no. 1, 69–82. A related discussion is found in Lawrence Kaplan's "Divine Promises—Conditional and Absolute," *Tradition* 18, no. 2 (Summer 1979) 35–43.

13. The literature on this topic is too diffuse for easy citation. A good example of diverse opinions is found in *Dimensions* 5, no. 3 (Spring 1971) 5–21. One of the earliest statements of the existentialist interpretation is found in Arthur A. Cohen, *The Natural and the Supernatural Jew* (New York, Pantheon, 1962) 179ff.

14. On the new traditionalism, see chapter 10, "A Theology of Modern Orthodoxy," in *Choices* (n. 7 above).

15. Eugene B. Borowitz, "The Changing Forms of Jewish Spirituality," *America* 140 (1979) 346–50.

16. Ibid.

17. Notice the section on "Moment Faiths" in the paper cited in n. 9 above.

18. As in a number of presently unpublished papers, including one delivered at a meeting in June 1981, "The Transformation of the Covenant."

19. Note how limited and how ambivalent their relation is to the *bat kol,* their closest counterpart to the biblical spirit of God: article "Bat Kol," *Encyclopedia Judaica* 4, 324.

20. *Ideas of Jewish History,* ed. Michael A. Meyer (New York: Behrman, 1974) xii, and note the tone of all the historians mentioned from Heinrich Graetz on.

21. Reeve Robert Brenner, *The Faith and Doubt of Holocaust Survivors* (New York: Free Press, 1980) 222ff.

22. Eugene B. Borowitz, "God and Man in Judaism Today," *Judaism* 13 (1974) 298–308.

23. For a fuller discussion, see chaps. 2 and 3 in *Choices* (n. 7 above).

24. He is treated in chap. 4 of *Choices.*

25. The best analysis of this material remains Maurice Friedman, *Martin Buber, The Life of Dialogue* (New York: Harper, 1960). For the early and late stages of Buber's thought on evil, see chaps. 15 and 16.

26. *The Sabbath* (New York: Abelard Schuman, 1952).

27. *Israel: An Echo of Eternity* (New York: Farrar, Straus and Giroux, 1969).

28. Nahum N. Glatzer, *Franz Rosenzweig: His Life and Thought* (New York: Schocken, 1953) 108ff.

29. Ibid. 285, where the theory is succinctly put. Its critical consequences are spelled out in the correspondence with Buber, reproduced in Franz Rosenzweig, *On Jewish Learning* (New York: Schocken, 1955) 109ff.

30. See my discussion on "The Problem of the Form of a Jewish Theology," *Hebrew Union College Annual* (Cinn.) 40–41 (1969–70) 391–408, where I discuss the similarity of structural form in Heschel and Rosenzweig.

31. For Rosenzweig, the material in n. 29 above is apt. For Buber, see his *Moses* (Oxford: East and West Library, 1946) 110ff.

32. New York: Seabury, 1978.

33. Philadelphia: Westminster, 1977.

34. Ibid., e.g., 100–101, 106–107.

35. See the Foreword to his *The Apostle's Creed in the Light of Today's Questions* (Philadelphia: Westminster, 1972).

36. *Human Nature* 104–105.

37. *Pirke Avot* 1.6.

17 / The Autonomous Jewish Self

1984

Questioners commonly challenge me with a Jewish version of the fallacy of misplaced confidence. For generations now, liberal Jews have made Western culture their surrogate for Torah—with disastrous results. While one might have accepted some Jewish sacrifice as the necessary accompaniment of a seismic shift to living in a new and better world, thinking in such other-directed terms in our situation seems ridiculous. Western civilization itself ails desperately. It not only does not merit being our religion, it seems likely to escape paganization only by the rebirth of the sort of moral devotion which faith in a commanding God can alone provide. Why then do liberal Jews not stop asking first what our society demands from them and attend instead to the claims that Judaism makes of all who wish to be authentic Jews?

Socially put, why are liberal Jews so half-hearted about their well-advertised return to traditional practices? Do we not know, no matter to what depth of conscious pride or embarrassment have caused us to repress it, that genuine Jewish piety means living by traditional Jewish law? If we are not ready to accept the whole law, then for the sake of the unity of all Israel, can we not now immediately move in one limited but critical area: to follow Orthodox Jewish law, in all its diversity, as our basis for Jewish marriages and divorces?

On rare occasions these challenges sound a metaphysical tone. Questioners cannot understand why Jews who acknowledge that religious duties are largely of human origin cannot simply accommodate those who know their standards are not their own but God's. How can liberal Jews utter an occasional absolute "no" when they proudly boast that all authority is substantially human and therefore open to revision?

My sort of liberal Jews will want to begin a response, I think, by carefully distinguishing between the failures of Western civilization and its lacking any value whatsoever. Many of the vital and creative aspects of contemporary Jewish life arose as a result of our emancipation. Jewish aesthetics has moved beyond ritual silver, manuscript illumination and synagogue music to embrace arts and styles that greatly enrich our Jewish lives. Jewish scholarship is not only fecund beyond our fondest expectations of but twenty years ago, it excites us intellectually through its use of a Western hermeneutic applied chronologically to texts examined critically. American Jewry exhibits an activism unique in the Diaspora Jewish experience. Zionism was the first great fruit of the fusion of the Western notion of social responsibility and the Jewish commitment to life. By now we consider it a premise of Jewish duty that we should help determine the course of our society and take political action for the State of Israel or Jews in peril. And—limiting this list to four examples—by adapting ourselves to America we have created a Jewish style which shows signs of being a worthy successor to other great amalgams of Jewish life and a host culture, such as Spanish and Polish Jewish life.

These and many other smaller triumphs exist because many Jews, against the advice of their leaders, believed that the spiritual survival of the Jewish community would never be assured by seeking to preserve Jewish life as isolated as possible from the newly opened up Western world. Rather, they knew that Jewish well-being depended on accepting the risks of entering the general society and actively seeking to benefit Jewish life from it. In the mid-nineteenth century—and even now in some quarters—this commitment to energetic involvement with Western civilization was seen as the death knell of Judaism. Today, a century or so later, the overwhelming majority of Jews, including a very substantial number of Orthodox Jews, is determined that they and their children shall have the best of both heritages. Liberal Jews like myself see in this historic transformation of Jewish community values a validation of our general sense of commitment to modern civilization and some of its central values.

The very most significant idea the Emancipation taught us, I venture to say, is the notion of the autonomous self. As we emerged from the ghetto, *shtetl* and *mellah*, we encountered a view of human nature that radically extended ideas which we had occasionally seen mentioned in our traditional texts. The Western world gave these old Jewish notions an emphasis and power the admittedly high Jewish sense of self had not come to. For the Enlightenment thinkers taught that human beings ought to make their own minds and consciences the *ultimate* basis of their decisions and actions. When they ceded to some external reality—tradition, convention, custom, class, society or even the church—the final right to tell them what they ought to do, they gave away the greatest human capacity: the ability to think for oneself. Instead of utterly depending on others, people need to educate themselves and develop their moral and esthetic faculties, so that they might then responsibly join with other people to freely determine the course of their common existence. Human dignity became identified with rational self-actualization rather than with faithful obedience. Liberals today have lost the optimism connected with that eighteenth century notion but we are far from ready to give up its high estimate of the human value of self-determination. If anything, our experience with the moral failure of every kind of institution and collective has forced us back on the self as the proper, ultimate touchstone of righteous existence.

The importation of the notion of the self into Jewish thought has proceeded under many guises and still remains incomplete. But, in practice, the masses of American Jews have made it the foundation of their relationship to Judaism. Our "non-observant Orthodox" affiliate with institutions pledged to the *halakhah* but, after listening respectfully to what the law requires, do "what is right in their own eyes." The new young traditionalists of whom we are so proud pick and choose their Jewish law from a three-volume catalog. Only the liberal Jews proclaim the autonomy of the self (in their transformed sense of that term, as we shall see) to be a fundamental principle for living Judaism today. When they perceive how much of the Jewish community, regardless of ideology, lives by the autonomous self, they feel confirmed in explicit championing of this Western notion.

Emancipated Jewry also enthusiastically adopted the Enlightenment assertion that ethical responsibility has a primary place in the functioning of the autonomous self. In matters concerning inter-human obligation an unparalleled imperative quality enters the life of the liberal Jew. Liberal Jewish duty extends far beyond ethics (in its several explications) but nothing else one must do manifests its supremely commanding power. It confronts us as a transcendent demand and lays an ultimate claim upon us. Not to grasp the compelling power of the ethical upon devout liberal Jews dooms one to misunderstand them. To be sure, Enlightenment thinkers spoke largely in terms of secular ethics (as in Kantian autonomy), and liberal Jews, in adopting their ideas, turned them into religious ones (thus substantially changing the Kantian autonomy). This, rather than mitigating the power of the ethical, only made it stronger.

Liberal Judaism proclaimed that a properly autonomous self exists essentially in response to the commanding power of ethics. The point needs emphasis. I wish to provide it by reminding you of the unanimous agreement of the great exemplars of modern Jewish thought in this matter. Our one great philosophic mind, Hermann Cohen, continued Kant's view that we hear the ethical command as a categorical imperative. The other path-breaking rationalist, Mordecai Kaplan, provides even stronger testimony to the sovereign power of the ethical claim. In Kaplan's naturalistic understanding of reason, the social group creates all significant human value—with one exception (not explained by the common canons of naturalism): moral law. A folk has the right to do anything with its culture that it deems proper (Kaplan's liberalism) except to contravene ethical standards. They remain so powerful that they constrain the otherwise omnipotent Kaplanian group. In both thinkers the self finds the ground and guarantee of ethics in its idea of God.

The non-rationalists also uphold this view of ethics, though one must understand them in their personalistic sense and not insist that because they are not Kantians they have no ethics at all. Martin Buber rejects the concept of a binding rational ethical law (and Kant's notion of autonomy) but he has a Buberian equivalent for it, the command which arises from genuine encounter. Whenever two persons truly meet, God is present as the third, enabling partner of their relationship. And every direct I-thou with God itself provides a mission on which we are sent. Because dialogue brings persons most fully into contact, it also most directly issues forth in a sense of duty to other human beings. The ethical imperative we carry with us as we leave our meeting is, then, our response to God. It comes with such imperative quality that even a received law should not be allowed to stand in its way if they differ. They may be antinomian but it clearly manifests a sense of ultimate religio-ethical claim.

Abraham Heschel's treatment of this theme—and certainly the fashion in which he lived—similarly relates the personal experience of the reality of God to the need for an ethical life. In Heschel's treatment of revelation, the ethical occupies a powerful place and in what little he wrote about the Holocaust, most of his remarks are addressed to our perverse use of our powers to do the good.

On no other single theme I can think of, not God, or the people of Israel, or revelation, or messianism, or law, or how we should think about these issues, do these thinkers so completely agree. For the liberal Jew then, ethics binds the self, regardless of the intellectual form in which one describes it. And, I hasten to add, it has a priority in Jewish duty over all other categories of Jewish responsibility, as necessary to a rounded Jewish life as they are. Despite the current disparagement of the old notion of Prophetic Judaism, the hierarchy of Jewish values proclaimed by many of the prophets still speaks to the religious perceptions of many liberal Jews.

Please note that for all these thinkers the old Enlightenment terms have significantly changed their meaning by being organically fixed in a religious context. For them, as for thoughtful liberal Jews of less intellectual distinction, the self is no longer fully understandable independent of God, and the autonomy of the self, primarily seen in ethical responsiveness, makes sense only in terms of the self's actualization of God's will since God is the source and standard of its own being.

I have not placed such stress upon the virtual identification of selfhood with religiously autonomous ethics so as to defend the old liberalism and its equation of Jewish duty with universal human ethics. That doctrine now appears to be less a timeless truth about Judaism than a response to the historic situation of liberal Jews in another day. If Judaism was to survive the Emancipation, acculturation was a spiritual duty. In that time one could well take the Jewishness of most Jews for granted. Hence the immediate task of liberal theologians was to clarify the ways in which Jews were not only permitted to be active participants in general culture but should see this as a new Jewish duty.

Living in a vastly different time, we have almost the diametrically opposite liberal Jewish theological agenda. Our universalism is largely secure, as our continuity at the university, in large cities and our subsequent secularization attests. Our new Jewish excitement comes from our turn to our particular roots. Liberal theologians now hear themselves summoned to recapture a compelling particularism without sacrificing the gains of the universalization of Judaism. Or, to translate that into my personalist language, we need to transform the older liberal general human self with its accretion of Jewish coloration into what I call the undivided Jewish self. Specifically, I wish to clarify some aspects of the Jewish self's "autonomy."

In putting the question this way, I have departed from Mordecai Kaplan's ingenious effort to make a Jewish rationalism commandingly particular. While I admire Kaplan's rounded sense of Jewish ethnicity, I believe that his sort of religious humanism cannot satisfactorily resolve the critical contemporary human problem, the need of a ground of value. I agree with those many thinkers who deny that any immanentism, even those called a "transnaturalism," can legitimately call us to prefer one aspect of nature over another and devote ourselves to it to the point of substantial self-sacrifice. Kaplan illogically attempts to use sociology prescriptively and contradicts much of our recent experience when he insists that collectives can properly command autonomous selves. Custom does have power but not to the point of empowering long-range imperatives. For several decades now we have continually been disillusioned by groups and institutions to the point where we greet their calls to sacrifice with considerable suspicion. The overarching symbol of this development is the American involvement in the Vietnam War. I must therefore leave it to others to clarify how the Kaplanian option can meet our ethical and spiritual needs and what limits it sets for community cooperation in the process.

For me, Buber took the important first step toward a new theology when he characterized the self as fundamentally relational. To put it starkly, Buber contends that one cannot be a proper self without a relationship to God, whether reached by a direct or an indirect I-thou encounter. The daring of this assertion may most easily be grasped by the contrast to Jean Paul Sartre for whom individuality remains utterly unrelievable. Buber's self is not only essentially social but involved with God. Thus, while retaining the experiential base of all liberalism, Buber radically breaks with humanism by pointing to God's role in every I-thou meeting.

The Buberian shift from liberal religion as *ideas* to religion as *relationship* further transforms the notion of autonomy. Because every relationship manifests distance as well as communion, the self retains its full identity even in its most intimate involvement with the other. Specifically, I-thou involvement creates command without heteronomy. Despite all that you and I now mean to one another, neither of us must now surrender to the other our power of self-determination. Yet because you are here with me, my self, formerly so potentially anarchic, now has a sense of what it must choose and do—and it knows God stands behind this "mission." For Buber, then, the "autonomy" of the self is fulfilled in relation to the other and God. This interpretation of religious experience is too individualistic for any orthodoxy and too other-involved for anarchy. Because Buber preserves autonomy while guiding it in terms of a social-Divine involvement, his thought has been highly prized by many contemporary liberal religious thinkers.

Buber was an enthusiastic particularist, in fact a cultural Zionist, for almost two decades before writing *I and Thou.* He believed all nations were addressed by God, though the Hebrews had uniquely responded to their summons. He served the Jewish people devotedly, not the least by recalling it to its responsibilities to God, particularly that of bringing reconciliation into Israeli-Arab relations. Yet Buber never clarified how he made his intellectual way from individual "command" to national duty. When pressed on this issue, he insisted on an uncompromising individualism with all its universalistic overtones.

To meet our particularist needs we must find a way to reshape Buber's relationally autonomous self so that it has a direct, primary, ethnic form. I suggest, prompted by some hints in Rosenzweig, that my sort of liberal Jew is constituted by existence in the Covenant. (The capital "C" usage distinguishes between the universal Noachide covenant and the particular Israelitic one.) A Jewish self is characterized not only by a grounding personal relationship with God but relates to God as part of the people of Israel's historic Covenant with God. Being a Jew, then, may begin with the individual, but Jewish personhood is structured by an utterly elemental participation in the Jewish historical experience of God. Jewish existence is not merely personal but communal and even public. In the healthy Jewish self one detects no place, no matter how deeply one searches, where one can find the old liberal schizoid split between the self and the Jew. One is a Jew, existentially.

In responding to God out of the Covenant situation, the relationally autonomous Jewish self acknowledges its essential historicity and sociality. One did not begin the Covenant and one is its conduit only as part of the people of Israel. In the Hebrew Covenant, tradition and community round out what the self of the Noachide covenant already recognizes as God's behest and the universal solidarity of humankind. With heritage and folk compelling values, with the Jewish service of God directed to historic continuity lasting until messianic days, the Covenanted self acknowledges the need for structure to Jewish existence. Yet this does not rise to the point of validating law in the traditional sense, for personal autonomy remains the cornerstone of this piety.

This matter is so important and generally so poorly understood that I would like to devote some space here to analyzing in some detail the dialectic of freedom and constraint in the liberal Jewish self.

The relational interpretation of the structure of Jewish selfhood I am suggesting here radically departs from the usual Jewish understandings. Traditionally, the Jewish self is firmly held within the *halakhah,* Jewish law. With modernity, liberals began to think of the Jewish legal process in terms of its social context. The folk, through its institutions, customs and folkways, could be seen as providing the forms for *Jewish* self-actualization, including a developing law. These two ways of interpreting the structure of Jewish existence have the advantage of furnishing us with common, public, objective standards of what it is to be a Jew. They do not "command" my sort of liberal Jew precisely because of their external, heteronomous nature. That is, I and many Jews like me can accept Jewish tradition as guiding us, indeed as an incomparably valuable resource, but not as overriding "conscience." Identifying our dignity as human beings with our autonomy, we are determined to think for ourselves. However, we are not general selves but Jewish selves. Thinking personalistically about our Jewishness, we identity our Jewish variety of self-structure in relational terms, a rather new way of envisioning authentic Jewish existence. Specifically, the Jewish self gives patterned continuity to its existence by a continual orientation to God as part of the people of Israel's historic Covenant. Four aspects of this situation deserve comment.

First, as noted above, the Jewish self is personally and primarily involved with God. Jewishness is lived out of a relationship with God which precedes, undergirds, and interfuses all the other relationships of the Jewish self. Where the biblical-rabbinic Jew had essentially a theocentric existence, the modern Jewish self may better be described as theo-related in ultimate depth. That being the case, the highest priority must today be given to the fight to overcome the pervasive agnosticism which resulted from the modernization of Jewry. Without a personal sense of involvement with God, this relational, Covenantal Jewish existence cannot be properly attained.

Second, and inextricably bound with the first, though subsidiary to it, is the Jewish self's participation in the Jewish people as part of its ongoing relation to God. All forms of radical individualism on the human level are negated by this stance. The Jewish self lives out the Covenant not only as a self in relation to God but as part of a living ethnic community. This people then seeks to transform its social relations as well as its individual lives in terms of its continuing close involvement with God. Jewish "autonomy" need not be sacrificed to what other Jews are now doing or think right, but the Jewish self will be seriously concerned with the community which is so great a part of its selfhood. Naturally, this individual autonomy will often be channeled and fulfilled through what the Jewish people has always done or now values. For the sake of community unity, the Jewish self will often undoubtedly sacrifice the exercise of personal standards. That most easily takes place when the demands are obviously necessary for community action—e.g., a folk, not a personal Jewish calendar—or when the demands are not seen as onerous, e.g., *Kiddush* over wine and not the whiskey or marijuana one might prefer. We shall deal with more significant clashes later.

Third, the Jewish self, through the Covenant is historically rooted as well as divinely and communally oriented. Modern Jews not only did not initiate the Covenant, they are not the first to live it. While social conditions and self-perceptions have greatly changed over the centuries, the basic relationship and the partners involved in it have remained the same. Human nature, personally and socially, has not appreciably altered since Bible times (as we so often note, reading ancient Jewish texts). Hence much of what Jews once did is likely to commend itself to us as what we ought to do. More, since their sense of the Covenant was comparatively fresh, strong and steadfast, where ours is often uncertain, weak and faltering, we will substantially rely on their guidance in determining our Jewish duty. But not to the point of dependency or passivity of will. Not only is our situation in many respects radically different from theirs but our identification of maturity with the proper exercise of agency (in Covenantal context for a Jew) requires us on occasion to dissent from what our tradition has taught or enjoined.

Fourth, the Jewish self, because of its intimate connections with God, folk and tradition, is sensitized to more than the present and its call to decision. All persons, as I see it, but certainly Jews, should put the immediate exercise of autonomy into the framework of attaining personal integrity. For a person lives in time, and the self persists as well as chooses. The soul which lives only in the present, with little connection to previous experience and minimal thought to the future, denies not only the chronological character of creatureliness but the most creative of human acts, to give wholeness to an entire life. Form, habit, institution and structure have a necessary role to play in such fulfillment of the self—as long as they continue to express what the individual, at some level of choice, still wills to do. And almost all of us, out of frailty or indecision, will often depend on previously chosen patterns to carry us through life, particularly its trials. But in the clash between a pressing, immediate insight and an old, once valuable but now empty practice, we will know ourselves authorized to break with the past and do acts which more appropriately express our deepest commitments.

With these theoretical matters clarified, let me now turn to the Jewish self's attitude to Jewish law. Since the Covenant must be lived, not just believed in or thought about, Jewish law has been the primary means of being an authentic Jewish self until modern times. As the effects of the Emancipation were increasingly internalized, the overwhelming majority of Jews insisted upon an autonomous relation to Jewish law, thereby utterly changing its character for them. But I am arguing that if they could relate to Jewish tradition as liberal Jewish selves and not merely as autonomous persons-in-general, they would find in Jewish law the single best source of guidance as to how they ought to live. That is, wanting to be true to themselves as persons—understood now immediately and not secondarily as *Jewish* persons and thus intimately involved in faithfulness to God, people and historic devotion—they would want their lives substantially to be structured by a continuing involvement with the prescription of Jewish law. But as *autonomous* Jewish persons, the provisions of the law would ultimately be tested by appeal to their conscientious individual Jewish understanding.

Over a decade ago, in *Choosing a Sex Ethic*[1] I gave an extended example of the way in which a Jew might candidly engage the choices confronting a mature, autonomous self in dialectical involvement with society and the variegated guidance provided by historic Jewish law. While some details of the judgments I made then seem to me now in need of revision, the fundamental delineation of the modern Jewish liberal decision-making process I provided there still seems to me fundamentally correct. Autonomy should not be subservient to the *halakhah* in sexual matters but at the same time, the law, in all its details, does not hesitate to make its claim on the committed autonomous Jewish self.

I suggest that, from a relational perspective, the Jewishness of the Jewish self should now be seen less in its obedient observance than in its authentically living in Covenant. Its Jewish acts result from their expressing that relationship. And, I would add, again following Rosenzweig, that everything one then did and not merely some delimited activities, would be Jewish. Against Rosenzweig, I do not see how, even in principle, Jewish law can be imposed on such a Jewish self. Rather, with autonomy essential to selfhood, I avidly espouse a pluralism of thought and action stemming from Jewish commitment. I also look forward to the day when enough Jewish selves autonomously choose to live in ways sufficiently similar that they can create common patterns among us. A richly personal yet Jewishly grounded and communally created Jewish style or way would be the autonomous Jewish self's equivalent of *"halakhah."* It would give us universalism without assimilation and a commanding particularism which has full respect for the dignity of the individual.

This multiplication of simultaneous responsibilities—to self, to God, to the Jewish past, present and future, and to humankind as a whole (through the Noachide covenant of which Jews remain a part)—obviously creates special problems for decision-makers. Facing any choice, one must take account of many commitments. And not infrequently there will be conflict among them. This constitutes a further reason for acknowledging the legitimacy, indeed the desirability of pluralistic Jewish practice and thought. More, we must remain continually open to the possibility that new and unanticipated forms may arise to express genuinely the imperatives which flow from existence in Covenant.

Does not this reassertion of liberalism's call for community openness make the character of the Covenant folk so shapeless that it hardly has distinct identity? Has not autonomy again manifested its anarchic and therefore ultimately un-Jewish character?

I cannot deny the risks involved in the path I am suggesting. Before saying they are too great to bear I want to direct our attention to one highly esteemed Western value I omitted from my previous list, namely, democracy. Liberal Jews passionately embrace what the Western world has taught us about the way in which people ought to conduct their societal life. The universalization of power by the enfranchisement of every citizen remains for all its faults and abuses the least humanly destructive form of government. Democracy calls for pluralism and tolerance of others' radically differing views, a concept which has produced social harmony unprecedented in human history. By contrast, wherever absolutisms have attained political power, human degradation has shortly followed, not infrequently in the name of the highest moral ends.

Liberalism's insistence on individualism will surely yield only a flabby sort of structure. But it will have no difficulty directly and organically authorizing and commending democracy. I do not see that the same is true of the orthodoxies I know or have read about. When one possesses the one absolute truth, how can one be expected to turn any significant power over to those who deny or oppose it?

The problem of an orthodox doctrine of democracy can only temporarily be settled pragmatically, that is, by arguing that because of the large number of unbelievers or the need to reach out to as many people as possible, one may expect that the true believers will practice democracy. Once the usefulness of the democracy ends, the absolutism will then naturally express itself. It will also not do to discuss how this or that tradition contains resources by means of which one might validate democracy. The hypothetical revisionism must yet make its way against the tradition's absolutistic beliefs, its history, established tradition, practice and ethos. Consider the situation in the Jewish community were the religious parties to come to full power in the State of Israel. Once their rule was consolidated, what would be the status of Noachides who refused to accept the Noachian laws as revealed by the Torah? What rights would Christians have? Or, a less questionable case of *ovde avodah zarah,* idol worshippers, *bakhti* Hindus and imagistic Buddhists? Though I have tried to be aware of contemporary Orthodox Jewish theoretical authentifications of democracy as desirable for a Jewish polity, particularly a Jewish state, only one is known to me, Michael Wyschogrod's paper on "Judaism and Conscience," which appeared in the Msr. John M. Oesterreicher *Festschrift, Standing before God.*[2] Let me summarize its argument.

Wyschogrod contends, convincingly to me, that despite some hints of a similar notion, a fully self-conscious concept of conscience does not appear in classic Jewish tradition. This follows consistently from the Jewish emphasis upon the affirmation of God's highly contentful revelation to the people of Israel. Judaism must certainly reject the autonomous conscience in its common, humanistic form, for, as Heidegger is used to show, it radically destroys obedience to anything other than ourselves. And I would add, precisely this separation of conscience from its transcendent source has been the intellectual cause of our gradual loss of a social consensus about the standards and nature of moral value.

Wyschogrod then carefully delineates a notion of conscience which might be acceptable to Judaism. Here the individual's sense of right is understood to be a faculty given humans by God so that they might discern and respond to God's will. Wyschogrod thus follows the philosophical path by which personal autonomy is fulfilled in theonomy, thereby avoiding the problem of a religious ethic being heteronomous.

He then sets about assimilating this notion to contemporary traditional Judaism. This he accomplishes by calling attention to the way in which the determination to remain Orthodox today must necessarily be made against the crowd. One can say, he suggests, that a significant measure of autonomy is involved in the continuing will to be a believing, practicing Jew. To be sure, in any possible conflict between the *halakhah* and the will, one sacrifices one's self-determination, our personal version of the binding of Isaac. And in the very sense that this can occasionally take place, one phenomenologically detects the role of autonomy within Orthodoxy.

Of particular interest, certainly in connection with the theme of this paper, are the motives Wyschogrod manifests for undertaking this unique intellectual enterprise. He acknowledges that the concept of autonomy has correctly pointed our attention to a critical locus of human dignity. Without some such self-actualization, we would be less the creatures that God formed us to be. Hence Orthodox Judaism needs to make room for the idea and function of conscience.

A practical consideration is also at work, one not explicitly stated but one suggested by the context in which this paper appears and by the consequences which follow from the argument. Consider the following breath-taking issue Wyschogrod carefully develops. If conscience may legitimately command one, may it still do so when we judge the person utilizing it to be acting in error? That is, if we adhere to an orthodoxy, we have an objective notion of God's true will. Shall we still grant conscience its rights when someone uses it against what we know is true and good? One cannot help but hear in such thinking the overtones of the old Catholic teaching that error has no rights.

But Wyschogrod strongly argues the opposite, that the individual conscience must be granted rights even when to us it appears to be acting in error. Not to do so would negate the very concept of conscience, for a heteronomous revelation would have effectively usurped our God-given right to think and judge for ourselves.

Wyschogrod's purpose in all this, I believe, is to try to make a theological place in Orthodox Judaism for Christians to be allowed to be Christians. He does not sacrifice the absoluteness of God's revelation but carefully provides room for individual conscience within it. Then those who cannot read its message plainly may still claim the right to go their deviant way. If I remember correctly, John Courtney Murray mounted an argument of this sort for many years within the Roman Catholic church to help it attain a positive attitude toward democracy and pluralism. His position was substantially adopted by Vatican Council II and now constitutes the church's official teaching. Perhaps the thought occurred to me because the central citation of Wyschogrod's argument about the right of the erring conscience is taken from Thomas Aquinas.

Wyschogrod makes only one stipulation about the employment of conscience other than genuineness. He requires serious, reverential study of God's revelation, the sacred texts of Judaism.

I shall be most interested to see what sort of reception Wyschogrod's argument receives in the Orthodox Jewish community. If accepted, it could provide a theoretical basis not only for interfaith but intrafaith understanding. Specifically, I believe the autonomous Jewish self I have described more than meets Wyschogrod's conditions for a conscience which Orthodoxy should respect even when it errs. The ethical sense of such liberal Jews is founded on theonomy, not humanism, and, because the Covenant sets the field of its perceptions, they are spiritually guided by classic Jewish texts. By Wyschogrod's standards, Orthodoxy should acknowledge the legitimacy of authentic Jewish liberalism despite its sinfulness. More, my Jewish Covenantalists can lay claim to even greater Jewish legitimacy. The Covenant clearly links them to the Jewish people and they are mandated to realize their Jewish selves in community. That goes far beyond Wyschogrod's demands—a further indication that his paper speaks to the question of Christian legitimacy. Of Jews who follow their conscience, it would seem reasonable to demand, certainly in a post-Holocaust time, not only reverence for God and study of texts, but passionate loyalty to the Covenant people.

One further point about Wyschogrod's paper—this rare effort to validate tolerance and democracy within Orthodoxy does so by arguing, against precedent, for a broad acceptance of the autonomy of the individual. If the well-known liberal move to the right could be met by this kind of Orthodox theoretical opening to the left, we might have another instance of the mutual redefinition of positions which often in the past has made possible greater human unity. In any event, we liberals will, at the least, see Wyschogrod's noble effort as further proof of our old contention that a vital contemporary Judaism must make greater place for the concept of personal autonomy than did our tradition in the past (though it requires reworking from its rigorous Enlightenment individualism to become the new autonomy of a Jewish self).

Experience further indicates that we are less likely to run into difficulty seeking communal agreement in practice than in theology. Different beliefs often lead to similar acts, as our joint work for the State of Israel, Soviet Jewry and *tzedakah* demonstrates. Liberal Jews enthusiastically participate in such communal activities, for they happily unite autonomy and Covenant responsibility. They become quite troubled, however, when their autonomous sense of their Covenant obligations conflicts with other views of Jewish duty. With regard to marriage and divorce practices, that means the *halakhah* as interpreted by the sages of contemporary Orthodoxy.

I think it will best serve my purpose of getting others to understand liberal Judaism better if, before turning to the contentious area of marriage law, I deal with one likely to arouse less emotion. This case should give us greater insight into the way a liberal as against a traditional *posek* might balance the conflicting claims of Jewish commitment.

J. David Bleich, in one of his summaries of recent *halakhic* literature[3] discussed the issue of dwarfism and the problems its treatment raises. The condition, troublesome to those who have it and often a heavy burden for their relatives, does not constitute a genuine threat to life, which would then merit the exceptional activities of *pikuah nefesh*, saving a life. Jewish law, it should also be noted, imposes no special disabilities upon dwarfs. Some urgency for the treatment of dwarfism arises from the greater than usual difficulty dwarfs have in conceiving children. They therefore not only merit help for general humanitarian and Jewish medical reasons but so as to enable the males more likely to fulfill their Jewish duty of procreation. However, the accepted therapy, growth hormone, must be collected from human corpses. *Poskim* (rabbinic decisors) must then seek to reconcile the laws of *kibud hamet* (honor for the dead) with the desirability of curing a distressing but non-life-threatening condition. Disturbed by the need to cut into the corpse, they give considerable attention as to how this must be done so as to create the least disfigurement. Ruling permissively they are able to find ways to maintain the law and its values while meeting a human need.

The autonomous Jewish self would face the situation somewhat differently. A corpse is surely entitled to respectful treatment. Indeed, in our day of lessening concern for the dead—fewer people appear to be saying *kaddish* and visiting graves—some special effort ought to be made to remind Jews that we cannot envision a self as utterly distinct from its body. While a corpse is surely far from a person, our psychosomatic sense of personhood requires us to give dead bodies reverential treatment.

However, when one thinks primarily in terms of selfhood, there cannot be any value comparison between, much less subordination of, the needs of a living person to a dead body. While the corpse exercises claims upon us, its proper honor must yield to the vastly more significant needs of the living. One can surely be a self and a dwarf, yet the selfsame psycho-somatic view of the self which authorizes honoring corpses requires us to recognize that dwarfism imposes very severe personal handicaps on its victims. Liberal Jews would then likely argue that the human suffering of the dwarf, not respect for the corpse, ought in this case be our primary consideration in determining our personal responsibility under the Covenant.

Fortunately, where dwarfism is involved there will be little difference in practice between traditionalists and liberals. But were rigorous *poskim* to impose such stringent conditions that the collection of pituitary glands was seriously impeded, liberal Jews would demur. We would not believe God would have us act so today to fulfill the Covenant. We might be in error but we could not follow the *halakhah* then if we were to fulfill what we know to be our Jewish duty.

Jewish marriage and divorce laws raise more directly ethical issues, as the two classic conflict cases, *agunah* (abandoned wife) and *mamzerut* (the category of "bastard"), indicate. Traditional Jews do not need liberals to tell them what agony these issues create. However, traditionalists are willing to sacrifice whatever stirrings of autonomous rebellion they may feel in such cases so that they may follow God's law. Liberal Jews, for whom autonomy tends to be ultimate, cannot easily take that course. They are far more likely to react in ethical indignation. In the name of proper legal procedure a woman can be debarred from remarrying and establishing a fully ramified Jewish home. Or, in compensation for a parental sin, a child is prevented from ever contracting a normal Jewish marriage. These ethical considerations already carry heavy Covenantal weight. They become overwhelming when we think of the Holocaust. Does much in Jewish life now take priority as an obligatory response to the Holocaust over contracting a Jewish marriage and creating a Jewish family? Yet also in the name of the Holocaust, liberal Jews are asked to accept traditional Jewish marriage and divorce law. While that will create more uniform practice in the Jewish community, it will necessarily also involve us in preventing some Jews from founding Jewish families!

To the autonomous Jewish self, the ethical and Covenantal damage done by the laws of *agunah* and *mamzerut* cannot be explained away by any form of mitigating defense. Our overwhelming sense of duty cannot be stilled by hearing that the decisors may be relied on to minimize drastically the numbers of *agunot* and *mamzerim,* or that we should consider the few unresolved cases a small price to pay for effecting the familial unity of the Jewish people. The fact is that, with all the compassion and legal creativity contemporary *poskim* display, there are *agunot* and *mamzerim*. And the legal disabilities are enforced on them whenever they come under Orthodox jurisdiction. For liberal Jews to adopt the contemporary Orthodox *halakhah* with regard to marriage and divorce means retroactively to validate the decisions already made and to put themselves in principle behind the possible creation of new *agunot* and *mamzerim*. As we understand our obligation to God under the Covenant, I do not see that we can do that. As I read our community, we believe God does not want Jews to relate to other Jews by categorizing and treating them as *agunot* and *mamzerim*. We cannot fulfill our Jewish responsibilities through a system which does so.

I am not suggesting that for the sake of community unity traditional Jews give up their understanding of God's law and the manner of its correct implementation. That would be a quite inconsistent application of the pluralism I have espoused. I do know that there are other Jewish laws which remain in full force but are, in practice, inoperable—an eye for an eye being the example we regularly cite to Christians. I have sufficient confidence in the resources of the *halakhah* and the creativity of contemporary *poskim* to believe that even the thorny problems of *agunah* and *mamzerut* could be solved once there is sufficient will to do so.

We face a far more difficult and complex issue when we deal with the question of women's rights in traditional Jewish marriage and divorce law. Because most liberal Jews perceive the equality of women as one of the great ethical issues of our time, we remain unpersuaded by all efforts to demonstrate the relative humanity of the *halakhah* in this area. That Jewish law has treated women better than many other legal systems have, that it has often made special provision to protect women from potential abuses of its male-oriented statutes, should inform Jewish pride about the inherent moral thrust in our heritage. To the autonomous Jewish self, all such apologetics do not validate continuing a system which badly discriminates against women. The feminist movement in Western culture has made us aware of how blind we Jews have been to our own ethical failings with regard to women. Acknowledging that, we would be untrue to our fundamental commitments were we to agree to operate by a law in which women are not fully equal legal agents with men.

I cannot take this issue further. I do not know what traditional authorities might do in this area and I am in no position to say what sorts of practices liberal Jews might accept for the sake of uniform communal practice. Liberal Jewish women will speak for themselves, and, considering how they have suffered at the hands of men, I do not expect them to be in a mood to compromise.

As a final contribution to this analysis of Covenantal decision-making I should like to make some generalizations concerning it. Should our various Covenant obligations appear to conflict, the duty to God—most compellingly, ethics—must take priority over our responsibilities to the

Jewish people or the dictates of Jewish tradition. I acknowledge only one regular exception to that rule, cases when the survival of the Jewish people is clearly at stake. Obviously, without the Jews, there can be no continuing Covenant relationship so Covenant, not universal ethics, provides the framework for my Jewish existence.

What should a Jew do when confronted by a conflict between a divinely imposed ethical responsibility and a duty upon which the survival of the Jewish people seems to rest? I cannot say. A true crisis of the soul occurs when two values we cherish ultimately can no longer be maintained simultaneously. And we call it a tragedy when, no matter what we decide, we must substantially sacrifice a value which has shaped our lives. May God spare us such choices. Or, failing that, may God then give us the wisdom and courage to face crisis with honest choice and stand by us when we have, as best we could, tried to do so.

My liberal subjectivity has now been exponentially amplified by this problem of a multiplicity of basic values. Nonetheless, I believe I can helpfully illustrate how the autonomous Jewish self might function in this situation by quickly sketching in my response to three diverse cases.

Many years ago, when I was breaking out of the old liberal identification of Judaism with universal ethics, it occurred to me that the Jewish duty to procreate can be objected to ethically. To bring a child into the world bearing the name Jew inevitably subjects that human being to special potential danger. All the joys and advantages of being a Jew cannot compensate for this ineradicable disability. Yet the Covenant absolutely depends on Jewish biologic-historic continuity until the messianic days come. For all its ethical difficulty then, I have no choice but to proclaim the Jewish duty to have children.

Why then do I resist establishing one community standard for Jewish marriages and divorces? Many in our community would say that the personal status of Jews will critically effect the survival of the Jewish people. But I read our situation differently. In my thought, the exceptional survival-category must be used as restrictively as *halakhah* uses *pikuah nefesh.* I am not convinced that the Jewish people will not survive at all without a uniform marriage and divorce law. Though the overwhelming majority of Jews worldwide have given up the authority of the *halakhah,* they still manifest a will to Jewish continuity. I agree that the Jewish people without one standard of practice in family matters will not continue as it did when it had such consensus—but even without it, the folk as such will survive. In this instance, I cannot therefore invoke the survival clause to overcome my sense of ethical obligation.

Then why will I not perform intermarriages? After all, in the contemporary situation, more than half the families formed by an intermarriage apparently try to live as Jews. Accepting their will to be Jewish as a means of Jewish survival would allow me to fulfill an ethical responsibility—that is, to serve two people who might seem humanly well-suited to one another despite their having different religions. I confess that I am moved by such arguments and know that my answer to this disturbing question may appear even more subjective than usual. In positive response to such people's Jewish concerns, I reach out to intermarried couples with warmth and gladly accept their children as Jews when through education and participation they manifest Covenant loyalty. I cannot go so far as to officiate at their wedding. To do this would give a false indication to them, and to the community, of my understanding of Covenant obligation. The relation between God and the Jewish people is mirrored, articulated and continued largely through family Judaism. As I see it, we must therefore necessarily prefer a family which fully espouses the Covenant to one which does so with inherent ambiguity. Moreover, I understand myself as a rabbi authorized to function only within the Covenant and on behalf of the Covenant.

My Reform Jewish colleagues who differ with me on this issue do so because they read the balance between ethics and Jewish survival differently than I do. They believe, erroneously in my opinion, that performing intermarriages will help win and bind these families to the Jewish people. Because I may well be wrong in this matter and because I respect their reading of their Covenant responsibility, I associate myself with them in full collegiality. My sense of liberal Jewish pluralism clearly encompasses this troubling disagreement.

Having devoted so much of this paper to my liberal certainties, I wanted to close it with an instance of my more characteristic tentativeness. We will not understand liberalism, at least not the sort which surfaces in my kind of liberal Judaism, without understanding the dialectic of confidence and hesitation which informs it. Perhaps with such insight we can find a way to move beyond community fragmentation to greater unity amid diversity.

NOTES

1. New York, 1969.
2. New York, 1981.
3. *Tradition*, vol. 18, No. 4 (Winter, 1980).

A WAY: THE POSTMODERN EXPLICATION OF JEWISH SELFHOOD

Insight may open up the past in new ways, but it does not thereby go on to become a creative force generating a fresh way of restructuring how we think. It was one thing for me to realize that individualistically founded thought would inevitably fail to appreciate the full social dimension of human responsibility. It was quite another thing to create a way of thinking that paid tribute to the dignity of self-determination while equally affirming the truth of the people of Israel's ongoing corporate relationship with God. Thus, nearly a decade passed until I was able to give my notion of the Jewish self book-length statement in *Renewing the Covenant: A Theology for the Postmodern Jew* (number 273 in the bibliography).

In that time, my continuing concern with applied theology turned away from issues of educational practice, though I did write two textbooks. One, in 1984, *Liberal Judaism* (number 215 in the bibliography), gave adults a thematic introduction to non-Orthodox Jewish theology. A year later, I wrote with my former student Naomi Patz an ideologically oriented work for children, *Explaining Reform Judaism* (number 229 in the bibliography). The major focus of my effort to refine my theologizing by reference to the living practice of Judaism in our time was now Jewish ethics. When Wayne State University Press expressed an interest in publishing a collection of my articles on various aspects of Jewish ethics, I was surprised how many I had done over the years. There are forty of them (seven previously unpublished) in their 1990 book *Exploring Jewish Ethics* (number 264 in the bibliography).

I have little doubt that this shift in my practical attention was connected with the turbulence of the times and a consequence of my 1970 founding of *Sh'ma, A Journal of Jewish Responsibility.* I remained its publisher and editor until 1993 (in no small part due to my neighbors Seymour Udell, *z"l*, who put his printing company at my disposal for its first three years, and Alicia Seeger, *z"l*, who graciously and efficiently managed its many administrative complexities). In that period of social activism and intense ethical debate, I was convinced that there needed to be an ongoing demonstration of Judaism's relevance to our public concerns. But I had learned enough about "Judaism" by then to know that speaking in its name had to be representatively multivoiced, not just "liberal," or "conservative," or "religious," or "secular," but dialogically inclusive of every responsible kind of voice. Like the texts of our tradition, it could serve our community best by the interplay of contesting interpretation, allowing the thoughtful Jewish reader to be enlightened by the rabbinic style of clarifying each point of view by pairing it with other points of view. That much was in place at the founding of *Sh'ma* and proved its worth as the little journal slowly found its uncommon voice and then its supportive public. It dawned on me only in the eighties that another cultural-intellectual transition was gaining strength, and that I had been slowly making my way into a postmodern way of thinking, a topic to which I shall return after two digressions.

Since I consider intergroup relations a special instance of applied ethics, two further papers in this section, number 22 on Orthodoxy and number 23 on (Zen) Buddhism (of the Kyoto School), can also be said to testify to my ethical interests. However, as the social ethos changed, I turned my attention to the individuals who are the ultimate agents of ethical purposes. The happy result of this turn to virtue ethics was the 1999 publication of *The Jewish Moral Virtues* (number 321 in the bibliography), done with my former student Frances Schwartz.

I also want to claim personal privilege for the maverick presence here of my study, "The Blessing over a Change of Wine" (paper 21). Above, in my introduction to the section A Glimpse and its article on computers and creative worship, I referred to the theologian's humanity as evidenced by a sense of humor. My halakhic essay on wine witnesses to two other important aspects of my life: friendship and wine. Nat Hess, *z"l*, my dear, older friend during the nearly half-century my wife, Estelle, and I lived in Port Washington, mentored me in the worlds of wine and Jewish leadership. In 1987, at the dinner celebrating his eightieth birthday, I presented him with this history of the legal arguments on whether a second, better-tasting wine at a meal should have a new blessing and what, if so, that should be. Alicia Seeger designed an elegant booklet containing this text, and eighty numbered copies were printed to serve as the party favor. Nat died as this collection was in preparation, and the study appears here in loving memory of him. And, to return to the living, it celebrates his old tasting partner's refusal to become an abstraction-making–machine, as attested by such things as co-founding the Wine Collectors' [tasting] Club at Edgehill, a life-care community in Stamford, Connecticut (where Estelle and I now happily reside).

My directly theological thinking did not subside after *Renewing the Covenant*. If anything, having made that statement allowed me to understand better the implications of my postmodernism and to apply it in previously unanticipated ways. Enough material soon became available that in 1999 I published *Judaism after Modernity: Papers from a Decade of Fruition* (number 322 in the bibliography). Two of the thirty-plus papers in that book appear in this volume, the previously mentioned one on Buddhism—which indicates how my resolute particularism nonetheless allows me to relate sympathetically yet with self-respect to a quite different faith—and a more exploratory effort with regard to God's role in healing, "Please, God, Heal Her, Please" (paper 24 here). In chapter 10 of *Renewing*, "What Does God Still Do?" I made a preliminary effort to break with the scientific insistence that natural causation was limited to physical-chemical activity. In a world where science had so widely come to be seen only as another "construction of reality" (if an extraordinarily useful one), healing services had spontaneously become endemic in the Jewish community. Surely, then, God as healer and not just as inspirer and presence requires some fresh statement, but it is just here that our language about what God still does is terribly inadequate. I therefore made a modest case in this paper for God as an effective agent in the healing process.

I have reserved my comments on my relationship to postmodernism until this point because the final selection of this section, "'*Im ba'et, eyma'*—Since You Object, Let Me Put It This Way" (paper 25 here—the title is a common term in the Talmud), is the only article in this collection that treats it directly. (More is said about it in connection with my effort at intellectual autobiography in the final section of this book.) I hope in this way to celebrate Peter Ochs's gathering of critiques of my theological book in a volume he cleverly titled *Reviewing the Covenant: Eugene B. Borowitz and the Postmodern Renewal of Jewish Theology* (SUNY Press, 2000). My concluding contribution to that volume was my response to the various academics there, good friends all, and is an effort to clarify just what my religious, atypical postmodernism entails.

Most of my critics were disturbed by my calling my thought "postmodern," though I quite self-consciously contravene a major premise of mainline postmodernism, premising my thought on Jewish faith as I do. Jacques Derrida, the founder of this new form of philosophy, effectively began his intellectual revolution by demonstrating the illogic of claiming any intellectual foundations for our thought. His deconstructionism heralded the end of all foundationalism, and he and his disciples have found creative ways of thinking usefully despite keeping that foundational insecurity in mind. How, then, could a thinker who insisted on beginning from a foundation of Jewish belief claim to be a postmodern? Having had my say on this topic in the paper mentioned above, I shall here only refer to another aspect of this development in my thinking.

Some decades earlier, when I had turned to existentialist categories to explicate my Jewish theology, I found myself facing the problem of how an avowedly atheistic philosophy could properly be utilized for a determinedly God-centered view of reality. Fortunately there were in those days numerous Christian theologians who also insisted that one could accept the postrationalistic stance of existentialism without also demanding that the free and unfettered human self be the only acceptable basis of contemporary thought. That is not our situation today; theologians in our time have a much more perplexing time finding ways to modify Derridean postmodernism to their religious purposes. In my case, something of my earlier experience in working with a reluctant philosophic point of view gave me sufficient qualms about calling my thought postmodern that I consciously did not make the subtitle of my *Renewing the Covenant "a postmodern Jewish theology,"* but only the less pretentious claim, *"a theology for the postmodern Jew."* I felt sufficiently at home with the postmodernism of the broad cultural movement, seeking to go beyond a defunct modernism that I identified myself with, but could not identify myself with Derridean philosophic orthodoxy. This sense of the legitimacy of my self-perception as a postmodernist intensified during the years covered by this period. That, I now believe, was engendered by my working from the Jewish "within" to the postmodern "without" while my critics wanted me to reverse that path—precisely the path that the modern Jewish thinkers had insisted was a methodological necessity for all sophisticated Jewish philosophy or theology. In resolutely rejecting that old path, I identify myself as a postmodern, albeit a member of its non-Derridean minority, a social situation not uncommon to a Jew.

18 / *Hillul Hashem:* A Universal Rubric in the *Halakhah*

1986

The need to rethink the theory of modern Jewish ethics arises from the loss of the meaning the liberals assigned to the words "Jewish" and "ethics." For Hermann Cohen and the many who utilized his ideas, the neo-Kantian definition of ethics determined the meaning of the word "Jewish." Today, the several competing versions of philosophic ethics all operate under a cloud of uncertainty, as Alasdair MacIntyre's widely discussed *After Virtue* (Notre Dame: University of Notre Dame Press, 1981) makes plain. Thus, one mode of reestablishing a compelling theory of Jewish ethics involves studying contemporary options in ethics and applying the most appealing of these to Judaism.

An alternate path explores the independent meaning the term "Jewish" should have in such a theory. Self-respect demands that it be given at least equal weight with Hellenic or Germanic philosophy, specifically, that they not be allowed to dictate what Judaism properly understands to be "the good and the right." From this perspective, mediation between Judaism and ethics begins from the Jewish side and does so in terms of authoritative Jewish teaching, namely, with concern for the *halakhah.*

Orthodox and postliberal Jews can easily share this approach to Jewish ethics though they are likely, in due course, to come to different conclusions about contemporary Jewish responsibility.[1] In doing so they must face the continuing difficulty generated by this procedure: how to reconcile a particular people's legal system with the sense of goodness available to all human beings.

This study arises as a continuation of my interest in this approach evidenced recently by a response to Aharon Lichtenstein's much-discussed paper, "Does Jewish Tradition Recognize an Ethic Independent of *Halakha*?"[2] There I pointed to the ambiguous and subordinate status of the "ethical moment" in *halakhah,* thus impugning the commanding power of Jewish ethics. Here I propose to study a specific halakhic provision which illumines Jewish law's relation to universal human moral judgment, namely the category *hillul hashem,* insofar as it shapes Jewish duty in terms of gentile opinion.

An inner theological dialectic lies behind the legal tension to be explored. God has given the Torah to one particular people, the Jews, and its rules distinguish between those who do and those who do not participate in the system. The same Torah indicates that God stands in a similar relationship, if a legally less demanding one, with all humankind, the children of Noah. Hence they may be said to have a legitimate basis for judging Jewish conduct.[3] The potential tension between what the Torah permits to Jews and a harsh evaluation gentiles might make of it creates the subset of the laws of *hillul hashem* to be studied. (On its meaning, see below.)

While the term *hillul hashem* does not occur in the Bible, its equivalents are found in several biblical books, with heavy concentrations in Leviticus and Ezekiel. The *peshat,* simple meaning, of these texts may be classified as moving from concrete acts of profanation, to those which directly or indirectly cast aspersions on God, and finally to an abstract sense of *hillul hashem.*

Since the book of Leviticus pays considerable attention to cultic acts which sanctify God—to the extent that various items can be called God's "holy things"—so, by extension, mishandling them profanes God. (Thus Lev. 21:6, 22:2, 32; Mal. 1:12; and perhaps Ezek. 20:39.) Idolatry—specifically, sacrificing one's child to Moloch—is a desecration (Lev. 18:21, 20:13). Ezekiel accuses certain women prophets of equivalent sacrilege (Ezek. 13:19). The theme also encompasses noncultic violations, of which swearing falsely by God's name is a similarly direct profanation (Lev. 19:12). And it includes unethical acts like a father and son having sexual relations with the same girl (Amos 2:7) and the Jerusalemites reneging on their solemn pact to free their Jewish slaves (Jer. 34:16). Ezekiel envisages this notion abstractly, and four times, in consecutive verses, proclaims God's determination to sanctify the Divine name which the people of Israel has profaned through its sinfulness (Ezek. 36:20–23).

The social dimension of several of these acts of profanation deserves particular attention. The heinousness of the sacrilege derives as much from what the act says about God to others, a public, as from its intrinsic profanity. The biblical authors consider God's social, corporate acknowledgment even more important than the equally indispensable private faith of individuals. The political term, king, so often used to refer to God, testifies to this social understanding of God's reality. Hence acts which imply that there is no God or which as good as do the same by testifying falsely to God's nature or commands, profane God's "name," that is, our understanding of God or, equally, God's reputation. Much of rabbinic teaching in this area derives from this social context.

A direct line runs from the Bible to the Talmud's teachings about *hillul hashem.*[4] Thus, since Jews are enjoined to sanctify God's name by martyrdom rather than commit murder, idolatry, or sexual offenses, failing to give up one's life then profanes God's name. So does rebelliously transgressing commands of the Torah. This identification of God with God's commands results in a significant rabbinic expansion of this theme, namely, that "important people," scholars being the chief case, must live by a higher standard than ordinary folk. People take rabbis and other such dignitaries as models for proper behavior. They therefore ought to avoid acts which the Torah otherwise permits but which, done by them, might lead to a lowering of communal standards and, in turn, to lesser sanctity in God's people, thus profaning its God.

A motif of particular importance for this investigation emerges from this preliminary survey. The concept of *hillul hashem* has extraordinary power.[5] When properly invoked, it can, so to speak, change the contours of Jewish duty. It does so by overriding a previous permission granted by the Torah and negating it, thus determining duty anew.

The *halakhah* contains such a possibility because its piety emphasizes the corporate dimension. Here the individual's "prior" options are limited to enhance the community's religious life and to safeguard it from sin. (With the Bible, the rabbis consider leading others to sin a qualitatively worse level of iniquity than is private transgression.) While the rabbis occasionally refer to the possibility of *hillul hashem* in private *(betzinah* or *beseter)*—of which the most notorious example is the advice to one overcome by lust to satisfy himself where he is not known—their overwhelming attention is given to acts in public *(befarhesiya* or *berabim).*[6]

Recognizing the cosmic importance the rabbis attached to the Jewish community and its practice of the Torah, the imperative, internal, social quality of *hillul hashem* seems quite logical. But considering the general corporate (as against individual) denigration of the gentiles, the *umot haolam* or *goyim*—who are usually identified as "wicked," and thus deserving of God's judgment—it comes as something of a surprise to discover that the same process operates in relation to them. The rabbis prohibit certain acts to Jews, not because the Torah proscribes them, but because of what doing them might lead gentiles to think or say.[7] In such cases, potential gentile opinion leads to a change in the "prior" contours of Jewish duty: hyperbolically, in some cases the gentiles "make" Torah.

In itself, this concern for the religious judgment of idolators is worthy of note. It testifies to the universalism implicit in *halakhah.* Of even greater interest, these prohibitions take precedence over Jewish economic loss, which the rabbis normally avoid in keeping with their principle, *hatorah hasah al memonam shel yisrael*, "the Torah has compassion on the funds of Jews." This unusual aspect of *halakhah,* with its intriguing parallels to recent ethical thinking about the universalizability of ethical judgment, deserves investigation.

Before proceeding, an important disclaimer must be made. In each instance to be studied, the majority of sages say Jewish law directly prohibits the act involved. They then rule that it carries a double opprobrium because it also constitutes *hillul hashem.* Here we are interested in the well-attested if minority usage of *hillul hashem* which some sages invoke to prohibit Jewish acts toward gentiles which they otherwise consider permissible. (It would also be of great interest if historians of the *halakhah* could elucidate the socio-temporal circumstances to which the rabbis may have been responding in these rulings.)

We may group the sixteen specific applications of *hillul hashem* we are studying into three categories: (1) the prohibition of acts directly disparaging God's honor or doing so by dishonoring the Jewish people; (2) the prohibition of possible stealing from gentiles whether direct or indirect; and (3) the prohibition of acts, national or individual, that might be perceived as deception.

Three acts fall into the first category. Only one is explicitly described as a direct affront to God: taking law cases to a gentile court.[8] This might be seen as testimony to the superiority of the gentiles' god or, with homiletic license, as indicating the denial of the God of Israel.[9] The other two cases dishonor the Jewish community: publicly taking charity from gentiles[10] and permitting gentile contractors to work for Jews on the Sabbath when it is clear that they are working for Jews, and gentiles do not permit work on their own Sabbath.[11]

The remaining cases, the overwhelming majority, concern thievery and deception. For *halakhah,* then, gentiles become a decisive factor in shaping the law mainly in ethical matters. The editors of the *Talmudic*

Encyclopedia consider the most embracing category of this theme *gezel hagoy*, "the robbery of gentiles." They not only treat it as the leading instance of the invocation of *hillul hashem* relative to gentiles[12] but they devote a substantial independent article to the topic.[13]

The problem is most easily confronted via a Tanaitic tradition cited in Y. B. K. 4.3. Two Romans, sent to learn all about Judaism, commented after having studied it that they admired Jewish law save for the provision that Jews are permitted to rob gentiles (perhaps, more narrowly, that Jews may keep what has been stolen from gentiles).[14] Thereupon Rabban Gamaliel prohibited the robbery of gentiles because it involved *hillul hashem*. Here not only do we have gentile opinion shaping Jewish duty (to the economic loss of Jews) but an indication that the permission once operated and the prohibition was instituted later. In any event, Jewish law proscribes the robbery of gentiles, whether because intrinsically forbidden by the Torah and doubly abominable as *hillul hashem*, or, according to some authorities, forbidden only under the latter rubric.

That would seem to settle the matter. Yet the robbery of gentiles arises in other specific matters which, for the sake of greater specificity, I consider below under the rubric of potential deception. A further set of problems arises probably because human cupidity is strong and Jews have been steadily persecuted. Thus, some authorities acknowledge that acts considered the robbery of gentiles might not become known, thus removing them from the prohibition of *hillul hashem*. But this means permitting such acts according to those sages who do not consider them intrinsically prohibited.[15]

Two prohibitions may be said to have been instituted to avoid even a gentile perception of Jewish theft. In the first instance, though Jews in the home of a Jewish owner may eat of that with which they are working, that practice is forbidden when the owner is gentile. He might conclude that Jewish laborers steal from their bosses.[16] In the second instance, a synagogue menorah which is the gift of a gentile may not be exchanged for anything else, even to perform a commandment, though that is possible for one donated by a Jew. And the sages explicitly note that invocation of *hillul hashem* is to prevent the gentile complaining about Jews appropriating his gift.[17]

Five cases, most of which traditionally are connected to the notion of *gezel hagoy*, seem to me better considered as forms of interpersonal deception. Thus, one may not lie to a gentile[18] or mislead him in negotiating to buy his slave.[19] A particularly intricate case involves *hafkaat halvaato*, the abrogation of a gentile's loan. In the original case, the loan was made by one gentile to another who then became the lender's slave until the loan was paid off. A Jew who purchases that slave should normally pay off the loan, but some authorities say Jews are not obligated to repay loans to gentiles.[20] Thus, Rashi, commenting on the talmudic text, says that this is not really *gezel hagoy,* only the refusal to give him back his money.[21] Sages following this legal line allow for keeping gentile money but consider this form of doing so less troubling a matter than outright *gezel hagoy.*

Hafkaat halvaato also arises analogously to other cases, described below (and, as we shall see, remains a living consideration for contemporary halakhic practice). The editors of the *Talmudic Encyclopedia* seem sensitive to the ethical problems involved in this issue. They therefore conspicuously feature an opinion that restricts this option, namely that of the Meiri, perhaps the leading traditional liberalizer of Jewish law regarding gentiles. In sum, once again the sages divide between those who hold *hafkaat halvaato* intrinsically forbidden and also a *hillul hashem,* and those who proscribe it only when it leads to a profanation of God's name.[22]

Two other forms of interpersonal deception are forbidden because of possible detrimental gentile opinion. One involves making a private condition when swearing an oath to a gentile under coercion, thus rendering it invalid.[23] The other concerns taking advantage of an error made by a gentile in the course of a negotiation.[24]

The five remaining cases seem more social in focus and if not prohibited might lead gentiles to consider Jews untrustworthy. A Jew may not oppress a gentile,[25] or keep something he has lost,[26] or deny him the testimony he seeks, even if this involves a loss to another Jew,[27] whenever such an act might lead to a profanation of God's name.

Perhaps the most troublesome of these issues is the avoidance of taxes imposed by a gentile government. While it is clear that "the law of the [gentile] country has the force of [Torah] law," a body of opinion clearly holds that in certain cases avoidance is permitted—but not if it might involve *hillul hashem.*[28] Finally, as the case of the Gibeonites made clear to the rabbis, the Jewish people may not break a treaty it has made with another people, even if false pretenses are involved, should that act result in the disparagement of the Jews and thus the profanation of God's name.[29]

One can therefore say about these sixteen instances that the evidence abundantly demonstrates that in certain cases, mainly ethical ones, gentile opinion can be a decisive, overriding factor in determining, even altering, *halakhah.* It would be of the greatest interest to know what constitutes the necessary warrants for invoking *hillul hashem* in a given case and what limits there are to its uncommon power. Nothing in the literature studied touches directly on the theory of the utilization of *hillul hashem.* Indeed, we do not find it characteristic of any given sage and it seems, on the surface, to be used with as much randomness as consistency.

So much is classic *halakhah.* To see how this motif might be of help to us in clarifying the nature of Jewish ethics today, it will help to take a brief look at its contemporary employment. A search made by the Institute for Computers in Jewish Life through the responsa program of the Bar-Ilan Center for Computers and Jewish Studies provided the necessary data. It generated a list of sources in which the term *hillul hashem* appeared in close association with either *goy* or *akum* (literally, "idolator"; legally, "non-Jew"—though hardly a happy association). In the works of three eminent respondents of our time, Yechiel Weinberg *(Seridei Esh),* Moshe Feinstein, *(Igrot Moshe),* and Eliezer Waldenberg *(Tzitz Eliezer),* seventeen possible *teshuvot* dealing with our topic occurred.[30] Of these, only eight were relevant to this study, the others either could not be found, had no reference to this topic, or related only to *hillul shabbat.*

Yechiel Weinberg is best represented in this sample, as five of his *teshuvot* deal with *hillul hashem* in relation to gentiles. He uses the term *hillul hashem* in these texts only in the citation or summary of the traditional dicta. The case topics are: (1) martyrdom (*Seridei Esh,* vol. 2, no. 79); (2) teaching gentiles Torah, where he adduces the case of the Romans (*Seridei Esh,* vol. 2, no. 90); (3) selling a synagogue seat to satisfy a debt, where the sale of synagogue property is discussed (*Seridei Esh,* vol. 3, no. 63); and (4) the robbery of gentiles (*Seridei Esh,* nos. 74–75—in the latter, beware of the misprint at the top of page 254 which indicates that this is responsum no. 57 rather than no. 75).

Only two responsa of Moshe Feinstein are relevant to this study. Both involve the issue of *gezel hagoy* with one merely mentioning the classic opinions (*Igrot Moshe, Yoreh Deah,* vol. 1, no. 103). The other is somewhat more interesting since it seems to be the only instance of this concept being used in a fresh application as against the citation of classic precedent (*Igrot Moshe, Hoshen Mishpat,* vol. 1, no. 82). He suggests that the sages did not absolutely require the return of a gentile's lost article because while voluntarily doing so can lead to sanctifying God's name among gentiles, having to do so might, on occasion, lead to *hillul hashem.*

It should be noted, however, that this unique example of a contemporary creative use of the concept of *hillul hashem* occurs in a theoretical discussion of the law of the rabbis living among idolators.

The one relevant *teshuvah* of Eliezer Waldenberg has special interest since the questioner proposes a new application of *hillul hashem.* Quite conscious of the concept's special power, he suggests that wearing his *tzitziyot* so that they are visible, rather than obscured by being under his other clothes, may lead gentiles to set inordinately high standards for his behavior (since most Jews are not this pious). This might lead to what he ingeniously calls *avak hillul hashem,* "a hint [literally, "the dust"] of a profanation of God's name" (*Tzitz [sic] Eliezer,* vol. 8 no. 3). Hence he inquires whether, since this does not involve either giving up the practice or altering it to avoid gentile mockery, he may wear his *tzitziyot* obscured. To which the answer is a firm negative, with the possibility of *avak hillul hashem* apparently of so little substance that Waldenberg never discusses it.

From this sample, limited in authorities and to the questions they have chosen to answer and publish, some tentative conclusions may be drawn. Apparently the major *poskim* of our time use the concept of *hillul hashem* only in the cases and contexts in which it came down to them. They do not seem to apply it to any new situations or in terms of any different perception of gentile opinion. Insofar as they are indicative of the broad sweep of contemporary *halakhah,* we may say that Jewish law internally recognizes that in certain instances, largely ethical, it should be governed authoritatively by gentile reactions to Jewish behavior or their perceptions thereof, if the sages, by standards and methods remaining obscure, deem such fresh legal determinations warranted.

At this point, liberal (and postliberal) Jews demur. For these authorities the Emancipation has changed nothing, and gentile opinions are still thought of as if there were no Jewish political equality amid functioning democracies. By the very grant of full civic status to Jews and the continuing effort to overcome the powerful vestiges of fifteen hundred years of legally established anti-Semitism, gentiles and their ethical opinions are worthy of very much more consideration than they were in pre-Emancipation times. The appeal to Jews of the Kantian insistence on the universalization of ethics rests on this intellectual-social basis. Rabbinic Judaism understood that "a decent respect to the opinions of mankind" can mandate Torah law. The changed behavior of gentiles toward Jews, and the continuing realities of Jewish equality, demand greater concern with and respect for the ethical judgments of those who are not Jewish.

The liberal concern with ethics stems from this religious perception. The search by postliberal thinkers for a new understanding of Jewish ethics may involve rejecting the liberals' insistence that Jewish obligation be universalizable. However, the new particularism does not invalidate the essential truth that Jews today must sanctify God's name in significant part by attending to universal, that is to gentile as well as Jewish, moral opinion.

Recent Jewish suffering at gentile hands bolsters rather than refutes this affirmation about the significance of gentile understandings of ethics. True, the Holocaust ended Jewish liberals' messianic enthusiasm at gentile goodwill. And the continuing manifestations of anti-Semitism must keep Jews wary, not only of our enemies but of our own wishful thinking. Such bitterly won realism does not constitute reason to deny that the Emancipation radically changed relations between Jews and gentiles. It raised universalism from a largely neglected human theoretical notion to an ideal which continues to exert powerful political pressure on much of humankind. If particularistic standards of ethical behavior are to be restored to supremacy, it will be difficult to argue that the German people had no right to do what it did; or, of equal significance today, that all humankind should have stood up to protest the barbaric German violation of fundamental human rights. More, if democracy cannot be trusted, not only is most of world Jewry unsafe but so is the State of Israel, whose survival depends on the continued health of free nations.

Let me illustrate the divergence of these two Jewish views of attention to gentile ethical judgments by showing how they affect or might affect one aspect of contemporary Jewish ethical responsibility, namely, a Jew's religious obligation to pay taxes to a non-Jewish government.

Herschel Schachter, professor of Talmud at Yeshiva University, devotes half of a recent study to this issue.[31] One might assume that the well-known talmudic principle *dina demalkhuta dina*, "the law of the country is [Torah] law," applies to taxation, a civil matter. The question is not that simple, and Schachter clarifies the background and substance of a significant difference of opinion on a gentile government's right to levy taxes. He writes, "This dispute . . . is not just a hair-splitting technicality. Upon the resolution hinges the major question of whether a Jew living under a non-Jewish government has to consider the laws of the land as legitimately binding [in Jewish law] upon him or not. . . . It is not necessary at this point to follow through to the end of the technical dispute; suffice it to record that practical *halakhah* generally accepts that the ruler does have certain legitimate powers over the individuals under his control, and that to some extent, as part of keeping the Torah, Jews must accept these restrictions or guidelines." (Note the qualification, "generally accepts," which allows a loophole that will grow at the next level of the discussion.)

Schachter then continues with a discussion of the sages' differing opinions as to the extent of the government's right to levy taxes.[32] Since the matter remains unresolved, he can only continue the discussion, "Assuming that the government has the legal right to levy taxes, and that the citizens are obligated to pay these taxes, *like any other debt that any individual owes to someone else*"[33] (emphasis added, as it returns us to the rabbinic notion of the Jew's right not to pay back a gentile loan). He then goes on to ask, "What would be the status [in Jewish law] of one who does not pay his taxes; or does not pay the full amount that he should legally be paying?"[34]

The difficulties now deepen. "If however it is a non-Jewish government to which one owes taxes. . . The Talmud clearly forbids 'gezel akum' stealing from a nochri *[sic]*, but 'hafka'as halva'oso' is allowed. That is to say that although theft from a nochri is forbidden, *not paying back* a debt which one owes to a nochri is not considered an act of gezel (theft). If this be the case, then the non-Jewish government has all the legal right to levy just and fair taxes; still, what is to forbid the individual from failure to pay his taxes on the grounds that 'hafka'as halva'oso' (nonpayment of a debt) of a nochri is allowed?"[35]

Schachter apparently cannot bring himself to translate the term *nochri*, which means "gentile" (literally, "stranger"). Reading the paragraph without the euphemism of the Hebrew term changes its ethical impact, precisely the question of gentile opinion (and perhaps that of poorly informed Jews as well who assume that Torah law is generally ethical and not discriminatory).[36]

He further notes that with the proliferation of small businesses the issue is a real one, but the sages do not definitively settle it. He continues, "To the question of whether it is permissible to operate a store and not collect or not pay sales tax, we find a mixed response."[37] He then explicates different views on this topic. He indicates, in one sentence, that the Vilna Gaon and "other Poskim" (though only *Kesef Mishneh* is cited in his note) permit nonpayment. Since there is no further citation, it is he who adds that "if one might possibly create a situation of 'chilul hashem' by not paying taxes, there is no doubt that the 'heter' [permission] of 'hafka'as halva'ah' [not repaying a gentile loan] of akum [here not 'nochri' but the old legal term for gentile, 'idolator'] does not apply. In the *rare instance* where (a) there is no question of signing a false statement, and (b) there is no possibility of causing a chilul hashem, this group of poskim does not consider it forbidden."[38] He then continues with a discussion of the opinion of those who insist on payment and, tellingly, raises the further issue of patronizing such an establishment, recording a statement of Rabbi J. B. Soloveitchik that it is forbidden.

To the postliberal Jewish ethical sensibility, appropriate reverence for the teaching of prior generations has here been carried too far. Almost every authority cited in Schachter's discussion lived under conditions of political inequality and discrimination, as well as in an economy of scarcity. Like the three contemporary respondents cited above, nothing in his discussion takes cognizance of the Emancipation and of the radically changed relations of Jews and gentiles.

Suppose, following the story of the Talmud of the Land of Israel, that gentiles, long told they cannot truly understand Judaism unless they understand *halakhah,* come to study it. And they learn that devout Jews in America are still guided by their sages to consider whether the American government does or does not have religious validity, does or does not have the right to tax them, and whether they, in turn, do or do not have an obligation to pay taxes, or indeed, to pay back gentile loans (if, of course, in the exercise of halakhic creativity they can be reasonably certain of not being detected and avoid *hillul hashem*)? Should not some contemporary Rabban Gamliel, indeed the halakhic community as a whole, rise up and decree that the very discussion of these matters in these terms, much less acting upon them, constitutes a *hillul hashem*?

But why wait for such a discovery and thus allow a grave sin to occur? Why not admit that in our changed situation, we ought to broaden our appreciation of human ethical opinion and, giving it greater scope than it once had in the life of Torah, allow it to override such elements of civil discrimination and inequality as have come down to us? The task of mediating between *halakhah* and ethics remains a difficult one for postliberals. But the fresh will to be guided by classic Jewish teaching must not be allowed to wipe out the truths of universal ethics on which, in fact, we build our Jewish existence day by day.

NOTES

1. I use the term "postliberal" to distinguish those non-Orthodox thinkers who consciously distance themselves from the earlier liberal equation of Jewish ethics with universal ethics (generally

formulated in a neo-Kantian structure) and who thus gave inadequate weight to the *halakhah's* independent striving for the good. The postliberals seek to remedy this by treating the classic Jewish legal sources with at least equal dignity.

2. Lichtenstein's paper is found in Marvin Fox, *Modern Jewish Ethics* (Columbus: Ohio State University Press, 1975). My response, "The Authority of the Ethical Impulse in Halakhah," appeared in *Studies in Jewish Philosophy,* vol. 2, and in somewhat different form in Jonathan V. Plaut, ed., *Through the Sound of Many Voices* (Toronto: Lester and Orpen Dennys, 1982). For the view that ethical considerations per se play no part in halakhic decisions, see David Weiss Halivni, "Can a Religious Law Be Immoral?" in *Perspectives on Jews and Judaism,* ed. Arthur Chiel (New York: Rabbinical Assembly, 1978).

3. See the admirable study by David Novak, *The Image of the Non-Jew in Judaism* (New York: Edward Mellen, 1983). I am not fully persuaded that the sources bear out the philosophical underpinnings that Novak finds in the origin and development of the category of Noachide law, but he has made a most impressive case for a considerable if implicit rationality in these laws.

4. This study of the halakhic sources on *hillul hashem* is based on the relevant articles in *Entziklopediyah Talmudit,* 17 vols. (Jerusalem: Talmudic Encyclopedia Institute, 1955–), henceforth ET, namely, "*goy*" (vol. 5), "*gezel hagoy*" (vol. 5), and, particularly, "*hillul hashem*" (vol. 15). My independent check of a number of the sources cited indicated that, other than what a historical-critical hermeneutic might add, the articles faithfully and intelligently represented the texts cited. For ease of reference, I shall therefore cite the rabbinic materials underlying my analyses by reference to the apposite encyclopedia column or footnote, all from the article "*hillul hashem*" unless otherwise specified.

5. ET, col. 347ff., the subsection on the "important person."

6. In keeping with the methodology of this study, I forbear from citing the many *aggadic* passages which testify, with the usual hyperbole, to the seriousness with which the rabbis deplored the sin of *hillul hashem.* See the collection in ET, col. 356ff.

7. ET, col. 344.

8. Many sages are quite explicit about this and make such statements as, "lest the gentiles say, 'The Jews have no Torah,'" (n. 160), "or they might say, 'Why did God choose thieves and deceivers to be His portion?'" (n. 161), or it might lead them to cast aspersions on the Jewish religion (n. 163).

9. ET, col. 347.

10. ET, n. 91.

11. ET, col. 356; cf. "*goy,*" vol. 6, col. 310.

12. ET, col. 355. The only *teshuvah* of David Hoffmann dealing with *hillul hashem* involved this sort of case (*Melamed Lehoil,* pt. 1, *Orah Hayyim* 35). We shall encounter another one below in our consideration of contemporary *teshuvot.*

13. ET, col. 351.

14. ET, vol. 5, col. 487ff. The article has nine columns of text with 134 notes in the usual condensed style of ET.

15. There are several variations of this story with the Romans making somewhat different complaints in them, e.g., *Sifre Deuteronomy,* ed. Louis Finkelstein, p. 401. The issue of the robbery of gentiles occurs only in the Talmud of the Land of Israel. Corroborative material, however, may be found in the discussions cited in B.M. 111b.

16. The issue of the robbery of a gentile becoming known is raised repeatedly by the sources cited in the article on *gezel hagoy.*

17. ET, col. 353, nn. 174–75.

18. ET, col 355, nn. 209–15.

19. ET, nn. 160–61.

20. ET, nn. 167–68.

21. ET, n. 169, but see the extended treatment in the article "*gezel hagoy,*" col. 493.

22. Ibid., nn. 97–98.

23. Ibid., nn. 102–103.

24. ET, "*hillul hashem,*" col. 353.

25. ET, n. 169, and see the long discussion in the article "*gezel hagoy,*" col: 494f., and see particularly n. 127 which is the case we are discussing.

26. ET, n. 170, and the discussion in the article "*gezel hagoy,*" nn. 108–11. The usual understanding of this is failure to pay one's debts. It may thus only be another way of putting the issue of *hafkaat halvaato,* but I have adduced it here for the sake of completeness.

27. ET, n. 169, and the discussion in the article "*goy,*" col. 359, nn. 153–57.

28. ET, nn. 216–17.

29. ET, article "*dina demalkhuta dina,*" vol. 7, col. 301.

30. ET, cols. 353ff.

31. I do not know what to make of the following statistical anomaly: though more *poskim* spoke of *hillul hashem* in relation to *goy* than to *akum* (six pages of printout to four), the bulk of the classic respondents used the former, less derogatory term while a much higher proportion of modern *poskim* (arbitrarily, those later than the Maharsham—Shalom Mordecai Shvadron, 1835–1911) used the latter term. In our sample, sixteen of the seventeen responsa were listed in the *akum teshuvot;* and the one indicated with the usage *goy* (though it did not appear in the cited sentence) could not be located due to a difficulty with the printout at that point (*Igrot Moshe,* possibly *Hoshen Mishpat,* vol. 3, no. 3).

32. "Dina De'malchusa Dina," *Journal of Holacha and Contemporary Society* 1, no. 1 (Spring 1981, Pesach 5741): 103ff.

33. Ibid., 107–11.

34. Ibid., 111.

35. Ibid.

36. Ibid., 112–13.

37. Ibid., 113.

38. Ibid., 113f.

19 / The Ideal Jew

1986

In this lecture I should like to pay tribute to the memories of two scholars who, in different ways, contributed to my intellectual growth. The one was Fritz Bamberger, Assistant to the President of the Hebrew Union College-Jewish Institute of Religion, who, while teaching modern Jewish thought at our school, exemplified much of the best of pre-Hitlerian German Jewry. The other was Gershom Scholem, surely one of the model Jewish scholars of this century. May their memories continue to be for widespread blessing.

Their paths and mine crossed one memorable evening. Fritz and his wife, Maria, invited my wife, Estelle, and me to dinner at their apartment with Gershom Scholem prior to his public lecture at our school. I do not know which aspect of that experience made the greatest impression upon me: the gracious hospitality of the Bambergers; the old, easy friendship of the two ex-Berliners; the openness of the world-famous savant to his young American admirers; the civilized range of the witty, erudite conversation; or the drama of the great scholar returning to the auditorium where, as a young man, he delivered the lectures that were originally published by the then Jewish Institute of Religion as *Major Trends in Jewish Mysticism.*

I

Whatever the case, I still clearly recall the extraordinary impact his lecture made upon me. He spoke that night about classic Judaism's model human beings and said "I do not think there can be any doubt as to what these types of the ideal Jew are."[1] Years later, his judgment still seems correct. He identified these ideals as the *talmid hakham,* the *tzaddik* and the *hasid*—terms too rich for easy translation but ones that may be rendered, the sage, the righteous and the pietist.

I should now like to extend Scholem's analysis in two directions: first, to add some nuances to his discussion of the past and, more important, to extend his thought into the present by speculating about the contemporary Jewish human ideal.

Scholem's premise was that "The basic tension in the religious society of Judaism is that between rational and emotional factors, rational and irrational forces. The ideal types formed by this society will necessarily reflect such tension." I see in this statement a reflection of Scholem's personal agenda, one powerfully formed by his response to German Jewish life. I, being part of the next generation and a product of American Jewry, see things differently. In part due to the acceptance of his work, in part because of historic events, the rational and irrational forces in Judaism, as in all humanity, seem to me more to co-exist than to be in radical tension. And, against his view, I find that to be true of the classic sources of Judaism, which he denominated the "talmudic and rabbinical forms to which Jewish philosophy or, for that matter, Jewish mysticism has added other dimensions without basically changing its substance."[2]

In that light, let me modify somewhat what Scholem said about the three ideal Jewish figures, particularly in terms of their depiction in talmudic and midrashic literature.

The first model he discusses is the *talmid hakham*, "the rabbinic scholar, or, as the extremely modest term would have to be translated literally: 'the pupil of a sage.'" He sees in this term "above all, an intellectual value and a value of a life of contemplation [as contrasted to activity]. What is asked of the scholar? A rational effort of the mind and its concentration."[3] After filling out his portrait of the sage, he sums up, "the decisive quality expected of him is his sobriety and rationality by which he is able to expound the values that have come down and been upheld by tradition, and his clarity of mind which makes him an educator, handing down those values to the next generation."[4]

This figure, I suggest, logically emerges from a distinctive characteristic of the Jewish religion, that God has given written as well as oral—as the rabbis insist—Torah, instructions, to the people of Israel. Since these include the possibility of their further elaboration, the person who knows the traditions and who can reliably interpret and apply them acquires high religious status.

Scholem emphasizes the academic character of the *talmid hakham* so heavily in order to dramatize his contrast with the *hasid*, whom

Scholem will depict as essentially an emotional type, a religious enthusiast. I think that rhetorical purpose leads Scholem to overstate the case, as three themes in talmudic literature make clear.

Scholem admits[5] that the *talmid hakham* is a community figure but then radically subordinates this role to the sage's personal intellectual activity. Talmudic texts are less one-sided for they describe him as being appointed by the community[6] and, whether or not officially installed to do so, performing various functions: as judge, preacher, teacher of students, decisor of various ritual issues, determiner of which vows one may be released from, and the agent of other such religious functions.[7] These surely require the exercise of rationality but hardly leave us with the sense of an ivory-tower intellectual as Scholem's description might.

Not the least aspect of being a community figure was serving as a role model. His disciples wanted to see how the master lived as well as to hear his teachings. And they then told their disciples what their masters did in the most diverse human situations. Their tales speak less of the sages as essentially sober, rational types, than of quite passionate men who regularly break into tears or otherwise give vent to their joy, distress or exasperation.

We see this quite plainly in the tales about Rabbi Akiba, whom Scholem describes "as the perfect embodiment of the type of which I am talking . . ."[8] True, he did keep public services to a limit when he led them, but in private he might begin his prayers in one end of a room and end them in another because of his many kneelings and prostrations.[9] He is also remembered as a practitioner of mysticism,[10] and when he preached at the funeral for his son Simeon, it is his humility, not his theodicy, which stands out.[11] Akiba was an extraordinary intellect but the Jewish tradition remembers him, like others whom it called *talmid hakham,* as a richly human personality.

Scholem says of the two remaining types, the *tzaddik* and the *hasid,* that "they are not judged by the quality of their intellectual penetration, but by the way in which they perform the discharge of their religious duties in action. They are, to put it briefly, ideals of the *active* [as against the contemplative] life." He then adds, "Of course, the types are not exclusive of each other. A scholar may well-nigh be a *tzaddik* or a *hasid* at the same time and vice versa. Each is to be judged by his own scale of values. If the *talmid hakham* represented an intellectual value in its perfection, the *tzaddik* or the *hasid* represents what we would call ethical values, values of the heart and of the deeds of man."[12] Moreover, while of the latter two types, there is "no clear-cut distinction and separation" and "very often the terms could be exchanged" in the middle ages, particularly in the *musar,* the pietistic literature, "the distinction between the two types becomes crystal clear."[13]

For all that, when Scholem describes the *tzaddik,* he does so in terms directly derived from the Talmud.[14] "The *tzaddik* is the Jew who tries to comply with the commandments of the Law. He would be a *tzaddik* in the eyes of God if, brought before His court, it would be found that he has fulfilled his duties at least more than fifty percent."[15] Further,

> He is the man who puts harmonious order into his life, or at least tries to do so and essentially succeeds. This order is the order of the Torah, an all-comprehensive ideal of harmony in the deeds and activities of men that leaves no room for extravagance . . . The *tzaddik,* let me put it in a sententious way, is the ideal of the *normal* Jew . . . In the moral sphere, indeed, the ideal of the *tzaddik* contains an element in common with the ideal of the scholar. This is the sobriety of the ideal, the absence of emotionalism. The Just Man is balanced in his actions, there is something deeply composed and cool-headed about him, however intense the passion to fulfill the Divine command that drives him may be. He does not lose control of himself.[16]

I believe that the notion of the *tzaddik* as the ideal for the ordinary Jew derives easily from Judaism as a religion of Torah. God's instructions, revealed to the people of Israel at Sinai and reinterpreted by the sages of each generation, focus upon the proper conduct of life. A Jew therefore serves God by trying to carry out God's behests, whether imparted as rule, ideal, model or folk intuition. The *tzaddik,* the one who has managed more often than not to carry out the Torah, thus becomes the common model for Jewish piety.

Scholem seems to me to distort the picture of the *tzaddik* by stressing his sobriety and level-headedness, and not giving equal weight to what he acknowledges as "the intense passion to fulfill the Divine commandment that drives him. . . ." Once again, what Scholem calls the classic epitome gives us a somewhat different picture than he has drawn. He says, "The classic manuals of Jewish morals describe such training for the state of *tzaddik,* none more stringently than the famous treatise *Mesillat Yesharim* [The Path of the Upright] . . . no doubt one of the noblest products of Hebrew literature."[17] Yet that book hardly deals with sober-sidedness in religion. Rather, after its introduction, its next four chapters teach about the virtue of "Watchfulness," its acquisition and the hindrances to practicing it. And the next four chapters focus on "Zeal" in the same way. These are less a call to harmoniousness than to religious drive.

The treatise says of the proper attitude toward the commandments, ". . . we should be as scrupulous with regard to the *mitzvot* and the worship of God as though we had to weigh gold or precious stones, for they are means to perfection and eternal worth."[18] Later, the desired combination of concern and control is nicely juxtaposed by the author, Moses Luzzatto, this way: "In short, a man should be attentive to his actions, and so watchful of his conduct that he will not tolerate in himself any bad or evil tendency, much less any actual sin or transgression. I consider it necessary for a man to conduct himself like a merchant who always takes stock of his affairs so that he may not go wrong in his reckoning."[19]

I think it difficult for us who live in a permissive religious time to appreciate the seriousness medieval believers would have brought to such words. They took God's sovereignty literally. Hence God's commands, and the rewards and punishments which they knew followed upon them, came to them with a compelling power we can hardly imagine. We can sense something of the spiritual distance between us in Luzzatto's teaching "that all decisions which incline toward leniency call for further examination. For although such leniency may be proper, it may, nevertheless, be a trick which the Evil Urge is playing upon us. Every tendency to be lenient should, therefore, be thoroughly looked into." But, in true Jewish spirit, Luzzatto does not teach asceticism. He concludes, "If, after such scrutiny, it still appears justified, it may certainly be considered good."[20]

Thus the properly zealous soul "moves with the swiftness of fire, and gives himself no rest until his object is attained. Note, further, that as enthusiasm calls forth zeal, so zeal calls forth enthusiasm, for when a man is engaged in the performance of a *mitzvah,* he feels that as he hastens his outward movements, his emotions are aroused and his enthusiasm waxes stronger. But if his bodily movements are sluggish, the movements of his spirit also become dull and lifeless."[21]

Thus, the *tzaddik* aimed at by the instructions of the *Mesillat Yesharim* is a far cry from what Scholem describes as "the family man and citizen of the community [who] measures his steps . . . weighs his actions . . . [and though he] resist[s] temptation, to prove his worth and to overcome great difficulties . . . nothing essentially extraordinary is asked of him." Luzzatto's *tzaddik*—and the Talmud's too, I would argue[22]—is something of an extremist, if only for taking religion so seriously and working at it so diligently.

For Scholem, the *talmid hakham* and the *tzaddik* are rational types while the third classic figure, the *hasid,* is essentially emotional.

> . . . the *hasid* is the exceptional type of man. He is the radical Jew, who, in trying to follow the spiritual call, goes to extremes . . . He is never content with the middle road, he does not count his steps. He is the enthusiast, whose radicalism and utter emotional commitment are not to be deterred by bourgeois consideration. [The latter, almost certainly, is a reference to the style of the *tzaddik* as Scholem understands him.] . . . Whatever he does, he does in a spirit of spontaneous exuberance and of supererogation . . . The *tzaddik* follows a law valid for all. I would say that he is the Jewish disciple of Kant in ethics. The *hasid* follows a law that is valid and binding only for himself . . . There is something non-conformist and even an element of holy anarchism in his nature. It is true, in his outward behavior he submits to the established law in all its rigor, but he transcends it by his spiritual fervor.[23]

Scholem's delineation of the *hasid* reaches a climax in the contrast he draws to the figure of the *tzaddik.* While he emphasizes strongly[24] that one might become a *tzaddik* through education, thus explaining the Jewish religious devotion to study, he says, "Whether you are a *hasid* or not is basically a matter of gift and character. It is a propensity which you have or have not. If you have it, you can develop it. But you cannot educate everybody to become a *hasid,* as in principle you could educate everybody to become a *tzaddik.*"[25]

Judaism's esteem for the *hasid,* I suggest, simply confirms all religion's effort to draw humankind to what Paul Tillich nicely termed ultimacy. Thus, in polytheism the various gods had unique powers and deserved to be served with special care and attention. In monotheism, however, the one God of all the universe shares that regard with no one; the single God thus properly demands our concentrated dedication. Since Jewish practice links the acknowledgement of God's unity with loving God with all one's heart, with all one's soul and with all one's might, some of the faithful will surely do so extravagantly.

What may be lost in Scholem's depiction is that the *hasid,* for all his extremism, remains a normative Jew, one whose life is structured by the Torah. Scholem himself often commented that Jewish mysticism, for all its interiority, is essentially law-abiding. Here his focus on the *hasid* as non-conformist enthusiast unfortunately underplays the balancing dialectic.

The matter is quite clear in the Talmud if only, as Scholem has noted, because many of the *talmidei hakhamim,* who were, of course, *tzaddikim,* are also called *hasid.*[26] The same is true of the description given in medieval Jewish literature. Recall that Scholem had said that no manual of training for the state of *tzaddik* did so "more stringently than the famous treatise *Mesillat Yesharim* . . . by the Italian poet and mystic

Moses Hayyim Luzzatto . . ."[27] But as to becoming a *hasid,* Scholem contends that Luzzatto "insists that all the advice or analysis which he can give is of no avail. The main thing is, according to him, that only those who have been vouchsafed a gift of Divine grace, who have a particular spark in their soul, may strive for the quality of a *hasid.*"[28]

I read the *Mesillat Yesharim* rather differently. To begin with, Luzzatto says directly that he is writing to train people to be *hasidim.* After complaining that while some people study science and others Torah, even in depth, he comments, "There are but few who study the nature of the love and the fear of God, of communion or any other phase of *hasidut,* saintliness. Yet the neglect of these studies is not due to their being regarded as inessential . . ." but because people consider them so commonplace that they feel one needn't spend much time on them.[29] Rather, though various practices pass for saintliness, they "fail to satisfy the intellect, and offer nothing to the understanding." His purpose is then summarized, "Although saintliness is latent in the character of every normal person, yet without cultivation it is sure to remain dormant . . . [it is] not so innate as to enable men to dispense with the effort needed to develop [it]."[30] Scholem's typology has obviously run ahead of his data.

Scholem does cite some material to show that Luzzatto considers *hasidut* a personal grace and hence uneducable. But the passages preceding his citation make the opposite point. Luzzatto has little use for the saintliness thought to come from performing certain pieties. Their practitioners "lack the power of true understanding and reflection *[ha'iyun vehahaskalah]*. They have neither troubled nor toiled to understand clearly and correctly the way of the Lord. . . . Saintliness should be reared upon great wisdom and upon the adjustment of conduct to the aims worthy of the truly wise. Only the wise can truly grasp the nature of saintliness."[31] If there remains any question about Luzzatto's belief that *hasidut* is rationally communicable to many people, it will help to remember that at this point he has already written seventeen chapters about its attainment, and his book continues for nine more.

Luzzatto gives a précis of his understanding of the *hasid,* one like that of Scholem, yet less anarchic in its spirituality.

> The *mitzvot* which are explicitly commanded are to him merely an indication of the purpose which is willed and desired by God. . . . Such a man will not say "It is enough that I do what I am expressly commanded," or, "I will fulfill only those duties which have been imposed upon me." On the contrary, he will say, "Now that I have discovered what God's purpose is, it will guide me in going beyond the prescribed commandment, and in cultivating

> those phases of the commandments which, so far as I may judge, are pleasing to Him." This is what is meant by affording happiness to the Creator. Accordingly, the principle of saintliness is that the scope of the observance of *mitzvot* should be enlarged. This applies to every possible aspect of the *mitzvot,* and to the circumstances under which they are to be observed.[32]

The extremism and radicality which Scholem stressed are found here but the nonconformity of Luzzatto's *hasid* is remarkably structured compared to what we have come to expect from apostles of religious enthusiasm.

Scholem concluded his lecture—and perhaps this thought led him to it—that, with the emergence of the Hasidic movement in the eighteenth century, these terms underwent a "very curious metamorphosis. Never would it have occurred to earlier generations . . . to give the title of *hasidim* to people who admired *hasidim.* But that is precisely what has happened here . . . a rather paradoxical, if not to say scandalous, usage of the word—and the true *hasidim,* those who live up to the [classic] ideal, now came to be called *tzaddikim* . . . A *tzaddik* in the hasidic sense has nothing to do with what the term meant in the traditional usage . . . but rather connotes the 'super-*hasid.*' "[33] This insight of Scholem's comes with startling effect, offering another example of the way in which new movements tend to co-opt old terms all the while redefining them. It is a stunning example of the idiosyncratic way religious traditions can transform themselves, which should caution students of religion that the same term may mean quite different things in different periods in a given faith. If so, how much the more is it possible that the same term used in different faiths is likely to have quite diverse meanings in each of them.

II

The insightfulness of Scholem's typology becomes clear when we apply it to modern times, which he did not. Jewish modernity arises with the Emancipation, the process beginning in the nineteenth century by which Jews were granted political rights in Europe and North America. Wherever Jews received equality they overwhelmingly abandoned ghetto life—created in response to 1,500 years of discrimination—and avidly embraced the broader cultural horizon of the welcoming society. Indeed, they often over-idealized its humanity, identifying their host nation with a commitment to universal human liberation and fulfillment.

In this radical shift of social horizon, the old ideals, *talmid hakham, tzaddik, hasid,* lost compelling appeal. They had been empowered by

Jewish faith exercised in a Jewish setting. Modern Jews lived primarily among non-Jews and largely adopted their human standards. Thus for newly enfranchised Jews—in my family as recent as my father's and mother's emigration from Poland and Hungary—attaining social competence took priority over Jewish achievement. Most American Jews, I am convinced, still have that hierarchy of values despite their recent revival of interest in their Jewishness.

A second significant social shift accompanied the first, namely, the loss of rabbinic authority. Modern Jews, happy in a democratic social order, increasingly, if often quietly, took on the dignity of religious self-determination. They would make up their own minds as to how they would live Jewishly and whose guidance (*sic*) they would accept.

A minority of Jews resisted these changes in the name of traditional Jewish faith. Their way of life was determined by God's gift of the Torah, interpreted for our age by contemporary sages, not by the gentile world and its culture heroes. The overwhelming majority of Jews, however, found unreconstructed Jewish faith no longer tenable. For them, modernization meant secularization, so even when they believed, they were surer of their questions than of their affirmations.

Scholem, studying pre-modern Jewish ideal types consulted the sacred books created by the religious elite. But to look for the contemporary equivalent of a Jewish ideal, we are better advised to turn to the people itself. I confess I do not know a methodologically defensible way of doing that, yet I believe it needs[34] to be attempted. What follows, then, proceeds from no sociological expertise but arises from my experience in and study of the Jewish community, both filtered through my intuition of the continuing existential validity of the Covenant.

Two academicians have recently essayed a similar task, seeking to characterize the Jewishness in which they were reared. Arnaldo Momigliano, celebrating the award of a Nobel prize to a fellow Italian Jew wrote,

> Jewish Italian society developed on its own lines—realistic, connected with business, comparatively open to foreign ideas, but fundamentally introspective, concerned with social justice and yet suspicious of too much novelty. Music, painting, literature, socialism and science became intense preoccupations of the Italian Jews. Profane music has been one of their interests since at least the Renaissance. Now we had composers such as Vittorio Tieti, Alberto Franchetti, Mario Castelnuovo-Tedesco, and Leone Sinigaglia. Painting was more of a novelty. Perhaps it is not chance that the socialist leader Emanuele Modigliani and the painter Amadeo Modigliani

> were brothers. Jewish scientists showed uncommon methodological preoccupations: two Jews, Eugenio Rignano and Frederico Enriquez, created that important international forum for scientific methodology, the periodical *Scientia.*
>
> How much this brooding, introspective mood contributed to the greatness of Italian mathematicians, physicists, chemists I can only guess, thinking as I do of some who were my relatives and friends. Where were the roots of the legendary mathematical imagination of Tullio Levi-Civita? Fascism was bound to exclude most of those Jews who had solid liberal or socialist traditions behind them; while economic interests led some Jews to direct involvement with fascism. One of the most honest Fascists was Gino Olivetti, the representative of industrial interests inside Fascism. Fascist ideological sympathies were also to be found among jurists . . . who wanted a reform of the Italian state on corporate lines.[35]

The ethos of modern German Jewry has been explored in greater depth by George Mosse in his Efroymson Lectures at the Hebrew Union College-Jewish Institute of Religion.[36] He argues convincingly for its encapsulation in the notion of *bildung.* That term, he notes,

> combines the meaning carried by the English word "education" with notions of character formation and moral education. Man must grow like a plant, as Herder put it, toward the unfolding of his personality until he becomes an harmonious, autonomous individual exemplifying both the continuing quest for knowledge and the moral imperative. . . . Such self-education was an inward process . . . [one which] did not refer to instinctual drives or emotional preferences but to the cultivation of reason and aesthetic taste. . . . Moreover, such self-cultivation was a continuous process which was never supposed to end during one's life. Surely here was an ideal ready-made for Jewish assimilation, because it transcended all differences of nationality and religion through the unfolding of the personality.[37]

Regardless of the regional variations among emancipated Jews, I suggest, to begin with, that the three classic ideals have powerfully maintained themselves, albeit in universalistic transformation. The *talmid hakham,* the talmudic sage, now became realized in the university professor—explaining the uncommon proportion of Jews in academia. The *hasid,* the religious extremist, now metamorphosed into the political radical, passionate about instituting the messianic age—another social role with statistical Jewish over-representation. The more common Jewish ideal, the *tzaddik,* the person striving for righteousness, now took the path of being a good citizen and neighbor, with particular emphasis on human welfare and culture—again providing the ethnic impetus for the uncommon involvement of Jews in these activities. Substantively, the old

Jewish models no longer move us; existentially, in accommodation to our new social situation, they still powerfully shape our lives.

These impressions can be taken a significant step further. American Jews, I suggest, have by now largely adopted a Yiddish[38] word to describe their contemporary ethnic ideal. It is the term *mentsh.* Put simply, a Jew may be a *talmid hakham, tzaddik* or *hasid* in the classic sense, or a professor, or radical, or good citizen or any combination thereof. But most of us are unlikely to esteem that Jew highly if he or she is not also a *mentsh,* a procedure indicating our adoption of a new and more significant human ideal.

What, then, is it to be a *mentsh*? As usual with such highly charged terms, no one exactly knows. And neither Yiddishists nor anthropologists have yet begun the process of unraveling its rich fabric of meanings. We shall have to proceed rather intuitively.

The word itself represents an intriguing and instructive tension. Denotatively, *mentsh* simply means "a person, a human being." Connotatively, it seems the equivalent of the English usage, "a *real* person," a phrase of similarly imprecise meaning. In the term *mentsh* the real and the ideal intersect. More important, the term's immediate reference is purely universalistic, pointing beyond Jewish standards to what anyone, anywhere ought to be. In this it shows its post-Emancipation provenance and commitment. But, of course, this is being expressed in Yiddish, as if to ground Jewish universalism in ethnicity, possibly even expressing the hope that Jewishness will give the Jew special, perhaps unique, insight into being human.

Joseph Landis has given this notion its most radical formulation, arguing that in the Yiddish language high humanity and folk particularity have become identical. In his paper entitled "Who Needs Yiddish?"[39] he says, "Dedicated as it thus was to the values of the head and the heart, to Torah and *maysim tovim* [good deeds], the Ashkenazi world was one whose ethic could indeed be called the ethic of *mentshlekhkayt.* In the word *mentsh* it found the summation of its strivings[40] . . . If Yiddish is, thus, the language in which *yidishkayt* uniquely expresses its *mentshlekhkayt,* it is also the language in which Jewish *mentshlekhkayt* expresses its religious *yidishkayt.*"[41]

The breadth of Landis's claim may be seen in his characterization of Yiddish literature. "At [its] moral center stands the ethic of Ashkenazic Jewry. Is there a Yiddish writer who does not ultimately affirm it? . . . Jews and their writers in Yiddish never lost faith in either man or life, never saw the world as a wasteland, never felt themselves alienated from man . . . Is there another literature . . . so entirely committed to man's emancipation, so entirely devoted to the values of *mentshlekhkayt* as Yiddish literature?" It comes as no surprise then that he concludes his paper with an argument for the Jewish necessity of Yiddish. "The greater the immersion in Yiddish and its works, the greater the distinctively Jewish qualities; and conversely, the further the remove from Yiddish the greater the distance from those qualities that characterize the most admirable expressions of Jewish being."[42]

Landis does not explain what he means by *mentshlekhkayt* and perhaps would suggest that we could only understand it by becoming literate in Yiddish. That might seem reasonable if Landis had at least considered the contrary evidence. Instead, he only displays those aspects of Yiddish which he admires and then passionately asserts that this constitutes its essence. As David Gold, Professor of Jewish Languages at the University of Haifa, has pointed out,[43] such an argument cannot stand academic scrutiny. Landis continually asserts as facts theses others find radically problematic. Moreover, how can one ever demonstrate that a given literature is to be identified with one of its themes rather than the myriad others it contains? To me, the fiction of the Nobel laureate Isaac Bashevis Singer, written in Yiddish and richly informed by the Jewish tradition, denies Landis's standards of *mentshlekhkayt.* It regularly focuses on people who are alienated and amoral, yet in whose pathetic humanity much of the modern world recognizes itself. Landis, I suggest, has told us more about his own deep *mentshlekhkayt* and his love of Yiddish than about the relations others might find between them.

A more precise discussion of the meaning of *mentsh* is found in Steven S. Schwarzschild's unpublished manuscript on Jewish language. He writes, "Even many who don't speak Yiddish know the Yiddish expression, '*Zai a mentsh!*' . . . What it does mean is: 'since you are biologically human, be also morally/intellectually human!' To say this in Yiddish no qualifying adjective is needed, unlike in German. '*Mentsh*' is *homo humanus* in one word, in one indivisible notion. In other words, the Yiddish noun carries with it, as part of its essential definition, an ethical component."[44] Schwarzschild "suggests" that the term *mentsh* echoes a talmudic statement and concludes that "Everything I said about the Yiddish '*mentsh*' is, therefore, not only a matter of 'the Ashkenazic ethos' [the reference is to Landis, whom Schwarzschild cites] but applies also, at least in this instance, to the Hebrew *ish.* And we are thus dealing with the ethos of Jewish language in general."[45]

Schwarzschild here correctly identifies one of the major connotations of the term *mentsh,* ethical behavior. Nothing so disturbs the contemporary Jew as an otherwise estimable community figure who is revealed to be morally culpable. Some recent notorious examples are: the non-observant Jew Abe Fortas, forced to resign from the Supreme Court for accepting a retainer from someone whose case might come before the court; Bernard Bergman, a leader in international orthodoxy, convicted of improper care of the aged in his nursing homes; and presently, Rabbi Meir Kahane, who espouses an anti-democratic Jewish politics.

A *mentsh* ought to have a strong sense of ethics, one which reaches out to all humankind and reflects the devotion to justice and compassion that animates every true human being. This ethical commitment has such power that often, when it clashes with a Jewish tradition, it transforms it, as is now happening with feminism, though somewhat grudgingly, to be sure. But it is by no means invincible. Sometimes, as with the issues of intermarriage and Palestinian rights, Jews will divide over what ought to be done, the majority remaining convinced that their commitment to their people's Covenant with God demands that Jewish particularity be given proper scope.

However, Schwarzschild's ethics has significantly different contours from the empathic humanism of Landis and the generalized sense of goodwill many people connect with the term. As a rationalist Jewish philosopher, Schwarzschild defines ethics in neo-Kantian terms, that is, as understood in the Marburg tradition of Hermann Cohen. Thus, his repeated use of the compound term "moral/intellectual" must be taken literally. For him, a *mentsh* is, ideally, someone who constructs an integrated understanding of the universe, utilizing a rationality which itself is ethically grounded, and who rigorously meets each moral challenge by the application of universal ethical reason. Few people using the Yiddish term *mentsh* have had anything like that notion of ethics in mind. Schwarzschild, I imagine, would grant that, but would find it irrelevant. He would merely insist that they should have—or perhaps unconsciously did—for only that understanding of it would bring rational integrity into the welter of Jewish experience. For a neo-Kantian, the empirical becomes comprehensible only in terms of a regulative idea.

The surmises of Landis and Schwarzschild must be deemed inadequate on two grounds. Both present elitist, believers' notions of what it must mean to be a *mentsh,* the one springing from Yiddishist ideology, the other from neo-Kantian certitude. Neither therefore felt the need to go to the people to inquire what, in a democratic, skeptical age, Jewish speakers implied when they used the word *mentsh.* A study of the term's use would surely seem the proper way to begin uncovering its probable meanings. No academic effort in that direction having yet been made,[46] I should like to present some preliminary, inexpert findings of my own.

Mentsh being so highly charged a term, it seemed likely that we would gain insight into its various connotations by looking at its use in folk expressions. I therefore consulted five collections of Yiddish folk sayings, one from early in the century, the encyclopedic Bernstein/Segel volume of 1908, the others coming from more recent decades.[47] This modest sample gives little support to either Landis's grandiloquent notion of *mentshlekhkayt* or to Schwarzschild's rationalistic rendering of the term *mentsh.*

Roughly a third of the adages listed under *mentsh* in the Bernstein/Segel anthology had some direct ethical content.[48] Some are simple lessons, for example: *"Iber dem hat Got dem mentshen gegeben tzve oyeren un ayn moyl, kidey er zol mer heren un veniger reden,"* "God gave a person two ears and one mouth so he should listen more and talk less";[49] and *"Der mentsh iz in zikh aleyn fernart,"* "One is often made a fool of by oneself alone."[50] A somewhat larger number encapsulate the sardonic reflections often associated with Yiddish. *"Der mentsh hot groyse oygen un zet nit zayn eygene feyler,"*[51] "A person has big eyes but doesn't see his own faults"; and *"Vos der mentsh tun zikh aleyn volten im kayn tzeyn sonim nit vintshen,"* "What a person does to himself, ten enemies wouldn't wish him."[52]

Of all the proverbs perused, only two can be said to invest the word *mentsh* with high humane or ethical content. "A *mentsh iz umetum a mentsh,"* literally, "A person is always a person," implying that one's innate worth remains regardless of events.[53] And "A *groysser oylem un nito keyn mentsh,"* "A great assembly, and no man in it!"[54]

From the Bernstein/Segel sample, then, one must conclude that *mentsh* is used overwhelmingly as a simple descriptive—human being, person—and not as an accepted ideal. The proverbs in the other sources I consulted similarly use the term *mentsh* in folk observations of human nature, about half of which may be called sardonic.[55] If *mentshlekhkayt* dominates the Yiddish language or carries the overtones of neo-Kantian morality, we should have more explicit indication of it than we have here. To the contrary, more maxims indicated how unethical one may expect people to be than the ethical humanhood they ought to manifest—and these near-cynical expressions are clearly observations, not exhortations to change. For example, "A *mentsh darf iber zikh kayn ergers nit hoben vi a mentshn,*" "A person can't have anything worse over him than another person";[56] "*Far Got hot men moyre—far mentshn muz men zikh hitn,*" "Fear God but beware of people";[57] and "*Got shtroft, der mentsh iz sikh noykem,*" "God punishes but people take revenge."[58] More positively, we can see *mentsh* used in its typical a-ethical sense in a maxim like, "*A mentsh mit gute maniren shlogt zikh durkh ale tiren,*" "A person with good manners can break through all doors."[59] Matisow calls our attention to the common Yiddish expression "*nit far keyn mentshn gedakht,*" "may—be unthinkable for any person." One of the phrases most frequently invoked to ward off possible danger, it carries no connotation of high humaneness or rational morality. Thus, his example is "*Un geven iz er a kaptsn, nit far keyn mentshn gedakht,*" "And he was a pauper—may it be unthinkable for any person."[60] Finally, though Landis and Schwarzschild both clinch their argument by pointing to the phrase "*Zai a mentsh,*" "Be a person!" it does not, as such, occur in these anthologies. What I did find was, "*Zai a mentsh, vest du zitzen in suke,*" literally, "Be a *mentsh* and you'll be able to sit in the Sukkah [during the Feast of Tabernacles]." The cryptic phrasing draws forth this comment from the anthologists, "This is what a mother says to her pampered little son: 'Behave properly and you'll be rewarded by [being allowed] to sit in the Sukkah.'"[61]

To me, the common use of the term *mentsh* speaks rather more of Jewish realism than of Jewish idealism, of *metshlekhkayt* as simple humanness not literary or moral/intellectual creativity. It exhibits, on the folk level, a modern shift of concern, away from the Torah and the God who gave it, to the human beings who must try to live it. At the least, it gives priority to exhibiting one's common humanity no matter what one's position or power. It also displays the new scepticism of modernist Jewish self-consciousness, one that deflates all sweeping claims to certainty with the evidence drawn from keeping a steady eye on people. I hear these overtones and more in such adages as "*A mentsh is doch nor a bosor vedom,*" "A person is only flesh and blood," which is to say something like, "People are only human."[62]

In the Yiddish, that sentiment has quite a different effect than in English. In our society we regularly aver to our humanity to excuse our failings. "I'm only human," has something of a pathetic tone, calling on the listener to acknowledge that people should not be expected to live up to high standards.

The Yiddish confession of our human weakness takes place in quite another context, for the one who utters it stands within the Jewish people and inherits its tradition. Its ethos still powerfully transmits even as it has transmuted its long tradition of commandment and aspiration. Among Jews, to be human is to strive to do one's duty and in that effort to attain one's dignity. And one knows that other Jews, though knowing you "are only human," will judge you by that standard. In this context, where a community strongly reinforces obligation, to say one is only human cannot function as a release from responsibility, as in our society we often hope it will, but only as a mitigation of our failing in what remain our legitimate responsibilities.

I think that in recent years psychotherapy has added much to the sense of realism we bring to the term *mentsh*[63] but enough has already been said to make my point. With the Emancipation, a new universalism, realism and skepticism came into the Jewish human ideal but it cannot be said to have displaced it so much as to have reshaped its reach to others and its understanding of self. Thus, one may hope that as long as Jews remain faithful to their heritage, their newfound humanism will not lead on to the relativism and aimlessness that so sadly characterize much of American life but to a newly refreshed *yidishkayt/mentshlekhkayt*. For a *mentsh*, it would seem, is only a post-Emancipation *tzaddik*,[64] a person more certain of human capacity and stupidity than of God's rules, one more concerned about everyday decency and compassion than about social conventions or institutional niceties, one as much a part of the global human race as of one's own wonderful people. The social and theological context has changed and with it the outer shape of the Jewish human ideal. But existentially, the underlying vision of what we are and ought to be remains remarkably the same.

NOTES

1. Scholem, Gershom, "Three Types of Jewish Piety," *Ariel*, No. 32, (1973), p. 5. All citations from Scholem are taken from this printing. The essay first appeared in the *Eranos Yearbook*, 1969.
2. All citations p. 6.
3. P. 7.
4. P. 9.
5. Briefly, at the bottom of pp. 8 and 9.
6. E.g., Y. Bekh end and Y. Taan 2.2.
7. E.g., Sifre Dt. 1.13, Er. 36b, Ber. 35a and 63b. The term *hakham* is most commonly used in connection with the giving of rulings.
8. P. 8.
9. Ber. 31a.
10. Hag. 14b.
11. Sem. 47b.
12. P. 10.
13. P. 11.
14. Kid. 40a–b.

15. P. 11.

16. P. 12. A somewhat similar figure is found in Hellenistic Judaism. David Winston describes one class in Philo's description of people as "those who are making gradual progress in virtue but are unable fully to attain it . . . Since this class undoubtedly comprises the bulk of humanity, it is somewhat disconcerting to find no explicit statement by Philo regarding their final disposition." *Logos and Mystical Theology in Philo of Alexandria,* HUC Press: 1985, p. 41.

17. P. 12.

18. *Mesillat Yesharim,* Moses Hayyim Luzzatto, translated by Mordecai Kaplan, Philadelphia: Jewish Publication Society of America, 1936 (hereafter: MY) p. 17. Note the duplication of *shehadikduk sheyidakdek* which makes the rendering "should be scrupulous" almost an understatement. While Kaplan's translation is somewhat loose by contemporary standards, it not only renders the text with reasonable accuracy but with a certain English fluency that commends it for continuing use.

19. MY p. 24.

20. MY p. 53. I have rendered the term *yezer* in the Kaplan translation as "urge."

21. MY p. 57. This statement begins with a reference to one "who is an ardent worshipper" *(asher tilahet nafsho),* thus, perhaps, seeming to refer to someone seeking a goal higher than that of a mere *tzaddik.* I shall return to that matter below. Here I only wish to indicate that for Luzzatto, a person only on the second level of his ten-step ladder to holiness must be concerned about generating considerable personal intensity. My point is that Scholem's account of the *tzaddik* does not sufficiently bring this out.

22. In rabbinic literature we have continual reference not only to the *tzaddik* but to the *tzaddik gamur,* "the complete *tzaddik.*" One can thus find implicit in the talmudic notion degrees of the state, an ordinary and an extraordinary, the one satisfied with a plurality of righteousness, the other driving toward perfection. An exchange between Bar He He and Hillel is instructive. The latter, for all his proverbial mildness, did not hesitate to apply the distinction made in Mal. 3:18 "between the righteous and the wicked, between one that serves God and one who does not," to the difference between someone who had repeated his new learning 101 times as against 100. Though both might be called a *tzaddik gamur,* the difference between them was as real as the difference in rates mule drivers charge for having to go eleven as against ten parasangs. Hag. 9b.

23. Pp. 18–19.

24. P. 9.

25. P. 21.

26. P. 10. R. Judah said that one who wishes to be a *hasid* should fulfill the laws of the tractates collected in the order Damages. Rava said the injunctions in the tractate of "The Fathers" (a figure of speech for the rabbinic masters). Others said those matters dealt with in the tractate Blessings. Kid. 30a.

27. P. 12.

28. P. 22.

29. MY p. 2.

30. MY p. 3.

31. MY pp. 144–45. Luzzatto's book is not a manual for the would be *tzaddik* but rather for one who wished to become a *hasid* and perhaps go beyond it some steps to holiness. Following an old rabbinic teaching, there are ten steps in Luzzatto's curriculum. As Scholem indicates, one needs to be a *tzaddik* in order to become a *hasid.* Thus in discussing Luzzatto's notion of the *tzaddik* as against that of Scholem, I cited only his early chapters, those dealing with stages one and two of the training, whereas he reserves saintliness for stage six. Much of late medieval Jewry seems to agree that *hasidut* can be cultivated by anyone, for Luzzatto's work became perhaps the most widely studied of all the medieval Jewish moral manuals.

32. MY p. 147.

33. P. 23.

34. Two factors confirm me in this method. The one is Jewish. The Covenant is made with the Jewish people, not with a given Jewish individual *per se.* Hence authentic if liberal Jewish thinking needs to proceed in terms of where the Covenant people, not merely the individual Jewish thinker, is to be found. I consider it a fundamental error of much liberal Jewish thought that it adopts, unthinkingly, the individualistic bias of philosophy or most Christian theology. It then never finds an easy way of understanding the appropriate claims of the Jewish people on the sovereign,

individual Jew. The second arises from a recognition that modernity has taught us some truths which Judaism ought to accept (not infrequently after Jewish criticism and refinement). One of these, in the religious realm, is that personal experience (itself tested by reason but not screened by it) offers our best access to ultimate reality. As a contemporary Jewish thinker I therefore work from this twofold, integrated stance.

35. "The Jews of Italy," Arnaldo Momigliano, *New York Review of Books,* Oct. 24, 1985, pp. 25–6.

36. Published as *German Jews beyond Judaism,* George L. Mosse, Bloomington: Indiana University Press and HUC Press, 1985. Note the title, which indicates the author's focus on the outward movement of modernizing German Jews.

37. Ibid., p. 3.

38. My efforts to see if there was an equivalent term among American Sephardi Jews produced few results. Rabbi Marc D. Angel, Rabbi of The Congregation Shearith Israel, The Spanish and Portuguese Synagogue, wrote in response to my query, "In Judeo-Spanish, the equivalent to 'mentsh' is 'benadam' [Hebrew for 'human being'], often pronounced 'benatham.' Obviously, it comes from the Hebrew. The word 'benadamlik' is used to refer to courtesy or consideration. I can't think of other terms that might be useful for your study. I have asked a friend here who knows Judeo-Spanish and I have also consulted a little Ladino-English dictionary. There may be other phrases but I am not familiar with them. Also, I do not know anything about Judeo-Arabic or other languages Sephardim have spoken." Letter of June 14, 1985.

39. "Who Needs Yiddish? A Study in Language and Ethics," Joseph C. Landis, *Never Say Die,* ed. Joshua Fishman. New York: Mouton, 1981. The essay originally appeared in *Judaism,* Vol. XIII, No. 4, Fall 1964. The subtitle must be taken literally.

40. *Never Say Die,* p. 357.

41. Ibid. p. 358.

42. Ibid. pp. 361–62. Note the poignancy of these remarks being made in English and even more so, their being reprinted nearly two decades later in the English section of a book on Yiddish.

43. See his review of *Never Say Die* in *Jewish Language Review,* 3, (1983), pp. 64–5. Professor Gold has been kind enough to supply me with references to his discussions of the ways in which the term *mentsh* has become part of Israeli Hebrew usage: *JLR,* 4, (1984), p. 235, and 5, (1985), pp. 456–57. For a similarly well-balanced view of the *Yiddishkayt-mentshlekhkayt* ideology, see Ruth R. Wisse, "The Politics of Yiddish," *Commentary,* Vol. 80, No. 1, July 1985, pp. 29ff.

44. Ms. p. 7. I am again indebted to my schoolmate and friend of over forty years, this time for sharing this extensive paper with me. Our relationship has flourished over the years precisely because we care enough about each other to criticize the other's thinking where it appears to be faulty.

45. Ms. p. 8.

46. I am grateful to Philip Miller, Librarian of the Hebrew Union College–Jewish Institute of Religion, New York, and Dina Abramowicz, Librarian of YIVO for their generous, gracious help, which pointed me toward such sources as existed and to others which we all hoped might turn out to be of greater value than actually was the case.

47. Ignaz Bernstein and B. W. Segel, *Juedische Sprichwoerter and Redensarten;* Warsaw: 1908. Hanan Aylati, ed., *Yiddish Proverbs;* New York: Schocken, 1949. Nahum Stuchkoff, *Der Oytzer fun der Yiddisher Shprakh;* YIVO, 1950. Shin. Esterson, *500 Gegramte Sprikhverter un Redensarten;* Jerusalem: 1963. James A. Matisoff, *Blessings, Curses, Hopes and Fears; Psycho-Ostensive Expressions in Yiddish;* Philadelphia: ISHI, 1979.

48. Op. cit., nos. 7, 9, 30 and 42, plus the examples cited below; additional sardonic ones are nos. 2, 16, 17, 22, 35 and 37, plus others fully cited. Pp. 164–67.

49. Ibid., no. 4. I bear the responsibility for the transliterations and translations.

50. Ibid., no. 23.

51. Ibid., no. 28.

52. Ibid., no. 36.

53. Ibid., no. 12.

54. Ayalti, no. 14, his transliteration and translation. Schwarzschild will find in this maxim additional basis for his suggestion, Ms. p. 7, that the Yiddish *mentsh* derives from the Hebrew *ish* based on Av. 2.6, "In a place where there is no man, strive to be [he prefers, to maintain proper Marburgian dynamism, 'become'] a man." I see no basis for this supposition in the traditional

understanding of the text. The classic Mishnah commentators ignore this phrase, and the ones given in the printings of the Talmud understand it as a restatement of one's common duty to be Jewishly observant; thus, *ish* means one who fulfills one's obligations stated in Torah, not merely one's ethical responsibilities. Maimonides, of course, gives this statement his usual metaphysical twist. See Av. 7a, where it is enumerated 2.5.

55. Of the 49 not otherwise cited Berenstein/Segel proverbs, I see the following as sardonic observations on human nature: nos. 11, 14, 18, 19, 21, 31 (which says there is no justice), 32 (which together with 34 and 47 contradict 9), 33, 38, 39 and 40 (which say there is little ethics), and 48. Much of the Stuchkoff maxim collection repeats statements from Berenstein/Segel. Where it presents fresh usages, they are more likely to be descriptive than ethically exhortive. Op. cit., pp. 163 col. b and 164 col. a.

56. No. 16. See also no. 3.

57. Ayalti, no. 276.

58. Ibid., no. 316. I would also include in this category Esterson no. 224.

59. Bernstein/Segel, no. 20.

60. Matisow, no. 129.

61. Bernstein/Segel, no 41.

62. Bernstein/Segel, no. 24.

63. I hope to be able to deal with this aspect of contemporary mentsh-hood in another context.

64. I think we can say about when this change in attitude reached conscious expression among Yiddishists. Ruth Wisse comments that *Yiddishkayt* "from the beginning of this century, and particularly in the period between the wars . . . began to assume a modern, ideological connotation," becoming a cultural process that "engenders *mentshlekhkayt,* humaneness," with the two eventually becoming identical terms. Op. cit., p. 29, col. a. I think she is speaking of an elitist development and that is one reason we find so little evidence of the ideological sense of *mentsh* in the sample of folk wisdom we examined. As she makes clear in her article, the generation descended from the immigrant Yiddish speakers largely abandoned the language. Insofar as they accepted the high-cultural notion of *yiddishkayt/mentshlekhkayt* they never had a chance to work it into the language they had grown up with but no longer used. Their continuing utilization of the Yiddish term *mentsh* seems then to express with particular power their desire to link the new ideal with their old idealism.

20 / The Critical Issue in the Quest for Social Justice: A Jewish View

1986

Though esteeming highly the spiritual worth of the individual, the Bible authors give priority to the corporate human relationship with God. I would speculate that they do so largely because they view humankind as essentially social. Looking at Adam, they have *Adonoi* say, "It is not good for man to be alone: I will make a fitting helpmate for him."[1] And the tower of Babel story comes to explain why the history of humankind is essentially a record of the conflict of peoples and nations.[2] Even the account of the Israelite patriarchs serves to introduce the emergence of the Hebrew nation and explain its possession of Canaan.[3] The historical books then tell what happened to the covenanted people, and the prophetic books criticize, threaten, remotivate, and redirect its efforts to create a communal life holy to God. Social ethics is obviously fundamental to the religion of the Bible.

We shall have little difficulty specifying the content of biblical social ethics as long as we see it as a body of abstract ideals. Can there be much doubt that the Bible, in all its diversity of authors, attitudes, voices, and concerns, unambiguously aspires to a time when people live together in plenty and not in poverty, in justice and not in oppression, in love and not in hatred, in peace and not in war?

Our difficulties in accepting and applying biblical social ethics arise as we move from the Bible's idealism to its profound human realism. Its writers accept as axiomatic the premise that human beings are no longer in the Garden of Eden because we are creatures who regularly will to sin. They see our stubborn, perverse rejection of God's will as the motive power of human history and the problem that God's loving, saving power must overcome. The biblical lawgivers, envisioning people this way, created statutes by which they might effectuate their God-inspired social ideal in their immediate, concrete social situation. The prophets, by divine revelation, clarified what God was doing in the particular local and international affairs of Jewish history.

In due course, direct revelation ceased in Israel, and altered social circumstances demanded a more appropriate statement of what God now wanted of the people of the Covenant. The rabbis in their unique way then continued the Bible's practical social concern in the exquisite details of talmudic law and the inspirational lessons of midrashic lore. That tradition of vision and application, of text and interpretation, of precedent and application, of enlargement and augmentation, of creative development and new enactment, goes on to the present day. A substantial body of classic Jewish writings treats ethical issues, and a not inconsiderable and growing contemporary literature seeks to apply them to our time.[4]

From this point on, the characterization of contemporary Jewish social ethics confronts two difficulties. The first of these it shares indistinguishably with the field of Christian ethics. The move from ethical ideal to specific injunction increases the pluralism of opinion among learned, thoughtful, faithful students of these matters. The classic differences over how idealistic we ought to try to be at this moment or how little we should settle for, human nature being so refractory, are exponentially multiplied today by the irremediable ambiguities created by the technical complexity of many social issues. How does one discover which economic theory provides the most reliable foundation for a program to lessen poverty, or which perception of military realities explains what hardware we require, or worse, how to combine the two of them in a time of "stagflation"?

More troubling than specifying content, I believe, is the challenge arising from those people who loyally come to the synagogue or church and consider social ethics in its broad sense peripheral if not irrelevant to their central spiritual concerns. This problem takes on special form today in the Jewish community but one which reflects the present situation of all biblical religions in America. I think I can best be of help in clarifying the central issue of biblical social ethics as well as of making plain the unique contours of contemporary Jewish religious thought by dealing with the metaethical rather than the material level of our question. I propose to expound and respond to the arguments of those who question why pious Jews in our time ought to have a major commitment to transforming society.

Like all our other visible, voluble pietistic movements, the American Jewish social quietists gain their strength largely in reaction to the liberal, activist interpretation of the Jewish social ethic which dominated our community for the first twenty years following World War II. One must keep in mind that our secularization had started earlier and proceeded more effectively than that of American Christians due to our heavy urbanization, our commitment to higher education, and our identification of the secular as the realm where we would meet less prejudice.[5] Liberalism had become the essence of Judaism for much of our community in a movement far more intense than the parallel Christian activity. Indeed, by the late 1960s, when this identification of Jewish social ethics with activist, liberal politics peaked, there had been over a century of unprecedented Jewish involvement in every cause for human betterment in which Jews had been permitted to participate. Surely this must be ranked among the proudest achievements of Jewish history. Not only did Jews devote themselves to the general welfare in strikingly large numbers, disproportionately so, and give creative leadership in almost every field they entered, they did so without long-established models to emulate but in spontaneous, enthusiastic response to their emancipation from centuries of a degraded social status.[6]

The rejection of Jewish social ethics as equivalent to liberal political activity has been gathering power for over a decade. It substantially derives from the universal American shift to the right.[7] With the American economy stagnating or in decline, the rising expectations of many once-quiescent groups in our society can no longer be met. Fierce competition for limited means has become common, and self-interest has increasingly replaced the common welfare as an immediate political concern. In this atmosphere, ethnics have turned to their roots rather than to the American future to find a sense of security, and old social coalitions have broken down as the groups seek greater gains for themselves. They have also lost their program of change. Increasingly people feel that liberalism did not and cannot resolve our social problems. Rather it created a host of new ones in the name of social improvement. To some extent this mood draws on the historic prejudices of Americans against various minority groups, for they are vulnerable and subject to attack in ways that were unthinkable a decade or so ago. Less debatably, the concern with the self and its satisfactions has for a growing number of people been understood in more isolated and less social a fashion than previously, the notorious narcissism of our times.

The American Jewish community reflects all these currents but does so in forms refracted by Jewish ethnic experience and values. Consider the issue of social class. Political liberalism had appealed to a community of acculturating immigrants who were poor in means, experience, and even opportunity but rich in hope. The overwhelming portion of the native-born, unretired American Jewish community is now solidly middle-class, and perhaps more of it is upper-class than any other religio-ethnic group. It may have had to make its way through a relatively unfair and discriminatory system, but its present status and privileges depend on the continuing functioning of that system. Today, by sharp contrast to fifty years ago, American Jewry has a stake in not greatly altering this country's socioeconomic structure.[8]

Moreover, a small but significant community role is now played by a relatively recent group of Jewish immigrants, those who arrived as refugees during the Hitler period or, more important, since then. A large proportion of this group had not previously come to the United States for religious reasons. The country was synonymous with assimilation and non-observance. In many cases, too, their form of Orthodoxy required limited participation in general society. Having survived the Holocaust and determined to continue their Jewish lives, they have little desire to learn from or accommodate to gentile ways. Their attacks on English-speaking, beardless, university-attending, American-oriented Orthodox Jews has mitigated much of the social concern visible among what, in the 1960s, came to be called "modern Orthodoxy."[9] Their presence and Jewish militance have posed a special challenge to what remains of the old, outer-directed American Jewish communal leadership. It had already been discredited by the heavy burden of guilt which historical reconsideration had fixed upon it for failing European Jewry during the Hitler years. American Jews had been so concerned to be part of the American war effort that they would not break ranks and press the special claims of the Jews the Nazis were murdering en masse. Worse, research disclosed that the liberal leaders the Jews had adulated had not cared enough for the Jewish victims to give such help as might have been possible, for example, bombing the death camps.

These special Jewish factors intensified the effect of the new general American ethnic assertiveness. As a result, many voices in the Jewish community began to oppose the dogmatic liberal identification of Jewish interests with those of all other American minorities.[10] The liberal political agenda, they charged, takes no account of the special needs of the Jews as a religio-ethnic group and ignores the unparalleled heritage of

Western anti-Semitism that still functions against this people. To hope governmental social and economic programs will create a society of such widespread contentment as to vitiate the old Jew-hatred is as naive as was the Jewish Communist dream that the proletarian state would eliminate anti-Semitism. To the contrary, liberal-sponsored programs like busing, affirmative action, and opposition to government aid to Jewish all-day schools directly lessen the chances of American Jews building a strong Jewish community life in the future.

The emerging Jewish right, as it has gained the economic strength and political sophistication to express its will—again paralleling Christian phenomena—has pressed a strong polemic against the Jewish authenticity of the Jewish liberals. By identifying Judaism with general ethics, they legitimated assimilation. Those who wanted to escape their Jewish identity could claim that by helping humankind they were, in fact, being good Jews. Generally they could be counted on to fight for the rights of every people except their own. Thus on the university campus, they impeded or fought the introduction of courses in Jewish studies. Consistent with their devotion to humanity, the liberals' Jewish religious practice tended to be minimal and their knowledge of Judaism superficial. Even the articles written by those who sought to show the harmony of Judaism and universal ethics are little more than a few biblical verses or rabbinic apothegms, often snatched from their context, utilized to Judaize a Western intellectual position. A Judaism which has no discipline and demands no sacrifice is unworthy of being called a religion. How then could such people speak authentically in Judaism's name and hope to apply its values to the problems of society as a whole?

Rather than pretentiously assert a Jewish mission to all humankind, Jewry should devote itself to what its millennial history best suits it for, sanctifying the lives of individuals and families. If Jews were properly observant, they would also be decent citizens. Devoting themselves mainly to the preservation and enhancement of their community, they could not help also being a positive force in society and making a major contribution to its welfare. Besides, in this time of social peril, Jews need to base their lives on the primary lesson of the Holocaust: in a crisis, no one else can be counted on to help Jews but other Jews. We are historically mandated and ethically entitled to make concern with our people's welfare the sovereign content of our social ethic.

This account of the ideology of the new Jewish right has thus far omitted one major factor which, in complicated ways, makes its appeal quite compelling, that is, the deep American Jewish concern for the State of Israel. No other Jewish cause remotely comes close to motivating American Jewry as does the survival of the Israeli state. It represents our people's primal, life-affirming response to the Holocaust and, in the face of excruciatingly difficult political pressures, exemplifies in its democratic, social-welfare orientation the age-old social values of Judaism. As the State of Israel perceives its needs, or better, as American Jewish leaders, eager not to repeat the failures of the Holocaust, understand their need to lobby for Israeli causes, the agenda of American political liberalism—domestic welfare—is soft and unrealistic. The major problems of our day are, rather, international. Hence America needs to become staunchly anti-Soviet and thus militarily unimpeachable.[11]

The reeducation of American Jewish leadership in this regard may well be dated to 1967. Lyndon Johnson informed a group summoned to the White House that if the State of Israel was to get the jet planes it desired, American Jews would have to stop backing the protests against the Vietnam War. Similarly, the lesson of the critical dependence of the Israeli army on the American arsenal for resupply in the decisive early days of the 1973 war was not lost on many American Jews. If the State of Israel is to survive, America must be militarily strong—and it would help if the Pentagon saw the American Jewish community as its backers.

From those days to the present, the rhetoric and formal organizational stands of most American Jewish organizations have shifted rightward, that is, general human concerns have essentially been displaced by ethnic and Israeli ones. This move has been justified by the ideology that Jewish concerns are the proper, authentic focus of a Jewish social ethic. It must be noted, however, that all this has not yet produced a clear-cut, major statistical reorientation in Jewish voting patterns, if the presidential elections of 1980 and 1984 have been rightly assessed.[12] The old liberal ethics of most American Jews has, in any case, surely lost its old élan and weakened to the point where it may well soon become empty. Historically, it is far too early to say what is likely to happen or when, and events in this century have been so unpredictable that speculation is most unwise.

Intellectually, the issue before Jews as individuals and as a community may be put this way: should the social ethic of contemporary Judaism as it concerns general society be achieved indirectly, as a side effect of particular Jewish observance, or should it be another major, direct, active concern of faithful Jews, comparable in some measure to their devotion to the Jewish community in its service of God?

I respond to this question speaking officially for myself alone, but articulating a position which I suggest many American Jews roughly share socially, though not perhaps theologically.

We too are deeply concerned about Jewish authenticity and therefore have no wish to gloss over the failings of doctrinaire Jewish liberalism. Any Jewish ethic worthy of that name cannot be purely universalistic, so concerned with humanity it has no interest in the Jewish people. Jews loyal to the Covenant with God must necessarily accept the responsibilities that places upon them to build their specific community and through it bring humankind to its messianic goal.

With all that, a word is in order in defense of a previous generation of Jewish universalists. They may have allowed their enthusiasm at the emancipation of the Jews to carry them too far in jettisoning Judaism's protective particularity. They should also have had a more realistic view of human nature and social change. For all that, their radicalism accomplished much for their less adventuresome fellow Jews. They articulated the ethic by which Jews still participate in general society, developed a style for Jewish involvement in general causes, accomplished much to improve human welfare, and served as living proof that one can be a proud Jew and thoroughly involved in the great social issues of our time. The challenge of their stance still cannot be ignored: will we long remain a vital community if in our democratic situation we try to reinstitute a ghetto orientation to Judaism?

By this brief digression I wish most emphatically to deny that the faults of Jewish liberalism totally invalidate its substance. The choice before us is not the either/or of a tarnished liberalism versus a refurbished, modernized traditionalism. Modern Orthodoxy and right-wing Conservatism, both strongly linked with the move to right-of-center or rightist political stands, would not exist had they not adopted much of the pioneering liberals' ideology. Right-wing Orthodoxy, as indicated by its fanatic, antipluralistic acts in the United States and the State of Israel, is too self-centered for most of us to accept it as an authentic Judaism for modern Jews. An excessive universalism need not be replaced by a particularism so overwhelming it has little direct interest in the pressing concerns of humankind. There are many Jews who counsel that we withdraw from the social arena except where Jewish interests are at stake or our allies in achieving them require our help. The older liberals have convinced many of us that Jews, having been welcomed as equals in society, should now understand that our faith demands of us that we share in seeking to meet the problems all human beings now confront even as we give special attention to the specific needs of our own people.

Our ethical choice hinges largely on our interpretation of our recent history. What does our experience of Emancipation from the ghetto mean to us? Ought it to bring us to introduce a major change in the traditional Jewish social ethic, making it more universally oriented and activist in seeking to attain its newly inclusive goals, or, in limited response to our new freedom, ought it to cause us only to extend when necessary our classic inner-oriented social ethic? On theological as well as practical grounds, I believe the Emancipation should influence our understanding of Judaism as profoundly as it now seems to us the destruction of the Second Temple did when it ushered in the era of rabbinic Judaism. Further, as I shall explain in due course, I do not consider the Holocaust to have invalidated the universal imperative of the Emancipation but, if anything, further to have reinforced it.

Let me begin my response on the practical level. The Jewish people, through its major centers in the State of Israel, the United States, and other free countries, has indissolubly linked its destiny with other free peoples. Should there be a major energy crisis, an economic collapse, radical atmospheric pollution, a global failure of democracy, an atomic war, the Jews will not escape unscathed. I cannot respond to such threats as easily as Jews of the ghetto era would have done by saying, as some Jews still do today, "What has all that to do with us? The people of Israel is eternal. God will guard us." Most of us live too intimately as part of Western society not to be deeply affected by its failures and successes, and all but the most self-isolated of our Hasidim would suffer significant spiritual dislocation if they could no longer live as free, emancipated Jews.

If so, we have a simple ethical responsibility to help those among whom we live shape our mutual destiny. Jews of other centuries were not allowed to share in the determination of their society's policies. We, having both the situation and the incentive, have become socially involved in ways unknown to other Jewries, and rightly so. Any retreat from this activist stance ought to be fought as inappropriate to our radically altered sociopolitical situation.

That argument can legitimately be extended. Having gained exceptionally from our freedom, as the result of great industry and application, to be sure, Jews have a special responsibility to give of their gains to society. To make a contribution only to the extent others do would seem too little on several counts. Most people do not give very much of themselves for the sake of society, one reason conditions are as bad as they are today. Many others, having benefited modestly from our social order, have neither the means, the energy, nor the know-how to do very much for anyone but themselves. It seems only morally right that those who have had greater success should give a greater proportion of their strength and their means to help those less fortunate. Then the Jews, who have fared spectacularly well in the United States, have a simple ethical responsibility to work for the common good in special devotion. And the long heritage of Jewish social concern should spur Jews on to bolster a society which makes it an important part of its life to promote the welfare of its indigent, handicapped, and otherwise deprived citizens.

On a more spiritual level, I want to argue that two of the great experiences of Diaspora Jewry in our time mandate a strong commitment to a universal ethic. In the first case, the Holocaust, I partially agree with the Jewish right. Jews ought to continue their exemplary response to the death of the 6,000,000 and the threat to all of us by vigorously upbuilding and furthering Jewish life today. I differ with those Jews who argue that the cruelty of the Nazis, the indifference of the "good Germans," and the callousness of the Allies' leaders demonstrate that Jews have no genuine share in Western society. We have been the classic outsider for millennia, they say, and despite surface changes we remain the great available victim.

I readily concede that Jews ought not to underestimate the continuing virulence of anti-Semitism or overestimate the changes wrought by some decades of democracy, goodwill, and ecumenism. But if we deny that a common standard of goodness applies between all human beings, strongly enough to command them to override their group concerns so as to respect the humanity of those their folk considers aliens, how can we fault the Germans for their bestial ethnocentrism? If there is no universal ethics which one should follow even under extraordinary social pressure, how can we condemn the Nazis and those who quietly went along with them? And if out of the bitterness of our suffering we insist upon the paramount importance of such interhuman responsibility, then how can we not exemplify it in our own lives? Instead of responding to the utter negativity of the Holocaust by confining our social concern largely to ourselves, thereby validating group moralities, we ought to demonstrate its evil by our own active concern for people far removed from our immediate situation.

I cannot leave the argument there. I do not see that we can insist today that the promise of the Emancipation finally be fulfilled by the

Western world if we do not ourselves resolutely affirm and live by universal ethical standards. We may claim rights among humankind because all people are part of one human family and ought to live in equal status, though that requires them to overcome millennial prejudices in which, as individuals and as classes, they have many vested interests. And, again, if we demand that others ought to effectuate that ideal, so should we who proclaim it, presumably because it is true and not merely because it now benefits us.

To me the Emancipation, for all its equivocation and unrealized promises, is a religious experience reminiscent in its own lesser way of the great revelatory exodus of our people from Egypt. Recent generations of Jews also passed from a long, painful "slavery" to a new freedom, and that passage should become a new motive for Jewish social behavior even as the ancient redemption motivated our people's social legislation—"you know the heart of the stranger, for you were strangers in the land of Egypt." Particularly as we begin to move personally away from that transition, we need to memorialize the experience of our release from the ghetto, *shtetl,* and *mellah* so that it can shape our social consciousness. Few people in our society know intimately what it means to suffer for centuries as pariahs and then come to positions of power and influence. Our own family histories teach us that a society is judged best by the way it treats its most powerless people, those the Bible once identified as the widow, the stranger, and the orphan. Today, Jews are in a unique position to identify with and help do something for such sufferers. We ought to accept that as our modern Jewish duty in order to be true to what we ourselves have endured and what we know we share with all other human beings.

In responding to the Holocaust and our Emancipation by dedication to action for the redemption of all humanity, I believe we can set a proper model of human behavior before all creatures. That is a far cry from the old liberal notion of the mission of Israel to all humankind, but in our contemporary confused and troubled human situation, it is hardly less an exaltation of the people of Israel's potential historic role. And its high estimation of the Jewish people comes from no assertion of Jewish spiritual superiority or expectations of what we shall actually accomplish, but only of what may result when we respond in Covenant faithfulness to what has happened to us.

Two pragmatic considerations seem to me to prompt the Jewish community to take an activist stance in social-ethical matters. The first is a reiteration of the classic modernist perception of the best long-range strategy for securing Jewish security, that Jews will fare better in a society more adequately meeting the needs of its citizens. If so, for their own sake, Jews ought to be involved in trying to overcome the major problems of the society. In doing so, they should be particularly concerned about the rights of underprivileged groups, for their treatment mirrors what may next happen to the Jews.

None of the recent traumas of Jewish history has changed the truth of these assertions. True, there are no guarantees of Jewish security; and Jews cannot do very much to change society or decisively alter its established patterns of inequity; and these social tasks do not nearly conduce to Jewish survival as much as will direct involvement in traditional Jewish responsibilities. Differently put, an outer-oriented Jewish social ethics ought not to take on the messianic dimensions for us that it did for a previous generation. Our hard-learned realism may temper our immediate expectations. It constitutes no reason to deny what our ideals and our enlightened self-interest motivate us to do with our lives.

I should like to suggest a second practical reason for not confining our energies largely to our own community. When we need political allies to help us fight for our cause should some Jewish interest be at stake, we shall be unlikely to find them or to find them receptive if we have not been available when they were carrying on their own struggle for greater social justice. Being a tiny minority in America—perhaps 5,800,000 in a population of over 220,000,000—we must depend on the goodwill of others in order to sway the democratic process. Our potential allies need to be able to count on us for regular aid. Better yet, we may best expect to gain the support we seek when the people we desire it from already stand in our debt for our having long been at their side in their fights.

We cannot, however, any longer assert unequivocally that the liberal rather than the conservative political program is necessarily the better or the more ethical way of achieving Judaism's vision of the good society. The old, dogmatic equation of Jewish ethics with political liberalism no longer is convincing. The transfer of religious ideals to concrete social plans always involves highly complex and contingent considerations. No point of view may reasonably claim that it invariably has the whole truth on such matters. Liberalism can assert a special affinity to biblical ethics because of its concern with benefiting the masses directly and its insistence on taking immediate social action to do so. Nonetheless, its recent record of ambiguous results has vitiated much of its theoretical promise and made it necessary to ask whether in any given instance the conservative option may not better effectuate our ethical goals. As with so much of our life, a revitalized Jewish social ethic must make room for a vigorous pluralism, in this case of political judgment, and out of a thoughtful dialectic over appropriate means, speak to the inquiring Jew.

In one fundamental respect, however, the liberal position seems to me to have special validity to anyone who takes the modern Jewish experience seriously. The Emancipation of the Jews did not come about by benignly waiting for internal developments, market forces, the private sector, or personal growth to grant Jews rights. It came by government initiative. Only in countries where governments acted and formally granted Jews equality and then demanded, if slowly, that their often unwilling citizenries live up to that grant, did Jews truly enter society. Unless Jews are prepared to deny the experience of their own families and ethnic group, they must emphatically reject the notion that government has no proper role in the moral improvement of the social order. Without resolute government leadership in furthering the goals of democracy—in America so closely linked to those of the Bible—the ethical dimensions of our social life may be counted on to contract. Human nature and social interaction being what they are, exploitation, injustice, and what the rabbis poignantly call "free hatred" will slowly but certainly strengthen their hold on our lives. Conservatives, who claim to be realists about human beings, ought to see that as clearly as they see the corruption of good government by those who must operate it. Whenever we are sensitive to the distance we still remain from our social ideals, we must ask what we can all do together, through government, the one "community" through which we all can act as one, to achieve them. And that is not to say that governmental action is always indicated because we consider it the only, the infallible, or the ultimate source of social transformation.

But for me and some other Jews, the most compelling reason for an activist Jewish social ethic is theological. The Emancipation has simply changed our view of what God wants of Jews in relation to all humankind. Or more precisely put, the changed horizon of effective Jewish social ethics exposed by the new scope given Jews for their lives has helped us realize that until recently Jews were only partially able to envisage and effectuate their duty to God. Having gained a broader vision of humankind, Jews like me can no longer delimit what we intuit God wants of us as overwhelmingly, if not exclusively, consisting of acts oriented to our own community.

The classic biblical and rabbinic chasm between Jews and gentiles does not yawn as deeply between us and our neighbors, and many bridges connect us with one another. We all stand before the same God. To be sure, we still find continuing merit, some would say cosmic significance, in sustaining our side of our people's distinctive Covenant with God. At the same time, we have come in ever more intimate ways to recognize our common humanity with gentiles. In very many ways, particularly in many moral and spiritual aspirations and not merely in our joint human needs, we are very much like one another. Working with one another, studying together, cooperating in various community projects, we cannot easily ignore how precious all humankind is to our God and therefore needs to be to us. And our personal postghetto perspective, so radically extended by our education outside of classic Jewish texts and now regularly stretched by the wonders of electronic communication and jet travel, keeps expanding. We can envisage a day when we consider the entire globe our neighborhood and everyone in it the neighbor we are called upon to love even as we love ourselves.

For us, proclaiming God is One must freshly mean appreciating and living out God's active care and concern for all human beings. Acting on that faith, we must devote ourselves in considerable measure to working with all people and not just with other Jews to make the sovereignty of God real on earth.

To this extent the Emancipation has been revelatory; it has given us a more extensive intuition of what God expects of us by having set us in these radically changed social circumstances. For all our disappointments and suffering in these near two centuries of freedom, Jews such as me still believe in the promise of the new, inclusive social order into which we have come and now comprise so integral a part. Authentically living by our people's Covenant with God in this time and place necessarily yields a conception of Jewish duty expanded from that which evolved in the previous fifteen hundred years of isolation, segregation, and persecution. And that has led some Jews to an activist Jewish social ethic which we believe our community as a whole will ignore or forget only at the cost of its great spiritual peril.

NOTES

1. Gen. 2:18.
2. Gen. 11:1–9.
3. Note the command as well as the promise in Gen. 12:1–3, the first mention of the Covenant relation and its entailments.
4. See the most helpful article by Sid Z. Leiman, "Jewish Ethics 1970–75: Retrospect and Prospect," *Religious Studies Review*, 2, no. 2 (April, 1976): 16–22. It not only provides a listing of all the relevant writings for those years, but includes translations and other materials dealing with

the history of Jewish ethics. I know of nothing comparable for the years since. Leiman's qualifications notwithstanding, I suggest that *Sh'ma, A Journal of Jewish Responsibility* remains the best way of remaining in touch with the scope and variety of contemporary Jewish ethical concerns, though I am not a disinterested observer.

5. So already my "The Postsecular Situation of Jewish Theology," *Theological Studies,* 31, no. 3 (September, 1970): 460–75.

6. Dawidowicz and Goldstein, "The American Jewish Liberal Tradition," in *The American Jewish Community,* ed. Marshall Sklare (New York: Behrman, 1974), and see the bibliography there on "The Politics of American Jewry," pp. 372f. Also Eugene B. Borowitz, *The Mask Jews Wear* (New York: Simon & Schuster, 1973), chaps. 2–4.

7. Much of what follows is speculative, but it is not uninformed or essentially ideological pleading. In general, minorities reflect majority trends; Jews, still quite eager to belong and not be thought too different, reflect majority currents faithfully if in idiosyncratic ways. Indeed, they are so sensitive to certain winds of social change that they often serve as a good indicator of the new directions most Americans will one day take, e.g., the almost universal adoption of contraception among modernized Jews in the 1920s.

8. Milton Himmelfarb, an astute observer of the American Jewish community and an early, trenchant critic of its unreflective liberalism (*The Jews of Modernity* [New York: Basic Books, 1973]), denies that a class shift is responsible for any Jewish voting change. Jews in poor, not well-to-do precincts are more likely to vote Republican. See his "Are Jews Becoming Republican," *Commentary* 72, no. 2 (August, 1981): 27–31, and Lucy Dawidowicz, "Politics, the Jews, and the '84 Election," *Commentary* 79, no. 2 (February, 1985): 25–30.

9. Because this sector of the community is inner-directed, where it publishes, it tends to do so in a Jewish language, Yiddish (*sic*), but not modern Hebrew. Being wary of the gentile world, it confines the full strength of its views to oral communication. Some sense of these subterranean attitudes may be gained from perusing the issues of the weekly English newspaper, the *Jewish Press.* A more accommodationist but still militantly rightist stance is taken by the *Jewish Observer,* the slick monthly publication of Agudath Israel, the somewhat non-Zionist Orthodox international religious organization.

10. For an early statement of a thoughtful revisionism, see Charles S. Liebman, *The Ambivalent American Jew* (Philadelphia: Jewish Publication Society, 1973), chaps. 7 and 8. In reading Jakob Petuchowski's "The Limits of Self-Sacrifice" (in *Modern Jewish Ethics* [Columbus: Ohio State University Press, 1975]), one should bear in mind that "self-sacrifice" means the liberal suggestion that Jews put devotion to the general welfare ahead of certain specific Jewish interests.

11. For a more detailed statement of the argument concerning the State of Israel plus a deeper analysis of those points on which I argue that the old liberalism needs to be modified, see my "Rethinking the Reform Jewish Attitude to Social Action," *Journal of Reform Judaism* 27, no. 4 (Fall 1980): 1–19.

12. See the data and attitudes of the articles cited in note 8.

21 / The Blessing over a Change of Wine: A Study in the Development of a Jewish Law Published in Honor of the Eightieth Birthday of Nathaniel E. Hess

1987

If you're like me, and want to pour the wine of joy,
Hear what I have to say.
I'll teach you pleasure's way, though you don't want to hear,
You friend of sighs and pain.
Five things there are that fill the hearts of men with joy,
And put my grief to flight:
A pretty girl, a garden, wine, the water's rush
In a canal, and song.

Samuel the Nagid (993–1056 C.E.)

INTRODUCTION

Wine had a special place in Jewish lives as far back as our records go. The Bible refers to it more than several hundred times; only water is mentioned as a beverage more frequently. Most of these biblical references celebrate the joy or esteem of wine, though not a few passages also call attention to its dangers. For all that, the well-known Jewish practice of reciting a blessing before drinking wine is not biblical, nor, for that matter, is any other blessing formula still in use. We first hear of the practice of "saying blessings" in the literature purporting to describe Jewish observance in the first and second centuries of the Common Era, that is, in rabbinic texts.

The sages of the Talmud devote considerable attention to the brief prayers they believe ought to be recited before enjoying various satisfactions, the *birkot hanehenin,* the blessings for delights, as they came to be known. The standard form of these brief prayers consists of a formulaic introduction and a varying conclusion. The blessings begin *barukh atah, adonai, elohenu, melekh haolam* . . . , literally, bless you, *Adonai* [God's ineffable name], our God, ruler of the universe . . . This is followed by a short phrase appropriate to the item about to be enjoyed, e.g., *bore pri haetz,* who creates (or, creator of) the fruit of the tree.

The familiar words of the opening create something of a problem for translators since it seems somewhat odd for us to bless God. Usually we think of God as giving us the goods we call "blessings" and we often call upon God to give us others, that is, to bless us. It hardly seems proper for us to suggest that, in some such sense of bestowal, we can "bless" God, the ultimate source of all the goodness we know. We therefore usually understand the word *barukh* in these texts as a term of thanks and praise. We are grateful for the pleasure that is soon to be ours and, acknowledging that it comes to us as a gift, we praise the donor.

When we, then, "bless" God, we do so quite directly, using the second person "You," and addressing God by name rather than abstraction, "God," or euphemism, "the Holy One." We then acknowledge that we do this as participants in our people's old relationship with God—"our God"—and indicate that we know we are addressing the One who orders all creation—the "ruler of the universe." The rabbis had a term for this opening formula, *shem umalkhut,* name and sovereignty. On occasion, some blessings were to be said without "name and sovereignty." Then *barukh* was immediately followed by the specific appropriate phrase, e.g., for bad news one says, *Barukh dayan haemet,* blessed be the judge of truth (or truthful judge). In rabbinic literature specific blessings are usually referred to merely by their closing phrase, e.g., the blessing "who creates the fruit of the tree." We shall meet that usage continually in the translations of the texts which occur below.

By directing Jews to utilize these formulae often during the day, the rabbis sought to link Jewish lives simply but closely to God, thus creating the characteristic form of everyday Jewish spirituality. And in their continuing concern about the specific circumstances when the blessings should or should not be said, the rabbis indicated the dignity with which they invested address to God and the importance of doing so in a proper form.

Our meager and ambiguous sources cannot clarify whether the rabbis created the blessing pattern or merely extended a ritual style that had grown up in prior centuries, specifically, sometime after the form of the Torah and the prophetic books was fixed about 400 B.C.E. In this paper, I propose to investigate the evolution of the law concerning a somewhat less known and observed rabbinic blessing, the one to be said when, after drinking one wine, one changes to another wine. This not only will cast considerable light on the dynamics of Jewish law generally, it seems an appropriate birthday offering to Nathaniel E. Hess, who, with his wife Marjory, has so often delighted guests at their table by accompanying notable meals with varied and elegant wines.

THE BASIC LAWS OF THE RABBIS

The Mishnah—edited about 200 C.E.—our earliest rabbinic source concerning blessings, gives wine a special status. "What benediction should one say for fruits? For the fruit of trees, one says [Bless You . . .] 'who creates the fruit of the tree'—except for wine, for over wine one says 'who creates the fruit of the vine' [as against table grapes for which one says 'fruit of the tree']" (Ber. 6.1). Typically, no explanation is given as to why this juice of a "tree" has a distinctive blessing, and it remains for the *gemara,* the discussion of the Mishnah which comprises the body of the Talmud, to provide one.

In the Babylonian Talmud—edited about 500 C.E.—the treatment of this Mishnah focuses on the similarities and differences between wine and oil, another valuable fruit extract but one for which no special blessing is given. (The closeness of the two may have been suggested by their coupling in Ter. 11.3.) After the *gemara* advances and rejects many reasons for wine's distinction, one is put forth that receives no refutation: wine is unique in having two great attributes; it sustains a person, as does food, and it also makes one joyous (Ps. 104.15) (Ber. 35b). Here, our sages, like those of other religions, seek to provide a reason for a custom practiced for many years. Typically, suggesting one that is not inconsistent with other practices is difficult but finally accomplished. Only, as we shall see below, such *post-facto* reasoning generally is flawed, stimulating other sages to advance explanations of their own.

The Mishnah gives no evidence of a blessing over a change of wine, and we come across this practice first in a text of the Talmud of the Land of Israel, the so-called Jerusalem Talmud, the *Yerushalmi.* (It was edited about 350 C.E.; citations from it are indicated by a "Y." preceding the tractate abbreviation.)

Near the conclusion of the Yerushalmi's *gemara* to chapter 6 of Mishnah tractate *Berakhot,* Blessings, the chapter which details the formulae to be recited for diverse matters, such as eating fruits, we come across an account of Judah the Nasi's special practice concerning wine. (He lived approximately from 135–220 C.E.) He was so renowned that he is generally referred to as *Rabi,* literally, my master, effectively "the Master *par excellence.*" He was the editor and authorizer of the Mishnah as well as head of the Jewish community in the Land of Israel and its representative to the Roman government. Any tale of his observance therefore comes with special weight. "Rabi would say a blessing over each jug [of wine] that he opened [successively at an occasion]. What would he say? R. Isaac Rovah [the Young?] reported that Rabi would say, '*Barukh Hatov Vehametiv,*' 'Blessed be the [one who is] good and does good [to others].'" This formula is already mentioned in the Mishnah, Ber. 9.2, as the appropriate response to rain or other good tidings. Rabi, apparently, found it relevant for those occasions when he opened extra containers of wine.

Rabi's reported practice seems not to have been common among the rabbis of prior generations else they would not have had to ask what formula he utilized. The same may be deduced from the text that follows it in the Yerushalmi, if it too is historical. "A tale about R. Akiba [c. 40–c. 135 C.E.] who made a banquet for his son Simon: over each jug of wine that he opened, he said a blessing, 'A good wine for the lives of the rabbis and their disciples'" (Y. Ber. 6.8). To us, Akiba's formula seems more a toast than what is explicitly described as saying a blessing—which indicates something of the textual problems we face when we seek to trace the origins and development of a religious practice.

The Babylonian Talmud, edited about a century and a half later, contains neither account. It says simply, "R. Joseph b. Aba reported that R. Yohanan [a generation later than Rabi in the Land of Israel] said, 'Even though they [the rabbis] ruled that one does not need to say the [usual] blessing [who creates the fruit of the vine] when there is a change of wine, one should say "Blessed is the [one] who is good and does good."'" Thus, what we had met as Rabi's own practice is for R. Yohanan a general rule for Jewish living.

A further condition is then attached to the practice, one of considerable significance to later sages. This passage in the *gemara* is part of a general discussion of the use of the blessing, *hatov vehametiv,* who is good and who does good, for short. The *gemara* insists that this blessing is reserved for occasions when goodness is shared between one person and others. Hence, this passage concludes, "Also here [with regard to a change of wine, the ruling assumes that] there are others in a group [who are] drinking together" (Ber. 59b).

A peripherally related ruling of R. Yohanan, which will become of significance in the later discussion of this practice, should be mentioned. He is reported to have said, "Both for a change of wine and for a change of place, one need not say a blessing." The seeming inconsistency with the text cited above can quickly be explained if we assume, as is customary, that the reference here is to the usual wine blessing, "who creates the fruit of the vine." One does not, R. Yohanan indicates, have to say that blessing again when there is a change of wine or when one has moved from one place to another, say during a long meal or banquet (Pes. 101a–b. Of some relevance, too, is Pes. 103a which discusses the law applying to a new cup of wine brought as part of saying the grace after meals. But this material does not become part of the halakhic discussion of our theme.).

These texts, for all that they are brief and somewhat cryptic, should indicate why the Jewish people has considered the Talmud(s) the foundation of its religious life. The Bible, of course, provides us with our fundamental beliefs and practices. But its history/calendar/law, on which later Jewish existence is based, provides few details about how we are to sanctify each day's activities. The Talmud does just that, amplifying old rites and indicating new ones, all the while theorizing about the bases upon which they rest. Countless specific discussions about such matters occur in the Talmud, some given extensive attention, others mentioned even more concisely than the few sentences we have concerning a change of wine.

THE LAW TO THE TIME OF MAIMONIDES

Jewish practice continued to grow and change in the post-talmudic era, sometimes in direct extension of rabbinic standards, sometimes in unanticipated ways. As in the gap between our biblical and rabbinic records, centuries can pass between relevant texts. What we then encounter as new concerns may long have been part of Jewish practice, and here happen to be mentioned, or they may have been relatively fresh developments. Moreover, some texts seem more a theoretical, scholarly analysis than a response to Jewish practice, and which is which is difficult to establish.

Among the earliest post-talmudic works seeking to present a rounded view of Jewish duty and its talmudic base is *Halakhot Gedolot,* the Great [Book of] Laws, a work ascribed to Simeon Kayyara, a scholar who lived in Babylonia, probably in the ninth century. Thus, about three centuries pass from the conclusion of the Talmud until the next treatise significantly mentioning our topic.

In the course of discussing the laws concerning *kiddush* and *havdalah,* the author mentions the rule for a change of wine as formulated by an unidentified Gaon. (The title, Gaon, was given to the heads of the two great Babylonian academies where the Talmud had been produced. Rulings from the Sura Academy—the other was at Pumbeditha—are often given in this text. Hence, one may conjecture that it is from a Gaon of Sura, perhaps Yehudai, who was in office 760–764 C.E. and who is frequently cited by the author.) "The law follows the practice of R. Huna that a change of wine does not require repeating the [usual] blessing but, rather, the blessing 'who is good and does good.'" The Gaon then adds a new dimension to the discussion, that of the quality of the wine. For he continues, "[A change of wine] from poor wine to good wine [requires saying the blessing] 'who is good and does good.' For the rule is established that a change of wine does not require [the usual] blessing but [the special blessing] 'who is good and does good'" (Hal. Ged., Pes. 101a, bottom). This reference of over a millennium ago is reminiscent of the contemporary practice of serving wines in order of their increasing quality.

Two further centuries pass until our next text. It brings us not only five hundred years or so past the completion of the Talmud but to a new geographic and cultural context, Europe. We find it, not surprisingly, in the commentary of Rashi (Solomon ben Isaac) to Ber. 59b, our central text in the Babylonian Talmud. Rashi lived from 1040–1105 C.E., mostly as a resident of Troyes, then capital of the district of Champagne, except for some years at the great study centers of the Rhenish (Franco-German) Jewish community. Though his commentary demonstrates his knowledge of agriculture, there is no scholarly basis for the contemporary Jewish oenophile's legend that he was a wine-maker.

In a concise manner Rashi helps the reader to follow the flow of the talmudic argument. Essentially, he fleshes it out—[note my own frequent use of brackets in translating these texts]. Here he typically amplifies the possibly cryptic words in the *gemara,* "[Because of a] change of wine . . ." saying, "If one is drinking wine during a meal [? feast] and another wine is brought which is better than the first, one should not say 'who creates the fruit of the vine.'" He does not need to specify what one does say, for the Talmudic text does that. Thus, by the eleventh century, the law of the special blessing was reasonably well established and Rashi followed the gaonic ruling that the superior quality of the succeeding wine was a condition for saying it.

Rashi's scholarship created a northern French center of Jewish study. Among its luminaries were the four sons of his daughter Jochebed and her husband, Meir, of whom Samuel (Rashbam, Samuel ben Meir, c. 1080–c. 1174) wrote about our topic. The Rashbam seems to have made his living from growing grapes and raising sheep. Among his halakhic writings are commentaries to sections of the Talmud for which his grandfather did not leave a final manuscript.

He speaks to our question at another talmudic reference to it, namely, at chapter 10 of the tractate *Pesahim,* where, in connection with the laws of *kiddush,* the law of a change of wine is mentioned. Rashbam writes, "If one is brought wine from another jug and it has a different taste, whether worse or better [than the first wine], one does not say the [usual] blessing but 'who is good . . . .'" He not only then cites the classic text from Ber. 59b but also adduces the material from the Yerushalmi concerning Rabi's practice of saying this blessing over each jug opened.

His uncharacteristically brief comment here contradicts that of his grandfather. Rashi had indicated that the second wine had to be of superior quality. Rashbam specifically notes that the blessing is to be said whether the succeeding wine is worse—note its precedence in the text—or better than the prior one. From his citation of the Yerushalmi text we may infer that he bases his ruling on Rabi's practice. The argument joined here over quantity versus quality as the condition for saying the blessing is an important focus of the succeeding literature.

The Rashbam was one of the founders of the school of study which gave rise to the talmudic comments known as the *tosafot,* literally, the additions. Their name arises from their unique method of talmudic analysis. Rashi's commentary had made the established interpretation of the Talmud so widely available—one only needed a manuscript of his notes to understand it rather than having to travel to a school to do so—that scholars could move beyond understanding a talmudic text to comparative study of its comments (e.g., Ber. 59b and Pes. 101a, or even two or more texts only analogously related). These originally oral arguments were eventually written down and collected. More than a hundred known Franco-German scholars were *tosafists* (authors of individual *tosafot*) and since most of the *tosafot* we have are anonymous, there must have been hundreds of others. All later Jewish legal study is based on the method of the *tosafot* and they are regularly published at the outside margin of a page of the (Babylonian) Talmud while Rashi is at the inside margin.

The same passage, Pes. 101a, which drew Rashbam's comment, also has one of the *tosafot,* and in its rich treatment of our topic we can see why this literature became so esteemed. The comment begins with a review of the literature, the central Talmud passage (Ber. 59b), Rashbam's comment to Pes. 101a and that of *Halakhot Gedolot.* It then turns to some lines of the Yerushalmi prior to the ones we cited above. There Abba bar Rav Huna is reported to have ruled, "New wine, old wine, one must bless; change of wine, one does not bless; change of place one must bless; lapse of attention is like a change of place [one must bless]." (I have allowed this text to stand in its cryptic crabbedness to illustrate the difficulty of determining its precise meaning.)

Two comments are in order before proceeding with the interpretation given by the *tosafot.* First, the citation from the Yerushalmi given here has the opening words in a different order than that of our printed versions (and the manuscripts on which they are based). Our present Yerushalmi text reads, "old wine, new wine, one must bless . . ." Since the tosafot draw major implications from their reading, this shift is critical—but one cannot be certain whether their text or ours has the original wording. Second, from parallel texts, Abba bar Rav Huna would seem to be talking about saying the customary blessing "who creates the fruit of the vine." That is, his ruling would seem to be: "[Whether the] wine is new or old, one must say [the usual] blessing over it. [However, when there is] a change of wine, one must not say [the usual] blessing. If one changes the place [where one is drinking, then before continuing drinking] one must say the [usual] blessing. And if one has had a lapse of attention, [the rule is] like that of changing one's place." And had this not been the usual interpretation of the passage, earlier authorities would likely have cited it in their discussions of a change of wine.

The *tosafot,* however, interpret the passage quite differently. "It means that he wishes to say that [when one goes from] a new wine to an old wine one needs to say a blessing because the old wine is better than the new but one does not say a blessing for changes of wine in general since one does not know that the second one is superior." This somewhat unexpected ruling supports Rashi's position that quality is a necessary condition for the blessing. Perhaps the introductory phrase, "he wishes to say," may hint that the *tosafot* was making an effort to find a talmudic passage backing Rashi's stand (which had only gaonic authority) against that of Rashbam (which had talmudic backing in the Yerushalmi).

Rashbam's position is certainly given proper credence, for there is immediate reference to Rabi's practice which, since he said the blessing "over every jug" he opened, appears to contradict the insistence on quality. The *tosafot,* having raised this possible objection to their position, now show how it can be countered—a good example of their method generally. They suggest that Rabi "said the blessing ['who is good' only] because he was not certain [of the condition of the wine in the next jug] but if he had known that it was inferior, no [blessing would have been said]. One might [further] suggest that even if the second was inferior he would have said the blessing because he was making the blessing because of the abundance of wines, as long as the succeeding wine was not unreasonably bad so that one could drink it only under coercion."

Clearly, we have wound up with a considerable acceptance of Rashbam's view. What had once been an insistence on quality alone has now given way to the priority of quantity as long as the loss of quality is not egregious. We may say that for the Gaon and Rashi, quality was a positive condition. The successor wine had to be better. The *tosafot* cannot insist on that in the face of Rashbam's talmudic authority to the contrary. So they accept his argument for quantity and make it the general rule. They then bring back the concern for quality by making it a secondary and negative consideration. The next wine, they rule, does not have to be better. It only must not be very much worse. Their mediation of Rashi's and Rashbam's views, complete with an effort to give everyone a share in the resultant decision, is typical of one major thrust in halakhic decision-making, the impetus to include and integrate.

Many later authorities follow this harmonization of views by the *tosafot,* often citing their exact words. It should be noted, however, that the *tosafot* have introduced a new issue to this topic, that of the age of the wine, whether new or old. While they make little more of this semi-qualitative factor, their exegesis provided a basis for later authorities to extend the conditions for saying the special blessing.

The comment of the *tosafot* then further clarifies the conditions for the blessing. "One must say the blessing 'who is good and does good' whether there is a meal or not. However, an individual is not required to make the blessing unless there is another person [drinking] with him" since the Talmud specifies that this formula is to be used only for a good in which others share.

These issues are further adumbrated in the *tosafot* to Ber. 59b. In this exegesis, to begin with, a change of wine is distinguished from having several kinds of bread or of meat because, as the Talmud indicates (Ber. 35b), wine alone both sustains and rejoices a person. Rashbam's comment to Pes. 101a is then given—but reversing the stand we have in our text! He is reported to have ruled that "specifically if the succeeding wine is superior one says the blessing 'who is good and who does good' but if it is [only of] equivalent [quality], no [special blessing is said]." This understanding of Rashbam as a protagonist of quality is then bolstered by citing the ruling of Abba bar Rav Huna on old wine after new (exactly in the language of our previous citation from the *tosafot*).

The complications are then multiplied by a reference to Rabenu Tam, Jacob ben Meir, another eminent Tosafist and Rashbam's brother. Rabenu Tam is said to have interpreted the Abba bar–Rav Huna passage somewhat differently. He ruled that the blessing is to be said "even if the later wine is not [highly esteemed] as long as it has not become unreasonably inferior." This reconciliation of the opposing positions is slightly different from that of the previous *tosafot.* The comment then continues by explaining why the account of Rabi's quantitative practice follows in the text. Rabi, it is suggested, "was not punctilious about whether the next [jug] was superior or not." One might also say that, despite the wording of the text, "new wine, [then] old wine," Rabi simply had a different position on this law. One could also integrate Rashbam's ruling [for quality] with this by saying that Rabi, though in doubt about the next jug's superiority, said the blessing should that turn out to be true. "But Rabenu Tam interpreted Rabi's practice as one that differed [from the quality ruling] as he explained." After all this, the *tosafot* laconically adds, "But other commentators [have explained] that the [words] 'new and old' refer to the blessing 'who creates the fruit of the vine' just like [the question of] change of place which follows [new wine, old wine] but we do not find this [explicitly] in our *gemara.*" This *tosafot,* which is not as clear as the prior one cited, did not become central to later rulings. The one to Pes. 101a did and this passage was interpreted in terms of its analysis.

There is a second relevant *tosafot* to the Ber. 59b passage which, let us remember, concluded with a ruling that the blessing "who is good" is said only when there is a group involved. "This is the law [even] if [only] his wife and children drink with him, but if he is alone, no [blessing 'who is good' is to be said]." The strong social nature of this practice is reinforced by a further ruling that a person drinking alone who has a change of wine may not even say the *sheheheyanu* blessing, which is reserved for good things that happen to one personally. The reason for this is that "we do not find that an individual says the *sheheheyanu* when in isolation."

We must now return to the conclusion of the *tosafot* to Pes. 101a and some material which seems somewhat bizarre in our cultural context. It is based on R. Mattena's statement that the blessing "who is good and who does good" was originally instituted (in the grace after meals) in relation to the battle of Betar, which ended Bar Kochba's rebellion against Rome, 135 C.E. (Ber. 48b).

Elsewhere, the Talmud reports that when Betar was conquered 80,000 men—and the women and children there with them—were slaughtered by the Romans, causing their blood to run into the Mediterranean, a Roman *mil* away. An early rabbinic text, understood to be related to this calamity, is then cited saying that "for seven years the gentiles fertilized [literally, harvested] their vineyards with the blood of Israel without having to use manure" (Git. 57a). The comment of the *tosafot* refers to this passage, saying "But surely one makes the [special] blessing over the wine because of the fertilization of their [the gentiles'] vineyards with the blood of Israel and says God 'is good' because [their corpses] did not rot and 'does good' because they [eventually] allowed them to be buried." The need to give a reason for a previously existing custom has here led to a historical (and exegetical) reason that explains things to the rabbis but seems quite odd to modern sensibilities.

The tosafistic comments display a considerable practical and theoretical elaboration of Jewish law concerning the blessing for a change of wine and we have no certain way of determining when or where this material originated. Nonetheless, the main lines of the halakhic discussion which followed the *tosafot* are fully prefigured in their writings.

One further source of this pre-Maimonidean period deserves mention, the *Sefer Haravyah.* Written in the thirteenth century by Eliezer the son of Joel of Bonn, the volume is, like *Halakhot Gedolot,* a discursive discussion of the law though its author is a tosafist who generally follows tosafistic rulings. In his discussion of chapter 6 of tractate *Berakhot* he adds a nice phrase to explain why wine has its own blessing and thus requires a blessing when a change of wine occurs. He says that because wine both sustains and rejoices the drinker it is "supremely distinguished" (*Siman* 98; p. 77 in the critical edition).

FROM MAIMONIDES TO THE SHULHAN ARUKH

The halakhic work of the Rambam, Moses the son of Maimon, 1135–1204, begins a radically new activity in Jewish jurisprudence, codification. Perhaps because of his philosophic training and interests, perhaps because of the influence of Moslem culture and Islamic models, he was not satisfied to continue making additions to the *halakhah* in the established patterns. He determined, apparently early in his life, to set forth, all-inclusively, all the laws which the sages had mandated down to his time. He did not propose to give a historical or a literary survey but a practical one, one which avoided all dialectics and simply gave the reader the law. To make it fully accessible, Maimonides wrote it in simple rabbinic Hebrew and eschewed the talmudic Aramaic in which the decisions may have once arisen. Most creatively, he also arranged the law thematically, by topic rather than by talmudic tractate. In the fourteen books of his code he takes us rather logically from basic Jewish beliefs to the coming of the Messiah.

The learning required to carry through this plan was immense, and few of the scholarly aids that we count on today were available: no libraries, few manuscripts (printing had not yet been invented), no indices or bibliographies, no sabbatical from his work as a physician or as spiritual head of Egyptian Jewry. The daring was no less impressive. Not since the time of the Mishnah had anyone sought to give a reasonably complete account of Jewish law, and Maimonides includes topics that the Mishnah touches on only peripherally if at all. Besides, there had been an enormous accumulation of Jewish discussion and decision in the nearly thousand years since the time of the Mishnah—as our theme, one rather marginal to everyday affairs, surely indicates.

The substantive issues were similarly daunting. For example, he could not give the law if he did not risk taking a stand on many issues—but some of these were still being debated. As a result, Maimonides' code did not lack for critics. They not only complained about his giving as law matters that they still considered open, they were equally disturbed because he never gave the sources for any of his rulings. (Commenting on Maimonides' code to clear up these problems thus later became a major scholarly activity.)

Maimonides refused to be cowed by these difficulties and with supreme assurance he entitled his work, *Mishneh Torah*, the Second Torah. In its introduction he calmly suggests that now one need not wander through many difficult discussions elsewhere to find the law but can simply find it here. To some extent, Maimonides partially accomplished his exalted goal. His erudition was so extensive and his arrangement of the law so compelling that, despite criticism, the *Mishneh Torah* became the foundation for all succeeding efforts at systematizing Jewish law. But it never came close to superseding the Talmud or to closing off the halakhic process. Prototypically, it was only another milestone, not the end of the road for Jewish jurisprudence.

We can catch a glimpse of Maimonides' genius in his treatment of our topic. He treats prayer in his second volume, called "The Book of Love," since he considers the duty to pray one aspect of the commandment to love God. One of its six sections is called *Hilkhot Berakhot,* the Laws of Blessings. Its fourth chapter deals with the regulations for the grace after meals which, in those days, often included an additional cup of wine. That, as we have noted above, suggests the possibility of a change of wine and, in *halakhah* 9, he writes, "When people are seated to drink wine and another kind of wine is brought to them—for example, if they were drinking red [wine] and they brought black [wine], or if they were drinking old [wine] and they brought new [wine]—they are not required to say the [usual] blessing over wine a second time. However, they should say the blessing, 'Blessed are You, *Adonai,* our God, ruler of the universe, who is good and does good.'"

Where the tosafists glory in expanding study through extensive analysis, Maimonides is practical, gloriously so in his two-sentence epitome of effective Jewish law in this area. He does this countless times in the *Mishneh Torah.* But we should not overlook the problems or hints hidden in his text. For one, he mentions the color of the wine, opening an issue which will engage later scholars. Morever, "black wine" is unknown to the prior sources and I have not been able to discover what he might be referring to. (Of course, some of our red wines, despite modern techniques of "fining" and thus of clarifying the wine, are quite dark indeed.) For another, on the matter that was so critical to the discussion of the *tosafot,* "new [then] old," Maimonides, usually quite meticulous about his language, says, "old and they brought new." This would usually indicate a lessening of quality, yet he mandates the special blessing for such a change. Either he had another reading in the Yerushalmi text—the one we have—or he wishes for other reasons to indicate that he considers quantity the only condition for the special blessing. Incidentally, his sharpest critic, Abraham ben David of Posquieres, 1120–1198, whose comments are almost always printed alongside the Maimonidean text, does not dissent from this Maimonidean ruling.

One other matter is of some importance. Maimonides rules that the blessing is to be said in the full form, with "name and sovereignty." He is the first to specify this though other writers may simply have taken it for granted as they did with "who creates the fruit of the vine." But this is the first text unambiguously to mandate the use of the full blessing formula.

The traditional styles of rabbinic discussion continued after Maimonides' *Mishneh Torah*. One of the most influential books circulating in the thirteenth century was the extensive work of Mordecai ben Hillel Hakohen, 1240?–1298, technically the *Sefer Hamordekhai*, usually known simply as the *Mordekhai*. The work became widely influential among Ashkenazi Jews and, in abridged form, also among Sefardi Jews. But its very popularity and usefulness seems to have led copyists and annotators to make changes in it to bring it up to date or make it accommodate other views of the law. The text as we now have it considers the change of wine in the two customary places, the passages of tractates *Berakhot* and *Pesahim* which mention this practice.

The *Mordekhai*'s comment to the former passage (*siman* 116) raises two issues. The one, being certain that others are partners in the enjoyment, is also discussed, though differently, in the *Pesahim* passage. Here, the author rules that the issue of whether one person may say the special blessing for everyone present, is decided according to the rules applied in this situation for saying the usual blessing over wine.

He then introduces us to a new problem, citing the *Sefer Haravyah*, though I did not see this material in our version of that text. "If they bring a bad wine and a good one simultaneously, one should immediately say the usual blessing over the good one, thus [by inclusion] exempting the bad one [from further blessing]. One should not say 'who creates the fruit of the vine' over the bad one first in order later to be able to say the blessing 'who is good and does good' and thus be able to multiply blessings. For the general rule is that one must bless the principle and desired thing first." It is a telling and characteristic dismissal of piety as merely the adding up of rites performed. It also reflects the concern of the rabbis that the multiplication of blessings might lead us to call on God's name with less reverence than is proper.

The *Mordekhai*'s comment to the *Pesahim* text is far more complex. Thus, after giving the basic law, the quality/quantity issue is reviewed, essentially following the argument in *tosafot* to this passage. Then, however, he introduces the question of the color of the wine as a substantive issue. "But when white wine [is involved in the change], one says the blessing 'who is good and who does good' even if it is greatly inferior to the first [wine] since it is healthier for the body than is red [wine] and therefore one says the blessing 'who is good and who does good.'" Today, we tend not to serve white wine after red, though Sauternes and other dessert wines would raise this question. Parenthetically, though we find some people sensitive to red wines and not to white, we have little data confirming the greater benefits of white wine. In any case, the *Mordekhai* has now extended the quality argument in a new direction.

The *Mordekhai* also develops the question of the company needed for the special blessing by calling attention to who should say the blessing. If each person having the additional wine said it, one might have the impression that they were individuals, thus invalidating the social ground for the blessing. Hence, he believes one person should say it for the group. A contrary opinion of Rabbenu Yehiel is then adduced which demonstrates that under certain circumstances one may say the blessing "who is good and does good" even when others are not clearly immediately involved. The author leaves this question unresolved.

The passage then reviews the reasons given for the recitation of this blessing, viz., the twin virtues of wine and its memorialization of the dead of Betar. In connection with the latter, the *Mordekhai* notes, "Therefore they instituted [this practice of the special blessing] for the wine since it is red like blood" (Pes., p. 35a). The *Sefer Haravyah* is then cited as ruling that the change from new wine to old wine requires one to say the usual blessing and not the special one. Specifically, the special blessing is reserved for cases where both wines are new or both are old and a new wine of that age is to be drunk. (I did not see this in our *Sefer Haravyah* text.) Abba bar Rav Huna's statement in the Yerushalmi is then adduced as the basis for this practice, indicating that he interprets it differently from the *tosafot* to Pes. 101a.

Spanish Jewish life also flourished in these centuries and its distinctive approach to the Talmud and halakhic questions may be said to have reached a peak in the work of Solomon ibn Adret. The Rashba, as he is generally known, lived from about 1235 to about 1310. His early life was spent as a banker to wealthy and well-situated clients, including the king of Aragon. He soon retired from business and, because of his exceptional scholarship, became the rabbi of Barcelona, a post he held for more than forty years. His influence not only extended over all of the Spanish community but over much of world Jewry, for he was one of the greatest *poskim,* decisors, of Jewish history. He wrote about one thousand responsa, many of which have been published and remain widely consulted. In due course his rulings were to have a significant effect on the positions Joseph Karo adopted in his classic code, the *Shulhan Arukh.*

The Rashba is equally renowned for his interpretations and amplifications of talmudic texts and these *novellae* or *hidushim* remain a significant guide to the meaning and entailments of the Talmud. In his remarks to tractate *Berakhot* he deals with the issue of a change of wine, doing so with the conciseness and direct logic which characterize his work. After a brief comment about the social context required for the blessing, he says "And one says a blessing for a change of wine whether the second one is better than the first or the first is better than the second, for the blessing is said only because of the abundance of the wine" as was Rabi's practice. He then indicates that Rashi has another position, insisting on quality as a condition of the special blessing. Thus, the two approaches to this question were placed unequivocally before the learned public, another good example of the unusual kind of "orthodoxy" found in classic Judaism. With Maimonides and the Rashba, two of the greatest Sefardic authorities, clearly on the side of quantity, this position could hardly be ignored.

Another Franco-German (and, hence, Ashkenazic) authority of this period, the Meiri (Menahem ben Samuel Meiri), 1249–1316, was born in Peripignan and spent his entire life there. He was a leading figure in Provencal talmudic creativity, with a comprehensive knowledge of prior literature and contemporary scholarship, and wrote copiously on every Jewish interest.

In his interpretation of the Talmud—it is too extensive to be called a "commentary"—he treats our theme in connection with the Mishnah on the blessing "who is good and does good." He specifies that a wine is "new" if it is less than forty days old (from the time of the harvest—much younger than any *nouveau* we might be offered). He then offers a third interpretation of the disputed Yerushalmi passage, saying that an old wine after a young one is blessed twice, first with the usual and then with the special blessings. This position has no echo in the later literature. He also indicates his agreement with "the French sages" who rejected the suggestion (Abraham ben David of Posquieres so ruled) that a change of bread also warrants the special blessing. The Meiri says of bread that "its proper making is in human hands," an argument which others later utilized.

Reemphasizing the issue of quality, he agrees that Rabi blessed each jug because each was better than the prior one. He concludes, "In general, what one brings [to the table to drink] from the bottom of the container as against [what one takes] at first is surely better than its predecessor, and thus it seems to me [that quality is the primary consideration]" (P. 210 in the critical edition).

He also raises a totally new issue, the relation of strong drink, our whiskey, to wine. If the whiskey is brought after the wine and its blessing, the whiskey does not receive its usual blessing ("by whose word all came to be"). Moreover, the Meiri denies that it, like a second wine, receives the blessing "who is good and does good." If the beverages are reversed and the wine follows the whiskey, "who is good and does good" is inappropriate since the wine still has not yet received its customary blessing, "who creates the fruit of the vine" (Idem.).

Despite the Meiri's definition of new wine, the *Kol Bo,* literally, everything is in it, an anonymous compendium of halakhic opinion of the late thirteenth or early fourteenth century, records another opinion. It says, "And the entire 30 days of its bubbling (fermentation?) it is called new [wine]." By either opinion the standards of drinkable wine were radically different in medieval times than they are today.

The *Talmudic Encyclopedia* indicates that the *Kol Bo* has more detailed language than the Meiri denying the special blessing for a change of bread. "Wine is produced by God's will and it is not [entirely] given into human power to make it good rather than bad. Consider, from one container of wine many can be made and one will be good and another bad. But as to bread, it is within human power to make it good or the opposite." Thus, special thanks to God for a change of wine is most appropriate. I was, however, unable to find this wording (E. T., 4.327, n. 164).

The Rosh, Asher ben Yehiel, c. 1250–1327, as person and author, sums up and extends the halakhic discussions of the Franco-German and Spanish sages. He lived most of his life in Worms and became the *de facto* spiritual head of German Jewry. Political unrest led him to move to Spain where, in unusual recognition of his eminence, he was made rabbi of Toledo and became a leader of the Spanish Jewish community. He thus encompassed the diverse worlds of Jewish law and creatively integrated them in a way that gave him a later authority near that of Maimonides.

In his running discussion of the Talmud, the *Piskei* (or *Hilkhot*) *Harosh,* he treats our topic in relation to the passage in *Berakhot.* He summarizes significant prior opinion, adding some interesting judgments of his own. Thus, like the *Mordekhai* but without reference to the work, he considers the blessing "who is good and does good" appropriate for a change of wine because "wine is like blood." He then introduces a new reason for a change of wine requiring a special blessing. Wine must be special for "we do not find song [associated] with anything but wine." He also agrees with the (again uncited) earlier work that when old wine follows new wine one must say over it "who creates the fruit of the vine." The Rosh comments, "It is not exempt [from the usual blessing] though 'who creates the fruit of the vine' was said over the new wine because it is considered a different kind [of wine] than the new [wine] for [aging] has changed it considerably for the better"—which, since he undoubtedly had red wine in mind, is our experience. He also accepts the ruling that if both wines are new or both are old, the blessing for a change of wine, 'who is good and who does good,' is not said. (*Pisekei Harosh,* Ber. ch. 9).

The Rosh's son, Jacob ben Asher, 1270?–1340, basing himself largely on his father's work, created a Maimonidean style thematic code called the *Arbaah Turim,* the Four Rows, because it was organized in four major sections. Popularly known as the *Turim* or *Tur,* we do not know exactly when it was completed. Unlike Maimonides' all-embracing code, it limits itself to practical Jewish law, omitting, for example, the laws concerning Temple sacrifices.

The author discusses the laws for a change of wine in the first section of his work, the *Orah Hayyim,* Life's Way, in the part devoted to the laws of blessings at a meal (*Tur,* O. H. 175). He summarizes the prior law with some new emphases. Thus, he agrees that each person may say the special blessing individually though it then appears they are not a company. He also adds some new ideas, indicating, for example, that the wine need not literally be "brought" to the table. If the two containers are already present when the usual blessing is said, one still says "who is good and who does good" before drinking the second wine. He also cites an unidentifiable authority for a ruling concerning two containers of wine from the same fermentation. If the wines were separated within forty days of being harvested, one treats them as if they were two kinds of wine and says the "who is good and does good" blessing. But if they were put into the two containers after forty days authorities differ as to what is appropriate since they seem to be truly of one kind.

The exceptional status of the *Arbaah Turim* in later Jewish jurisprudence—the *Shulhan Arukh* follows its divisions and section numbers—may largely have been due to the extraordinary commentary Joseph Karo wrote to it. Karo, 1488–1575, is most widely known as the author of the code the *Shulhan Arukh,* the Ordered Table, which still functions as the classic presentation of Jewish law. But Karo's major work, in his own estimation and that of rabbinic scholars, was his *Beit Yosef*, the House of Joseph, his commentary to the *Tur*.

As a child, Karo was a refugee of the Spanish-Portugese expulsions of Jews who then spent much of his life in Turkey. He felt keenly the need to bring greater order into the Jewish practice of his day, so greatly disrupted by a century or more of turmoil. Another code, he seems to have reasoned, would not have undisputed scholarly authority and thus would only add to the welter of opinion. Instead, he determined to write an analytic, developmental commentary on Jewish law, one so faithful to its historic sources and evolution that its conclusions could hardly be rejected. He took twenty years to complete the task, finishing it in 1542 in the Land of Israel, in Safed, where he then served as head of the community. He accomplished his task so well that many consider this work unmatched in rabbinic literature for its integration of masterful knowledge and legal acuity.

Karo's comment to the *Tur* paragraph dealing with a change of wine exemplifies the excellence attributed to the *Beit Yosef*. He reviews the major writers and arguments and discusses pertinent comments by others, some of whom wrote in the two centuries between the appearance of the *Tur* and his commentary. His statement of the different views is clear and he does not hesitate to give his own opinion, often in decisive language. His "comment" is the lengthiest and most extensive treatment of this topic we have thus far encountered. A number of its fresh contributions to the discussion deserve our attention.

Some authorities, he notes, have the custom of not saying the special blessing if they have had the opportunity to drink the second wine during the preceding thirty days. Others only say it if the recently tasted wine is of distinguished quality, some combining the special quality and time requirements. But Karo notes that even authors who record this practice admit that there is no good basis for it, hence he says one should not be concerned about their opinion.

In a copy of the *Mordekhai* he found a ruling that an innkeeper and a traveler should not say the blessing "who is good and does good" because they are not truly partners in the good of a change of wine. Karo calls this ridiculous, without basis in its supposed source, unattested elsewhere and not, he carefully notes, in an old copy of the *Mordekhai* he consulted.

On the controversy about new and old wines, he is similarly decisive. He understands Maimonides to have clarified and simplified the issue, ruling that a shift between two kinds of wines mandates the blessing "who is good and who does good," it being immaterial "whether both are new or old or one is new and the other is old." He then concludes tellingly, "And that is the universal practice," indicating the silent yet sometimes decisive influence that community observance had on the evolution of Jewish law.

He reports that another authority had discovered a ruling that if the first wine had been completely finished, then the special blessing is not to be recited on the succeeding wine since, technically, there is then no special abundance of wine. Karo responds, "There is no reason for this. Surely there has been an abundance of wine so one must say the blessing." By contrast, he approves of the French explanation for not saying the special blessing over a change of bread—that good wine, unlike bread, is in God's hands. Moreover, "it is customary for people who eat to have two different kinds of bread. Thus, when they say their initial blessing, they have all the [coming] kinds of bread in mind. But wine, since it is not customary to drink two kinds during one meal, has the [special] blessing 'who is good and who does good'" (B. Y., Tur O. H., Gyshom 175).

FROM THE SHULHAN ARUKH TO THE TWENTIETH CENTURY

The developments of the preceding 1,500 years are summed up in the provisions of Joseph Karo's great code, the Shulhan Arukh, Orah Hayyim, 175.1–6:

> 175. The Laws of the Blessing "Who Is Good and Who Does Good" over Wine. This section contains six paragraphs.
>
> 1. If they bring them [the diners] another wine, they do not recite the blessing "who creates the fruit of the vine" but rather make the blessing "who is good and who does good" over it. *[At this point a comment by Moses Isserles, the Rema, is found in the text. Perhaps the outstanding halakhist of Polish Jewry in the sixteenth century—a period some historians consider that community's intellectual peak—Isserles wrote a commentary to Karo's* Beit Yosef, *providing the Ashkenazic customs and interpretations where these differed from Karo's Sefardic rulings. He then abbreviated this for a commentary to Karo's* Shulhan Arukh, *the Ordered Table, which he entitled the* Mapah, *the Tablecloth. Without this addition it is unlikely Karo's code could have been as widely accepted among Ashkenazi Jews as it came to be. The* Mapah *is now regularly printed interspersed in the text of the* Shulhan Arukh *and will be indicated in this translation by the use of parentheses and the introductory word "Rema."]* (Rema: But specifically, this applies only when they [the wines] were both not present before them

simultaneously when the original blessing was said. For if they were [present], one only need say "who creates the fruit of the vine," as is explained in paragraph 3.)

2. In general, they recite the blessing "who is good and who does good" at every change of wine even though they do not know that the second is better than the first as long as they do not know that it is worse than it. (Rema: It makes no difference whether they are both new wines or one is new and one old or even if one is drinking it within 30 days [of the harvest]. Some say that if one has first drunk red wine and white wine is brought, even though it is much worse [than the red], the blessing "who is good and does good" is said because it is healthier for the body than the red.)

3. If they bring a bad and a good wine together one should immediately say the blessing "who creates the fruit of the vine" over the good one, thus exempting the bad one [from additional blessing]. One should not do it in reverse order so as to say the blessing "who is good and who does good" afterward. For, as a matter of principle, one should say a blessing over the primary and choice [item] first.

4. One should not say the blessing "who is good and who does good" unless another person will be joining in the drinking. For this is its meaning, "good" refers to [the good of] the reciter [of the blessing] and "does good" [refers] to [the good of] the other [person]. This is the law if his wife and children are with him but if he is alone he should not [say the blessing].

5. If many people are participating in a festive meal, each one should say the [blessing] "who is good and who does good" and one person should not say the blessing for all of them for we fear lest the windpipe open up before the gullet when they respond "Amen." (Rema: But if they are seated in order to drink but not eat, then one may say the blessing for them all.)

6. The wines of two containers but of one kind: if they had been put into separate containers within 40 days of the grape harvest, [the wines] are considered as if they were of two kinds and one should say [the blessing] "who is good and who does good." But if they had been put into their containers after 40 days [from the grape harvest] one does not say the ["who is good and does good"] blessing over them since they are one kind of wine.

Some role in the eventual eminence of the *Shulhan Arukh* must be attributed to the rapid growth of Jewish printing in the sixteenth century. It made Jewish study no longer dependent on access to manuscripts and the possession of a prodigious memory. Of course, printing also tended to fix texts that had heretofore been somewhat fluid, e.g. the *Mordekhai,* hence it tended to constrain a certain prior freedom. Moreover, as we now regularly discover, printers were not always discriminating in the choice of manuscripts with which they worked or unfailingly accurate in reproducing them. In any case, from this century on, the new technology of manuscript reproduction substantially affected the development of Jewish law.

Contemporaneous with Joseph Karo and a co-resident in Safed for some years was the former head of the Egyptian Jewish community, Radbaz, David ben Solomon ibn Abi Zimra, 1479–1573. During his lengthy communal service, questions were addressed to him from all over the Jewish world and many of his responses to them were later published. Such responsa, *teshuvot,* had been a major factor in the growth of Jewish jurisprudence ever since the eighth and ninth centuries when the genre was developed by the heads of the Babylonian talmudic academies. We have not had occasion yet to cite a responsum and these by Radbaz not only are intrinsically interesting but help round out our introduction to the literature of halakhic development.

Radbaz was asked if the blessing "who is good and who does good" is to be recited when a company runs out of the first wine and a second is therefore brought to them. Radbaz cites a source which knows of such a ruling but is doubtful about it since more of the initial wine may be available but, rather than serve it, another wine is brought to the table. However, one might also reason that in such a situation they are not drinking out of a desire to change wines but out of necessity, so to speak. This would make the initial negative ruling plausible, Radbaz thinks, and he commends it as a reasonable middle way of dealing with this problem (Responsa Vol. 4, no. 1,195 or 125).

Another of his *teshuvot* casts a bit of a shadow on Jewish hospitality in the sixteenth century. The inquirer wishes to know whether one who does not share the second wine with the guests but drinks it alone may recite the blessing "who is good and who does good." Radbaz responds that while there is some debate on the matter, he sees no sense in the reasoning purported to justify a selfish drinker. Rather he rules, "Indeed, I say to you that such a one may not say the blessing 'who is good and who does good'" (Vol. 1, no. 228).

When Radbaz left Egypt for the Land of Israel, he was succeeded as head of the community by Bezalel Ashkenazi, 1520–1591/4. Probably as a result of a local controversy which reduced the powers of his office, he too emigrated to the Land of Israel where he became the chief rabbi of Jerusalem. Over his lifetime he was an avid collector, copier and editor of old halakhic manuscripts. These served as the basis for his extensive legalistic commentary to the Talmud, the *Shitah Mekubetzet,* the Anthological System. His brief comment to Ber. 59b adds a slightly different note to the quality/quantity controversy. Upholding the position that the blessing is said because of the abundance of wine, he notes, "Even if one does not know whether the succeeding wine is good or not, [the reason for serving] many wines [is] in order to drink [of them] even if one does not drink [of] them [all] immediately." That gives added reason for gratitude when one turns to a succeeding wine (Sh. Mek. Ber. 59b, p. 33a).

The *Shulhan Arukh* had many critics, most of whom felt its treatments of the law were too brief. The result was a number of competing codes, one of the most influential of which was Mordecai Jaffe's *Levush Malkhut*, the Garment of Majesty, generally called simply the *Levush*. Jaffe, c. 1535–1612, served as a rabbi and *yeshivah* head in Prague, Venice, Grodno, Kremeniec and Posen, vitae testifying not only to his eminence but to the troubles that now befell Central European Jewry. He gives a nice subjective interpretation of the special blessing's second phrase "who does good." I bless God who does good "for me with this additional wine, [one] which God has given me. [Therefore] blessed be God for this graciousness" (Lev., Hil. Seud., 175.1). He agrees with the consensus on the quantity standard with the usual exception, that a bad second wine should not elicit a blessing. He considers white wine always superior to red because of its health benefit (175.2). As we can see, there is little to distinguish the *Levush* from the *Shulhan Arukh* on this topic.

Another halakhic luminary of this period was Yom Tov Lipmann Heller, 1579–1654, whose commentary to the Mishnah became so widely influential that it has become customary to print it in the margin opposite that of Ovadiah Bertinoro, the "Rashi" of the Mishnah. Among Heller's many other writings was a series of relatively brief notes to the Talmud, oriented more to elucidating the law than clarifying the wording. He adds an interesting sidelight to the reasons given for saying the blessing "who is good and who does good." One might think that relating wine to the blood of the dead of Betar limits the special blessing to a change involving red wine. Heller writes, "But the term 'wine' generally was [=meant] red [wine to the rabbis]. This [limitation to one kind] caused no controversy for they instituted [the blessing] over all wine [white and red]." Thus, Heller acknowledges a flaw in the old reason for the custom, that it explains only half the practice. He must then compensate for this by saying, in effect, that the rule is arbitrary. Such is often the fate of new reasons chasing old customs.

By the seventeenth century the status of the *Shulhan Arukh* was well established and it gave rise to an important new form of halakhic literature, commentaries to it, in whole or in part. One of the most authoritative of these, though it deals only with the laws presented in the *Orah*

Hayyim is the Magen Avraham, the Shield of Abraham, of Abraham Abele Gombiner, c. 1637–1683.

In his notes to Section 175, where the laws of a change of wine are given, he largely concentrates on the issue of who truly may be said to be a partner in one's "good." Gombiner's contribution, other than a fine summary, is his ruling, "If the householder sets the container [of wine] on the table, as is customary at great meals [with many guests], then all are equal in the 'good' and it is as if they owned a share [of the wine]. Hence they say the blessing 'who is good and who does good'" (M. A., 175.4).

By the eighteenth century the law in this area is reasonably well settled: quantity is determinative, except when the succeeding wine is known to be clearly inferior. But scholars continue to observe the mitzvah of studying the law, seeking to find new facets of God's Torah. Thus, the Lithuanian sage Moses ben Simeon Margoliot, d. 1781, in his commentary to the Yerushalmi, gives an extensive review of the discussions based on the passage concerning the new and old wine. He apparently finds Rabi's practice too indiscriminatingly quantitative, leading him to a new interpretation of it. "It seems reasonable that Rabi had very many of the different varieties of wine and for that reason he said the blessing over each container he opened. For with varieties [of wine] it is customary to set them [before the company] each one by itself even though there occasionally are many containers of one variety. Usually when people are drinking wine from one container and they open another container to drink from it, it is probably either because it is of another variety or it is superior to the first that they open the other to bring it to the table." Since Rabi is reported to have "opened" and not merely brought the containers to the table, it is likely that the new wines were superior. And it is also possible that he was doing all this to teach the students the *halakhah* in this matter.

An occasional effort has been made to provide the community with an updated *Shulhan Arukh.* While no one has succeeded in that high ambition, a number of such texts have become authoritative works for later halakhists. One notable such attempt, the *Shulhan Arukh of the Rav,* was authored by Shneur Zalman of Lyady, 1745–1813, the founder of Habad Hasidism, popularly known as Lubavitch Hasidism. He is reported to have been set to this task in 1770 by his *rebbe,* Dov Baer, the Maggid of Mezirech. Though he worked on it for many years, only a small part was published during his lifetime with about a third of the manuscript appearing after his death, the rest having been lost in a fire.

Shneur Zalman largely repeats the laws of the *Shulhan Arukh,* though adding some subtle touches of his own. Thus, in discussing why wine has a second blessing, the only reason he gives is that it rejoices (omitting the usual cognate "it sustains") but here, going beyond his predecessors, he specifies intriguingly, "For it rejoices God and people." He also tilts the standard for saying the second blessing toward the side of quality, ruling, "But if one knows that the second is inferior to the first, one should not say over it the blessing 'who is good and does good,' even if it is only slightly inferior"—as against his predecessors' concern only for a marked inferiority (Sh. Ar. Harav, O. H., 175.1).

This concern for quality is further indicated by his discussion of red and white wine. "If one is drinking white wine and then red [wine is brought to be drunk], if one knows that the red wine is somewhat superior [to the white], one says the [special] blessing. However, one does not automatically [do so] for the white is much healthier for the body." Of course, here the issue of quality is not related to taste but to health. But taste too is a consideration, as he continues, "It should not be necessary to emphasize that if one is drinking old wine and then new [wine is brought to be drunk] that one does not automatically say a blessing over it unless it is known to have a superior flavor like the old [wine]" (ibid., 175.2)

One further such nuance is pertinent, since it relates to Nathaniel Hess's occasional practice. Prior authorities only spoke in terms of a "later" or "succeeding" wine. Shneur Zalman is the first to specify, "if people are brought a third kind of wine, they once again say the blessing, 'who is good and who does good' as long as [third and other later wines] were not consciously included when they said the blessing over the second wine" (ibid., 175.5).

The last work to be considered here was published just after Nathaniel Hess was born. It is the six-volume commentary to the *Orah Hayyim* section of the *Shulhan Arukh,* which was completed in 1907 by one of the great personalities and scholars of recent times, Israel Meir Hakohen, 1838–1933. He is more popularly known as the *Hafetz Hayyim,* the title of his first, anonymously published, extraordinarily influential book. Its title, literally, Who Loves Life, hardly indicates its content, a detailed analysis of Jewish law concerning the sin of gossip.

His commentary, the *Mishnah Berurah,* the Clarified Mishnah, provides us with a new explanation of the special blessing formula. "Various books have given a reason for this wording. It is clear that people need to hold back somewhat from the pleasures of this world. Wine surely brings one to joy but it can also bring one to irresponsibility. Therefore, they [the rabbis] ordained this wording 'who is good and who does good' for everyone knows that the blessing 'who is good and who does good' was instituted as part of the grace after meals because the dead of Betar were allowed to be buried. [Saying] this [blessing], one will remember the day of [one's own] death and thus not be tempted to have over much wine" (M. B., O. H. 175.2, the bracketed data).

We also find here a recommendation for the Passover *seder* when four cups of wine are to be drunk. "In principle, it is good on Passover night not to drink from another variety of wine during the meal so as not to have to say over it the blessing 'who is good and who does good.' Then one would seem, perhaps, as if one had added to the [required four] cups. But if one is thirsty and desires to drink from it [another variety], one may say the blessing 'who is good and who does good' over it" (idem.).

Since the quality standard might still raise some doubts in the mind of the one offering the wine, some strategies for avoiding saying an unnecessary blessing are suggested. "In general, it is good to be zealous [about one's duty] when one has some prior doubt about which wine is good. To start, one should remove one wine from the table and after this say the blessing 'who creates the fruit of the vine' over the [remaining] one. Afterward, one can say the blessing 'who is good' over the second one and thus be free of all doubts." He then cites some support for this view (ibid, 175.3).

A further refinement is also added to the issue of the partnership in the good. "Many recent authorities likewise agree that one should not say the blessing 'who is good and who does good' unless [at least] the two of them drink from two wines. But if two drink only from the first wine and only one drinks from the second wine, or *vice versa,* the special blessing is not to be said." The time of the blessing is also considered. "Recent authorities have written that one can say the blessing 'who is good' after-the-fact. That is, if one has [already] drunk but then remembers [not saying the blessing] and has some wine in one's mouth though one has swallowed [most of] it, one should say the blessing. But if one remembers [the lapse] after having drunk [it completely], it is not appropriate to say the [special] blessing" (ibid., 175.4).

Thus, by the twentieth century, Jewish law has a well-established consensus about the proper response to a change of wine. When a successor wine is to be drunk, one should say a blessing to God for it: "Bless You, *Adonai,* our God, ruler of the universe, who is good and who does good." One says the blessing in appreciation of the abundance of wine to drink, a delight one needs no educated palate to appreciate. Sensibly, one refrains from saying the blessing if one knows that the new is quite bad. One also does not say it if one is alone or if others present are not also drinking—confirming the wine-lover's experience that good wine is enhanced by appreciative company. Surely this Jewish practice ought to be more widely known to our generation with its consuming interest in good food and drink. And may it soon be widely practiced!

Much might yet be said about this theme in Jewish law, another reason among the many why Jewish study is a lifelong responsibility. May all who read this paper be granted a full hundred and twenty years which they fill with this and other *mitzvot.* And may they have the joy of witnessing forty more years of abundant blessing and fulfillment granted to Nathaniel E. Hess.

The days of cold are past and days
Of spring have buried winter's rains.
The doves are sighted in our land;
They flock to every lofty bough.
So friends, be true and keep your word.
Come quickly, do not disappoint a friend.
But come into my garden. There are
Roses scented as with myrrh to pluck,
And drink with me, amid the buds and birds
Assembled there to sing the summer's praise,
Wine, red as my tears for loss
Of friends, or red as the blush on lovers' cheeks.

Samuel the Nagid (993–1056 C.E.)

My thanks to Prof. Raymond Scheindlin for permission to use his translation of these poems by Samuel the Nagid.

22 / Co-Existing with Orthodox Jews

1987

Orthodox spokesmen have often proposed a simple solution to the problem of Jewish unity. They suggest that, since we Progressive Jews adapt to so much else in the modern world, we agree for the sake of Jewish unity to accept classic Jewish law in all matters related to Jewish identity. The analogy to *kashrut* serves as a paradigm for this argument. "You can eat in my house but I cannot eat in yours. Why do you not then agree to follow our practice?"

In my experience, thoughtful traditionalists—the extremists, intellectual and moral, of both camps being omitted from this discussion—often cannot see the element of religious principle in Progressive Judaism. From their perspective, there doesn't appear to be any. The classic Jewish sources focus on faith in terms of practice rather than belief, but many observances central to traditional Judaism—Shabbat, *kashrut,* Jewish marriage, Hebrew *davening*—seem to have little meaning to many Progressive Jews, some even feeling free to discard them altogether. Thus it appears puzzling that the vaunted flexibility of Progressive Jews cannot, for the sake of the Jewish people, embrace at least some few disciplines of classic Jewish law.

Our first task, then, is explanatory: to indicate that what others perceive as our rejection of Judaism, arises from what we see as an even deeper level of Jewish belief and devotion. It is not enough merely to point to the changes that Jews instituted in response to shifting historic circumstances. That once controversial notion of ours has largely become the common property of all modernized Jews. The critical issue then becomes not whether Jews ever ought to change, or even the rate of that change, but the criteria and, in turn, the structures for reshaping Jewish duty. In sum, the issues between us are not descriptive but normative, not how the Halacha functioned but how our meta-halachic commitments indicate it now ought to function.

ELUCIDATING THE CONTRADICTORY VIEWS OF COMMANDMENT

In all our theological variety, we Progressive Jews mostly agree that the primal ethical thrust of classic Judaism now demands greater weight than it once had in determining our Jewish obligations. And its immediate consequence is a greatly increased regard for the dignity of the individual Jew, that is, for the Jewish "conscience." As a result, wherever human welfare is involved, we hear an ultimate command being laid upon us which demands priority in our Jewish living. We do not thereby deny the indispensability of symbolizing all the other dimensions of our historic faith. We only know that sanctifying human relations is our primary Jewish responsibility and thus a major criterion of the life of prayer, ritual, and study which inspires and guides us in our messianic service. We also are convinced that this heightened concern for persons must begin with each individual Jew's unique capacity for religious experience and understanding.

Many Progressive Jews abuse the freedom we esteem. But we do not consider the continuing ubiquity of sin a refutation of our ideal. Surely no useful lesson in comparative Judaism will result from comparing the most admirably sincere Orthodox Jews with the most vulgarly nonobservant in our midst. I have no fear of the result of our comparing the pious elites of our movements with one another, or, for that matter, seeing what we would learn by similarly studying those among both groups who claim our name but refuse our respective disciplines.

If we are to argue our theories in terms of what best contributes to the survival of the Jews, I am convinced that we Progressive Jews have taken the right risks. In a time when people are overwhelmingly educated and socialized to think for themselves, only a Judaism that demonstrates ultimate respect for the conscientious decisions of individuals can long hope to survive and flourish. To me, that is not merely a pragmatic consideration but a faith I find expressed in the Torah when it says we are "created in the image of God." To be a person has come to mean exercising self-determination. Thus all human beings, including Jews, need to be given adequate scope for the exercise of personal autonomy and the grounding which will enable them to do so with mature responsibility.

Two emphases would help make plain to others that these commitments obligate us even as Halacha does other Jews. First, of course, is our actions. We would make our case to the Jewish world more convincingly if our pious elite were larger and its activity more visible. Obviously, that goal commends itself intrinsically, but in the context of this discussion it will also help to keep its political significance in mind. Second, other Jews would better understand the depth of our religiosity if, instead of talking about human feelings or needs, we would speak of what God wants. Note the circumlocutions I resorted to above in stating our religious case, "primal, highest, essential, intuition, ultimate." I utilized such humanistic terminology so that as many people as possible would feel comfortable with my survey of our common belief. Historically, such language was a new midrashic style we created to make Judaism believable again in a day when God and Torah had so overwhelmed Jewish consciousness that human initiative had stultified.

But ours is no time in which to idealize human capabilities in such a way that we remain embarrassed to speak directly of God. We modernists may envisage God differently. Nonetheless, we all assert that the imperative power of the ethical and the inalienable dignity of the individual are not merely our human idea or hope but a result of who God is and what God has done. Formally, we do not speak of God and duty differently than do other Jews. We, too, assert that our obligations derive from what we believe God wants us to do. And our Progressive Jewish versions of Jewish responsibility derive from our several perceptions of how God wants us to live the Covenant today. Put in those terms, the common language of our tradition and the true language of our faith, few people would ask us to deny our sense of God and Torah for the sake of a less disputatious Jewish community.

That having been established, we must face a harsh reality: if conscience is to be respected, we cannot ask Orthodoxy to violate its own faith and accept Progressive Judaism, *de jure*, as a fully equivalent, if alternative, interpretation of Judaism.

Setting aside all considerations of power, as we did when considering our own case, let us continue to focus on the question of belief. Theologically, Orthodoxy cannot recognize the teaching of Progressive Judaism as valid. The basic, authoritative Jewish texts of Jewish law clearly classify our modernist reinterpretation of Judaism as our tradition's equivalent of heresy, *apikorsut*. Ideally, it can never be condoned.

On both sides, then, the protagonists stand on principle—and the stands are irreconcilable. Were that not the case, our problem might already be moving toward resolution as a result of a little good will or dialogue.

FINDING A JEWISH WAY NEVERTHELESS

Yet for all their intractability, I do not believe our difficulties are beyond substantial amelioration. Both sides have a deep, though subsidiary, faith that might now help us overcome the present impasse: their commitment to *Ahavat Yisrael,* the love of the Jewish people and of individual Jews. The higher politics, that is, political action as a climax of our social ethics, might, with God's help, find a way to move us from this common ideal to a pattern of mutually acceptable existence.

As a matter of Halacha, Leviticus's commandment to love your "neighbor"—literally, your "fellow-Jew"—as yourself is conditional upon that Jew's observance of the commandments. Two contemporary realities tend to mitigate this restrictive reading of the law. First, we all remain deeply wounded by the Holocaust. Enough Jews have already been lost in this generation, making almost all of us desirous of finding ways to keep us from losing more. Second, most modernized Jews prize the benefits pluralism has brought to social relationships. Even groups that cannot easily validate granting rights to those espousing error appreciate the human security and social opportunity tolerance has brought to minority-group existence. So, too, in our community, experience with democracy has taught us the virtues of finding ways to live with Jews with whose beliefs and lifestyle we may radically disagree.

Somewhat hesitantly, I wish to suggest that a third factor may also give us some measure of hope, namely that while neither group is without substantial power, neither is strong enough to force the other to its will. While there are great regional variations and each group draws on different strengths, we have a rough balance of power among us. Orthodoxy demands respect for its unbroken tradition, its venerable institutions, its sages' impressive learning, its adherents' dedication and self-sacrifice and the not unambiguous value of its many fanatics. With all that, if we inquire about the faith people actually live, Orthodoxy appeals to but a small minority of Jews.

Progressive Judaism may lack centuries of experience to authenticate its modernized Torah. Nonetheless, it bespeaks the unarticulated faith of most contemporary Jews, regardless of their institutional affiliation. They want to be Jews but they also want their Judaism to manifest what they have found precious in modernity: democracy, pluralism, the dignity of each person, and the virtue of not insisting that one generation's social arrangements cannot be changed by those that follow it. On all these counts, they know Progressive Judaism is right even when they cannot publicly admit it. Their tacit assent is our greatest political asset.

With neither group able to enforce its view on the other, realism may lead them to permit their love of Jews to guide them to some mutually acceptable accommodation.

It will not do, however, to suggest that this process can be hastened by asking Orthodox and Progressive Jews to subordinate their special interests to the needs of *Kelal Yisrael,* Jewry as a whole. That appeal seriously misconstrues the present impasse. Neither group believes Jewish unity is the overriding Jewish value. Had *Kelal Yisrael* been our most significant concern, we would never have brought Progressive Judaism into being, for its creation seriously divided the Jewish community by defying the accepted community leadership and the established traditions of our people. The same is true of Zionism, our movement's secular counterpart. If further proof is needed, should Meir Kahane ever become Prime Minister of the State of Israel, no fervent appeals to *Kelal Yisrael* will keep the overwhelming majority of modernized Jews from dissociating themselves from his administration.

The concept of *Kelal Yisrael* has even less weight in traditional Judaism. Neither the Bible nor Rabbinic literature significantly employs the term. Rather, its recent currency derives from secular Jews who, having abandoned God and Torah, love the Jewish folk enough to make it their supreme value. Believing Jews—and here Progressive and Orthodox Jews stand as one—will seek the good of the Jewish people not in some low though common denominator but in terms of what they believe God wants of this people.

A critical concern of classic Jewish social theory—accommodation to reality—may also give us some hope in this quest. The Torah reflects a transcendent idealism. But it is meant to be lived by real people in real history. Hence, though it demands holiness, it also seeks ways to make its ideals practical and livable.

Over the centuries the Halacha, the Jewish legal tradition, demonstrated an extraordinary capacity for finding the fine line between God's lofty demands and the Jewish community's actual capabilities. Indeed, Progressive Judaism became a necessity only as that genius faltered before the unparalleled challenges of the Emancipation. In any case, Rabbinic Judaism commends the piety of a certain species of compromise. It must not make Jews cynics by its easy sacrifice of our ideals, as the Hellenists once did. Yet it also may not aim for such purity that it becomes unrealistic, like that self-destructive sect that left Jerusalem for a holiness attainable only in Dead Sea isolation.

The move to compromise fuels extremist indignation at the betrayal of principle. In this dispute we may confidently expect the prophetic voices in Progressive Judaism and the super-pious among the Orthodox will righteously spurn any proposed middle way. At their best, they will remind us of the ideals that any arrangement will, in part, have sacrificed. But human and Jewish history assure us that such radical efforts to implement God's fullest demands now cannot build a community or keep it alive in history. Jews may be inspired by their prophets and *Chasidim* but Judaism is the creation of rabbis. We work at the higher politics by way of their measured idealism. So we do not ask our leaders to devise practices even our fringe groups will find acceptable but only ones the bulk of our community feels it can support with full Jewish integrity.

In pursuit of this goal our leaders must give special consideration to one group among us, Jewish women. Equal Jewish rights having so long been denied them that they are properly sensitive about their status, particularly in matters relating to Jewish identity, and they are rightly touchy about who presumes to speak and rule on them. There still being few women in positions of genuine power among us, we must ask our leaders to make certain that feminist Jewish concerns receive due consideration as we move toward Jewish unity. Lest males once again create the structures of female existence, we must, in turn, ask feminists for some specific guidance. Even though their major energies must still be given to confronting a community slow to change, we shall need to know which aspects of traditional Jewish practice they might, for the sake of unity, abide.

I do not see that the substance of any possible arrangements with the Orthodox can be worked out in public. If anything, the media, with their preference for controversy and their practice of provocation, are a hindrance to the resolution of contentious issues. Even in private it should be clear that neither side will negotiate matters of principle. But since doctrines always co-exist with administrative variation, it may be possible to find or create some significant areas of mutual activity. At the very least, people who respect one another's piety and power will want to learn from one another something of the other group's concerns and openness. That might make it possible for each group, independently, to adopt a course of action that the other could live with. Perhaps the most useful thing we can do in public is to indicate our sincere, if principled, devotion to seeking a reasonable accommodation with one another. I can, I think, best contribute to that process by considering an example or two of the specific sort of issues that might arise and how we might usefully approach them.

FACING SOME REALITIES OF COMPROMISE

The late, great *posek,* Harav Moshe Feinstein, *zichrono livracha,* issued a daring halachic ruling that weddings conducted by Progressive rabbis do not create what the Halacha considers a marriage. Superficially, that seems an egregious insult to our rabbinate and the many Jewish families its rites have consecrated. Yet the Jewish legal effect of Reb Moshe's ruling has quite another tone. It as good as ends the halachic problems created by our wedding ceremonies. Couples married by us would not need a traditional *get* should they divorce. More important, their children by a subsequent marriage are not *mamzerim,* the Jewish bastardy which bars marriage to a kosher Jew. Other authorities disagreed with Reb Moshe's conclusions and insisted that Jewish law must consider our wedding ceremonies legally binding, thus leaving the evil consequences intact.

In my case, Reb Moshe's juridic analysis and conclusion correspond, in fact, with my subjective intent and resulting practice. I do not seek to perform "halachically valid" wedding ceremonies (in the technical sense of that phrase, its only proper sense, I believe).

I imagine some people will disparage the integrity of any rabbi who says he has no interest in performing a "proper Jewish" wedding ceremony. Their attack utterly misconstrues my meaning and misperceives my purpose. I take Reb Moshe's legal language literally, which is generally what legal writers wish their readers to do. At a wedding I do not seek to act as an agent of the traditional Jewish legal system conducting a juridically valid ceremony that thereby renders the couple subject to its provisions covering marriage and descent. Were that my intention I should do many things I, in fact, do not do. Thus, I should carefully investigate whether the witnesses to the *ketuba* are halachically fit to execute this document and I should insist upon an act of *kinyan* by the groom to formalize his serious legal intent in this transaction. I not only dispense with these and other serious legal matters, I do not make a great effort to become expert in this aspect of Jewish law. I would gladly agree to the understanding that no Jews married by me should ever have to issue or receive a traditional *get* or have a child who might be given the status *mamzer.*

All of this, to my way of thinking about Judaism, has little to do with the *Jewish* legitimacy I seek to convey by a wedding ceremony. To me, Jewish authenticity arises from a Jew's continuing personal appropriation of the people of Israel's Covenant with God, not in following specific juridic procedures by which Jews in prior ages and today have sought to express it. I hope by the marital rites I conduct to help two Jews sanctify their personal relationship as the most basic level of their people's historic, ongoing Covenant with God. To accomplish that personalist-ethnic-spiritual task, I study what Jews once did and now do in such rites, utilizing whatever I and other rabbinic colleagues have found useful in our tradition and creating new forms where present needs remain unfulfilled.

From my Progressive theological perspective, I deny that there is anything Jewishly *inauthentic* about my practice for all that it is technically unhalachic. But if it will help to reduce barriers between Orthodox and Progressive Jews, I will gladly indicate on whatever *ketuba*-like document I sign that the rites to which it attests were not meant to create a halachically valid marriage. (Were a formula to that effect added to the Hebrew text, it could have legal effect without generally confusing most of our laity about our religious goals.) To me, such a practice would represent so slight a compromise of principle and so great a gain in Jewish unity that I would not hesitate to commend it to my colleagues.

Of course, wherever possible, I prefer, as a continuer of our people's Covenant with God, to utilize its classic, halachic forms to do so. They often express today, as they have for ages, the living reality of our ongoing relationship with God. But in the cases where they do not, loyalty to God takes precedence over faithfulness to legal procedure.

I do not assume that if we made a few adjustments to Jewish law, like adjusting our practice to Reb Moshe's ruling, and if there were some independent halachic flexibility by the Orthodox, we could easily overcome our present difficulties. Much of what stands between us is emotional, not rational, and our passions are intensified by our various investments of power and ego. Consider another possible compromise we might be called upon to make.

We have long taught that ritual practices should not be invested with the high significance we bring to ethical concerns. If, then, a difference in ritual tended to separate us from most of the household of Israel, we should not find changing it very troublesome. Yet apply that reasoning to the custom of some elements in Progressive Judaism to pray bareheaded. That practice is not only different from that of almost all other Jews but also distasteful to many of them—a fact we know and adapt to without much difficulty, for example, when we are at Progressive services in the State of Israel. Praying bareheaded once symbolized our desire to be fully integrated into Western civilization. But that social goal having largely been achieved, most of us today give higher priority to affirming our place as Jews among the *Jewish* people as a whole. I think it clear that our contemporary Jewish goals would best be met and Jewish unity considerably advanced if all Progressive Jews prayed with covered heads. So much for the logic of the case.

But were we to advance such a suggestion—it could be no more than that in Progressive Judaism—it would arouse passionate objections: "We weren't brought up that way"; "We aren't used to wearing skull-caps"; "It feels uncomfortable, even embarrassing"; "The old usage defined us and now we're becoming Orthodox"; "Why must we do all the changing?"; "Why can't we simply let things alone?" I think there are good, rational responses to each of those comments. I doubt that they will have much effect until the emotional backlash created by the proposal has been overcome—if ever. So this small step toward greater Jewish unity would likely engender considerable dissension among us. We must not underestimate the power of emotion in religious affairs.

If that is true of Jews who believe in the value of Jewish change, how much the more may we expect that various Orthodox Jews will greet their sages' possible halachic creativity with hurt and outrage. As I understand their mood, they bring to these issues a deep-seated resentment against non-observant Jewry. It abandoned Halacha for the benefits of Western civilization, now shown to be largely spiritually bankrupt, and in the name of its new, superior way of life isolated the Orthodox and as good as discriminated against Orthodoxy. For the first time in the more than a millennium since Rabbinic Judaism became widely accepted, the pious have had to defend Jewish law against the practice of Jews—and now these one-time uncaring others ask those who have faithfully preserved the tradition to suggest modifications of it. Such suggestions are likely to raise deep emotional responses. And where Orthodoxy enjoys privilege and an established community position, the passion to maintain them will greatly intensify the feelings.

I have concentrated so on the fearsome challenges we face because I think easy optimism and subsequent disappointment may lead us to despair of making any progress. But I do not consider these dauntingly difficult issues of practical social ethics insoluble. Rather, I believe that realistic people of good will and fertile imagination may yet find ways to resolve them. In this century, with its often dismal human record, two people from religions other than ours, Mahatma Gandhi and Martin Luther King, *chasidei umot ha-olam,* righteous gentiles indeed, have shown us that higher politics remains possible despite the harsh realities of power and the ugly strength of prejudice. What Jews now need is leaders who show their moral courage and political sagacity, creating out of what can be done a faithful reflection of what ought to be done.

No one can give our leaders a rule by which to distinguish an unworthy compromise or an overly idealistic demand from what, as best we can figure it out, God wants of us in our particular here-and-now. That is where their leadership as well as their character and faith will be tested.

May I also suggest that, in a way, the heavy burdens our leaders carry differ only in scope from those each of us shoulders in his or her own life? God calls us all to be holy not in some general, abstract spiritual way but in the humdrum particularities of making money and spending it, of working with some people and against the designs of others, of loving and hating and being indifferent, of the situations we are stuck with and those we can create to our will. Our Judaism seeks to make us realists who are not cynical, idealists who are not fools. But we, facing the hundred compromises each day requires, must ultimately proceed on our own, mediating between God's demand for holiness and the particularity of the creation in which God bids us work it out. We, too, each in our own spheres, must practice the higher politics, the high art of living Torah.

23 / Dynamic Sunyata and the God Whose Glory Fills the Universe

1992

My response to Prof. Masao Abe is divided into two disparate yet related sections. The first, though lengthier and theologically more substantive, is intimately, perhaps decisively, related to the second, which is shorter and more practical.

I

Having long puzzled about how to explain Judaism adequately in English terms—the language being so substantially shaped by Christianity—I greatly admire Masao Abe's accomplishment in conveying his Buddhist understanding of ultimate reality. The problems facing him are far more daunting than those confronting Jewish theologians, for he does not share a common Scripture and God with Christians as Jews do. Decreasing the linguistic barriers to greater understanding, as Masao Abe has so well done here, seems to me one of the most realistic and important aims of interfaith dialogue.

He also shows commendable openness to his dialogue partners' thought, not only seeking to learn from them but then integrating these insights into his statement of his distinctive Zen philosophy. Moreover, while not repressing the issues that Christianity and Judaism raise for his own thought and belief, he can firmly indicate his considerable questions concerning them. He thus admirably demonstrates the potentially transformative moral power of interfaith dialogue.

Though his primary discussion is with Christianity, Abe also seeks to understand how Jewish thinkers have come to terms with the Holocaust, hoping in this way to initiate Buddhist-Jewish dialogue. It is to the best of my knowledge, the first step in direct academic exchange between these faiths, though Leo Baeck and Martin Buber had written about Buddhism many decades ago.[1] I feel privileged to be invited to enter into dialogue with Professor Abe.

There are many matters on which I can find Jewish points of agreement with him: individual responsibility is substantially corporate; an exaggerated thirst for life and attachment to things is a major source of evil; people need insight into a reality that is beyond the everyday and it is as much dependent upon "grace" (my discomfort with the Christian overtones of this term is so great that I had to signal it) as upon will and act; "salvation" might come at any moment, thus the present can be heavy with significance; "thingification" easily bars the way to true understanding; and much more. Yet, since holistic context radically shapes the distinctive significance of a specific theme in a given faith, all these points of agreement point us toward a more fundamental disagreement. Thus, if I may make a disinterested academic observation, Abe's reinterpretation of Christ's kenosis seems to me quite utterly to transform it from what I have understood contemporary Christian theologians to be saying; I therefore look forward to seeing how they respond to him.

The heart of the Jewish-Buddhist discussion may be approached most easily by beginning with the second of the two questions Abe asks of Jewish thinkers at the conclusion of his discussion of the Holocaust. He inquires: "If the rupture caused by the Holocaust is not a rupture of this or that way of philosophical or theological thinking, but of thought itself, how is *Tikkun,* that is, a mending of the rupture, possible?" To Abe as a Buddhist, "mending," *Tikkun,* has to do with thought or understanding, in a Mahayana sense, to be sure. That follows logically from his insight into the human situation and its remedy. *Avidya,* ignorance, is the fundamental evil, and thus enlightenment, *vidya,* true understanding, is its "mending." If, then, thought itself has been ruptured, the indispensable remedy is no longer available and all appears lost. How, then, can Jews still speak meaningfully of *Tikkun* after the Holocaust?

Abe's question is based on a citation from the writings of Emil Fackenheim and it will help to read it again. Fackenheim writes, "For the first time in this work *[To Mend the World],* we are faced with the possibility that the Holocaust may be a radical rupture in history—and that among things ruptured may be not just this or that way of philosophical or theological thinking, but thought itself." I understand Fackenheim to be saying that the Holocaust may be "a radical rupture in history," one so comprehensive that "among things ruptured" is thought—which is to say that the meaning of the Holocaust, *among other things,* exceeds the capacities of the intellectual activities the West calls philosophy or theology.

What, besides cognitive construction, does Fackenheim feel is now decisively challenged? More significantly than philosophizing, this qualitatively unique evil radically throws into doubt the Jewish people's very Covenant with God and the way of life it authorizes—and by extension it also threatens the covenant between God and all humankind, the children of Noah. The ultimate issue is not how we can now think, though that is important to *homo sapiens.* Rather, it is how we might now mend our covenant relationship with God so that the essential *Tikkun,* the mending of human history, can take place. In its Jewish context, *Tikkun* is attained by how one (everyone) lives, not primarily by what understanding they achieve. Thus, as Fackenheim has emphasized, Jews have "coped" (to use Abe's verb) with the radical rupture of the Holocaust by rededicating themselves to living in Covenant. Not the least significant part of this *Tikkun* has been their insistence on not merely continuing their inherited religious way of life but on creating various new-old ways to live in Covenant. Thus, Fackenheim's own hope for *Tikkun* is not based on an elevation of insight but by our building our lives, as best we can, on the example of those Jews and gentiles whose deeds demonstrated that the death camps could not destroy their spirit.

It should be emphasized that neither philosophy nor theology is the basis for identifying the critical Jewish response to the Holocaust. Instead, the surprisingly positive activity of the Jewish community in the post-Holocaust period finally forced Jewish thinkers to reflect on its meaning. They did not lead or even significantly direct the Jewish people's response to the horror. In fact, it took them about two decades to confront directly the questions raised by the Holocaust. Only then, after the living responses were well established, did the thinkers' ideas begin to have a significant impact upon our community.

It is still not clear to me whether the Christian death-of-God movement and, probably more important, its underlying cultural ferment were more responsible for bringing Holocaust theology into being than any indigenous demand by Jews for a fresh statement of their faith.[2] Jewish thinkers did confront this challenge. At their best, they sought to understand, learn from and interpret what the Jewish community had been going through—and it is on this secondary level that they have had their influence in reshaping Jewish life. In these observations I am, of course, reflecting my own understanding of Judaism as the enduring Covenant between God and the Jewish people, hence a religion as much of the group as of, at least to liberals, individuals. Unlike the Descartean bent of Western philosophy, I believe Jewish thinkers must constantly seek to think out of communal Jewish experience, seeking as best they can to understand its significance, though they must also do so out of their specific individuality.

Some comparative considerations may be helpful at this point. For Judaism the fundamental human concern is not redemption from sin. The God we stand in Covenant with "knows our frame and remembers that we are dust" and thus, as the prior verses say, directly has compassion upon us and forgives our sins (Ps. 103:8–14). This God can be heard by Ezekiel calling the people of Israel to repentance by saying climactically, "I have no pleasure in the death of him that dieth, says *Adonai*, God, therefore turn yourselves and live" (Ezekiel 18:32). Having no doctrine of original sin, Jews believe that the responsibility and the capacity to turn from evil is given not only to Jews but to all humankind, as the example of the Ninevites in the book of Jonah demonstrates. We further believe that people, Noachites or Israelites alike, are not fundamentally ignorant of how they ought to live, because God has given us instruction (Torah) to that end and, in various ways, continues to do so. One requires no unusual intellectual or spiritual gift to know [illegible] usual case how one ought to live. One learns it as much if not more from one's family and community as from one's formal religious training and from the great teachers of each generation. Thus, believing Jews are not surprised to discover genuine religion and morality, in quite diverse forms to be sure, among many peoples and faiths. For Judaism, the primary human task is creating holiness through righteous living. The responsible deed, the one that simultaneously acknowledges God, others, time, place, nature, and self in Covenantal fulfillment, not only mends the torn but fulfills the promise inherent in existence.

What is at stake here is precisely the level of seriousness with which one should take this ethical/spiritual human capacity. For Masao Abe it is a deeply felt and humanly quite significant matter, one whose importance may certainly not be trivialized. But it is only the second level of the three dimensions of his thought. Thus he knows that all issues are properly and legitimately understood *ultimately* from the vantage point of the third dimension, which is that of a trans-human fundamental dimension represented by religious faith or awakening—that is, dynamic Sunyata. In it, all such dualities as good and evil, holy and profane, are overcome and transcended. By contrast, in the classic Jewish understanding, ultimate reality has indelible quality; God is holy—and that means, most closely, that God is good. There is nothing more ultimate. And because God is holy/good,[3] Jews are to be holy/good, which means to do holy/good deeds and create a holy/good human order, which ultimately embraces nature in its fulfillment, with God's help.

Because the holy/good deed has such ultimacy, Jews have made it their primary concern and have now enhanced this traditional activism with the dynamism of modern self-assertion. This existential commitment has provided the motive power for the extraordinary Jewish contribution to modern civilization. Even Jews estranged from their religious tradition tend to measure their worth by what they do for humankind. As a consequence, the almost unanimous response of Jewish thinkers and lay people to the Holocaust has been to try to act to frustrate its goals and prevent its replication. Negatively, that means opposing evil wherever one sees it; positively, it means fostering goodness to the extent that one can. And this form of *Tikkun* has been the most important Jewish response to the Holocaust.

Leo Baeck, the one Jewish theologian (liberal, to be sure) to have been in a concentration camp during the Holocaust and to have survived, wrote these lines as part of the conclusion to his post-Holocaust book of theology:

> The great task of dark days, and the greater one of bright hours, was to keep faith with the expectation. Man waits for God, and God waits for man. The promise and the demand speak here, both in one: the grace of the commandment and the commandment of grace. Both are one in the One God. Around the One God there is concealment. He does not reveal Himself, but He reveals the commandment and the grace . . . Every people can be chosen for a history, for a share in the history of humanity. Each is a question which God has asked, and each people must answer. But more history has been assigned to this people than to any other people. God's question speaks stronger here . . . It is so easy to remain a slave, and it is so difficult to become a free man. But this people can only exist in the full seriousness of its task. It can only exist in this freedom which reaches beyond all other freedoms.[4]

With this worldview, the caring Jewish community will overwhelmingly reject the suggestion that, for all the trauma connected with the Holocaust, we ought to understand that it ultimately has no significance; or, to put it more directly, that ultimately there is no utterly fundamental distinction between the Nazi death camp operators and their victims. For most Jews, a response to the encompassing evils of our day—world hunger, political tyranny, religious intolerance and warfare, the threat of nuclear destruction—cannot properly be made with a consciousness that they are truly second-level concerns, that bringing people to a higher level of understanding is the most significant way to face them. And I cannot imagine them agreeing that the ultimate response to the Nazis would have been for Jews to raise their consciousness from a radically moral to a higher, postmoral level.

Does this then mean, as Masao Abe inquires in his first question, that the Holocaust is an isolated event entirely unrelated to other events in the world and history and thereby has a fixed, enduring absolute evil nature? And if the latter is true, how can the Jewish people come to terms with the Holocaust and with God, who ultimately allowed the Holocaust to occur? In some sense the answer seems reasonably unequivocal: Even Fackenheim, the thinker who has made the strongest case for the qualitative uniqueness of the Holocaust, does not suggest that it was "an isolated event entirely unrelated to other events in the world and history." He and the rest of the Jewish community would not be so sensitive to the Christian background of Nazi anti-Semitism if they thought the Holocaust so unhistorical, nor would they be so concerned that it retain a place in human consciousness to spur people to do the good. Does it, then, have a fixed, enduring, absolute evil nature? Yes and no. It is, as far as we can tell, uniquely significant in telling us about human evil. Until some other, more horrific event occurs—Heaven forfend—and as long as memory recalls it, no small matter to Jews, it seems "fixed [and] enduring." But is it "absolute"? If Abe means, Does it carry the same ultimacy that, for him, Sunyata does and Jewish holiness does not? then I must say, No. In my understanding of Judaism, only God is "absolute," though I would assert that only in a metaphorical, weak sense. (Were God a strong absolute, as Bradley indicated, there could be no creation and no independent human will.)[5] And insofar as the "absolute" God is holy/good, the Holocaust is enduringly evil.

In that event, to continue with the question, "how can [the] Jewish people come to terms with God, who ultimately allowed the Holocaust to occur?" Here, I think, the phrase "come to terms" requires a more intellectual response than the one I gave in my previous discussion of how we "coped." I believe a brief discussion of Holocaust theology and the Jewish community's response to it will be most instructive for clarifying Judaism's distinctive affirmations as I understand them.

To the best of my knowledge only one Jew who has written extensively on the Holocaust, Richard L. Rubenstein, has followed the logic of the problem of evil to the conclusion that God cannot be good. He suggests that, after the Holocaust, God ought better to be understood as

> the Holy Nothingness, known to mystics of all ages, out of which we have come and to which we shall ultimately return . . . The limitations of finitude can be overcome only when we return to the Nothingness out of which we have been thrust. In the final analysis, omnipotent Nothingness is Lord of all creation .[6]

While Rubenstein has not developed this notion fully, there is much in what he did write concerning it that might lead Masao Abe to fruitful dialogue with him.

The Jewish community agreed with Rubenstein that the Holocaust posed a radical challenge to its inherited or reappropriated tradition. But his conception of God found few echoes in what then developed into Holocaust theology. I think it is clear why: it did not provide a ground for qualitatively distinguishing between Nazis and Jews. It had explained logically why "God" could "ultimately allow the holocaust to occur" but had done so only by denying that there was any ultimate reason for being morally outraged to begin with; if ultimate reality is morally neutral—and perhaps negative since Rubenstein calls death the only Messiah[7]—one has as much right to be a Nazi as a Jew. That way of "coming to terms" with the Holocaust was, for all its logical rigor and grim courage, antithetical to the fundamental religious intuition of the Jewish community.

I cannot recall a Jewish thinker who has dealt with Holocaust theodicy who has not begun with a vigorous reassertion of the so-called "free-will defense." Consistent with what has been said above, most Jews see the Holocaust as an indictment of humankind, specifically of the Nazis for their demonic use of their freedom. For the Jews I know, theological speculation must not be allowed to shift the primary responsibility for the evil from the Nazis to God. Some human beings, often after considerable deliberation, decided to carry out the Holocaust—and many renewed that decision day after day for years. They were the worst. But in a similar but qualitatively different human failure, the Western democracies and even Jewish community leadership did not do what they could to stop or protest the Holocaust; the human guilt is proportional to the human power. While Jews may have been aghast that God would have allowed human freedom to proceed to such evil lengths, no one seriously suggested that a good God should have deprived people of their freedom or, almost the same thing, severely limited its effective scope. The holy/good deed can only come from a free person. That notion is so central to the Jewish intuition of ultimate reality that humankind's action and nature, not God's, must be the primary level of the discussion.

Those Jews who sought a rational understanding of how God could allow the Holocaust found their solution by denying God has encompassing power. They had no difficulty producing numerous citations from rabbinic literature in which God is depicted as limited. Moreover, the notion of a finite, perhaps growing God, had considerable appeal because it heightened the moral responsibility of humankind. One could not now sink into passivity, throwing oneself utterly into God's saving hands and abandoning what one might have done to save oneself and the world. It is a concept that has brought much solace to Jews in a troubled time, and, universalized and popularized in Harold Kushner's *When Bad Things Happen to Good People* (New York: Schocken), it has been a healing balm to many troubled Americans.

Surprisingly, considering the alleged rationality of the contemporary Jewish community, the idea of a limited God has not become dominant. For all its helpfulness and logical clarity, it seems to many people to create as many new problems as it resolves old ones. On the human level, it leaves people with no cosmic recourse when they are sorely stricken and have exhausted their human power struggling against their ills. God may then be a co-sufferer but God is also as helpless as we are and thus cannot offer much solace. And it is not clear in a post-Holocaust age that we can count on humankind to perfect God's limitations, since we have so many of our own. How, then, will the Messiah come and history be redeemed from mere neutrality or worse? Moreover, on the ontological level, troublesome questions are raised by the power that is not in God's hands. Is there a force or being over against what we had understood to be the one God? And how shall we now transcend our rationality and have faith that despite God's limited power, God's goodness will ultimately prevail in our universe?

Such questions or their human equivalents have, paradoxically enough, engendered a significant return to the God of the Covenant who, we were told two decades ago, was dead, at least in our time. A minority among us, but an unabating one, is in the midst of a probing spiritual quest. As I have analyzed this movement over the years,[8] it has seemed to me to have been generated by a search for a more adequate ground of value. Once, the high human quality that modern Jews have so prized seemed common to all rational, educated, cultured people; thus humanism could be a substitute for religious faith. In recent years, human frailty and perversity, institutional failure, cultural vacuity, and philosophy's inability to mandate substantive ethics, have increasingly threatened to make our civilization amoral or worse. To be more in touch with what one ultimately believes, to find greater power to resist, as one knows one must, these corrosive social forces—perhaps even to harness them for human betterment—people have turned to traditional religious belief. Sophisticates who once would have found that unthinkable, given the attractions of radically autonomous human reason and Nietzschean self-assertion, now find those alternatives largely discredited. They have few moral credentials to present to a generation concerned with value. If anything, they are more the problem to be overcome than a proper standard for its solution.

How do these almost-traditional Jewish believers "come to terms" with the Holocaust? Unable to sacrifice God's goodness, or power, or deny the reality of evil, they reluctantly sacrifice the certainty of logic in the face of what they know to be the ultimate commanding power of living in holy goodness. They believe, in their fashion, even though they do not understand in any ultimate way. Like classic Jewish pietists, they hope the goodness of God day by day will set the context for their confrontation with evil. Creating that day-to-day appreciation of God's continual giving goodness is more important to them than understanding the theological ground of the limit case of gross suffering.

Perhaps such a piety, even in its modern guises, sounds strange for a people so proud of its intellectuality. But there is a certain classic Jewish reticence to probe too deeply into God. Christian theologians like Jurgen Moltmann find it congruent with their trinitarian faith to speak of what transpires in God's interior. Masao Abe suggests that from his Buddhist perspective they ought to move on to "the still greater interior of the interior." On this score, the central tradition of the Jewish people has been resolutely agnostic. It does not know much about God's essence because, as a religion of revelation, God did not say much about it. In recent generations, as thinkers have reinterpreted revelation in terms of human religious experience, this aspect of Jewish awe has, if anything, been strengthened. Almost all Jewish thinkers readily acknowledge that they have little knowledge of Godself though they claim empowering understanding of how God wants us to live. The power of the holy/good deed remains that strong among us.

There is an important exception to this characterization of Judaism—namely, Jewish mysticism—and a brief consideration of its career is in order. Our earliest records of the Jewish mystical tradition—from the time of early rabbinic literature—and its first books focus on how God created the universe and exercises power through it: quite roughly, the classic concerns called *maaseh vereshit* and *maaseh merkavah,* "the work of creation" and "the work of [God's] chariot" (as per Ezekiel 1). We hear of heavenly palaces and angelic beings, even of the dimensions of God's "body," but not about God's inner life.

About a millennium later, theosophy had emerged as a major Jewish mystical concern with the appearance of the Zohar, the classic work of the Jewish mystical tradition, at the end of the thirteenth century C.E. Strongly influenced by medieval Jewish rationalism's emphasis on unity, the author of the Zohar knows God to be, in utter identity and unbroken unity, both *En Sof* and *Sefirot.* The former term translates easily as "without end"—but thus, if the meaning is taken rigorously, God is the one about whom nothing at all can be said, not even, in a way, this, since saying inevitably suggests limits. Some mystics have even gone on to call God, in this understanding, "Nothing." But they and other Jewish theosophists also radically affirmed that the *En Sof* is also the *Sefirot,* the ten "spheres" of interactive divine energy whose configurations and interplay may be described by a range of metaphors so daring and so grossly material they sometimes leave moderns aghast.

In the sixteenth century, Isaac Luria extended the notion of God's pervasive unity to the extent that creation could only be accomplished by God's "contraction" (a sort of "emptying"?) to make "room" for the universe. Two centuries later, the Maggid of Mezeritch, the second-generation leader of the new Hasidic movement, mystically knew that God alone was truly real, and thus in his teaching, a clear distinction between a "relative" human level of affairs and an "absolute" divine one holds sway. Much Hasidic doctrine still features this understanding, though the extent to which it remains part of esoteric as against the folksy, exoteric instruction given by Hasidism is unclear. And, it should be noted, for all this doctrine of two levels of reality, Hasidim have been most faithful in their observance of even the minutiae of Jewish law and custom. Masao Abe should find much in this development in Jewish mysticism that is congenial to him though its sense of ultimate reality is that of pervasive fullness rather than that of dialectical emptying.

The bulk of the Jewish community, however, continues to reject such mysticism. Most Orthodox Jews find its teachings about God suspiciously unlike those of the Bible and the Talmud. These Jewish classics accept the reality of creation and the ultimate significance of the holy act. They find this inherited tradition not only self-commending but fully coherent with their experience. Jewish liberals generally find the enveloping mystical sense of God at variance with their own sporadic, tentative religious experience. More critically, knowing God so intimately, Jewish mysticism tends to bend human freedom utterly to God's will. But what if, as in the case of women's rights, people find they must trust their own sense of the holy/good more than the regulations and customs, indeed more than the "revelation," they have inherited? Again, the primacy of the sense of proper human value reasserts itself and insists upon its central place in any affirmations that are to be made about God. I believe that religious sensitivity is at the root of the general community rejection of asserting God is All-in-All, thereby entailing, ultimately, that there is no real evil—not even the Holocaust. Modernized Jews may wish to make increasing room for God in their lives, but, as I understand them, they do not propose thereby to wipe out but to empower what they know to be demanded of humankind: "Seek good and not evil, that ye may live; and so *Adonai,* the God of hosts, will be with you, as you say. Hate evil, love good, and establish justice in the gate" (Amos 5:14–15).

II

I reproduce here the letter I wrote Masao Abe upon reading his paper:

> Dear Professor Abe,
>
> Ever since I first read a paper of yours many years ago in *Religious Studies* I have followed your writings with great interest (most recently in vol. 14, no. 3 of *Japanese Religions*). It was therefore with great pleasure that I accepted John Cobb's gracious invitation to be a Jewish respondent to your paper "Kenotic God and Dynamic Sunyata."
>
> Beginning my study of it, I was drawn up short by the places where you cite Nietzsche from *Beyond Good and Evil* dividing history into premoral, moral and postmoral periods. You then indicate that he "identifies the first stage of history" with "primitive religions." The following breathtaking statement then appears: "It may be said that this first stage corresponds to the time of the Old Testament which relates stories of this kind of sacrifice in such cases, as Abraham and Isaac. The second state of human history indicates the time of the New Testament and the Christian era following it . . ."
>
> In this context, "the time of the Old Testament," and thus the "Old Testament" itself, and thus the Judaism derived from it are identified with pre-moral religion. Only "the time of the New Testament," and thus the New Testament itself, and thus the Christianity derived from it, are identified with moral religion. The sentence thus perpetuates one of the worst religious canards of Western civilization, one which is a major root of the

anti-Semitism that has finally come to be seen as an ugly, discrediting blotch on Christian religious claims.

You specify, "it may be said . . ." By whom? You do not ascribe this to Nietzsche and no note number concludes the paragraph. My cursory survey of the context of *Beyond Good and Evil* did not reveal Nietzsche as its author. In fact, in section 52, some paragraphs before section 55 which you cite, he is relatively positive about the "Old Testament," calling it the great book of justice.

Of course, such statements "may be said"—but they should not be said. If they are said, they should not be repeated. And if they are repeated, they should be clearly repudiated by those doing so.

I can imagine that even if I spent many years seeking to understand Buddhism and the Asian culture in which it arose and now flourishes, I might well blunder in speaking of them despite my best efforts to be faithful to their finest representation. What astonishes me is that the four academics to whom you express gratitude for their suggestions did not call the offensiveness of this material to your attention.

I look forward to hearing from you about this matter.

Due to travel and relocation, Professor Abe was unable to respond to my letter until shortly before this book was to be edited and put into production. While he was then willing to rewrite the portion of the paper in question based on my criticism, it seemed wiser, at this late date, not to prepare a revision of the manuscript already seen by seven other respondents. At Professor Cobb's suggestion, he proposed that the original text be left standing, that I make my criticism of his presentation of Nietzsche's view of the three stages of human history and he would make his response to it in his rejoinder to all the respondents. I agreed to this arrangement.

I wish only to append three brief comments. First, in a discussion of this matter, Milton Himmelfarb was kind enough to point out a historical inaccuracy. The charge that Judaism is "premoral" is not part of classic Christian theological anti-Semitism but is a creation of post-Enlightenment anti-Semitism—and a typical example of secularization, I might add. Second, while it is only one sentence in a demanding, lengthy paper, it will be of some interest to me to see whether any of the Christian theologians responding in this volume noted and reacted to the statement I found so offensive. Finally, in my reading about Buddhism I have occasionally wondered whether Buddhists writing in English mean by such terms as "right conduct" and "right speech" (two major aspects of *sila,* the moral component of the Noble Eightfold Path), or even the more general "compassion," what Jews generally mean by these terms. I shall be less uncertain reading Professor Abe's response.

NOTES

1. Leo Baeck, in *The Essence of Judaism* (New York: Schocken, 1961), describes the Buddhism of apparently "static" Sunyata as the typological opposite of Judaism; Buber compares and contrasts Zen Buddhism and Hasidic Judaism in his essay, "The Place of Hasidism in the History of Religion," *The Origin and Meaning of Hasidism* (New York: Horizon, 1972).

2. See my *Choices in Modem Jewish Thought* (West Orange, N.J.: Behrman, 1983) chapter 9, "Confronting the Holocaust," particularly pp. 187–90.

3. I am not satisfied with either the term "holy" or "good" by itself to convey the quality of the mandated, desired Jewish act. "Holy" alone often carries the connotations of "churchy," or of a segregated spirituality. "Good" is too easily secularized into humanistic ethics. The fulfilled Jewish act is more life-involved than the one, more God-oriented than the other. This dilemma surfaces in another way in trying to translate the term *tzedakah.* We variously render it as "righteousness" or "justice," but it is as likely to mean "faithfulness, reliability" and it comes to mean what English calls "charity" *(caritas).*

4. Baeck, *This People Israel* (Holt, Rinehart, Winston, 1964), pp. 397 and 402.

5. I discuss the equivocal applicability of the term "absolute" to the God of Judaism in my paper "Liberal Judaism's Effort to Invalidate Relativism Without Mandating Orthodoxy," in *Go and Study: Essays in Honor of Alfred Jospe* (B'nai B'rith Hillel).

6. Richard L. Rubenstein, *After Auschwitz* (Indianapolis, Ind.: Bobbs Merrill, 1966), p. 154.

7. Ibid, pp. 184, 198.

8. While this topic is found in many of my articles over the past two decades it was the fundamental theme of my analysis of the situation of American Jewry in *The Mask Jews Wear* (New York: Simon and Schuster, 1973) when Jewish discussions of the death of God were at their height. See particularly the afterword and compare the chapter on the 1980s in the second edition published by Sh'ma, Inc. See the later statements at the end of chapters 2 and 3 in part two of my *Liberal Judaism* (New York: Union of American Hebrew Congregations, 1984).

24 / "Please, God, Heal Her, Please"

1997

[The conference began on the day of Yitzhak Rabin's funeral. As I was the first speaker on the formal program, I began as follows: The Torah says—here I read the text of Genesis 35:28, dealing with Isaac's death and burial. I continued, *Al tikri ken, ela Va-yigva Yitzhak va-yamat, va-ye'asef el amav, ve hu lo zaken u-seva yamim, va-yikberu oto edom ve-yisrael banav.* Let us pray that from today's funeral, in which so many participated wholeheartedly, peace will gain new strength. But this is not a conference on mourning, though it is filled with mourners. We are here to speak not of metaphorically broken hearts but of the many real ailments which afflict us and what Judaism can do to help heal them. So it is to that we now turn.]

Two experiences, thirty years apart, frame these ruminations.

In 1963, I and some others addressed groups at the Central Conference of American Rabbis convention seeking to persuade the Reform rabbis to replace their establishment rationalism with existentially oriented thought. My presentation was entitled "Faith and Method in Modern Jewish Theology." Its plea to acknowledge the primacy of faith in our Judaism was greeted with an incredulity typified by the question of a colleague somewhat older than me. Restraining his sarcasm, he said that he doubted that I now wanted us to begin reciting the *Refa'enu* instead of relying on the science of medicine. I wonder if today, a spry eighty-four-year-old, he has changed his attitude. Back then he nimbly expressed the wall of separation dividing the clinic and the synagogue, an attitude still stoutly supported by many Jews today.

In recent months my practice of many years standing, praying the *Refa'enu* and other prayers for the healing of specific people I know, has been especially fervent. My overriding concern has been someone whose affliction has not lessened despite extensive consultation. All else having failed, a highly risky operation of uncertain promise was undertaken. That made me pray with even greater intensity. The operation failed and the prognosis is now uncertain. Though saddened to some primal depth, I have not relented and continue to ask God to heal this hurting soul.

Thirty years ago my practice would have caused most modernized Jews to shudder or shrug. Today, many in our community will, I trust, reach out to me in empathy.

Consider: six years ago, when Rachel Cowan first broached the idea of a project on Judaism and healing, it wasn't clear if any Jews cared, or were doing anything, or could learn something useful if they met to share what knowledge and experience they had accumulated. This assembly, co-sponsored by two great American Jewish institutions, has had to turn worthy applicants away for lack of space, and it is only the first of about a half-dozen such meetings whose mailings have reached me.

What brought about this radical change of ethos? Why has a skeptical community become one in which a sizable minority eagerly seeks to learn about and practice Judaism's counsel for the work of healing? Let me spin out a theological hypothesis which explains this development to me and which you can test against your own experience and the rich data of the sessions soon to begin.

Thirty years ago my colleague felt certain he could refute faith's role in a modern Judaism by reminding us of the absurdity of asking God to heal the sick. Whence did his dogmatic liberalism arise? Not out of his Jewish knowledge, for he knew the halakhic texts requiring us to recite the *Refa'enu* daily (e.g., B.T. Megillah 17b, Avodah Zarah 8a). Biblical prayers for healing are difficult to ignore, the most famous probably being Moses' astonishingly concise, five-word plea that Miriam be cured of leprosy, "*El, na, refa na, lah*" (Num. 12:13). R. Eliezer is reported to have reminded his disciples of it as their proper model for brevity in Jewish prayer (B. T., Berakhot 34a). In his petition, Moses dispenses with the customary sequence of praise, request, and thanks, while also eschewing any artistic embellishment. He knows God heals, so he asks God to do so. Yet not exactly, for he doesn't "ask" at all but, employing that odd usage of Jewish prayer of which Heinemann reminded us, he addresses God with an imperative, "Heal, please."[1]

By linear Greek standards, the Jewish attitude toward medicine defies logic. When a teacher upholds Judaism's strong sense of God's providence, he says that the Master of the Universe is the source of illness. In that mood, too, God is the only legitimate physician. Exodus 15:26, "I, Adonai, am your healer," is its classic text, and Asa, king of Israel, who sought the help of human physicians rather than God, is its whipping-boy (2 Chron. 16:12). Yet that attitude coexisted with the notorious old Jewish esteem for physicians and love of medicine. The rabbis of the Talmud, often pictured as powerful healers, frequently rest their bio-ethical halakhah on the determinations of medical experts, and themselves pass on treatments for a variety of afflictions.

These paradoxical views may explain the slenderness of the rabbis' proof that the Torah—God—commands physicians to heal the sick, namely, the duplication of the verb "to heal" in the list of damages that one who injured another must pay (Exod. 21:19, B. T. Bava Kamma 25a). The classic Jewish theology of medicine is dialectical. God sends illness—often as punishment for sin—yet God also commands doctors, and by extension all of us, to cure those ailments. This is the most dramatic example I know of rabbinic theology's view that there is not just one but two effective sources of energy in the universe, God and people. God, being God, may act independently; people, having only derivative, "imaged," status, may not. They act with God, but the way the human and divine energies intertwine in our world is beyond our sorting out.

We call this bipartite notion of agency "covenant," and the resulting nonlinear quality of rabbinic theology arises from this covenantal dialectic, as I have termed it. As various unnamed talmudic sages said, God rules, but *olam ke-minhago noheg,* "the universe goes its accustomed way" (B. T. Avodah Zarah 54b). Accepting the partnership of the human and the divine may well be the theological root of the historical anomaly Shatzmiller points out, that medieval Jewry had no religious difficulty accepting new medical procedures based on changing scientific knowledge.[2]

What agitated my colleague was not the Jewishness of prayers for healing but their clash with modernity. They implied that God acted in the natural order as an effective cause, a notion that violated science and thus the modernization of Judaism, which had accommodated to it. In that worldview, natural events occurred only for mechanical or electrochemical reasons. These might eventually be given mathematical form, thus proving that such processes, like their mathematical delineations, had inherent necessity, obviating the need for God or other supernatural forces. In short, modern causation was immanent, so God was irrelevant except as invoked by the still pious to explain nature's origin, order, and values or the occasional experience of a numinous presence.

This modern God could no longer be asked to heal, a task now in the hands of the medical team. At best, God lay behind the orderliness assumed by treatment and research, the values which moved people to seek and apply them, and the presence which might give patients and caretakers a psychosomatic boost. That vision frames the prayer for the sick provided in the Reform *Rabbi's Manual* of 1961:

> In this hour of her great need, our hearts go out to our sister______. Bestow on her Thy help and healing. Guide her physicians, Thy servants. Give them understanding hearts, skilled and tender hands. Sustain her dear ones with faith in Thy goodness and love. May she find constant strength and comfort in Thee, O God, now and evermore.[3]

Believing more than that, I want a richer text, but I could begin my praying here.

This limitation of God's effective role to the psyche of the ill or their caregivers was the accepted ideology of modernized Jews some generations back, and most people still fall back on it when speaking of this topic. Here is some of a prayer for the sick in the home prayerbook published by the CCAR last year:

> In sickness I turn to You, O God, for comfort and help. Strengthen within me the wondrous power of healing that You have implanted in Your children. Guide my doctors and nurses that they may speed my recovery. Let my dear ones find comfort and courage in the knowledge that You are with us at all times, in sickness as in health. May my sickness not weaken my faith in You, nor diminish my love for others. From my illness may I gain a fuller sympathy for all who suffer. I praise You, O God, the Source of healing.[4]

These words touch me more deeply not just because they were written for private prayer while the text in the *Rabbi's Manual* was for use at a congregational service. The new book also sounds a fresh and important note: respect for the power of healing that resides in each person, a topic I shall return to later. Now, I only want to note the 1994 prayer's continuity with that of 1961. God still does not heal, as Jews once thought God did, but is, at best, the God of healing, the backdrop for the processes by which people naturally induce the restoration of health.

Mordecai Kaplan's naturalism lent a certain clarity to this perspective. Writing to a hypothetical sufferer from infantile paralysis he says:

> When the doctor relieves your pain, when he helps you to get back more strength and better control over your muscles, it is with the intelligence that

> God gives him. When you use braces and other devices that help you get around and do some of the things you want to do their manufacture is due to the intelligence and the concern for your welfare, that God puts into the minds of those who make these devices. Do not feel that God does not care for you. He is helping you now in many ways, and He will continue to help you. Maybe some day you will be restored by His help to perfect health. But if that does not happen, it is not because God does not love you. If He does not grant you all that you pray for, He will find other ways of enabling you to enjoy life. Be thankful to God for all the love and care that people show toward you, since all of that is part of God's love, and do not hesitate to ask God for further help. If the people around you are intelligent and loving, that help will come to you.[5]

In these and other such passages, Kaplan speaks for all those Jews for whom science still explains reality. But it is just this erosion of the old certainty paradigm which has deeply shaken us in the past decade or so. Everywhere we turn these days—economics, nutrition, politics, therapy—what once was authoritative is now, at best, a plausible construction of reality. In medicine, we no longer regard doctors, even the greatest experts, as gods. We know them and their helpers to be fallible, and the most humane of them share with their patients the limits of what they know and might be able to do. The infant in me wants my physician to tell me exactly what I have and how long it will take me to get over it, if I can; but the adult in me responds better to a caring discussion of the likelihoods of my condition.

These days, too, we do not smugly scorn alternative forms of treatment as quackery. MDs now commit the onetime heresy of going to a chiropractor, some obstetricians have collegial relations with midwives, and acupuncture and herbal medicine, with no scientific basis the West can fathom, often have effects exceeding mere psychosomatic expectations.

I am not saying that medicine has been discredited and that I now refuse an occasional sonogram or have substituted *tai chi* for my daily dose of beta, calcium, and angiotensin inhibitors. Medical science still remains our best way of fulfilling the commandment to "guard our souls" and stay healthy (Deut. 4:15, B. T. Berakhot 32b). What is at stake, rather, is whether medicine, and science generally, still adamantly insists on a monopoly of insight into nature. But increasingly, medical personnel and institutions welcome religion as bringing to their work an independent, significant understanding of people and the universe. Not infrequently, too, it is we Jewish leaders who are the recalcitrant ones, stubbornly holding on to a prior generation's achievement of allowing hard-nosed science to restrict what Judaism could still teach and do. I guess we are afraid of returning to the magic and superstition which once characterized much of the premodern Jewish healing style. However, we need not trash every aspect of modernity as we make our transition from a modern to a postmodern Judaism. That paradigm shift, from the modern to the postmodern, is the theological realignment which is the tectonic source of the rising interest in Judaism's role in healing.

Exactly what postmodern Judaism commends in this area is, typically enough, disputed, a delightfully consistent indication that postmodernity has diverse potential. Once, piety's place in therapy could only be justified by humanistic motives, the ethical and the psychological. The new view I discern adds to these, at the least, an appreciation of the mysterious, nonempirical ways in which the mind—better, the soul—affects the body. Many now believe that what transpires in our depths, and not only in our unconscious minds, influences our organs and limbs for good and ill. With the old empirical censor silenced, we can stop filtering out those fleeting intuitions we have of our inner healing power, and, redirecting our spiritual energies, we can newly employ our primal curative capacities. And some people, for reasons utterly beyond us, can do this so well that they can reach out and cure others. All grandiosity aside, we do not yet know our own power.

But as long as we speak only of what humans do—even using the word "God" but meaning only human activity—we will not appreciate the depth of the new religious involvement in healing. Jewish postmodernity, confounding the Nietzschean pronouncements of modern secularity, centers on God, the One we sense to be utterly independent of us yet simultaneously intimately involved with us. A reverse *tzimtzum* is underway. Modernity expanded human agency so fully that there was little space left in our universe for a God-not-ourselves. Now, with science demythologized and culture unable to command worthy values, messianic humanism seems utterly unrealistic.

Chastened by the human record in this past half-century, people accept the self-contraction that contrition mandates. The *tzimtzum* resulting from humankind's new humility has left space in our world for God, and we, conscious of our limitations and the reality of our new/old God, are groping for better ways to let God's presence and God's power into our lives more fully.

Consider the prevalence of services for healing and healers or the efforts to provide prayer and meditative material for the ill. Or think of the increasingly popular Clinical Pastoral Education programs for clergy, which seek to blend the insights of psychotherapy with the uncanny reach of religious practice and belief. In these and other activities, God's being there with us bestows on us a certain increase in our power that is a consecration of self and a model for what we are sent to do with others. Twice, Deuteronomy Rabbah (6:13) refers to this bipartite exercise of power, interpreting Moses' opening plea on behalf of his sister, "*El na,*" "Please, God," as saying, "If You will heal her, that is good; but if not, I will heal her." And Radak, interpreting Jeremiah 17:14, the source of the *Refa'enu* prayer, says that the pain and injury from which he asked relief were really his own sense of shame and accursedness. It is no diminution of what we can do to reach for what God might also do that laboratories cannot depict. Hesitantly shedding the old constricted rationalism, gropingly moving as our new experience of bipartite covenant guides us, we have begun turning to God for what God might independently do for the ill. And sometimes we find that God heals in ways we must call God's own.

Not always. I am still praying fervently that God cure that dear soul whose recent operation failed. Of course I want God to infuse with new power and unfaltering endurance those superbly informed and deeply feeling souls who stand that watch. I also ask my Intimate Other, the One who has so often granted me the little healing of presence, to accept my anger and my frustration, and raise me from my bitterness and gloom that I may see my duty and do it. For years the balm of knowing that God was with me has kept me faithful in my liturgical vigil for the sick I regularly pray for. But for some time now, I have sought more. I want God to heal them. "*Refa, na.*" God being God and I being me, a believing Jew, I can no longer ask for anything less than God's independent action to stop this suffering and to restore today's list to health. "*El na, refa na.*" "Please, God, heal, please." I may not be as blunt or as peremptory with God as Moses was, but, niceties aside, that is the burden of my postmodern praying. And no matter how many times my prayer has not been granted, no matter how many years now my Alzheimer's patient has sunk deeper into physicality, I resolutely come back and pray it again. Not for me that curious modern trait, that when the prayers for healing "fail," we bitterly attack God, but when they succeed, as mine often have, all the praise and gratitude go to the caregivers and some, perhaps, to the patient.

No, I do not know how God can be an efficient cause in the natural order—but I do know that in our culture "how" questions can only be satisfactorily answered in the empirical terms of science, a mode of description which bars God. Yes, I am unhappy that I cannot integrate the scientific view of causation with my conviction that God can independently heal—but I know that these days all we have to work with are the fragments of various broken systems. When I was young, I was taught to glory in amplifying certainty; today, the maturity I esteem enables one to live humanely despite the enveloping uncertainties. My kind of postmodern Jew treads warily between pooh-poohing science and kowtowing to it, and seeks with every capacity of mind and soul to approach ever closer to the ideal Unity without denying the realism that befits an era awash in disillusion.

I know no easy rule for negotiating the narrow ridge of postmodern Jewish existence, but I can suggest a helpful exercise. Shall we bring back amulets? That is, shall we enlist the aid of various angels or heavenly powers or of a particularly efficacious name of God to cure the sick? The rabbis believed that amulets healed and allowed wearing efficacious ones as an exception to the strict Shabbat halakhah about adornments. Shall we now move on from prayer and rite and meditation to amulets, and begin seeking expert writers? Sometime ago I would have dismissed this notion with a snort if not a tirade invoking Maimonides. Today, with a nod to the Rashba and Nahmanides, I cannot be so dogmatic, yet despite my hard-gained openness, I am not ready for amulets. Such scientific explanation as still influences my faith militates against my doing so.

But my postmodern faith does not always hint at a closet rationalism. The second request of the *Refa'enu* prayer, *hoshienu ve-nivashe'a,* "Save us, and we shall be saved," links healing to salvation: Every cure is a small redemption, surely an underground reason why Jews in disproportionate numbers spend their lives doing therapy. They want to help usher in the Messiah.

What we but taste now, the rabbis foresaw fulfilled in the promised future. Resh Lakish is repeatedly cited as teaching that there is no Gehenna in the world-to-come, but the sun, released from its sheath, fiercely punishes the wicked. However, as Malachi 3:19 teaches, "Unto you who fear my Name, the sun of righteousness will arise with healing on its wings" (B. T. Avodah Zarah 3b–4a). In Exodus Rabbah (14:21), an anonymous exegesis of Isaiah's eschatological promise specifies as part of the first of God's ten innovations then that "when anyone is sick, God will order the sun to heal them." Do you not, as I do, long for that world without sickness, pain, and suffering? I have no difficulty envisioning God's goodness joined to God's power to re-create the world so that we all can sit under our vines and fig trees in good health. Until that day we must live in the hope of this messianic healing and recollect it as we work at the everyday redemptions of *refuat ha-nefesh, refuat ha guf*, healing of soul, healing of body.

NOTES

1. *Ha-Tefillah bi-Tekufat ha-Tannaim ve-ha-Amoraim* (Jerusalem: Magnes Press, 1966).
2. *Jews, Medicine and Medieval Society* (Berkeley: University of California Press, 1995), chap. 1 *passim.*
3. *Rabbi's Manual* (New York: Central Conference of American Rabbis, 1961), p. 55.
4. *On the Doorposts of Your House,* Chaim Stem, ed. (New York: Central Conference of American Rabbis, 1994), p. 153.
5. *Questions Jews Ask: Reconstructionist Answers* (New York: Reconstructionist Press, 1956), pp. 119–20.

25 / *"Im ba'et, eyma"*—Since You Object, Let Me Put It This Way

2000

All authors hope someone reads them and finds their work engaging. And they dream of having insightful, accomplished people so taken with their effort that they will then want to write about it. Having learned and benefited for years from the work of the friends whose response to *Renewing the Covenant* is presented here, [in *Reviewing the Covenant: Eugene B. Borowitz and the Postmodern Renewal of Jewish Thought*, Suny, 2000] I am deeply touched by their kindness to me personally and by their searching responses to my ideas. May the Shekhinah long rest upon us all as we carry on this effort at contemporary Torah. Thank you, colleagues; thank you, God.

It will help me to respond to the specific issues raised by my colleagues if I first briefly indicate what I think I was doing in my book, for that is the conceptual context of what I now have to say. Some facts about me personally also have a bearing on my approach to these matters, so I will begin there.

I am a rabbi, a seminary professor, and my primary reference group is not the secular academy, but the believing, practicing community of non-Orthodox Jews, no matter which label they apply to themselves. That will help to explain why *Renewing the Covenant* is a work of apologetic theology. That is, it seeks to mediate between believers like myself and those who are inquirers, perhaps semi- or occasional-believers. Norbert—following Susan's lead, I cannot, comfortably call a friend of nearly forty years "Samuelson" merely because a stuffy old academic convention thinks that's dignified—Norbert correctly indicates that I also seek to create a bridge between academic thinking about belief and the minority of believing non-Orthodox Jews who seriously want to think about their faith, a sub-community critical to the ethos of every group.[1] Apologetics seem inevitably to disappoint people in each of the communities addressed. Some outsiders always complain that you haven't properly accepted their truth. Some insiders feel you haven't been true enough to the faith (David Novak and Susan Handelman), while others feel you might have used a more effective way of accomplishing the task (Edith Wyschogrod, Tom Ogeltree and Norbert, with Yudit Greenberg in both groups, and Peter trying to show what makes us all an intellectual family). Essentially, what we are debating in this book is what might constitute the most effective apologetic language for our time.

The apologetic argument of *Renewing the Covenant* proceeds in two unequal steps. The first describes the experiential basis for contemporary belief, chapters 1–3. In these pages, I do not analyze personal religious experience as has been the typical academic and prior non-Orthodox Jewish theological procedure. Rather, in keeping with my understanding of Judaism as the Covenant between God and the people Israel, I seek to lay bare the communal spiritual path of the Jewish people in the second half of the twentieth century, underground though most of it has been. In sum, the Jews, as part of Western civilization's turn from messianic modernism but particularly because of the Holocaust, came to a new openness to God (the contemporary search for "spirituality") and acknowledgment of the importance of Jewish peoplehood. These two pillars of renewed Jewish faith, God, and Israel (the people), derive from a root intuition: "*Regardless of what the world knows or cares, anything that mitigates the categorical distinction between the S.S. death camp operators and their Jewish victims violates our most fundamental contemporary experience and contravenes a central mandate of our tradition*" (The italics are in the original, one of only six sentences so distinguished in *Renewing the Covenant* (p. 43); all page references given in the body of this paper are to this book). This affirmation of a value inherent in the universe is the foundation of Jewish life today. Derridean postmodernism denies such a faith credence; that is the major reason I am not a Derridean postmodern.

The second, longer part of the apologetic case consists of an analysis and synthesis of the beliefs uncovered in our recent experience, God, chapters 4–10, and the people Israel, chapters 11–16. This consideration of God and Israel allows me to enunciate my radical recontextualization of the general self as the Jewish self. These foundations being set, I can move on to the classic task of a Jewish theology, creating a theory of sacred obligation, a meta-*halakhah*, in my case the delineation of what the contents page (vii) announces as "A Postliberal Theology of Jewish Duty." This is described in the section on Torah, chapters 17–20, with the last of these bringing all these strands together in a rare, systematic analysis of non-Orthodox Jewish decision-making. Its five integrated principles are presented in initial, italicized statements:

> First, the Jewish self lives personally and primarily in involvement with the one God of the universe (p. 289). . . . Second, a Jewish relationship with God inextricably binds selfhood and ethnicity, with its multiple ties of land, language, history, traditions, fate, and faith (pp. 289–90). . . . Third, against the common self's concentration on immediacy, the Covenant renders the Jewish self radically historical (p. 291). . . . Fourth, though the Jewish self lives the present out of the past, it necessarily orients itself to the future (p. 292). . . . Fifth, yet despite the others with whom it is so intimately intertwined—God and the Jewish people, present, past, and future—it is as a single self in its full individuality that the Jewish self exists in Covenant (p. 293).

Keeping this plan in mind will, I believe, lend greater coherence to my comments on the specific issues raised by my readers.

IN RESPONSE TO MY COLLEAGUES

Four words have proved troublesome in my communicating my meaning. The least disruptive of these may be "Absolute," which I use in one of my discussions of God. Far more contentious has been my applying the label "postmodern" to my thinking. Neither of them, however, has worked as much mischief as have the related terms "self" and "autonomy." Would that when I wrote this book I had known Peirce's logical category of "vagueness," so tellingly outlined for us by Peter, for I might have mitigated these difficulties by announcing that it guided me.[2] Despite the difficulties these terms have engendered I continue to find a certain justification for having employed them. What it means to be a "postmodern," and certain side-issues connected with the term, are so significant for the rest of what I have to say that I shall begin with this broad-ranging topic.

WHAT LABEL SHOULD I SPORT?

The best justification for a taxonomy of thinkers in our time may be that philosophers who work by different methods (who are of different "schools") cannot easily talk to one another about fundamental matters without first indicating their philosophic "faith." That people are often seriously misled by these classificatory names has not made labeling obsolete because the information/opinion glut makes these shortcuts to understanding all the more useful. I begin, then, with the thinker's standard disclaimer: I am not my label(s); I am, of course, me, and so notorious a defender of thinking for oneself should surely be allowed even more than the usual distance from the reductionism of classification [*sic*].

I begin with a marginal matter, whether I am "a Reform Jewish" thinker. This comes to mind particularly because of a recent exchange of articles with Elliot Dorff, whose recent review of *Renewing the Covenant* insisted that its true meaning could be discovered only in terms of the ideology of the Reform movement.[3] Since the (invidious) stereotyping of Reform Jews may lurk in the background of others' interpretation of what I wrote, I want to begin my response to my critics by citing a bit of what I said to Elliot: "I do not know how I can persuade you that 'I am not now and never have been a card-carrying Reform ideologue.' . . . I have always tried to think academically about Jewish belief and its consequences. None of my models—Cohen, Baeck, Kaplan, Buber, Rosenzweig and Heschel—ever did their thinking as part of a movement, or in the context of its ideology. They simply tried to think through the truth of Judaism in their day as best they could understand it, and I have spent my life trying to emulate them. I attempted to nail down my meaning in *Renewing the Covenant* by mostly speaking about 'non-Orthodox' Jews. When I mean Reform Jews there or anywhere, I say so."[4]

As to whether I am a "postmodern," a topic of considerable comment and difference of opinion among these readers, it depends, of course, on your taxonomic standards. Tom suggests that I'm probably better off thinking of myself as a "chastened modern," which description of me is certainly true. It was that cognitive and, in my case, Jewish "suffering" (to use Peter's term), that pushed me to go beyond modernity. Edith makes a strong case that my use of the term is intellectually inappropriate and will mislead thoughtful people as to my kind of thinking. She has such stature as thinker and leader in this area that she may well be right. Was it an unconscious ambivalence about this title that caused me not to utilize "postmodern" to refer to myself or my thought in my book's title but to refer in its subtitle to the cultural situation of my readers? The critical issue, of course, is whether it makes any sense to speak of a non-Derridean postmodern community of reflective communication. A number of the colleagues gathered here think it does and, emboldened by their agreement, I stand by my original self-identification and respectfully reject Edith's reproof.

Not long after *Renewing the Covenant* was published, I learned to specify what I thought entitled me to speak of myself as a (non-Derridean) postmodern. In two critical respects, I reject and radically revise modernist "doctrine." Modernists from Kant on made the individual human the independent basis for truth, and thus, to validate religion, they had to seek ways of moving from their human certainties to God's possible reality and nature. But religious postmoderns like me know persons to be inseparable from God, their ground, and truth as what emerges between God and people. (The fundamentalists say it comes almost entirely from God to humans, while the non-Orthodox say, in various balances, it is more two-sided than that.) Modernists also knew that truth was necessarily universal, and thus, if they wished to give some validity to a particular group, they had to demonstrate to what extent this particular group reflected universal truth. But postmoderns like me know that all truth begins in particularity, and any universal one might affirm derives from that particular base. (Heretically enough, I also insisted that one premise of modernity was too true to be denied a place in the foundations of my—our—postmodernity: the close identification of human dignity with the exercise of a significant measure of self-determination. See below.)[5]

I must, however, confess that the issue of philosophic label is not very important to me. As Susan says, the critical term for us is "Jew" and we will use whatever intellectual language now least inadequately describes what we "know" that to be. So I was once a boy rationalist, evolved into a religious existentialist and, seeing its inadequacies, began to identify myself as a postmodern thinker. Let a more satisfactory way of talking about Jewish truth appear in our culture and I shall, I hope, have the intellectual courage to embrace it, temporarily, to be sure.

For me then, as for David and Susan, Torah truth, as best we understand it, is primary and it is the criterion for the apologetic language we will utilize—another radical break with the modernists. So again risking terminological static, I call myself a Jewish "theologian" in an effort to signal to my readers that my thinking is governed by my Jewish faith. Philosophy in recent decades has insisted that it alone was the rightful arbiter of truth. It therefore as good as dictated to modernist Jewish thinkers what might now properly be included in their Judaism, generally with radically reductionist results, *pace* Norbert, but I shall return to this theme again. I can understand how Jews of a critically philosophic bent might well become Derridean postmoderns and then see what Jewish sense that made possible, like Edith's stunningly creative use of Lyotard. But the image of Israel as silent victim straining for language to challenge its Accuser is one that says more about the hermeneut than about any significant reality I discern in the people Israel today. We are, however, still at the beginning of the Derridean evocation of Jewish meaning, and, though my Jewish faith precludes my joining that interpretive enterprise, I look forward to the spiritual stimulation that the emerging Derridean description of Jewish faith and duty will provide.

Several of the non-Derrideans, who include me in the postmodern camp, wonder if I am not more residually modern than I realize. Two things must be said in that regard. First, I do not mean by the "post" in postmodern that everything modern must be put behind us. I, and the people Israel, continue to owe modernity too much to do such a thing. The process of modernization gave Jews freedom from the ghetto, equality of opportunity, and unparalleled security for our community. It taught us the extraordinary value of pluralism, the preciousness of individual rights, and the sacred dignity of substantial self-determination. Indeed, I proudly proclaim that the third premise in my kind of postmodernist thinking about Judaism is (a radically recontextualized understanding of) "autonomy." I do not seek to hide from my residual modernism but openly question whether postmodernity should really qualify as an independent, sixth stage in the long history of Jewish spiritual development (p.4, pp. 49f and the references cited in note 5). Nonetheless, my hybridized thinking is so fundamentally other-than-modern, that I think the term "postmodern" will usefully call to the attention of other "chastened moderns" the deep change of perspective and attitude now arising among us.

It seems to me that the appearance of a strong modern color to my thought is magnified because I am engaged in apologetics, a task which requires one to communicate with "suffering" moderns in the only language that still makes sense to them, despite their cognitive dissonance with it. This problem first forced itself upon me in 1967 when I was writing my book on Jewish sex ethics for college students. I could not hope to address them in my nascent language of Covenant faith and hope they would long continue reading, so I tried to find an idiom congenial to them that would also engage them in full seriousness. But I finally couldn't stand the self-repression and concluded the work by addressing them in the accents of Jewish faith.[6]

I did not have the systemic sophistication in 1967 to realize that the problem of standing at the boundary explained the curious logical break in the "argument" of *God in Search of Man* by Abraham Heschel.[7] Most of the first third of the book, on God, speaks the language of human experience with such eloquence that four decades plus later people find it speaks to their innermost being. But once Heschel draws his readers into the presence of the living God, he moves to the other side of the theological table and begins a continuing polemic against relying on human experience, rather than on the revelation of God he has led them to. That reversal, so crucial to his faith and his purpose in writing, regularly shocks readers who, snug in their modernity, anticipate that like other Jewish teachers he will indicate how radical amazement fits into their modernity and congenially modifies Jewish tradition. But he doesn't do so, and that is why, though many quote Heschel's sentences, few Jews have adopted his theology as a whole.

In much of *Renewing the Covenant,* I speak to searching still-modernist Jews in their terms: those of "self," "autonomy" and "universalism." However, I do not concede the primacy of universalism and then try to validate particularity. I see no way one can do that and arrive at the primacy of particularity, which I take to be the Jewish and post-modern truth. My strategy is to undermine the three foundations of the universalizing modernist faith. I do this by arguing against the goodness of human nature, the discrete individuality of persons and the identification of truth with universals (chapters 11, 12, and 13, respectively). This allows me to ease them into my revision of "the self" as "the Jewish self." Perhaps I stay with my apologetic language too long, but I am hopeful that the cumulative transformation of my language will set the context of my getting there rather than vice versa, as often seems to me the experience of the reviewers in this book.

Norbert suggests that I should not equate modernity with a rationalism that Yudit nicely calls "linear." He speculates that I am really involved in an ongoing polemic against the thought of my late, lamented friend Steven S. Schwarzschild but have, in fact, misunderstood him. He then sketches in a picture of a Kantian probabilism which would yield a rationalism far more humane than the categorical one I so disdain. Passing quickly over the rational certainty of Kantian regulative ideals and emphasizing the imprecise judgments which necessarily ensue when the ideals are applied to real cases in the contingent world, Norbert argues that rationalism only claims that it is the best way of reaching our inevitably limited practical decisions. The Steven I knew would have quickly gone into one of his consciously self-indulgent tirades at the idea that he was a Kantian for essentially pragmatic reasons, namely, as Norbert puts it, that since no thinking can give us certainty, then "nothing is more likely to lead us to correct judgments (in science and ethics) than [Kantian] reasoning." Steven, like the creator of "pure" reason, and so forth, hated any hint of pragmatism. For him reason required or commanded us, and even in the realm of historical decisions, he, like most of my Germanic teachers, felt that a good measure of the "categorical imperative" passed over into his practical judgments. If there was a Cohenian neo-Kantian probabilist around in the heyday of modernism, I never ran into one. And if a biographical note is permitted, once Steven's brief, student-days' flirtation with Rosenzweig passed over, we never discussed the foundational clash between his rationalism and my non-rationalism, though an occasional loving barb on that divide did fly between us. To have done so would have destroyed our friendship since Steven insisted on being taken on his own terms; a position which he would have been happy to defend as rationally required, although he would have done so with a mischievous smile. I shall return to Norbert's explication of what I take to be a "chastened" rationalism when I respond to the questions about my discussion of Israel.

THAT TROUBLESOME TERM, "THE SELF"

David and Susan are only more emphatic than Yudit and Peter in charging that I give the individual too much freedom in relation to God. A good deal of their unease arises from my frequent references to "autonomy," a term their philosophical sophistication necessarily connects with Kant and its meaning in his thought. For Kantians "autonomy" indicates that the self alone gives the (moral) law, not God or anyone else, though Cohenian neo-Kantianism rushes in to show how God, as the most foundational idea in the rational worldview, undergirds the moral law and is closely identified with it. My postmodern thinking asserts something quite different. I claim that people are, on their own, incompetent to legislate the basic laws by which they ought to live. They are similarly ill-equipped to bring the Messiah by their own action, as the Kantian liberal Jews grandly professed. I speak of a God who is real in His/Her own right and is not merely the grandest of my rational ideas. I further insist this God commands people, albeit nonverbally, and, as best we can put it, has input into our lives by coming into relationship with us. How, then, as David warned me years ago, can I use the term "autonomy" to describe an aspect of my God-human relationship and not expect to be taken as a neo-Kantian semi-secularist masquerading as something else?

Perhaps my difficulty in this respect is that I suffer from a failure of imagination. I have not been able to find another term which succinctly points to the truth which almost all modernized Jews take to be the core of their existence: that their humanity demands that, in some significant measure, they think for themselves. They have learned this from modern social life, and its telling symbol for them is the right to vote. Most of these Jews have never seriously heard of Kant, and they will glaze over if you try discussing heteronomy and autonomy, suggesting theonomy as the way to resolve the ethical dilemma this contrast poses. And, having heard of religious frauds, who in the name of God have gotten people to do terrible things, they reserve the right to judge for themselves any religious claim to having the truth to which they should accede. In short, they believe God gave them freedom to think and wants them to use it in determining their Jewish duty in a more proactive way than traditional Judaism allowed/allows.

Against Buber's championing of the "I" in determining the law, Susan calls on us to follow Rosenzweig's recommended response to God, "*Hineni,*" "Here I am." Rosenzweig declares that the Law as a whole is binding upon us. The semi-believers I am addressing, Susan, may be able to join Rosenzweig in acknowledging God's "authority," but they will cherish that Rosenzweig who also taught, as you know, that the self retains some rights even in its acquiescence to God. For he gave sufficient credence to the nomos-making dignity of the self that he found it necessary to validate the Law by calling on us to turn what came to us as *Gesetz,* an objective statement of law, into *Gebot,* a command addressed to each of us personally. And he famously, if cryptically, indicated that one need not do what, at the most serious level, one was not "able" to do.

Even the modestly "liberal" Rosenzweig, I suggest, grants too much to the Law and too little to us for most of us to follow him. If the law the sages are teaching is entirely binding upon us in principle, then, to give a telling example, God does not want women to be full members of a *minyan.* An increasing majority of modernized Jews know, by their own judgment, that such discriminatory rulings are better charged to human invention than to God's revelation via the sages. It is this authority of the self—which I limit by the recontextualization Covenant selfhood lays upon it—for which I need a term (I shall later return to the topic of the law in my comments on Torah).

My apologetic problem, then, is finding a word for the significant, but not exclusive, enfranchisement of persons in determining their/our Jewish duty.[8] Yes, the Kantian associations of "autonomy" give too much power to the "autos," the single self, but I can think of no better word to protect the self's legitimate role in law-making. It would be tedious to regularly put quotation marks around it, "autonomy," and eccentric to write it ?auto?nomy, or with dashes through the "auto," ~~auto~~nomy, though this might qualify as a visual postmodern doubling. So I risked retaining the term, hoping that people would see how differently it functions when Covenantalized. I consider the reinterpretation of selfhood—which still has a measure of legislative authority for us—as Jewish selfhood in which individuality cannot be separated from its relation to God as one of the people of Israel's Covenant relationship with God—to be the most creative and important thing I accomplished in *Renewing the Covenant.* That is to say, I do not see how we can have a Jewishly satisfactory "Theology of Postliberal Duty" with the old "autonomy," yet we need to make some place in such a new understanding for our sense of the sacredness of our ability to think/choose for ourselves. So I crafted a system which did that.

Let me be specific by pointing again to my epitome of my theory of how non-Orthodox Jews today ought to determine their Jewish obligations. I prefaced these on page 288 with a general statement of why the modernist, Kantian, or Buberian ideal of a universalized self needed to be replaced by the ideal of a "Jewish self." Because of its Jewishness, that self was not an isolate, but was necessarily involved as one of five co-functioning factors involved in the "law"-making process. Of these, the real God I had previously delineated, was the first and dominant participant (p. 289). Fully three of the five factors were devoted to the people of Israel's significance in the process: as contemporary reference community; as bearer of a vast repository of prior Covenant-duty deliberations; and as a people pointing toward the Messiah. Only then, fifth, do I speak of the continuing place of the self. "Fifth, yet despite the others with whom it is so intimately intertwined—God and the Jewish people, past present and future—it is as a single soul in its full individuality that the Jewish self exists in Covenant" (p. 293, italicized in the original). When I said "a single soul in its full individuality," I was thinking not just of the remnant of ?auto?nomy we still rightly insist upon, but of the precious individuality of all those historical Jewish "characters" whose very idiosyncrasy Jews have long cherished. It did not occur to me after all I had written about the Jewish self and what that very sentence says about the soul "intimately intertwined" with God and the Jewish people, that readers could still think I meant by it something like that notorious caricature of a Reform Jew, a person who did what they personally pleased. And how any philosopher reading these words could find this a heavily Kantian "autonomy" is a tribute to the way the past impedes the creative present.[9]

Again, let me note my surprise that my early statements (in the chapters on God) seeking to clarify what remained of individual human power in the presence of the transcendent God determined what some readers thought I was doing in my later transformation of selfhood into Jewish selfhood. The people I was addressing would have been uncomprehending had I tried from the first to talk to them about the Jewish self, and I would have lost them. I needed first to develop my argument for particularity, and then clarify what I meant by Israel before I could begin trying to wean them away from a central idea of contemporary culture, that there is a general selfhood. I thought that my crowning, final statement of my theology would put the prior pieces transformingly into place. I am now chastened by the fact that my strategy has not worked out well with a good number of these sophisticated readers. Such are the perils of apologetics.

The selfhood issue particularly troubles Tom. He feels that despite my devoting a chapter to "The Social Side of Selfhood" (chapter 12), and my giving the community three places of the five in my calculus of decision-making, I do not seem to appreciate how socially determined the self is. "The central point is that I cannot simply opt out of the formative bonds that figure in my moral identity and still hold onto my moral autonomy. I can exercise my free conscience in opposition to the teachings of my formative community only by means of resources also supplied by that community. . . . When I become alienated from the community that formed me, my moral autonomy is itself at risk. . . . In fact, my alienation from my primary community of reference is, more than likely, a reflection of the fact that other attachments . . . have already gained preeminent importance in my life." So he believes that I ought to spend more time on "the critical retrieval and mediation of the normative traditions that constitute Jewish particularity."

To a considerable extent I agree with Tom, and clarifying this will also allow me to highlight our differences. I agree that in the usual case one's morality is substantially formed by one's "primary" community, and that one cannot "simply" leave it and still easily hold on to one's moral self. Yet that, as I read Jewish history, is just about what the mass of modernizing Jews did when they left their essentially inner-oriented ghetto or *shtetl* identities and opted for the world of urban, educated, secularized Western culture as their primary "moralizing" community. Of course this involved a good deal of boundary-crossing pain, but this was not undertaken and endured on the basis of anything previously visible in the pre-modern Jewish community, but because something deep in their human nature indicated its value. Something vaguely similar occurred when they gave up their formative national environments and immigrated to countries with a rather different ethos, and then when they gladly gave up the formative powers of the lower class for the middle class and beyond. Anyone who has tried to work in the Jewish community in recent generations knows that, until recently, the only hope of promoting Jewish life was to show how Judaism fit in with its primary values—those of a humanizing slice of secular Western society.

I derive two lessons from this applicable to Tom's critique. First, that for all the sociality of selves, they also have an inner power to transcend their group—a rather phenomenal one in the rare cases of prophets and saints. In the more common case, they can radically shift groups and transform their "selves." Let me call attention to a term in Tom's tradition which points to a special case of this, "conversion," that human/divine power which makes it possible for pagans to find a radically "new being" by becoming Christians. Something human and vaguely similar to that happened when Jews, utterly uncoerced, opted to transform their lives in societies with radically different value concerns against what their traditional communities taught them and their communal leaders advised. I should add that I am unacquainted with Tom's theology of conversion and look forward to learning how it relates to this discussion.

Second, the primary value-forming community of the Jews whom I am addressing is neither that of traditional Judaism nor that of one of its modern reinterpretations. The non-Orthodox communities—and to a considerable extent people who affiliate with "centrist" Orthodox communities—almost always keep their Jewishness secondary to the larger social worlds to which their parents adapted. So when I am speaking to the Jewish public in terms of "self" and "autonomy," I am doing so in the accents of their primary moral community, "chastened" though they have been by their affiliation with humanizing American secularity. Nor do I see this secondariness of Jewishness in the free countries soon disappearing. No new "hot" intellectual or spiritual movement breaks out in America these days without our soon hearing of the large number of

Jews who have become its devotees. So my modest "attention to the critical retrieval and mediation of the normative traditions that constitute Jewish particularity" is, as I understand it, in keeping with Tom's sense of the power of the social in individual life.

However, Tom's positive project intrigues me sufficiently that I should like to take a lightning stab at it. To begin with, I think this task of the retrieval of "normative traditions" would be rather easier for Christians than for Jews, since the church has a tradition of creeds and of classic doctrinal statements to draw on. Jews have nothing truly similar. But let me hazard an informed guess about our "normative traditions of particularity." Positively, they are God's choosing us from among all peoples to receive God's Torah and the resulting *halakhic* structure which expressed its mandates in Jewish life. But to these shaping beliefs we must add the ongoing, negative experience of anti-Semitism, the social experience which long made and kept Jews Jewish. None of these "traditions" is highly effective among us today. Most modernized Jews do not believe in Jewish chosenness, and they do not observe Jewish law as law, but only as a resource from which they select those practices they think will enhance their American lives. Fortunately, anti-Semitism continues to decline in the Western world, though only a dreamer would suggest that it no longer exists. But Jew-hatred is less a threat to our continuity these days than is the general acceptance of Jews which makes intermarriage and its assimilation so rife.

Renewing the Covenant is faithful to its title. It seeks to reinstate God's reality (chapters 3–10), to substitute Covenant for chosenness (so after the preparation of chapters 11–13 the delineations of chapters 14–16), and thence create a structure of duty-making that can replace the abandoned legal system (chapters 17–20). It hopes to so establish the cogency of these beliefs that a growing, eventually critical minority of Jews will want to live by them because of their truth, and not because some enemy will not let them be anything else.

SOME WORDS ABOUT THE INEFFABLE ONE

My terminological *teshuvuh*, repentance, must now proceed to my calling God an/the Absolute, albeit a Weak Absolute. My philosophic colleagues are aghast at my oxymoron and would like me to provide some conceptual clarity of the description of God as Absolute. Alas, I was being midrashic/heuristic, not spinning out tightly cognitive claims. I had argued in the experiential section that revulsion against the immorality of our times had sparked a new search for the Ground of our values. I wanted a term that, as an old *aggadah* put the need to penetrate the usual complacency, would "smash into the ear" of the hearer. If relativism is the evil to be opposed, then we needed to find its opposite, or at least the ground of non-relativism, what is termed in common parlance an "absolute." Used figuratively, "absolute" usefully marks the rather desperate search of people these days to find something stable to hold on to: to hold on to, no matter how bizarre it may be and no matter how costly (in dollars and cents, too). Jews, those fervent modernizers, show the same phenomenon. By calling God an absolute I only meant to call attention to the importance of the anchoring function of God in our lives. Any postmodern Jewish view of God, in my view, would have to provide for God's effectively exercising this role.

However, to connect God with a reasonably stable commandingness opens God to the modernist fear that God's grounding greatness will as good as wipe out persons. To refute this, I sought to call attention to biblical and rabbinic Judaism's unselfconscious paradoxical insistence that the One Ruler-God of all the universes nonetheless created a real world, and in it gave people the astonishing freedom to obey or to defy God. So borrowing a philosophic usage, I added "weak," in the sense of "don't push the substantive term too far," to the term "Absolute." That makes good Jewish theological sense and seemed to me sufficiently evocative that it might "shatter the ear" of my readers, but for philosophers it makes no sense. It is, I believe, a good instance of the translation problem we have when we seek to move between these related but disparate disciplines.

A somewhat similar problem arose in relation to my suggestion that God's redemptive power is sometimes seen in historical events in our time. Yudit and Edith particularly are troubled by this (as I think many in the Jewish community are). They want to know how I can say that God is involved with particularly beneficent events, and then not also involve God in the terrible things that happen in history. Classically, Judaism has said that God is involved in both, and that creates the problem: the incompatibility of the good God and horrible evils. The Bible already knew that justice was a limited answer indeed, and the rabbis taught that the life of the world to come would compensate for the lack of justice in this world. But, overwhelmingly, believing Jews were able to accept the fact that there are some things that we just cannot understand, probably because they were grateful for all the goodness they did in fact receive, beginning with life. The pious live, not always easily, with God's inscrutability. Philosophers care too much about rationality to accept that "answer." And they cannot easily accommodate the insight of believers old and current that, if the clumsy locution is permitted, history is "lumpy" and God's saving acts are sporadic. In several places in *Renewing the Covenant,* I have tried to explain why, after considerable reflection, I take this stand.[10] Now the gap between what philosophers consider intelligible speech and what religionists know must truthfully be said, widens to the point where discussion is difficult indeed.

This necessarily brings us to a discussion of the place of the Holocaust in contemporary Jewish theology. A number of my critics believe that since those terrible days we must operate with "a displaced and decentered faith." This phrase and its equivalents are frequently repeated by thinkers today, and they convey the understanding that since the Holocaust, we cannot believe in God as we once did. I demur from this position. I do not believe God is the central problem of post-Holocaust theology—a radical revisionism which I sought to justify in chapter 3 of *Renewing the Covenant.* None of my critics represented here have found this interpretation worthy of comment or refutation. Nonetheless, the matter is so important to assessing how the Holocaust should influence our religious thinking, I think it important to restate my case, even briefly.

Belief in God cannot die for people who don't really believe in God's existence to begin with, and who had already given up the idea of God's retribution as far back as the Kishinev pogroms of 1903 and 1905. By mid-century, the overwhelming majority of modernized Jews were agnostic if not atheist. What they believed in, what functioned as their "god," was not *Adonai* but humankind and its capacities. They built their lives on education, politics, business and culture—not the God of the 613 commandments. As the century drew toward an end they began to realize, in a subterranean, postmodern way, that their secular "god" had failed them and that a messianic faith in humankind is ludicrous. What was "displaced and decentered" in our effective faith was not God, but human power, that is, the ethos of modernity—and out of that recognition, the widespread religious search and postmodern spiritual longings of our time emerged. That is why I do not make the Holocaust, or the problem of theodicy, central to my thinking about God, though it is fundamental to my teaching about human nature and our need for God's help. I urge anyone reading these lines to make their own judgment of the case I have presented in chapter 3 of my book.

I could have as good as written the previous paragraph nearly a decade ago, when I was completing the manuscript of *Renewing the Covenant.* The intervening years have only confirmed my view. The Holocaust, once at the forefront of Jewish writing, is rarely a living theological issue today. As the second editions of some of the old radical books appear, their authors now share their second thoughts about what they once proclaimed and that, if nothing else, should give us pause in our continuing to mouth the old slogans about the Holocaust.[11] It is not that we are forgetting the Holocaust, but simply that we have begun to do what Jews have always done with a great historic event: we have begun to ritualize it. And I include in that ritualization the rhetoric we still use when we do discuss it. Old phrases and images reappear, old emotions are evoked and relived, the past and present are momentarily joined, and, having heeded the command "to remember," we go back to what are now the living questions of our existence. And among caring Jews of diverse temperaments and labels, that live agenda often centers on building a personal relationship with God, as incredible as that would have sounded in the heyday of the death-of-God movement.

THE PEOPLE ISRAEL

Yudit asks why I do not give more attention to the State of Israel and its ongoing place in covenanted lives. Since I am a religious rather than a secular Zionist, I devote myself to the primary task: determining what Jewish faith is in our times. Only with that in place can one hope to know what our relationship might be to the Land of Israel, to the State of Israel, and to the community living upon it. This not being a book in which I move very far from theoretical issues to practical ones, I limited myself to one paragraph on the State of Israel which I hope readers will find as rich in meaning as I do (p. 290). Some time after the book appeared I was asked to give my views on "What Is Reform Religious Zionism?" And that paper connects my theology with our immediate obligations theoretical and practical.[12]

Yudit also wondered why I do not explain why exactly a general self, who happens to be Jewish, should strive to become a Jewish self. Once one grants the premises of Enlightenment rationality—the individualistic self and truth as universals—I do not see how it is ever possible to make a case for the value of the particular that does not relegate it to second best. Why detour through an old, self-serving particular, when one can find groups that try to move as directly as they can to the universal goal? And why then also take on the oddity and disability of Jewishness in Western culture? Those assimilationist questions have bedeviled Jewish thinkers in this century who have accepted the supremacy of modernity, and attempted to build a robust Judaism from the foundations of universal human reason or experience. That is why I framed my case first as an attack on the universalist counterfaith (chapters 11–13), and only then tried to show the admirable character of the Jewish people in relationship to God, each other, and humankind (chapters 14–16).

Norbert suggests that there is now a rationalism that no longer atomizes individuals, but sees them relationally. It therefore gives rational credence to collectivities, and not merely to individuals. That certainly would provide us with an argument for the validity of particular groups, such as the people Israel. But, in typical philosophic fashion, it would do this for all groups universally. So the particular Jewish group would again be only another possibility for satisfying that rational need. Any other collective that satisfied the rational standards for relationality would, in that sense, be similarly commended. We are left again, though on a new level, with the problem of getting from philosophy's universalism to the unique significance of Jewishness.

This matter is critical to my determination not to be a philosopher in the present philosophic climate. In some bedrock, primal fashion, I and others like me know that the existence of the Jewish people in Covenant with God is a matter of unique cosmic significance. Any way of thinking that doesn't readily allow me to express and validate that truth cannot be the medium by which I will explain Judaism to others. Until someone creates a rationalism that can give particularity a primacy Jewishness has in my life, I cannot be a first-level rationalist. (But as my writing makes clear, I am a devoted second-level rationalizer, trying to think as hard and as clearly as I can about my first-level experience. Philosophers, of course, deny there can be "experience" without its already containing some mental structuring that can make something into my "experience." In effect, then, everything must begin with philosophy. For my rejoinder, see chapter 19 of *Renewing*.)

Let me only briefly add to this that most rationalism is resolutely secular and so constructed that the Covenanting God of Israel is as good as ruled out *ab initio.* I also cannot accept a system of thought which will devalue, if not rule out, what I and others like me know to be the ultimate ground of our existence. So I practice theology but, in the present intellectual situation, not philosophical theology.

TORAH, GOD'S INSTRUCTION

If Judaism values *praxis,* what we do, more than it values *doxis,* what we say about what we believe, then the questions David, Yudit, and others have raised about relationship's ability to command and, in addition, to generate law, are central ones for my enterprise. The topics are closely related but it will be necessary for me to focus on them somewhat separately.

Anyone who has long been in a relationship with another—neighboring, friendship, work—will surely have realized that involvement generates responsibility and that the more intimate and long-standing the relationship, the more it commands me. The paradigm case is marriage. The spouse commands simply by being spouse rather than stranger, and does so more compellingly than does a neighbor, friend or coworker with whom I have a relationship. When the demand is put into words, its specificity and the fact of its being spoken to me gives it great urgency. But even when no word is spoken, one knows that there are things one must, and others one must not do. In that situation, you may be uncertain what exactly you ought to do or how best to go about it—the advantages of the verbal—but you know that you must respond to the unverbalized command. Often, we discover, such unarticulated demands have a greater power than the spoken ones, for there is something particularly reproachful about the spouse's cries, "You should have known what to do," or, "If I had to tell you it wouldn't be the same thing," or "If you really loved me, you would have known."

This telling experience furnishes us with a metaphor for what happens between us and God in the Covenant. No wonder Rosenzweig spoke of revelation as love. When through the religious life one builds an intense and long-lasting intimacy with God, one knows one "must" not stain the relationship by one's behavior, but one "must" rather dedicate oneself to acting as the loved One would want us to. (That is the general case—but we should not forget, as Yehudah Hanasi once wailed, "Some people win the life of the world to come in an instant while others must spend their whole lives striving to attain it and never know whether they have.")

I suppose that is another reason that I am a theologian. I want to clear away the intellectual rubbish that so often keeps us from allowing a budding relationship with God to mature. And I want to provide as fine an understanding of the Covenant as a relationship as I can so that people will not only be attracted to it in theory, but enter into it as a bond which directs their lives. Ideas are not the only, or often even the best way of carrying on this "dating service" but, without them, I think a community as educated and critical as ours is will not be willing to "commit."

Relationship commands, but it is too personalistic to yield what we normally think of as law, the enduring-evolving, clearly specified norms of what we must regularly do or else carry a burden of guilt and/or punishment. What is at stake between the two views is not merely the vagueness of relationship and the specificity and objectivity of law, but the intensity of the urgency to act connected with each kind of command. In fact, can relationship get people to act as well as law can? We cannot answer that question by dismissing the former as too easy to subvert, for no system is people proof, and the law, too, is regularly subverted by literalists, positivists, and other less elegant sinners. We will, I believe, get a better picture of what each viewpoint can and cannot do by leaving off comparisons of who fails in each and turning to a case to illuminate this difference of approach.

Assume, that after a reasonably energetic effort, a tenth man is not forthcoming to complete a *minyan* and people will start to leave if we delay any further. What shall we do about the person who came to say *kaddish*? The Law is clear. For all our concern for the mourner, he cannot say the mourner's *kaddish* as part of the service. That is what Susan and Soloveitchik mean when they refer to "sacrifice" as an ingredient of Jewish duty. There are things which have long been difficult to understand in Jewish Law, but God's behests have such an urgency to them that we set aside our qualms and do them. Thus, while I do not know how Susan feels about sitting behind the *mehitzah,* which divides the sexes in her centrist Orthodox *shul,* when she comes to the synagogue, that is where she will sit; it is the Law. Thus, too, the mourner will understand why he could not say *kaddish* in this unfortunate circumstance, but he and the rest of the people there will know they have fulfilled the centuries-old ruling and acted with a Jewish authenticity any observant Jew will admire. In a society as shifting and unstable as ours, these are virtues to cherish.

Yet if I recall David's position of some years ago correctly, there are rare occasions when he, who like Susan gladly wears the "yoke of the Kingdom of Heaven," might break with the Law. Say that, as in cases of *mamzerut, halakhic* illegitimacy, the Law is blatantly unethical, punishing the innocent offspring for the sin of the parents, and no classic *halakhic* device avails to declare that there really is no case. In such an extreme case, David, most reluctantly to be sure, would not follow the classic *halakhah.* But he would be most stringent in limiting what qualified as a case of "blatantly unethical" Jewish law. It does not include allowing a gathering of nine men to carry on a service with the mourner's *kaddish.* I raise this matter only to indicate that so redoubtable a champion of Jewish law as David once acknowledged that in quite exceptional circumstances it might be necessary to exercise extra-halakhic moral authority.

For a large and, in my view, increasing majority of modernized Jews, feminism is the issue that mandates the need to revise or even break with the Law as it is understood by the sages of that community of Jews who are most devoted to its study and practice. To these Jews who insist on thinking about the Law's purposes, it seems plain that, in the case given above, should a woman be available to join the prayers she should be counted in the *minyan* so that *kaddish* could be said. Indeed, women should be counted in *minyanim* regularly, and be as required to say *kaddish* as men now are. All such changes would act to strengthen the living Covenant relationship. Many believe that they can use the term "*halakhah*" for these revisionist rulings; others believe that co-opting a traditional title obscures the contemporary relational authority behind them, and does violence to what the term "*halakhah*" traditionally meant. In any case, to ask all women to accept the lesser status that traditional law effectively assigns to women, is to demand more of a "sacrifice" than seems compatible with Covenant as the relationship between God and the entire Jewish people.

I find that Peter's suggestion that we think of our duties in terms of Kadushin's "value concepts" pushes us too far to the permissive pole of the duty spectrum. Kadushin, after all, was working with *aggadah,* lore, rather than *halakhah,* law and, while *aggadic* statements do have a certain limited authority for believing Jews, they do not come with anything like the rigor associated with the notion of command. Moreover, thinking of praxis in terms of value concepts is made more troubling by Kadushin's insistence that their meaning is always indeterminate. I may be reading too little into Peter's suggestion, but I am sensitive to this issue because of our spate of writers who, in their eagerness to co-opt the term *halakhah* for their non-Orthodoxy, regularly so empty it of legal forcefulness that their "*halakhah*" effectively retains only *aggadic* authority, despite its more stringent-sounding label.

Were I the rabbi of the nine-person [*sic*] non-*minyan,* and the mourner asked if we could have the service anyway so she/he could recite the mourner's *kaddish,* I would think of the Law in order to see if it reasonably clarified the present Covenantal imperative. Clearly tradition would prohibit it, but a great many caring Jews in our community today would think it a shame that a mourner who came to synagogue to say *kaddish* was denied that possibility because of what they would call "a technicality." They, like me personally, could not imagine God frowning on us because of our untraditional effort to have nine people, not ten, symbolize the Jewish community seeking liturgically to renew its ancient Covenant, as well as allow our neighbor to fulfill her/his special responsibility in that regard. But if the group present, understanding the situation, was willing to go ahead, I would lead that service. Someone else utilizing the same Covenantal calculus might rule differently, but that is the pluralism that this kind of goal-oriented reasoning encourages.

If *keva,* the regularity, of Jewish law is critical to us, I do not see how we can ever achieve that without a firm belief that God stands behind just these words, this ruling and the dialectical system which gave birth to it—ten men, not nine, or not nine and a woman. Without that dogmatic faith, other rationales for the Law will produce only tepid results. Most Jews are too critical and questioning to accept classic Jewish law as binding because they are told it is, if not God's revelation, the established historic structure of Jewish living. This position and its corollaries have thus far failed to produce communities who live by even a modernized Jewish law, as Conservative Jewish leaders regularly ruefully acknowledge. In my opinion, the theological root of the difficulty for the non-dogmatic theories is the depth of our commitment to the religious validity of the self's rightful part in any rule-making. Only a living relationship with God, I insist, can hope to demand that we work out our individuality as part of the Jewish people's Covenant with God.

The great contribution of Covenantalized decision-making will not be *keva,* but its emphasis on *kavannah,* intention. What transpires between us—God-Israel-me—is here a matter of consciousness as well as of act. When our doing grows out of a consciousness of self-in-relation, that inwardness will shape our persons as well as be a commanding power in our doing. At the moment, Covenant relatedness is largely a matter individual Jews feel privately. Yet I would hope that we will soon see the day when there are communities of Jews who share enough of this Covenantal sensibility that they will want to move beyond the isolation that many Jewish selves feel in our time, to the formulation of communal norms for Covenanted Jewish living (p. 294). I do not think that will ever likely become "law" but it would flesh out the communal aspect of Covenantal existence and add another layer of urgency to being a praxis Jew.

RENEWING THIS CONVERSATION

Several of the colleagues have commented on my book's failure to show the Jewish textual basis on which my thought rests, while others wish I had indicated more clearly what sort of practice this theology entails and how Covenantal reasoning leads to it.

As to the missing texts, I am unable to resolve the methodological problem which besets us all with regard to texts and contemporary thought. No matter how many citations one adduces, they can merely illustrate a possible relation of some aspects of our tradition to the new thinking. That is because we have no way of determining what they all say, or how to give a representative sample of them or indicate their essence. None of these possibilities carries much credence, so all textual citation remains a thinker's selection of what she/he finds relevant in the tradition and testifies more to the thinker's hermeneutic than to "the normative" ideas in the tradition (whose existence is another hotly debated notion among us). In this situation I have thought it wiser to clarify my hermeneutic than to gather texts to demonstrate its putative Jewishness. I also hoped that various of my briefer writings would indicate my roots in rabbinic literature, and my way of learning from it. In the winter of 1999, the Jewish Publication Society will publish my and Francie Schwartz's book, *The Jewish Moral Virtues,* which, in typical *musar* fashion, is highly textual and ranges across the entire Jewish tradition. That will give my readers some greater indication of my relationship to the Jewish sources. And as I indicate in the preface to *Renewing the Covenant* (pp. x–xi), I hope that one day my decades-long study of *aggadic* discourse will see the light.

As my theological work was coming to systematic fruition, I began testing out various of its notions in one area of *praxis,* Jewish ethics. A collection of many of my papers in this area was published in 1990 by Wayne State University Press under the title, *Exploring Jewish Ethics.* A better indication of how my mature theology relates to decision-making may be found in the results of a seminar I conducted for a number of years, in which students rendered a decision on a current ethical issue of concern to them, based on the five-point schema I had outlined in the last chapter of *Renewing the Covenant.* Fourteen publishable student studies resulted from that course, and these were published by

Behrman House in 1994 as *Reform Jewish Ethics and the Halakhah: An Experiment in Decision Making.* While these are my students' papers, not my own, the approach to reading *halakhic* (mostly) texts is strongly guided, occasionally in dissent, by my viewpoint. Thus, this volume may be said to open a window on how my theology would work in practice.

God, rain blessing on Peter Ochs for his dedication to furthering Jewish thought in our time, and for his imaginative effort here to push post-modern thinking about Judaism another step ahead.

And to You, dear God, I say "Blessed are You" for all you have done to sustain me to this day.

NOTES

1. On the notion of a Liberal Jewish elite, see the chapter on "Jews Who Do; Jews Who Don't" in my *Liberal Judaism* (New York: UAHC, 1984), pp. 459–67.

2. Not long after the publication of *Renewing the Covenant,* when giving some lectures at the University of San Francisco, I gave as one reason for my finding postmodernism congenial: "I am grateful to postmodern discourse for authorizing those who admit they cannot give reasonably unambiguous voice to the *logos* to speak their truth, sloppy in structure as it may seem to some. This structural untidiness is abetted by my writing with conscious imprecision, a choice designed to warn my reader that my theology does not allow for geometric clarity." *Our Way to a Postmodern Judaism: Three Lectures* (San Francisco: University of San Francisco, Swig Dept. of Jewish Studies, 1992), p. 38.

3. Elliot insisted that, regardless of what I said in *Renewing the Covenant,* it must be understood as a statement of Reform Jewish ideology. Note his subtitle: "Autonomy vs. Community: The Ongoing Reform/Conservative Difference," *Conservative Judaism,* Vol. XLVIII, No. 2 (Winter 1996): 64–68. My response and Elliot's rejoinder appeared as "The Reform Judaism of *Renewing the Covenant*" and "Matters of Degree and Kind" in *Conservative Judaism,* Vol. L, No. 1 (Fall 1997). (The issues were dated to maintain the consecutive publication of the journal but they actually appeared at a considerably later date.)

4. Ibid., p. 62.

5. This self-understanding appeared about the same time in two publications in slightly different form: *Choices in Modern Jewish Thought,* 2nd ed. (W. Orange, N.J.: Behrman House, 1995), pp. 288ff, and *The Human Condition: The Alexander Schindler Festschrift,* ed. Aaron Hirt-Mannheimer (New York: UAHC, 1995) as part of my paper, "Reform: Modern Movement in a Postmodern Era?"

6. See Eugene B. Borowitz, *Choosing a Sex Ethic: A Jewish Inquiry* (New York: Schocken Books, 1968), pp. 116–20.

7. Abraham Heschel, *God in Search of Man* (Philadelphia: Jewish Publication Society, 1956).

8. The issue cannot be that individuality has no place at all in traditional Judaism. Even Heschel, the defender of the accuracy and empathic passivity of the prophets, acknowledges that they express God's truth in terms of their individual personalities and styles. Halakhic decisors are regularly described as having *shitot,* individualized systems of reading the tradition. I discussed how this functions in Conservative Judaism in my response to Elliot Dorff, "Autonomy vs. Community: The Ongoing Reform/Conservative Difference," *Conservative Judaism,* pp. 64–65.

9. The most egregious misreading of that sentence was Ellen Umansky's. Because I spoke of the self in its full individuality, she accused me of not having progressed beyond classic Reform Judaism. Her astonishing misreading was compounded by her gerrymandering of my statement. She omitted its first word, "Fifth," the one which indicated how I had recontextualized selfhood to give it a properly postmodern, Jewish relational situation and made it the Jewish Covenant self. My appreciation of her ideas was not enhanced by her suggestion that we now ought to move on to a

theology where selves and religion were thought of relationally, a matter central to my writing for some decades. "Zionism and Reform Judaism: A Theological Reassessment," *Journal of Reform Zionism,* vol. I, no. 1 (March 1993): 44–50. My response appeared as a lengthy endnote, no. 4, in my own contribution to these discussions, "What Is Reform Religious Zionism?" *Journal of Reform Zionism,* vol. II (March 1995): 24–30.

10. See Borowitz, *Renewing the Covenant,* pp. 123–25, 128, and 131 on the limited God; and pp. 148–50 on retribution.

11. Most notable is Richard L. Rubenstein's preface to the second edition of *After Auschwitz,* 2nd ed. (Baltimore: Johns Hopkins University Press, 1992), pp. xi–xiii; see also the quite different tone of the preface to the second edition of Emil Fackenheim's *To Mend the World* (Bloomington: Indiana University Press, 1994), pp. xi–xxv.

12. Eugene B. Borowitz, *Journal of Reform Zionism,* vol. II (March 1995): 24–30.

A PAUSE: TO LOOK BACK BEFORE MOVING ON

I have not often taken much time to think about my life and its development. My personal and intellectual life have generally been so full of activities and projects that my thinking has been mostly present- and future-oriented. Had it not been for two most flattering invitations, I should have stayed far away from autobiography, even in the restricted intellectual domain to which they summoned me.

The first request came from Professor Robert M. Seltzer, director of the Jewish Social Studies Program at Hunter College of the City University of New York. He kindly invited me to deliver the second Anne Bass Schneider Lecture, in which scholars are asked to reflect on the interplay of their lives with their academic work. Though I had done an occasional, relatively informal piece on some aspect of my spiritual development, this invitation required that I do something far more searching and analytical. After my oral presentation, Dr. Seltzer, evidencing his historian's interests, asked me to expand my original text, and the result was published as "A Life of Jewish Learning: In Search of a Theology of Judaism (paper 26 here).

After a statement of such length and detail, I thought that study would be my final foray into an alien intellectual realm. Then I had the great joy of being invited by Dr. Ellen Frankel, editor and CEO of The Jewish Publication Society (on behalf of its Editorial Committee) to publish a collection of my studies over the years as a volume in its Scholar of Distinction series. That should not normally have further involved me in autobiography, but my work over the years is a record of the development of an academic discipline—modern Jewish religious thought—as well as the evolution of a particular stance—postmodern Jewish theology—in that field. Merely to reprint my old papers without situating them in the developing intellectual situation in which they arose would be to deprive them of a major part of their significance. Hence I asked, in these pages introducing each section of this book, to be allowed to extend my remarks in my Hunter College lecture and to let the specific comments generated by the papers in this volume undergird what I had said there.

I freely admit that I have learned much about my intellectual development from undertaking this task and, as always, have no idea how these insights will play themselves out in my future writing. For I am, as ever, busy with new projects as well as some unfinished old ones. The twenty-first century has turned out to be a busy time of writing and publication for me, of which my investigation "'Halakhah' in Reform Jewish Usage: Historic Background and Current Discourse" (paper 27 here) is a warrant. For a scholar, the ongoing process of learning and teaching allows one to touch the hem of eternity.

26 / A Life of Jewish Learning: In Search of a Theology of Judaism

2000

Bob Seltzer and I first encountered each other half a century ago at his family's St. Louis synagogue. Newly hatched from rabbinical school, I was the assistant rabbi there, and, as was typical in those days, I had been asked to start and run a youth group. Bob was a member of that high-school-age group and I remember him as bright, sensitive and somewhat shy, but one of those kids of such promise that you cannot help wondering what they will make of themselves. In Bob's case I have been able to keep some track and have watched with admiration his emergence as a historian of Eastern European Jewry and his broader work on Judaism entire as well as his significant leadership of various Jewish intellectual enterprises. So it was with very great pleasure indeed that I received his invitation to give this lecture. I cannot imagine that his extending this honor to a student of theology was without some qualms on his part or that of various of his colleagues. The relationship between the university, particularly those which are government sponsored, and the discipline which speaks of religious faith from within the circle of belief, has long been a troubled one, a difficulty exacerbated by those Jewish faculty members who want their Judaism to be resolutely non-religious. Having taught Jewish thought at various secular universities over the years, I think such worries can easily be overstated. In any case, I pay tribute to his courage in overriding those issues and welcoming me to this platform.

The particular terms of this lectureship call for a still somewhat uncommon academic mix of biography with serious intellectual work. I see in this a tribute to the cultural shift in thinking about thinking which characterizes our time and loosely goes by the name "postmodernism." The charge laid on me has led me to an insight which I suggest is the *grundmotif* of this lecture. Somehow I have managed to traverse the second half of the twentieth century as a culturally involved, socially engaged, serious intellectual, indeed, a Jewish religious thinker, of all things, and yet have lived essentially without notable angst or crisis. As I look back over the past fifty years or so, it seems to me that my religious intellectual life has been a relatively organic development, one not untroubled or unperplexed, but, by contrast to what many other writers report, a relatively straightforward and unbroken development.

This absence of radical theological or personal spiritual crisis was not due to any of the usual causes of religious certainty. I do not recall ever having had an enveloping mystical vision or a conversion experience; I did not grow up in a household suffused with religiosity or characterized by rich observance or Jewish learning; and from what I have read of some other people's religious lives, I cannot claim a naturally saintly demeanor or a congenitally intense sense of personal piety. Unlike most of my Jewish neighbors and friends, I do appear to have a more lively and acted-upon sense of the reality and presence of God. Otherwise, I seem to me to have been always a rather normal, if bookish, Midwestern American Jew. When, as the years have gone by, I wondered why I wasn't as radically troubled by various events as were numbers of people whom I highly esteemed, I have thought this simply might be a failing of mine. But my efforts to be a religious rebel or to contend with God never lasted long. They seemed unauthentic to me. So, though I couldn't then come up with a clear understanding of why I was right to do so, I persisted in my way. Perhaps others will find in the mental story that follows an explanation for my curious life experience.

Taking heuristic license, I shall speak about five distinct and largely successive themes in my intellectual development.[1] Life, of course, is not that neat and my head has often seemed to me an untidy closet, overflowing with a jumble of ideas, one which regularly defied every effort to tidy it up. Still, since my long-term focus has been on systematic theology, I am accustomed to the guilt of over-simplifying in the desire to make the broad truth stand out. I shall here, as often elsewhere, paint with a very wide brush.

In my first stage I sought to give a rational construction of Jewish truth but quickly ran afoul of the insoluble problems of epistemology. These systemic difficulties made it impossible to know with any certainty that our religious beliefs were true. That did not turn me into a secularist, as happened to so many others, but this, second led me to existentialism as a means of explicating Judaism. Thinking existentially pointed us beyond pure cognition to what it might mean to conceptualize in terms of the whole self and thus opened up valuable ways of talking about God. Unfortunately this philosophy also emphasized human generality, thus again posing a barrier to integrating Jewish particularity with the reality of a personally known God. Seeking to resolve this critical issue, I, third, began giving considerable attention to what we might assert about the role of the social in contemporary Judaism—a topic that, as I shall explain later, had to include why the founding of the State of Israel took only a subsidiary role in my theology. At the same time, fourth, I was deepening my sense of what God might still mean to us and why the question of the Holocaust meant something quite different to me than what it had in most Holocaust theology. All of which came to a climax, fifth, in my current postmodernism, a stance which has finally provided me with a cultural language with which to set before the thinking community a fresh, systematic statement of a richly ramified Jewish belief.

Let me immediately connect with this intellectual agenda two personal experiences which seem to undergird my march through these various phases. The one may be my earliest childhood memory. I remember going with my father and grandfather, both immigrants from Eastern Europe, to a small, Lower East Side traditional synagogue for an evening *Simhat Torah* service. I have a vague sense of being given a flag and marching around with it. Something about that evening seems to have made an indelible, favorable impression on me and I have long associated it with my primal sense that there is something profoundly good and true about Judaism. Did I come to feel that way because at no other time I can recall did I do anything with my father and grandfather, a man, I must add, I did not much care for? We moved to Columbus, Ohio, when I was six or seven—but whether the *Simhat Torah* experience was before or after that I cannot say, so I do not know whether it had anything to do with a special or a rather ordinary trip to Manhattan.

The other experience is connected with my growing up in the Midwest. My father, who loved being with Jews, discovered that there was only one way to associate with them in the Ohio *galut,* exile, and that was to belong to and attend a synagogue. As a result, we often went to the local Conservative synagogue, the logical gathering place for modernizing East European Jews like my parents. There, and everywhere else in Columbus Jewish life, I found that no one ever explained Judaism very well. Despite my regular dismay that teachers, rabbis, and visiting speakers made Judaism seem rather dumb, I never wavered from my judgment that Judaism had to be better than that. I swore to myself that if I ever had the chance I would give it a properly intelligent explanation.

My impulse to be a latter-day Maimonides seemed most unlikely of realization because, though people often said that I should become a rabbi, that, in typical post-immigrant fashion, was the last thing any reasonably bright, upwardly aspiring young American Jewish boy would do. I did maintain a number of Jewish interests after Bar Mitzvah and confirmation until I got to the university, Ohio State, in 1940—I was sixteen—but once there I could not find much at Hillel that appealed to me. Jewish studies, needless to say, didn't exist in those days, and this major school of 15,000 students had just one Jewish professor, in marketing, typically enough.

THE BOY RATIONALIST'S EPISTEMOLOGICAL DISAPPOINTMENT

I came to the university as an enthusiastic devotee of the ethos of modernity: reason was the best, indeed the only guide to truth and value, and the university was the instrument by which one acquired its variegated teaching. Though I had received a glimpse of how one might give a sophisticated exposition of Judaism from Manuel Brandt, the instructor in my synagogue's high-school class, Judaism was far from the forefront of my attention. For all my inner regard for Judaism, it was the irresistibly attractive and convincing ideas of the general culture that filled my imagination. In that, I simply mirrored the goals of my generation. I became a philosophy major and, in due course, was permitted to enlarge that concentration to include the social sciences. I fervently anticipated the immense human benefits that would result from applying the scientific method to all issues of human concern and I scorned those old-fashioned types who refused to use their minds rigorously.

Yet before long my polemical rationalism was brought up short by my fundamental commitment to the reality of value in the universe. The usual shorthand for this is moral value or ethics, but, as best as I can recollect my sensibility then, I had in mind something broader than the good one should do. It centered rather on the kind of person one should be. Of course, that certainly demanded substantial ethical dedication but it aspired somewhat higher by attaching us to a broad ideal of high human quality. Even in today's more embracing diction that sounds rather fuzzy and had I tried to articulate it in the heyday of rationalism, it surely would have been dismissed as simply laughable. Nonetheless, I was convinced then, and remain so today, that this vision of the reality of value was not ultimately a mere act of personal whim, volition, or projection, or simply a social construct, for all that self and society shaped it in their fashion. I knew that value inhered in the universe, and this insight became the criterion by which I began evaluating the adequacy of the various systems of thought for which my teachers and fellow students were proselytizing. Of course, other standards also influenced me. Nonetheless, I firmly believe that the issue of the ground of value was central for me in those undergraduate days.

I was certain enough about my commitments to reject the pragmatism which was so powerful an intellectual force in the university culture then. In my practical, naive way, I could not understand why, by strictly pragmatic standards, Hitler would not be entitled to try the hypothesis that Germany would function better as an exclusively Aryan enterprise and see, by whatever means efficiently led to that end, if this social vision worked. As a result, for a short period I became a Platonic idealist, attracted to its notion that The Good was the highest of all ideals and thus at the heart of reality. But I could not find a contemporary exponent of philosophical idealism who made much sense to me. Equally troubling was the fact that no philosopher who reasoned in this fashion had much general intellectual acceptance. I did not want to talk a philosophic language that only I and a few others thought could explain things. I wanted to be able to converse with some significant portion of our society. (I now recognize the slippery nature of seeking social acceptance, for I long suffered from it in the years that I spoke the lonely language of theology to a Jewish community that was resolutely secular and agnostic.) When I concluded that philosophical idealism was not rationalistic enough for the mid-century intellectual temper, I knew I would have to find a radically different manner of talking about the truth.

A decade plus later, this same value benchmark reasserted itself in my rejection of linguistic analysis or the philosophy of language which swept through the English speaking academic world in the 1950s. This movement prided itself on its rigorous rationality and certainly taught us how many of our intellectual problems were due to tangles in our language and the way we used it. But the linguistic analysts insisted that, to be meaningful, statements had to be empirically verifiable or, as consistency later required them to put it, that statements had to be empirically falsifiable. By that criterion, the entire realm of ethics had to be considered rationally devoid of meaning, non-sense, as some polemicists put it, and ethical statements relegated to the realm of mere emotive utterance. Many of these philosophers were themselves people of fine character, ones you probably could have counted on in a time of persecution, but they either did not see or did not much care what their demotion of ethics to the realm of personal or social preference might engender if widely accepted. Because I cared profoundly about social consequences, I was something of a pragmatist, but surely one who evaluated our suggested duties by how well they conformed to my idealistic ontology, a stance which, I would now contend, is typical of much halakhic reasoning.

My break with philosophy and the adequacy of rationalism can easily be traced back to a specific experience at the university, one so memorable and vivid that it was as close as I have ever come to a conversion. I hasten to add that it had no religious aura about it but was more like what I imagine happens when an animal sheds its old skin. The event was accompanied by sensations of strangeness, newness, freedom, and hope, and an eagerness to set out on a new path. That was, I take it, a self-conscious experience of powerful growth.

What transpired was mundane enough. As an advanced undergraduate, I was granted admission to a graduate seminar on epistemology offered by a visiting professor from Johns Hopkins. Since little could be more basic to a philosophic quest than a rational understanding of how we know what we know, I entered the course with great interest and considerable timidity. The nub of the sessions soon turned out to be the conflict between epistemological dualism and epistemological monism. That is, we usually naively assume, in some pre-Kantian fashion, that our minds can make contact with the world outside us so that our ideas are an accurate reflection of what is "out there." That assumes two distinct entities, the mind and the world, and thus involves a dualism of knowing. However, mind/world reasoning engenders a paralyzing problem: how does a quite material world get into our consciousness as immaterial ideas? This leads other philosophers to argue that all cognition is only the mind's patterning and that, rationally speaking, we have no evidence at all that there is a world "out there." To be fully consistent, we must say there is only mind and, as it were, a monism of knowing. Of course, this abandonment of any possibility of knowing a real world is attacked by other philosophers as an intolerable solipsism.

The arguments for dualism and for monism went back and forth in the seminar. We read thinkers who propounded one or the other view, and the students then would deepen the inquiry by espousing one or another position. The mental exercise was impressive and initially quite exhilarating. But after some weeks it became apparent to me that we would reach no decision. Indeed, by the rationalistic premises of the discussion, we could not reach a decision. Walking to my car one afternoon after class, I realized that if I became a philosopher I would never know with rational certainty how I knew what I knew. In fact, for the rest of my life I would keep debating this issue or finding ways to evade it. Today this is part of the widespread attack on Cartesian rationality, which, by its privileging of doubt and individual judgment, is finally self-destructive. There is little of true human significance that can be put into "clear and distinct" ideas, so certainty, that great initial promise of rationalism, becomes unattainable. The world and human duty were far too real to me to devote my life primarily to a discipline in which one could never know the truth, particularly the truth of value on which I and our community based our lives.[2]

Permit me an addendum, one I believe important to understanding why my rejection of a universalizing rationality as the prime shaper of our Judaism remained a major theme in my work. As the years went by and my consciousness of the depth of my particular Jewishness rose, it reinforced my early demotion of rationalist thinking to a secondary role in my theologizing.[3] Classically, modern Jewish philosophers have made one's rationality and its concomitant universalism primary. As a result, their thought necessarily rendered particular Jewishness of secondary value even though the thinkers often made valiant efforts to give Judaism validity by exposing and lauding its universal message. Alas, Judaism always comes off second best in this kind of thinking. As a result, modern sophisticates over the decades have self-righteously disdained their Jewishness (and its special responsibilities and social disabilities), for the general culture's humanistic lifestyle which directly focuses on the universal goals rather than being encumbered by their ghetto-ish incarnation, Jewish practice. Radically put, the primacy of rationalism makes Judaism dispensable, at least in principle. Even Mordecai Kaplan, the great exponent of the naturalistic virtue of particularity, was forced by his Durkheimian premises to as good as concede this point in his book *The Future of the American Jew.* In his adulation of the religionization of democratic nationhood, he can only point to the present ethical shortsightedness of American national vision as providing a temporary, counterbalancing role for the historic religions.[4] The implication is clear: should the American civilization ever develop a full-fledged religious culture, as he hoped and trusted it would, there would be no need to remain a Jew.[5]

If, however, one believes, as I came to understand I did, that there is something cosmically valid about Judaism and hence it is not dispensable, then any philosophy which continues the old identification of truth primarily with universals will necessarily be unacceptable.[6] This issue lies behind the century-long argument over whether the discipline should be "the philosophy of Judaism," or "Jewish philosophy." In a "philosophy of Judaism," one seeks to show how a rational truth which has been established by academic philosophers can be found in the particular literature and practices of the Jewish religion. "Jewish philosophy," by contrast begins with the premise that Judaism has some particular insight into reality which the philosopher now seeks to explicate to inquirers in the terms of some culturally accepted rationalism. This perennial modern conflict surfaced again at a recent meeting of the American Academy of Religion. With special apologies for this shameless simplification of their highly nuanced and impressively sophisticated presentations, Lenn Goodman argued the case for a contemporary philosophy of Judaism (one which was fully conscious of the value of Jewish particularity); David Novak made a case for Jewish philosophy based on a prior commitment to God's revelation at Sinai; and Norbert Samuelson presented a non-revelational case for Jewish philosophy based upon a prior commitment to Judaism, its texts and its tradition of reasoning. For all my admiration of these colleagues and their instructive work, I deny the ability of any contemporary philosophic rationality to provide an adequate statement of Judaism's particular content.

Something similar needs to be said about employing "ethics" as well as "tradition" as major factors in explaining how one goes about one's non-Orthodox decision-making. I learned this, in good part, from my own error in this regard. In my very early article, "Toward a Theology of Reform Jewish Practice,"[7] I followed a common liberal track by simply setting ethics and tradition side by side as determinants of what we should do. I did not then see that the major problem of our decision-making arose at those places where the universal insistence of ethics clashed with the particular demands of Jewish tradition. The ethical cannot, on its own terms, accept any compromise or diminution of its claims; anything less is unethical. But there are instances where the demands of Jewish tradition cannot be subordinated to the hegemony of ethics without grave danger to the entire fabric of Judaism. Intermarriage is the classic case, and, depending on what one sees as basic to the edifice of Judaism, decisors will differ as to when they allow the tradition to say "No" to what ethics commands. To resolve this difficulty, non-Orthodox traditionalists like Jakob Petuchowski, z"l, Elliot Dorff, and Moshe Zemer, will generally try to argue that the *halakhah* itself contains an ethical concern (and that in something of a modern sense of "ethics"). That flies in the face of all in classic Jewish law which is resolutely a-ethical or even un-ethical, including its insistence that private conscience must almost always bend to the stated law.[8] I can only applaud the goals of such thinkers even as I often agree with their decisions. We do need to give major priority in Jewish duty to what ethics tells us about the unique importance of persons as persons, but I do not think we can ever theoretically integrate that well with our sense of the particularity of Judaism's truth as long as we do not substantially recast our thinking, something I believe postmodern Jewish categories now finally allow us to do.[9] And that returns me to my story.

I had moved through the university with some speed and was, at eighteen and a half, into my senior year of courses. But I had also exhausted all my allegedly sensible career options. My course in advanced algebra seemed to me terribly sterile so I couldn't press ahead with becoming an atomic physicist, and while I liked chemistry, the lab work was too devoid of human contact for me to become a chemist. I gave up on medicine after an intensive summer's study of zoology and I rejected law, despite some tempting offers from some very well-connected Jews, because I feared that I couldn't pursue justice as an adversary whose goal was winning cases. Teaching philosophy had been my last and best hope of putting all my interests together and when that collapsed, I fell back on the rabbinic option that had so often been urged upon me and which I had investigated as far back as when I graduated high school.

In 1942 I entered the Hebrew Union College in Cincinnati, with the specific interest of studying Jewish theology. I already used that troublesome term, "theology," because I didn't know what else to call my interest in an abstract, systematic statement of the content of Jewish belief and the reasons for believing in it. I soon learned how odd most of my schoolmates found my focus on belief and its exposition. Those students who rose above simple careerism were devoted either to social justice (as it was called before activism demanded another name) or to "Zionism," that is, a non-ideological passion for the Jewish people and its particular future. All were praxis-oriented, sturdy exemplars of American pragmatism and champions of the ideology that the Jewish emphasis on mitzvah meant that what you did counted, not what you believed. It did not take much psychological acumen to see that this stance justified their living, as did most of American Jewry, in peace with their agnosticism.

My teachers were not only mostly believers but they were also impressively learned, emulators of that pioneering modern Jewish scholar, the historian Leopold Zunz. They had a quasi-Hegelian trust in the explanatory power of historic development to resolve all modern issues of belief. This naive trust in the persuasive power of a historical treatment of ideas animates and thus makes unusable, the first great English book of Jewish theology, Kaufmann Kohler's work by that name. True, we had a Professor of Jewish Theology, Samuel Cohon, as fine a Jew and human being as there was at the Hebrew Union College. When I had advanced enough to take his major course, I self-confidently pressed him to face up to the critical difference between the history of an idea and the reasons why one should still believe it. My attack, which lasted through several sessions, opened a breach between us that only some years of maturation and a considerable growth in humility on my part managed to mend. If the oddity of an avoidance of theology at a theological school seems strange, let me also point out that it took a long time for American Jews generally to get over their antipathy toward questions of belief and the term "theology." Thus, in 1962, when I wrote an article for *Commentary* on "The Jewish Need for Theology," it evoked a response from that redoubtable philosophic analyst, Sidney Morgenbesser, asserting that theology was not Jewish and that all self-respecting moderns would reject any effort to coerce Jewish belief. I responded that Judaism certainly did not have the equivalent of Christian dogmatic theology but it certainly had an aggadic tradition of seeking to clarify Jewish faith.[10] I wish the language of "meta-ethics" and such terms had been common then as I should have been able to make a much better case for theology by saying it is our meta-*halakhah*, the belief which impels and guides our duties—another example of my life-long concern with the ground of our values.

In sum, at the College I again found myself in the situation where I knew Judaism was very much better than the way my teachers were explaining it to me. Fortunately I soon found a friend who shared my odd interest, Arnold Jacob Wolf, a fifth-generation American Jew and a scion of a family which had known distinguished Reform rabbis. Though we never studied in the typical *chevrusa* (yeshivah study partner) style, we became spiritual companions and mentors to one another in a way that has continued on to the present day. We were soon joined by Steven Schwarzschild, z"l, whose rich Germanic culture and razor-sharp neo-Kantian mind, honed by the socialist Marxism of the Frankfurt School, gave our triumvirate a fizzy continental intellectuality that constituted our real rabbinic-school education.

This late-1940s-early-1950s emergence of a minority of Reform Jews interested in theology, among whom must be named our predecessor, Lou Silberman, our contemporary, Jakob Petuchowski, z"l, and the most distinguished of the émigrés from the Hochschule fur die Wissenschaft des Judentums, Emil Fackenheim, was matched at the Jewish Theological Seminary then in such figures as Seymour Siegel, z"l, Herschel Matt, z"l, Byron Sherwin, and David Silverman. These men and others became the core of a small, path-breaking community of theological concern that had no predecessor in American Jewish life and, as a collective, has had no successors. I leave it to the historians to explain this phenomenon, one made more notable by the fact that its early documents are driven by neither of the factors that Jewish writers always invoke when speaking of recent Jewish thought: the Holocaust and/or the founding of the State of Israel.

The kind of theology that concerned us in those days was not narrowly intellectual. Its natural corollary was a new Jewish pietism, with the thinker taking God, the people of Israel, and Jewish practice very much more seriously and personally than had heretofore been the case. While the standard Jewish concerns of the day, Zionism, study, and social action, now received a new impetus and tone, in my life it led to a lifelong dedication to the practice of prayer with *kavvanah,* intention. For us, and for me, God was not merely a curiously complicated conceptual challenge but a reality in whose presence one had to stand with regularity, doing so as one of the people of Israel encountering God. To this day, praying in one or another of the modernized traditional modalities of Jewish piety is a significant part of my daily regimen. With its unpredictable highs and lows, it is also an unceasing spiritual challenge and a difficult and humbling one, at that. It is not called *avodah,* labor, for nothing.

THE PROMISE AND PROBLEMS OF EXISTENTIALISM

I left the College after ordination in 1948 disappointed that the Faculty did not want to grant me a fellowship to stay and do graduate study. It was, I believe, the only time a student aspiring to a doctorate has been so denied. But two special resources accompanied me then. I had married just before my senior year and I was to learn from the gifted, exceptional Estelle, my wife now of 52-plus years, what it means to live in a covenant of mutuality. I never use the words "covenant" or "partnership" that she does not stand behind them. *Vehamaskil yavin* (and the wise will know all that implies). And I took with me to my St. Louis position the inklings of a new direction in thinking, one that was yet quite indistinct but in which Buber and Rosenzweig, of whom I shall say more later, were my uncertain guides. Greater clarity did not begin to come until, after two years of congregational service, I received the fellowship I had once been denied and we returned to the College so I could study for the newly established Ph.D. degree. My tenure was too brief for that, only one year, for when the Korean War broke out it was my turn to serve as a chaplain, having been deferred from military service in World War II. Fortunately we were stationed stateside for the two-year stint and I was able to complete my first earned doctorate, in the College's *in absentia* D.H.L. program. My dissertation was in the area of rabbinic theology. Because of my anti-philosophic stand, I did not want to follow the more common path of studying the medieval Jewish philosophers and then using their thought as a basis for contemporary Jewish thought. I turned rather to the creators of our Judaism, the rabbis, to study in detail what they said theologically and how they expressed their belief in a non-Hellenic diction (the latter a topic I have studied for years and that still intrigues me).[11]

While a resident graduate student I had been able to read rather widely and I discovered that there was in that period a culturally significant language I might use to give a non-rationalistic exposition of Judaism: existentialism. The existentialist thinkers knew the critical truth that our most fundamental sense of reality does not sensibly arise from pure reason but from what it means to be a self, a person, a living being, or, as they technically epitomized it, that our existence precedes our essence.

Two things made me hesitate about adopting the existentialist approach to truth. The first was that its primary exemplars, Sartre and Jaspers, were committed atheists and as resolutely secular as the typical rationalist philosopher. However, the patron saint of this fresh way of thinking was Søren Kierkegaard and there could be little question about his authentic religiosity. As it turned out, there was also a more recent body of writing which could be called religious existentialism, and my first book, a decade plus later, was devoted to describing these thinkers and arguing that Franz Rosenzweig and Martin Buber were entitled to a place in their number.[12] My second reservation about espousing this position arose from the easy identification of religious existentialism with its Christian exemplification. True to their tradition, Christian thinkers regularly utilized the existentialist analysis of the human condition to make a case for sin as a necessary concomitant of humanhood which only God's grace could then overcome. In keeping with classic Jewish teaching, however, neither Rosenzweig nor Buber was as pessimistic about human existence and reconciliation with God. Rather they pointed to the way all human beings—and not just Jews—might encounter God directly and without a mediator.

Arnold Wolf and I had discovered Buber while we were rabbinical students, no thanks to our teachers who were too rationalistic to even mention his name in class. I can still visualize the dowdy copy of *I and Thou* in its old, green binding which Arnold retrieved from our library stacks and which began our conversion to a non-rationalistic pattern of religious thinking. We then avidly read everything of his that appeared in English. A British publication, Buber's commentary on much of the Torah, entitled *Moses,* had a major effect on us.[13] It showed one could read the Bible without deprecating critical scholarship but nonetheless taking its religiosity seriously, that is, in Buber's fashion, not censoring out the reality of God's presence in the story. We then devoured the early Buber books of the newly established American branch of the Schocken publishing program, the two volumes of *The Hasidic Tales* and, even more thrillingly, the collection of papers entitled, *Israel and the World.*[14] In these varied essays we could see how the theory enunciated in *I and Thou* could be applied to problems as real as Jewish education, Zionism, and Jewish life generally.

Situating Buber and Rosenzweig in the existentialist stream of modern religious thought allowed us to signal that we were not alone in rejecting the primacy of rationalism and provided us with a culturally significant way of communicating the content of our kind of Judaism. That seems relatively easy to say today when non-rationalism seems almost to dominate our culture. But in the 1950s and early 1960s it was anathema to the resolutely rationalistic non-Orthodox establishment as, in a lesser way, it was to the American Jewish ethos. Let me emphasize here that assigning reason a role secondary to some prior reality does not mean abandoning rationality altogether. If anything, I believe that we non-rationalists have a particular obligation to be as clear and explicit as our basic stance allows us to be. Such subsidiary rationality is one of our few safeguards against the many astonishingly irresponsible non-rational notions we regularly hear about these days. To be sure, thinking which begins from a non-rational base can never reach the kind of certainty that rationalism once promised and which still allures many people. Not a small number of the orthodoxies of our time have flourished because of their attraction to people who cannot bear having to live with a certain measure of risk. Existentialists cannot even mitigate that vulnerability by supplying their adherents with a (rational) rule for recognizing when we have reached the limits of necessary uncertainty. The secondary use of reason prevents it from containing the unknown, but that should not cause us to belittle how valuable its limited applicability remains.

This lecture exemplifies what reason can do even when relegated to a secondary role. My students over the decades have received this procedure in strikingly different ways. Thirty years ago, I was much too non-rational and pious for them. In the last decade plus, they often rebel at my insistence upon their thinking hard and doing so based on a considerable body of knowledge. After all, isn't religion ultimately about what it is that they, as they say, "simply know," or "deeply feel"? Similarly, encountering my persistence at analysis and argument, some classify me as an, ugh!, rationalist. I do not know whether I am too compulsive about the need to think clearly about what we believe but cannot rationally explicate. I only know that I have yet to find a more responsible way to refine my religiosity.

To revert, for a moment, to rationalistic categories, Buber's non-rational thinking resolved two critical problems for me. The first was the epistemological issue: how could one "know"—in the special, certainty-seeking sense of that term—that God was real. At the cost of limiting what rationality could accomplish, Buber had given up on what I-it certainty could say about persons and God. He had, however, called our attention to the reality that these days we have two ways of knowing, not only the familiar I-it mode but an even more significant one, that of the I-thou. In this non-rationalistic manner of knowing, the full sense of quality and value is made plain. We know God as persons are known, not as things are known, and to identify a thing with God is idolatry, even if the thing is an idea. However, we can find God, better, meet God, in direct and indirect encounters with God which are closely analogous to our moments of true relationships with persons. This dualistic, now I-it, now I-thou, epistemology deeply offends the rationalists, those dogmatists of the I-it and worshipers of concepts. Regardless, as the years have gone by and the personal has, for most of us, greatly expanded beyond the cognitive, what Buber said has come to make increasing sense.

Buber also served us mightily, as did Rosenzweig quite independently, by clarifying what it might mean to take revelation, God's input into our lives and history, quite seriously, but not in an orthodox fashion. Rationalists reinterpreted revelation as some form of human discovery or growth, and the more confidence one had in human beings and their capacities the more value one could attach to this notion of Torah as largely human insight.

Buber and Rosenzweig had a real God, so they did not need to rest all the burden of religious truth on the power of human discovery. But they also had such modern respect for people that they could not honestly diminish the human role in revelation as much as did the traditional orthodoxies. They taught, rather, that the best metaphor for God's input is not verbal communication—stories and laws and counsel—but only interpersonal presence. In friendship or love it is the other's presence that, even without words, commands us. Such relationships send us into the world to tasks we must define for ourselves, whether as individuals or as communities—for groups, too, can relate to an Other. Often what we wordlessly know we must do is to be loyal to our past together, but our relationship may also prompt us to a creative response to this moment. Rosenzweig pointed to love as the human counterpart to such non-verbal commanding. As any faithful friend or serious lover knows, the beloved's unspoken demand of us has great authority indeed. Love, too, is the concrete reality behind the Buberian notion of relationship, a word which he, more than anyone in this century, has given such valence that it is now bandied about even in advertising slogans.

Permit me here a comment about why my recent writing has made so little direct reference to feminist thinkers. Partially, as I have written,[15] it is from a hesitancy to engage in inter-gendered discourse until women suggest the standards which they think are appropriate for discussions across the gender divide. Having long waited for such guidance but not found it, I am more recently of the opinion that these standards will have to emerge out of our discussions. In larger part my reticence has come from my acceptance of the ethical truth of the feminist denunciation of male sexism, a chastisement I have sought to act upon in my writing and behavior. My response to the few feminist thinkers who have gone beyond the indictment of our sinful treatment of women to state what the feminist experience now positively directs us all to do has a more theoretical character. Having for nearly half a century been a committed Buberian, in my life as in my thought, much feminist teaching about the importance of persons and real relationships, of community and its newly personalized structures, sounds quite reminiscent to me. I hear in this thinking a restatement of what Buber was saying decades ago (though his language follows the sexist conventions of his day). The content of what he says, and not just the German or English usages, makes plain that the "thou" is always necessarily beyond gender. Thus far, I have heard little that goes beyond Buber, but I look forward to the instruction I shall yet receive from feminist thinkers on this and many other matters.

There are problems with Buber's position. Nonetheless, I regularly find that the Buber attacked for his individualism is a caricature of the man's life and thought, one often based on reading little more than the heady opening pages of *I and Thou.* Buber has an extensive, compelling social vision. He passionately believed in community and, by his thinking, helped liberate that term from its institutional understanding to make it a more personal, relational ideal. He was a Zionist at the turn of the twentieth century and the first editor of the World Zionist Congress cultural magazine. After World War I he was one of the intellectual leaders of the interfaith religious socialist movement in Europe. At the Hebrew University, the Orthodox would only stop objecting to his appointment to the faculty if his title had nothing to do with religion, so he was, with good reason, appointed Professor of Social Philosophy. Buber has a strong theory of the relationship between religion and society as well as law. Any open-minded person can see that if they will take the pains to read the last dozen or so pages of *I and Thou,* the discussion of the illegitimacy of Korah's rebellion in the book on *Moses,* and his 1936 polemic against Kierkegaard in the essay "The Question to the Single One," collected in the volume *Between Man and Man.*[16] It is this Buber, the social thinker, who alone ought properly to be criticized.

Buber's social vision must be resisted, I believe, because of his insistence that even as one of a genuine community, one should determine one's duty as a pure "I" in relation to the group's common (thou) center. Thus, the deciding self needs to shake off the very social bonds that he has otherwise commended. Theoretically, one detects here a vestige of Kantian autonomy, now taken a step beyond its old rational/secular isolation but nonetheless loyal to the hegemony of the newly relational individual. Practically, this is Buber's response to the various forms of collectivism which he saw threatening the individual, fears which were only to become more evident as the twentieth century moved into its middle third. And he augmented these by his judgments that, in the Jewish community, the ethos of Orthodoxy and the compulsive propriety of Liberal Judaism oppressively interposed barriers between Jews' "I's" and the Eternal Thou.

Let me quickly summarize the gains and problems of the existentialist Judaism that as the 1960s wore on, forced me to begin a further search for a better, that is, a less inadequate language of Jewish theology. Buber, to give the prime example, restores a real God to us, but one who now has sufficient regard for human freedom such that people become partners in revelation. Though this takes us a quantum leap beyond rationalistic, humano-centric religion, it leaves the Jewishly concerned with a problem. As it were, Buber has brought a living sense of God's reality back into our post-ghetto Judaism. But leaving it at that makes us only *B'nai Noah,* children of Noah, sharers in God's covenant with all humankind. But because Buber's thought does not somehow raise *Yisrael,* Israel, the Jewish people, to a role of near equivalent authority, it does not yet help us understand what is involved in being *B'nai Yisrael,* children of Israel, sharers in God's Covenant with the Jewish People.

In due course I would identify my struggle to transcend Buber and Rosenzweig as the problem of a theology of *"halakhah,"* of what non-Orthodox Jews believed that should impel them to observe more than, as we still called it then, the Moral Law. Rosenzweig simply dogmatized that law was necessary and could not explain how that jibed with his insistence that revelation was a partnered activity, one in which we were not to be coerced. Buber more consistently held on to the existential self, but this position reduced communal duty to how the individual group member presently responded to the group's norms. In practice, Buber's individualism justified modernizing Jews in shucking off the social eccentricity of identifiably Jewish acts and, at best, having a personal, perhaps humanitarian, relationship with God. But I knew with gradually increasing clarity that the truth of Judaism inhered in its particularity and not merely in its universalism. Therefore, what our community now required was a theology of non-Orthodox Jewish duty, particular as well as universal.

All of the foregoing reflects how the central concern of Jewish religious thinking began a sea-change in this period. Ever since we came out of the ghetto the driving issue of Jewish life had been "How can we, who still somehow want to stay Jewish, be authentically modern?" With the rise of Jewish social integration in the 1950s, some people began asking, "Since we are so fully modern, what might it mean for us now also to be authentically Jewish?" In the sixties, the rise of our Holocaust consciousness and the possibility of another major Jewish destruction in Israel's Six-Day War, made most of our community realize how much we still cared about our Jewishness. Both these influences were magnified by our increasing disenchantment with the United States as a moral society. Despite a federal civil rights law, our race relations were deplorable, and, despite widespread objection to our war in Vietnam, our country persisted in fighting it. We began losing the bedrock foundation of our modern Jewish faith: that Western civilization was utterly superior to Judaism. It became increasingly evident that modernity, too, had deeply serious problems, and Judaism now commended itself to us as a valuable corrective to our society's ills.

This must not be exaggerated. What was a crack in the cultural facade and has since become a vast breach has not persuaded the vast majority of ordinary Jews to give up their utterly primary allegiance to the modern world. Contemporary Jews disagree strongly on what constitutes the proper balance between modernity and Jewishness. Very many of us remain unrepentantly dedicated to the agenda of modernity, content to have our children and grandchildren be fine human beings, worthy *B'nai Noah*. As a result, such Jews are often, as Leslie Fiedler so memorably termed them, their family's "terminal Jews." But there is also among us a not insignificant minority who think differently, people who divine that something cosmic would be lost if the people of Israel dwindled into insipidity or became a living museum piece. Something like that latter view, an intuition I can trace back as far as my struggles with a student sermon I had to give in 1948, made me years later move beyond religious existentialism in search of a compelling theology of ethical-and-more-than-ethical Jewish duty.

Was I sensing, animal-like, the tremors gathering along the tectonic plates that made Western civilization seem so solidly established? For in these post–World War II decades our culture lurched from heady self-confidence to increasing self-doubt and initiated a radical realignment of what had been its glory in secularity and its disdain for serious religious belief. So a fuller appreciation of who God was and what God may still be said to do developed alongside my strengthening Jewish consciousness. During the seventies and early eighties, these concerns were surely intertwined—the forerunner of what I would later call a needed

Jewish "holism"[17]—yet in what follows I will, for clarity's sake, treat the issues of community and God separately.

AM (PEOPLE) AND SELF

Humanly, I came to my mature decades benefiting from some wonderful accomplishments, those memorable events and relationships whose direct influence on my thought I must leave to others to elucidate. Estelle and I had produced and raised three wonderful daughters, and nothing had been more fundamental to my daily life, not even, I believe, my intense dedication to my demanding, multifaceted activities. I would like to believe that they all appreciated the priority I tried to give to the family and hope that this made it somewhat easier for Estelle and the children to have respect for my love of my work. A single practice perhaps best epitomizes this. For many years my home office was on our first floor so that the children, coming home from school, felt it natural to come by and say "Hello" or chat with me. I almost always immediately stopped what I was doing and spent some time talking to them before they were off to something else and I could resume my work; to this day, when Estelle returns from an outing, I regularly stop what I am doing and spend a little time with her to see how things went, only then heading back to my office. Obviously my growing sense of community was given greater reality by these years of being-there, schlepping, attending, appreciating, trusting, worrying, and all the rest that goes by the name of "familial love." And, if I may jump some years, when our children had grown, Estelle became a psychoanalyst in private practice, a faculty member at two psychoanalytic institutes and Dean of Curriculum at one of them. That immensely enriched our relationship and led me on to new depths of understanding myself and human variability.

In 1953, after my two years of chaplaincy service, we had settled in Port Washington, New York, and though we moved twice in that community, making seven moves in nine years of marriage, we finally bought a large old house where, to our surprise, we lived for forty-two fulfilling years. I was the first full-time rabbi of the newly founded Reform congregation in our reasonably posh Long Island suburb, and when I left the congregation after four memorable years of service, we remained dues-paying members of that synagogue and quiet participants in its life. When I have thought or written about what I consider typical of the American Jewish community, it is my neighbors and friends of Port

Washington whom I first have had in mind, though the realities of the many other communities I have been in over the years have enlarged my sense of what really has been going on.

During the four exciting, even tumultuous years I was a pulpit rabbi, I became involved in the joint doctoral program of Columbia University and Union Theological Seminary, majoring in philosophy of religion. I found that work enormously stimulating and broadening. It began a lifelong interest in Christian theology and, to a lesser extent, the religious thinking of other faiths and the academic philosophy of religion. My long involvement in interfaith discussions among theologians traces back to that wonderful experience.[18] I managed to complete the program as an A.B.D. ("All But Dissertation") before an invitation in 1957 to become the Associate and then the national Director of Education for the Reform movement at the Union of American Hebrew Congregations (the UAHC). That experience, in turn, led to much of my writing on Jewish education and gave me a very special view of the realities of American Jewish community life.[19] One of the conditions of my appointment was that I get a doctorate in education. Fortunately, many of my Columbia-Union credits were transferable to the Teachers College program in philosophy of education, which I completed in 1958. For my doctoral project there I tried writing up the theology of Judaism which I felt should undergird the work of teachers in Reform Jewish schools. It was my first effort at writing up a full-scale, systematic statement of Jewish belief, and while it qualified me for my degree, I knew the effort was premature and so I abandoned it without qualm and moved on to find a riper understanding. (My second aborted effort came in 1970, I believe, when I had my first sabbatical from the HUC-JIR. I spent each morning writing an opus that would give intellectual credence to my beliefs, but, as those months came to an end, I knew that, despite its bulk, it went nowhere. Again, I never bothered to re-read or try to revise that manuscript; mainly, I suppose, because it had taught me what I still didn't know and couldn't do. These two good-sized manuscripts now repose with my other papers at the American Jewish Archives.)

My next five years planning for our educational work in the United States and Canada allowed me to work with a broad range of people across the continent. I was also involved with the UAHC staff on joint projects for our movement and with the representatives of other Jewish and non-Jewish movements or community institutions. I happily became the publisher and editor of the UAHC's broad-ranging educational publications, an activity that had already attracted me as a rabbinic student.

A good deal of my early writing was related to education, and its frequent theological interest—which defined the goals of our work—gave it a unique emphasis in this field. Education being so intimately connected with socialization, I could not help but continually be confronting the question of the relation of our ideal community to our real community.

In 1962 an early dream of mine was fulfilled when I became a full-time member of the Hebrew Union College–Jewish Institute of Religion faculty. Initially, my primary function was to teach education, with Jewish religious thought as a minor area of specialization. But I came to the College with the understanding that eventually I would mainly be devoting my time to theology, as in fact happened. Aside from the warm human contacts it provided, teaching gave me two precious new opportunities. The first was time—time in which to read and think and write, a luxury which only those of us who have tried to do those things while carrying on other full-time jobs may be able fully to appreciate. The other was the chance to work out my thought with my students. I have long believed that the most important rule of education is "Don't waste the students' time," so preparing for my sessions on Jewish thought became an important laboratory for me, one fully complemented by the response of my students to what we read and I presented. Even after thirty-seven years of full-time teaching, both these gifts of faculty status remain immeasurably precious to me.

The upheaval of the 1960s drove me into another project whose length of endurance and breadth of consequence I could not envision when I began it: the founding of *Sh'ma, A Journal of Jewish Responsibility.* It bothered me deeply that while people regularly prated of the relevance of Judaism to contemporary affairs, few ever tried to demonstrate what that might mean in our roiling social situation. By then political conservatives had stated their ethical (often their Jewish) case with such cogency that it would have been ludicrous for someone with my sense of community to act as if one could say "Jewish ethics" and assume that would simply mean what *The Nation* or *The New Republic* stood for. As in the Talmud, "the Jewish view" would now have to emerge more from the dialectic of thoughtful, informed Jewish opinions, expressed side by side, than from merely stating one point of view. My vision was confirmed when only one person on the political right refused my invitation to join our ethically polyglot group of Contributing Editors (seeing in my proposal another liberal plot to co-opt conservatism to its pink-ish purposes) and another soon left us when I raised some questions about the quality of a submission. Over the years, several people on the right similarly withdrew, not wishing to give any credence to utterances from the left, despite the efforts I continually made to enlist writers and contributing editors from the conservative political position. In only one respect, I feel, did my own chastened liberalism affect the magazine: it remained resolutely committed to pluralism, a standard most neo-con journals, Jewish and otherwise, still regularly consider a sign of moral weakness. (After he had published, by invitation, in *Sh'ma* I asked Meir Kahane in a not-for-publication letter, whether I would be allowed to publish my journal in a state he led, and he responded that as I lived up to my ideals so he would live up to his. *Lehavdil*, in distinction, thanks to Buber's teaching about relationship, I had little difficulty accepting learned, conscientious difference of opinion amongst us.) Over the years, particularly as the journal established itself as a forum of thoughtful debate, the rate of acceptances of my invitation to write articles always remained very high. I was always pleasantly surprised at this, because my invitations often included asking writers of lead articles to tell me which of their position's critics they respected so that I could then invite them to respond to the articles. And we allowed no rejoinders except, if memory serves me, in one instance.

This private, "underground" little magazine—published without institutional support or "angel," except for the help in its first three years of a generous printer-friend—soon created a kind of idealized community of Jewish interest among its customary 5,500 subscribers. For twenty-three years, I served as its Editor and Publisher, with the indispensable administrative help of my gracious, able neighbor, Alicia Seeger, of blessed memory indeed. The contact this gave me on many levels with the real people who make up "the Jewish community" undoubtedly gave a broadening reality to my thinking about what it means that our folk stands in living Covenant with God. Though I have not been directly involved in *Sh'ma* since 1993, I continue to run into people who want me to know that they still remember fondly the community of readers/discussers that another time created. Their kindly reminiscences help me reinforce my dream of and dedication to Judaism's social calling.

Sh'ma was another channel for my continuing interest in Jewish ethics, which had by now become the main area of Jewish practice in which I sought to apply my maturing theological ideas. This had a twofold effect on my more abstract reflection. Considering the practical consequences of my thoughts helped me to understand more deeply what it was that I was espousing. And having to face the reaction of our community to a concrete proposal for its action gave me a more solid sense of what it meant to be thinking as one of a people (see below) and not merely as an isolated mind.[20] My first substantial statement in this area, the book *Choosing a Sex Ethic,* appeared in 1969 and my most recent book, with Frances W. Schwartz, is on *The Jewish Moral Virtues.*[21]

The intellectual side of all this biographical approach to community focuses on my response to the two major social ideologies of the post-mid-century period, Zionism (which classically spoke in resolutely secular terms) and Reconstructionism (which sought to move beyond political Zionism to a theory of humanistic-religious Jewishness).

The leaders of Zionism built their social constructs on the modern European theory of nationalism. By making group identity critical to Jewish modernization, their views gave our community its strongest theory of the nature of the Jewish people, one whose appeal was amplified by its utterly urgent practical significance due to the rise of Nazism and the bitter reality of the Holocaust.

The notion of Jewishness as another secular national enterprise has never had much appeal to Diaspora Jews. Such "Zionism" as world Jewry has manifested is humanitarian (to save Jews who need to emigrate)—or philanthropic (to help the State of Israel support its needy immigrants and meet its social problems)—or political-familial (to support the Israelis against their international enemies). By contrast, world Jewry has steadfastly refused to perform the two central Zionist *mitzvot: aliyah,* to immigrate to the Homeland, and learning and using modern Hebrew. That explains, I believe, why, regardless of what some observers would like to have been the case, the founding of the State of Israel was not a major event in the Midwestern Jewish communities in which I lived in the late 1940s. Furthermore, the living significance of the State of Israel in the New York suburbs where I resided in the fifties and sixties was modest indeed. Only when the Six-Day War evoked the possibility of the destruction of the State of Israel did anything approaching passionate identification with the Israelis come into being. Even then, while fund-raising and political action burgeoned, *aliyah* and Hebraism did not.

The limits of our new enthusiasm for the State of Israel were tested in the seventies over the issue of how American Jews should give voice to their growing sentiment that the Israelis ought to be more vigorous in their pursuit of peace and more humane in their treatment of the Palestinian Arabs whose land they had acquired. I was a moderate peacenik in the seventies and it was no fun being ostracized by the American

Jewish establishment and its hangers-on for our ethically based criticism of the State of Israel. It was small consolation later when what had once been decried as heresy became, after the incursion into Lebanon in the eighties, what our establishment leaders began calling a sign of the maturity of our relation to the State of Israel.

The theoretical issue, for the few of us who cared about such matters, was now unmistakable. By nationalistic standards, as some right-wing Diaspora Zionists argued, why shouldn't we conquer territory and rule over it for our national benefit as other nations have often done? Overwhelmingly, Diaspora Jews have rejected such arguments because they have insisted that being Jewish had to do with a certain quality of human behavior. Turning its back on Ahad Ha-Am, Israeli and Zionist leadership has preferred the pragmatism of politics to facing up to the intimate connection between Jewishness and value that many Israelis and most Diaspora Jews take for granted. That failure, among others, has recently led Israeli as well as Diaspora thinkers to discuss what has come to be called "post-Zionism." Some Israelis have even dared to suggest that their country ought to be a multinational, democratic state rather than a specifically Jewish one.[22] Often, it seems that little remains of Zionist theory today other than a desire to keep asking what Zionism might still mean to us.

Mordecai Kaplan's genius created a theory of Jewish peoplehood that, while utterly rejecting the belief in our chosenness, integrated Zionist peoplehood with a religious sense of the high human quality demanded by Judaism. He did this by infusing his naturalistic, anti-revelational vision of Jewish civilization with a thoroughgoing commitment to humanistic ethics and religiosity. Sociological observation and theory had demonstrated that all peoples naturally tended to create cultures in which religion is the binding element of their value systems. The Jewish folk, as it needed to turn its attention to the various aspects of its civilization that modernization had caused us to repress, now also had to revive the religious aspect of its social life in harmony with the humanistic ethos of general culture. He argued, without chauvinism, that the Jews were particularly empowered by their rich moral heritage to restate their religio-ethical ideal today in terms of the universal ethical human task.

At mid-century, *The Reconstructionist*, the Kaplanians' journal, was one of the few places where one could encounter people who thought hard about what Jewishness might mean to moderns. Though I had enjoyed reading it ever since my rabbinic school days, I never became a

Reconstructionist. Kaplan's thought seemed to me philosophically naive about the source of our values, claiming that they were as inherent in the universe as the physical laws that scientists discovered. Just like my HUC historian professors, his theory of Jewish duty sought, without further argument, to turn a description (that by sociologists of so-called "primitive cultures") into a prescriptive way of life, authoritative for secular moderns.

In his recent book, *Rethinking Modern Judaism,* Arnold Eisen has given us a far more sophisticated version of this effort to use sociology as the basis of a new theory of Jewish ethical-and-more-than-ethical-duty. Eisen makes a subtle case for a performative approach to Jewish practice, that is, that *doing* more likely creates its own sense of the authority of the deed than does a theory of authority that *enjoins* the doing. Though he acknowledges that God or God's surrogate must be mentioned in the Jewish practice, the effectiveness of doing the act, he contends, makes moot the reality that American Jews attach to such symbols, which he believes is modest to non-existent. Thus, by attending to actual motives to Jewish practice—social integration/distinction; symbolic explanation; nostalgia; ultimacy; and "tradition"—we have our best hope of reinvigorating communal Jewish practice.[23]

I would agree that there is a large sector of American Jews who still profess the agnosticism typical of modernism, or at least are most comfortable when speaking its familiar language. Many more Jews still find it difficult to speak directly about God or their personal relationship with God. Nonetheless, several things persuade me that this anthropological approach to Jewish social responsibility crucially needs to be amplified by a directly theological understanding. Consider the practical issue. If ritual and nostalgia-writ-large are so performatively effective, why is it that they have not, in themselves, created a major body of observant American Jews? Moreover, I find it difficult to believe that people who seem to question so many things and exercise so strong a sense of judgment about what they will and won't do can long go on using words like God as the major referent of what they are doing without asking what they mean or stand for. Kaplan and Eisen want to avoid the theological issues by being functionalists, hoping that by attending to how things work and have effects they can evade the thorny issues of why we should bother doing them. I, in contrast, remain convinced that the critical issue of our time is the ground of our values and, thus, of our duties. While the two approaches could complement one another nicely, the theological approach is more congenial to this blending than is the functionalist.

Eisen's own personal position is not as rigorously humanist as that of Kaplan, though operationally he seeks to make room in the Jewish community for those of little or no belief. Why, I wonder, does he make no mention of the opposite contemporary social development, of the continuing strength and the growing practice of Jews who are in search of greater spirituality? Thus, to give a ritual example, prayers for healing and healing services now seem to be utterly widespread among American Jews simply because people were religiously ready for them. They would have seemed ludicrous in the days when we dogmatically insisted that whatever Divine Power we could acknowledge has no direct effect on our lives. One can, of course, perform such ritual acts without a graduate degree in theology but if some shift had not taken place in our old modernist distance from God, we could not now find virtue in them as some congregations and rabbis still refuse to do.

Where Eisen has suggested that our overwhelmingly non-Orthodox community can be healthy as long as it lives by benign nostalgia, others have argued that it requires a significant dose of *halakhah,* religious law. My recent exchange of views on this topic with Elliot Dorff indicates my sense of the limits of this approach.[24] What was at stake between us and is, in my view, a critical question for all non-Orthodox theologies of duty, is what sort of authority we attach to the notion of "law." Elliot felt that by "authority" I meant enforcement and pointed to the case of Prohibition which was law without being fully enforceable. Hence, he argued, we can have effective Jewish law even without any social sanctions behind it. The issue, as I see it, is not whether a dictum is enforceable but whether people consider it "law" or something possessing a different kind of authority. What I had called attention to, I thought, was the difference between the kind of compelling power Judaism vests in the *aggadah* as against that of the *halakhah.* The *aggadah* clearly is Oral Torah and therefore one should take its dicta quite seriously. However, it does not have such authority that Jews are obligated to carry out aggadic prescriptions. That is, they do not have the sense that they really "must" or "ought" to do what a given aggadist advocates, though they know they might be well advised to follow it. Not so the *halakhah* which, once it is fixed, whether by tradition or one's *rav,* must be carried out whether one likes the ruling or not. True, unfortunately, all Jews are to some extent sinners. So what makes this law is not that people always actually carry it out, but that they believe that, regardless of personal predilection, this deed should be done. They therefore regard not doing so as some kind of malefaction, in short, a sin. Thus, a special sense of power or compulsion attaches to law, and this is what makes it "law." The term *"halakhah"* classically carries this kind of authority, though it does so in its own special systemic fashion.

Heteronomous prescription, as the observant Orthodox readily demonstrate, can build and vivify a community. However, its sense of what one must do, regardless of moral twinges or the press of Judaism's other values, can also make for the continuing Jewish/human reality of the *agunah* problem and the continuing lack of a solution for it. I do not see that we can gain a liberally acceptable sense of compelling duty by evading the issue of the source of its authority and merely asserting, as Dorff and other Conservative thinkers have, that one simply cannot have Judaism without *halakhah,* rules for proper Jewish behavior. Dorff goes beyond such assertive positivism and happily recounts the many reasons why the law commends itself to our volition. That is, he tries to help us understand why we should choose to have "law," particularly the flexible Conservative version of it—a strategy which I read as effectively turning *halakhah,* required duty, into *aggadah,* valuable counsel. It is his tribute to the religious significance of the strong sense of self with which modernity imbued us. As I observe the community, I find that Jews take making up their own minds as so basic to their existence that, regardless of denominational label, they will, once off the rabbi's turf, think about their rabbi's or their movement's halakhic rulings only to submit them to a higher authority, their conscientious best judgment. Tikvah Frymer-Kensky's sophisticated ethico-communitarian approach to this question even more openly abandons the power of law as law, yet seeks to co-opt the dignity of the term while effectively turning it into aggadic wisdom.[25]

I agree that we shall have no robust Jewish practice unless we can find a way to endow our communal observances with a certain measure of independent authority. I do not see how that can be done without bringing God and our community's relation to God into our reckoning. That will lead me, shortly, into my discussion of God. Before doing that I should like to point to two significant ways in which my growing sense of community in this period affected my thinking.

The first of these was methodological. Ever since the writings of Kant and Schleiermacher, in their different ways, modern theorizing about religious truth has begun from human experience rather than from Divine revelation. Moreover, the starting point was always the individual, and that inevitably made groups of secondary value. But Judaism is essentially a group experience and activity, though one with a strong appreciation and tradition of individual personalities. Hence, rather than begin my theologizing with some variety of individual experience, as most previous non-Orthodox thinkers had done, I realized that I ought rather to found it on the collective religious experience of the Jewish people in our time. Not having either prophetic inspiration or an academic discipline by which to read the soul of a group, I have imaginatively waded into the sea of our recent history, up to my nostrils as it were, and then tried to set forth how, at our deepest level, we have been affected by recent decades. The resulting insight has been the spiritual-social foundation of my theological work. I shall return to this topic below when I speak about God.

The second way community affected my thinking derived from my participation in American Jewish life on many different levels. What I found there served as a reality check on my theorizing, indicating whether or not what I was trying to say made communal sense and where, in the face of communal satisfaction, I knew I needed to dissent. Once again, the dialectic between my pragmatism and my idealism asserted itself. Temple membership, attendance at services, and Torah study classes, sending our children through our synagogue school, listening carefully to what people said, and watching what they actually did about their Jewishness, all served as a balance to my voracious reading and unceasing reflection. In sum, living as another Jew among Jews (and non-Jews) has been a major resource for my theologizing.

WHEN HUMAN *TZIMTZUM* MAKES ROOM FOR GOD

I had not anticipated that trying to think out of communal experience would lead me to an enhanced understanding of our way to God. Clarifying Buber's personalistic approach to reality had long seemed to me an effective means of helping a thoughtful minority of Jews develop or deepen a relationship with God. However, as the seventies became the eighties it became increasingly clear to me that the death-of-God thinkers had radically misread our social drift. Instead of God fading from the scene and humanism triumphing, a substantial turn to religion was evident throughout Western civilization and, as part of that development, in the Jewish community as well. The Havurah movement flourished by making small-group liturgy more meaningful to people than services in large, formal institutions could, and Jewish mysticism became a flourishing interest and practice among us. In more recent years this development has burgeoned in the widespread concern about spirituality and the concomitant efforts to vitalize the private religious lives of Jews. Some people still talk about the Holocaust as a challenge to believing in God, but no one, with the possible exception of David Blumenthal, has had anything fresh to say on that topic for many years now. Such Holocaust theologizing as does surface seems more a ritual repetition than a fresh spiritual concern. This communal experience cried out for interpretation.

My diagnosis of the situation stemmed from a curious fact about the argument for the death of God. It forthrightly asserted that the utter injustice of the Holocaust made it impossible to believe any longer in the God of Jewish tradition who rewarded good and punished evil. The logic was impeccable but it had little to do with the spiritual situation of modern Jewry. As Elie Wiesel has pointed out, traditionalists were more likely to retain their faith in the death camps than were the liberals of every stripe. And as for modernized Jews, no Jewish thinker, beginning with Moses Mendelssohn, had tried to defend the old Deuteronomic sense of tight Divine justice. Rather, with science increasingly describing how the world operated, modern Jewish views of God for the past two hundred years or so have denied that God has a hands-on relation to human history as our pre-Enlightenment thinkers still believed. When, at the beginning of the twentieth century, the Kishinev pogroms shocked the civilized world and world Jewry, there were no modern Jewish voices which judged that depravity to be God's punishment of a wicked Jewry. Rather, many Jews called for Jewish training for self-defense and many more went about organizing themselves internationally to put political pressure on the Russian government. They took it for granted that human action, not God's retribution, immediately determined history. This secularized view of history was endemic among us, as world Jewry modernized and politicized itself. Thus, the God who was declared dead after the Holocaust was not the God of our largely agnostic community.

What then lay behind this curious anomaly of a community of unbelievers disturbed about the proclamation of God's demise? Another development provided a clue. A number of death-of-God thinkers had argued that we should not be fearful because God was gone. If anything, it liberated us from dependency on the Divine and let us more maturely assume full responsibility for what transpired among us. Clearly, as Kant had long since taught us, the loss of God would make no difference to our ethics, for these quite independently stemmed from our rationality, not from God's revelation. Interestingly enough, Richard Rubenstein, the leading Jewish death-of-God theologian, was too perceptive to rely on this modernist dogma. In the post-Kantian era which had swept European philosophy after World War I, rationality came to be restricted to what could be tightly demonstrated. With rationality more a matter of tight reasoning than of any given content, one could no longer assert, as the Kantians confidently had, that every rational person would know why they must be ethical. (I have previously alluded to a similar line of reasoning in the philosophic linguistic analysts after World War II.)

However, if reason no longer demanded we be ethical, what did? Rousseau and other Enlighteners believed in the essential goodness of human nature and sought to release it from its social trammels so that it could finally express itself in high human decency. But how could one have such an optimistic faith in human nature after the Holocaust? Rubenstein bluntly acknowledged with the atheist existentialists (and the scientific materialists) that the world was devoid of value and it was only we humans who willfully imposed our varying senses of right and wrong upon it. But this intellectual collapse of an independent foundation for our ethics contradicted the general condemnation of the Nazis as utterly evil in their mass murder of Jews and others. They should have known better, we insist. But why? What now justified our soul-searing protests against the Holocaust? The meta-ethical questions refuse to give us peace: where do our values come from? What still commands human decency and is the criterion of our human worth?

All this intellectual ferment was paralleled by a growing social recognition that modernity, which had heralded personal freedom as the new route to salvation, had betrayed us. Drugs, violence, sexual license, and family abuses may have been some of the more dramatic symptoms of our social malaise, but the growing gap between the rich and the not-rich, the self-centeredness that made marriage hazardous and family and social life precarious, the meaninglessness and depression that strangely accompanied our extraordinary economic well-being all put the lie to the messianic promise of modernity. This crisis in values was the spiritual root of the resurgence of religious fundamentalism all over Western civilization. Suddenly it seemed that only the religious right of the Abrahamic faiths offered the commanding standards and reinforcing community that modernity now more and more seemed unable to mandate and socially exemplify. Among Jews, this impulse gave new and unanticipated vitality to Orthodoxy, most strikingly in the particular appeal of those of its sub-groups who gloried in refusing to accommodate to modernity.

However, anomaly piled atop anomaly because the various fundamentalisms, despite their great appeal, were able to achieve only a limited acceptance, more in politically tinged Moslem cultures, less in Christian societies, and even less in the Jewish community. Most Westerners seem to agree that, for all modernity's faults, it has given us one lasting insight into reality, namely, that personal human dignity largely means being entitled to substantially make up one's own mind about what one will believe and do. To put it theologically, we see our "autonomy" as a most precious gift of God's, even though we have learned from the chastisements of modernity that we must radically rework the ego-centric understanding which Kant and other Enlighteners gave that term.

Pondering our persistent ethical commitment despite its loss of intellectual and social grounds, I finally realized that we had been looking at the alleged death of God in upside-down fashion. Its solution required that we turn Feuerbach on his head. His famous nineteenth-century dictum about God had grandly opined that all our statements about God are really statements about humankind and how we view ourselves. In an era when Western humanity was exhilarated by the prospect of its apparently limitless capacities, he as good as put humankind in God's place. But, now, in the sobering reappraisal of human nature required by the Holocaust, to assert that God was dead really meant that what had really died for us in the Holocaust was not Judaism's God but our exalted modern view of ourselves and our capabilities. We have been forced to acknowledge that we are not as smart or as good as we thought we were or, at least, could become. Worst of all, our confident proclamation that we alone would bring the Messianic Age is ludicrous for people who still cannot get their lives, their families, and certainly any of their great institutions to any near-ideal level. The late twentieth century has indeed been a time of the loss of the faith we moderns passionately espoused, of ourselves as the only god worth following. That was disturbing indeed and such a blow to our egos that we hid our psychic turmoil behind the soothing modern notion of the death of God. Now that our overblown human self-idolization has died, it has made possible a healing human *tzimtzum,* a self-contraction that has made some room for God in our lives. I believe we come to God these days primarily as the ground of our values and, in a non-Orthodox but nonetheless compelling fashion, as the "commander" of our way of life.

Something similar could now also be said of the value of Jewish tradition and practice to us. Once we realized we were not always smarter than our forebears, once we admitted that our individuality had its limits and our community might yet have much to teach us, particularly how to judge that which should be rejected or fought in our society, Jewishness took on a new value to many Jews. And with a real God involved not only with us as persons but with our people—as well as, from a Jewish point of view, with all other peoples—the concept of Covenant, of having a personal and folk relationship with God, as against merely a concept of God, became deeply appealing.

By the end of the seventies this growing torrent of ideas and assertions now cried out for systematic statement and, providentially, it seemed to me, I found a new cultural language, postmodernism, which permitted me to give this new theology a properly nuanced yet fully systematic statement.

SPEAKING OF JUDAISM IN THE ACCENTS OF POSTMODERNISM

If my biographical comments have become fewer as this paper has approached the present, it is because, as I see it, the impelling events which pushed me in certain directions now mostly lie behind me. Yes, children have grown and left our home and area (but not our circle of living love). Grandchildren have appeared to let us see the cycle of Jewish continuity play itself out. We are clearly older, less vigorous, more threatened by those depredations of age that have taken many friends from us. We now live in a senior life-care community where we find the limited responsibilities of managing and operating a household quite liberating. Estelle has retired from her practice while I remain full-time at my teaching and writing, both of which continue to give me great joy. And while my energies at seventy-five are not what they once were, I am still poised to do new projects while fending off other appealing ideas. Yet none of this has, in any way that I can detect, significantly influenced or deflected the line of thought that I enunciated early in the 1990s and have further developed over this decade. I must leave it to whatever historian may one day glance in my direction to say more than that.

As my Jewish religious sensibilities began to come together in the late seventies and early eighties, I could not help hearing about a complex of ideas and attitudes associated with the name of Jacques Derrida. Philosophical deconstruction quickly made a certain sense to me as its anti-foundationalism seemed a deeper level of my own judgment that reason had to be a secondary instrument of the search for wisdom and not its prime generator and developer. I also appreciated the postmodern emphasis on thinkers being self-conscious about their particularity, a view which jibed well with my own sense of the non-universal truth of Judaism. When I added to these factors the postmodern tolerance of various styles of self-expression, I became persuaded that this cultural style could provide a cogent manner of discourse with which to speak of Jewish belief today.

As with existentialism years before, I soon realized that I could not accept this new intellectuality in its common guise but only in one of its peripheral forms. The advocates of postmodernism are post-foundationalist, that is, they deny that thinking properly begins from certain rational premises which then structure the inferences that follow. Deconstructionalism further points out that classical cognition is a contradiction in terms, for words refuse to mean just one thing in an argument, and thought regularly doubles back on itself in self-denial. But Derrida and his followers do not exempt ethics and the realm of values from this deconstruction; thus, they deny the possibility of a thinking stability to moral judgments. In practice, these postmoderns, with Derrida himself the chief example, do not hesitate to make ethical pronouncements, often doing so with considerable passion. But it is certainly not clear, despite some intriguing attempts, how one could arrive at a postmodern, Derridean ethics which is more than purely personal preference. Surely our revulsion at Nazi bestiality and the countless other ethically revolting acts which have made up so much of recent history arises from a more fundamental basis than whim. For this and other such reasons, I, like a number of other writers, think of myself as a non-Derridean postmodern.

This claim to be part of the family of postmoderns but not of Derridean derivation has drawn the academic criticism that a refusal to stand in the line of Derridean thought denies one the right to call oneself a postmodern. That is an odd charge indeed for a community that claims to be non-foundational.

There is much in the postmodern stance, however, which makes it a congenial language for speaking about religious faith. It easily countenances a pattern of thought which mixes certainty and uncertainty. It knows that certain kinds of assertions must always remain fuzzy while others can be made relatively clear. It tolerates a balance between that which is relatively fixed in the thought and that which remains open to fresh imagination or insight. It can live with a mix of risk and security in a given pattern of thought. However, what mostly makes it appeal to me is its radical insistence that particularity precedes universality. No one can think in complete transcendence of time, place, class, race, folk, culture, body, and, most tellingly, as the feminist thinkers have taught us, gender. Yet we once considered it a major breach of academic etiquette for writers to use the word "I" in a formal academic paper as if no biography lurked behind what they advocated. Today, postmodernism bestows a new dignity on particularity, allowing us, on the social level, to assert that our folk, Israel, is nearly as significant in our Judaism as is the one God.

Ten plus years have passed since I began to give these thoughts systematic statement in *Renewing the Covenant: A Theology for the Postmodern Jew.* As I labored over that book, I was continually surprised that my articulating one aspect of my thought required me to think about and set down aspects of it that I had not consciously worked on before. Whole chapters forced themselves upon me as I sought to fill out the case I was making for viewing Judaism in just this way. When I had finished the book I was grateful for what the laboring had made possible, a newly mature stage to my thinking. Since then, it has occasionally struck me, as I have read this work with my students, that it often has a richer, truer theological diction than I have ever reached before.

After the book appeared, I had some fleeting anxiety that, having so fully explicated my postmodern vision of Judaism, my theological stream had run dry. The near decade since that time has happily proved me wrong. My systematic statement has, in fact, turned into a platform rather than a ceiling. Again and again it has empowered me to go deeper into what I did discuss there or delve into areas to which I had not previously turned my attention. Much of this recent development is on display in my book of earlier this year, *Judaism after Modernity: Papers from a Decade of Fruition.*[26] In particular, that volume indicates how much I have learned from responding to my critics. A good example of this process, now based on a more formal, academic critique of *Renewing the Covenant* by a broad range of colleagues, will appear in a volume, neatly entitled *Reviewing the Covenant.* My interest in Jewish ethics has also not abated, and, working with a lay student of mine, Frances Weinman Schwartz, I was also able to publish this year our effort at creating a contemporary style of *musar* literature in a work on *The Jewish Moral Virtues.* It makes a new/old case for twenty-four ethical *midot* which our sages and folk wisdom have classically commended to us.[27]

I remain, then, a work in progress and I have been honored indeed to give you this account of my thought and life thus far.

NOTES

1. I shall not generally cite those of my writings which illustrate the developments I shall be tracing. Fortunately, in celebration of my seventy-fifth birthday, Amy Helfman, Associate Librarian of the Klau HUC-JIR Library in New York, was kind enough to do a bibliography of my writing over the years. Her paper is entitled "A Life in Covenant: The Complete Works of Eugene B. Borowitz, 1944–1999." It is a fine commentary to this lecture and is available on line at www.huc.edu under my name in the faculty section. Some hard copies of her work are available by sending a self-addressed envelope to The Samek Institute, HUC-JIR, 1 W. 4th Street, Room 518, New York, NY 10012–1186.

2. While this most probably took place in spring 1942, it was not until 1957 that one of my publications gives evidence of this transition. My paper to the Central Conference of American Rabbis entitled, as per their invitation, "The Idea of God," is framed in the classic terms of the rationalistic Judaism which had always been the intellectual backbone of Reform Judaism. In my paper, however, I, without realizing how revolutionary the act was, turned what was a general, philosophic inquiry—a proper concept of Divinity—into a particularistic, existential question—how will we recognize a Jewish idea of God when we encounter one?—giving Kaplan and Buber as my two, partially overlapping, partially disagreeing, examples. "The Idea of God," *CCAR Yearbook* 67 (1957): 174–186. Note how much of this topic is taken up in what follows in the Schneider Lecture [reprinted here as paper 3].

3. For an early statement of my emerging holistic view, one more notable for what it accepts and what it rejects rather than for how one gets from the negative to the positive stage, see "On Celebrating Sinai," *CCAR Journal* 13, no. 6 (June 1966), pp. 12–23 [reprinted here as paper 9].

4. He summarizes this ongoing repetition of this theme, democracy as the new national religiosity, at the end of the book. *The Future of the American Jew* (New York: The Macmillan Co., 1948), pp. 518–522.

5. Ibid., pp. 437, the last two words, and 438. The preceding two pages set the context.

6. This becomes a significant theme in my argument in *Renewing the Covenant.* Norbert Samuelson seeks to save a place for philosophizing about modern Judaism by arguing that there are rationalisms today which are hospitable to God. But he cannot then make a case that they, based as they are on universalism, can validate a rich Jewish particularism. His critique of my thought and my response to him (and my other critics) appears in *Reviewing the Covenant* (Albany: SUNY Press, 2000). [My response to his suggestion is found in my paper in that volume, reprinted here as paper 25.]

7. *CCAR Journal,* 8, no. 1 (April, 1960), pp. 27–33.

8. Aharon Lichtenstein, a major figure in contemporary Orthodoxy, wrote a widely read article on "Does Jewish Tradition Recognize an Ethic Independent of Halakha?" and argued that, while it does not recognize such an outside source of duty, it has an internal thrust in a somewhat similar legal direction. His careful reasoning, however, culminates in assigning most of the ethical teaching to the *aggadah,* which, of course, does not have the compelling authority of the *halakhah.* See my article, "The Authority of the Ethical Impulse in *Halakhah,*" in *Through the Sound of Many Voices,* ed. Jonathan Plant (Toronto: Lester & Orpen Dennys, 1982). It is reprinted in my *Exploring Jewish Ethics* (Detroit: Wayne State University Press, 1990) as "On the Ethical Moment in *Halakhah,*" paper no. 15 [and here also as paper 15].

9. On one level, this is the nub of the entire argument of *Renewing the Covenant* and its climactic chapter 20.

10. *Commentary,* 33 (August 1962), pp. 138–44. The correspondence appeared about two months later.

11. Ever since I encountered Wittgenstein's notion of "language games" some forty years ago, I have wondered how one might describe the language game in which the rabbis allowed themselves to speak directly of Jewish belief, the *aggadah.* On and off since then, I have read and done research on that ever-expanding topic. I now have some hope of bringing that long-enduring investigation to a written conclusion. I have been wrong about this several times before, though, I believe,

I have good reason now for my optimism. For a previous reference to this aspect of my work and its relation to my theological statement there, see *Renewing the Covenant,* pp. x–xi.

12. *A Layman's Introduction to Religious Existentialism* (Philadelphia: Westminster Press, 1965).

13. *Moses* (Oxford, UK: East and West Library, 1946).

14. *Tales of the Hasidim: The Early Masters* (New York: Schocken Books, 1947), *Tales of the Hasidim: The Later Masters* (New York: Schocken Books, 1948), *Israel and the World: Essays in a Time of Crisis* (New York: Schocken Books, 1948).

15. *Renewing the Covenant* (Philadelphia: Jewish Publication Society, 1991), p. xii.

16. *Between Man and Man* (New York: The Macmillan Company, 1948), pp. 40–82.

17. *Renewing the Covenant,* chapter 4.

18. In the summer of 1946, 1 recall having to interrupt my budding relationship with Estelle to spend two weeks teaching Judaism at a Methodist summer encampment (an experience which had quite an influence on my work two years later establishing the Leadership Training Institutes of the National Federation of Temple Youth). So too much of my first book, *A Layman's Introduction to Religious Existentialism,* was devoted to Christian thinkers. For some of my recent work in this area, see papers nos. 33–40 in *Exploring Jewish Ethics* (Detroit: Wayne University Press, 1990). Note there the expansion of my involvement to include an exchange with one of the foremost Western teachers of Zen Buddhism, Masao Abe [reprinted here as paper 23], and my reflections in paper no. 40 on the problems and value of such interfaith discussions.

19. As the Helfman bibliography bears out, hardly a year went by in the decade from 1956 on that I did not have a publication dealing with education. In the same period, I was, from 1957–62 the Editor of the Union's quarterly education journal, *The Jewish Teacher.*

20. I discuss my consciousness of this connection of theology and practice in the preface to *Renewing the Covenant,* p. xi and its context.

21. *Choosing a Sex Ethic* (New York: Schocken Books, 1969); *The Jewish Moral Virtues* (Philadelphia: Jewish Publication Society, 1999). Most of my ethical papers in the intervening years are gathered in *Exploring Jewish Ethics* (Detroit: Wayne State University Press, 1990).

22. See the detailed, comprehensive volume by Lawrence Silberstein, *The Post-Zionism Debates* (New York: Routledge, 1999).

23. Eisen, Arnold, *Rethinking Modern Judaism* (Chicago: University of Chicago Press, 1998), particularly the summary pages, 246–263.

24. Dorff' s original article, "Autonomy vs. Community: The Ongoing Reform/Conservative Difference," appeared in *Conservative Judaism,* Vol. XLVIII, No. 2 (Winter 1966). My rejoinder, "The Reform Judaism of Renewing the Covenant," and his response, "Matters of Degree and Kind," appeared in *Conservative Judaism,* Vol. L, No. 1, (Fall 1997). Both issues were quite late and the dates on them substantially precede the actual publication.

25. "Toward a Liberal Theory of Halakha," *Tikkun,* Vol. 10, No. 4, and see particularly pp. 44ff.

26. *Judaism after Modernity: Papers from a Decade of Fruition* (Lanham, MD: University Press of America, 1999).

27. *The Jewish Moral Virtues* (Philadelphia: The Jewish Publication Society, 1999).

27 / *"Halakhah"* in Reform Jewish Usage: Historic Background and Current Discourse

2002

Reform Judaism equally espouses freedom and tradition. In recent decades, as freedom has appeared to overstep its proper bounds, Reform Jews have increasingly used the term *"halakhah,"* Jewish law, in their efforts to redress the balance between their movement's central affirmations.[1] This effort has been complicated, I believe, by a failure to distinguish between the four major shades of meaning given the term. Since these clearly reflect the history that produced them, they will be better understood after a survey of the relevant Reform Jewish past.

I

The clash of beliefs over *halakhah* in its traditional sense of religious law was motivated and shaped by the Emancipation. Jewish laymen became convinced that their rabbinic leadership would resist accommodating the established, ghettoized, pre-Emancipation patterns of Jewish observance to their happy new social situation. Empowered by modernity's emphasis on human initiative, they boldly struck out on their own, believing that seeking fresh ways to worship and serve God could not be inimical to true Jewish belief. Ever since those days of pious radicalism, a commitment to freedom has been central to Reform Judaism. Despite the many divergent views of what the right to change properly meant, there was frank acknowledgment that this new affirmation of freedom in Judaism yoked two contrary impulses. Reform Judaism may glory in the enfranchisement of the self but it remains only adjectivally Reform; it is nominatively Judaism,[2] and that means a religious tradition that is fundamentally an inherited (or, in the minority case, adopted), historical, corporate practice of faithfulness to God. This tension between freedom and tradition has given us our 200-year history of non-Orthodox anxiety—and not in Reform Judaism alone[3]—over what constitutes an authentic modern Jewishness.

This tension cannot easily be mitigated since Jews from biblical times on have believed that law—*mitzvah, halakhah*—is central to their pact with God. But with the advent of the Emancipation, most Jews who modernized, worldwide, largely abandoned the practice of Jewish law as law, and denied its authority over them as Jews. Those who were committed to some kind of Jewish continuity asserted that some of its old observances were ethically mandated or emotionally rewarding or socially valuable. But once they had embraced an instrumental attitude toward the law, its particulars no longer carried the sense of necessity or urgency that gives "the law" its uniqueness. They no longer felt "bound" to follow the tradition's spiritual strategy of binding freedom by law. Nonetheless, when they found it desirable to do so, they would, in their own way, follow one or another of its precepts. As the generations passed, the leaders of this modernizing Jewry have been continually pained by their people's continual abuse of freedom, their making it an excuse to do less and less, thereby creating what is often called *hefkerut,* anarchy.

The working out of the Reform Jewish version of this non-Orthodox dilemma is most helpfully seen from that moment in 1889 when Isaac Mayer Wise founded the Central Conference of Americans Rabbis (the CCAR). One spur to that effort was the radical declaration about modern Judaism issued in 1885 by a private group of Reform rabbis meeting in Pittsburgh. Wise, in his first presidential address to the CCAR, made his intentions for the group unmistakably clear, and his remarks will serve as the standard by which we may judge the century-plus progress of Reform Judaism toward it.

> The united Rabbis of America [the Central Conference of American Rabbis] have undoubtedly the right—also according to Talmudical teachings—to declare and decide, anyhow for our country, with its peculiar circumstances, unforeseen anywhere, which of our religious forms, institutions, observances, usages, customs, ordinances and prescriptions are still living factors in our religious, ethical and intellectual life, and which are so no longer and ought to be replaced by more adequate means to give expression to the spirit of Judaism and to reveal its character of universal religion. It is undoubtedly

> the duty and right of the united rabbis to protect Judaism against stagnation and each individual rabbi against the attacks frequently made upon every one who proposes any reform measure. Let the attack be made hereafter on the Conference and let the honor of the individual be preserved intact. *All reforms ought to go into practice on the authority of the Conference, not only to protect the individual rabbi, but to protect Judaism against presumptuous innovations and the precipitations of rash and inconsiderate men. The Conference is the lawful authority in all matters of form.*[4] (Emphasis added.)

Wise's resolution of the freedom paradox may be characterized as "administrative," to have the body of rabbis as a whole take the responsibility of deciding what should and shouldn't be done. Collective action would lend those decisions special authority and perhaps historical weight. Then, should various individuals lead their congregations in a radically uncommon direction, people would recognize this as sheer idiosyncrasy. Moreover, any rabbi following a Conference norm who was attacked by his laity would be shielded by the power of a collective rabbinic decision (a realistic hope even today).

This strategy of Isaac Mayer Wise worked fairly well for about a decade. During those years, the Conference reached agreement on a number of pressing practical matters, most notably publishing a prayer book for modern synagogue services and another volume to provide contemporary music for them. Joseph Silverman, in his President's Message to the Conference in 1903, lists fifteen other accomplishments of the Conference he deemed significant and concluded his list with an open-ended "etc."[5] But this appearance of a growing consensus of practice and opinion is deceptive. Already in the previous year, he had called for "a Synod or a Sanhedrin" which might make it possible for the Conference "to be that central body . . . to give a decisive interpretation of Jewish law and practice."[6] Obviously it did not, in fact, have the authority Wise had hoped it would muster.

Whatever hope there might have been that the Conference could serve as a "lawful authority" came to an end as a result of the controversy over "the Sabbath question," as it was called. From 1902 until 1904 (with echoes in 1905) the rabbis debated what practice Reform congregations should make the focus of their Sabbath observance. Some defended the traditional Saturday morning observance, others the Friday night service (which Wise had originated) and, most contentious of all, others, in keeping with American custom, advocated a Sunday morning service. The rabbis were so deeply divided on this issue that, to preserve the

Conference and all the good it could do short of seeking to become a legislative body, it seemed prudent to stop trying to rule corporately on issues of observance. Rabbi Moses Gries pithily summed up the situation during a 1903 discussion, "You have declared that we have no legislative authority," and in this comment he was only echoing what numbers of colleagues had already said in their own way.[7] What the members in those years called "individualism" so permeated the Conference that above the major papers printed in the Year Books from 1903 to 1906 is a notice in small type, "The writer alone is responsible for views expressed in this article."[8] Note the irony: the Conference having been founded to protect individuals from attack now sought corporate protection from the views of its members.

One positive result of this controversy was the founding of the CCAR Responsa Committee. This instrumentality remained relatively inactive until after World War II. It will, however, be useful in understanding the changes that came into the Reform ethos later if we clarify how Reform rabbis tended generally to approach the issue of Jewish duty in this pre-World War II period.

In the latter part of the nineteenth century and well into the mid–twentieth century Reform rabbis thought of themselves as protagonists of Prophetic Judaism. Their understanding of this perspective awaits appropriate historical study but something still can usefully be said about how this view affected rabbinic (and thoughtful lay) decision-making. In those days, liberal scholars and rabbis read the prophets as valuing ethics over ritual and reaching for a universal horizon of responsibility rather than a particular one. It was argued that this biblical teaching—which more recent scholars have seen as Kantian eisegesis—had understandably become covert during the many centuries in which Jews lived in cultures that held them in contempt. Now that Jews lived in societies in which their equality appeared increasingly to be a reality, the ethical universalism of the prophets could be discerned and proclaimed—an agenda that, not coincidentally, coincided nicely with the social goals of post-Emancipation Jewry. In brief, the Kantian Moral Law now replaced the classic Jewish Oral Law.

This altered sense of compelling duty carried with it a new system for validating action and not merely a different body of texts to cite. Its adherents saw the prophets, even those who wrote no texts, such as Nathan and Elijah, or even Abraham, confronting God about Sodom and Gommorah, as providing a model of personalized Jewish religious decision-making. As Jeremiah puts it, "I said, 'I will not mention Him, I will not speak His name again'—but in my heart there was a raging fire, one shut up in my bones. I could not hold it in, I was helpless" (Jer. 20.9). Inner conviction forced the prophets to criticize their society for its faults and to call their miscreant people to a more Godly way of life. To a generation in transition this sounded very much like what modernity proclaimed to be the compelling power of reason, a universal human capacity in which ethical duty became a categorical imperative. Simply put, Prophetic Judaism enfranchised the enlightened conscience. Today, in our vulgar privatistic mood with its cynicism about rationalistic ethics, this appeal to personal inner guidance seems dangerously permissive. Prior modern generations, however, lived in a Germany or an America whose ethos adulated rationality and reinforced it with a rather rigid social decorum.[9]

With the rationally informed conscience the basis of Reform Jewish practice, it is no wonder that the CCAR Responsa Committee, its one remnant of classic Jewish decision-making, was relatively inactive until past mid-century. To be sure, from its inception in 1906 this body has had a most uncommon parliamentary status, one apparently befitting the largely negative Reform Jewish attitude to heteronomous rules. The Committee is a formal instrumentality of the CCAR, and its responsa identify themselves as such. Reports of its committee business are published in the Conference's Yearbook and often one or two of its responsa in the preceding year. However, none of its responsa are official statements of the Conference corporately. Rather each is understood to be the opinion of, and carries the authority only of, the person who signed it, though the person who authored (or, more recently, the committee as a whole which voted to accept it) does so as someone designated for that task by the Conference.[10]

By 1929 an interest in ritual and religious practice had so manifested itself among Reform Jews that the Conference passed a resolution looking toward the establishment with the Union of American Hebrew Congregations of a joint Committee on Ceremonies. Once established, it put forward various initiatives with regard to observance.[11] After World War II, although some rabbis published their individual guides to Reform Jewish practice,[12] the movement as a whole resisted efforts initiated within the Union to create some sort of corporate guide to religious observance.[13] In the Conference, however, the Responsa Committee gradually began to give some leadership in this area.[14]

This transition is intimately connected with the person and prestige of Solomon B. Freehof. His love of rabbinic literature had led him to become a professor at the Hebrew Union College and only later a congregational rabbi. In 1944, when he was not yet on the CCAR Responsa Committee, he published the first of two small volumes entitled *Reform Jewish Practice and Its Rabbinic Background* (Cincinnati: HUC Press, 1944). The second appeared in 1952. His method in this volume was entirely descriptive which befitted the purpose he gave for doing this work.

> It has been the consistent attitude of Reform that practices should be modified to meet the needs of the times . . . Therefore many new practices develop constantly. Often they are a modification of some older Jewish practice which had hitherto been entirely neglected and which now it is felt can be reconstructed and serve to instruct and inspire. It is, therefore, of interest to Reform Jews to learn more of the vast treasury of Jewish practice in the past so that from it material for new observances may be derived . . . In this way Reform Jews may see their observances against the background of tradition.[15]

This volume and its successor helped broaden the Reform openness to halakhic literature.

Freehof was appointed a member of the CCAR Responsa Committee only in 1947 and became its chairman in 1955, moving on now from description to guidance.[16] His interest in responding to questions of practice came at a time when American Jewry was increasingly interested in Jewish authenticity. This combination helped turn an ineffectual CCAR instrumentality into an increasingly significant source of Reform Jewish teaching about practice. Freehof brought two other highly valued characteristics to his leadership in this area. First, he made it quite clear that he had no desire to introduce a sense of mandated direction to Reform Jews. As he famously put it in the introduction to his first volume of responsa (as CCAR Responsa Committee Chairman), "the law is authoritative enough to influence us, but not so completely as to control us. The rabbinic law is our *guidance not governance*" (emphasis added).[17] Second, in the roughly twenty years that Freehof wrote responsa, his general aim was to supply rabbinic reasons justifying modernization. He expressed it this way in the second volume of his responsa,

> . . . we are inclined for emotional reasons to say "yes" whenever possible . . . Whenever it is impossible to say "yes," the law not permitting it, then we know that the law, if contrary to our modern conscience, will not continue to be observed . . . whatever in the great legal literature can inspire us, what-

> ever can help organize our life, we gladly study, happily accept, and proudly observe.[18]

He was not rigid about this and occasionally insisted upon the law as against current practice, a shift of method which awaits a detailed study of his activity in providing guidance.[19]

Freehof kept publishing responsa until 1980. In the years that followed, a much remarked-upon interest in a deeper Jewish spirituality manifested itself among a significant minority of Reform Jews and with it a desire for a richer pattern of Jewish observance. Not surprisingly, a new tone slowly emerged in the Responsa Committee's decisions. The responsa begin to attend more closely to the demands of the classic *halakhah* so that instead of regularly providing an *asmakhta,* a pretext/proof-text, for contemporary innovation, the decisions occasionally evidenced a certain hesitancy or even negativity toward radical change. Recently, for example, in a matter many members of the Conference felt deeply about, the Responsa Committee, responding to an inquiry, ruled against rabbis conducting same-sex wedding ceremonies, but the Conference plenary later passed a compromise resolution affirming the right of members to exercise their consciences in doing so.

A caveat must be sounded concerning this greater Reform interest in the *halakhah.* No one knows the extent to which Reform rabbis or the Reform laity attach some level of obligation to do what either the CCAR Responsa Committee rules or what the highly occasional resolutions on practice of the Central Conference of American Rabbis commend. Absent any hard data, I think we may safely speculate that the CCAR Responsa Committee, the closest thing Reform Jews have to a halakhic process, remains for them an esteemed source of guidance, no more, albeit a more traditionalistic one than it once was.[20]

II

In recent years, one hears more frequently and, perhaps, with more intensity, a restatement of Isaac Mayer Wise's desire "to protect Judaism against presumptuous innovations and the precipitations of rash and inconsiderate" people, namely, "What Reform Judaism needs is *halakhah.*" The layers of meaning and intention which people impute to this emotionally laden term could perhaps best be clarified by the fieldwork of a team of cultural anthropologists practiced in the art of thick description. In the meantime, useful insight can be gained by an informal taxonomy of the different connotations of the term in Reform Jewish discourse. My schematization discloses four distinct nodes of meaning with the later levels building upon the former ones. Though the edges of these categories are blurry, even this rough catalog should help us understand better why our discussions in this area are often difficult. I have tried to bring some measure of clarity to this analysis by limiting my data to the writings of thoughtful colleagues in this area. I hope I have not exacerbated the communication problem by my simplification of their richly nuanced work in my pursuit of a global sense of this realm of discourse.

When Reform Jews in recent years have said, "What Reform Judaism needs is *halakhah*," they meant, at the first and simplest level, that Reform Judaism cannot be understood or practiced as a biblical religion, a notion that an unreflective sense of Prophetic Judaism might suggest.[21] *Halakhah* used in this way means "rabbinic literature," specifically, that part of it which indicates what Jews ought to do. In thinking about Jewish duty in our time, one needs, at the very least, to understand the writings in which most of our practice was first elaborated and, subsequently, developed. In the early usage of the term this way, one connected with the writings of Solomon B. Freehof, there seems to be little more weight than that placed upon the term.[22] In more recent discussion one quickly picks up the hope that knowledge of the *halakhah* will serve as a check to the "presumptuous innovations and the precipitations of rash and inconsiderate men." At the least, it should give one pause in going against significant concerns of Jewish law, and, at the best, it may serve as a motive for adopting traditional practice. Unfortunately, it is commonplace of all efforts to educate for character that knowledge does not easily translate into will and action.

A second, more substantive level of meaning redefines *halakhah* and, by giving it a new, non-traditional meaning, co-opts the term and its positive Jewish associations for non-Orthodox purposes. Freehof, continuing a century-old strategy of liberal theoreticians, contends his decision-making method is halakhic in that it utilizes a classic halakhic technique for allowing change, namely, that *minhag*, custom, can become law. This permits him to utilize such legal material as can be discovered to justify current Reform Jewish practice.[23]

John Rayner, the intellectual leader and religious guide of Liberal Judaism in Great Britain, reworks the concept in terms of its function, suggesting it is our Jewish term for what we understand God wants us to do (a redefinition echoed in that of Mark Washofsky,[24] who will be discussed below). Since this is clearly what the Reform thinkers are pointing to in their efforts to guide Jewish practice, Rayner believes that simple self-respect demands we recognize this Reform literature as *halakhah*. An unwary reader of Rachel Adler's work may infer from her identification of *halakhah* with praxis that she believes something similar. In common usage, praxis denotes the activities which rightly derive from a given theory as contrasted to its abstract elaboration,[25] but Adler has made clear that her sense of the term has a kinship with its Marxist understanding, a position we shall also discuss below.

Rayner clarifies his own meaning and the distinctive focus of his guidance by first giving us a theological analysis of what it can mean today to "understand what God wants of us." He argues that all we can know with reasonable certainty of God's will for us is our ethical duties, so while our ritual activities serve important instrumental goals, they do not carry the same religious authority as does God's moral law.[26] Moshe Zemer, whose views, too, will be discussed below, similarly identifies the *halakhah* as an ethical activity, arguing that just this quality made the earlier *halakhah* so strongly creative.[27] Students of the history of Jewish law can best evaluate the cogency of this strong claim, one which goes far beyond the usual non-Orthodox assertion that an ethical motif is a significant aspect of the halakhic process.[28]

Before moving on to the third level of usage, two observations appear apt. First, though these theoreticians often speak about halakhic change, they are generally silent about the conserving and disciplinary aspects of the *halakhah*, the mechanisms which, in fact, regularly set the limits for its developmental thrust. This selective vision suggests that they have given us less an academically reliable historical depiction of the halakhic process than an ideological understanding of it, one they share with their fellow-believers. As typically happens, young movements advocating substantial change co-opt the highly charged terms of their less flexible progenitors and reinterpret them so as to validate and valorize their radical activities, in this instance, redefining and claiming the hallowed term *halakhah* so as to defeat a number of its classic concerns.

A second observation reinforces this sense of anomaly. In the 1960s, Gunther Plaut, who advocated a positive Reform posture toward *halakhah*, nonetheless deemed it important to face candidly the terminological problem of this position. Acknowledging that the Reform Jewish use of the term as "practice by consent" deviated from its classic connotation as "practice become law," he proposed that Reform Jews call their version of *halakhah* by a related term, "*halicha*" [his transliteration then].[29] Had this proposal been widely accepted, it would have made clear that when Reform Jews used a Hebrew term to characterize their approach to observance, they did not mean it to convey the sense of required duty customarily associated with the term *halakhah*. Yet, for all its ethical validity, Plaut's suggestion was almost totally ignored.

There is no simple explanation for this recent Reform devotion to the term *halakhah*, albeit after substantial redefinition. In large part, it has come from appreciating how deeply modern Jewish practice, for all the non-observance, remains rooted in the *halakhah*. Some of it also comes from the shift in Reform self-image which places more weight on our being part of *k'lal Yisrael*, the Jewish people entire, and the resulting desire to share in the extraordinary intellectual and spiritual energy the Jewish people has historically invested in the halakhic process. This desire for greater continuity may also be a response to the claim, "There can be no Judaism without *halakhah*" (though this dismisses the thousand-year-plus era of biblical Judaism and the near two hundred years of modern Jewry's refusal to be bound by *halakhah* while nonetheless creating new kinds of Jewish loyalty). It also seems clear to me that this practice comes, if unconsciously, from the perennial desire to counterbalance the Reform emphasis on religious freedom with some measure of obligation. Reform teachers, it seems to me, hope that by calling their guidance about observance "*halakhah*," they will subliminally endow it with an aura of religious urgency.

All of these motives are at work on the third level of use when *halakhah* is taken to mean continuity with the traditional Jewish mode of decision-making, one substantially informed by classic Jewish legal literature, attentive to its precedents, responsive to some of its concerns, and, perhaps, utilizing its classic teaching-form, the responsum. When deliberating about a question of proper practice, proponents of this usage will not be satisfied with reasoning that primarily flows from biblical, midrashic or modern views on the issue, though they may be strongly influenced by them. Rather, they want "texts" that indicate what "the *halakhah*" said on this matter. Where there is dissent from the accepted Jewish legal position, they think it important to clarify why this is so and what halakhic grounds, if any, might undergird the new stance. Advocates of this approach do not pretend that their Reform views ought to be given the authority attached to those of a traditional *posek*, decisor, yet they want it to carry the title "*halakhah*," in their redefinition of its meaning. Nostalgia alone does not, I believe, entirely explain this incongruous passion; one must add to it the unconscious hope that the term will carry with it some small measure of Jewish religious discipline.

As our chief example in this area, let us consider Rachel Adler's creation of a contemporary marriage document. For her, authentic Jewish practice ought to be understood in terms of a construct of modern social theory, "praxis." She defines a praxis as "a holistic embodiment in action at a particular time of the values and commitments inherent to a particular story."[30] The redefinition in place, she then immediately asserts, "Orthodoxy cannot have a monopoly on *halakhah,* because no form of Judaism can endure without one [a praxis]; there would be no way to live it out." Adler has emphasized that she uses the term praxis in the special sense which Marxist theoreticians have attached to it.[31] Though the sources she cites in this regard do not clarify the special connotations she attaches to "praxis," some of its chief characteristics may be surmised. For Adler, a proper praxis shapes our lives in terms of the story-belief we affirm. For the same reason it will be revolutionary and creative, not accepting prior practices or institutions which, as we now read our old tale, we see clashing with it. Yet, because our praxis is a social instrumentality, it will also have a conserving aspect, respecting those aspects of its traditional praxis which still bring the old truth into contemporary lives. And it must be pluralistic, our readings of our grounding myth and our imaginative ways of bringing it into our lives being so diverse.

How then does her vision of praxis inform her transforming the *ketubbah,* the traditional halakhic marriage contract, into a *brit ahuvim,* a lovers' covenant? In revolutionary fashion, she uproots a central instrument of Jewish marital law, a legal realm that most traditional halakhists have defended against change. Yet the *ketubbah* is fundamentally a sexist document and one based on the law for the acquisition of a chattel. A generation that understands the Jewish story to be essentially concerned with justice for everyone and the creation of loving relationships surely demands some radical action be taken. So Adler, with admirable learning and imagination, creates one based on the halakhic instruments for establishing a partnership, thus, incidentally illustrating how, in her sense of praxis, a conservative social tendency operates in dialectic with its radical thrust.

What can we learn from the lengths to which she goes to provide a *halakhah*-based structure for her new marriage document? With *halakhah* now meaning Jewish praxis, the initial answer would be, "because no form of Judaism can endure without one." However, if

North American Reform Judaism has existed in an organized form for over a century and a quarter (the movement being decades older), it must have had a praxis to give it such endurance. That praxis grew from understanding the Jewish story primarily as the emergence of prophetic ethics, and thus yielding a way of life in which ethics became obligation as moral law but rituals were only optional, instrumental resources. (John Rayner's view of *halakhah* has recently shown the continuing vitality of this Jewish vision.) Why then doesn't Adler follow traditional Reform praxis of radically abandoning unethical Jewish laws, in this case, the *ketubbah,* and, if the couple desires a wedding document, create one, with or without a halakhic base, that they will find meaningful? Apparently something in the nature of *halakhah* or her reading of the Jewish story requires her to go beyond revolutionary praxis to create a new wedding document on a substantially halakhic basis but it is not presently clear what that impetus is.

The writings of Moshe Zemer and Mark Washofsky follow a somewhat similar pattern. In Zemer's case, his Reform commitment to the *halakhah* is largely conditioned by the needs of the special community he serves. As an Israeli Reform rabbi, he seeks to demonstrate to Israelis convinced that the halakhic process is inflexible and largely frozen in time, that Jewish religious teaching can speak valuably to their modern ethical sensibilities.[32] He redefines *halakhah* as "ethical in its very essence."[33] He can then indict contemporary Orthodox decisors for their unwillingness to boldly resolve ethical issues in the law. However, applying his special vision of the process, he exploits every opening provided by past and present halakhists to assert a halakhic basis for a liberal position on issues such as the status of women, the treatment of gentiles, and end-of-life decisions.

Zemer does not, however, include in his recent book examples of why his position does not require him to radically change restrictive halakhic rulings on such ethically charged matters such as interfaith marriage, same-sex marriage, and patrilineal Jewish identity. Where the North American Reform rabbinate respectfully accepts collegial performance of the first two practices and has as a body much more fully embraced the third, the Israeli Reform rabbinate has dissented from the stance of the CCAR on these issues. We would have had fuller insight into Zemer's understanding of halakhic reasoning if his book had also indicated what prompts his rejection of positions which many of his North American Reform colleagues believe conscience requires them to accept, though doing so leads to their radically rejecting the classic *halakhah*. The most he has said in this regard is that his work seeks to respond "to a contemporary Jew who feels a bond to the codified *halakhah*" but he has not yet explicated just how strong and motivating he believes that bond to be or why others should adopt it.[34] Nonetheless, reference to such a "bond" indicates that Zemer's extensive halakhic argumentation seeks to give his decisions a certain normative power they would not otherwise have.

Mark Washofsky writes so clearly and cogently on this topic that it will be best to allow him to speak for himself.

> . . . this tradition within which we [Reform Jews] define our Jewishness is a fundamentally halakhic one. It is in the literature of the *halakhah* that the tradition . . . works out its answers to the eternal question: what precisely does God, our Partner in covenant, want us to *do*? . . . If we Reform Jews regard ourselves as students of Torah and our religious practices as part of that tradition, then we, too, must continue to take part in the conversation of *halakhah*, learning and speaking the language in which the tradition creates our practices, gives them shape and bequeaths them to us.[35]

By italicizing the word "do," Washofsky has indicated his intention. His scholarship in the area of Jewish law and his application of it in writing for Reform Jews both in this volume and as Chair of the CCAR Responsa Committee is dedicated to providing substantive guidance on what Reform Jews ought to do.

He is forthright about the three major differences between traditional and Reform halakhic determinations:

> First, and foremost, Reform responsa are not "authoritative": the answers they reach are in no way binding or obligatory . . . a responsum is essentially an argument, a reasoned attempt to justify one particular course of action . . . it seeks to win its point through persuasion . . . [it] is just this sort of argument, directed at a particular audience: Reform Jews committed to listening for the voice of Jewish tradition and to applying its message to the religious issues before them. . . . [second] We see *halakhah* as a discourse, an ongoing conversation through which we arrive at an understanding, however tentative, of what God and Torah require of us . . . [third, for us] Torah, if it is to serve us as a sure source of religious truth, cannot exist in the absence of certain essential moral and ethical commitments . . . gender equality . . . the moral equality of all humankind . . . [and] the possibility and desirability of religious innovation and creativity . . . while our responsa seek to uphold traditional halakhic approaches whenever fitting, we reserve to ourselves the right to decide when they do not fit . . . [and] modify or reject those interpretations in favor of others that better reflect our religious mind and heart.[36]

I do not know of a more persuasive statement of how, in living practice, one can simultaneously affirm the paradoxical Reform Jewish commitment to freedom and tradition.[37] Other Reform Jews, however, find even this dialectical commitment to religious freedom excessive and this produces a fourth sense of the term *halakhah,* one calling for rulings which set limits to religious innovation.

While few of the laity or clergy have been willing to expound this rhetoric in print, we can gauge its tenor by looking at the writings of Walter Jacob, a former Chair of the CCAR Responsa Committee (further identified in note 16). In his earlier stage he followed the irenic path of his mentor, Solomon Freehof. By 1982, however, he expressed a more forceful attitude when addressing a CCAR session discussing rabbinic authority. He said then, "Both the rabbi and the congregation are autonomous, yet in a sense a member, by joining a congregation, signifies acceptance of the authority of the rabbi for guidance and inspiration. The rabbi has also made an implied contract through the ordination he has received and the rabbinic body which he has decided to join. Despite this high degree of individualism, we have surrendered authority in another unique direction to conferences and conventions . . ."[38] Yet in his concluding comments (concerning CCAR responsa) he acknowledged that "all such decisions [by us] seek to provide guidance for the individual, and we hope they will be followed."[39] A year later, in his introduction to a comprehensive collection of CCAR responsa, he reiterated this moderate position, saying, "The authority of the Central Conference of American Rabbis and its Responsa Committee lies in its ability to persuade and reach a consensus." But in the 1987 introduction to a volume of his responsa, the tone shifted. Discussing the changing mood of American Jewry he wrote, "We are no longer satisfied with guidance but seek governance. It is the duty of liberal Jews to perform *mitzvot* on a regular basis as a part of their life." This reversal of Freehof's oft-quoted maxim was particularly striking, coming as it did from his long-time associate and successor. The tone carried over to the conclusion of his presentation. "Responsa are one way in which our rabbinic group, the Central Conference of American Rabbis, has set limits and defined its borders. These limits may have seemed vague a century ago; as responsa have appeared over several generations, they have become clearer."[40] His opinion hardened over the next few years. In a one-page opinion piece in the Fall 1992 *Reform Judaism,* he seven times called for a standard of governance. Indeed, he demanded we choose "between a Reform Judaism that provides *guidance* or one that provides *governance*. . . . Let us...make *mitzvot* and *halachah* a reality in the life of every Reform Jew" (emphasis in the original). This strong stance evoked little or no response, and to the best of my knowledge, this was as far as Jacob took his call for governance. In 1994 another full-scale call for discipline was made to the CCAR. Elyse Goldstein, responding to a paper on issues of Jewish personal status, made the case for Reform Jewish standards.

> I simply do not understand why communities of rabbis like those in Toronto and Boston . . . cannot create and enforce communal standards. In Toronto we not only "encourage" the *mikveh* [ritual bath] and *hatafat dam* [drop of blood drawn from previously circumcised males undergoing conversion] or circumcision—we *require* it—all of us, as a rabbinic body, whether or not we agree with it as individuals . . . to convert to Reform Judaism is to accept a branch of Judaism with standards, religious vision and religious leadership. Let's not disappoint them. It is as simple as that.[41]

Thus far Goldstein's proposal, for all that it is limited to local rabbinic initiatives, has, as far as I know, evoked no positive action.

The bold calls of these writers rarely use the highly charged term *halakhah*, but their euphemisms "governance" and "standards" echo in other people's advocacy of a Reform *halakhah*. But for all the greater feel for Jewish tradition among Reform Jews, there is little evidence that they are yet willing to accept heteronomous rules for living their religious lives. That certainly seemed to be the message of the recent broad-scale uproar among the Reform laity and rabbinate. They were responding to what they perceived as an effort by the 1998 leadership of the CCAR to commit them to a new standard of religious observance in their early drafts of a contemporary statement of the principles of Reform Judaism. Our people seemed to be saying that they will not have their religious self-determination infringed upon even though they are often newly serious about what the Jewish tradition can still say to them.

III

Understanding more precisely what we Reform Jews mean when we use the term *halakhah* is unlikely to substantially advance the quality of our Jewish living. Most people are more shaped by doing and subsequent reflection than by working out a mature theology of duty by which they then seek to live. Thus, we shall properly look to those who are deeply concerned about the advisability of specific acts to help us in our ongoing effort to give Jewish religious depth to our existence. To the extent that they are able to make their teaching "persuasive," as many of them state their goal to be, they will give us a most valuable and needed leadership.

Yet, as they have indicated, they can only hope to persuade those who are open to the voice of the Jewish tradition as read in the light of contemporary Jewish religious experience. Increasing the number of Jews who have that openness is, thus, the corollary task of Reform Jewish leadership, and it is a liturgical-theological one. With God already back in Reform religious experience, the less difficult task is helping our people become increasingly sensitive to what the Presence of God "requires" of them. The more complex, because counter-cultural, challenge is helping people transcend a rigid individualism so enamored of conscience that it belittled peoplehood and tradition. Feminism and much other thinking should by now have taught us that the self is necessarily as social as it is individual. When we can get our adherents to see themselves fundamentally as Jews as well as persons, sharers in their people's historic Covenant with God, we may hope their recontextualized "autonomy" will prompt them to listen to their people's guidance as well as to the individual, still, small voice within.[42] With the caring, doing minority among our people persisting and slowly growing, that is not an unrealistic agenda.[43]

NOTES

1. I am thinking here of the topic's movement from the periphery to something like the center of Reform Jewish discussion. I recall what a sense of surprise greeted me when, at a 1955 Reconstructionist-sponsored rabbinic meeting, I spoke on "Reform's Interest in *Halakhah,*" a speech which shortly thereafter appeared in *The Reconstructionist* 21, no. 20 (February l0, 1956).

2. Dr. Chanan Brichto first called this linguistic distinction to my attention.

3. See, for example, my exchange with Elliot Dorff in the pages of *Conservative Judaism* concerning his review of *Renewing the Covenant*. My response, "The Reform Judaism of Renewing the Covenant," vol. 50, no. 1, Fall 1997, occasioned a rejoinder by him in the same issue which, to my eyes, only indicated the great overlap between the Reform and Conservative views of duty.

4. *Central Conference of American Rabbis, Year Book*, Vol. I, New York: (CCAR Press 5651–1890) reprinting with Vols. II and III, 1958, p. 19. Not by chance is this paragraph introduced by a side-bar identifying these remarks as about "The Importance of the Conference." (These volumes all had the Hebrew date until 1914 and were entitled Yearbook beginning in 1915. There was a sudden reversion in 1953 when the front cover of the volume said "Year Book" though the spine had it as "Yearbook." This anomalous usage continued until 1961.)

5. *CCAR Year Book* 1903–5663, pp. 20f.

6. *CCAR Year Book* 1902–5662, p. 37 in a section of his address entitled "The Scope and Authority of the Conference."

7. *CCAR Year Book* 1903–5663, p. 87. So, too, Rabbi Jacob Voorsanger calls it humiliating that the Conference "can only engage in academical discussions," p. 55, and Rabbi Joseph Silverman says that "The Conference has thus far been only a literary and deliberative body whose influence has only been suggestive and advisory," p. 26f.

8. *CCAR Year Book* 1902–5662. Since 1906 that rule has become so accepted a part of CCAR discourse it does not need to be mentioned. Thus, though I find it superfluous to do so for insiders, lest any outsider misunderstand me, I declare: though I have long taught at its seminary and been active in the intellectual life of the Reform movement, I make no claim that this paper somehow speaks for Reform Judaism or the CCAR. For my views on the disjunction between movement ideology and individual theological formulations, see my response to Elliot Dorff's review of *Renewing the Covenant*, "The Reform Judaism of Renewing the Covenant," op. cit.

9. Thus, in 1948, after my ordination, my wife, Estelle, and I moved to St. Louis where I was to be the assistant rabbi in a large, suburban Reform temple. My graduation from the Hebrew Union College and some interviews demonstrated that I had a proper sense of values. Now we needed to get properly outfitted for services. The senior rabbi had decided to give up wearing a frock coat (a "Prince Albert") in the pulpit, and so I only needed a double-breasted, charcoal gray jacket and gray striped trousers. Estelle learned it was no longer necessary to wear or carry gloves at services, but a proper hat was still expected of women in temple. And this regimen was considered a liberalization of the old, stuffy ways! In such a time, it seemed reasonable to believe that reason reinforced by social constraint could channel human freedom.

10. Another personal experience may help clarify this anomalous status. In 1948, I attended my first meeting of the Central Conference of American Rabbis, held that year in Kansas City. As I remember it, the Responsa Committee chairman had been invited to present a sample of its work at one of the plenary sessions. When he concluded reading a responsum, a member rabbi asked for the floor and began discussing what we had just heard. Almost immediately, a point of order was raised by Rabbi Jonah B. Wise, the son of Isaac Mayer. He said something like, "Mr. President, may I remind you that it is the rule of the Conference that responsa may be read [to the Conference in session] but not discussed." The President concurring, the would-be discussant resumed his seat and the session moved on to other business. I have never been able to find the source of that rule but I retain a vivid memory of that occasion which was my introduction to the uncommon nature of the CCAR Responsa Committee. However, though the 1948 Yearbook does list me and Jonah B. Wise as attending, it has no mention of a Responsa Committee report. There were also none in the prior and succeeding years. In 1950 there was such a report (pp. 107ff.). And it is followed by a vigorous discussion. I assume that was because the report that year was a response to a specific Conference resolution of 1948 asking the Responsa Committee to report back to the Conference on the issue of euthanasia. Only in 1953, with the new chairmanship of Solomon B. Freehof, did an annual report become customary (pp. 123ff.) and but these are not followed by discussion.

11. Several of these key initiatives are discussed in Michael Meyer's *Response to Modernity, a History of the Reform Movement in Judaism*. (New York: Oxford, 1988), pp. 322–25. See also his discussion of the special role of Solomon B. Freehof there.

12. One of the earliest and most discussed was Frederic A. Doppelt and David Polish, *A Guide for Reform Jews* (New York: Bloch Publishing Co., 1957). Others that aroused national attention were Abraham J. Feldman, *A Guide for Reform Jews* (New York: Bloch Publishing Co., 1962) and Stanley R. Brav, *A Guide to Religious Practice* (Cincinnati: The Temple, 1962).

13. *Response to Modernity*, op. cit., p. 376.

14. For a good orientation to what transpired, see *Response to Modernity*, op. cit. pp. 375f.

15. Op. cit., p. 14.

16. Walter Jacob, who was Freehof's associate and successor in the congregation the latter long served (and succeeded him as chairman of the CCAR Responsa Committee) has written about this scholarly aspect of Freehof's life against the background of the history of the CCAR Responsa Committee in "Solomon B. Freehof and the *Halachah*, an Appreciation," in *Solomon B. Freehof: Reform Responsa for our Time*, (Cincinnati: HUC Press, 1977).

17. *Reform Responsa* (Cincinnati: HUC Press, 1960), p. 22.

18. He is comparing the Reform stance to that of the Orthodox decisors who, he says, regularly prefer to say "no." *Recent Reform Responsa* (Cincinnati: HUC Press, 1963), pp. 12f.

19. Such a study is currently the HUC-JIR doctoral project of Rabbi Joan Friedman, whose paper "A Critique of Solomon B. Freehof's Concept of *Minhag* and Reform Jewish Practice," at the 2000 AJS conference provided a foretaste of such a detailed view of his method.

20. Some personal experience in this area may also be relevant. From the mid-1980s, I conducted a seminar for students on Reform Jewish ethics and the *halakhah*. The particular goal of the course was to have students, while working on a specific practical problem of their own choosing,

confront the dialectic of opinion in the classic *halakhah* as well as in the contemporary clash between conservative and liberal ethics to see how these various views affected them when it came to reaching a decision. Fourteen papers produced by the students were deemed worthy of publication and I invited Prof. Louis Newman of Carleton College to introduce the collection. While he was taken with the seriousness and commitment of the student authors, his general impression was that most of them found it difficult to give the *halakhah* the proper weight that he believed even non-Orthodox Jews should ascribe to it. See his essay, "Learning to be Led: Reflections on Reform Judaism and the *Halakhah*," *Reform Jewish Ethics and the Halakhah*, ed. Eugene B. Borowitz (W. Orange, NJ: Behrman House, 1994), pp. xiiiff.

21. So the burden of the opening pages of Freehof's first volume of responsa, *Reform Responsa*, (Cincinnati: HUC Press, 1960), pp. 3f. and see also p. 15.

22. So, for example, in his second volume of responsa, his interpretation of the growing flow of questions to the CCAR Responsa Committee. *Recent Reform Responsa* (Cincinnati: HUC Press, 1963), pp. 7f. He carefully delimits the new interest in halakhic literature in his third volume of responsa, *Current Reform Responsa* (Cincinnati: HUC Press, 1969), pp. 2–7 and note his concluding sentences.

23. Rabbi Joan Friedman's unpublished paper, cited above in note 19, documents his use of the concept *minhag* and faults him for violating the classic Jewish sense of the meaning of the term in his expositions. It seems to me that Freehof is clear that he is not seeking to use the term *minhag* as Jewish tradition did but in a specifically Reform Jewish reading of the history of Jewish law. As he indicates, he does not write for traditionalists and specifically calls his rulings "Reform" responsa. See his earliest work, *Reform Responsa*, op. cit., p. 23. This entire second-level reinterpretation of the term *halakhah* strikes me as a good example of the way in which ideology is regularly a factor in the reading of texts, something like those misreadings which Harold Bloom famously argued have been a prime source of our cultural creativity.

24. He writes, "We do not, however, identify *halakhah* as a set of crystallized rules or as the consensus opinion held among today's Orthodox rabbis. We see *halakhah* as a discourse, an ongoing conversation through which we arrive at an understanding, however tentative, of what God and Torah require of us." Mark Washofsky, *Jewish Living: A Guide to Contemporary Reform Practice* (New York: UAHC, 2001), p. xxiii.

25. *The Cambridge Dictionary of Philosophy*, ed. Robert Audi (New York: Cambridge University Press, 1995), pp. 638f.

26. His book, *Jewish Religious Law: A Progressive Perspective* (New York: Berghahn Books, 1998), contains a number of his recent lectures on this topic and brings them to a rounded statement of his views. It is helpful to keep in mind the eight qualities he believes a comprehensive Reform *halakhah* would evidence, p. 42, particularly when he makes his strong case for Reform study and use of the classic halakhic literature, p. 64. His theological analysis is given in chapters 6, 7 and 8 of this work. His statement on ethics begins this exposition, pp. 54f., but he rejects the exclusively ethical interpretation of Reform duty which some still espouse, p. 56. From this he builds to his own *Via Media*, as he terms it, "Between Antinomianism and Conservatism," the title of chapter 7.

27. He titles his book on Reform Jewish practice *Evolving Halakhah*. Its third chapter gives his theory of *halakhah* and begins, "*Halakhah* as it developed was an evolving ethical system that found ways to cope with the particular conditions of each generation." *Evolving Halakhah* (Woodstock, VT: Jewish Lights Publishing, 1999), p. 37.

28. When my monograph, "A Life of Learning: In Search of a Theology of Judaism,"(New York: Hunter College, 2000) appeared, Zemer wrote me, challenging my assertion on page 10 that the halakhic system is "resolutely a-ethical or unethical." I responded in a letter which I will gladly make available to interested colleagues who will send a stamped, self-addressed envelope to me at HUC-JIR, 1 W. 4 St., NY, NY 10012. A more authoritative treatment of the issue is to be found in David Weiss Halivni, "Can a Religious Law be Immoral?" *Perspectives on Jews and Judaism: Essays in Honor of Wolfe Kelman*, ed. Arthur A. Chiel (New York: Rabbinical Assembly, 1978).

29. "The *Halacha* of Reform," *Contemporary Reform Jewish Thought*, ed. Bernard Martin (New York: CCAR Press, 1968), pp. 88–103.

30. All in italics in the original. *Engendering Judaism* (Philadelphia: Jewish Publication Society, 1998), p. 26.

31. When I presented a highly preliminary version of this paper at the HUC-JIR conference on "The Modern Study of *Halakhah*," March, 2001, Adler, in response, stressed this and directed

me to the footnote in her book where this is explained. There, she presents a somewhat broader view, stating that her usage "has obvious kinships with the Marxian use of the term 'revolutionary praxis' . . . with Christian liberation praxis, . . . and with the reappropriation of Aristotelian *phronesis*, practical wisdom . . ." citing relevant literature for each. *Engendering Judaism*, op. cit., n. 17, p. 225, relative to text on p. 26.

32. See the Introduction to *Evolving Halakhah: A Progressive Approach to Jewish Law* (Woodstock,VT: Jewish Lights Publishing, 1999), pp. 21f.

33. Op. cit., p. xxii. See also chapter three, "The Essence of Evolving *Halakhah*," pp. 37ff. which begins, "*Halakhah* as it developed was an evolving ethical system that found ways to cope with the particular conditions of each generation." The two issues he then raises are not directed to the adequacy of his historical judgment but to current issues in applying his thesis.

34. Op. cit., p. 37. He does however cite approvingly Louis Jacobs's opinion that for the non-Orthodox Jew "The ultimate authority . . . is the historical experience of the people of Israel . . ." Op. cit., p. 44. (Jacobs is one of a number of Conservative Jewish thinkers with whose views on the law Zemer obviously feels great sympathy.) This standard does not help us very much, however, for without further qualification of "experience" we would have to say that Jews since the Emancipation have had the experience of radically denying the binding quality of the *halakhah* and yet, in some identifiable way, remaining Jews.

35. *Jewish Living* (New York: UAHC Press, 2001), p. xxif. This section of the Introduction to the book is entitled, "Reform Judaism and the *Halakhah*."

36. Op. cit., pp. xxii–xxv.

37. If this theoretical stance is to become the living reality of the Reform movement, it depends on enlarging the community of "Reform Jews committed to listening for the voice of Jewish tradition and to applying its message . . ." Fortunately, the shifting ethos of Western civilization in recent decades has brought many Jews to this perspective. I have tried to provide a theological interpretation of this shift and of the theology of Jewish duty which ought to animate it, in my *Renewing the Covenant* (Philadelphia: Jewish Publication Society, 1991), chapters 2 and 3 analyze the social transition, with the remainder of the book devoted, as the Contents pages indicate (vii and viii), to "A Postliberal Theology of Jewish Duty."

38. *CCAR Yearbook*, 1982, Part Two, "Rabbinic Authority." (New York: CCAR Press, 1982), pp. 34f.

39. Op. cit., p. 36.

40. *Contemporary American Reform Responsa* (New York: CCAR Press, 1987), p. xxi.

41. *CCAR Yearbook* (New York: CCAR Press, 1994), p. 71.

42. While my *Renewing the Covenant*, op. cit., is first concerned to establish who/what this God is with whom we stand in relationship, its more uncommon feature is the effort to help the modernized Jew, fixated on the (individualistic) self, recognize how inadequate a picture this is of human beings in general and of Jews, in particular. See chapters 11–13, which lay the foundation for what I call "the Jewish self." This construct then allows me to move on to a theory of the people of Israel's relationship with God, the Covenant, chapters 14–16, and thence to a full theology of contemporary Jewish duty, based on this recontextualization of the self, chapters 17–20. My argument about freedom and tradition reaches a climax on page 294 and is briefly applied to five practical issues in the concluding pages of the book.

43. I am deeply indebted to Rabbi A. Stanley Dreyfus for his meticulous, critical reading of a penultimate draft of this paper and to Shoshana Nyer for her research assistance.

Glossary

Aggada—Narrative or homiletic writings of rabbinic literature, as opposed to *halakhah*, legal texts.

Agunah/Aguno—A woman "chained" either to a husband who is missing or one who refuses to divorce her.

Ahavat Yisrael—"Love of Israel," the Jewish virtue of loving other Jews and the Jewish people as a whole.

Akum—Acronym for gentiles; see also *Goy, Nochri, Umot ha-olam.*

Aliyah—"To go up"; a verb used for moving to and settling in the Land of Israel.

Am—"People," one of the most commonly used biblical and rabbinic terms to describe the Jews as a social group.

Apikorsut—The rabbinic term roughly equivalent to the Christian term "heresy."

Arbaah Turim—Fourteenth-century Jewish law code by Jacob ben Asher reflecting the Ashkenazi, the central and north European, legal tradition.

Avidya—Sanskrit for "ignorance," a term variously used by Hindu and Buddhist teachers to refer to the major impediment to our release from endless reincarnation.

Avodah—"Labor, service," figuratively the term for Jewish prayer services.

Beit Yosef—The title of the great sixteenth-century commentary to the *Arbaah Turim* by Joseph Karo who wrote the final classic Jewish law code, the *Shulchan Arukh.*

Bildung—The German virtue of being a cultured, learned person.

Birchat hashachar—The blessings for a Jew to recite each day when arising.

Birchot hanehenin—The term for those blessings said over various enjoyments.

Brit—"Covenant," the relationship between people and God; it also refers to the circumcision ceremony for Jewish males on the eighth day after birth.

Chanuko/Chanukah—The eight-day December holiday celebrating the Jewish victory over the Syrians early in the second century B.C.E.

Chasidei umot ha-olam—"The righteous among the [gentile] nations" who, Judaism teaches, are assured of a share in the life of the world to come.

Chevrusa—Yiddish term for a person or group with whom one studies.

Chuppah v'kiddushin—"Canopy and sanctification rites," the essence of the Jewish wedding ceremony.

Dat—"Law," the medieval Hebrew term for religion.

Davening—"Praying," the Yiddish term for reciting the Jewish prayer service.

Diaspora—Jewish communities outside the Land of Israel.

Din—"Law," particularly the specifics of Jewish duty.

Dina demalkhuta dina—"The Law of the State is [Torah] Law" for Jews when it relates to general commercial and political affairs.

Epistemological—Philosophic term relating to how we know what we claim to know.

Galut—"Exile," the classic Jewish term for the condition of Jews living off the Land of Israel.

Gaon—"Excellency," the title originally of the head of a talmudic academy in Babylonia, later applied to any great Jewish scholar.

Gehenna—A term derived from a Jerusalem place name, which by rabbinic times had the connotations of "Hell."

Goi/Goy/pl. Goyim—"Nation/s" in Hebrew; later a Yiddish term for gentiles.

Grundmotif—German philosophical term for a premise basic to one's thinking.

Hafetz Hayyim—Title of the early book establishing the scholarly reputation of Israel Meir Hakohen, eminent nineteenth- and twentieth-century East European *halakhic* and moral authority.

Halacha/Halachah/Halakhah—Literally, "the walking," the Hebrew term for Jewish law.

Hasid/pl. Hasidim—Literally "Pious one," but currently used as the term for an adherent of Hasidism.

Hasidut—"Hasidism," the Jewish mystical movement of the early eighteenth century that emphasized joy and community.

Havdalah—"Difference, separation," specifically the ceremony concluding Shabbat with blessings over wine, spices, and the distinctive braided candle.

Havurot—Small face-to-face groups for prayer and study.

Hermeneutics—The study of the theory of interpreting a "text," broadly understood.

Heter—A permissive ruling in a commonly stringent area of Jewish law.

Heteronomy—A source of rules other than one's own reason and conscience.

Hidushim (=Novellae)—Scholarly notes extending previous understandings of the Talmud.

Hillul hashem—"Desecration of the Name," doing or saying something that defames God in any way.

Homontaschen—"Haman's Pockets," Yiddish term for the three-cornered, filled pastry eaten by Ashkenazic Jews in connection with the Purim festival.

Kabbalists/Cabbalists—Jewish mystics devoted to the esoteric teachings developed from the eleventh century to our own time.

Kaddish—Jewish prayer in praise of God, associated now with memorializing one's dead.

Karaite—A follower of the sect developed in the eighth century that rejected rabbinic interpretation in favor of creating a biblically centered Judaism.

Kashrut—The Jewish dietary laws and practice.

Kavannah/Kavvanah—The intention that ideally ought to accompany Jewish observance.

Kelal Yisrael—The Jewish people entire.

Ketuba/Ketubbah—The Jewish marriage contract.

Keva—The fixed and regular in Jewish practice, as contrasted to *Kavannah*.

Kibbutz—An Israeli communal settlement whose members work for and live off of communal property.

Kibud hamet—The respect due to a corpse according to Jewish law and morality.

Kivyachol—"As it were," a term employed by the rabbis to signal that they are about to say something about God, which they do not wish us to take literally.

L'havdil/Lehavdil—A device in Jewish rhetoric to distinguish different states, e. g., the dead and the living.

Lifnim mishurat hadin—"Within the legal limit," a rabbinic phrase used in praise of those who, reaching for a higher standard, do not exercise their full legal rights against others.

Ma'aseh B(V)ereshit—"The Creation Work," one of the two classic domains of Jewish mystical thought, this one centered on the events of the creation of the world.

Ma'aseh Merkavah—"The Chariot Work," one of the two classic domains of Jewish mystical thought, this one centered on Ezekiel's description of God's chariot.

Maasim Tovim—"Good deeds."

Mamzerut/pl. Mamzerim—The Jewish legal equivalent of bastardy.

Matan Torah—"The Giving of Torah," generally, the revelation at Sinai.

Mehitzah—The dividing screen between men and women in a traditional Jewish synagogue.

Meiri—Shortened form of the name of Meir of Rothenberg, eminent legal authority of thirteenth-century Germany.

Meliorism—The ethical approach that accepts gradual progress as the best course of action.

Mellah—The North African Jewish quarter, the equivalent of the European ghetto.

Mentsh—Yiddish term for a truly good person.

Mentshlekhkayt—The quality of living of those who may be called a "*mentsh*."

Mesillat Yesharim—"The Path of the Upright," the eighteenth-century classic of Jewish religio-moral wisdom.

Midot—Literally, "Measures," used in medieval writing as the Hebrew term for "virtues."

Midrash—Homiletic or exegetic interpretation of biblical text.

Minyan—The ten adult male Jews who, in traditional synagogues, make up the quorum needed for full worship.

Mishnah—The legal compendium compiled in Palestine about 200 C.E., discussion of which serves as the basis of the Talmud.

Mishneh Torah—The first of the three classic Jewish law codes, this one compiled by Maimonides in the twelfth century. See also, *Arbaah Turim* and *Shulchan Arukh*.

Mitzvah/Mitzvo/pl. Mitzvot—A "commandment," but also, figuratively, a good deed.

Musaf—"Addition," in the Temple, the extra holy day sacrifices and in the synagogue the special additional prayer section in a Shabbat or festival morning service.

Musar—Pietistic ethical teaching, most notably as a genre of medieval Jewish literature.

Nebbach—Yiddish term connoting "What a pity!" mostly used ironically.

Noachides—The non-Jewish descendants of Noah, i. e., humankind, who, according to Jewish teaching, fulfill their covenant with God by following seven commandments.

Nochri—"Foreigner," a common term for a gentile. See *Akum*.

Novellae—Latin term carried over into English for *Hidushim*, as explained above.

Olam ke-minhago noheg—"The world operates in its fashion," the rabbinic notion akin to natural law.

Orach Hayyim—"The Way of Life," one of the four major sections of the *Arbaah Turim* and the *Shulchan Arukh*.

Ovde avodah zarah—Literally, "those who practice idol worship," in rabbinic literature the legal category for most gentiles. See *Akum*.

Peshat—The simple, straightforward meaning of a phrase or story.

Pharisee—Adherent of the religio-political group of, roughly, the last two centuries B.C.E. and the first century C.E. closely linked to the sages of rabbinic literature. See Sadducee.

Pikuah nefesh—Literally "Saving of a soul," used in halakhic writing to denote the critical importance in Judaism of saving a life.

Piyyutim—"Poems," particularly the poetry written as additions to Jewish liturgy.

Posek/pl. Poskim—Term for someone who renders halakhic decisions.

Pru ur'vu—"Be fruitful and multiply," the first commandment of the Torah.

Purim—The Jewish holiday described in the Book of Esther that celebrates the Jewish victory over Haman and his plot to destroy the Jews of Persia.

Rav—"Master," the title bestowed by teaching masters on worthy, learned disciples.

R'fuo—"Healing."

Rishonim—The sages who were active in the period before the *Shulchan Arukh*.

Rosh Hashono/Hashanah—Literally "the head of the year," name for the Jewish new year.

Sadducee—Adherent of the religio-political group opposed to the Pharisees. It died out in the period after the destruction of the Temple, 70 C.E.

Shacharit—The morning service.

Shavuot—One of the three Jewish pilgrimage holidays, this one celebrating the barley harvest and the time of the giving of the Torah.

Sheheheyanu—The blessing said when doing something for the first time or the first time in at least a year.

Shekhinah—Rabbinic name for God's Indwelling Presence, personified in feminine, nurturing terms.

Shem umalkhut—"Name and Sovereignty," a legal formula for a full blessing.

Shevirah—"Shattering," the second major event in Isaac Luria's sixteenth-century mystic creation myth, the smashing of the vessels originally meant to contain all creation. See also *Tikkun* and *Tzimtzum*.

Sh'liach tzibbur—"Messenger of the community," a cantor or other prayer leader.

Shofar—The ram's horn blown on *Rosh Hashanah*.

Shtetl—The Yiddish term for a primarily Jewish village in Eastern Europe.

Shulchan Aruch/Shulhan Arukh—"The Prepared Table," the third classic medieval Jewish law code, compiled by Joseph Karo in the sixteenth century. It has not been superseded. See also *Mishneh Torah* and *Arbaah Turim*.

Simchat Torah—"The Joy of Torah," the holiday which concludes the fall harvest celebration, *Sukkot*, and greets the conclusion of the synagogue reading of the Torah scroll and its immediate resumption from the beginning.

Sivan—Late spring month in the Jewish calendar in which the *Shavuot* festival occurs, celebrating the barley harvest and the giving of the Torah.

Solipsism—the pattern of thinking in which one is so centered on oneself that it is not clear how other people can be given due regard.

Sukkah—Temporary hut erected during *Sukkot*, the festival of Tabernacles, which celebrates the fall harvest, beginning five days after Yom Kippur, the Day of Atonement.

Talmid Hakham—"Disciple of a Sage," the modest term used for one learned in Torah.

Talmud Torah—"Torah Study," in Judaism God's commandment and a spiritual activity.

Talmud Yerushalmi—"The Jerusalem *Talmud*," brought together about 400 C.E. and of auxiliary authority to the Babylonian Talmud of two centuries or so later.

Tannaim—The generic term for the sages of the period leading up to the Mishnah. Some scholars credit them with creating the form of post-biblical Judaism that, with evolution, remains basic to all Jewish religious life.

Tathata—Term in some versions of Buddhism for the postenlightenment insight that "that's just the way things are."

Tefillin—"Phylacteries," the square leather boxes with straps, one each tied to arm and head, for the morning service, containing the following biblical passages: Exod. 13:1–10, 13:11–16; Deut. 6:4–9, 11:13–21.

Teshuvah/T'shuvah/pl. Teshuvot—"Repentance," the Jewish practice after sinning. More specifically, an "answer," particularly a formal rabbinic legal response to a halakhic inquiry.

Theonomy—The special form of heteronomy in which the other doing the commanding is God.

Tikkun—Literally, "repair." Currently most often used in *tikkun olam*, "repair of the universe," the third term of Isaac Luria's sixteenth-century mystic creation myth, referring to the acts of mystic intention by which Jewish observance restores the broken creation. See also *Shevirah* and *Tzimtzum*.

Tur—Shortened name for the second classic medieval law code, the *Arbaah Turim* or its author.

Tzaddik/pl. Tzaddikim—"A righteous person," generally the ideal for ordinary Jews but used in Hasidism (see *Hasidut*) as a title for the leaders of its subgroups.

Tz'dakah—Charity.

Tzimtzum—"Contraction," the first of the three major events in Isaac Luria's sixteenth-century mystic creation myth, the omnipresent God's contraction to make room for creation.

Tzitziyot/Tzitzit—The "fringes" which, in Num. 15:37–41, male Jews are commanded to have on four-cornered garments.

Umot ha-olam—"Nations of the World," a rabbinic term for gentiles collectively. See also *Akum*.

Vidya—Buddhist term for religious understanding. See its contrary, *Avidya*.

Yahrzeit/Yohrtsayt—Yiddish term for the anniversary of a close relative's death. See also *Kaddish*.

Yidishkayt—Yiddish abstraction for the "Jewishness" of cultural or personal style, particularly in one of its East European modes.
Zekhut—(Religious) "Merit" earned by doing a *mitzvah.*
Zichrono livracha (z"l)—"May their memory be for a blessing," a phrase term said after mentioning the name of someone respected who has died.

Bibliography of the Writings of Eugene B. Borowitz

COMPILED BY AMY W. HELFMAN*

1944

1. Review of *The Stream of Religious Life,* by Dorothy Alofsin, *Hebrew Union College Monthly* (February 1944): 18.
2. "Waldo Frank and the Jew in Our Day," *Hebrew Union College Monthly* (December 1944): 19–20.

1945

3. "In the Beginning," "Records of the Ages," "All Work and No Play," "That for Which We Stand," and "Teachers of Our Teachers," *The Jewish Layman* 20, no. 2: 4–19.
4. "Reform's Bridge to the Future," *Liberal Judaism* 12, no. 12 (April 1945): 20–25.
5. Review of *Germany's Stepchildren,* by Solomon Liptzin, *Hebrew Union College Monthly* (February 1945): 18.
6. Review of *One God, the Ways We Worship Him,* by Florence Mary Fitch, *Hebrew Union College Monthly* (May 1945): 12.
7. Review of *Poems by A. M. Klein, Hebrew Union College Monthly* (May 1945): 12.
8. Review of *The Relevance of the Bible,* by H. H. Rowley, *Hebrew Union College Monthly* (May 1945): 12.

1946

9. "Comment" [weekly column], *Ohio Jewish Chronicle*, 23 August–18 October 1946.
10. Review of *One Destiny*, by Sholem Asch, *Chicago Jewish Forum* 4, no. 3 (Spring 1946): 210–11.
11. Review of *A Partisan Guide to the Jewish Problem*, by Milton Steinberg, *Hebrew Union College Monthly* (January 1946): 16.
12. "Sermon Silhouette [for] Eugene B. Borowitz," *Hebrew Union College Monthly* (January 1946): 14.

1948

13. (In collaboration with Rav A. Soloff and Arnold J. Wolf). *Ring Around a Haman: A Purim Play*. Cincinnati: n.p., 1948.

1949

14. Eretz [pseud.], "The Rabbi Who Assists." *Hebrew Union College Quarterly* 36, no. 2 (June, second quarter 1949): 4–6.
15. "To Publicize the Miracle" [pamphlet], St. Louis, MO: Shaare Emeth Congregation.
16. "Mass Contests As a Chanuko Stimulant." *The Jewish Teacher* 18, no. 1 (November 1949): 1–4.

1950

17. (In collaboration with Rav A. Soloff and Arnold J. Wolf). *Kings or Better: A Purim Play*. Cincinnati: Union of American Hebrew Congregations, 1950.
18. "Theological Conference: Cincinnati, 1950," *Commentary* 19 (June 1950): 567–72.

1952

19. "Mommy, Why Can't I Have a Christmas Tree?" [response], *American Judaism* 2, no. 1 (November 1952): 12.
20. (In collaboration with Arnold J. Wolf). *Postscript to Purim [a play]*. New York: Union of American Hebrew Congregations, 1952.

20a. (In collaboration with Sam Fishman and Irwin Rich), "Annie Get Your Fun," *The Youth Leader*, Vol. XIII, No. 1, Spring 1952.

1956

21. "Creating Commitment in Our Religious Schools," *The Jewish Teacher* 24, no. 3 (March 1956): 7–12. Reprinted in *Judaism and the Jewish School*, edited by Judah Pilch and Meir Ben Horin. New York: Bloch, 1966.

22. "Reform's Interest in Halakhah," *The Reconstructionist* 21, no. 20 (February 10, 1956): 9–13.

22a. "Questions and Answers for Quiz Programmes," (with Bernard Hooker), *The Jewish Youth Group*, John D. Rayner and Henry F. Skirball, eds., London: World Union for Progressive Judaism, 1956.

22b. Review of *The Still Small Voice, The Story of Jewish Ethics, Book One, The Jewish Teacher,* Vol. XXIV, No. 4, May 1956.

1957

23. "The Idea of God," *CCAR Yearbook* 67 (1957): 174–186. Reprinted in *Reform Judaism: A Historical Perspective*, edited by Joseph L. Blau. New York: Ktav, 1973.

23a. Review of *Theodor Herzl, a Portrait for This Age,* ed. Ludwig Lewisohn, *The Jewish Teacher,* Vol. XXV, No. 2, Jan. 1957.

1958

24. "Have You Seen the Messiah?" [editorial], *The Jewish Teacher* 27, no. 1 (November 1958): 2.

25. "The Idea of God," *The Reconstructionist* 24, no. 7 (May 16, 1958): 14–19. Based on the 1957 speech to the CCAR (23), this includes a reply from Mordecai Kaplan.

26. "Reconstructionism in Reform Judaism," *The Reconstructionist* 24, no. 1 (February 21, 1958): 26–28.

27. "Theology and Jewish Education," *Religious Education* 53, no. 5 (September–October 1958): 418–21.

1959

28. "Existentialism's Meaning for Judaism," *Commentary* 28 (November 1959): 414–20.

29. "An Existentialist View of God," *Jewish Heritage* 2, no. 2 (Fall 1959): 5–9.

30. *An Outline of the Curriculum for the Jewish Religious School Recommended by the Commission on Jewish Education*. New York: Union of American Hebrew Congregations, 1959, 1960, 1962.

31. "Teaching the Knowledge of God," *The Jewish Teacher* 27, no. 3 (March 1959): 21–26.

32. "Why Do We Teach?" [editorial], *The Jewish Teacher* 27, no. 3 (March 1959): 2.

1960

33. "Down With Fun-day School" [editorial], *The Jewish Teacher* 29, no. 1 (October 1960): 2.

34. "Toward a Theology of Reform Jewish Practice," *CCAR Journal* 8, no. 1 (April 1960): 27–33.

1961

35. "Crisis Theology and the Jewish Community," *Commentary* 32 (July 1961): 36–42. (Correspondence regarding this article appeared in the November 1961 issue, p. 440–41.) Reprinted in condensed form as "A Theology for Modern Judaism" in *The Jewish Digest,* Feb. 1962.
36. "Hillel's 5th 'Little Book'" [review of *Faith and Reason*, by Samuel H. Bergman], *National Jewish Monthly* 75, no. 10 (June 1961): 24.
37. "A Jewish View of Education." In *Philosophies of Education,* edited by Philip H. Phenix. New York: John Wiley, 1961.
38. "Love." In *D'var Torah*. [New York:] National Federation of Temple Brotherhoods, 1961.
39. "Problems Facing Jewish Educational Philosophy in the Sixties," *American Jewish Yearbook* 62 (1961): 145–163.
40. "The Realities Are Changing!" [editorial], *The Jewish Teacher* 30, no. 1 (October 1961): 2.
41. Review of *Martin Buber: Religious Existentialist,* by Malcom (*sic*) Diamond. *The Jewish Teacher* 30, no. 2 (December 1961): 18.
42. Review of *Religious Education*, edited by Marvin J. Taylor, *The Jewish Teacher* 30, no. 1 (October 1961): 24.
43. "Solving the Theological Problems Involved in Teaching the Bible," *The Jewish Teacher* 29, no. 4 (April 1961): 10–14.
44. "Who Is Israel?" *Jewish Heritage* 4, no. 2 (Fall 1961): 5–10.

1962

45. "A Comment" [response to article by Norman Frimer], *Judaism* 11, no. 2 (Spring 1962): 154–5.
46. "The Editor's Bookshelf," *The Jewish Teacher* 30, no. 3 (February 1962): 18.
46a. Review of *A Faith for Moderns, Robert Gordis, CCAR Journal,* Vol. X, No. 1, issue 37, (April 1962).
47. "The Jewish Need for Theology," *Commentary* 33 (August 1962): 138–44. Reprinted in *Relevants*, edited by Edward Quinn and John Dolan. New York: Free Press, 1970. Reprinted in condensed form as "Folk and Faith," in *The Jewish Digest,* Vol. VIII, No. 3, (March 1963).
48. "Judaic Roots of Modern Education." *Heritage of American Education,* edited by Richard E. Gross. Boston: Allyn and Bacon, 1962. An excerpt from this chapter appeared as "The Decisive Moment in the History of Jewish Education," *The Jewish Teacher* 30, no. 3 (February 1962): 16–17.

1963

49. Ben Hamon [pseud.], "The Reform Rabbis Debate Theology," *Judaism* 12, no. 4 (Fall 1963): 479–486.
50. "Faith and Method in Modern Jewish Theology," *CCAR Yearbook* 73 (1963): 215–228.
51. "Jewish Education Is an Act of Faith," *The Jewish Teacher* 31, no. 4 (April 1963): 21–22.
52. Review of *Evangelical Theology: An Introduction,* by Karl Barth, *The Jewish Teacher* 31, no. 4 (April 1963): 28.
53. Review of *Existentialism and Religious Liberalism,* by John F. Hayward and *The Retreat to Commitment,* by William Warren Bartley, *The Jewish Teacher* 31, no. 4 (April 1963): 28.
54. Review of *The Natural and the Supernatural Jew,* by Arthur A. Cohen, *The Jewish Teacher* 31, no. 4 (April 1963): 31.
55. Review of *The Nature of Man in Theological and Psychological Perspective,* edited by Simon Doniger, *The Jewish Teacher* 31, no. 4 (April 1963): 28.
56. Review of *The Story of Jewish Philosophy,* by Joseph L. Blau, *The Jewish Teacher* 31, no. 4 (April 1963): 30.
57. "Two Modern Approaches to God," *Jewish Heritage* 6, no. 2 (Fall 1963): 10–16.

1964

58. "Creative Worship in the Computer Age," *American Judaism* 14, no. 1 (Fall 1964): 48–49. Published in condensed form as "Judaism and the Computer," *Jewish Digest* 10 (February 1965): 69–71.
59. "Jewish Faith and the Jewish Future." *Great Jewish Ideas,* edited by Abraham E. Millgram. Washington, DC: B'nai Brith, 1964.
60. "Martin Buber under Attack" [precis of a lecture], *Congregation Habonim Bulletin*, May 1964.
61. "On Dealing with Doubt," *The Jewish Teacher* 33, no. 2 (December 1964): 15–18.
62. "Recent Books on Theology, 1963–4," *CCAR Journal* 12, no. 3 (October 1964): 84–85.
63. Review of *Problematic Rebel,* by Maurice S. Friedman, *Conservative Judaism* 18, no. 3 (Summer 1964): 69–71.
64. "Subjectivity and the Halachic Process," *Judaism* 13, no. 2 (Spring 1964): 211–219.
65. "Tension in Reform Judaism," *The Christian Century* 81, no. 23 (June 3, 1964): 729–32.
66. "Theological Issues in the New Torah Translation," *Judaism* 13, no. 3 (Summer 1964): 335–45.
67. "The Trick Is to Keep at It" [excerpts from a speech given at BBYO's 1st Annual Eastern Judaism Institute], *In Review*. Washington, DC: B'nai Brith Youth Organization, 1964.

68. "Unity and Reality in Mordecai Kaplan's View of God," *Jewish Education* 34, no. 2 (Winter, 1964): 96–103.
69. "Why Don't We Pray in Our Synagogues?" *Keeping Posted* 10, no. 5 (December 1964): 5.
70. "Why We Went," *Christian Century* 81, no. 35 (August 26, 1964): 1061–2.

1965

71. *A Layman's Introduction to Religious Existentialism.* Philadelphia: Westminster Press, 1965.
72. "Believing Jews and Jewish Writers," *Judaism* 14, no. 2 (Spring 1965): 172–186.
73. "Bonhoeffer's World Comes of Age," *Judaism* 14, no. 1 (Winter 1965): 81–87.
74. "Individual and Community in Jewish Prayer," *Rediscovering Judaism*, edited by Arnold J. Wolf. Chicago: Quadrangle, 1965. Reprinted in *Gates of Understanding*, edited by Lawrence A. Hoffman. [New York:] Central Conference of American Rabbis and Union of American Hebrew Congregations, 1977.
75. "A Jewish-Catholic Colloquy," *Congress Biweekly* 32, no. 5 (March 1, 1965): 7–8.
76. "Jewish Theology: Milton Steinberg and After," *The Reconstructionist* 31, no. 7 (May 14, 1965): 7–14.
77. "Judaism in Transition" [report on CBC broadcast], *CBC Times* 18, no. 4 (July 24, 1965): 6–7.
78. "The Openness of Catholic Theology," *Judaism* 14, no. 2 (Spring 1965): 212–19.
79. Participant in symposium, "The Quest for Jewish Values—Part II: Questions for Thinking Jews," *Jewish Heritage* 8, no. 1 (Summer 1965): 28–43.
80. "Teilhard de Chardin," *Judaism* 14, no. 3 (Summer 1965): 330–8.

1966

81. "Christkillers No More: Jewish Education and the Second Vatican Council," *Religious Education* 61, no. 5 (October 1966): 344–8.
82. "God-Is-Dead Theology," *Judaism* 15, no. 1 (Winter 1966): 85–94. Reprinted in *The Meaning of the Death of God,* edited by Bernard Murchland. New York: Random House, 1967.
83. "The Legacy of Martin Buber," *Union Seminary Quarterly Review* 22, no. 1 (November 1966): 3–17.
84. "On Celebrating Sinai," *CCAR Journal* 13, no. 6 (June 1966): 12–23.
85. "On the 'Commentary' Symposium: Alternatives in Creating a Jewish Apologetic," *Judaism* 15, no. 4 (Fall 1966): 458–465.
86. "On the New Morality," *Judaism* 15, no. 3 (Summer 1966): 329–336.
87. "Recent Books on Theology, 1964–65," *CCAR Journal* 13, no. 1 (January 1966): 75–80.

88. Response in "The State of Jewish Belief: A Symposium," *Commentary* 42 (August 1966): 80–82.
89. "Toward Jewish Religious Unity: A Symposium" [discussion comments], *Judaism* 15, no. 2 (Spring 1966): 158–59.
90. "The Typological Theology of Rabbi Joseph Baer Soloveitchik," *Judaism* 15, no. 2 (Spring, 1966): 203–10.
91. "Utilizing Programmed Instruction in Teaching the Reading of Hebrew," *The Jewish Teacher* 34, no. 4 (April 1966): 28–30.
91a. Excerpt of "The Synagogue in American Life and Its Future," *Dimensions and Horizons for Jewish Life in America,* Philip Goodman, ed., New York: National Jewish Welfare Board, 1966.
91b. "Responsible Parenthood," Discussant, *The Vatican Council and the World of Today*, Providence: Brown University, 1966.

1967

92. "A Call for Ecumenical Polemics," *Religious Education* 62, no. 2 (March–April 1967): 107–12.
93. *Facing Up to It* [pamphlet]. London: Reform Synagogues of Great Britain, 1967.
94. Introduction to *Essays,* by Henry Slonimsky. Chicago: Quadrangle Books, 1967.
95. "Jewish Values in the Post-Holocaust Future: A Symposium" [discussion comments], *Judaism* 16, no. 3 (Summer 1967): 293–94.
96. "Judaism and Christianity" [excerpt from *Commentary* symposium (88)], *The Sign* 46, no. 11 (June 1967): 42–43.
97. (In collaboration with Walter Wurzberger). *Judaism and the Interfaith Movement*. New York: Synagogue Council of America, n.d. [Papers presented at a conference, February 22, 1967].
98. "Our Teenagers Tomorrow," *Living Judaism* 1, no. 4 (Summer 1967): 104–108. Reprinted with two other lectures in *Facing Up to It*.
99. "Recent Books on Theology 1965–66," *CCAR Journal* 14, no. 3 (June 1967): 71–76.
100. Editor, *The Story of Prophecy* by Hannah Grad Goodman. New York: Behrman House, 1967.

1968

101. *A New Jewish Theology in the Making*. Philadelphia: Westminster Press, 1968.
102. "Autonomy versus Tradition," *CCAR Journal* 15, no. 2 (April 1968): 32–43. Reprinted in *Exploring Jewish Ethics*.
103. "Confronting Secularity." In *The Paradox of Religious Secularity*, edited by Katharine Hargrove, R.S.C.J. Englewood Cliffs, NJ: Prentice-Hall, 1968.
104. "Contemporary Forces and Trends," *JWB Circle* 23:4 (June 1968): 2+.

105. "Hope Jewish and Hope Secular," *Judaism* 17, no. 2 (Spring 1968): 131–47. Reprinted in *The Future As the Presence of Shared Hope*, edited by Maryellen Muckenhirn. New York: Sheed and Ward, 1968. A revised version appeared in *Exploring Jewish Ethics* as "Hope Jewish and Hope Secular, a Response to Jürgen Moltmann."
106. "Judaism and the Secular State," *Journal of Religion* 48, no. 1 (January 1968): 22–34. An expanded version appeared in *Religion and Public Education*, edited by Theodore Sizer. Boston: Houghton Mifflin, 1967. This version was reprinted in *Exploring Jewish Ethics*.
107. "Mashma'uto ha-datit shel tayatron ha-absurd," *Prozdor* 11–12 (Tishri 5768): 120–23. Translated from chapter nine of *A Layman's Introduction to Religious Existentialism*.
108. "Recent Books on Theology," *CCAR Journal* 15, no. 4 (October 1968): 90–98.

1969

109. *Choosing a Sex Ethic*. New York: Schocken, 1969. A two-part excerpt from this book was published as "Choosing a Sex Ethic," *National Jewish Monthly* 84, no. 6 (February 1970): 25–34, and "Speaking Personally," *National Jewish Monthly* 84, no. 7 (March 1970): 58–64.
110. *How Can a Jew Speak of Faith Today?* Philadelphia: Westminster Press, 1969.
111. "Autonomy and Institutions"[three lectures with comments], *Pacific Association of Reform Rabbis, Yearbook* 13 (1969): 37–71.
112. "The Future of Rabbinic Training in America: A Symposium" [response], *Judaism* 18, no. 4 (Fall 1969): 404–405.
113. Panelist, *20 Years Later: The Impact of Israel on American Jewry*. New York: American Histadrut Cultural Exchange Institute, 1969.
114. "Recent Books on Theology," *CCAR Journal* 16, no. 3 (June 1969): 54–60.
115. Review of *Birth Control in Jewish Law*, by David M. Feldman. *National Jewish Monthly* 83 (March 1969): 88–89.
116. Review of *God of Daniel S*, by Alan Miller. *New York Times*, 26 October 1969, sec. 7, p. 73. (Letter from Rabbi Ira Eisenstein in response to this review appeared in *New York Times*, 23 November 1969, sec. 7, p. 46.)
117. Review of *Portnoy's Complaint*, by Philip Roth. *Dimensions* 3, no. 4 (Summer, 1969): 48–50.

1970

118. "Aspects of Jewish Theology." *Image of the Jews*. Washington, DC: Anti-Defamation League, 1970.
119. "At the Beginning," *Sh'ma* 1/1 (November 9, 1970): 5–7.
120. "Jewish Theology Faces the 1970's," *The Annals of the American Academy of Political and Social Science* 387 (January 1970): 22–29. Also published in condensed form as "The 614th Commandment," *Jewish Digest* 16 (January

1971): 23–31. Published in Hebrew as "Machshevet ha-emunah ha-yehudit b'Amerikah b'sof esor v'al saf esor." In *Hagut Ivrit b'Amerikah,* edited by Menahem Zohori, Arieh Tartakower, and Chaim Ormian. Tel Aviv: Brit Ivrit Olamit/Yavneh, 1973.
121. "Marriage, Broadway Style," *Sh'ma,* Trial Issue 2 (June 9, 1970), n.p.
122. "On Refusing to Be Radicalized," *Sh'ma,* Trial Issue 2 (June 9, 1970), n.p.
123. "The Postsecular Situation of Jewish Theology," *Theological Studies* 31, no. 3 (September 1970): 460–475.
124. "The Problem of the Form of a Jewish Theology," *Hebrew Union College Annual* 40-41 (1969–70): 391–408
125. "Restructuring the Rabbinate: An Open Letter to Dr. Theodore I. Lenn," *CCAR Journal* 17, no. 3 (June 1970): 59–64.
126. Review of *Judaism and Christianity*, edited by W. O. E. Osterley, H. M. Loewe, and E. H. Rosenthal. *Religious Education* 65:3 (May 1970): 299–300.
127. "The Year in Judaism," *New York Times,* 15 March 1970, sec. 7, p. 8+. 1971.
128. "Another Man's Calm" [reply to letter from Roland B. Gittelsohn], *Sh'ma* 1/13 (April 30, 1971): 101–102.
129. "The Dialectic of Jewish Particularity," *Journal of Ecumenical Studies* 8, no. 3 (Summer 1971): 560–74.
130. "Education Is Not I-Thou," *Religious Education* 66, no. 5 (September–October 1971): 326–31.
131. "Friendship," "Love, Post-Biblical; Love of God, Man's; Love of Neighbor," and "Theocracy." *Encyclopedia Judaica*. Jerusalem: Keter Publishing House Ltd., 1971.
132. "Have You Read *Commentary* Lately?" *Sh'ma* 1/11 (April 2, 1971): 81–83.
133. "The Living God and the Dying Religious Style," *When Yesterday Becomes Tomorrow*. New York: Congregation Emanu-El of the City of New York, 1971.
134. "Modern Faith versus Jewish Style," *Judaism* 20, no. 3 (Summer 1971): 313–19.
135. "Power and Reality in Conservative Judaism," *Sh'ma* 1/20 (November 19, 1971): 155–59.
136. "Reform Judaism's Coming Power Struggle," *Sh'ma* 1/10 (March 19, 1971): 75–79.
137. Review of *The Star of Redemption*, by Franz Rosenzweig, trans. William Hallo. *New York Times,* 3 October 1971, sec. 7, p. 33.
138. "A Spate of Recent Books on Modern Jewish Thought," *JWB Circle* 26:5 (October 1971), sec. 2, p. 1+.
139. "Technology and Its Problems" in "The Object of Human Invention Is to Make Us Humane," *Think* 37:1 (January 1971): 26.

1972

140. "New Jewish Cultural Horizons," *JWB Circle* 27, no. 3 (April–May 1972): 9+.

141. "Nixon vs. McGovern: What Is Your View?" and "The Electoral Priorities for a Jew," *Sh'ma* 2/36 (September 1, 1972): 121, 122–23.
142. "Politics—the Art of the Impossible," *Worldview* 15, no. 10 (October 1972): 4.

1973

143. *The Mask Jews Wear*. New York: Simon and Schuster, 1973.
144. "Abraham Joshua Heschel, Model," *Sh'ma* 3/46 (January 19, 1973): 41–42.
145. "Covenant Theology—Another Look," *Worldview* 16, no. 3 (March 1973): 21–27.
146. "Emil Fackenheim—Beyond Existentialism?" *Judaica Book News* 3, no. 2 (Spring 1973): 30–31.
147. "Nixon's Budget and the New Jewish Ethics," *Sh'ma* 3/48 (February 16, 1973): 58–59.
148. "On Being a Reform Jew Today," *CCAR Journal* 20, no. 3 (Summer 1973): 55–61.
149. "Our New (Old?) Agenda," *Sh'ma* 4/61 (November 16, 1973): 8.
150. "A Silence Which Gives No Consent," *Sh'ma* 3/56 (September 7, 1973): 121–22.

1974

151. "Abraham Joshua Heschel: An Extremist but Not a Fanatic," *JWB Circle* 29, no. 3 (April–May 1974): 5+.
152. "The Career of Jewish Existentialism," *Jewish Book Annual* 32 (5735/1974–75): 44–49.
153. "Comments [on lecture, "Baeck's and Buber's Social and Political Thought"]." In *Leo Baeck Memorial Conference on Jewish Social Thought*. New York: American Federation of Jews from Central Europe, 1974.
154. "God and Man in Judaism Today: A Reform Perspective," *Judaism* 23, no. 3 (Summer 1974): 298–308.
155. "The Israelis and Us, the New Distance," *Sh'ma* 5/82 (November 29, 1974): 172–5. Published in Hebrew as "Ha-Yisraelim v'anachnu—ha-marchek hechadash," *T'futzot Yisrael* 13, no. 3 (July–September 1975): 37–44.
156. "The New Year and Our Bad Mood," *Sh'ma* 4/77 (September 20, 1974): 129–30.
157. "Religion and America's Moral Crisis," *Worldview* 17, no. 11 (November 1974): 52–56. Reprinted in *Exploring Jewish Ethics*.
158. Review of *A Passion for Truth,* by Abraham Joshua Heschel, *New York Times,* 13 January 1974, sec. 7, p. 22.
159. "Rise of the Modern Marrano" [excerpt from *The Mask Jews Wear*], *Jewish Digest* 19 (January 1974): 14–24.
160. "Tzimtzum—A Mystic Model for Contemporary Leadership," *Religious Education* 69, no. 6 (November–December 1974): 687–700. Reprinted in

Exploring Jewish Ethics. Reprinted in *What We Know about Jewish Education,* edited by Stuart L. Kelman. Los Angeles: Torah Aura, 1992.

1975

161. "After One Hundred Issues," *Sh'ma* 5/100 (October 31, 1975): 319–20.
162. "Arik Brauer's Visions of the Jewish Past," *National Jewish Monthly* 89 (March 1975): 2–7.
163. "The Chosen People Concept As It Affects Life in the Diaspora," *Journal of Ecumenical Studies* 12, no. 4 (Fall 1975): 553–68.
164. "What Knowledge Does Judaism Think It Possesses?" *Biblical Studies in Contemporary Thought*, edited by Miriam Ward. Burlington, VT: Trinity College Bible Institute, 1975.
165. "The Will to Fight—The Will to Live," *Sh'ma* 5/92 (April 18, 1975): 250.

1976

166a. "For Dissent on Israeli Policy—Part 1," *Sh'ma* 6/116 (September 3, 1976): 123–27.
166b. "For Dissent on Israeli Policy—Part 2," *Sh'ma* 6/117 (September 17, 1976): 129–33. Articles were simultaneously published as "Are American Jews Allowed to Dissent on the Policies of Israel Governments?" *Israel Horizons* 24, no. 8 (October 1976): 14–19.
167. "Jews As Closet Agnostics," *Moment* 1, no. 3 (March 1976): 69–70. Also published in condensed form in *Jewish Digest* 22 (October 1976): 14–16.
168. "The Old Woman As Meta-Question: A Religionist's Reflections on Nozick's View of the State," *Journal of the American Academy of Religion* 44, no. 3 (September 1976): 503–15. Reprinted in *Exploring Jewish Ethics* as "Individualistic Ethics: A Dispute with Robert Nozick."
169. "The Prospects for Jewish Denominationalism," *Conservative Judaism* 30, no. 4 (Summer 1976): 64–74. Reprinted in *Exploring Jewish Ethics*.

1977

170. "Anti-Semitism and the Christologies of Barth, Berkouwer and Pannenberg," *Dialog, a Journal of Theology* 16 (Winter 1977): 38–41 [see also: "Retraction about Pannenberg," *Dialog, a Journal of Theology* 16 (Spring 1977): 81.]. Reprinted in *Christianity and Judaism,* edited by Richard W. Rousseau, Scranton, PA: Ridge Row Press, 1983.
171. "A Call for Poor to Act on Conscience," *Sh'ma* 8/143 (December 9, 1977): 200–202.
172. "Facing the Future of Jewish Education," *Jewish Education* 45, no. 2 (Spring 1977): 33–40.
173. "An Introduction to Our Commentary" and "Preface," *CCAR Journal* 24, no. 2 (Spring 1977): 3–5, 13–17.

174. Letter to the Editor, *Lilith* 1, no. 4 (Fall/Winter 1977-78): 3–4.
175. "Liberal Jewish Theology in a Time of Uncertainty," *CCAR Yearbook* 87 (1977): 124–170.
176. "Philip Roth: Coming Home to Moralism," *JWB Circle* (December 1977), sec. 2, p. 1–2.

1978

177. *Reform Judaism Today*. New York: Behrman House, 1977-78.
178. "Buber and His Jewish Critics," *Sh'ma* 8/152 (April 14, 1978), n.p.
179. "Feeding Our Minds, Not Our Bodies?" *Sh'ma* 8/150 (March 17, 1978): 81–82. [Purim issue]
180. "Humanism and Religious Belief in Martin Buber," *Thought* 53, no. 210 (September 1978): 320–28.
181. "Judaism in America Today," *The Christian Century* 95, no. 36 (November 8, 1978): 1066–70. Reprinted as "Judaism Today: Survival and Authenticity" in *Where the Spirit Leads,* edited by Martin Marty. Atlanta: John Knox Press, 1980.
182. "The Lure and Limits of Universalizing Our Faith." *Christian Faith in a Religiously Plural World,* edited by Donald G. Dawe and John B. Carman. Maryknoll: Orbis, 1978.
183. Editor, *A Second Look: An Anthology of Articles by Sh'ma Editors Which Appeared in Other Journals and Which They Would Like to Share with* Sh'ma's *Readers.* Port Washington, NY: Sh'ma [Inc.], 1978.

1979

184. *Understanding Judaism.* [textbook] New York: Union of American Hebrew Congregations, 1979. (Portuguese translation, *Compreendendo O Judaismo*, 1986.)
185. "The Changing Forms of Jewish Spirituality," *America* 140, no. 16 (April 28, 1979): 346–51.
186. "The Liberal Jews in Search of an 'Absolute!'" *Cross Currents* 29, no. 1 (Spring 1979): 9–14.
187. "A New Building, a New Task," *Founders Day Addresses*. Cincinnati: HUC-JIR, 1979.
188. "Quest for Spirituality" [contributor to symposium], *Reform Judaism* 8:3 (December 1979): 6–7.
189. "Theology in Grade Nine" [discussion with students], *Keeping Posted* 25, no. 3: 5–6.
190. (In collaboration with Edya Arzt). *What Judaism Offers: A Teaching Guide on Jewish Spirituality*. Published by the Baltimore Board of Jewish Education in cooperation with the American Association for Jewish Education. Winter 1979.
191. "What We Learned from the 1970s, II" [symposium], *Sh'ma* 10/185 (January 11, 1979): 37–38.

1980

192. *Contemporary Christologies: A Jewish Response*. New York/Ramsey, NJ: Paulist Press, 1980.
193. "Affirming Transcendence: Beyond the Old Liberalism and the New Orthodoxies," *The Reconstructionist* 46, no. 6 (October 1980): 7–17.
194. "After Ten Years," *Sh'ma* 10/200 (October 31, 1980): 158–60.
195. "Beyond Immanence: How Shall Liberal Jews Educate for Spirituality?" *Religious Education* 75, no. 4 (July–August 1980): 387–408.
196. Discussant of paper, "A Strategy for Judging the Adequacy of Business Ethics." *Ethics and Corporate Responsibility,* New York: HUC-JIR, 1980. Reprinted in *Exploring Jewish Ethics* as "The Role of Shame in Business Ethics."
197. "How Are You Thinking about Voting?" *Sh'ma* 10/200 (October 31, 1980): 154–55.
198. "Liberal Judaism's Effort to Invalidate Relativism without Mandating Orthodoxy." *Go and Study, Essays and Studies in Honor of Alfred Jospe,* edited by Samuel Z. Fishman and Raphael Jospe. Washington, DC: B'nai Brith Hillel Foundation, 1980.
199. Response in the symposium on "Liberalism and the Jews," *Commentary* 69 (January 1980): 23–24.
200. "Rethinking the Reform Jewish Theory of Social Action," *Journal of Reform Judaism* 27, no. 4 (Fall 1980): 1–19. Reprinted in *Exploring Jewish Ethics*.
201. "A Super-Commentary," *Sh'ma* 10/188 (February 22, 1980): 60–61. [Purim issue]

1981

202. "Reassessing Our Stance after the AWACS," *Sh'ma* 12/224 (December 25, 1981): 29–30.
203. Response in the symposium on "What Is Shaping My Theology?" *Commonweal* 108, no. 2 (January 30, 1981): 50, 52.
204. (In collaboration with Estelle Borowitz)."Talking with Children about Sex." *The Jewish Family Book,* edited by Kathy Green and Sharon Strassfeld. New York: Bantam, 1981.
205. "We Are One—with Japanese-Americans!" *Sh'ma* 12/222 (November 27, 1981): 9–10.

1982

206. "About This Special Issue on Lebanon" [introduction and reply], *Sh'ma* 12/236 (September 3, 1982): 121, 123.
207. "The Authority of the Ethical Impulse in *Halakhah*." *Through the Sound of Many Voices: Writings Contributed on the Occasion of the 70th Birthday of W. Gunther Plaut,* edited by Jonathan Plaut. Toronto: Lester and Orpen Dennys, 1982. Reprinted in *Studies in Jewish Philosophy,* edited by Norbert M. Samuelson. Lanham, MD: University Press of America, 1987. Reprinted

in *Exploring Jewish Ethics* as "On the Ethical Moment in *Halakhah:* A Disagreement with Aharon Lichtenstein."

208. "Harvard Divinity School Convocation Address," *Harvard Theological Review* 75, no. 3 (July 1982): 267–74. Reprinted in *Exploring Jewish Ethics* as "Toward a More Moral Social Order." Also published as "Lessons for Our Society from the Days of Awe," *Harvard Divinity Bulletin*, December 1982–January 1983, n.p.
209. Introduction to *Gates of Freedom: A Passover Haggadah,* by Chaim Stern. Bedford, NY: New Star Press, 1982.
210. "Reading the Jewish Tradition on Marital Sexuality," *Journal of Reform Judaism,* 29, no. 3 (Summer 1982): 1–15. Reprinted in *Exploring Jewish Ethics*.
211. Review of *Abraham and the Contemporary Mind*, by Silvano Arieti. *Theology Today* 39 (April 1982): 96–98.
211a. *A Curricular Approach for the 1980s*. West Orange: Behrman House Catalog for the Jewish School 1982–83, 1982, pp. 33, 47, 65, 79.
212. "The Shame of American Jewry," *Sh'ma* 12/239 (October 15, 1982): 155–56.

1983

213. *Choices in Modern Jewish Thought: A Partisan Guide.* New York: Behrman House, 1983. Second expanded edition, 1995.
214. "Emil Fackenheim As Lurianic Philosopher" [review of *To Mend the World*], *Sh'ma* 13/254 (May 13, 1983): 109–11.

1984

215. *Liberal Judaism*. New York: Union of American Hebrew Congregations, 1984. Excerpts from the chapter "What Do We Expect in the Messianic Age?" were reprinted in *Reform Judaism,* Spring, 1999.
216. "The Autonomous Jewish Self," *Modern Judaism* 4, no. 1 (February 1984): 40–56. Reprinted in *Exploring Jewish Ethics*.
217. "The Autonomous Self and the Commanding Community," *Theological Studies* 45, no. 1 (March 1984): 34–56. Reprinted in *Exploring Jewish Ethics*.
218. "The Covenant, a Century of Modernization," *Sh'ma* 14/272 (April 13, 1984): 93–94.
219. "The Inner World of a Rabbi—My Spirituality," *CCAR Yearbook* 94 (1984): 46–48. Reprinted in *Judaism after Modernity*. A slightly abridged version appeared as "My Inner World," *Sh'ma* 14/277 (September 21, 1984): 131–32.
220. "On the Jewish Obsession with History." In *Religious Pluralism,* Boston University Studies in Philosophy and Religion 5, edited by Lee Rouner. South Bend, IN: University of Notre Dame Press, 1984. A revision of this article was published as "Recent Historic Events: Jewish and Christian Interpretations," *Theological Studies* 44, no. 2 (June 1983): 221–40. This

version was reprinted in *Exploring Jewish Ethics* as "Judaism and Christianity on Recent Historic Events."
221. "Religious Values in a Secular Society," *Journal of Ecumenical Studies* 21, no. 3 (Summer 1984): 536–47. Revised version appeared as "Beyond the Secular City," *Moment* 10, no. 9 (September 1985): 17–22. This version was reprinted in *Exploring Jewish Ethics*.
222. "Rethinking Good and Evil" [review of *Evil and the Morality of God* by Harold Schulweis], *Moment* 9, no. 10 (October 1984): 57–59.
223. "This Land Is Our Land: What It Begat," *Moment* 9, no. 5 (May 1984): 55–58. Reprinted in *Exploring Jewish Ethics*.
224. "What Must We Reform Jews Do?" [excerpt from *Liberal Judaism*], *Reform Judaism* 12 (Spring 1984): 10–11.

1985

225. "After Fifteen Years—My View," *Sh'ma* 15/300 (November 1, 1985): 156–58.
226. "Beyond Ethnos and Ethos: The Faith of American Jews." *Proceedings of the Institute for Distinguished Community Leaders*. [Waltham, MA:] Brandeis University, July 21–23, 1985.
227. "Borowitz on Rackman on Feminism," *Sh'ma* 15/298 (October 4, 1985): 139–40.
228. "The Dilemma of Contemporary Jewish Ethics, a Lecture by Eugene B. Borowitz" [transcribed and edited by Rosie Hurwitz], *Religion* (Lawrence, Kansas) 22, no. 3 (July 1985): 1–4.
229. (In collaboration with Naomi Patz). *Explaining Reform Judaism*. [textbook] New York: Behrman House, 1985.

1986

230. "The Critical Issue in the Quest for Social Justice: A Jewish View." *Contemporary Ethical Issues in the Jewish and Christian Traditions*, edited by Frederick E. Greenspahn. New York: Ktav, 1986. Reprinted in *Exploring Jewish Ethics* as "Social Justice, the Liberal Jewish Case."
231. "Freedom" and "Reason." In *Contemporary Jewish Religious Thought*, edited by Arthur A. Cohen and Paul Mendes-Flohr. New York: Scribners, 1986. The essay "Freedom" was reprinted in *Exploring Jewish Ethics* as "Freedom: The Metamorphoses of a Jewish Value."
232. "Harav Moshe Feinstein, *z"l*," *Sh'ma* 16/312 (April 18, 1986): 93.
233. "*Hillul Hashem:* A Universalistic Rubric in Halakhic Ethics." In *The Life of Covenant*, edited by Joseph A. Edelheit. Chicago: Spertus College of Judaica Press, 1986. Reprinted in *Studies in Jewish Philosophy*, edited by Norbert M. Samuelson. Lanham, MD: University Press of America, 1987. Also reprinted in *Exploring Jewish Ethics* as "*Hillul Hashem:* A Universal Rubric in the *Halakhah*."
234. *The Ideal Jew*. The B. G. Rudolph Lectures in Judaic Studies. Syracuse: Syracuse University, 1986. Reprinted in *Judaism in the Modern World*,

edited by Alan L. Berger. New York: New York University Press, 1994. An abridged version appeared in *Exploring Jewish Ethics*.

235. "Jewish Ethics." *The Westminster Dictionary of Christian Ethics*, edited by James Childress and John Macquarrie. Philadelphia: Westminster Press, 1986. Reprinted in *Exploring Jewish Ethics*.
236. "Mourning the Death of the Shuttle Crew," *Sh'ma* 16/308 (February 21, 1986): 62–63.
237. "Religion Book Week: Critic's Choices—Eugene Borowitz," *Commonweal* 113, no. 4 (February 28, 1986): 121–22.
238. "Tzedakah, a Jewish 'rumor of angels,'" *Sh'ma* 16/317 (September 19, 1986): 130–35.

1987

239. "Between Anarchy and Fanaticism: Religious Freedom's Challenge," *The Christian Century* 104, no. 21 (July 15–22, 1987): 619–22. A fuller version of this paper was published in *Exploring Jewish Ethics*.
240. *The Blessing over a Change of Wine, a Study in the Development of a Jewish Law.* Port Washington: Sh'ma, Inc., 1987.
241. "Co-Existing with Orthodox Jews," *Journal of Reform Judaism* 34, no. 3 (Summer 1987): 53–62. Reprinted in *Exploring Jewish Ethics*. A fuller version of this paper was published as "At the Intersection of Theology and Politics," *European Judaism* 24, no. 2 (Autumn 1991): 31–37.
242. "Encounter and Dialogue among the World's Religions [Judaism]," *Bulletin—Center for the Study of World Religions, Harvard University* 13, no. 1 (Winter 1987): 3–6.
243. "Judaism." *The Encyclopedia of Religion*, edited by Mircea Eliade. New York: Macmillan, 1987. Reprinted in *Judaism A People and Its History*, edited by Robert M. Seltzer, New York: Macmillan, 1989. Reprinted in *Judaism after Modernity* as "Continuity and Creativity in the History of the Jewish Religion."
244. "His Majesty's Opposition, As It Were." *The Seminary at 100*, edited by Nina Beth Cardin and David Silverman. New York: Jewish Theological Seminary of America, 1987.
245. "Jesus the Jew in the Light of the Jewish-Christian Dialogue" and "The Challenge of Jesus the Jew for the Church," *Proceedings of the Center for Jewish-Christian Learning* 2 (Spring 1987): 16–18 and 24–26. A revised version of "The Challenge of Jesus the Jew for the Church" appeared as "How Is the Church to Confront Jesus' Jewishness?" *Moment* 14, no. 3 (April 1989): 40–47+. Both papers were reprinted in *Exploring Jewish Ethics*.
246. "Separate Jews and Their Universal God," *Manna* 17 (Autumn 1987): 16.
247. "Struggling for the Soul of Reform Judaism." Introduction to *Yamim Nora'im: Sinai Sermons*, by Eugene J. Lipman. Washington, DC: Temple Sinai, 1987.

247a. Editor (in collaboration with Sharon Sobel and Beth Klafter), *A Bibliography of Contemporary Jewish Thought*, New York: HUC-JIR, 1987.

1988

248. "How Special, This People We Love" and "What Might We Mean by 'And Who Is Like Your People Israel, a Unique Nation of the World'?" *Proceedings of the Institute for Distinguished Community Leaders.* [Waltham, MA:] Brandeis University, July 25–27, 1988.
249. "Jewish Meta-Ethics and Business Ethics," *Sh'ma* 18/350 (March 18, 1988): 75–79. Reprinted in *Exploring Jewish Ethics.*
250. "Mentshhood," *Present Tense* 15, no. 6 (September–October 1988): 46–49. An abridged version of this paper appeared in *Exploring Jewish Ethics* as "Being a *Mentsh,* the Psychological Aspect."
251. "Paul Cowan, *zecher tzadik livracha,*" *Sh'ma* 18/359 (October 14, 1988): 145.
252. "The Proper Aims of Theological Exchange [letter]," *Sh'ma* 18/348 (February 19, 1988): 64.
253. "Psychotherapy and Religion: Appropriate Expectations," *Religious Education* 83, no. 4 (Fall 1988): 562–70.
254. (In collaboration with Sherry Blumberg). "Religious Pluralism: A Jewish Perspective." *Religious Pluralism and Religious Education,* edited by Norma H. Thompson. Birmingham: Religious Education Press, 1988. Reprinted in *Judaism after Modernity.*
255. "Seymour Siegel, *zecher tzadik livracha,*" *Sh'ma* 18/350 (March 18, 1988): 73.
256. "Temptation in a Capitalist Context," *Sh'ma* 18/358 (September 30, 1988): 139–42. Reprinted in *Exploring Jewish Ethics.*
257. Editor, *Ehad: The Many Meanings of God Is One.* Port Washington, NY: Sh'ma, 1988.
257a. Editor, *Reform Jewish Ethics and the Halakhah, No. 1,* New York: HUC-JIR, 1988.

1989

258. "Even More than God?" Foreword to *Loving the Torah More than God?* by Frans Jozef van Beeck, S. J. Chicago: Loyola University Press, 1989. Reprinted in *Judaism after Modernity.*
259. "Liberalism vs. Orthodoxies on Pluralism," *Sh'ma* 19/365 (January 6, 1989): 28–30.
260. "Nora Levin, *zecher tzadeket livracha,*" *Sh'ma* 20/382 (November 24, 1989): 9.
261. "On Homosexuality and the Rabbinate, a Covenantal Response." *Homosexuality, the Rabbinate, and Liberal Judaism: Papers prepared for the Ad-Hoc Committee on Homosexuality and the Rabbinate.* New York: Central Conference of American Rabbis, June, 1989. Reprinted with an added statement in *Exploring Jewish Ethics.*
262. "Heeding Ecclesiastes at Long Last," in "Woody Allen Counts the Wages of Sin" [essays about film, *Crimes and Misdemeanors*], *New York Times,* 15 October 1989, sec. 2, p. 15–16.

263. "Steven S. Schwarzschild, *z"l,*" *Sh'ma* 20/384 (December 22, 1989): 25.
263a. Editor, *Reform Jewish Ethics and the Halakhah, No. 2*, New York: HUC-JIR, 1989.

1990

264. *Exploring Jewish Ethics*. Detroit: Wayne State University Press, 1990.
265. "The Concept of Covenant in Reform Judaism." In *Berit Mila in the Reform Context,* edited by Lewis M. Barth. No city: Berit Mila Board of Reform Judaism, 1990. Reprinted in *Judaism after Modernity* as "Covenant."
266. "Covenant Theology." *What Happens after I Die?* by Rifat Sonsino and Daniel B. Syme. New York: UAHC Press, 1990. Reprinted in *Judaism after Modernity* as "Life after Death."
267. "Dynamic Sunyata and the God Whose Glory Fills the Universe." *The Emptying God,* edited by John B. Cobb Jr. and Christopher Ives, Maryknoll: Orbis, 1990. Reprinted in *Exploring Jewish Ethics* as "Buddhist and Jewish Ethics, a Response to Masao Abe."
268. "Maturity," *Manna,* no. 29 (Autumn 1990): n.p. [on first page of insert, "Manna Theology Supplement"].
269. "NFTY after Fifty Years" [letter], *Journal of Reform Judaism,* 37, no. 2 (Spring 1990): 71–73.
270. "On the Passing of the Ethnic Era," *Sh'ma* 20/397 (September 21, 1990): 122–24.
271. Participant in symposium, "Fundamentalism: Current Issues in the Jewish-Christian Dialogue," *Proceedings of the Center for Jewish-Christian Learning* 5 (Spring 1990): 7–21.
272. "The Torah, Written and Oral, and Human Rights: Foundations and Deficiencies." *The Ethics of World Religions and Human Rights,* edited by Hans Küng and Jürgen Moltmann. Philadelphia: Trinity Press International, 1990. [Series: *Concilium* (1990), 2]. Reprinted in *Judaism after Modernity* as "Human Rights."
272a. Editor, *Reform Jewish Ethics and the Halakhah, No. 3*, New York: HUC-JIR, 1990.

1991

273. *Renewing the Covenant: A Theology for the Postmodern Jew*. Philadelphia: Jewish Publication Society, 1991.
274. "A Theological Response to Orthodoxies." *A Traditional Quest,* edited by Dan Cohn-Sherbok. Sheffield: JSOT Press, 1991. Another version of chapter 17 of *Renewing the Covenant,* which also appeared as "The Enduring Truth of Religious Liberalism" in *The Fundamentalist Phenomenon,* edited by Norman J. Cohen. Grand Rapids: Eerdmans, 1990.
275. "Belief and Morality," *Reform Judaism* 20, no. 1 (Fall 1991): 28–29.

276. "Rethinking Our Holocaust Consciousness," *Judaism* 40, no. 4 (Fall 1991): 389–406. Version of chapter 3 of *Renewing the Covenant*.
277. "The War in Iraq: A Note from the Editor," *Sh'ma* 21/407 (February 8, 1991): 49.

1992

278. "Autonomy and Community." *Autonomy and Judaism,* edited by Daniel H. Frank. Albany, NY: State University of New York Press, 1992. Revised version of paper originally given at the 10th annual conference of the Academy for Jewish Philosophy, held June 4–5, 1989, at the Reconstructionist Rabbinical College. Later revised to be chapter 18 of *Renewing the Covenant*.
279. *A Buddhist-Jewish Dialogue between Profs. Masao Abe and Eugene B. Borowitz*. Port Washington: Sh'ma, 1992. [Includes materials by both authors from *The Emptying God* (267), plus rejoinders by both men.]
280. "Fully Human, Fully Jewish." *Aus Zweier Zeugen Mund: Festschrift für Pnina Navè Levinson und Nathan Peter Levinson,* edited by Julius H. Schoeps. Gerlingen, Germany: Bleicher, 1992. Adapted version of chapter 13 of *Renewing the Covenant*.
281. "The Holocaust and Meaning: An Exchange [correspondence with Frans Jozef van Beeck, S. J.]," *Cross Currents* 42, no. 3 (Fall 1992): 417–24. Reprinted in *Judaism after Modernity*.
282. "How I Read Myself—and My Critics," *Sh'ma* 22/426 (January 24, 1992): 47–48.
283. "Jewish Thought—on the Emergence of a Genre," *Jewish Book Annual* 50 (1992–3, 5753): 62–70. Reprinted in *Judaism after Modernity* as "American Jewish Modernity Comes to Self-Consciousness."
284. "On Viewing the Chagall Murals: Two Notes," *Sh'ma* 23/444 (December 25, 1992): 31.
285. "Our Jewishness under Threat," *Manna,* no. 36 (Summer 1992): 8–9.
286. *Our Way to a Postmodern Judaism: Three Lectures*. San Francisco: University of San Francisco, 1992. A revised version of these lectures appears in *Judaism after Modernity* as "The Way to a Postmodern Jewish Theology."
287. "Reform Perspectives on God" [letter], *Reform Judaism* 20, no. 3 (Spring 1992): 65.
287a. Editor (in collaboration with Andrea L. Weiss), *A Bibliography of Contemporary Jewish Thought,* 1992 edition, New York: HUC-JIR, 1992.

1993

288. "Alicia Seeger, in Tribute," *Sh'ma* 23/452 (April 16, 1993): 96.
289. "Buddhism and Judaism: Some Further Considerations" [with reply from Masao Abe], *Buddhist-Christian Studies* 13 (1993): 223–31. Reprinted in *Judaism after Modernity*.

290. "A Hearty Welcome to Our New Editors," *Sh'ma* 23/447 (February 5, 1993): 49.
291. "Jottings from an Editor's Desk," *Sh'ma* 23/449 (March 5, 1993): 65. [Purim issue]
292. "Justice Ginsburg, Another 'Terminal Jew'," *Sh'ma* 24/457 (September 17, 1993): 7–8.
293. "Looking Backward, Looking Forward," *Sh'ma* 23/455 (May 28, 1993): 113–15.
294. "Zur Problematik des interreligiösen Dialogs aus der Sicht des Judentums." In *Weltfrieden durch Religionsfrieden: Antworten aus den Weltreligionen,* edited by Hans Küng and Karl-Josef Kuschel. Munich: Piper, 1993. Paper for the UNESCO colloquium on "World Religions, Human Rights, and World Peace." Previously published in English as "Finding a Way to Peace among Religions, a Response to Hans Küng" in *Exploring Jewish Ethics.*

1994

295. "Crisis and Confidence: Psalm 90." *Healing of Soul, Healing of Body,* edited by Simkha Y. Weintraub. Woodstock, VT: Jewish Lights, 1994. Reprinted in *Judaism after Modernity.*
296. "Human Aspiration, the Lessons of the Century," *European Judaism* 27, no. 1 (Spring 1994): 52–62. Reprinted in *Judaism after Modernity* as "Money."
297. "Virtual Judaism on CD-ROM Now Available," *Open Lion* 2, no. 1 (Winter 1994): n.p. [Behrman House newsletter, Purim issue.]
298. Editor, *Reform Jewish Ethics and the Halakhah.* West Orange, NJ: Behrman House, 1994. Borowitz's introduction ("From Cognitive Dissonance to Creative Groping") and "concluding reflection" ("Toward a Postmodern Jewish Ethics") from this volume were reprinted in *Judaism after Modernity.*

1995

299. "Abraham J. Heschel: Thinking about Our Teacher." *What Kind of God?* edited by Betty R. Rubenstein and Michael Berenbaum. Lanham, MD: University Press of America, 1995. Reprinted in *Judaism after Modernity.*
300. "Apostasy from Judaism Today," *Modern Theology* 11, no. 2 (April 1995): 173–79. Reprinted in *Judaism after Modernity.*
301. "In Tribute to Jacob Neusner," *Sh'ma* 25/491 (March 31, 1995): 6–8.
302. (In collaboration with Kerry Olitzky). "A Jewish Perspective." *Aging, Spirituality, and Religion,* edited by Melvin A. Kimble, et al. Minneapolis: Fortress Press, 1995. Reprinted in *Judaism after Modernity* as "Aging."
303. "Reform Judaism: Modern Movement in a Postmodern Era?" *The Jewish Condition: Essays on Contemporary Judaism Honoring Rabbi Alexander M. Schindler,* edited by Aron Hirt-Manheimer. New York: UAHC Press, 1995. Reprinted in *Judaism after Modernity* as "Postmodernity and the

Quintessential Modern Jewish Religious Movement." A revised version of this essay was published as "Future of Reform—More God, More Jewish, More Humble," *Manna*, no. 50 (Winter 1996): 18–22.

304. "Ta Sh'ma," *Sh'ma* 26/502 (November 24, 1995): 7.
305. "What Is Reform Religious Zionism?" *Journal of Reform Zionism* 2 (March 1995/Adar II 5755): 24–30. Reprinted in *Judaism after Modernity* as "Zionism." This paper was also reprinted in *Zionism: The Sequel,* edited by Carol Diament. New York: Hadassah, the Women's Zionist Organization of America, 1998. An earlier version appeared in *CCAR Yearbook* 104 (1994): 73–78.

1996

306. "Are We Too Soft on Apostates?" *Reform Judaism* 24, no. 4 (Summer 1996): 54–5+. Reprinted in *Judaism after Modernity.*
307. "The Crux of Liberal Jewish Thought: Personal Autonomy," *Journal of Psychology and Judaism* 20, no. 1 (Spring 1996): 40–41.
308. Foreword to *Judaism and Spiritual Ethics,* by Niles E. Goldstein and Steven S. Mason. New York: UAHC Press, 1996.
309. "My Father's Spirituality and Mine." In *Entrances to Holiness.* Sudbury, MA: Congregation Beth El, 1996. Also appears in *Paths of Faithfulness,* edited by Carol Ochs, Kerry Olitzky, and Joshua Saltzman. Hoboken, NJ: Ktav, 1997. Reprinted in *Judaism after Modernity.*
310. "A Vital Zionism: Rubrics for Discussion," *Elu v'Elu*, no. 1 (September 1996): 4–5.
311. "What Does the Halakhah Say about . . . ? Joseph Karo's Preface to the *Beit Yosef*," *CCAR Journal* 43, no. 2 (Spring/Summer 1996): 51–58. Reprinted in *Judaism after Modernity.*

1997

312. "How a Discipline Became Established," *CCAR Journal* 44, no. 2 (Spring 1997): 65–70. Reprinted in *Judaism after Modernity* as "My Way beyond Modernity."
313. *Please, God, Heal Her, Please.* Healing and Judaism Monograph Series, eds. Kerry M. Olitzky and Nancy Weiner, no. 1. [New York:] National Center for Jewish Healing, 1997. Reprinted in *Judaism after Modernity.*
314. "The Reform Judaism of *Renewing the Covenant,*" *Conservative Judaism* 50, no. 1 (Fall 1997): 61–65.
315. "Response to the Gift of 'Not a Festschrift,'" and "My Pursuit of Prayerfulness." *Jewish Spiritual Journeys,* edited by Lawrence A. Hoffman and Arnold J. Wolf. West Orange, NJ: Behrman House, 1997. Both essays were reprinted in *Judaism after Modernity.*
315a. Editor (in collaboration with Daniel A. Lehrman), *A Bibliography of Contemporary Jewish Thought,* 1997 edition, New York: HUC-JIR, 1997.

1998

316. "Contemporary Reform Judaism Speaks: Finding a Jewish View of the 'Just Society.'" *Signposts on the Way of Torah*, edited by Jacob Neusner. Belmont, CA: Wadsworth, 1998. Reprinted in *Judaism after Modernity* as "Finding a Jewish View of a Just Economy."
317. Foreword to *Unfinished Rabbi, Selected Writings of Arnold Jacob Wolf*, by Arnold Jacob Wolf. Chicago: Ivan R. Dee, 1998. Reprinted in *Judaism after Modernity*.
318. "Masao Abe's Challenge to Modern Jewish Theology." *Masao Abe: A Zen Life of Dialogue*, edited by Donald W. Mitchell. New York: Charles E. Tuttle Co., 1998. Reprinted in *Judaism after Modernity*. Published in German as "Ein Loblied auf die intellektuelle Freundschaft," in *Das Leben leise wieder lernen: jüdisches und christliches Selbstverständnis nach der Schoah*, edited by Ekkehard W. Stegemann. Stuttgart: Verlag W. Kohlhammer, 1997.
319. Personal Statement and Biography for CCAR Honorary Membership.
320. Editor, *Theological Terms in the Talmud: A First Book*. [New York:] The Ilona Samek Institute at HUC-JIR, 1998.

1999

321. (In collaboration with Frances Schwartz). *The Jewish Moral Virtues*. Philadelphia: Jewish Publication Society, 1999.
322. *Judaism after Modernity: Papers from a Decade of Fruition*. Lanham, MD: University Press of America, 1999.
323a. "Respecting Limits in Pluralism," *Sh'ma*, Vol. 29, Number 561, April 1999.
324a. "Abraham Joshua Heschel: Prophet of Social Activism," in *No Religion Is an Island: The Nostra-Aetate Dialogues*, Edward Bristow, ed. New York: Fordham University Press, 1999.
325a. "The Rabbi and Personal Jewish Virtues," (with Frances W. Schwartz), *CCAR Journal: A Reform Jewish Quarterly*, Winter 1999.
326a. "Foreword," *Teaching Jewish Virtues*, Susan Freeman, Denver: A. R. E. Publishing, 1999.

2000

327a. "Eugene Borowitz Reflects on Jacob Behrman, Writing, and Editing," *Open Lion*, Vol. 7, Issue 1, Fall 2000.
328a. *A Life of Jewish Learning: In Search of a Theology of Judaism*. The Hunter College Jewish Social Studies Program. Occasional Papers in Jewish History and Thought, No. 12. The Anne Bass Schneider Lecture in Jewish Studies. New York: Hunter College of the City of New York, 2000.
329a. Associate Editor to Peter Ochs, *Reviewing the Covenant: Eugene B. Borowitz and the Postmodern Renewal of Jewish Theology*, SUNY Press, 2000. 2002.
330a. "The Postmodern Mood in the Synagogue, a Symposium" (with Jacqueline Mates-Muchin), *CCAR Journal: A Reform Jewish Quarterly*, Winter, 2002.

331a. "Covenant and Chosenness." *Great Jewish Ideas*. United Federation of Chicago accepted for publication.
332a. "Textual Reasoning and Jewish Philosophy: The Next Phase of Jewish Postmodernity?" a revised version of paper no. 13 in *Judaism after Modernity*. Textual Reasoning, Peter Ochs and Nancy Levene, eds. Eerdmans, 2002.
333a. "*Halakhah* in Reform Jewish Usage: Historic Background and Current Discourse." *CCAR Journal: A Reform Jewish Quarterly*.

*Entries marked with an "a" are additions by Eugene B. Borowitz.

Index